INTERNATIONAL BUSINESS
FIRM AND ENVIRONMENT

McGraw-Hill Series in Management

Fred Luthans and Keith Davis, *Consulting Editors*

Allen: The Management Profession
Benton: Supervision and Management
Buchele: The Management of Business and Public Organizations
Cleland and King: Management: A Systems Approach
Cleland and King: Systems Analysis and Project Management
Dale: Management: Theory and Practice
Davis and Frederick: Business and Society: Management, Public Policy, Ethics
Davis and Newstrom: Human Behavior at Work: Organization Behavior
Davis and Newstrom: Organizational Behavior: Readings and Exercises
Del Mar: Operations and Industrial Management: Designing and Managing for
  Productivity
Dobler, Lee, and Burt: Purchasing and Materials Management: Text and Cases
Dunn and Rachel: Wage and Salary Administration: Total Compensation Systems
Feldman and Arnold: Managing Individual and Group Behavior in Organizations
Finch, Jones, and Litterer: Managing for Organizational Effectiveness: An Experimental
  Approach
Flippo: Personnel Management
Gerloff: Organizational Theory and Design: A Strategic Approach for Management
Glueck and Jauch: Business Policy and Strategic Management
Glueck and Jauch: Strategic Management and Business Policy
Glueck and Snyder: Readings in Business Policy and Strategy from *Business Week*
Hampton: Contemporary Management
Hicks and Gullett: Management
Hicks and Gullett: Modern Business Management: A Systems and Environmental
  Approach
Hicks and Gullett: Organizations: Theory and Behavior
Johnson, Kast, and Rosenzweig: The Theory and Management of Systems
Karlins: The Human Use of Human Resources
Kast and Rosenzweig: Experiential Exercises and Cases in Management
Kast and Rosenzweig: Organization and Management: A Systems and Contingency
  Approach
Knudson, Woodworth, and Bell: Management: An Experiential Approach
Koontz, O'Donnell, and Weihrich: Essentials of Management
Koontz, O'Donnell, and Weihrich: Management
Koontz, O'Donnell, and Weihrich: Management: A Book of Readings
Levin, McLaughlin, Lamone, and Kottas: Production/Operations Management:
  Contemporary Policy for Managing Operating Systems
Luthans: Introduction to Management: A Contingency Approach
Luthans: Organizational Behavior
Luthans and Thompson: Contemporary Readings in Organizational Behavior
McNichols: Executive Policy and Strategic Planning
McNichols: Policymaking and Executive Action
Maier: Problem-Solving Discussions and Conferences: Leadership Methods and Skills
Margulies and Raia: Conceptual Foundations of Organizational Development

INTERNATIONAL BUSINESS

FIRM AND ENVIRONMENT

Alan M. Rugman

Dalhousie University

Donald J. Lecraw

University of Western Ontario

Laurence D. Booth

University of Toronto

McGRAW-HILL BOOK COMPANY

New York   St. Louis   San Francisco   Auckland   Bogotá
Hamburg   Johannesburg   London   Madrid   Mexico   Montreal   New Delhi
Panama   Paris   São Paulo   Singapore   Sydney   Tokyo   Toronto

This book was set in Times Roman by The Saybrook Press.
The editors were John R. Meyer and Sheila H. Gillams;
the production supervisor was Leroy A. Young.
The cover was designed by Anne Canevari Green.
The drawings were done by Volt Information Sciences, Inc.
Halliday Lithograph Corporation was printer and binder.

INTERNATIONAL BUSINESS
Firm and Environment

2 3 4 5 6 7 8 9 0   HALHAL   8 9 8 7

ISBN 0-07-054274-0

Library of Congress Cataloging in Publication Data

Rugman, Alan M.
    International business.

    (McGraw-Hill series in management)
    Bibliography: p.
    Includes indexes.
    1. International business enterprises.   I. Lecraw,
Donald J.   II. Booth, Laurence D.   III. Title.
IV. Series.
HD2755.5.R835   1985   658'.049   84-15482
ISBN 0-07-054274-0

CONTENTS

PREFACE

SPECIAL FEATURES OF THE BOOK

The subtitle, *Firm and Environment*, explains the focus of *International Business*. A business student or manager needs to know about the relevant international aspects of the business. The puzzle is, what is relevant? The environment of international business is vast and, left unstructured, virtually impossible to comprehend, let alone document and explain in any book. Some focus is required, to crystallize understanding. Such a structure can come through analysis of the firm operating in the international environment.

The multinational enterprise is the leading actor on the stage of international business. This type of firm today accounts for the greater part of international transactions. A modern international business textbook needs to explain the reasons for this recent growth of the multinational enterprise and then relate this analysis to issues of management and policy. The power of the multinational enterprise draws the attention of governments and regulators as well as competition from rivals. These issues, along with the strategic planning of the multinational enterprise and the operation of its functional areas, are all aspects of the firm in the international environment that require study in a comprehensive treatment of international business.

This textbook on international business offers students and instructors a new approach to the subject. While it covers the same topics as other texts in the field, the key subject of the multinational enterprise is explored here in much greater depth, using a more powerful conceptual foundation than has been available so far. The conceptual model developed is applied to understand the management of international business. It is then used as a practical basis for the treatment of the international dimension of the key functional areas of finance, marketing, production, and human resource management. The theory of the multinational enterprise is developed early in the book and is applied to the issues of global strategic planning and decision making in the functional areas and to the discussion of conflicts between government and multinationals.

This books expands upon the existing works in international business, but pursues the new theoretical foundations of the field in greater depth than other texts. At the same time, coverage of relevant aspects of the international environment is included. Many fresh insights into the field of international business are drawn out by the new analysis. The text also includes many relevant managerial, policy, and practical applications, as well as several new cases. Students specializing in particular topics can both test their understanding of the materials and pursue them further through the use of key words, discussion questions, and references to essential reading in the end of book bibliography. Future revised editions will update these materials, building on the conceptual framework of the book, which will remain as a powerful tool of analysis.

The field of international business is large and growing. As U.S. business schools move ahead to internationalize their curricula, more and more universities and colleges are offering courses on international business. To satisfy requirements of the American Assembly of the Collegiate School of Business, all students in business programs must be exposed to the international dimension of business. This AACSB accreditation requirement is normally satisfied by offering a basic course in international business. This book caters to this expanding need with a text that can stand on its own as an introduction to the field of international business or as an essential supplement to the functional area courses, for example, in international finance, international marketing, human resource management, and international business policy. These area courses lack the unified treatment of the multinational enterprise and all its strategic elements that only such a specialized international business text as this one can provide.

Aimed primarily for M.B.A. students in the United States and Canada, the book will also be suitable for juniors and seniors specializing in business administration and commerce. On an international level it will be suitable for graduate courses in international business and for undergraduates specializing in this area or taking a general course to supplement work in international economics, international politics, or international law and history.

ORGANIZATION OF THE BOOK

The distinguishing feature of this textbook is that it builds an explanation of relevant environmental factors upon the solid foundations of an understanding of the key instrument of international business—the multinational enterprise. As a result, this book is more analytical than competing books which are now widely recognized as being deficient in their use of the modern theory of the multinational enterprise. With the maturing of the field of international business, it is now possible to include many more theoretical principles in a textbook and use them for a deeper discussion of policy issues and the decision-making activities of management.

The conceptual theme of the book is developed extensively in the early chapters to explain the motivation, operation, and performance of the multinational enterprise (MNE). The theory developed is then applied in an interdisciplinary manner to analyze cross-cultural conflicts, trade and payments, choice of foreign entry mode, and such policy issues as the conflict between nation states and the MNE, codes of conduct for the MNEs, technology transfer, transfer pricing, taxation, and regulation of the MNE.

The second half of the text applies the new conceptual framework to analyze strategic planning and its relevance for the major functional areas of the MNE: finance, marketing, production, and the management of human resources. Indeed, the topic of strategic management in a globally competitive world becomes a major focus of the latter part of the book, where the functional chapters are treated not just in an international dimension but also in a strategic manner. This throws fresh light on such issues as centralization of control, organizational structure, control of the R and D function, Japanese style management, conflicts between governments and multinationals, the north-south dialogue, and international integration.

The book incorporates summaries of original theoretical and empirical work undertaken by the authors on some of these topics. Mainly it surveys the extensive data and results of other scholars in the fast-growing field of international business. Most of the text deals with managerial applications of international business, with practical problems and issues being highlighted throughout the book. A separate Instructor's Manual with guides to the cases and questions, as well as discussion questions and testing materials, is available.

This text is written specifically for a student audience, and we shall be pleased to receive comments, from both students and their instructors, about their experiences in using this book to study the fascinating field of international business.

NOTE ON FURTHER REFERENCES

A textbook writer is variously regarded as a brilliant synthesizer of vast, disparate literature or as a thief. To those colleagues who believe that their ideas have been stolen and not specifically acknowledged in the text, we apologize. As the field of international business develops a stronger conceptual and empirical core, it is becoming increasingly difficult to recognize the significant contributions of all contemporary writers. This book would be more like an annotated bibliography than a textbook if the valuable contributions of all the 1400 members of the Academy of International Business were listed. To partially compensate we have included a bibliography at the end of the book. These references should help to guide the interested reader toward a deeper and richer understanding of particular subjects found to be of interest.

ACKNOWLEDGMENTS

The quality of this book was much enhanced by the excellent research assistance of Kathy Peach, John McIlveen, Jocelyn Bennett, Jennifer Barr, Heather Cochrane, and others associated with the Dalhousie Centre for International Business Studies over the 1981 to 1984 period. While at the Centre, Dr. David Komus assisted in the preparation of tables in Chapters 1 and 6. Pat Zwicker literally typed and corrected thousands of pages of manuscript on the word processor before we finally got it right. Pat is to be commended for the excellent quality of her work under constant pressure.

Many colleagues have provided stimulating comments and advice, including Thomas Houston, Philip Rosson, Andy Peacock, and Dick Chesley (all of Dalhousie University), Edwin Miller (University of Michigan), John O'Shaughnessy, Steve Robock, and Ian Giddy (Columbia Business School), and David Rutenberg (Queen's University). We are especially grateful to the reviewers of various draft chapters of this book: Sarkis J. Khoury (University of Notre Dame), Ali Fatami (Kansas State University), Fritz Rieger (Oklahoma State University), Fred Luthans (University of Nebraska–Lincoln), Arvind K. Jain (McGill University), Robert Grosse (University of Miami), Richard W. Moxon (University of Washington), Bruce Kogut (University of Pennsylvania/Wharton School), Stephen W. Miller (St. Louis University), and Robert Z. Aliber (Williams College). Their penetrating insights greatly improved both the content and the presentation of the book.

Many helpful comments have been received from students in international business courses using drafts of this book at the Columbia Business School and at Dalhousie University. Their insights have been invaluable.

A comprehensive book on international business covers too broad a sweep for any one author to be an expert in each area. The brainchild of Rugman, this book required the help of experienced coauthors to achieve balance and depth in its coverage. Don Lecraw was the primary author for Part Four, and Laurence Booth for the finance chapters. Johny K. Johansson prepared the marketing chapter. This is, however, truly a coauthored effort, and synergistic benefits arose from the extensive interaction of all participants.

The authors wish to acknowledge the research and financial support provided by the Dalhousie Centre for International Business Studies and its funding agencies of the government of Canada.

Alan M. Rugman
Donald J. Lecraw
Laurence D. Booth

INTERNATIONAL BUSINESS
FIRM AND ENVIRONMENT

PART ONE

THE NATURE OF INTERNATIONAL BUSINESS: MULTINATIONAL ENTERPRISES AND TRADE

INTRODUCTION TO INTERNATIONAL BUSINESS

THE FOUNDATIONS OF INTERNATIONAL BUSINESS

This book concerns multinationals and their internal markets. The student who reads it will learn that the activities of multinationals are explained by the process of "internalization." This concept is the building block for the chapters that explain the international aspects of the functional areas of the multinational enterprise and the ways in which it interacts with governments.

The organization of a textbook on international business can proceed in either of at least two ways: (1) by placing the major concepts of each functional area (marketing, policy, finance, etc.) in an international dimension and then attempting to integrate them such that their relevance for international business management is clear or (2) by developing a distinctive concept of international business which builds upon the student's knowledge of the other core fields of business but does not repeat it.

This book follows the latter approach. It does so by identifying the multinational enterprise (MNE) as the most important organization of the international business field. The actions, growth, and economic impact of the MNE are examined in their own right. The MNE is then contrasted with other forms of international business activity such as exporting, joint ventures, licensing, or similar contractual agreements. Trade, business activity in export markets, offshore assembly, and other aspects of international business activity are also covered, but in less detail than the MNE. Analysis of the ways in which the MNE reacts to restrictions on international trade, licensing, and investment is a key conceptual method followed in the text.

At the outset, the analytical foundations required to understand the role of the MNE are developed in some detail, so that the operations of the internal market of the MNE can be fully understood. These foundations of international business draw much of their inspiration from the fields of economics and finance. This is a natural development since the models in these fields are well developed and their techniques are easily adapted to the study of international business. However, other areas of business such as marketing, management, and human resource management are not neglected. A knowledge of how to operate these functional areas and solve the management problems of the MNE stems largely from an analysis of its internal market.

A supplementary theme in the book is to examine relevant parts of the environment of international business. The managers of the MNE need to understand the political regulations and cultural environments within which the MNE operates. The unique ability of the MNE to cross national boundaries and produce abroad is explained in the context of a world system characterized by environmental constraints, natural market imperfections, and government regulations. The conflicts between MNEs and governments of home and host nations are reexamined in the light of the paradigm of internalization, developed in the text as the foundation of international business.

This text is not an encyclopedia of international business. No book could attempt to catalog all the actual and potential items of relevance to international business activity. Instead, this text cuts through the plethora of detail by concentrating on an analytical framework which underlies the day-to-day operations of international business. This analytical focus provides the manager of an organization engaged in international business with the tools necessary to make informed decisions about foreign sales, production, organization, and strategic planning of the firm. Frequent use of this framework of analysis throughout the text in the examination of real-world management problems and policy issues ensures its relevance.

Analytical techniques for international business management have been developed only recently; indeed, the theory is still not well understood by many professionals in the field. In this text, the various strands of analysis are drawn together to generate a new body of theory. Experts in any one of the areas of economics, finance, marketing, production, and management will recognize particular models from their disciplines, but the criterion used for selection of a model in this text is the contribution it can make to the development of a relevant theory of international business, which can be applied to increase the efficiency of MNEs in their worldwide operations.

It may appear at first glance that the coverage of this book is too comprehensive for a one-semester text. In fact, only the key analytical concepts from each field are used here; often the details are merely sketched in. The reader interested in a full explanation of the paradigms of each field can find them in the appropriate core texts of the field. The goal of this text is to explain the new theory of international business and apply it in analysis of relevant practical managerial and public policy issues. The development of these analytical foundations of international business is the substance of what follows in this text.

THE FIELD OF INTERNATIONAL BUSINESS

The key areas of the field of international business need to be evaluated against the ultimate objective of efficient management of the MNE. This involves the determination of optimal policies in the main functional areas of management: production, human resource management, marketing policy and strategy, and financial management. The application of strategic planning to formulate the business policy of the MNE involves integration of these four functional areas.

To develop an understanding of efficiency, it is first necessary to study essential theoretical concepts relevant to international business management. The conceptual issues are simplified by dividing them into two categories: real (nonfinancial) and financial. Under the "real" side of theory in the International Business (IB) course we study trade theory and then the theory of the MNE, including the reasons for choice of entry mode. The "financial" side of theory involves discussion of environmental factors affecting the MNE such as foreign exchange (FX) rates, the balance of payments, and the international monetary system. It also involves study of internal decisions affecting the MNE, such as its appropriate cost of capital and the opportunities for international diversification.

Finally, the subject of international business must consider explicitly the major role of government in its relationships with the MNE and other firms engaged in international business. It is vitally important to understand the reasons for such policies and the optimal way of reacting to them. To this end, it is necessary to understand the philosophy of international agencies and foreign governments. These are part of the environment facing the MNE, as are the cultural, political, legal, social, and economic systems of nations in which the MNE operates. Clearly it is vital to recognize and understand the environments within which business is to be conducted, and for MNEs this is a more complex task than for domestic firms.

Figure 1-1 is an illustration of these principles. This graphic describes how this particular book is organized. First, the upper half of Figure 1-1 reveals the major division between environmental and company variables. The environmental variables are exogenous (outside) the firm, while the company-specific variables are endogenous (inside) the firm. Information about both sets of factors together is required for the MNE to organize its management functions, shown in the lower part of Figure 1-1. The ultimate control, organization, and strategic planning by the MNE of its four critical functions determine how successfully it can incorporate the basic information about environmental and company factors.

There are several major themes in this book:

1 The reasons why free trade is efficient and the operations of firms engaged in international trade.

2 The reasons why tariffs are inefficient, the national costs of inefficiency and reactions by firms to these inefficiencies.

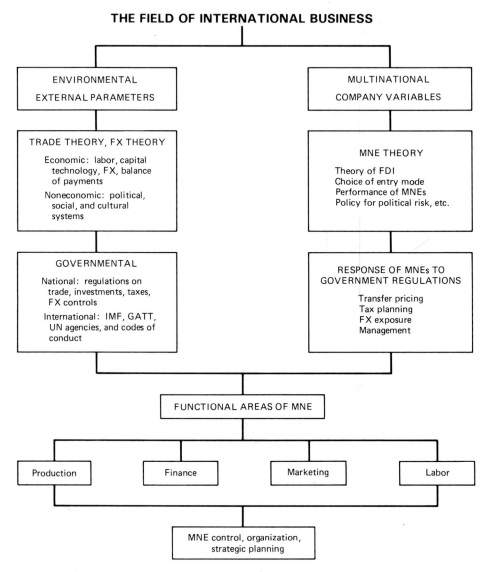

FIGURE 1-1
Major topics in international business.

3 The reasons why foreign direct investment takes place and why multinationals exist as responses to inefficient markets and environmental constraints.

4 The reasons why foreign direct investment occurs instead of exporting or licensing.

5 The regulation of foreign direct investment and the emergence of MNEs from Japan, Europe, Canada, and middle-income countries.

6 The problems of international finance: foreign exchange rates and exposure and what multinationals can do about them.

7 The ways to run the MNE efficiently in its operations in production, marketing, finance, and human resources.

DEFINITION OF THE MULTINATIONAL ENTERPRISE (MNE)

The difference between a domestic corporation and the MNE is that the latter operates across national boundaries. More specifically, the MNE produces abroad as well as at home. International production is the essence of multinationality. It involves a corporation in the establishment of foreign susidiaries, and such a firm is referred to by its acronym, MNE.[1]

The number of nations in which a corporation must be involved in to be classified as an MNE is another issue, and one which can be answered only in relation to the nature of the problem being addressed. Some scholars have suggested that production in at least one foreign nation is all that is required for qualification as an MNE.[2] The firm then controls income and generates assets in more than the home nation and is involved in one foreign market. Yet, since some economies, such as those of Canada and the United States, are highly correlated in their economic activity, other scholars have advocated that the definition of an MNE be restricted to firms with operations in six or more foreign nations.[3] This latter definition appears to be safer, if more conservative, and is the one followed here.

Another approach is to use the ratio of foreign (F) to total (T) operations.[4] The F/T ratio is readily available from corporation annual reports, or directories and surveys of MNEs, and can be calculated for sales, assets, employees, and so on. Firms with an F/T ratio greater than some arbitrary number, such as 30 percent, or 25 percent, can be classified as MNEs. One problem with the F/T ratio is that the available data do not always permit a distinction to be made between exports (X) and sales by overseas subsidiaries (S). The F consists of the sum of X plus S,

---

[1]Foreign production is defined to include the production of physical goods and foreign investment in such service sectors as finance, insurance, construction, transportation, communication, and retail trade. Foreign production does not include international trade in technology, trademarks, patents, or franchises to unaffiliated foreigners, even though such international trade in intangible assets is a large part of international business.

[2]Authors who support this definition, stating that *foreign production* in one or more nations is the nature of the MNE, are: John H. Dunning, "The Determinants of International Production," *Oxford Economic Papers* 25 (November 1973):289−336; Neil Hood and Stephen Young, *The Economics of Multinational Enterprise*, London: Longman, 1979.

[3]As defined by the Harvard Business School multinational enterprise research project, the MNE is a corporation on *Fortune*'s 1967 list of the 500 largest U.S. firms with manufacturing subsidiaries in six or more nations. See Raymond Vernon, *Sovereignty at Bay: The Multinational Spread of United States Enterprises*, New York: Basic Books, 1971.

[4]Nicholas Bruck and Francis Lees, "Foreign Investment, Capital Controls and the Balance of Payments," *The Bulletin*, New York University: Graduate School of Business Administration, Institute of Finance, No. 48−9 (April 1968); and Alan M. Rugman, *International Diversification and the Multinational Enterprise*, Lexington: D. C. Heath, 1979.

whereas, clearly, only the S is wanted in a satisfactory measure of F/T. To minimize this problem, in this book MNEs are defined by the production in number of countries method and also the F/T method.

A third method for defining MNEs is by the attitude of the management team of the corporation. The work of Perlmutter (1969) suggested three types of management view: ethnocentric, polycentric, and geocentric.[5] Ethnocentric corporations are home-country-oriented, so the MNE does not appear here. A polycentric corporation has international operations but no integration of these in a systematic manner. It is host-country-oriented. A true MNE is geocentric; it has a world orientation. It integrates worldwide operations and has a global planning strategy which serves the interest of the stakeholders in the nations in which it operates. This definition of the MNE is not as readily quantifiable as the F/T or number of countries method, so it is not used much in this book. However, it is important for international management policy and strategy and is used in later sections.

It is also worthwhile to distinguish between portfolio investment and foreign direct investment. Portfolio investment is purely financial investment; no control over the asset is involved. Examples of portfolio investments are the use of foreign bonds, other interest-bearing assets, or small investments in equities via the stock market. In contrast, foreign direct investment (FDI) involves control; the main example is an equity investment in a significant share of the outstanding stock. It is a moot point at which level of equity ownership control is established. The U.S. Department of Commerce defines FDI as any equity investment greater than 10 percent in a foreign corporation.[6] In Canada and other nations the ratio is variable and often higher than 10 percent, depending on the assessment of effective control.

THE NATURE OF WORLD TRADE AND INVESTMENTS

The United States is the world's largest foreign investor, accounting for over 40 percent of the stock of FDI investment in 1979. Exhibit 1-1 shows the countries that receive U.S. foreign direct investment. The western European market countries together account for over 40 percent of total U.S. FDI. Not surprising is the importance of Canada, the closest high-income nation, as a host country (20.7 percent). The next-largest recipient is the United Kingdom (13.2 percent). There is considerable U.S. investment in Latin America but very little (only 3 percent) in Japan.

Exhibit 1-1 illustrates several other points. First, American firms have far greater amounts invested in developed countries than in developing ones. This is consistent with the idea that FDI is complementary to foreign trade. The industrialized nations invest primarily in each other and they also do most of the world's

[5]Howard V. Perlmutter, "The Tortuous Evolution of the Multinational Corporation," *Columbia Journal of World Business* 4:9 – 18 (January-February 1969). This classification is also used in: David P. Rutenberg, *Multinational Management*, Boston: Little Brown, 1982.

[6]Neil Hood and Stephen Young, *The Economics of Multinational Enterprise*, London: Longman, 1979 require 25 percent of the share capital of the foreign enterprise to be owned by the parent.

trade among themselves. Second, the major type of U.S. FDI is in manufacturing industries. Approximately 40 percent of foreign investment is in manufacturing, reflecting a technological knowledge advantage held by many U.S. firms.

The United States has recently become the most important and largest host country to foreign direct investment. (This phenomenon is called *reverse investment.*) Exhibit 1-2 shows that Canada, the United Kingdom, and the Netherlands account for one-half of such foreign direct investment into the United States. Noteworthy is the substantial foreign direct investment by the Netherlands at 22.5 percent. This is to a large extent due to the involvement of Royal Dutch-Shell in the United States. Japanese involvement at 7.7 percent is more than double the percentage of U.S. investment in Japan. This is not surprising, since Japan is a small host country to FDI, with a policy of encouraging licensing rather than involvement by MNEs.

EXHIBIT 1-1
U.S. FOREIGN AND DIRECT INVESTMENT ABROAD AT YEAR END 1981

| | All industries | | Manufacturing, |
	$US millions	Percentage	$US millions
All countries	227,342		92,480
Canada	46,957	20.7	19,658
Europe	101,318	44.6	45,534
United Kingdom	30,086	13.2	8,052
France	9,102	4.0	5,501
Germany	16,077	7.1	10,312
Netherlands	8,775	3.9	3,203
Switzerland	12,437	5.5	997
Rest	24,841	10.9	17,469
Japan	6,807	3.0	3,277
Australia, New Zealand, and South Africa	12,030	5.3	4,694
Other western hemisphere	38,883	17.1	15,762
Brazil	8,253	3.6	5,420
Mexico	6,962	3.1	5,140
Bermuda	10,353	4.6	15
Other	13,355	5.9	5,187
Other Africa	4,282	1.9	448
Middle East	1,958	0.9	197
Other Asia and Pacific	10,986	4.8	2,902
International unallocated	4,122	1.8	—

Source: Survey of Current Business, U.S. Department of Commerce, Bureau of Economic Analysis, 62.2:8, (August 1982):22.

EXHIBIT 1-2
U.S. FOREIGN DIRECT INVESTMENT AT YEAR END 1981

	All industries, $US millions	Percentage	Manufacturing, $US millions
All countries	89,759		29,533
Canada	12,212	13.6	5,787
Europe	57,705	64.3	19,016
United Kingdom	15,527	17.3	5,910
France	5,844	6.5	1,815
Germany	7,067	7.9	2,917
Netherlands*	20,177	22.5	4,604
Switzerland	4,368	4.9	2,731
Rest	4,722	5.3	1,039
Japan	6,887	7.7	1,111
Other western hemisphere	8,352	9.3	3,314
Other	4,603	5.1	305

*51.8 percent of the Netherlands' FDI in the United States is in the petroleum industry.
Source: Survey of Current Business, U.S. Department of Commerce, Bureau of Economic Analysis, 62.2:8, (August 1982):37.

The growing amount of FDI in the United States is due to its large market potential; abundant raw materials; falling labor costs relative to other high-income countries; and in the late seventies, to restrictions on trade in some products. These country-specific factors which encourage FDI are discussed in later chapters. Another important factor in the flow of FDI into the United States is the growing strength of non-U.S. multinationals. The firm-specific advantages of European, Japanese, and Canadian MNEs which enable them to invest in the United States are also discussed in later sections.

Since the end of World War II, the international sector of the world economy has experienced increasing growth as both world trade and foreign production have expanded more rapidly than world GNP. The future outlook is for this rapid growth to ease off as host countries implement restrictive national policies, particularly in the resource area.

Exhibit 1-3 presents data on world trade for 1979. It can be seen that for the world as a whole, exports must equal imports, but the two are not necessarily equal for any one country. With a few exceptions, most countries import slightly more than they export, reflecting a need for raw materials. The outstanding exceptions are the Middle-East oil countries that export far more than they import.

One measure of the importance of a country in total world trade is its share of world trade. The United States, with 12.7 percent, holds the largest share, followed by Germany, Japan, and France. The U.S. share of world trade has steadily declined over the last two decades. As a percentage of GNP, overall trade in the United States accounted for only 9.6 percent in 1981, indicating that exports

EXHIBIT 1-3
THE RELATIVE IMPORTANCE OF TRADE IN LEADING NATIONS

Country	Imports as a percent of GNP 1981	Exports as a percent of GNP 1981	Percentage of world imports 1981	Percentage of world exports 1981
United States	10.4	9.6	14.3	12.7
Canada	27.7	29.0	3.7	4.0
United Kingdom	24.4	27.2	5.4	5.6
Austria	43.3	42.8	1.1	0.8
Belgium	68.7	65.2	3.3	3.0
Denmark	37.5	38.1	0.9	0.9
France	22.9*	20.9*	6.3	5.8
Germany	31.4	32.1	8.7	9.6
Italy	28.4	24.9	4.8	4.1
Netherlands	54.8	58.5	3.5	3.7
Spain	20.2	18.0	1.7	1.1
Sweden	31.2	30.9	1.5	1.6
Japan	16.0	16.6	7.5	8.3
Australia	19.2	16.0	1.4	1.2
Hong Kong	—	—	1.3	1.5
Korea	45.6	41.4	1.4	1.2
Singapore	220.7	167.8	1.4	1.1
Brazil	9.4	9.1	1.3	1.3
Oil-exporting countries	—	—	8.4	14.8
Indonesia	19.2	27.0	0.7	1.2
Iran	15.0	24.8	0.7	0.6
Iraq	—	—	1.0	0.6
Kuwait	—	—	0.4	0.9
Libya	42.4	57.5†	0.8	0.8
Nigeria	—	—	1.1	1.1
Saudi Arabia	30.4	69.6	1.8	6.2

*Data for 1980.
†Data for 1978.
Source: International Monetary Fund, International Financial Statistics, 36:5, (May 1983).

are small in relation to the size of the economy. This export share increased by almost 100 percent in the 1970s. The relatively small export share is explained in part by the large size of the U.S. market, which allows firms to realize economies of scale in production without exporting. This scale advantage does not occur to a small, open country such as Belgium, unless it exports, and, indeed, exports are over 60 percent of Belgium's GNP. In addition, many U.S. firms are more active in FDI than exporting, a situation which is analyzed later.

The market economies of western Europe together account for 34 percent of world trade. The foreign trade of the EEC exceeds that of any one country, making it the largest trading area in the world. One-half of EEC trade is intra-community trade among the ten member nations. The population of the EEC is greater than that of the United States or the Soviet Union, and the level of production is equal to that in the United States. Also significant to note is the fact that the oil-producing countries of the Middle East account for approximately 10 percent of world trade.

Some nations have imports and exports substantially greater than 100 percent of their GNP. Singapore, for example, has imports of 221 percent and exports of 168 percent of GNP. This is due to the nature of trade and, more especially, to Singapore's role as an offshore assembly platform, that is, a trading nation that exports most of its production and requires corresponding imports to support production. Other nations that act as trade entrepôts are Hong Kong and Taiwan.

World trade and foreign production are integrating the world's economies at an increasing rate. The ratio of U.S. exports to GNP nearly doubled during the decade ending 1980. At the same time, the United States' share of world trade declined by a third. While world trade is becoming more important to the American economy, therefore, the share of U.S. trade in total world trade is becoming less important as other nations expand their international sectors. The growth of trade is being experienced in most western industrialized nations. Like the United States, they are also experiencing declines in their world trade shares, confirming the growth of trade by the OPEC nations and the Pacific rim nations.

Exhibit 1-4 illustrates the rapid growth in FDI abroad. The figures in the table represent the stock of FDI; this is a snapshot, at one moment in time, of the nation's accumulated stock of FDI. In the 12-year period from 1967 to 1978, the stock of FDI abroad increased 225 percent, from a total of $114.1 billion to $369.3 billion. These dollar amounts are not adjusted to account for inflation or appreciation in value of stock, so the real increase is probably greater. Comparisons over time reveal the erosion of the U.S. and British positions, with both countries showing a decline in the percentage of FDI abroad. In sharp contrast is the rapid growth of FDI from West Germany and Japan; their stock of FDI increased by ten and eighteen times respectively over the period. Switzerland also shows a strong growth in its stock of direct investment (five times). This significant growth has occurred partly because Switzerland is a country offering attractive tax and financial opportunities for outward direct investment; it is not due primarily to the activity of indigenous Swiss firms.

Over the past two decades there have been many changes in the pattern of foreign direct investment. The former dominance of the United States and United Kingdom as a result of their technological superiority and balance of payments surpluses has declined. Rapid postwar growth in western Europe and Japan due to a strong economic recovery and their strengthening currencies has resulted in a change in the sourcing of FDI. Indeed, European and Japanese-based MNEs have been growing more rapidly than U.S. or British MNEs, especially the British, in the last decade.

Two patterns have emerged recently in foreign direct investment abroad. First

EXHIBIT 1-4
STOCK OF DIRECT INVESTMENT ABROAD OF DEVELOPED MARKET ECONOMIES,
BY MAJOR COUNTRY OF ORIGIN, 1967 TO 1978

Country of origin	Billions of dollars end of				Percentage of distribution			
	1967	1971	1975	1978	1967	1971	1975	1978
United States	56.6	82.8	124.1	168.1	49.6	49.3	47.2	45.5
United Kingdom	17.5	23.7	30.4	41.1	15.3	14.1	11.6	11.1
Germany, Federal Republic of	3.0	7.3	16.0	31.8	2.6	4.3	6.1	8.6
Japan*	1.5	4.4	15.9	26.8	1.3	2.6	6.0	7.3
Switzerland	5.0	9.5	17.6	24.6	4.4	5.7	6.7	6.7
Netherlands	11.0	13.8	19.0	23.7	9.6	8.2	7.2	6.4
France	6.0	7.3	11.1	14.9	5.3	4.3	4.2	4.0
Canada	3.7	6.5	10.4	13.6	3.2	3.9	4.0	3.7
Sweden	1.7	2.4	4.4	6.0	1.5	1.4	1.7	1.6
Belgium-Luxembourg	2.0	2.4	3.6	5.4	1.8	1.4	1.4	1.5
Italy	2.1	3.0	3.3	3.3	1.8	1.8	1.3	0.9
Total above	110.1	163.1	255.8	359.3	96.5	97.0	97.3	97.3
All other (estimate)†	4.0	5.0	7.2	10.0	3.5	3.0	2.7	2.7
Grand total	114.1	168.1	263.0	369.3	100.0	100.0	100.0	100.0

*Fiscal year beginning April 1 of the year indicated on the basis of cumulative annual flows of direct investment as reported to the International Monetary Fund.

†Includes Austria, Denmark, Norway, Finland, Portugal, Spain, Australia, New Zealand, and South Africa. For 1978: data not available for Denmark and South Africa.

Source: United Nations, Economic and Social Council, *Transnational Corporations in World Development: A Re-examination* (UN, 1978: 05692).

is the increase in activity by third world MNEs. Firms in developing countries, such as Brazil, Hong Kong, Singapore, India, and Mexico, have been investing abroad in other third world nations. Second, the oil-exporting developing countries of OPEC have recently started to make major capital investments in other countries, but few data are available from these nations. Such new investment trends are contributing to a more diversified pattern of worldwide foreign direct investment abroad.

In general, there are few available data on trends of foreign investments from and in the Soviet Union and eastern European nations.

THE WORLD'S LARGEST MNEs

The dominance of MNEs in international investment is such that by 1976, MNEs accounted for one-half of investment abroad. More important, the sources of FDI are concentrated within a limited number of corporations; there are only about 450 MNEs in the world of any significant size. Comparisons over time show a slight erosion of the U.S. and British dominance and rapid growth from Japan, West Germany, and Switzerland.

Exhibits 1-5 through 1-9 identify the largest U.S., European, Japanese, Canadian, and third world multinationals and present data regarding their degree of multinationality. This multinationality is expressed by three ratios: S, which represents sales by foreign subsidiaries to total sales; X, which represents exports to total sales; and F/T, which is the ratio of foreign (S + X) sales to total sales.

Exhibit 1-5 examines the fifty largest U.S. multinationals. Petroleum and motor vehicle producers are the largest of the U.S. multinationals and can be seen to

EXHIBIT 1-5
IDENTIFICATION OF THE FIFTY LARGEST U.S. MNEs

Rank	Firm	Industry	Sales, $US millions	S	X	F/T
1	Exxon	Petroleum	79,106	74	—	74
2	General Motors	Motor vehicles and parts	66,311	25	—	25
3	Mobil	Petroleum	44,721	63	—	63
4	Ford Motor	Motor vehicles and parts	43,514	44	—	44
5	Texaco	Petroleum	38,350	62	—	62
6	Standard Oil of California	Petroleum	29,948	57	—	57
7	Gulf Oil	Petroleum	23,910	47	—	47
8	International Business Machines (IBM)	Office equipment	22,863	53	—	53
9	General Electric	Electrical appliances	22,461	20	12	32
10	Standard Oil (Ind.)	Petroleum	18,610	21	—	21
11	International Telephone and Telegraph	Electrical appliances	17,197	52[†]	—	52
15	Conoco (formerly Continental Oil)	Petroleum	12,648	37	—	37
16	E. I. duPont de Nemours	Chemicals	12,572	18[‡]	14	32
17	Chrysler	Motor vehicles and parts	12,002	19[§]	—	19
18	Tenneco	Petroleum	11,209	23	—	23
20	Sun Company, Inc.	Petroleum	10,666	29[†]	—	29[†]
21	Occidental Petroleum	Petroleum	9,555	47	5	52
22	Phillips Petroleum	Petroleum	9,503	21	3	24
23	Procter & Gamble	Soaps and cosmetics	9,330	30[†]	1[†]	31[†]
24	Dow Chemical	Chemicals	9,255	51	13	64
25	Union Carbide	Chemicals	9,177	32[†]	5[†]	37[†]
26	United Technologies	Aerospace	9,053	21[†]	16[†]	37[†]
27	International Harvester	Industrial and farm equipment	8,392	21[†‡]	6[†]	27[†]
28	Goodyear Tire &					

EXHIBIT 1-5
(*continued*)

Rank	Firm	Industry	Sales, $US millions	S	X	F/T
	Rubber	Rubber	8,239	36†	—	36†
29	Boeing	Aerospace	8,131			
30	Eastman Kodak	Photographic equipment	8,028	25†‡	13†	38†
33	Caterpillar	Industrial and farm equipment	7,613	18†	30†	48†
34	Union Oil of California	Petroleum	7,568	23	—	23
35	Beatrice Foods	Food	7,468	22†	—	22†
37	Westinghouse Electric	Electrical appliances	7,332	13	12	25
39	R. J. Reynolds Ind.	Tobacco	7,113	23	5	28
40	Xerox	Scientific instruments	7,027	47	—	47
45	Rockwell International	Aerospace	6,466	13	9	22
46	Kraft Incorporated	Food	6,433	28†	—	28†
48	Monsanto	Chemicals	6,193	28†	6†	34†
49	Philip Morris	Tobacco	6,144	19‡	6	25
50	General Foods	Food	5,472	26†	—	26†
51	Minnesota Mining and Manufacturing	Scientific instruments	5,440	39	—	39
53	Firestone Tire and Rubber	Rubber	5,284	35	—	35
54	McDonnell Douglas	Aerospace	5,279			
55	W. R. Grace	Chemicals	5,267	30	—	30
57	PepsiCo. Incorporated	Beverages	5,091	21†	—	21†
59	Coca-Cola	Beverages	4,961	46†	—	46†
60	Deere & Company	Industrial and farm equipment	4,933	18†‡	12	30†
61	Colgate Palmolive	Soaps and cosmetics	4,831	57†	0	57†
66	International Paper	Paper	4,605	22†	6†	28†
67	Ralston Purina Co.	Food	4,601	25†	—	25†
68	TRW, Inc.	Motor vehicles and parts	4,560	30	5	35
69	Allied Chemical Corp.	Chemicals	4,539	20†	8†	28†
71	Weyerhaeuser	Paper	4,423	9	22	31

Definitions: ranking is by sales for 1979, from *Fortune 500*.

Abbreviations: S = sales by subsidiaries, for 1979, as percent of total sales; X = exports by parent firm, for 1979, as percent of total sales; F/T = ratio of foreign (F) to total (T) sales. Rank number: 1979 rank of the MNE in *Fortune*'s "Directory of the 500 Largest U.S. Industrial Corporations."

†Uses information for 1978.

‡The figure reported in the source included exports, which have been deducted in this table to obtain a figure for sales by subsidiaries.

§Was 28 in 1976.

Sources: *Fortune*'s "Directory of the 500 Largest U.S. Industrial Corporations"; Stopford, J. M., J. H. Dunning and K. O. Haberich, *The World Directory of Multinational Enterprises, London: Macmillan, 1980 (for data on F/T).*

EXHIBIT 1-6
IDENTIFICATION OF 50 LARGEST EUROPEAN MNEs

Rank	Firm	Country	Industry	Sales, $US millions	S	X	F/T
1	Royal Dutch-Shell	Netherlands-U.K.	Petroleum	59,417	—	—	—
2	British Petroleum	Britain	Petroleum	38,713	78[b]	7	85
3	Unilever	Netherlands-U.K.	Food products	21,749	33[c]	5	38
4	ENI	Italy	Petroleum	18,985	25[b]	10	35
5	Fiat	Italy	Motor vehicles	18,300	—	—	—
6	Compagnie Française des Pétroles	France	Petroleum	17,305	56[g]	6	62
7	Peugeot-Citroën	France	Motor vehicles	17,270	28[d]	19[d]	47[d]
8	Volkswagenwerk	Germany	Motor vehicles	16,766	22[e,f]	41[g]	63
9	Philips	Netherlands	Electronics, appliances	16,576	91	—	91
10	Régie Nationale des Usines Renault	France	Motor vehicles	16,117	45	40	85[h]
11	Siemens	Germany	Electronics, appliances	15,070	12[b]	39	51
12	Daimler-Benz	Germany	Motor vehicles	14,942	15[e]	38[g]	53
13	Hoechst	Germany	Chemicals	14,785	33[e,f]	34[g]	67
14	Bayer	Germany	Chemicals	14,196	51[b]	20	71
15	BASF	Germany	Chemicals	14,139	20[d]	25[d]	45[d]
18	Thyssen	Germany	Steel and industrial products	13,637	12[b]	35	47
19	Societé Nationale Elf Aquitaine	France	Petroleum	13,386	24[f]	—	—
20	Nestlé	Switzerland	Food products, beverages	13,017	—	—	97
25	Imperial Chemical Industries	Britain	Chemicals	11,391	51	21	72
28	B. A. T. Industries	Britain	Tobacco	9,479	84	3	87
29	Ruhrkohle	Germany	Mining—coal	8,857	—	20[d]	
30	Saint-Gobain-Pont-à-Mousson	France	Building materials, metal products	8,355	50[f]	11	61
32	Compagnie Generale d'Èlectricité	France	Electronics, appliances	8,234	9[d]	28[d]	37[d]
33	Montedison	Italy	Chemicals	8,199	13[d]	28[d]	41[d]
35	Pechiney-Ugine-Kuhlmann	France	Metal refining, aluminum, steel	7,961	25g	27	52
36	Rhône-Poulenc	France	Chemicals	7,944	29g	30	59
38	Petrofina	Belgium	Petroleum	7,827	—	—	—
40	Thomson-Brandt	France	Electronics, Appliances	7,056	8	29	37
41	Friedrich Krupp	Germany	Metal refining—steel; industrial equipment	6,981	10	30[g]	40
44	Mannesmann	Germany	Industrial equipment, metal products	6,825	25[i]	45[g]	70

EXHIBIT 1-6
(*continued*)

Rank	Firm	Country	Industry	Sales, $US millions	S	X	F/T
46	AEG-Telefunken	Germany	Electronics, appliances	6,513	15^b	31	46
47	ESTEL	Netherlands	Metal refining—steel, metal products	6,503	—	—	37^d
49	Schneider	France	Industrial equipment metal refining—steel	6,412	—	—	59
50	British Steel	Britain	Metal refining—steel	6,385	7	18	25
51	DSM	Netherlands	Chemicals	6,359	15^f	44	59
52	BL	Britain	Motor vehicles	6,345	14^b	30	44
53	Michelin	France	Rubber products	6,244	—	—	54^d
55	Akzo Group	Netherlands	Chemicals	5,992	66g	22	88
59	Ciba-Geigy	Switzerland	Chemicals, pharmaceuticals	5,950	64^d	34^d	98^d
60	Robert Bosch	Germany	Motor vehicle parts, electronics, appliances	5,899	13^b	36^j	49
63	Gutehoffnungshutte	Germany	Industrial and transport equipment	5,758	—	44	—
65	Volvo	Sweden	Motor vehicles	5,475	28^b	47	75
67	Rio Tinto-Zinc	Britain	Mining	5,340	68	5	73
68	Brown Boveri	Switzerland	Electrical equipment	5,293	26	74	100^k
73	General Electric Co.	Britain	Industrial equipment, electronics	4,855	21	26	47
81	Metallgesellschaft	Germany	Metal refining, non ferrous	4,244	47	—	—
82	Guest, Keen & Nettlefolds	Britain	Motor vehicle parts	4,161	31	13	44
83	Solvay & Cie SA	Belgium	Chemicals	4,128	—	—	90
89	Salzgitter	Germany	Metal refining—steel; ship building	3,869	—	39	—
90	BSN-Gervais Danone	France	Food products, building materials	3,866	43	—	—

Definitions: ranking is by sales for 1979, from *Fortune 500*. Sales have been converted to U.S. dollars using an exchange rate based on the average rate in the official exchange market during each company's fiscal year, ending December 31, 1979.

Abbreviations: S = sales by all foreign subsidiaries, for 1978, as percent of total sales; X = exports of parent firm, for 1978, as a percent of total sales. Rank number: 1979 Rank of the European MNE in *Fortune's Directory of the 500 Largest Industrial Corporations Outside the U.S.*

[b]The figure reported in the source included exports, which have been deducted in this table to obtain a figure for sales by subsidiaries.

[c]Excludes sales in EEC.

[d]Figures from United Nations, Economic and Social Council. *Transnational Corporations in World Development: A Re-examination* (UN, 1978: 05692), for 1976.

[e]By foreign subsidiaries Welt, i.e., German and foreign majority-owned subsidiaries.

[f]Figure includes all exports; any intragroup exports are therefore included with direct exports (from home country).

[g]Exports Welt.

[h]The F/T ratio may be incorrect, since the UN source identified F/T for 1976 as 45.

[i]By foreign subsidiaries Konzern (net).

[j]Exports (Konzern).

[k]Includes Switzerland (home country).

Sources: Stopford, John M., John H. Dunning, and Klaus O. Haberich, *The World Directory of Multinational Enterprises*, London: Macmillan, 1980; United Nations, Economic and Social Council, *Transnational Corporations in World Development: A Re-examination* (UN, 1978: 05692).

dominate the top ten positions. While the F/T ratios of most U.S. multinationals are below 50 percent, those of the petroleum firms are much higher as a result of the high level of sales by foreign subsidiaries.

Exhibit 1-6 identifies the fifty largest European MNEs. As with the U.S. MNEs, the group is dominated by petroleum and motor vehicle producers. Total sales for the top ten are 38 percent lower than those for the top ten U.S. MNEs. The European MNEs are as multinational as the U.S. MNEs, since their F/T ratios are equally high. Indeed, the frequency of F/T ratios over 50 percent is greater among the European MNEs than it is among the U.S. MNEs.

It can be seen that many of the fifty MNEs in Exhibit 1-6 are German-based. This is not surprising, considering Germany's rapid industrial growth since the end of World War II.

Besides U.S. and European MNEs there has been a remarkable growth of MNEs based in other nations, including small nations such as Canada. However, the most significant development has been the recent emergence of Japanese MNEs. These MNEs are supplementing the traditional Japanese strengths in exporting. Japan's surge in overseas production can be appreciated when it is realized that in the 5-year period from 1975 to 1980, Japanese foreign investment doubled and is expected to quadruple during the 1980s. This remarkable acceleration in investment is helping to reshape the role of international business and trade in the world economic system.

Exhibit 1-7 identifies the twenty largest Japanese MNEs. Japanese MNEs are not as large as American or European MNEs. The largest Japanese MNE, Toyota Motor, had sales of $14,012 million ($US) in 1979, which did not rank it with the top ten MNEs in the United States or Europe. Japanese industry is dominated by motor vehicle and electronics producers and metal-refining processors. In comparison to the largest U.S. and European MNEs, the largest Japanese firms are not as multinational, as shown by their smaller F/T ratios. This is to be expected as Japan is in an expansionary, developmental phase and its firms are just starting the process of becoming multinational, first by exporting (note the low S relative to X) and more recently by foreign direct investment.

Exhibit 1-8 identifies the ten largest Canadian multinational enterprises (those with sales exceeding one billion U.S. dollars). From the data presented, several interesting points can be observed. The high degree of multinationality of these firms is striking. Seven of the ten have F/T ratios greater than 75 percent. This is probably explained by the small size of the Canadian (home) market relative to foreign markets.

In terms of sales, the Canadian MNEs are signficantly smaller than the largest MNEs in the United States, Europe, or Japan. Alcan Aluminum, Canada's largest MNE, does not rank within the top fifty in the United States and ranks well down the European and Japanese lists.

From Exhibit 1-8 it can be seen that the majority of Canadian MNEs are resource based, reflecting Canada's traditional comparative advantage in resource products. In contrast, MNEs based in the United States, Europe, and Japan are more involved in secondary manufacturing and high technology.

EXHIBIT 1-7
IDENTIFICATION OF THE TWENTY LARGEST JAPANESE MNEs

Rank	Firm	Industry	Sales, $US millions	S	X	F/T
17	Toyota Motor	Motor vehicles	14,012	—	35	35
21	Nissan Motor	Motor vehicles	12,652	25	41	66
22	Hitachi	Electronics, appliances	12,633	4	17	21
23	Nippon Steel	Metal refining-steel	12,595	1	31	32
24	Mitsubishi Heavy Industries	Motor vehicles, industrial equipment	11,960	1	33	34
26	Matsushita Electric Industrial	Electronics, appliances	11,128	—	31	31
57	Nippon Kokan	Metal refining—steel	5,971	—	34	34
66	Sumitomo Metal Industries	Metal refining—steel	5,342	3	44	47
70	Honda Motor	Motor vehicles	5,019	—	—	64
74	Kawasaki Steel	Metal refining—steel	4,795	1	36	37
78	Kobe Steel	Metal refining—steel	4,411	14	23	37
85	Ishikawajima-Harima Heavy Industry	Industrial equipment, shipbuilding	4,011	48*	—	48*
87	Nippon Electric	Electronics, appliances	3,943	8	25	33
91	Toyo Kogyo	Motor vehicles	3,860	14	46	60
108	Sanyo Electric	Electronics, appliances	3,414	—	55	55
122	Isuzu Motors	Motor vehicles	3,040	5	34	39
124	Sony	Electronics, appliances	2,973	—	—	59
128	Kawasaki Heavy Industries	Industrial equipment, shipbuilding; transportation equipment	2,875	12	36	48
141	Bridgestone Tire	Rubber products	2,655	7	24	31
150	Komatsu	Industrial and farm equipment	2,557	—	41	41

Definitions: ranking is by sales for 1979, from *Fortune* 500. Sales have been converted to U.S. dollars using an exchange rate based on the average rate in the official exchange market during each company's fiscal year, ending December 31, 1979.

Abbreviations: S = sales by all foreign subsidiaries, for 1976, as percent of total sales; X = exports of parent firm, for 1976, as percent of total sales. Rank number: 1979 rank of the Japanese MNE in *Fortune*'s "Directory of the 500 Largest Industrial Corporations Outside the U.S."

*Figures from Stopford, John M., John H. Dunning, and Klaus O. Haberich, *The World Directory of Multinational Enterprises*, London: Macmillan, 1980.

Sources: *Fortune*, various issues; "Directory of the 500 Largest Industrial Corporations Outside the U.S."; Stopford, John M., John H. Dunning, Klaus O. Haberich, *The World Directory of Multinational Enterprises*, London: Macmillan, 1980; United Nations Economic and Social Council, *Transnational Corporations in World Development: A Re-examination* (UN, 1978: 05692).

Also noteworthy is the ranking of the firms. The tenth largest Canadian MNE is ranked thirty-fourth in the list of large firms in Canada. This spread is explained by the significant number of foreign owned (namely, U.S.) subsidiaries in Canada, many of which are ranked at the top of the Canadian list.

Finally, Exhibit 1-9 reports data on the size, nationality, and industry of the twenty-four largest third world MNEs, that is, those with sales exceeding one

EXHIBIT 1-8
IDENTIFICATION OF THE TEN LARGEST CANADIAN MNEs

Rank	Firm	Industry	Sales, $US millions	S	X	F/T
79	Alcan Aluminum	Metals	4,381	76	6	82*
125	Massey-Ferguson	Farm equipment	2,973	87	7	94*
154	Inco	Metals	2,489	50	40	90*
185	Noranda Mines	Metals	2,121	—	—	75†
216	MacMillan Bloedel	Paper and wood products	1,861	49	31	80*
241	Northern Telecom	Electrical appliances	1,622	41	10	51*
243	Seagram	Beverages	1,608	23	71	94†
266	Moore	Paper and wood products	1,541	91‡	—	91*
313	Domtar	Paper and wood products	1,277	—	—	30
319	Abitibi-Price	Paper and wood products	1,256	15	47	62*

Definitions: ranking is by sales for 1979, from *Fortune 500*. Sales have been converted to U.S. dollars using an exchange rate based on the average rate in the official exchange market during each company's fiscal year, ending December 31, 1979.
  Abbreviations: S = sales by all foreign subsidiaries, for 1978, as percent of total sales; X = exports of parent firm, for 1978, as percent of total sales. Rank number: 1979 rank of the Canadian MNE in *Fortune's* "Directory of the 500 Largest Industrial Corporations Outside the U.S."
  *Figures from Stopford, John M., John H. Dunning, and Klaus O. Haberich, *The World Directory of Multinational Enterprises*, London: Macmillan, 1980; otherwise obtained from annual reports.
  †Figures from Litvak, I. A., and C. J. Maule, *The Canadian Multinationals*, Toronto: Butterworths, 1981.
  ‡Includes exports by subsidiaries.
  Sources: Annual reports.
Stopford, John M., John H. Dunning, and Klaus O. Haberich, *The World Directory of Multinational Enterprises*, London: Macmillan, 1980 (otherwise obtained from annual reports).
Litvak, I. A., and C. J. Maule, *The Canadian Multinationals*, Toronto: Butterworths, 1981.
United Nations Economic and Social Council, *Transnational Corporations in World Development: A Re-examination* (UN, 1978: 05692).
Rugman, Alan M., "Canadian Multinationals and Developing Countries," in *Multinationals and Technology Transfer: The Canadian Experience*, Alan M. Rugman (ed.), New York: Praeger, 1983.

billion U.S. dollars. Excluded from this list are MNEs from the Netherlands Antilles, South Africa, and Israel. Some of the third world MNEs are large; the largest, Petróleos de Venezuela is ranked higher than the largest MNE from either Japan or Canada. It is twenty-ninth on the *Fortune* list of the "Largest Industrial Companies in the World."

The industrial mix of the third world MNEs is a special blend of the other tables thus far presented. Petroleum firms dominate the list with eight of the top eleven firms and ten overall, as they do in the European and U.S. cases. The major difference, however, is that virtually all of these petroleum MNEs are state-owned, whereas only four, all European, are state-owned in Exhibits 1-5 and 1-6. Metal refining is the next-largest category with seven MNEs. This is similar to the Japanese MNEs where firms in metal refining are the dominant group along with motor vehicles and electronics. Finally, there are four mining MNEs similar to the structure of the resource-based Canadian MNEs. The remaining third world MNEs are diversified.

EXHIBIT 1-9
IDENTIFICATION OF THE TWENTY-FOUR LARGEST THIRD WORLD MULTINATIONALS

Rank	Firm	Industry	Country	Sales, $US millions
16	Petróleos de Venezuela	Petroleum	Venezuela	14,116
27	Petrobrás	Petroleum	Brazil	10,279
39	Pemex	Petroleum	Mexico	7,279
80	Hyundai Group	Shipbuilding, transportation	South Korea	4,304
84	YPF	Petroleum	Argentina	4,118
93	Kuwait National Petroleum	Petroleum	Kuwait	3,832
104	Indian Oil	Petroleum	India	3,533
109	Samsung Group	Food products, industrial equipment, electronics, textiles	South Korea	3,410
119	Chinese Petroleum	Petroleum	Taiwan	3,098
142	Haci Omer Sabanci Holding	Textiles	Turkey	2,629
165	Korea Oil	Petroleum	South Korea	2,316
190	CODELCO-CHILE	Mining, metal refining—copper	Chile	2,071
211	Zambia Industrial & Mining	Mining, metal refining—copper	Zambia	1,886
227	Lucky Group	Petroleum, electronics, appliances	South Korea	1,760
228	Steel Authority of India	Metal refining—steel	India	1,758
253	Koç Holding	Motor vehicles, electronics	Turkey	1,570
258	Hyosung Group	Textiles, motor vehicles	South Korea	1,558
262	Philippine National Oil	Petroleum	Philippines	1,547
271	GECAMINES	Mining—copper, cobalt, zinc	Zaire	1,495
285	Vale do Rio Doce	Mining—iron	Brazil	1,409
299	Grupe Industrial Alpha	Metal refining—steel, chemicals	Mexico	1,324
321	Pohang Iron and Steel	Metal refining—steel	South Korea	1,250
334	KUKjE (ICC)	Rubber, metal refining—steel	South Korea	1,189
374	Siderúrgica Nacional	Metal refining—steel	Brazil	1,105

Source: Fortune, "The Fortune International 500," August 1980.

Thirteen countries are represented by the third world MNEs. However, eight have only single representatives, and these are in resources with five in petroleum and three in mining. South Korea predominates on the list with seven entries. South Korean MNEs are diversified as a group and individually and resemble the industrial mix of Japan's top twenty MNEs.

It will be extremely interesting to observe the future growth of these types of third world MNEs. They may either become vehicles for the development of their home nations or they may be subjected to greater competitive rivalry from the MNEs of the advanced nations.

SUMMARY

While many forms of international business activity exist, the focus of this text is the multinational enterprise. The MNE is distinguished from a domestic corporation by its ability to operate across national boundaries. This ability is necessitated by the existence of market imperfections. The success of the MNE in overcoming market imperfections by their operations across national boundaries is one of the major issues addressed in the book.

Another important theme is the efficient management of the MNE. This leads to practical guidelines for the operation of the four functional areas of the MNE: marketing, finance, production, and human resources. In order to understand the concept of efficiency in international business management, it is necessary to study both the internal factors affecting the MNE and the environment in which it operates.

A number of methods are used to classify MNEs. The method used here is the F/T ratio, which expresses multinationality as the ratio of foreign (F) to total (T) operations. The type of operations in which MNEs are involved is FDI, in which control over the foreign subsidiary is maintained by the MNE.

An examination of world trade and investment reveals that the United States is not only the largest foreign investor, but that it is also host to more FDI than any other country and holds the largest share of world trade. Recently, however, this dominant position has been eroded, and the positions of West Germany and Japan have improved rapidly.

International trade and investment are now dominated by MNEs. Indeed, a limited number of MNEs control the majority of foreign investment. Petroleum and motor vehicle producers tend to hold the top-ranking positions for both U.S. and European MNEs. In addition to the high-ranking U.S. and European MNEs, attention will be paid in this book to rapid growth of MNEs in small nations such as Canada and Japan.

KEY WORDS

Multinational enterprise (MNE)	Ethnocentric
F/T ratio	Polycentric
Portfolio investment	Geocentric
Foreign direct investment (FDI)	Country-specific factors
Market imperfections	Degree of multinationality
Internalization	

QUESTIONS

1 Identify the differences which exist between domestic business and international business. Distinquish between exogenous and endogenous variables and give examples of each. In what ways can a businessperson prepare for a career in international business management?

2 What is the essence of multinationality, as described in this chapter? Elaborate upon the several definitions which exist for an MNE. In your answer, describe how Perlmutter's managerial types enter into the definition of an MNE.

3 Describe the changing nature of FDI in the United States. In your answer, discuss the growth of FDI from countries such as Japan and West Germany. What factors have contributed to this growth? What new patterns are emerging in FDI?

4 The world's largest multinationals have been outlined in Exhibits 1-5 to 1-9. Describe why they are MNEs. In your answer, draw on the data given and also on the other definitions of an MNE. What are some possible explanations for the differences among Canadian, U.S., and Japanese MNEs?

Exercise: Look up Fortune's Annual directory of the largest 1000 U.S. industrial corporations in the May issues and the largest non-U.S. industrial corporations in the August issues. Pick several of the largest 100 U.S. and non-U.S. firms, and find out if they are MNEs. To do this you may need to refer to the annual reports of the companies concerned or a good company directory, in order to calculate the F/T ratio or another indicator of multinationality.

CHAPTER 2

INTERNATIONAL TRADE

THE IMPORTANCE OF INTERNATIONAL TRADE

This chapter examines two fundamental questions of international business: (1) what factors determine the extent, composition, sources, and destination of trade and (2) what the effects of trade are on exporting and importing firms and on the world at large. The initial analysis of these questions is at the macro level; the implications for firms engaged in exporting and importing and those that compete with imports are described later in the chapter. The objective of this chapter is to foster an understanding of international trade from the viewpoint of an international manager.

An understanding of the determinants and effects of international trade is important for managers. International trade is a vital component of the economies of all countries. The expansion of trade is related to the economic growth of nations and the world economy itself. Trade leads to structural shifts in the economic organization of countries, and this provides new opportunities to firms, workers, and consumers. In short, the ability of a nation to seize export opportunities and respond to imports is a major determinant of its national economic performance.

International trade is usually the first phase of international operations of a firm. Trade then leads to other modes of international operation: joint ventures, foreign direct investment (FDI), and licensing. The value of world trade far outpaces that of the other modes of international operations. Total world trade was almost $4 *trillion* in 1981 compared to a flow of FDI of about $40 *billion* (on a stock of $500 billion). During the postwar period, world trade expanded continuously in value and volume. Only in 1981 did international trade begin to decline. This was a consequence of the world economic recession and the new protectionist policies being adopted in many countries. Until this situation is reversed, the economies of all trading nations, and the fortunes of individual firms within them, will continue to decline.

It is important for nations, individuals, and firms to understand the basis of trade. Everyone has a stake in world trade, and it is necessary to respond constructively, not destructively, to changes in the world trade environment. The analysis of trade contained in this chapter can help the reader to develop an understanding of the determinants of trade flows in the real world and of the gains and losses that trade brings to nations and firms.

Trade theory is also important since it forms one of the conceptual pillars on which this book builds the theory and practice of international business. In a world with full information, perfect competition, and no barriers to trade, international business would require only a study of international trade and international capital movements. Foreign direct investment and licensing would not arise as modes of international operations. To the extent that the real world differs from the stylized model of free trade and perfect competition developed here, FDI and licensing become important methods of operating internationally.

When trade does not occur as a result of such natural market imperfections as transaction costs or artificially created barriers (such as tariffs), opportunities arise for international managers to benefit from FDI and contractual arrangements. Conversely, when economic conditions move toward freer trade and perfect competition, international trade becomes the more efficient method of operating internationally. Examples of such trends in international business abound.

Recently, Japanese trading companies have increased their direct investments in the United States and Europe in response to increasing trade protection (of both the tariff and nontariff type). Some U.S. multinational enterprises have withdrawn from foreign direct investments in response to the erosion of their competitive positions [such as firm-specific advantages (FSAs) in proprietary technology]. International trade, therefore, is an integral part of international business. An understanding of the forces that drive and distort trade is fundamental for international business operations.

This chapter develops models that explain the basis and effects of trade. It starts with the earliest and simplest theories of trade and moves toward more recent and more realistic models. The older models of trade are included since many government policy and business decisions are formulated (often unwittingly) in relation to such theories. This can lead to questionable government policies and inefficient business decisions.

Chapter 3 introduces tariffs and nontariff barriers to trade into the model of trade. It illustrates their effects on national welfare, efficiency, and business decisions. Chapter 10 describes and analyzes the international organizations that influence world trade and international business.

THEORIES OF TRADE

Theory of Mercantilism

The system of mercantilism prevailed in Europe during the seventeenth and eighteenth centuries when modern nation states were beginning to develop. The logic of the mercantilistic theory of trade is as follows. The power and strength of a nation, and especially its government, increase as the nation's wealth increases. The wealth of a nation (and its rulers) increases as the amount of gold it possesses increases. Exports increase a nation's gold stock as they generate inflows of gold, while imports reduce the gold stock as gold is lost to the nation. Mercantilists conclude that exports are "good" and should be promoted while imports are "bad" and should be impeded. According to this theory, the state is much like an individual whose well-being and power increase with wealth, where wealth is decreased by spending (imports) and increased by revenues (exports).

Support for the mercantilistic view of the world was not difficult to find. Rulers without gold could not pay soldiers to enforce their positions against the many internal or external usurpers that beset them. Nations without gold could neither fend off foreign attack nor press their national interests beyond their borders. Gold was the mechanism used to mobilize real resources to protect and extend the nation's interests.

Additional support for the mercantilistic system, and policies based on this theory, was found in the impact of trade on domestic production and employment. Exports demonstrably increased domestic production and provided jobs for domestic workers while imports were seen to replace domestic production and force workers out of jobs. Trade policy was designed to maximize the interest of the state rather than of particular groups within society.

Arguments against mercantilism, based on the impossibility of all nations simultaneously pursuing export promotion and import restriction policies, were thrust aside. It was thought that since strong individuals and businesses could increase their wealth by producing and selling more, strong nations should do the same. The wealth of weak, stupid, or profligate nations would decline. The mercantilistic theory was thus produced by and supportive of the political economy of the times.

Mercantilistic thinking persists today in less extreme terms. Countries that consistently import more than they export and deplete their reserves of gold (foreign exchange) find themselves in a weak position, at the mercy of foreign powers, banks, and sometimes foreign troops. Examples of such countries are Mexico, Poland, Argentina, and Brazil. Their economies lie in shambles for want of foreign exchange; they are forced to follow economic policies dictated from abroad, and their leaders face diminished political support or even forced resignation.

A notable example of recent mercantilistic policy is found in France under the leadership of General Charles de Gaulle. In an effort to wrest world economic leadership and power away from the United States, de Gaulle instituted policies to increase French exports and impede imports, especially of American products.

He further insisted that the payments deficit of the United States with France be paid in gold. This mercantilistic policy has been followed, to a lesser degree, by de Gaulle's successors.

What, then, is wrong with mercantilistic trade theory and policy? Two fallacies lie at the center of the mercantilistic theory. It is incorrect to believe that gold, or any other asset, has a value in and of itself. Gold, or other assets, has value only when it is used or traded for other consumption or production goods.[1] If a nation exchanges productive assets and consumption goods in order to accumulate gold, it is decreasing its productive capacity and national welfare in exchange for an idle resource, that is, a product that cannot be consumed or used in production.

The second and more telling fallacy in the mercantilistic theory lies in its failure to recognize the potential gains in economic welfare (efficiency) that arise from the comparative advantage (specialization) of using the nation's resources in the most efficient manner. Even if the objective of a nation were to increase its gold stock, an emphasis on exporting and import substitution is the wrong policy prescription. At any one point in time, a nation has a limited stock of human, capital, technological, and natural resources.[2] If a nation allocates these resources inefficiently, its economic well-being is less than optimal since resources are diverted from more efficient to less efficient uses.

An extreme example (yet one that actually happened) can be cited. When Canada fostered the development of a domestic pineapple industry, it diverted land, labor, and capital from more efficient uses elsewhere. For these pineapples to be marketed in Canada, pineapples from abroad had to be excluded. Canada would have been better off if the resources devoted to pineapple production had been diverted to the production of wheat in which that country has a comparative advantage. Some of this wheat could have been exported in exchange for more than a sufficient quantity of pineapples. We move on to explain the reasons for this in the next sections.

Arguments against mercantilistic theory and policy, similar to the one above, were advanced by the classical economists Adam Smith and David Ricardo. Smith argued that the consumption of real goods could be increased by free trade and that the accumulation of gold for its own sake was pointless. These concepts are explained by Smith's theory of absolute advantage.[3]

Theory of Absolute Advantage

The concept of absolute advantage is intuitively appealing. It states that by specializing in the production of the good at which a nation is most efficient, the nation can increase its welfare through international trade.

---

[1]Gold can potentially be used as a medium of exchange or as a store of value, but these uses depend on its value in terms of other productive goods.

[2]The case in which resources expand over time and the expansion which is influenced by trade are discussed later in the chapter.

[3]Adam Smith, *An Inquiry into the Nature and Cause of the Wealth of Nations*, London, 1776.

A simple example illustrates this point. Let us assume that two nations, North and South, are both able to produce two goods, cloth and grain. Assume further that labor is the only scarce factor of production and hence the only cost of production.

LABOR COST (HOURS) OF PRODUCTION FOR ONE UNIT

	Cloth	Grain
North	10	20
South	20	10

Note that a nation is doing well if it has a *low* number of labor-hours per unit of production, as these represent *costs* of production. It is clear that North has an absolute advantage in the production of cloth, since the cost requires only 10 labor-hours, compared to 20 labor-hours in South. Similarly, South has an absolute advantage in the production of grain which it produces at a cost of 10 labor-hours, compared to 20 labor-hours in North.

Both countries gain by trade. If they specialize and exchange cloth for grain at a relative price ratio of 1:1, North can employ more of its resources to produce cloth, and South, more of its resources to produce grain. North can import one unit of grain in exchange for one unit of cloth, thereby "paying," in effect, only 10 labor-hours for one unit of grain. If it had produced the grain itself, North would have used 20 labor-hours, so it gains 10 labor-hours from the trade. In a similar fashion South gains from trade when it imports one unit of cloth in exchange for the export of one unit of grain. The effective cost to South for one unit of cloth is only the 10 labor-hours required to make its one unit of grain.

The theory of absolute advantage, as originally formulated, does not predict the exchange ratio between cloth and grain once trade is opened, nor does it resolve the division of the gains from trade between the two countries. The example assumed an international price ratio of 1:1, but this ratio (P_{cloth} to P_{grain}) could lie between 2:1 (the pretrade price ratio in South) and 1:2 (the pretrade price ratio in North). For determination of the relative price ratio under trade, the total resources of each country (total labor-hours available per year) and the tastes of each country must be known. In turn, this determines the relative gains from trade for each country.

Recent work incorporating each country's relative preference in the consumption of cloth or grain, has shown that the larger one country is relative to the other, the greater is the likelihood of the after-trade price ratio approaching the pretrade price ratio of the larger country. In this situation, the gains from trade are smaller for the larger country.[4]

Even this simple model of absolute advantage has several dramatic implications. First, there are unambiguous gains from trade provided there are different costs of production for cloth and grain in the two countries before trade. Second, the more a country is able to specialize in the production of the good it produces

[4]Hauthakker's results on this were published in 1976.

relatively efficiently, the greater are its potential gains in national welfare. This conclusion is in direct contradiction to the mercantilistic theory. Third, if the objective of a country were to accumulate gold, its best strategy would still be to trade freely, but then for the government to tax away the gains from trade (in the form of cloth and wheat) and exchange these goods for gold. Fourth, *within* one country the gains from trade are rarely evenly distributed by the competitive market. This last implication is illustrated by the following example.

Prior to trade, if grain producers in North worked 20 hours, they would produce one unit of grain that could be exchanged for two units of cloth. After trade, the grain producers who remain can exchange only one unit of grain for *one* unit of cloth. The remaining grain producers are worse off under trade. Cloth producers in North, however, work 10 hours, produce one unit of cloth and exchange it for one unit of grain, whereas previously they received only a half unit of grain. They are better off. If grain producers in North switch to cloth production, their 20 hours of labor results in production of two units of cloth, which they can exchange for two units of grain. They are better off under international trade. As long as North does not specialize completely in cloth, there will be gainers (cloth producers and also grain producers who switched to cloth) and losers, those who continue as grain producers.

Since the nation as a whole benefits from trade, the gainers could compensate the losers, and there would still be a surplus to be distributed in some way. If compensation does not take place, however, the losers (continuing grain producers) have an incentive to try to prevent the country from opening itself up to trade. This problem, which the model of absolute advantage highlights, has plagued attempts by government to move toward a free trade policy by reducing barriers to trade.

A more complicated picture of the determinants and effects of trade emerges when one of the trading partners has an absolute advantage in the production of both goods. Trade under these conditions still brings gains, as David Ricardo first demonstrated in his theory of comparative advantage.[5]

Theory of Comparative Advantage

Ricardo's model is useful in illustrating the gains from trade from comparative advantage. In terms of our previous example of two countries, North and South, and two commodities, cloth and grain, Ricardo's model can be illustrated as follows:

LABOR COST (HOURS) OF PRODUCTION FOR ONE UNIT

	Cloth	Grain
North	50	100
South	200	200

[5]David Ricardo, *Principles of Political Economy*, London, 1817.

In this example North has an absolute advantage in the production of both cloth and grain, so it would appear at first sight that trade is unprofitable, or at least that incentives for exchange no longer exist. Yet trade is still advantageous to both nations, provided the *relative* costs of production differ in the two countries.

Before trade, in North one unit of cloth costs (50/100) hours of grain, so one unit of cloth can be exchanged for one half unit of grain. In North, the price of cloth is half the price of grain. In South one unit of cloth costs (200/200) hours of grain or one grain unit. In South the price of cloth equals the price of grain. If North can import more than a half unit of grain for one unit of cloth, it will gain from trade. Similarly, if South can import one unit of cloth for less than one unit of grain, it will also gain from trade. These *relative* price ratios set the boundaries for trade. Trade is profitable between price ratios (price of cloth to price of grain) of 0.5 and 1.

For example, at an international price ratio of two-thirds, North gains from trade. It can import one unit of grain in return for exporting one and a half units of cloth. Because it costs North only 50 hours of labor to produce the unit of cloth, its effective cost under trade for one unit of imported grain is 75 labor-hours. Under pretrade conditions it costs North 100 labor-hours to produce one unit of grain. Similarly, South gains from trade. It imports one unit of cloth in exchange for two-thirds units of grain. Prior to trade, South spent 200 labor-hours to produce the one unit of cloth. Through trade its effective cost for one unit of cloth is (2/3 × 200), that is 133 labor-hours—cheaper than the domestic production cost of 200 labor-hours. Under these conditions, North will tend to specialize in the production of cloth and South will tend to specialize in the production of grain.

This example leads to a general principle. There are gains from trade whenever the *relative* price ratios of two goods differ under international exchange from what they would be under conditions of no trade. Such domestic conditions are often called *autarky*. Free trade is superior to autarky. Trade provides greater economic output and consumption to the trade partners jointly as they specialize in production, exporting the good in which they have a comparative advantage and importing the good in which they have a comparative disadvantage.

The general conclusions of the theory of comparative advantage are the same as those for the theory of absolute advantage. In addition, the theory of comparative advantage demonstrates that countries jointly benefit from trade (under the assumptions of the model) even if one country has an absolute advantage in the production of *both* goods. Total world efficiency and consumption increase under free trade.

As with the theory of absolute advantage (as formulated by Adam Smith), Ricardo's theory of comparative advantage does not answer the question of the distribution of gains between the two countries, nor the distribution of gains and losses between grain producers and cloth producers within each country. No country will *lose* under free trade; that is, no country's overall welfare is decreased, or else it would not trade, but in theory at least, all the gains could accrue to one country and to only one group within that country.

The concept of efficiency and its application to international trade can now be explored in a more formal model of the gains from trade.

GAINS FROM TRADE

Efficiency in a Nation

Nations are complex organizations. Thousands of business, economic, financial, marketing, and human resource decisions are made at any point in time. To simplify the great mass of behavioral and economic decisions that affect business activity, it is convenient to reduce these factors into two categories: production and consumption. This yields a simplified model of the real world which is easy to understand and useful for analytical purposes.

The production side of each nation's business represents all goods and services extracted, processed, manufactured, and distributed by members of its society. It is the supply side of the economy. The other category of a nation's business is the demand side and represents the consumption of all the output coming from the supply side. The individual tastes and preferences of all the consumers in the nation are represented on the demand side.

Equilibrium quantities and prices of all consumption and production are set by the competitive market system, where the invisible hand of Adam Smith guides the allocation of resources and the distribution of output and consumption in the most efficient manner. As will be seen later, a similar optimal situation can be achieved when firms use their internal markets to overcome imperfections in their external markets for factors of production and goods and services. Chandler has called the act of making a market within a firm the visible hand.[6]

At this time it is not necessary to pursue the subject of internal markets or its application to multinational enterprises as exemplified in the theory of internalization. This topic is discussed in Chapters 5 and 6. Instead, we shall revert to the situation of a Smithian laissez-faire, free-market, capitalist system. To be specific, the remainder of this chapter is based on the assumption that a nation allocates factors of production and distributes goods and services through competitive markets in an efficient manner. This simplification of the complex production and consumption sides of a nation's economy is necessary for purposes of exposition. Trade theorists have extended this basic model to incorporate more complex and realistic assumptions, but the basic thrust of their reasoning remains the same, as do the conclusions of their models.

The major purpose of this section is to demonstrate that once a nation is achieving efficient output and consumption, it is usually feasible and beneficial for the nation to increase its welfare through trade. Under trade each nation specializes according to its comparative advantage, as discussed earlier. A country is encouraged to specialize by the attractive prices being offered for its export good

---

[6]Alfred D. Chandler, Jr., *The Visible Hand*, Harvard University Press, 1977.

if international prices (the terms of trade) differ from the relative prices of the goods in a nontrade situation.

With no trade, the relative prices of goods in each country usually differ as a result of different resource bases, levels of income, preferences among goods, and production technologies in each nation. Autarkic relative prices always differ between countries; thus gains from trade are possible. The theories of Smith and Ricardo support this conclusion in a world in which labor is the only factor of production and there are constant returns to scale. (For instance, in North laborers can produce one unit of cloth with 50 hours of labor or a half unit of grain with the same labor-hours, regardless of the level of output.) The neoclassical model of trade can be extended to incorporate multiple factors of production, decreasing returns to scale, and multiple outputs.[7] In the simple form discussed here the model assumes two factors of production (capital and labor), decreasing returns to scale, and two outputs (e.g., grain and cloth). This simple model incorporates difficult concepts, but the insights revealed about the gains from trade are worth the effort.

The Closed Economy

Figure 2-1 is a basic graphical description of efficient production in a closed economy. It is a theoretical simplification of a complex economic system, but one which is useful in introducing the principle of efficiency. The theoretical model can be extended from a closed to an open (trading) economy, a procedure which illustrates in a dramatic manner that there are gains from trade.

In Figure 2-1 the two axes are labeled X and Y. These represent quantities of the two goods (or services) produced by the nation. To make the analysis intuitively more appealing, it is perhaps convenient to consider X as representing agricultural-type goods, such as grain, and Y as representing manufactured goods, such as cloth.

The production possibilities frontier is bounded by TT'. This transformation frontier shows the outer limits of combinations of both goods X and Y that can be produced in this economy. For example, if the country were to specialize completely in the production of agricultural goods, it would produce OT' of good X and none of good Y. Alternatively, this society could devote all its resources to the production of good Y, in which case it would produce OT of Y and no X. More realistically, an economy will produce some combination of goods X and Y. If it is efficient, it will produce somewhere along the TT' transformation frontier.

The production possibilities frontier TT' is bowed outward from the origin in Figure 2-1 according to the assumption that there are decreasing returns to scale in production of both X and Y. Note that as the production combination moves from OT toward OT', increasing amounts of Y must be given up in order to produce the

---

[7]The model can be extended to constant and increasing returns to scale. The implications of these more complex models concerning these effects of trade are similar to the ones presented here.

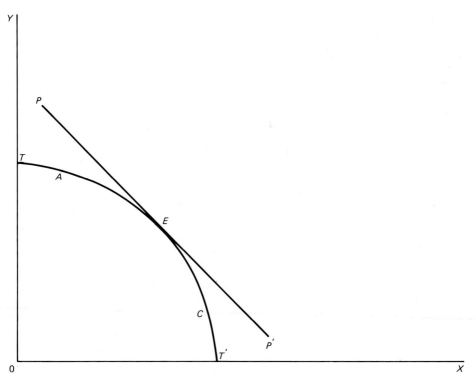

FIGURE 2-1
Output in a closed economy. The production possibilities curve *TT'* is the boundary for efficient combinations of products of goods *X* and *Y*. The price line *PP'* is tangent to it at point *E*.

same increase in output of X. This means that the opportunity cost of producing more X increases as the economy moves from T to T' by increasing production of X at the expense of reducing production of Y. The slope of the production possibility frontier TT' is the marginal rate of transformation of Y into X, the MRT_{YX}.

If the economy is efficient, it will operate somewhere along TT' since to the left of TT' output of both X and Y can be increased. The economy cannot produce combinations of X and Y to the right of TT'. The position along TT' at which the economy operates is determined by the relative prices of X and Y in the market. This conclusion can be illustrated by a simple example. Suppose that $P_X = 1$ and $P_Y = 2$ ($P_X/P_Y = \frac{1}{2}$). If the economy is at point A, firms can increase production of X by four units but must decrease production of Y by one unit, that is, $MRT_{XY} = \frac{1}{4}$. At point A, firms could increase total revenue by reducing production of Y by one unit, thereby enabling them to increase production of X by four units:

$$
\begin{aligned}
\Delta R &= \Delta Q_X P_X + \Delta Q_Y P_Y \\
&= 4 \times 1 + (-1)\,(2) = 2
\end{aligned}
$$

As firms move to seize this opportunity to increase profits, output of X would increase and output of Y decrease and the economy would move toward point E along TT'. Similarly, if the economy were at point C where $MRT = 4$, firms would find it profitable to increase production of Y and reduce that of X.

In a competitive market economy, the relative prices of the goods in the market determine how much of each good will be produced. The efforts of individual firms in the market to increase profits will lead the economy to produce at point E, producing X_E of X and Y_E of Y. Note that at point E the $MRT_{YX} = P_X/P_Y$; that is, the slope of the production possibilities frontier equals the ratio P_X to P_Y. At point E the domestic price line PP' is tangent to TT'.

In the stylized world of the model, consumers are able to maximize their welfare. They do this by using information on their tastes, subject to the constraints of their income levels and of the relative prices of X and Y in the market. The generalized tastes (preferences) of consumers for combinations of X and Y can be represented by social indifference curves as in Figure 2-2. Consumers are

FIGURE 2-2
Consumption in a closed economy. Only one of the set of social indifference curves is tangent to price line PP'. This is indifference curve I_1I_1', which is tangent at point E. There is a higher level of social welfare achieved at E than at either points F or D, as these both lie on a lower social indifference curve.

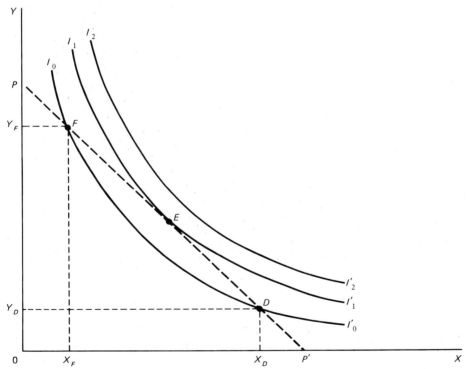

equally satisfied when they are consuming combinations of X and Y along any indifference curve, such as I_0I_0'. For example, they are indifferent to consuming at point D (OX_D, OY_D) compared to point F (OX_F, OY_F). Yet at point E on I_1I_1', consumers are better off than on any point on the former curve, I_0I_0'. If consumers have fixed income G they can consume any quantity of X and Y to the left of price line PP' such that:

$$G \geqslant P_X X + P_Y Y$$

Note that all the indifference curves are negatively sloped and are bowed toward the origin. This shape reflects a diminishing marginal rate of substitution, indicating that the rate at which consumers are willing to substitute more of one good for less of another diminishes as more of one good is consumed relative to the other. To use an example, if my consumption of grain is high, but I have very few clothes, then I will be willing to give up more grain to obtain clothes than when I am starving but have many clothes. The marginal rate of substitution of Y for X (MRS_{YX}) in consumption is the slope of an indifference curve such as I_1I_1'. As more X is consumed relative to Y along I_1I_1', the MRS decreases.

Consumers with limited incomes can consume any amounts of X and Y provided the sum of the price times quantity combination is less than or equal to this limit:

$$P_X Q_X + P_Y Q_Y \leqslant \text{Income}$$

The line PP' in Figure 2-2 represents the prices which would be charged for all combinations of quantities of production of X and Y, given no production possibilities limitations. The slope PP' is P_X/P_Y. In order to maximize their satisfaction, consumers would select the combination of X and Y which lies on the indifference curve furthest from the origin but is also equal to their income. This is the point of tangency of PP' and I_1I_1'. At this point they will consume quantity X_E of good X and quantity Y_E of good Y. They cannot afford to consume on I_2I_2' and can have more satisfaction than on I_0I_0'. Thus a point of equilibrium is reached at point E, where the $MRS = P_X/P_Y$.

The total nature of the (closed) economy is now apparent. Figure 2-3 combines the production frontier TT' and the consumers' indifference curves. Given the production possibilities of the economy and its social indifference curves, consumers will maximize satisfaction at point E. Producers will also maximize profits at point E, which is the most efficient situation for producers and consumers of this nation. If the economy were at A, either producers or consumers, or both, would find that the prevailing price ratio allows them to be better off by moving to E as consumers demand more X and less Y (bidding up P_X relative to P_Y) and producers produce more X and less Y in response to the change in relative price. Only at E does $MRS = MRT = P_X/P_Y$ for the closed economy. Efficiency in both production and consumption is maximized.

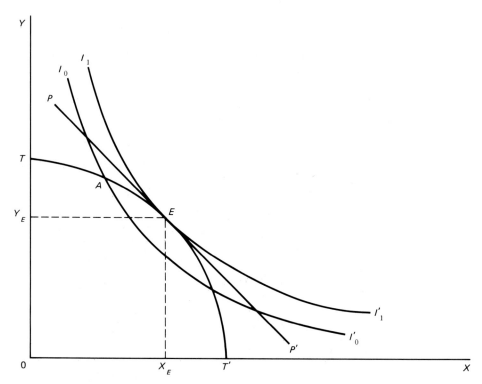

FIGURE 2-3
Output and consumption in a closed economy. Both production and consumption are maximized
in this model at point E. Here production possibilities curve TT′ is tangent to the highest available social indifference curve I_1I_1'. At E the optimal domestic price line is PP′.

The Open Economy

This same nation can experience a gain from trade. This gain occurs whenever the
international price line has a slope different from that of the domestic price line.
For simplicity let us assume that the nation being studied is a small country, so that
its internal prices are fixed, that is, are "set exogenously," as economists say. We
shall also concentrate, for the time being, on the "real," that is, the nonmonetary
side of the economy; thus exchange rates are not considered. They are introduced
later in Chapter 8 when we discuss the international financial environment.

When the nation opens itself up to trade, it faces international prices $P_W P_W'$ as
in Figure 2-4. Domestic firms produce to maximize profits given these international prices, and consumers simultaneously maximize their satisfaction in relation to these prices, just as both groups did in the closed economy. Producers
now produce at point $J(X_J,Y_J)$, and consumers consume at point $K(X_K,Y_K)$.
With free trade $MRT = MRS = P^T{}_X/P^T{}_Y$ as before, and the economy is efficient
in production and consumption. But the society as a whole is better off (because

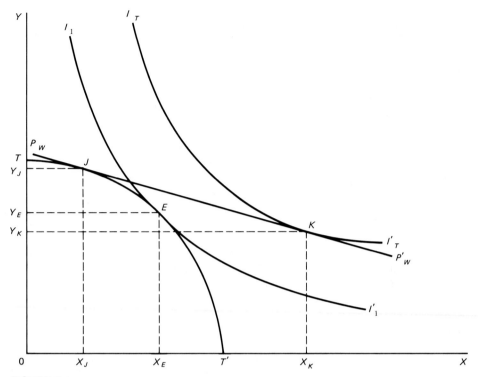

FIGURE 2-4
Efficient production and consumption in an open economy facing international prices. Before trade, the economy produces at E (X_E, Y_E) with welfare $I_1 I_1'$. Under trade with a new world price $P_W P_W'$, the economy produces at J and consumes at K. It exports $Y_J - Y_K$ and imports $X_K - X_J$. Welfare is increased to $I_T I_T'$.

$I_T I_T'$ is above $I_1 I_1'$). The nation's producers are still on TT' (as they must be), but consumers have moved above it. How can this be? Essentially, the nation trades the good for which it has a comparative advantage (good Y) for goods in which it is at a comparative disadvantage (good X) at international prices. The nation produces Y_J of Y, consumes Y_K, and exports $Y_J - Y_K$. It produces X_J of X, consumes X_K, and imports $X_K - X_J$. Trade is in balance:

$$\text{Exports} \quad = \quad \text{Imports}$$
$$P_Y(Y_J - Y_K) \ = \ P_X(X_K - X_J)$$

In this model, *if* a nation's exports and imports do not affect world prices (P_X/P_Y is fixed), it will always gain from opening itself up to free trade. This conclusion is true *regardless* of the shape of the production frontier (as long as it is bowed away from the origin), the tastes of consumers (provided their indifference curves are bowed toward the origin), or relative international prices (so long as they are fixed and differ from those of the nation before trade). This result is both powerful and useful for managers and others involved in trade.

The model can also be used to demonstrate the gainers and losers in an economy when it opens itself to trade. In the example in the preceding paragraph, producers of Y, the exported good, will receive higher profits from the higher prices they receive for X. Conversely, producers of X will lose and some will go out of business and become producers of Y (possibly at lower profits). Workers in the X and Y industries will similarly be affected. Consumers will face higher prices for Y relative to X after trade. Those who value Y highly relative to X will suffer a loss of consumer surplus.

A simple extension of this basic model can be used to show which product will be imported and which will be exported. This analysis was developed by the Norwegian economist Eli Heckscher and his student Bertin Ohlin (a Nobel Prize winner in 1977).[8] Consider two countries, North and South, which produce two products, X and Y, using two factors of production, capital and labor. Assume that the production of Y is relatively more capital intensive than the production of X and that North has relatively abundant capital resources while South is relatively labor abundant. For simplicity, assume that the people of North and South have the same tastes. Such a "world economy" is represented in Figure 2-5. The shapes of North and South's production possibility frontiers reflect the factor endowments of the nations. They show that North could potentially produce more Y than could South (since production of Y is capital-intensive and North is capital-abundant) and South could potentially produce more X than North.

Prior to trade, North produces and consumes at point C and South at point D. Pretrade, the price of X relative to Y is higher in North than in South. (Why is this true?) With free trade the international price line is $P_W P_W'$, and both countries have moved to the same higher indifference curve at point E. North has expanded production of Y by producing at point F, and South has expanded production of X by producing at point G. North exports Y in exchange for imports of X from South.

This simple diagram leads to an important conclusion: under free trade, each country exports the product that uses intensively its relatively abundant factor and imports the product that uses intensively its relatively scarce factor. This is the Heckscher-Ohlin theorem. In North, producers and workers in capital-intensive industry Y will gain relatively and absolutely compared to producers and workers in the X sector.

The implications of this model can be extended even further if several assumptions are made about the production technology of X and Y and the economies and tastes in North and South.[9] Wolfgang Stolter and Paul Samuelson showed in 1941:

---

[8] Eli F. Heckscher, "The Effects of Foreign Trade on the Distribution of Income," *Economisc Tidskrift*, 1919; Bertin Ohlin, *Interregional and International Trade,* Harvard University Press, 1933.

[9] In order for this model to be theoretically correct, the following assumptions must be made: a country produces two goods using two factors of production; neither good is an input for the other; competition prevails; factor supplies are given, no factor is unemployed, and factors are mobile between industry; one good is labor-intensive and the other capital-intensive; and opening trade changes the relative prices of the two goods.

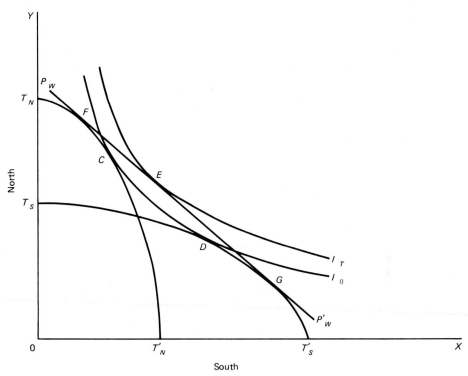

FIGURE 2-5
Determinants of trade and income distribution. Before trade, the capital-abundant country (North) produces at C (relatively more of the capital-intensive good Y) and the labor-abundant country (South) produces at D (relatively more of labor-intensive good X). Pretrade, both countries have welfare I_0. After trade, North produces at F, imports good X, and exports good Y. After trade, South produces at G, imports goods Y, and exports good X. Welfare has risen to I_T for both nations.

Moving from no trade to free trade unambiguously raises the returns to the factor of production used intensively in the exported product and lowers returns to the factor used intensively in the imported product.[10]

In the preceding example, owners of capital in North will receive higher returns after trade (and labor lower wages) while in South capital owners will receive lower returns and labor higher wages. This conclusion is intuitively appealing. North is essentially exporting capital embodied in Y, thereby decreasing the supply of capital relative to labor. This increases the price of capital and lowers the price (wages) of labor. The reverse is true for South.

[10]Wolfgang F. Stolter and Paul A. Samuelson, "Protection and Real Wages," *Review of Economic Studies* (November 1941).

In the late 1940s, Samuelson extended these results (with additional simplifying assumptions) and found that:

Free trade will equalize not only the prices of the traded goods, but all factor prices as well, i.e., under free trade the returns to capital, and land and all wage rates will be the same in all countries.[11]

From this analysis of the winners and losers under free trade (in these simplified models), the *central* conclusion of the analysis bears repeating: *trade increases overall national welfare*, but these gains are not distributed evenly among the owners of factors of production, among different producers, or among the different consumers.

MORE REALISTIC MODELS OF TRADE

The models of the determinants and effects of trade presented to this point have, by necessity, been highly stylized simplifications of the real world. Over the past 40 years, economists have researched the implications of these models by changing the assumptions on which they rest, thereby making them more realistic. Broadly summarized, these improved models have led to conclusions that moderate the force of the conclusions of the simpler models. Yet they do not, in general, change their central thrust: free trade brings welfare gains to the nation as a whole. This section describes the most important of these modifications to the basic trade model and their implications concerning the determinants and effects of trade. Chapter 3 analyzes the impact of trade restrictions on welfare and income distribution.

The basic trade model assumes that *adjustment* to trade is costless, in the sense that resources can move quickly and freely to new uses in the transition process. In the real world, however, adjustment is slow and painful. In North, plant and equipment and (skilled) labor are reallocated from industry X to industry Y. This is a difficult process as plant and equipment are scrapped when they are no longer economically viable, since they no longer earn a profit and the human capital, the labor, used to produce X is reduced or made obsolete entirely. Geographic relocation is necessary within a country, and it brings with it social and political costs. During the adjustment process, in the contracting sector, plant and equipment are idle and labor unemployed. In the expanding sector plant and equipment strain at capacity, sales and profits boom, and labor earns high wages and overtime. Moreover, the very businesses and workers that benefit least (lose the most) from free trade are the very ones that must bear the adjustment costs.

[11]Paul A. Samuelson, "International Trade and the Equalization of Factor Prices," *Economic Journal* (June 1948); "International Factor Price Equalization Once Again," *Economic Journal* (June 1949).

Adjustment costs occur primarily in the short run, while the full gains from trade are only realized in the long run. On a discounted basis, the short-run costs loom large compared to the long-run gains. These costs are highly visible and often highly concentrated—bankrupt firms and unemployed labor (in the X industry). The gains are more diffused—higher national income and increased value of consumption spread among a wide number of consumers. These problems are similar in many respects to those caused by technological change which caused the Luddites to smash textile machinery in England in 1811 to 1816. More recently such adjustment costs have caused concern about the impact of the "automated office" on employment of women. Yet the solution is *not* to block free trade (or technological change), but to mitigate the adjustment costs of such change and redistribute the net benefits more evenly. The capitalist, free enterprise, market system can perform badly in the redistribution of benefits from winners to losers and in reducing transition costs. Only when compensation is workable and long-run factor mobility is assured is it possible to claim unambiguous gains from trade.

The basic trade model assumes that world prices are not affected by a country's imports and exports (i.e., the country faced *fixed* world prices). Obviously, if the country is large (or several similar countries are taken together), exports will drive down the price of the exported product on world markets and imports will drive up world prices. These effects of trade on world prices can be incorporated into a modified model, although the geometry or algebra becomes more complicated. Two conclusions arise from such modifications: (1) the greater the response of world prices to a country's exports and imports, the smaller are the gains from trade; and (2) if a country's exports and imports affect world prices, it can increase its *own* welfare by reducing exports and imports through tariffs. The country gains from these trade restrictions, but total world welfare declines. (This subject is addressed in Chapter 3 under the heading "Optimum Tariffs.")

The basic trade model is static, so it does not consider growth through technical progress or increases in factors of production. The real-world effects of trade on growth are many and complex. Trade can reduce monopoly power; spur technological progress; and, through its effects on income, change growth rates and consumer preferences. One notable example of the welfare *reducing* effect of trade is the case of "immiserizing" growth. By this is meant that *if* for some reason (technological progress, increased population, etc.) a country's capacity to produce its exportable product grows over time, and *if* its increased exports reduce world prices sufficiently, it is possible for the country's welfare to be reduced, over time, by trade. Immiserizing growth may be a problem for some less developed countries if the growth of exports of some natural resource products and manufactured goods have driven down world prices such that output gains have been more than offset by price declines.

In the basic trade model imports and exports expand simultaneously toward the trade equilibrium position. In the real world domestic producers in the exporting industry of one country usually cannot expand production and exports as fast as world production of the imported good can penetrate the country's market. A short-run trade deficit almost inevitably occurs. This deficit may adversely affect growth, the price level, employment, capital formation, and external debt. These are short-run costs of adjusting to trade and must be evaluated against trade's long-run benefits.

In summary, these modifications to the basic theory complicate the analysis of the determinants and effects of trade. However, the thrust of the conclusions remains the same:

1 Trade increases national welfare, but the gains and losses due to trade are not evenly distributed.

2 Trade enables a country to expand production and to export goods in which it has a comparative advantage. These are goods using its relatively abundant factor intensively.

3 Adjustment to trade entails real, short-run costs that must be balanced against the real gains from trade.

EMPIRICAL RELEVANCE OF THE TRADE MODEL

Trade theory is not a useful tool in formulating public policy or business decisions if it cannot predict the course and effects of events in the real world. A theory can be questioned on two grounds. First, its internal consistency and assumptions can be examined, as was done in the last section. The basic model generally stands up well to this examination. Second, its predictions and implications can be tested against real-world observations. This section examines the results of such tests.

The basic trade model of Heckscher-Ohlin and Samuelson received a setback with the empirical work of Leontief in the mid-1950s. On the basis of an input-output analysis of the U.S. economy, Leontief concluded that U.S. exporting industries were more labor-intensive than its importing-competing industries. Yet trade theory predicts the United States to be a capital-abundant, labor-scarce country. If this were true, the trade model would predict that the United States should export capital-intensive products and import labor-intensive goods. What was going on? Trade economists rushed into a frenzy of theoretical and empirical research to resolve the *Leontief paradox*.

First Leontief replicated his study using better and more appropriate data. The Leontief paradox remained. Trade theorists then went back and examined the many assumptions of the basic trade model and introduced more sophistication into the equations. Three key factors were identified that might resolve the paradox while retaining the basic model:

1 *Government-imposed trade barriers.* The world of international trade is not a free trade world. Yet the trade model assumed a free trade final equilibrium. For example, the United States tended to restrict imports of labor-intensive products while encouraging capital intensive imports (especially natural resources).

2 *Natural resources.* The United States was a net importer of minerals and forest products. These products are intensive not only in natural resources (often with significant economic rents), but also in capital. The United States was a net exporter of farm products, products intensive in land and labor. When these factors of production were included in the model and the empirical tests performed, the paradox was reduced in size.

3 *Human capital and skills.* Capital is invested in education and training of labor as well as in plant and equipment. In the 1950s, American workers in general had a higher level of education, skills, and training than the workers of its trading partners. This relatively high level of human capital should have been included in the capital intensity of its exported goods when the tests were performed. Statistics showed that the United States exported goods that were intensive in skills and human capital and imported goods with low skill and human capital intensities. An American worker was more productive than an Indian worker, so the export of "labor"-intensive goods from the United States was really an export of human capital-intensive goods.

The flood of theoretical and empirical research directed at resolving the Leontief paradox has deepened and extended our knowledge of international trade. Ironically, recent research by Edward Leamer has shown that Leontief's test of the trade theory was incorrect and that when the correct test was performed, the paradox did not occur![12]

One of the research thrusts in developing the theory of trade in response to the Leontief paradox was to study the role of technology in trade. The classical trade model assumed that information on processes and products was freely available to all, which was an unrealistic assumption. In 1966, Raymond Vernon of the Harvard Business School published the *product life cycle* theory of international trade and investment.[13]

Vernon began with the proposition that new products and processes are developed and introduced in response to cost and demand conditions in the innovator's local market. Initially, demand is limited and insensitive to price (inelastic). Production of new products is skill and knowledge-intensive, and involves short production runs, frequent modifications and, hence, low physical capital intensity. As demand expands at home and later abroad, the innovating firm exports abroad. Over time, demand expands in all markets and becomes more price sensitive. Product modifications are fewer.

At a later stage, product and process technologies become diffused and production begins abroad, often by MNEs based in the innovating country. In this stage, production runs are longer (to satisfy high demand) and capital intensive (to reduce costs). In the final stage producers abroad are now cost-competitive in the innovator's market due to their lower labor costs, and export back to the originating country which becomes a net importer. This flow of trade over time is illustrated in Figure 2-6.

---

[12]Edward Leamer, "The Leontief Paradox Reconsidered," *Journal of Political Economy* 3 (1980).
  [13]Raymond Vernon, "International Trade and International Investment in the Product Cycle," *Quarterly Journal of Economics* (May 1966).

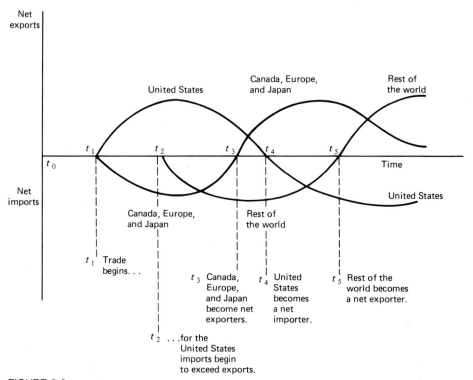

FIGURE 2-6
Trade flows over the product cycle. [Adapted *from Louis T. Wells (ed.). The Product Life Cycle and International Trade. Boston: Division of Research, Harvard Business School, 1972.*]

The product life cycle model provided an excellent explanation of world trade patterns in manufactured products in the early post−World War II period. Labor-saving product and process innovations occurred and were introduced in the United States due to its large, high-income, high-wage market. The United States exported new research and development (R and D) and skill-intensive products in exchange for more standardized, older products that were produced by capital-intensive production processes abroad. Not only did the product life cycle theory explain trade flows, it explained outward foreign direct investment by U.S.-based MNEs. The model showed that U.S.-based MNEs had invested abroad to capitalize on their firm-specific advantages in technology, capital, and management when these markets became threatened by competitors.

Over time, several factors have reduced the technological superiority of some U.S.-based MNEs. As world income has risen relative to that in the United States and trade barriers were reduced, more and more innovations have been developed and introduced outside the United States. Technological capabilities outside the United States have increased so that new product and process technology can be rapidly transferred at relatively low cost outside the originating country. Other product cycles have begun to originate outside the United States based on size and resource conserving innovations (Japan) and quality and design (Europe). By the mid-1970s the movement of many products over the cycle often became so rapid that exports from the innovating countries did not occur, and imports from abroad, based on lower production costs due to lower wage labor, soon followed their initial introduction.

With the spread of technological capabilities and the lowering of trade barriers in many industries, world conditions now more closely approximate those in the classic trade model. Recent tests of this model support its conclusions and thereby support the validity and usefulness of the model itself.[14]

INTRAINDUSTRY TRADE

To this point in the chapter the analysis has shown that a country exports products for which it has a comparative advantage and imports those for which it is at a comparative disadvantage. In this model a country would never simultaneously import and export the same product. Yet when actual trade patterns are observed, there is a high degree of intraindustry trade between nations: France both imports and exports textiles, Germany both imports and exports wines and grain, Switzerland both imports and exports watches, and the United States both imports and exports many fruits and vegetables. The theory of intraindustry trade has been developed to explain such trade patterns.

Part of the phenomenon of intraindustry trade is due to problems of definition and product classification. Much of international trade is in differentiated products, which although classified to the same product group in the trade statistics, are often quite different and embody different intensities. France exports high-quality, high-fashion, skill-intensive textile products and imports low-quality, standard textiles with high intensities of low-skill labor. Germany imports red wines and exports white wines. Switzerland imports low-price digital watches and exports high-price mechanical ones. Europe imports some types and qualities of grains and exports others.

Intraindustry trade, as a result of product differentiation, was analyzed by Grubel and Lloyd (1975). They define intraindustry trade in industry i as the total of its exports (X) plus imports (M) less the amount of net exports. The index of intraindustry trade R_i is

$$R_i = [(X_i + M_i) - |X_i - M_i|] \frac{\times 100}{(X_i + M_i)}$$

The second term $|X_i - M_i|$ is net exports, or conventional interindustry trade.

---

[14]Vernon has described this "death" of the product life cycle in "The Product Cycle Hypothesis in a New International Environment," *Oxford Bulletin of Economics and Statistics* 41 (November 1979).

The index is 1 when exports equal imports and 0 when a country either only exports or only imports a product. For Australia, it was 0.06 (a low level of intraindustry trade) for ski boots (a seven-digit SIC class), 0.15 for footwear with leather uppers and soles of rubber or plastic (the five-digit class), 0.20 for shoes (the three-digit class), 0.26 for footwear (the two-digit class), and 0.43 for miscellaneous manufactured articles (the one-digit class). The measure of intraindustry trade increased with increasing levels of aggregation. For ten major industrialized countries, it averaged 0.48 in 1967, ranging from 0.66 for chemicals to 0.30 for mineral fuels and lubricants. The more differentiated are the products within an industry, the greater the potential for intraindustry trade.

For intraindustry trade arising from differentiated products, a country's natural resources (including climate and geography) may give it a comparative advantage in one product subclass, but not in others; an example is Germany regarding white wine. Consumer preferences in one country can also lead firms to develop firm-specific advantages (FSAs) in one product subclass. Fashion consciousness in France led to the development of the high-fashion clothing industry in France based on immobile factors of production such as designers and crafters. France then can export high-fashion clothing, even though garment manufacture is highly labor-intensive and wages are high in France. Similarly, high-fashion shoes are exported from Switzerland and Italy. If a country's specific assets are dissipated through technology transfer, however, the country can lose its comparative advantage and cease to export. As discussed here and in Chapter 5, the product life cycle theory of trade and investment is essentially a model of intraindustry trade and investment based on the development and dissipation of firm-specific assets in differentiated products.

Economies of scale may also give a country a cost advantage in one product subclass. The United States was a major exporter of specialty roller bearings since its large market allowed American firms to achieve economies of scale in these low-demand products which were difficult to achieve for competitors in smaller countries. At the same time, the United States imported standardized roller bearings from other countries since the high demand for these products allowed firms abroad to achieve economies of scale even when they produced largely for domestic consumption. Intraindustry trade based on economies of scale has decreased over time as tariff barriers have fallen since firms in small countries can get down along their cost curves by producing for newly accessible export markets.

Even for totally homogeneous products, however, there may be intraindustry trade as a result of transportation costs, storage costs, selling costs, and information costs.

Transportation Costs

There are transportation costs for shipping goods from the producer to the ultimate consumer. For some products the delivered price of the product may be lower when supplied from a nearby region of another country rather than from a distant region of the country even though *production* costs are lower at home.

Lumber is imported into the northeastern United States from Canada yet shipped from Washington State to Japan; Canada imports steel from Japan into Vancouver and exports it from Hamilton, Ontario.

Storage Costs

When a product is consumed at a time different from that when it is produced, the price to the consumer must include storage costs. For food products, production is seasonal, so that price can be reduced by reducing storage costs if the good can be exported at harvest and imported during the off-season. For example, the United States exports oranges in April and imports them in December.

Selling and Information Costs

A country may specialize in packaging, storing, shipping, and insuring goods it imports and selling them on export markets. This is called *entrepôt trade*. In Singapore, for example, gross exports (including exports of products previously imported) is well over 100 percent of GNP, as was shown in Table 1-3.

IMPLICATIONS FOR BUSINESS

The theory and evidence of international trade have important implications for business. Economic agents—firms, labor, owners of capital and land, and consumers—all seek to maximize the returns to their scarce resources. Since trade increases overall welfare, unless it is restricted by nonmarket forces, such as government, it will expand as these agents pursue the opportunities that trade presents. Government, in its role as protector of the public interest, also has an incentive to foster trade to increase national welfare. If an individual business aligns itself with the process of international trade, market forces will work for it and the firm will prosper. If it does not, those same forces will work against it; it will decline unless government intervenes.

Investment in "sunrise" industries, in which the nation has a comparative advantage because of its factor supplies and costs, has a greater chance of success than investment in comparatively disadvantaged ("sunset") industries. Of course, firms and workers in these latter industries have every incentive to lobby government to restrict trade. If trade restrictions are imposed, the industries still survive for a time. They exist, however, only as long as the dam of government protection can withstand the flood of world trade and the national and international protests of those hurt by these trade restrictions.

Three trends in the international trade environment are important for international business: tariff barriers are continuing to be reduced (despite neoprotectionism); transportation and communication costs as a percent of shipping value are decreasing; and the speed of technological diffusion is increasing. All three trends facilitate trade by reducing natural and government-imposed trade barriers. Industries and individual products that were once sheltered from competition from international trade are increasingly exposed. This evolving trade environment presents both threats and opportunities for managers in all countries. If they respond to threats by obstructing trade, not only will national and world welfare be reduced, but their firms will ultimately decline. Only if managers respond to the opportunities of trade by investing in plant equipment and R and D in industries in which the nation has a comparative advantage, will their businesses flourish.

More than far-sighted business decisions are necessary. The burden of adjustment to trade must be shared evenly. Such a conclusion is reached on practical grounds. If some groups lose from trade, they will lobby government for increased protection and trade will be impeded, to the detriment of potential winners and the nation as a whole. Capital and labor will remain tied up in inefficient uses and will not flow to more productive ones. The cost of capital and labor will rise in industries with a comparative advantage, and their competitiveness on international markets will decrease. Measures for retraining workers and employing capital can be expanded.

It makes no sense to advocate free trade unless funds are available to facilitate adjustment. Political pressure from labor and business in declining sectors will ultimately force trade restrictions, to the detriment of the nation as a whole, unless the principles of trade theory outlined in this chapter are fully understood and implemented. The manager of a firm involved in international business is, of course, not responsible for the implementation of these principles. This is the job of government. However, a clear understanding of the environment of international trade is a starting point for international business activity.

SUMMARY

To fully understand international business, it is necessary to examine both the determinants and effects of international trade. Many theories have been developed to explain world trade. All of them agree that free trade is efficient and that there are gains to trade. This has an obvious implication for managers, namely, that international business is socially useful.

According to the mercantilists, trade, in particular exports, will increase a country's gold reserves, thereby increasing its wealth. Adam Smith, on the other hand, in his theory of absolute advantage, held that a nation could increase its welfare by exporting goods in which it had specialized in production and importing those in which it had an absolute disadvantage. Finally, Ricardo's theory of comparative advantage illustrated that even if a country had an absolute advantage in the production of several goods, as long as the relative costs of production differed, trade would still be advantageous to both nations.

Even when a nation has achieved efficiency in a closed economy, it can still experience a gain from trade. The Heckscher-Ohlin theorem states that international trade occurs when each nation produces and exports that good which uses intensively its relatively abundant factor, resources (land or capital), and labor. In return, the nation imports goods that use its relatively scarce factors internally.

Empirical testing by Leontief of this basic trade model, produced a paradox since the United States appeared to export labor-intensive goods. The resolution of the Leontief paradox resulted in an extended knowledge of the models of international trade. It was found that the United States actually exported human capital-intensive products.

The product life cycle theory explains not only the reason for international trade, but also the more realistic patterns of multinational enterprise activity that recent world trade has followed. This type of intrafirm trade by multinationals has been increasing in recent years, and the principles of international trade need to be amended to take account of intraindustry trade.

In Part 2 of the book we shall develop a model of multinational activity which has close parallels to the theory of trade discussed here. But first it is necessary to examine, in Chapter 3, some of the barriers to trade which give rise to multinationals.

KEY WORDS

Mercantilistic theory
Absolute advantage
Comparative advantage
Autarky
Invisible hand
Visible hand
Closed economy
Production possibilities curve
Social indifference curve

Diminishing MRS
Exogenously set prices
Heckscher-Ohlin theorem
"Immizerizing" growth
Leontief paradox
Product life cycle theory
Intraindustry trade
Sunrise industry

QUESTIONS

1   Briefly discuss the theory of mercantilism. How is the level of imports and exports related to this theory? Give an example of this theory as it exists today. What are the fallacies of mercantilism? Can you think of any examples?

2   Briefly state Smith's concept of absolute advantage. What are the implications of this theory? Give examples where applicable. Why is this theory a threat to free trade?

3   Contrast Ricardo's theory of comparative advantage with Smith's theory of absolute advantage. What is the common conclusion of both these theories? What is the general principle underlying both of these models? Discuss the downfall of these theories.

4   How do the "more realistic" models of trade, as described in the chapter, differ from those previously discussed? What are the costs and benefits which are ignored in basic trade models? In light of these problems, how can real gains from trade be realized?

5   Describe, briefly, the Leontief paradox. What factors could be used to resolve the paradox? Explain. Has the theory been proved correct?

6   Describe the product life cycle theory. Use a graph to illustrate the theory. How does this theory relate to the firm-specific advantages of MNEs? Give examples of countries which have gone through stages of the product life cycle theory.

7   Explain the concept of intraindustry trade. If comparative advantage states that a nation will export its specialty goods, why does intraindustry trade occur? Give examples of this form of trade.

8   Discuss the practical implications of trade theory. What are the three trends which are important for business? How must international managers react to these trends?

Exercise: Graph the production possibilities curve $Y^2 = 25 - X^2$.

a   What is the significance of any particular point on the curve $(X, Y = 4,3)$?

b   Given the social indifference curve $I_0 = Y^2 = 156.25/X^2$, does this indicate an open or closed economy? Explain.

c   At what combination of goods X and Y is production and consumption maximized?

d   What are the "gains from trade?" Be specific in terms of domestic production, consumption, imports, and exports of goods X and Y.

BARRIERS TO TRADE

The principles of the benefits of free trade are well known but are less widely accepted in practice. Yet every nation in the world acts to impede the free flow of trade. As barriers to trade are a fact of the international economic environment, international managers must be knowledgeable about their causes and impacts on international operations. This chapter analyzes the effects of barriers to trade on (1) the level and distribution of national and international income, (2) the flows of international trade, and (3) the location of production and investment.

The analysis reveals both threats and opportunities posed by trade barriers. International managers must consider these when making strategic and tactical decisions. Managers concerned about the effect of trade restrictions on their business operations can also act to change and shape their environment by lobbying government to raise or lower barriers to trade. The final section of the chapter analyzes the politics of the economic reasons (demand and supply) for trade barriers.

TARIFFS AND INEFFICIENCY

In this section we shall investigate the economic aspects of a tariff, the most common instrument used by governments to protect the home market from trade. We shall see that there are alternative policies, such as taxes and subsidies, which achieve the same objectives, but at a lower cost in terms of social welfare.

In Chapter 2 it was demonstrated that free trade leads to the efficient allocation of resources at both the national and international levels. This occurs when:

$$MRT = MRS = \text{relative price ratio of the traded goods}$$

This equality holds because an international price line, derived according to comparative advantage, is available to equalize the production and consumption sides of the economy. If a tariff is imposed on the imported good X in the form of a customs duty, the price of good X increases relative to that of good Y. In terms of Figure 2-4, a tariff leads to a relative price line steeper than that of the free trade price line, $P_W P_W'$. The tariff-distorted price line cannot keep the slopes of the production possibilities curve MRT equal to the slope of a social indifference curve MRS. Therefore, the efficiency condition that $MRT = MRS$ is violated and the tariff is inefficient.

The proof of the distorting effect of a tariff is too technical for a book on international business, and the interested reader is referred to one of the textbooks on international economics recommended in the Bibliography. For our purposes, the conclusion that a tariff decreases the efficiency of the allocation of resources and reduces national welfare is all that is required. If international prices are fixed, a tariff is inefficient; it prevents the full benefits of free trade from being realized. The free trade price line is often called the *terms of trade*, so the tariff generally serves to worsen the nation's terms of trade. We now move on to explore the implications of this inefficiency in more detail.

COSTS OF THE TARIFF

Figure 3-1 is a partial equilibrium diagram which serves to explain the essential reasons why imposition of a tariff leads to inefficient resource allocation. The vertical axis (ordinate) now represents the price of good X, and the horizontal axis (abscissa) indicates the quantity of good X. The tariff is imposed in the form of a customs duty. The effect is to increase the price of the imported good to domestic consumers.

Line $P_W P_W'$ in Figure 3-1 represents the free trade world price ratio for a country facing exogenously determined terms of trade (as assumed at the start of Chapter 2 and in this section). At the free trade price the domestic supply and demand curves for good X, shown as S_X and D_X respectively, indicate that OA of the good will be produced at home while OB is consumed at home. The gap is AB. This is the amount of good X coming from abroad to satisfy domestic consumption of OB at the world price $P_W P_W'$. Thus consumers are supplied from two sources: domestic producers in the amount OA plus a foreign supply of AB.

Political pressure for a tariff usually arises from the owners or workers in the import competing industry. In this example the home producers of good X will ask for a tariff to reduce the imports of AB. They want to substitute domestic production for imports, that is, to reduce the quantity AB. If a prohibitive tariff is imposed, the price will rise to OH, where domestic supply and demand are equal. However, total consumption of good X will fall and national welfare will be reduced.

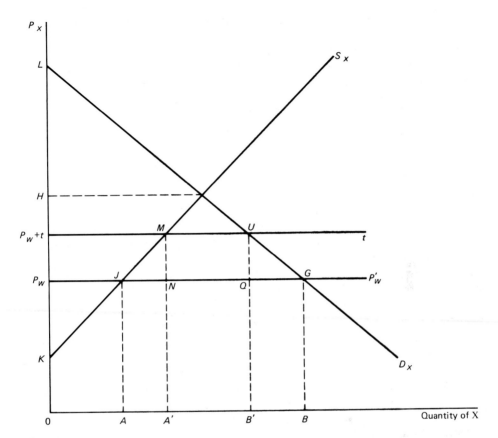

FIGURE 3-1
The effects of a tariff. A tariffs of t leads to increased production of AA', decreased consumption of $B'B$, government revenue of $MNQU$, and welfare losses of MNJ plus GUQ.

To consider this last point, let us take an intermediate tariff t which raises the price of imports to $P_W + t$. At this price, compared to free trade, domestic production increases to OA' and consumption demand falls to OB'. The gap to be filled by imports falls to $A'B'$. Thus the results of the tariff have been to replace $AA' + B'B$ of imports by increased domestic production AA' but at the cost to the nation's consumers of reduced consumption of good X in the amount of $B'B$. Is the substitution of domestic for foreign production worth the cost of reduced consumption? The answer is usually no.

To understand why there are usually economic costs to a tariff, it is necessary to introduce the concepts of consumer surplus and producer surplus. As shown in Figure 3-1, consumer surplus occurs at the old world price of P_W whenever the demand curve is above the price level $P_W P'_W$. The area of consumer surplus is triangle $P_W GL$. This surplus occurs since each and every point on the demand curve represents the "willingness to pay" for good X by individuals in society. As the price set in the market is P_W, there is a surplus realized by consumers up to the equilibrium quantity of OB. After that point, of course, consumers are not willing to pay for good X at equilibrium price P_W, so there is no demand after OB. Producer surplus occurs in an analogous manner. At world price $P_W P'_W$ the domestic producers would be willing to supply quantity OA at the various prices depicted by their upward-sloping supply curve. Since the price actually received is P_W, there is an area of producer surplus of $P_W JK$.

There are several interesting implications of the imposition of a tariff. Once the price rises to $P_W + t$, it is immediately apparent that there is a loss of consumer surplus of the trapezoid area $(P_W + t)P_W GU$. This has some redistributional impact, since producers now benefit at the expense of consumers, but the total effect is usually more than offset by the net loss of consumer surplus. Second, the area $MNQU$ represents tariff revenue. This tax (realized from tariff t) is paid on the reduced amount of imports $A'B'$ and is collected by the customs authority on behalf of the government. These funds represent a transfer from the consumer to the government with the use of the tariff revenue now being determined by the government.

The two remaining areas are the net costs of the tariff. Triangle UQG represents the consumption cost of the tariff, an uncompensated loss of consumer surplus as some consumers stop buying X. Triangle MJN represents the production cost of the tariff. This loss occurs as quantity AA' of good X is now produced at higher cost by domestic producers, whereas this quantity previously was available at the world price P_W. Resources are reallocated by the tariff from more efficient industries to the X industry. The sum of the two triangles is the total cost of the tariff, the consumption cost UQG plus the production cost MJN. These are the welfare costs of protection. They demonstrate that a tariff is inefficient. Such costs are not incurred under free trade. The steeper (more price inelastic) the demand curve and the supply curve for the product, the smaller are these welfare loss triangles, and the smaller the impact of the tariff on national welfare.

A similar analysis can be made of the effect of an export duty on welfare if the world price of the exported good does not change in response to the country's exports. (Try it!) Tariffs or other barriers to trade applied by the exporting country were not widely used (except in some low income countries) until quite recently. They are discouraged by the General Agreement on Tariffs and Trade ($GATT$). Following the success of OPEC (at least from the point of view of its members), there has been a worldwide impetus toward restricting exports to improve the terms of trade by raising the world price of the exported product. This effect of export restraints is discussed in the next section on optimum tariffs.

Many economists have used the concepts of welfare loss triangles to estimate the costs of the tariff for various nations and industries. These studies are difficult to perform in a methodologically correct way. Among other things, the demand and supply curves for each product must be estimated, which is not an easy task. The partial equilibrium analysis presented above, in which only one imported good is considered, is not the appropriate tool for analysis at the aggregate national level. The effect of a tariff on the price of one product spills over into the prices of other products, especially if the product is used as an input for further production. These studies do not look at the *dynamic* effects of tariffs since the model used for estimation is static. The important effect of free international trade on domestic productivity in import-competing industries is also usually neglected. The effects of other barriers to trade (quotas, "buy national" laws, etc.) are seldom calculated, but studies have shown that these effects are at least as important as the tariff effect.

These and many other caveats aside, the welfare loss due to tariffs has been calculated by use of the formula:

$$\frac{\text{Net loss}}{\text{GNP}} = \tfrac{1}{2}(\text{percent of tariff}) \times (\text{percent change in imports}) \times \frac{\text{import value}}{\text{GNP}}$$

When the percent welfare loss is calculated by this method, it is usually small. If a country's average tariff were 10 percent, the elasticity of demand for imports were 0.2, and the import share of GNP were 10 percent (reasonable figures), the loss would be 1 percent of GNP, not a large percentage effect, but enough to pay for many hospitals, schools, and other desirable social goods. Estimates of this static welfare loss for individual countries range from less than 0.1 percent (for the United States) up to 4 percent for small, protected countries with high import ratios, such as Canada. It is possible that these estimates understate the welfare losses due to trade restraints if all their effects are taken into account.[1]

One final comment is in order before moving on. The bulk of most countries' imports (such as raw materials, many agricultural products, and petroleum) enter duty-free. Use of the average tariff rate for all imports greatly understates the welfare loss on some individual products imported over high tariff barriers. Tariffs (and quotas) on some textile imports are an extreme example. For these products the welfare loss can approach 30 percent of domestic production—a high price to pay for protection.

EFFECTIVE AND NOMINAL TARIFFS

The *nominal* tariffs charged on imports are analyzed in this chapter. Nominal tariffs are not an appropriate (or accurate) measure of the protection given domestic industry by a tariff. A better measure is the rate of *effective* tariffs. The effective tariff, or better yet, the effective rate of protection, is defined as the percentage by which value added at domestic prices exceeds value added at world prices. The formula for the effective tariff rate is given as

$$e_j = \frac{V' - V}{V} \qquad (3-1)$$

---

[1]See one of the trade texts listed in the Bibliography for a more extensive analysis of these effects and their impacts.

where e_j is the effective tariff rate on product j, V is the value added at world prices under free trade, and V' is the value added at domestic prices.

"Value added" is defined as the value of further processing required to manufacture the finished good from its input(s) [or raw material state(s)]. That is, the processing of inputs into finished goods "adds value." Consider the example illustrated in Figure 3-2. The nominal tariff rate on unstrung pearls is 20 percent, and the nominal rate on strung pearls (a finished necklace) is higher, at 50 percent, to protect domestic stringing.

Thus the value added at world prices is $25 ($100 − 75), while the value added at domestic prices must be adjusted for the tariff rates on finished goods and inputs: ($100 × 1.50) − ($75 × 1.20) = $60. According to equation (3-1), the effective tariff rate is 140 percent [(60 − 25)/25] versus a nominal tariff rate of 50

FIGURE 3-2
Nominal and effective tariffs. Inputs of unstrung pearls are $75 and face a tariff of 20 percent. Stringing pearls for a necklace costs $25 in labor and return on capital; then a 50 percent nominal tariff on pearl necklaces would give effective protection of 14 percent, (60 − 25)/25.

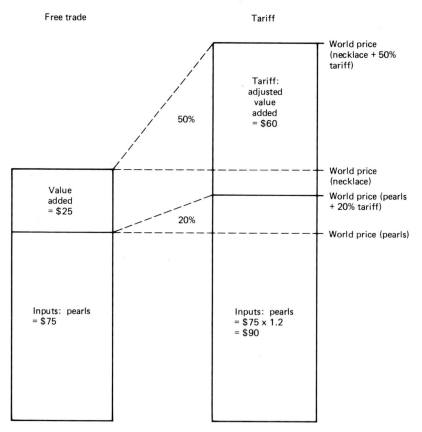

percent. The domestic pearl stringing industry could be 140 percent less efficient than its foreign competitors and still compete in the domestic market.[2]

Effective tariffs are usually higher than nominal tariffs since tariffs in most nations increase with the level of processing. Effective tariffs can be lower than nominal tariffs and even negative in some cases. In Canada the pulp and paper industry imports some of its machinery over high tariffs but must sell its output to the United States, often over trade barriers. Consequently, this industry faces *negative* effective tariffs and must be *more* efficient than producers abroad.

Calculation of the effective rate of tariffs for a country is not easy. A ranking of a nation's industries by relative rates of effective protection from tariffs and non-tariff barriers gives a good indication of relative efficiency compared to the rest of the world. A low or negative effective tariff in an industry makes it more efficient than one that requires a high effective tariff.

Trade negotiations focus on *nominal* tariffs. A reduction in the nominal tariff of a given percent usually implies a greater percentage reduction in the effective tariff. In the preceding example, if tariffs on pearl necklaces are reduced from 50 percent to 25 percent, the effective tariff would be reduced from 140 percent to 40 percent. The domestic necklace industry could be only 40 percent less efficient than its competitors abroad and still survive.

OPTIMUM TARIFFS

One of the crucial assumptions in the preceding analysis of the welfare loss due to tariffs was that world prices for imports and exports were not affected by a country's supply of exports or demand for imports. For a large country such as the United States or for several countries taken together as a group, this assumption must be modified. The demand by the United States for imported coffee, for example, is a substantial percent of world demand and raises world coffee prices. Similarly, the supply by the United States of wheat on world markets lowers world wheat prices. Under these conditions it *may* be possible for the United States to increase its welfare by imposing "optimum" tariffs on imports and exports.

The analysis of optimum tariffs in an international trade context is similar to the analysis of a monopolist and monopsonist in the domestic market. A monopolist can increase its profits by restricting output to the point at which marginal cost

---

[2]A more comprehensive formula, in which the prices of inputs and finished goods need not be adjusted by the nominal tariffs, is

$$e_j = \frac{t_j - \Sigma a_i t_i}{1 - \Sigma a_i}$$

where t_j is the tariff rate on finished goods, t_i is the tariff rate on inputs, and a_i is the percentage value of input per unit of finished good (i.e., the inverse of the value added). The sigma sign recognizes that many inputs may go into a single finished good rather than our simple one input example. This equation is derived by substituting the free-trade value added $V = 1 - \Sigma a_i$, and the protected value added $V' = (1 + t_f) - \Sigma a_i(1 + t_i)$, into equation (3-1) and simplifying.

MC = marginal revenue MR and raising prices at that volume up to the demand curve.[3] The monopolist gains, but there is a welfare loss to society as a whole. Similarly, the welfare gain to the exporting country by imposing an export duty to restrict exports and raise world prices is more than offset by the welfare loss by the rest of the world. In the domestic market, a monopsonist can increase profits by reducing demand for factors of production and driving down their prices. Again society as a whole loses. Similarly, a nation may impose an optimum tariff on imports to increase national welfare, but only at the expense of world welfare.

Arguably, a nation should be concerned only about its own welfare in its policy decisions. Even if this nationalistic viewpoint is maintained, however, the other nations whose welfare has been reduced may well retaliate by restricting their own trade to influence world prices. If this happens, a trade war may ensue, to the detriment of all. Beggar-thy-neighbor trade policies exacerbated world economic conditions during the Great Depression. In the 1980s, there is a significant possibility (some say a probability) that such policies may again flourish—with similar results.

Following the success of OPEC, other groups of commodity-exporting coun-tries have attempted to form cartels to raise export prices. In general these have not been successful, as witnessed by warehouses jammed with coffee (in Brazil) and churches pressed into service to store sugar (in the Philippines). The condi-tions necessary for a cartel to succeed and the related subject of world commodity buffer stocks are described in another section of this chapter.

The major problem in imposing optimal tariffs and duties to increase national welfare lies in the threat of retaliation by the nation's trading partners since their welfare is reduced by more than the gain to the nation imposing the optimum tariff or duty. Thus OPEC was able to enforce its price increases by threatening to cut off vital oil supplies. This case is an anomaly. If there is retaliation for setting an optimal tariff, in general, no country wins and every country loses.

ALTERNATIVES TO TARIFFS TO PROMOTE DOMESTIC PRODUCTION

Some of the distortions and welfare losses imposed by the tariff can be avoided by alternative measures. For example, by applying the same situation as in the previous section, some of the costs of a tariff can be overcome by the selective use of taxes and subsidies. This case is illustrated in Figure 3-3.

In Figure 3-3 we again start off from a free trade situation where the world price is set exogenously at $P_W P_W'$. As observed before, home production is OA, imports are AB, and total domestic consumption of good X is OB. Now to achieve the same increase in domestic output of good X as under the tariff, that is, additional production of the amount AA', it is possible to use an al-ternative economic policy to the tariff. Such a policy is a subsidy.

---

[3]The height of the optimum tariff is equal to the reciprocal of the foreign supply elasticity.

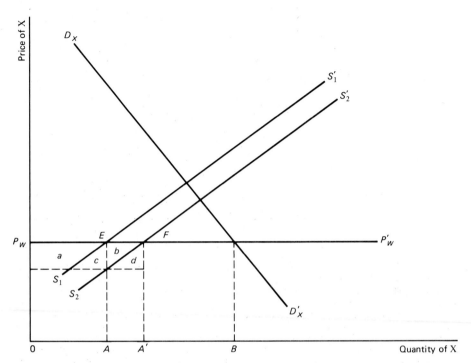

FIGURE 3-3
Welfare losses from a direct subsidy. Welfare losses from a direct subsidy of *EF* per unit lead domestic producers of *X* to expand output from *OA* to *OA'*, the tariff-protected output. Welfare loss is area *d*.

A direct subsidy to the producers of good X results in subsidized output of EF per unit output and will allow increased output of good X at each and every price level, since $S_1 S_1'$ has been shifted to the right to $S_2 S_2'$. By retaining the world price level at $P_W P_W'$, therefore, a subsidy has the effect of shifting the domestic supply curve $S_1 S_1'$ to the right. The new supply curve is $S_2 S_2'$, and it demonstrates that domestic production of good X increases by AA' under the subsidy since it cuts the world price line at point F. This has an identical effect on home production as the tariff analyzed in Figure 3-1, yet the reduction in consumer surplus due to the tariff is avoided since the price of good X is still $P_W P_W'$.

To complete the analysis, it is necessary to realize that subsidies are not free goods. The government must generate revenues of $b + c + d$ to pay home producers to be inefficient. The net welfare loss is area d, since area a is the producers' surplus before the subsidy and areas $b + c$ are a gain of producers' surplus. The payments for the subsidy can come from either the general revenues of the government, at a cost to all the members of society, or from the consumers of good X. In the latter case a head tax is imposed on consumers of X. This head tax will reduce income of all consumers. Since consumers still face a world price of $P_W P_W'$, they will continue to consume at B so there will be no welfare loss from the head tax. If consumption of X is taxed, to finance the subsidy to X producers, $D_X D_X'$ shifts to the left, consumer surplus is reduced, and there is a deadweight welfare loss.

A head tax-subsidy system is superior to a tariff in that it achieves identical effects of increased home production but at lower welfare costs. Producers have gained at the expense of the populace, who now must pay a highly regressive head tax. This analysis demonstrates an important general principle in economics: a policy should be direct rather than indirect. If expansion of domestic production of good X is the target, the appropriate policy is a direct subsidy (financed by a head tax) rather than second-best policies, such as tariffs, which affect consumer prices and consumption.

National governments, however, most often use tariffs or other trade barriers to subsidize domestic production. Although the preceding analysis shows clearly that subsidies financed out of general revenues lead to lower welfare losses, subsidies to producers are not used more frequently for obvious reasons. A direct subsidy requires money, and governments are typically short of revenue. Governments that raise taxes, especially taxes to subsidize producers, are subject to rebuke by their constituents. Moreover, the stigma of direct subsidies is not appreciated by their recipients. Such subsidies can easily be identified and cut when government budgets are under pressure. Consumers have difficulty in perceiving the direct impact of tariffs on the prices they pay, so they are less apt to protest for their removal. Tariffs are also a source of revenue for government and a particularly important one in many less developed countries. All these factors usually lead government to rely on tariffs to subsidize domestic industry indirectly (with increases in government revenue) rather than to subsidize them directly (with increased government outflows).

OTHER ARGUMENTS FOR TRADE RESTRICTIONS

The optimum tariff argument can be invoked to support the erection of barriers to trade. Under certain conditions such tariffs can improve national welfare. In the United States, for example, the terms of trade effect of tariffs (as they approach the optimum) can compensate for an adverse effect on efficiency and welfare. During the last round of the GATT negotiations, the Tokyo round, presentations advocating tariffs did not use the optimum tariff argument, although tariffs on some products were already *below* the optimum level from the viewpoint of welfare in the United States. Negotiators for the United States were willing to trade off welfare losses to achieve gains from the reduction of tariffs imposed by their trading partners. This rationale is the converse of another argument for not imposing optimum tariffs, namely, a "threat of retaliation."

Arguments for trade restrictions based on protection of domestic industries are more prevalent. The analysis in the preceding section demonstrated that there are better means of protecting these industries than trade protection. Although such alternatives have lower welfare costs, they are often politically unattractive. A host of other arguments have been advanced by proponents of trade restrictions. One of the most widely used is the infant industry argument.

Infant Industries

Some industries have significant economies of scale in production, marketing, research and development (R and D), finance, general management, or international operations. To compete in these industries in the domestic market, let alone internationally, a firm must operate above some often large, minimum efficient scale. New firms do not suddenly spring into existence at large scale without substantial startup costs in learning by doing and market penetration. In the short run, this makes them uncompetitive with established producers.

When these conditions prevail, how can a nation foster the development of firms in industries in which it has a long-run comparative advantage? The infant industry argument for trade restrictions states that government may protect its infant industries by restricting trade to secure the domestic market for them until they are grown up and can fend for themselves against the established producers at home and abroad. The argument can be extended to include direct and indirect subsidies, particularly for export. Essentially, the infant industry argument advocates short-term welfare reduction in exchange for long-term welfare gains. This rationale for protection dates back at least as far as Alexander Hamilton, who argued for protection of the infant textile industry in the United States.

Historically, protection of infant industries at a critical stage of development has been effective in several countries, most notably the United States and Japan. Infant industries in these nations have grown up and become efficient and internationally competitive. There are several problems, however, with the theory and practice of protection based on such an industrial development scenario.

In protecting infant industries, the nation is trading off real short-term losses in welfare against expected future gains. Two questions arise. First, if these firms will be viable in the future, why does the capital market not provide funds to support them in the expectation of future returns? Possibly there are other distortions in the economy that prevent the resource allocation process from funding these new industries. The objection to this defense is that when externalities exist (such as economies of scale), there is a natural incentive for firms to merge and take advantage of this externality through internalization. By internalization of market imperfections within the firms they can grow naturally and increase national economic efficiency. There is no need for government intervention.

Second, what skills does government possess in evaluating the present and future comparative advantage of the country that will enable it to forecast future "winners" better than the market? Again, a rationale based on market distortions and risk sharing could be involved. It may be incorrect, however, to cite past "successes" of infant industry policies as support for following them in the present. On a *discounted* basis, trading of short-term costs against long term benefits may decrease national welfare on a net present value basis. Figure 3-4 illustrates this point. It is not only necessary for the price line *OH* to fall to equal the world price *OW*, which is achieved at time *OM*. In addition, the home price must fall below *OW* such that area *B* (on a discounted basis) can compensate for area *A*. In citing the successes of infant industries, current benefits are noticed while past costs are often forgotten. This has happened even when Japan's success with infant industries is regarded with awe and admiration. The costs to Japan of high internal domestic prices and losses of consumer welfare are forgotten.

There are implementation problems in protecting infant industries, especially for small countries. Unless these industries can attain scale efficiency so that they can eventually be competitive, i.e., unless they can and will grow up, they will need continued protection and will create a continual drain on national welfare. In

FIGURE 3-4
The infant industry argument. If the world price of good *X is OW,* the infant industry argument is that higher-cost domestic production, starting at price *OH,* is justified not only if home prices first fall to equal world prices after time period *OM* but also when a more stringent condition is met. The second requirement is that the high cost over *A* be fully compensated by an equivalent time discounted area *B.*

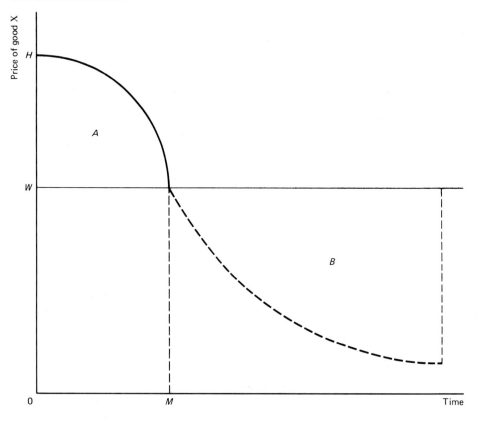

the short run, infant firms in protected industry may be able to exercise quasi-monopoly power, set prices above the competitive level, earn excess returns, and be inefficient. As long as government protects them, they have little incentive to operate or price efficiently, and provided they are not efficient, government protection is necessary for their survival.

Protection also invites foreign MNEs to set up "miniature replica" branch plants. Canada is the archetypical example of this situation. One hundred and twenty five years of protecting infant industries has resulted in a concentrated, small scale, largely foreign-owned manufacturing sector which is unwilling and unable to compete internationally. Moves to reduce this protection are met with protests that industry will be decimated and that foreign firms will withdraw from Canada.

Even if the firms in the industry do grow up and mature, it is difficult to know when to reduce protection. Certainly the firms (and their employees) will resist policies that would expose them to foreign competition. This problem can be resolved only *if* government initially states that the protection will be reduced over time, *if* the time path of the reduction is scheduled prior to investment, *if* the schedule is correct, and *if* the government adheres to it. All these "ifs" are rarely realized in practice, so the nation loses.

The Old Industry Argument

A related argument to the infant industry argument for protection is often advanced by firms in established industries, which are facing increased competition from abroad. It advocates temporary protection from new, efficient foreign producers. This breathing space is to be used to modernize. The steel, automobile, and textile industries in the United States have advocated protection on this basis. This argument is easily dismissed. If these firms are perceived as being able to become efficient and profitable again, the capital market will respond to such short-term capital requirements and government protection will not be necessary.

Externalities

Arguments for protection based on externalities often combine social, cultural, and nationalistic factors with economic ones. They are difficult to quantify and analyze rationally and can be subject to abuse. Arguments range from the preservation of the family farm to having an industrial strategy. There is a social value imputed to them beyond their economic value. Canada, for example, has a large natural resource base that gives it a comparative advantage in many resource products and resource-based industries. The cry is often heard, however, that Canadians should not remain "hewers of wood and drawers of water," but should be provided with white collar industrial jobs fitting their level of income and education. Protection of the manufacturing sector is advocated on this basis. Similarly, Canada's aspirations for a national cultural identity have led it to protect its domestic arts, broadcasting, and other media from foreign competition. As explained earlier, such objectives of national sovereignty can be achieved in a more efficient manner by direct subsidies.

Nationalism also rears its head. A favorite example is the rhetorical question, "Do you want our national flag made out of foreign textiles?"[4] Protection to foster self-sufficiency for national defense is also advocated. While the ability of the United States to produce and transport arms and equipment was a crucial factor in the Allied victory in World War II and the lack of matching capacity hastened the defeat of Germany and Japan, it is difficult to envisage a war in the future whose outcome will hinge on the prolonged mass movement of people and equipment. If high-technology industries are required to provide a base for defense, contracting such sectors for them can be better fostered by a subsidy rather than a tariff.

This dismissal of the arguments for protection does not mean that they are either unimportant or incorrect. Economic and trade theories shed light only on the inefficient aspects of tariffs. It points out that the declared benefits of protectionist policies must be evaluated carefully against (often unforeseen) economic consequences. Evaluation of the costs and benefits of protection for social, cultural, political, and national defense reasons is complex, and rational analysis is difficult. This void leaves the stage open for resolution of the issues based on political bargaining power and logrolling, often wrapped in grandiose rhetoric far removed from the realm of economic efficiency.

Income Distribution

Free international trade allocates resources on an international and national basis in the most efficient way. The distributional effects of free trade can be cruel to some and generous to others. The private enterprise, free market system rewards value received, since factors of production receive their marginal revenue products. The question of whether this is a fair or equitable way to distribute income is beyond the scope of this book.[5] Trade influences the distribution of income between factors of production, industries, firms, workers, consumers, regions, and countries. Those hurt by trade often lobby government to restrict it, although often their rationale focuses on other effects of trade, not their own reduced economic circumstances. As shown in the previous section, it would be economically better to compensate the losers directly rather than through trade protection.

Cries are often heard for trade protection based on "unfair" competition from abroad. The call is for "fair" trade, not free trade. It is "unfair" for national industries and their workers to have to compete with "cheap labor, modern industry, or subsidized exports" abroad. The question of why it is fair to protect domestic workers earning $10/per hour at the expense of foreign workers earning

---

[4]Similarly, Merrill Lynch was criticized for filming its "We're bullish on America" commercials in Mexico.

[5]Compare this to the Marxist statement, "From each according to his abilities, to each according to his needs."

$0.50 per hour is seldom articulated, much less answered. In the United States over the past 20 years, the largest gains in real income for workers, executives, and owners have been in capital-intensive, oligopolistic, unionized industries. These are the very industries who now protest most loudly about "unfair" trade and demand protection, at the expense of their fellow consumers.

Economic Stability

Trade integrates a nation into the world economy in which prices, particularly commodities prices, are often unstable. Trade may introduce instability into the domestic market and (arguably) increases risk. Government could vary the level of protection (e.g., variable import tariffs or export duties) to even out these price swings. Such policies could increase the stability of the returns to factors of production and reduce adjustment costs and risk. If this stability is, indeed, of value, there is a question of why futures markets or buffer stocks have not been formed to provide this valued service.

One of the hottest topics in international trade and development economics is the international regulation of commodities' prices between floor and ceiling limits to set prices at a stable, "fair" level. These proposals are surrounded by controversy on theoretical and practical grounds: what constitutes a fair price, how production and export markets will be allocated among producers and how this allocation will be controlled, who should pay the administrative costs and the costs of creating and financing the necessary buffer stocks, whether these quasi-cartels will use their power to raise prices, what is a "fair" price, and how control and payments should be allocated among producing and consuming nations. Although these questions cannot be resolved quickly, there is a trend in the international trade environment toward increased involvement in trade by national governments and international organizations. Regulation of trade flows and prices outside the market system will become an increasingly important factor in international business.

Protection as a Bargaining Chip

Trade negotiations usually involve the reduction of the level of protection by one nation in exchange for reductions by that nation's trading partners. The "bargaining chip" rationale for trade restrictions argues that unilateral relinquishment of these chips results in reduction of the nation's bargaining strength in future negotiations. This argument is akin to President Reagan's proposition, "We must arm in order to be more effective in negotiating arms reductions" and has all the strengths and weaknesses of that proposition, with the difference that trade restrictions can be applied quickly whereas an arms buildup requires time. The threat by the United States to use the "food weapon" against OPEC countries highlights the similarities between the two propositions. Unilateral reduction of trade barriers increases national welfare; multilateral reduction can be achieved only by trading reductions in trade barriers and not by some other means (defense agreements, financial transfers, etc.); thus the bargaining chip rationale has some validity.

In summary, on the grounds of economic efficiency, the arguments for trade protection are ill-founded (with the exception in some restricted cases of the optimal tariff and infant industry arguments). The arguments may have validity on other grounds, but how these other factors should be evaluated to determine the effects of protection on national welfare is difficult and uncertain at best and subject to unscrupulous manipulation at worst. To return to the message in the earlier section entitled "Alternatives to Tariffs," *any* of the goals that can be achieved through trade restrictions can be achieved at lower cost (more efficiently) by more direct policies. Protection of the domestic textile industry to ensure that the national flag is made of domestic cloth is far more costly than a direct subsidy of flag protection.

NONTARIFF BARRIERS TO TRADE

The economic effects of nontariff barriers (NTBs) to trade are roughly similar to those of tariffs; that is, they are inefficient distortions which reduce potential gains from trade. There is a wide range of NTBs, as can be seen in Exhibit 3-1. Nontariff barriers have gained prominence in recent years as they have become more visible and more important. Nations have resorted to them more frequently for protection in lieu of tariffs. For example, the *average* U.S. tariff rate was reduced from an all-time high of 60 percent in 1932 to 12 to 15 percent during the 20 years following World War II to about 5 percent by 1980. Nontariff barriers remained largely intact until the 1970s, when their use increased. The Tokyo round of the GATT negotiations devoted considerable attention to reducing NTBs. The negotiators listed over 800 NTBs used by the member countries.

Some of these NTBs were not imposed by nations to deliberately interfere with trade. Sometimes they arose out of domestic policy and economic management. Examples include tax breaks to reduce regional income disparities or regulations designed to increase local purchasing or employment. These then resulted in a type of indirect export subsidy. Yet other NTBs are more blatant devices which restrict imports or foster exports.

The most frequently used NTBs are now discussed in more detail.

Quotas

Quotas are the most important NTBs. Returning to Figure 3-1, instead of imposing a tariff on good X, a quota could be set on imports to restrict them to $A'B'$. Domestic production would increase to OA' and prices would rise to $PW + t$. Government would lose tariff revenues $MNQU$ unless it could auction off the quota to foreign exporters or domestic importers. In theory the quota could be sold for exactly $MNQU$. If the national government assigns the quota to the government of its trading partner or foreign exporters as compensation, however, this revenue is lost to the nation and welfare is reduced below that of a tariff. If the

EXHIBIT 3-1
NONTARIFF BARRIERS TO TRADE

Specific limitations	Customs-administrative rules	Government participation	Import charges
Quotas (including voluntary)	Valuation systems	Procurement policies	Import deposits
Import licenses	Antidumping rules	Export subsidies and incentives	Supplementary duties
Foreign-domestic ratios	Tariff classifications	Countervailing duties	Import credits
Minimum import price limits	Documentation needed	Domestic assistance programs	Variable levies
Embargoes	Fees	Trade-diverting aids	Border levies
Bilateral agreements	Disparities in quality and testing standards		
Orderly marketing agreements	Packaging, labeling, marketing standards		

firms in the domestic market have market power, under a quota they can simply subtract the quota from their downward-sloping demand curve, reducing output to the point at which $MC = MR$ (with the quota) and price up to the modified demand curve. In this case, a quota decreases national welfare more than the equivalent tariff, whatever procedure the government uses in distributing quota rights.

Historically, the GATT has prohibited import quotas except on agricultural products, as emergency measures, or when a country has short-run balance of payments problems. Countries have circumvented this regulation most notably for textiles, footwear, and automobiles by negotiating (imposing) "voluntary export restraint agreements." In general, business would rather be protected by quotas than tariffs. Under quotas, if future domestic demand is known, business can subtract the quota and have a reasonable idea of their future production levels. Under tariffs, domestic producers must estimate the elasticity of the demand curve for imported products *and* the future movements in world prices. On the other hand, if domestic demand declines (as it has for autos, textiles, and footwear), a fixed quota will take up a larger percent of the depressed domestic market, whereas under a tariff domestic producers are largely unaffected. (To see this differential effect, refer back to Figure 3-1 and shift LD_x to the left assuming a tariff or quota.)

Buy National Restrictions

"Buy national" regulations require national governments to give preference to domestic producers, sometimes to the complete exclusion of foreign firms. This NTB has been particularly irksome to American businesspeople since in the United States the telephone, telegraph, electricity generation and transmission, airlines, and railroad industries are privately owned (and open to bids from importers) while they are government-owned in most of the United States' trading partners (and closed to American bids). This market for American exports was estimated at $50 billion per year. On the other hand, the United States has a wide range of "Buy American" regulations at the national and state levels which discriminate against foreign producers. Procurement of products for national defense is sometimes limited to American producers or requires a high price discount below the U.S. price for foreign suppliers.

During the Tokyo round of the GATT negotiations, a mild code to open up government contracts to foreign suppliers was negotiated. Now at least governments must publicize large procurement contracts and accept foreign bids. Governments, however, are still not required to make public the winner's bid price or its basis for selecting the winning bid.

Customs Valuation

During the Tokyo round, considerable progress was made in the area of customs valuation for duty. Value for duty is now generally on the invoice cost, even for intrafirm trade between related subsidiaries of MNEs, unless transfer price manipulation can be demonstrated. The latitude of customs to reclassify products was also reduced. Prior to this agreement, some countries had highly idiosyncratic valuation procedures. In the United States, there were nine valuation systems prior to the Tokyo round.

Technical Barriers

Product and process standards for health, welfare, safety, quality, size, and measurements can impede trade by excluding "nonstandard" products. Testing and certification procedures, such as testing only in the importing country and on-site plant inspections, were (and still are to a lesser extent) cumbersome, time-consuming, and expensive. These costs must be borne by the exporter *prior* to any foreign sales. National governments have the right and duty to protect their citizens by setting standards to prevent the sale of hazardous or shoddy products. Standards can be used not only to ensure quality and performance, but also to impede trade. Japan excluded American-made baseball bats from the market because they did not meet the Japanese standard. No product produced outside Japan (even products made by foreign subsidiaries of Japanese MNEs) could bear the certification stamp of the Japanese Industrial Standard (JIS) or Japanese Agricultural Standard (JAS), and sale in Japan without the JIS or JAS logo was difficult. At one time the new regulations for automobile safety in the United States required bumpers to be above the height practical for imported subcompact cars. The new code on technical barriers to trade requires consultation between trading partners before a standard that impedes trade is put in place. The code also requires that testing and certification procedures treat imports and domestic goods equally and that the importing country accept certification to standard in the exporting country.

Subsidies, Countervailing Duties, and Antidumping Legislation

The GATT allows importing countries to protect domestic producers from unfair competition by imposing additional duties on products that have received export subsidies or are "dumped" at low prices. Before the duties are imposed, the country must show that its domestic industry has suffered "material" injury by dumped or subsidized imports. Although products at these artificially low prices provide consumers in the importing country with a "good buy," such competition is thought to be "unfair" to domestic producers. Domestic producers particularly object to dumping and subsidized imports if the domestic market of the exporting country is closed to them.

The Toyko round developed a code on countervailing duties and antidumping duties that expedited the process of determining whether exports had been dumped or subsidized and whether the domestic industry had been injured. This subject is exceedingly complex.

If the EEC remits value-added taxes on exports, is this a subsidy? (No.) If Canada subsidizes production in one of its depressed regions for domestic purposes, are the exports of a subsidized firm subject to countervail? (Yes.)

If the British government finances the huge losses British Steel incurred by selling at home and abroad at prices below full cost, are its exports subject to antidumping or countervailing duties? (Maybe, sometimes.)

How is "material" injury defined—detectable, minimal, significant, or the major cause of injury (among other causes), and how is it measured—decreased sales or profits, less than projected profits and sales, or excess capacity?

These questions will keep international trade lawyers and consultants busy in the years ahead.

Agricultural Products

Trade in agricultural products is highly regulated by quotas and fixed and variable tariffs. Domestic producers are often highly subsidized both directly and by artificially high domestic prices behind trade barriers. Agricultural exports are often subsidized as well. The EEC flatly refused to discuss its Common Agricultural Policy (CAP) at the Tokyo round. The CAP sets variable tariffs on imports to maintain high domestic prices by excluding or impeding imports. Moreover, revenues from these tariffs are used to subsidize exports. The CAP infuriates American agricultural producers since it not only reduces their exports to the large European market, but also reduces world prices and gives them "unfair" competition in third-country markets. The United States is not without guilt in this area, however, since it subsidizes the export of many agricultural products.

Export Restraints

Over the vigorous objections of natural resource-exporting countries, the Tokyo Round moved to tighten the conditions under which exports could be restrained. In general, world tariffs increase with the level of processing (e.g., import duties increase as copper is processed from concentrate to blister, to refined copper, to copper wire and bars, to copper pots and pans). This tariff structure makes upgrading of natural resources in the producing country difficult. During the Tokyo round natural resource-producing countries were largely unsuccessful in their attempts to harmonize tariffs on a sectoral basis to increase their ability to upgrade prior to export. They argued successfully for their right to restrict exports to induce further domestic processing.

Export Cartels and OPEC   Since 1973, the impact of OPEC on world oil prices has focused the glare of world attention on export cartels. Export cartels are neither new nor confined to OPEC, however. In 1974 a study by the Organization for Economic Cooperation and Development (OECD) identified 489 national export cartels and 100 international export cartels in six OECD countries.[6] Although only 2 to 5 percent of the total exports of these countries were covered by cartel agreements, in some industries high percentages of exports were made by cartels. In 1962 American exports of sulfur (86.1 percent), motion picture and television films (80.0 percent), carbon black (69.8 percent), phosphate (44.7 percent), and potash (24.4 percent) were by cartels, and these products held a dominant position in world markets.[7] Even nations whose laws prohibit cartels from selling on the domestic market (such as the United States and Canada) condone and sometimes even encourage cartels for exports.

The strict definition of a cartel is a group of producers who limit total output by allocating production quotas among themselves to influence the price of their produce. According to this definition, the OPEC cartel is not a cartel. Before 1982, OPEC did not allocate production quotas among its members, and in 1982 and 1983, when it tried to do so, the result was complete failure. Instead, four countries within the cartel, Saudi Arabia, Kuwait, Libya, and the United Arab Emirates, have acted as price leaders and individually regulated their production to set and defend the price of oil at the price they thought was best for them, a price far above the competitive level. The other members of OPEC pumped as much oil as their production capacity and international constraints permitted. In 1982 and 1983, when the downturn in the world economy, conservation measures, and increased output by OPEC and non-OPEC producers led to a surplus of oil on world markets at the posted price, the four OPEC price leaders reduced production by 60 percent from 1979 levels. The surplus continued and there was widespread price cutting by some OPEC countries. In early 1983 an attempt by Saudi Arabia to negotiate production quotas and cutbacks for all members resulted in failure and world oil prices fell sharply.

Cartels are inherently unstable, particularly in the long run. The many conditions necessary for a successful cartel are listed in Exhibit 3-2. These conditions fall into four groups: supply, demand, price, and group cohesion. For a cartel to be effective, it must control a large percent of world supply. As a group, they must be able to regulate total cartel supply in the face of changing world conditions. Control is easier if resources and production are concentrated among a few producers; if production levels can be changed easily and at low cost; if output can be stored without loss; and if production, trade levels, and prices are easily monitored. Short- and long-run demand should be inelastic with few substitutes and few opportunities for conservation. Over time, the revenue requirements of the members should be similar, to facilitate setting an optimum price. In OPEC, Saudi Arabia desired a relatively low cartel price in order to discourage long-run substitution, conservation, and technological progress. Nigeria, Iran, Indonesia,

---

[6]The United States (38 in total), the United Kingdom (288), Spain (6), the Netherlands (20), Japan (167), and Germany (70).

[7]United States Federal Commission Economics Report on Webb Pomerene Associations: Staff Report to the Federal Trade Commission, Washington, DC, 1967.

EXHIBIT 3-2
CHARACTERISTICS OF A SUCCESSFUL CARTEL

Supply	Concentrated in a few countries
	Inelastic short- and long-run supply
	Undifferentiated products
	Production easily controlled
	Low storage and spoilage costs
	Few opportunities for new production technology
	Trade flows easily monitored
Demand	Inelastic in both short and long run
	No close substitutes
	No conservation opportunities
	No technological opportunities in developing substitutes or in conservation
	Stable
Price	Easily monitored
	A consensus on price objectives
	Price of the product a small component of price of final consumption
Membership	Common culture, race, religion, language, political system
	Common economic philosophy toward restrictive business practices

and Venezuela wanted a relatively high price to maximize short-term revenues. Cooperation in a cartel is facilitated if the members possess common characteristics, such as language, religion, political philosophy, or race.

These conditions are extraordinarily difficult to find. The International Bauxite Association raised royalties by 400 percent during 1974 through 1980. Morocco and Tunisia raised the price of phosphate by 400 percent between mid-1972 and the end of 1974. Banana exporters failed in their attempts, for obvious reasons. South Africa succeeded for a long period in maintaining diamond prices at high levels. On *economic* grounds, there is a potential for cartels in gold (South Africa and the Soviet Union), uranium (Canada, South Africa, and Australia), nickel (Canada), and wheat (Canada, the United States, Argentina, and Australia). The problems in forming cartels in these products are largely political. There is less potential for coffee and sugar (high supply elasticity), rubber (high demand elasticity), copper, and tin (high supply elasticity and differing revenue requirements among producing countries). If world resources are depleted in the future for specific products, then new cartels may be formed.

COUNTERTRADE

Countertrade is essentially barter trade in which the exporting firm receives payment in terms of products produced in the importing country. Countertrade forms a major component of east-west trade (e.g., western pipeline products and technology in exchange for Russian natural gas). It is also important in the aircraft industry (e.g., the purchase of Boeing 747s by British Airways if Boeing uses Rolls Royce engines) and in defense products (e.g., the purchase of American jet fighters by Canada if some of the parts are sourced in Canada). In the early 1980s, some low- and middle-income countries have turned to countertrade to try to balance their trade accounts.

With one exception, countertrade decreases the efficiency of world trade since it substitutes barter for exchange of goods by the price system. For example, a U.S. exporter of machinery to Indonesia may have to take payment in an "equivalent value" of palm oil or rattan. The exporting firm will then either have to sell these products for which it has no expertise itself or sell them through a broker or other firm. Some party to the trade—exporter, importer, or consumer—must bear these additional costs. Despite these obvious inefficiencies, countertrade appears likely to become an increasingly important factor in the international trade environment of the 1980s.

There is, however, one situation in which countertrade *may* be beneficial. For example, if a U.S. producer of textile machinery exports to China and agrees to take payment in the form of textile products, importers in the United States may perceive a lower risk of variability in product quality and delivery schedules (as a result of American technology and management), and the Chinese may perceive a lower risk of product failure in buying the machinery since the selling firm will not be "paid" unless the machinery performs to specifications.

With this exception, countertrade increases the inefficiencies in the world trade system, thus increasing costs and decreasing trade volume. Even in the case discussed here, if China sources textile machinery based on whether the exporter will take payment in textiles, inappropriate sourcing and sales can occur. For these reasons, international organizations such as the OECD have actively tried to discourage countertrade.

TRADE IN SERVICES

International trade in services has received relatively little attention from government, from trade economists, or during trade negotiations. Reliable statistics are seldom collected. But as high-income countries have moved toward a service economy, trade in service has grown and become a significant component of the current accounts of many countries. In 1981 the United States exported goods worth $236 billion and imported goods worth $264 billion. It exported $136.6 billion and imported $97 billion in "other goods and services." Its trade surplus in services of $39 billion offset its trade deficit of $28 billion to yield a current account surplus. In 1980 the United States had a surplus in service flows of $6.2 billion in fees and royalties and $25.7 billion in income from investment.

The flow of services internationally is highly regulated. Internationally traded services such as banking, investment income, insurance, media, transportation, advertising, accounting, travel, and technology licensing are subject to a host of national and international regulations for economic, social, cultural, and political reasons. Trade in services largely falls outside the mandate of the GATT. One of the major trade questions for the 1980s and 1990s will be the regulation of trade in services. Will services be brought into the GATT so that reductions in impediments in service flows can be traded for reductions in barriers to the flow of goods? The United States, as the largest exporter and importer of services (and the largest *net* exporter), supports this proposal. Alternatively, a new organization similar to GATT could be founded to facilitate negotiations on barriers to trade in services and to regulate this trade. The United States views this proposal as a second best (but a far second best) alternative since it is already relatively open to trade in services and hence has few bargaining chips.

Whatever forum is used, negotiating reductions in barriers to trade in services will be difficult, complex, and lengthy. The barriers are often difficult to list, much less quantify for purposes of negotiation. The issues are often *highly* charged and not subject to rational analysis. For example, Canada imposes Canadian content requirements on television, radio, and print media to foster a "national cultural identity"; to protect its cultural heritage; and to protect the domestic arts, theater, and movie industries. A government that reduced these trade barriers or even agreed to negotiate regarding them would be hung in effigy with the (protected) Canadian media heading the pack. Negotiations over even such purely economic service flows as technology will be difficult since net technology importers, especially some developing countries, believe that technology, once generated, should be a free public good and should be transferred to the host country at the low marginal cost of transfer.

FREE TRADE ZONES

A free trade zone is a designated area where importers can defer payment of customs duty while further processing of products takes place. Thus the free trade zone serves as an "offshore assembly plant," employing local workers and using local financing for a tax-exempt commercial activity. The economic activity in a free trade zone takes place in a restricted area such as an industrial park, since this land is often being supplied at a subsidized rate by a local host government interested in the potential employment benefits of the free trade zone.

To be effective, free trade zones must be strategically located either at or near an international port, on major shipping routes, or with easy access to a major airport. Important factors in the location of a free trade zone include the availability of utilities, banking and telecommunications services, and the availability of a commercial infrastructure.

Between 300 and 400 free trade zones exist in the world today, often encompassing entire cities (e.g., Hong Kong and Singapore). More than two-thirds are situated in developing countries, and most future growth of these zones is expected to occur there. In 1980, over 10 percent of world trade passed through these zones, with free trade zone activity accounting for 6 million jobs. By 1985, it is estimated that free trade zones may be handling more than 20 percent of worldwide trade; this is a significant portion of economic activity, especially relevant for small open trading nations.

The advantages offered by free trade zones are numerous and are mutually beneficial to all the stakeholders. For private firms, free trade zones offer three major attractions. First, the firm pays only the customs duty (tariff) when the goods are ready to market. Second, manufacturing costs are lower (e.g., labor and capital are cheaper) in a free trade zone, as no taxes (corporate or income) are levied. Third, while in the zone, the manufacturer has the opportunity to repackage the goods, grade them, and check for spoilage, thus reducing waste. Customs duties are only paid on the goods finally removed from the zone. Secondary benefits to firms occur in the reduction of insurance premiums (since these are based on duty-free values), the reduction of fines for improperly marked merchandise (since the goods can be inspected in a zone prior to customs scrutiny), and the added protection against theft (resulting from reduced security measures).

On the state and local level, advantages can be realized in terms of increased employment, diversification of industry, and promotion of commercial services. On a more global level, free trade zones enable domestic importing companies to compete more readily with foreign producers or subsidiaries of multinational enterprises, thereby increasing participation in world trade. Favorable effects are felt on the balance of payments since more economic activity occurs and net capital outflow is reduced. Finally, there is an improved climate for business, since a free trade zone reduces bureaucracy with savings to business capital currently inaccessible because of the delay in paying duties and tariffs. A free trade zone is a step toward free trade and can be an important signal by government to business that the economy is being opened up. Opportunity replaces regulation and growth of economic activity should result.

Before the establishment of more free trade zones becomes fully accepted and encouraged, governments must be convinced of their many economic benefits. Free trade zones are a vital necessity if nations are to remain competitive on an international scale. Not only will existing companies benefit from their use, but new industries will be attracted, keeping up the same benefits of world trade.

SUMMARY

International trade never has been and never can be free. At most, freer trade can be an objective toward which countries individually and as a group strive. Through government-to-government negotiations and by natural forces—lower transportation and communication costs, technology diffusion, increased capital, and labor flows—the world is moving toward freer trade. Just as freer trade presents threats and opportunities to business, so, too, does the restriction of trade. The level and type of trade restrictions shift the mode of international business operation among trade, licensing, foreign direct investment, countertrade, and international loans. An understanding of the determinants and effects of trade and restrictions on trade is vital for the practicing international manager.

KEY WORDS

Terms of trade
Effective tariff
Value added
Threat of retaliation
Infant industries argument
Bargaining chip

Nontariff barriers
Cartel
Countertrade
Free trade zones
Technical barriers

QUESTIONS

1 The chapter discusses three types of tariffs: nominal, effective, and optimum. Describe how each of these differs. Which type of tariff indicates greater efficiency? What problems are inherent in using optimal tariffs?

2 How can the welfare losses described in the first question be avoided? If possible, use a diagram to illustrate your answer. Explain. What is meant by the statement: A policy should be direct rather than indirect? If this is true, why are subsidies not used more often?

3 What is the basic premise of the infant industry argument? Discuss the problems inherent in this theory. Use a graph, where possible, to illustrate your answer. How can these problems be resolved?

4 The converse to the infant industry argument is the "old industry argument." Describe this concept. Why can it be dismissed so easily?

5 Nontariff barriers have become increasingly predominant in recent years. Four major categories of nontariff barriers are outlined in this chapter. Briefly describe these categories, giving examples of each. Discuss, in greater detail, two examples of nontariff barriers.

6 The impact of cartels, such as OPEC, is widely known. Define a cartel. What are the conditions necessary for a cartel? What products offer potential for cartels? If you were a consultant for a leading firm in one of these industries, what arguments would you present regarding the formation of a cartel?

Exercise A: Demonstrate, in graphical form, how the tariff is inefficient. Discuss the impact upon production, consumption, revenue, and national welfare. What are the effects on both producers and consumers?

Exercise B: Evaluate the following: The textile industry states that although it is protected by a tariff of 20 percent, it must use imported cloth which comprises 40 percent of its total cost under free trade. It must pay a tariff duty of 15 percent on this cloth. Hence it argues that it receives 5 percent (20 − 15 percent) protection.

CASE: The Dumping of Polish Golf Carts

One problem of east-west trade is the difference in the underlying economic systems of the two types of societies. Poland is a country burdened with heavy foreign debt, so the development of export markets is a national priority. Because of its centrally planned system, the state will have a presence in many of Poland's exports, even in such quixotic products as golf carts.

In the late 1960s, golf became extremely popular in the United States, with golf carts in great demand. Several European countries were sought by an American importer to produce the carts since they offered inexpensive alternatives to the costly American product. Of the four countries considered (Yugoslavia, Bulgaria, East Germany, and Poland), Poland was chosen for its lower duties (most favored nation status) and experience in manufacturing operations.

In the early 1970s Pzetel, a Polish manufacturer of light aircraft, won a contract to produce 10,000 golf carts per year. When Pzetel's partner in the United States went bankrupt, the company set up its own importer-distributor, Melex, USA. Melex was highly successful, selling 1000 carts in 1971 and 3000 in 1972. Demand grew rapidly, with production doubling after 1972.

The selling price was $1000 to $1200, about $400 less than its American counterpart. As Melex's sale doubled, American producers grew angrier, filing an official complaint with the U.S. Treasury Department in 1974. The charge was "dumping"—selling goods in international markets for less than their home price or cost of production in the home nation.

The U.S. Customs Department invoked a compensatory duty of $150 per unit on all carts shipped in 1975. Although two Canadian firms had closed since Melex began operations, Pzetel fought the ruling, denying any responsibility for their competitors' failure. The issue lay in determining whether the carts were sold at less than fair market value.

Three methods are used for this: selling below home-country prices; selling below the cost of production; and a system of reconstructed values, which involves comparison of Polish manufacturing costs with those of another western European country.

None of these was appropriate for Melex. There was no Polish price as all golf carts were sold in the United States. The cost of production could not be used since Poland is a socialist country and prices are not market-determined. The final problem was in finding a comparable country. The U.S. Treasury chose a small Canadian manufacturer as a reference point, but its cost structures were hardly a replica of Poland's.

In 1977 the method of comparability was tried. This concept, similar to reconstructed prices, compares Polish costs to what those costs would be in a western economy at a similar stage of development. Spain was chosen as a comparable nation. Poland opened its books to U.S. Customs inspection, and the newly constructed price was found to be only $10 more than the actual price. Although the U.S. Treasury Department accepted this finding, problems still exist.

Subsequent cases (e.g., Harley Davidson, a division of A. M. F. Corporation) attest to the fact that a more conclusive method of determining fair market value and dumping must be found. The feat of antidumping action has created a barrier to the free flow of east-west trade.

QUESTIONS

1 Define "dumping." To whom is it a problem, and to whom is it not?

2 Identify and describe three methods of finding the true economic price of a dumped product.

3 Under what economic conditions might it be rational for a firm to charge different prices for the same product in different nations? Is this dumping?

4 What other commodities in east-west trade do you consider to be involved in dumping?

PART # TWO

THE FIRM IN THE INTERNATIONAL ENVIRONMENT

CHAPTER 4

INTERNATIONAL BUSINESS BY NONMULTINATIONALS

THE ROLE OF EXPORTING

This chapter on exporting provides a linkage between the country-specific environmental factors just considered and the more firm-specific factors that will concern us for most of the remainder of the book. We now have an understanding of the principles of efficiency arising from a situation of free trade and the real-world problems that other aspects of government policy impose to constrain the potential benefits of trade. Now these concepts from international trade need to be turned into relevant business guidelines.

It is remarkably difficult for a firm about to become engaged in international business to know when to stop scanning the global environment and to turn principles into practice. In this part of the book we provide a framework for such a business agenda.

This chapter considers the problem of how to operate a firm in the complex international environment from the viewpoint of a person or firm just about to go international. We shall discuss the export and other foreign opportunities and risks facing a smaller or inexperienced firm about to enter international business. This chapter on nonmultinationals will also include an introductory analysis of alternatives to exporting such as joint ventures, turnkey projects, and licensing.

Chapter 5 develops an important model suitable for multinational enterprises, large and small. This model focuses on the internal markets of the MNE and thereby develops the theory of *internal*ization. This contrasts with the concept of *international*ization discussed in the present chapter. Finally, Chapter 6 concludes this part of the book by providing more rigorous standards in the appropriate choice of entry mode for a global business with a strategic interest in protecting the special firm-specific advantages it has developed.

HOW TO GO INTERNATIONAL

Finding Foreign Markets

The beginning of exporting for most small business and nontrading companies consists of the receipt of unsolicited orders from a customer abroad. From such apparently small beginnings empires can be built. For example, Toyota's exports to Europe started back in the fifties on the initiative of a Danish auto dealer who went to Japan to buy a few trial cars.

As unsolicited orders increase in number, the firm might find itself with an export share which demands more and more attention from management. As exports become an integral part of the business, there is naturally less tendency to sit back and wait for orders. The firm starts thinking about actively exploring foreign markets.

The first steps in this process are usually quite tentative. The firm might hire an "export manager" to take care of the paperwork, add staff if the work increases (i.e., if the export sales are growing), and possibly develop over time a full-grown export sales division. This process usually takes several years, however. During those years, the exporting group of the business must take care of many matters such as shipping, documentation, finance, and servicing sales agents abroad.

One obvious place to look for further sales is in the countries where orders are already originating. There might be other customers with similar needs to whom it would be relatively easy to sell, considering the fact that the channels of distribution have already been established. Alternatively, the exporter should look at countries similar to the ones already in the fold, especially countries which are close to the firm's main base of operations, the home country. The similarity in terms of product requirements and tastes coupled with usually lower transportation costs have made this "cultural" or "psychological" proximity one of the key factors in explaining how firms choose export markets.

For evaluation of the market potential in these candidate countries, there are usually several useful sources. In the United States, probably the quickest and least expensive way for the inexperienced firm to begin is through the export trade specialist in the nearest Department of Commerce district office. The specialist will be able to determine whether similar products are being exported to these countries already, by whom, and in what amounts. Other countries can be explored with the help of the *Global Market Surveys* and the *Country Market Surveys* which the office has access to.

The identified countries can be studied in greater detail through the *Overseas Business Reports*, which provide basic background data on each specific country. These publications cover the economic conditions, trade regulations, market factors, and trade with various countries. The district office will also be able to identify addresses of potential distributors and for a nominal fee will provide a computer search across countries, product areas, and types of leads, such as calls for tenders (invitations to quote), agents and distributors, and so on.

Most countries have some information system of a similar nature sponsored by either the government or the trade associations. Alternatively, the consulates of the respective countries might be useful in organizing initial contracts. For exporters to Japan, the Japan External Trade Organization (JETRO) maintains offices in many countries around the world and is able to provide quite specific information on a product basis about conditions in the Japanese market.

Price Quotations

Of immediate concern to the fledgling exporter, even as unsolicited orders flow in, is the problem of quoting the "right" price. The problem is not so much what the optimal price is—usually the firm might want to cover additional risks by setting price slightly higher than in the domestic market, or, alternatively, where the foreign market is deemed to be of great future potential, a lower "penetration" price might be most appropriate. The problem is rather that in quoting the prices, the price escalation due to tariffs, fees, and transportation needs to be considered.

The simplest and least effective solution is to quote free on board (FOB) factory, which means that the customer has to pay all charges once the product has left the plant. One small extension is FOB ship, where the manufacturer loads the product on the appropriate means of transportation (rail, ship, truck, etc.) and the customer pays all remaining charges. A similar quotation is free along side (FAS), port of exit, where the product is priced for delivery to the customer on the dock.

A more marketing-oriented quote is the cost, insurance, and freight (CIF), where the seller assumes the responsibility for the three cost items to a designated foreign port, possibly the customer's own warehouse. Lesser involvement is represented by C&F, where the insurance is paid by the buyer.

Many variations of these quotation procedures are possible. The main question to keep in mind is the degree to which the risks and costs are to be divided between the seller and the buyer. Successful exporters have learned that it is usually better to quote a higher price which includes these CIF factors rather than shifting the burden over to the buyer. The reader should remember the concept of the firm-specific advantages (FSAs) and the lowering of transaction costs here. With increased experience in exporting, it will be more efficient for the seller to quote CIF rather than FOB, and it also makes good marketing sense.

Payments

Quoting a price is one thing—getting paid is another. Because of the geographic separation, sellers will do well to carefully consider the options available to protect themselves against default.

There are essentially five methods of payment: cash in advance, open account, consignment, letters of credit, and documentary drafts. *Cash in advance* is an option that places a heavy burden on the buyer and should be used only when initial orders are filled and the export business is judged relatively unimportant to the seller.

An *open account* is the opposite of cash in advance. Here the seller assumes all risks, and this option should be used only when the credit standing of the buyer is high. This type of payment is applicable in particular with a long-standing relationship and where the customer is a large, well-established firm.

Consignment refers to the case where payments are made only as the goods are sold by the buyer. This method is particularly applicable where the seller is interested in testing a new market and is eager to have a distributor carry the product. It is usually an interim option, to be renegotiated once a more precise evaluation of the potential of the market is possible.

The most common payment options in exporting are letters of credit and documentary drafts. Here the payment is made contingent on the receipt by the buyer of the goods in the specified condition. The letter of credit is issued by the buyer's bank, which promises to pay the seller once certain stipulations have been fulfilled. The *documentary draft* is simpler and cheaper, and the bank agrees to pay the seller on presentation of the draft (through the seller's own bank connection) or after a certain date (sight draft versus time draft, respectively).

The *letter of credit* (LC) follows a rather intricate course through the facilitating institutions. An example is given in Figure 4-1. After the initial agreement about the sale, the seller sends a document (usually an invoice) to the buyer (Seoul Furniture Co.). On receipt, the buyer contacts a South Korean bank, and an LC (confirmed by the seller's bank) is sent to the seller (East Coast Manufacturing). On receipt of this LC, the seller arranges for the shipment of the merchandise and collects the bill of lading (BL). In such a case the LC stipulates payment after 90 days, but the seller has the option of discounting the LC against immediate money in any other bank (Canadian Commonwealth). This bank requests payment from the Seoul bank on the basis of the LC and the shipping documents. Finally, the Korean bank will be paid by the buyer at time of maturity (after the 90-day period).

Variations on this scheme are possible. For example, it is common for the LC to stipulate payment only after the buyer has received the merchandise in good condition. The basic principle follows the example in Figure 4-1 rather closely.

Financing

Because of the difficulties for many buyers in paying cash in advance and the many risks involved in doing so, the question of financing of a sales transaction often becomes important in export operations. The LC arrangement is only one example of how a bank might help to finance a purchase. (The example given in Figure 4-1 shows how the Seoul bank in fact has given the buyer a 90-day loan.) In most countries banks will be a prime source for trade financing, often for longer periods than 90 days, but there are usually other sources available.

Government assistance is one source of financing. In most countries there are government funds available in one form or another for the financing of exports. In the United States the Export-Import Bank is a government institution which not only offers direct loans for large projects and equipment sales requiring long-term financing (over 5 years) such as commercial aircraft and power plants, but also

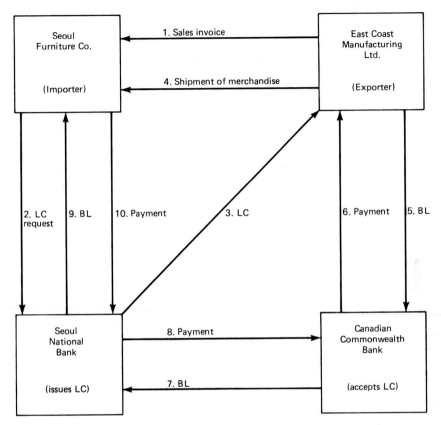

FIGURE 4-1
Exporting under a confirmed time letter of credit.

provides medium-term (181 days to 5 years) and long-term guarantees for commercial bank financing.

For short-term (up to 180 days) and medium-term protection, the U.S. government also offers an insurance program, the Foreign Credit Insurance Association (FCIA), a combine of about 50 insurance companies which insures against political and commercial risk for up to 95 percent of the loss.

Most countries also offer some form of exporting incentive consisting of tax relief on export earnings. In some cases the Japanese government has waived tax liability on such revenues. In the United States the 1971 Revenue Act (amended in 1976) created a special corporate entity called Domestic International Sales Corporation (DISC). Under this charter an exporter may be able to create a subsidiary for its export business and defer up to 50 percent of the net income derived from export sales.

For many exporters to low- and middle-income countries, the financing question is the most important competitive consideration. Many of these countries can only buy certain products, particularly investment goods, if the seller can provide attractive, long-term financing. With international competition running at an all-time high, export financing considerations provide the kind of competitive advantages that can make or break a sale. In this respect many of the Japanese trading companies who have a strong financial base are at an advantage over many smaller exporters whose individual resources cannot match such competition. In fact, a major source of Japan's country-specific advantage (CSA) is based on the ability of Japanese companies to marshal financial resources for the huge projects often required in the developing nations.

Shipping Procedures

The physical handling and shipping of the merchandise often requires fairly detailed knowledge which most exporters would rather not spend the time and money to learn. Instead, *freight forwarders* specializing in overseas shipments can be used to handle exports. These independent agencies will generally serve as the exporter's traffic department.

The shipping documents which are needed for customs and payment procedures include the bill of lading (BL), which specifies the exact nature of the goods and the assignment of responsibility for its shipment to the buyer's country. In many cases the seller also needs an export license, depending on the product and the country of destination. Insurance certificates, certificates of origin, and inspection certificates are some of the additional documents that might be needed.

The freight forwarder will be able to handle the dispatch of the merchandise and the paperwork involved, and also advise on the possible types of vessel and handling that are most appropriate (e.g., containerization). Some forwarders can handle air and railroad shipments in addition to ocean shipping, but there are also specialized agents for each means of transportation. The choice between these various agents is usually based on the fees charged and the reputation of the agent. Once a reliable agent has been found, a long-term relationship is often developed which minimizes the transaction costs involved in renegotiating each particular shipment.

EXTERNAL EXPORT DEPARTMENTS

The exporter eventually finds it useful to rely exclusively on a more comprehensive form of facilitating agent, such as an export management company or a trading company. This procedure simplifies matters a great deal for the exporter and makes the employment of in-house personnel unnecessary. Accordingly, this is usually the preferred mode of operation when exporting occupies a relatively minor portion of the total business.

Export Management Companies (EMCs)

Export management companies are independent businesses which act as the export departments for several noncompetitive manufacturers. They carry out the basic functions involved in generating export sales, including procedural matters. They also do research on market potential in various countries and exhibit the client's products at trade shows around the globe. They are generally empowered to transact business in the name of the client manufacturer and are paid on the basis of a commission on the sales amounts transacted. In many cases they will also take outright ownership to certain products, in fact serving as the client's customer and then reselling the products in the various countries abroad. As the EMCs develop their contacts in different countries they will possess a decisive firm-specific advantage which enables them to spot new opportunities for products other than the ones they sell. The outright ownership option is then exercised when they decide to take on the business risk (and return) themselves.

Because it is possible for the EMCs to develop their own businesses, the exporter who sees a great potential in the foreign markets might do well to work closely with these organizations and perhaps limit involvement to the early stages of market penetration. As the exporter develops more of a know-how in the export business (and as the export group in the organization grows), it might be profitable to be able to assume more and more of the middleman's functions in-house.

Export Consortia

Another type of comprehensive organization quite common in certain countries (e.g., Canada) is the voluntary cooperation of several noncompetitive manufacturers in exporting consortia. These are groups of cooperating businesses whose individual size might be small but who together form a rather large organization. The consortia serve to generate returns-to-scale savings in developing expertise for handling certain types of products and certain groups of countries of particular relevance to the members. They are similar to producers' co-ops (cooperatives) and carry out much of the administrative work necessary for exports. They also carry out some of the basic market assessments as they are requested by member firms.

General Trading Companies

The most conspicuous institutions providing comprehensive service are the general trading companies. The British and Dutch trading companies were closely identified with the colonial policies of their home nations. Indeed, it has been argued that the British East India Company was one of the world's first multinational enterprises and that it ran India more efficiently than did any subsequent administration. Today these trading companies have passed away, to be replaced by several based in South Korea and Brazil. The U.S. Congress has passed a law to allow the creation of American Trading Companies, but the most important today by far are the famous Japanese monoliths.

The names of Mitsubishi, Mitsui, Marubeni, and others are known around the world. For many years their presence has meant exceedingly strong and tenacious competition for non-Japanese businesses. The names and rankings of the ten largest *sogo shoshas* are given in Exhibit 4-1.

With the outstanding success of the Japanese in various export markets, the role of *sogo shoshas* has expanded from a national focus to a more global and multi-national outlook. As a consequence, the Japanese trading companies are being viewed increasingly as a resource in facilitating and managing trade flows also involving non-Japanese principals. Any presumptive exporter or importer needs to consider the assistance of these giants of world trade.

The most basic function of the large trading company is to facilitate exchange between buyers and sellers in different countries. This middleman position, however, has been considerably augmented during the last 20 years or so. With a worldwide network of people and communication units, the trading company can be counted on to identify and appraise potential buyers of Japanese products in almost any country in the world. They can also supply the workers to transact the business, including people with procedural and negotiating knowledge for that particular country. *Sogo shoshas* also provide the means of transportation, and will, if necessary, accept financial liability for the shipment. They are willing and able to provide after-service in many cases, thereby offering buyer and seller the insurance which protects against the jeopardy of international transactions.

An example of the unusual degree to which the trading company can accept responsibility for the product is the case of Toyota's export of trucks to Algeria. The company judged the market too small for the costly provision of the necessary service and parts organization needed to back up their product. Therefore, they

EXHIBIT 4-1
THE TEN LARGEST GENERAL
TRADING COMPANIES IN JAPAN

1	Mitsubishi Corporation
2	Mitsui & Company, Ltd.
3	Marubeni Corporation
4	C. Itoh & Company, Ltd.*
5	Sumitomo Shohi Kaisha, Ltd.
6	Nissho-Iwai Company, Ltd.
7	Tomen, Ltd.
8	Kanematsu-Gosho, Ltd.
9	Nichimen Company, Ltd.
10	Ataka & Company, Ltd.*

*Merged in 1977.

contracted with the Mitsubishi corporation for it to take charge of their whole marketing operation in the country.

In recent years trading companies have gradually come to accept greater responsibility for the various functions involved in international trade. They now serve as partners in joint ventures, provide financing for the development of raw material deposits, and assist in third-country trade negotiations which do not directly involve Japanese companies. With their pool of skilled and knowledgeable personnel in different parts of the world, they are well qualified to provide a liaison function in multilateral negotiations and to identify potential participants in international joint ventures. In many cases they serve a banking role made possible by their close connections with several banks, with at least one major bank belonging to their industry group.

At times their vast information network also serves political needs. A favorite story among Japanese trading companies is the alleged fact that the trading companies were first to break the news about the Iranian revolution, beating out even the American CIA.

Among the large companies mainly responsible for the Japanese exports in major product categories, the use of trading companies varies considerably. Steel companies, for example, use trading companies extensively, with some—such as Nippon Steel, the largest steel producer in the world—employing several *sogo shoshas* in a competitive fashion to check the reliability of the information provided and to obtain the best possible deal.

The Sony corporation, on the other hand, relies little on trading companies, preferring to establish its own subsidiary sales offices in export markets. The higher the technology embodied in the products, the lower will be reliance on the *sogo shoshas*. This has caused some pessimism in trading companies about their relative role in future Japanese exports. So far, however, there has been little evidence of such a decline in quantitative terms. In response to this threat, Mitsubishi, the largest Japanese trading company has begun to market branded consumer products under its own name: color film, televisions, and automobiles.

THE *INTERNATIONAL*IZATION PROCESS

It is time now to pull together some of the major strands that have been discussed so far in this chapter. We need to pick out a few general principles which can act as guidelines for nonmultinationals when they go international. Since the process of becoming international is fairly simple, we emerge with a descriptive rather than a predictive model. Yet it is useful to flag the key items of interest at this stage before moving on to study the more complicated behavior of MNEs.

The role of exporting and similar sales efforts abroad can be related to the penetration of foreign markets by alternative strategies such as licensing, joint venture activity, and foreign direct investment (FDI). This is the process of *international*ization, which can be contrasted with the theory of *internal*ization, which will be developed in Chapter 5.

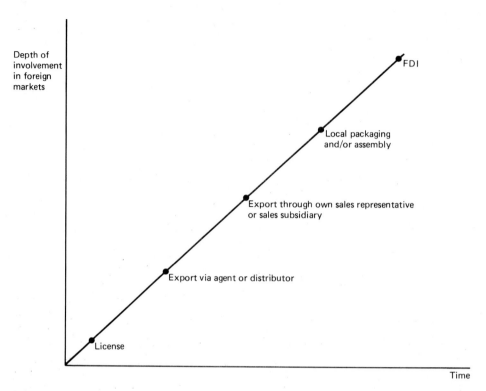

FIGURE 4-2
Entry into foreign markets: the internationalization process.

Figure 4-2 outlines the typical process by which a firm producing a standardized product will seek to involve itself in a foreign market. In this internationalization process the firm regards foreign markets as risky, since these markets are unknown to it. In terms of the special costs of doing business across national boundaries, to be introduced in Chapter 6, the firm faces export marketing costs. To avoid such information costs and risk, its strategy is to go abroad at a slow and cautious pace, often using the services of specialists in international trade outside the firm. Over time, familiarity with the foreign environment will reduce the information costs and help to alleviate the perceived risks of foreign involvement.

Initially the firm may seek to avoid the risks of foreign involvement by arranging a licensing deal. This strategy is most suitable for a standardized product where there is no risk of dissipation of the firm's technological advantage. Otherwise, licensing will be reserved for a much later stage of entry. Indeed, when it is important for the firm to retain control over its firm-specific advantage in technology (as in internalization theory), licensing will come as the last mode of entry (as shown in Chapter 6). The firms involved in internationalization, on the other hand, typically are not concerned about losing their firm-specific advantages.

Rather, they want to avoid exposure to an uncertain foreign environment. Abstracting from the licensing option (and the more complex problem of joint ventures), the other types of foreign entry for a firm are as follows.

1 The firm sees potential extra sales by exporting and uses a local agent or distributor to enter a particular market. Often the firm uses exporting as a "vent" for its surplus production and may have no long-run commitment to the international market. If it does well abroad, however, it may then set up its own local sales representative or marketing subsidiary, in the hope of securing a more stable stream of export sales.

2 As exports come to represent a larger share of sales, the firm may increase its capacity to serve the export market. This stage marks an important departure for the firm from simply viewing exports as a marginal contributor to sales volume or as a vent for surplus in times of excess capacity. At this stage the firm will often set up a separate export department to manage foreign sales and production for such markets and product design and the production process itself may be modified to tailor products for export markets.

3 After the firm has become more familiar with the local market, some of the uncertainty associated with foreign involvement has been overcome. Now the firm may begin to move on the foreign production side. Initially it may start to use host-country workers to engage in local assembly and packaging of its product lines. This is a crucial step, since the firm is now involved in the host-country factor market and must deal with such environmental variables as wage rates, cultural attitudes, and worker expectations in its new labor force.

4 The final stage of foreign involvement comes when the firm has generated sufficient knowledge about the host country to overcome its perceptions of risk. Because it is more familiar with the host-country environment, it may now consider a foreign direct investment activity. In this it produces the entire product line in the host nation and sells its output there, or it may even be able to reexport back to the home country. These decisions depend on the relative country-specific costs, for example, if labor is inexpensive in the host nation (as in southeast Asia), more exporting takes place than if it is expensive (as in western Europe and the United States).

It has become clear that the internationalization process is more complicated than it seems at first glance. Like all generalizations, this schematic path of export commitment relies on simplifications. In reality, the process of foreign entry is sufficiently complicated to depend on a careful weighing of firm-specific and country-specific factors.

OTHER FORMS OF INTERNATIONAL BUSINESS ACTIVITY

Joint Ventures

Joint ventures are usually undertaken by one MNE and a local partner. The MNE brings its firm-specific advantage (in knowledge, technology, or capital) to the operation while the host-country partner traditionally brings knowledge of the local environment. Usually the MNE chooses a partner that is not an MNE itself. This arrangement helps to ensure the stability of the joint venture from the viewpoint of the MNE since it not only provides host country-specific knowledge, but also facilitates relationships with host governments.

On some occasions a joint venture in the international context results in a company owned by more than one MNE. If there are many MNEs sharing ownership, the joint venture is usually referred to as a *consortium*. Joint ventures are commonly used in projects for which no single firm has the ability to commit large amounts of capital, the necessary technology is lodged in several firms, and there is a desire to spread the risk of an uncertain project.

In addition to these considerations, the MNE has other reasons for participating in joint ventures: (1) the host government may legislate or pressure the MNE into accepting an indigenous partner, (2) the MNE may require a partner in order to obtain knowledge of the new and unfamiliar host-country environment, and (3) the local partner may give the MNE access to channels of distribution otherwise denied it or can help to open up access to local raw materials and other resources. This is especially true when the local partner has good lines of communication to the host government.

Usually joint ventures between MNEs involve MNEs which are complementary rather than competing. These MNEs use the same raw material inputs for the manufacture of noncompeting products. Joint venture partners are generally of similar size although Japanese MNEs tend to be larger than their partners. Similar size enhances the stability of the joint venture, since the relative importance of the project to each MNE (and hence the effort contributed to its success) is the same.

The most important consideration in a joint venture is the selection of the partner(s). Sharing management is difficult, so careful consideration must be given to finding a partner that has complementary skills and with whom the MNE can work. The MNE will have to decide whether a passive or active partner is needed. When protection of the MNE's firm-specific advantage is essential, a passive partner is preferred. The joint venture partners should decide on the management sharing system as part of the final agreement, complete with a contingency plan in the event that poor performance results.

Killing (1982) classified joint ventures into three categories: shared management, dominant management by one partner, and independent management from either partner. Killing found that independent management outperformed the others and shared management had the poorest performance. This suggests a positive relationship in a joint venture framework between performance and independence from parent companies. It also demonstrates the adverse effects on performance resulting from management conflicts inherent in different organizational and cultural attitudes in a joint venture. Joint ventures with the poorest performance record and the highest instability are those in which ownership and control are shared equally between the partners. These ventures may operate successfully when conditions are good but may split apart along ownership lines when problems arise.

Turnkey Projects

A turnkey project is a package deal in which the MNE constructs a production facility and provides training for the personnel necessary to operate it, such that the facility is ready to begin operations on the completion of the project. Usually turnkey projects are for production of a standardized product. Thus, a turnkey project involves the sale of what will be a fully operational production facility. The MNE provides a package deal to a host-nation firm or government. On occasion, during the negotiations over the project, the MNE may decide or be forced to retain a small share of the project.

The turnkey project can be an alternative to exporting or to MNE activity when a host government has imposed restrictions on these modalities. In addition, the host nation's market may be too small or the risk of foreign direct investment too great to warrant investment by the MNE. An added benefit to the turnkey project for the MNE is that it can become the supplier of future factor inputs. The MNE can also expect to license additional managerial or technological expertise to the host nation. However, the MNE must give up some control to the host government (which usually owns the facility). For this reason the MNE risks dissipation of its firm-specific advantage. The MNE must determine whether the plant and personnel involved in the turnkey project can eventually become an international competitor against the MNE before it enters into such a venture.

Licensing and Other Contractual Arrangements

Most licensing arrangements provide for the use of an MNE's technology, patents, trademarks, or other firm-specific advantages (FSAs) by a foreign firm in exchange for a fee. The fee usually includes a minimum payment and may also include a percentage of the foreign firm's sales or profits arising from the use of the license.

There are a number of environmental reasons why the MNE may prefer licensing to other modes of entry. The host government may prohibit FDI. The risk of nationalization or foreign control, once in, may be too great. The size of the host market may not be large enough to warrant FDI. Similarly, on occasion, the required economies of scale may not be attainable. Finally, production may be too cumbersome in a host nation which may lack factor inputs in sufficient quantities at reasonable prices. The host nation's labor climate may be incompatible, or intense local competition may reduce the attractiveness of the investment.

There are also reasons internal to the MNE why licensing should be avoided as an entry mode. First and foremost is the risk of dissipation of the MNE's knowledge advantage. The licensee as the buyer of knowledge will acquire at least part of the MNE's FSA in knowledge through licensing arrangements. The MNE should be certain that the licensee will not become a competitor in the future. The licensee sometimes creates fallouts of new technology based on the licensed knowledge, and hence the MNE should contractually ensure that it has access to such developments. Any form of licensing involves the MNE in an association with the licensee. The worldwide reputation of the MNE may suffer if the licensee cannot reach the desired product standards and quality or if it engages in questionable activities.

For small firms that have developed an FSA in product or process technology, licensing can offer an attractive opportunity to earn additional profits without the commitment of capital and managerial resources which are often required for exporting or FDI. Small firms often have no interest in international operations and are not concerned with the dissipation of their FSAs to firms in the markets abroad. They regard the licensing fee as an unexpected bonus from their activities in their national market.

Licensing is not restricted to unrelated foreign firms. License fees or management fees charged are another means of repatriating profits from joint ventures and foreign subsidiaries in the event of capital controls. There are also other forms of licensing which amount to sublicenses: management contracts, franchising, and contract manufacturing (see Exhibit 4-2).

Management contracts provide for the licensing of managerial expertise in specified areas. Management contracts allow the MNE to better control the amount of knowledge that is divulged, and through its influence on the foreign firm's management, the MNE may obtain other benefits such as becoming the supplier of factor inputs. Management contracts also help to ensure quality control and provide international experience for the firm's executives.

In a *franchising* arrangement, the MNE is a supplier of a package of goods and services and often a brand name to the licensee. A proven success formula in operations and marketing is also usually included. Since the licensee uses the MNE's brand name and international promotion, the risk to the MNE's reputation is particularly acute with this type of contractual arrangement.

Contract manufacturing is the reverse situation of a franchise as the MNE pays the license fee. As mentioned, the MNE may not perceive the host market as warranting FDI, so instead production is contracted out to a local firm and the product is marketed under the MNE's brand name. As in franchising, however, quality control is essential to protect the MNE's reputation. Contract manufacturing is also used as a pre-FDI market test. As no investment in production facilities is required, the risk of market acceptance failure is lower. Foreign direct invest-

---

EXHIBIT 4-2

FORMS OF LICENSING	
Basic license:	Contractual arrangement whereby the MNE, for a fee, allows its technology, patents, or trademarks to be used by another firm.
Management contract:	Contractual arrangement whereby the MNE, for a fee, provides management expertise in specified areas to another firm.
Franchising:	Contractual arrangement whereby the MNE, for a fee, acts as a supplier and allows another firm to sell its products or services.
Contract manufacturing:	Contractual arrangement whereby the MNE will pay the fee to a local producer to manufacture its product under the MNE's brand name.

ment may occur later once the market acceptance and size have been determined.

To summarize, licensing occurs when access to foreign markets is limited, the market potential is insufficient to warrant FDI or as a pre-FDI market test strategy, or when the firm's commitment to the international market is limited. The greatest risk to the MNE from licensing is the risk of dissipation of its FSA in knowledge so that the licensee can operate without the MNE or even become a competitor. The production of the MNE's knowledge advantage is fundamental to the theory of internalization, as we shall see in Chapter 5.

SUMMARY

This chapter has presented two main sets of material on nonmultinationals. One has been concerned with the "nitty-gritty" of exporting, the agencies and information sources that the exporter can make use of either through external arrangements, such as hiring a general trading company, or through internal personnel hired once the export business has grown sufficiently large. The second part of this chapter centered on other types of nonmultinational activity such as joint ventures, turnkey operations, and licensing. It explained the process of internationalization, in contrast to the process of internalization, to be discussed in Chapter 5.

The reader should be reminded that more of the export marketing function is discussed in the chapter on marketing management (Chapter 15), where it is assumed that the firm is ready to pursue a full-blown marketing program in a country market abroad. This latter case generally assumes that some FDI has taken place, if not in production, at least in marketing, so that the marketing effort can in fact be controlled by the seller. In the present chapter, the focus has been on "pure" exporting, where all marketing (and production) activities must perform at an "arm's-length" distance to the market. In such a case the marketing tactics of the firm revolve around the capability of the distributor in the foreign country, while the major strategic questions are what countries to enter and how rapidly to expand.

KEY WORDS

Internationalization	Export license
FOB factory	Export management companies
FAS, port of exit	Export consortia
Cost, insurance, freight	*Sogo shoshas*
Letters of credit	Joint ventures
Export-import bank	Turnkey projects
Foreign Credit Insurance Association	Licensing
Domestic International Sales Corporation	Management contracts
Freight forwarder	Franchising
Bill of lading	Contract Manufacturing

QUESTIONS

1 Chapter 4 opens with a discussion of the items concerning a firm in the initial phases of exporting. One of the most important is payment. Five methods are described for which the exporter can be paid. Discuss these. If possible, use a diagram to illustrate your answer.

2 Financing is a critical component in export operations. Discuss the various forms of assistance and agencies available to exporters in this area. Is it possible to have a CSA in financing?

3 What are export management companies? Identify their firm-specific advantage. Is there any risk in the use of export management companies? How can this risk be lessened, if at all?

4 Discuss the role of the general trading company. Define *sogo shosha* in your answer and discuss the functions of the *sogoshosha*. Give an example, if possible. Under what condition(s) would reliance on *sogoshoshas* be minimal?

5 Discuss the process of internationalization. Use a diagram to illustrate your answer. How does risk change each stage of the process?

6 Several other forms of international business activity are described in this chapter. Discuss one of these in detail. Why would the MNE use this form of operation? What are the important considerations in this type of international business?

7 Why would an MNE choose licensing over other forms of activity? Conversely, why would licensing not be preferable? Discuss the different forms of licensing available to a firm.

Exercise: Go through a selection of annual reports, and map out gradual expansion into foreign markets for one exporting company. On the basis of the information in these reports, would you characterize the company as a country-centered, gradual exporter or as an MNE with a global strategy? Make sure you pay attention to possible shifts in emphasis between home and foreign markets.

CHAPTER 5

BUILDING A THEORY OF THE MULTINATIONAL ENTERPRISE

INTRODUCTION

The multinational enterprise (MNE) has become an important organization in the second half of the twentieth century. As was observed in Chapter 1, it dominates world trade and investments. Here we explore the reasons for the multinationality of production, a development which is at the core of international business studies.

We shall see that firms undertake foreign production and become MNEs in situations in which exporting or licensing is either theoretically impossible or practically infeasible. Firms become MNEs in general, where foreign production is preferable to the other alternative methods of servicing foreign markets. In this chapter MNEs are contrasted with the exporting mode just developed in Chapter 4 on alternatives to MNEs.

The conceptual alternatives to the MNE, and the MNEs themselves, are examined against a background of environmental variables, many of which are assumed constant for reasons of simplicity in modeling. Where necessary, these parameters are relaxed and added into the work. This method of analysis throws light on the future of the MNEs in a world in which their economic, political, and social environments are constantly changing and their relationships with governments are subject to constant public scrutiny.

The principles of efficiency, introduced in Chapter 2 in a free trade context, are used here to analyze situations in which trade is practically unavailable or theoretically impossible. At this stage MNEs are examined as complete organizations; this approach is necessary for determination of their basic raison d'être. At a later stage the functional areas within the MNEs are examined individually in more detail. Here we need an initial overview of the fundamental rationale of the MNE; this is an essential bridge between theory and practice.

It will be demonstrated that the MNE is a logical alternative to free trade. Indeed, under the types of market imperfections studied in this chapter, there is a symmetrical relationship between the regular markets of free trade and the internal markets within MNEs.

FREE TRADE OR MNEs

The symmetry between free trade and the MNE is demonstrated in Figure 5-1. In a world of perfect markets, international business would be carried out through free trade. Under such conditions a course in international business would consist of a study of international economics: importing and exporting and finance. All international exchange would be through trade, with exporting and importing undertaken according to the general principles of comparative advantage, explained earlier in Chapter 2.

This simple model of the international economy does not exist in the real world. Instead, for most products there are at least some barriers to free trade. These market imperfections serve to reduce the potential gains from free trade that would otherwise occur in such an efficient model of production and exchange.

There are two types of market imperfections: those imposed by government regulations and those occurring naturally. An example of a government-imposed regulation is a tariff on imports, discussed in Chapter 3. Such interventions into the free market cause distortions in the world economy and impose welfare losses on trading nations. Tariffs have effects similar to quotas, taxes on traded goods, foreign exchange controls, immigration laws, and other regulations affecting trade in goods or factors of production. Firms (or countries) in monopoly or quasimonopoly positions for a product can also distort trade patterns, output, and price and impose costs on the world economy.

In a similar fashion, the effects of natural market imperfections also impair market efficiency. Such market imperfections arise in the pricing of knowledge (as explained in the following paragraphs) and in the circumstances which lead to transaction costs preventing the competitive market from developing. Three major types of transaction costs are (1) buyer and seller uncertainty, (2) quality control, and (3) the difficulty of making a sales contract in a situation of uncertainty and imperfect information. These transaction costs are examined in more detail in the following paragraphs.

As can be seen in Figure 5-1, the natural and "unnatural" market imperfections together serve to block free trade and reduce the gains from trade. Some of these imperfections can be overcome by using the internal markets of MNEs instead of the external international market. Indeed, both natural imperfections and government-imposed regulations act as incentives for MNEs to create and use their internal markets to transfer goods and services through trade, licensing, and foreign direct investment. The MNEs are vehicles which bypass bottlenecks to the international transfer and exchange of goods, materials, and people.

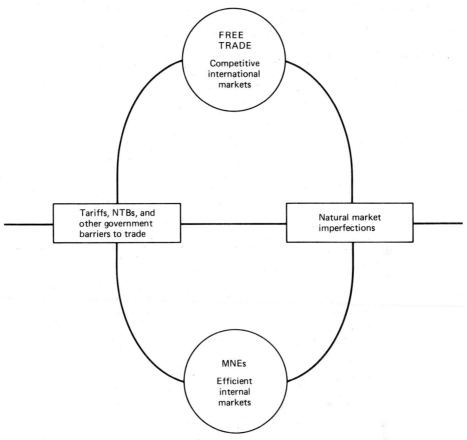

FIGURE 5-1
The world economic system.

In this manner MNEs are replacements for free trade when the trade is impeded by market imperfections. Foreign direct investment substitutes for trade in goods and services. In the same way that we found free trade to be efficient, we can show that MNEs increase efficiency when free trade is blocked, and that the two situations are symmetrical. The objective of this chapter, then, is to develop a theory of the MNE in which the role of the internal markets of MNEs is central. Chapter 6 then examines the choice between exporting, through markets external to the firm, foreign direct investment by the internal markets of the MNE and methods of entry to foreign markets where control is not retained, such as in a joint venture, or by licensing.

ELEMENTS OF A SIMPLE MODEL OF MNEs

From the viewpoint of the MNE, Figure 5-2 indicates that its strategic and tactical planning stems from an assessment of both environmental and internal factors.

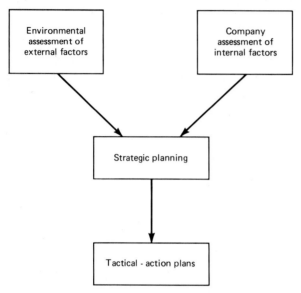

FIGURE 5-2
Global strategy of MNE—how to enter international business. The MNE needs to consider two sets of variables in order to engage in effective decision making about its global strategy. First, it needs to scan a multitude of environmental factors, best regarded as parameters (i.e., external) to the firm. Second, it needs to assess its own internal factors.

First, we examine the environmental factors. It is best to recognize that most environmental factors are beyond the control of managers and the MNE. This observation is equivalent to assuming that the environmental variables faced by the MNE are exogenous parameters to the firm. This is a useful assumption, especially for short-run, tactical planning.

In practice there is little that the MNE can do to make fundamental changes in the economic, political, social, and cultural environment within which it operates. For example, popular mythology to the contrary, there are relatively few recent examples of MNEs exerting political power such as was done by ITT in Chile, United Fruit in Central America, and oil firms in the Middle East in pre-OPEC days. Direct intervention in host nations by MNEs is now a rare event.

There are at least two sets of environmental variables of concern to the MNE, those that occur in the home and in relevant host nations in which the MNE operates. All we need to do, then, to implement a useful model, is to make the simplifying assumption that MNEs cannot alter these environmental factors during the decision-making period being considered.

The second set of factors to be assessed are those within the control of the MNE. These internal, or company, variables are determined by management on a daily basis as it decides on the appropriate mix of labor, capital, technology, and other factor inputs used to produce the goods and services made by the firm. The organizational structure and style of the company are also determined internally, as are other elements in its production and marketing divisions.

To engage in strategic planning, the MNE must consider both environmental and company factors. The key decision to be made in its strategic planning is the decision to enter foreign markets and the appropriate choice of entry mode with which it will service these markets. This decision requires that the MNE choose between the major categories of exporting, foreign direct investment, and licensing. It can prove to be an expensive mistake to make the wrong strategic decision.

The MNE also formulates tactical plans to deal with its short-run problems. Tactical planning deals with shorter-run operational and managerial decisions. It involves optimization of the production, financing, marketing, and labor functions, subject to the overall strategic planning of the MNE.

Tactical action plans are usually more flexible and less costly to revise than strategic plans. In the MNE, tactical planning of the product line is complicated by cross-border production flows, labor and capital flows, and the regulations imposed by at least two sets of governments. Line management is very challenging and presents opportunities to have a significant impact on the bottom line of the MNE.

Both tactical and strategic planning are affected by environmental and company variables identified in the preceding paragraphs. Exhibit 5-1 is now required to give a more detailed classification of the environmental and company variables and to explain their interrelationships.

Environmental Variables

In the literature on the theory of the MNE, the environmental variables are often referred to as *country-specific advantages* (CSAs) or *location-specific factors*; both terms refer to the same notion. The CSAs are the variables affecting the nation as a whole. There are three types of environmental variables of interest to us: economic, noneconomic, and governmental.

Economic Variables

Economic variables make up a nation's aggregate production function, where this is defined to include all the factor inputs available in the society. For simplicity these are usually modeled as labor (L) and capital (K). In more sophisticated models other factors can be brought in for analysis; these include technology (TECH), availability of natural resources (RES), and management skills (MGMT). The latter is sometimes referred to as a type of human capital.

Noneconomic Variables

In addition to economic variables, the country-specific factors also include the entire set of political, cultural, and social variables of each nation. The importance of these noneconomic variables to the operations of the MNE will differ from country to country. This implies that an MNE faces a distinct group of environmental conditions, risks, and opportunities in each country in which it operates.

EXHIBIT 5-1
TWO SETS OF VARIABLES IN A MODEL OF THE MNE

Environmental	Company
Country-specific Location-specific	Firm-specific Ownership-specific
These are the variables in a nation's aggregate production function (L, K, Tech, Mgmt) and also include its political-cultural system + government	These are special advantages of MNE (e.g., knowledge, Mgmt, marketing, R and D skills), and also strategic planning skills

The environmental variables are external parameters; i.e., exogenous variables given to the firm. The MNE cannot influence them. Instead, the MNE attempts to maintain a special firm-specific advantage, for example in knowledge, technology, or management skills.

In reality, of course, every country indeed has a unique set of country (location)-specific factors; no two national sets of economic and noneconomic factors are identical. The differences in weights, or values, attached to each variable serve to generate a unique set of characteristics for each country. The MNE needs to recognize such differences between nations. To some extent, a firm engaged in international business will be able to generalize across cultures, political systems, religious groups, and social values to minimize the additional costs of foreign direct investment over production in the home country, but the firm should not forget the special nature of each nation's country-specific factors.

Governmental Variables

Even when economic and noneconomic variables have been considered, the firm has not monitored all the potential environmental factors facing it, since there is a final country-specific factor to be accounted for separately. This is the government (G) of the nation under consideration. Both home and host governmental variables affect the MNE.

Each nation has its own special brand of politician. The politicians reflect the location-specific factors of the nation and even add to them in a special way. There is always variety in government intervention with international business. Indeed, there may be several levels of government involved in aspects of international business. For example, entry into a foreign nation may involve dealing with local municipal harbor authorities, federal transportation officials, state (regional or provincial) agencies responsible for distributional and production requirements, and a broad spectrum of federal laws and regulations affecting international trade and investments.

To begin building a model of the MNE, it is a practical necessity to take into account these variables. Multinational enterprises must respond to the economic, political, and cultural environments of nations, rather than determine them. Indeed, such environmental variables are decided on by home and host residents rather than by MNEs. From the viewpoint of the MNE, therefore, the country-specific factors are given as exogenous variables.

In subsequent chapters, some of the environmental factors are studied in more detail. In fact, some of them can be endogenized in the model, i.e. treated as determined within the model. This occurs once the simple theory of MNEs has been built up. This modification is presented in Chapter 14, where the relationship between the strategy of the MNE and governments is developed. Such a further examination of the fixed environmental system, with which it is necessary to commence the model, can occur only after the basic model is established, as we are doing in this chapter.

FIRM-SPECIFIC ADVANTAGES

Exhibit 5-1 also outlines in more detail the second set of variables required to build a theory of MNEs. These are the MNE's firm-specific advantages (FSAs). These are company variables, sometimes called, in the literature, *ownership-specific factors*.

These are the internal advantages possessed by MNEs. Each MNE has its own unique firm-specific advantages which give it a competitive advantage relative to other firms. To be sure, there may be little difference in firm-specific advantages between members of an oligopoly or MNEs in nearly competitive conditions. Yet each MNE is a monopolist to the extent that it has its own company name and its own unique method of organizing its internal market. Every MNE attempts to differentiate its product from those of rival firms. Each MNE protects its firm-specific advantages by retaining ownership over them until the risk of dissipation is commensurate with payments for licensing or other types of contractual arrangements.

What, then, are these firm-specific advantages of MNEs? They arise when the MNE has developed special know-how or a core skill that is unavailable to others and cannot be duplicated by them, except in the long run and at high cost. In many cases such firm-specific advantages arise from R and D expenditures which lead to the production of a new type of product, the development of a new production process, or a more efficient or effective means of organizing the production process. In other cases, innovation and adaptation of techniques to the special circumstances of the MNE can lead to differentiated product lines, thereby generating a firm-specific advantage in marketing or distribution.

The core skill of the MNE can be some element of its management structure, marketing techniques, or overall strategic planning that leads to a firm-specific advantage. These firm-specific advantages are modeled as endogenous to the MNEs, since their internal markets permit the MNEs to control them.

One objective of the management of the internal market of the MNE is to establish property rights over the firm-specific advantage so that it is not dissipated to other firms. A firm may be able to utilize its FSAs to compete in several nations. The ownership of the core skill in its internal market is, itself, an asset to the MNE. It protects this asset by producing abroad similar goods as in the home market and using its foreign subsidiaries to monitor, meter, and regulate the use of the firm-specific advantage abroad. The internal market of the MNE permits it to maximize its worldwide earnings without dissipation of this invaluable asset.

REASONS FOR INTERNALIZATION

Exhibit 5-2 demonstrates in more detail the reasons for internalization by MNEs. It is a development of Figure 5-1, where market imperfections were first identified as barriers to trade. It is necessary now to consider natural market imperfections in more detail, especially the difficulty of the MNE in appropriating a return on its investment in skills, techniques, information, and knowledge. Government-induced market imperfections are also discussed. Both types together induce internalization.

The first type of natural market imperfection to be discussed is knowledge; this is know-how or information in the broadest sense. Knowledge is acquired by companies by either research and development, or as a by-product of their normal operations. Knowledge occurs in many forms, but discussion of it is simplified if, at this stage, we generalize and treat any special firm-specific information, skill, technique, or technology as knowledge.

EXHIBIT 5-2
REASONS FOR INTERNALIZATION

Natural market imperfections	Unnatural market imperfections
Pricing of public good, e.g., knowledge	Government-imposed, e.g.: Tariff
Transaction costs	Foreign exchange control
Buyer uncertainty	Regulations on FDI
Quality control	
Difficulty in making a contract	

Both natural market imperfections and unnatural market imperfections induce internalization by MNEs.

Knowledge Advantage of MNEs

Knowledge is a product which is difficult to price on a regular market. Knowledge is usually found in the form of an intermediate good, rather than a final good; it is essential in the development, production, distribution, and sales of products. Knowledge is often firm-specific; that is, it is developed by an individual company as part of the firm's ongoing efforts to manufacture a better product, or to provide a better or cheaper service to its customers.

As an intermediate product, knowledge is an intangible asset to a firm. It is difficult for the firm to know the value of its knowledge. Because of this uncertainty, the firm attempts to establish property rights over the knowledge which it has developed. The best way for the firm to do this is to use its knowledge on its internal market rather than sell it on the highly imperfect external market for knowledge. This permits the firm to control the use of its own knowledge advantage. Such control permits the firm to arrange for the optimal rate of exploitation of its knowledge advantage since it forestalls potential competitors, at home or abroad, from gaining access to its knowledge advantage and thereby weakening its competitve position.

While the necessity of internalizing knowledge applies to both domestic and multinational firms, the latter have taken internalization to its logical conclusion by internalizing operations across national boundaries. The MNE, with a knowledge advantage, uses its internal market to service consumers in many nations with the product lines and services that the MNE controls.

Usually the firm-specific advantages of MNEs are developed in response to conditions in their home countries. For example, technology-intensive MNEs typically engage in R and D in their home countries to develop new products and processes for operations and sales in their home countries. Once the MNE has developed, tested, and successfully sold the product at home, it will be introduced abroad either through exports or by production in one of the MNE's subsidiaries. The network of wholly owned subsidiaries positioned around the world to capture local and regional markets is the hallmark of foreign direct investment by MNEs in manufacturing industries. The most common type of firm-specific advantage of these horizontally integrated MNEs is knowledge. It is only through their internal markets that such MNEs can monitor, regulate, and meter the use around the world of their knowledge advantages.

Knowledge as a Public Good

The efficient pricing of knowledge cannot take place on an external market since it is a public good. A public good is defined as one where consumption of it by one party does not prevent consumption of it by other parties. Exhibit 5-3 illustrates this concept. Besides knowledge, other examples of a public good are a lighthouse beam, a public park, a road, or a bridge. Yet all of these can become private goods if certain conditions prevail, as we shall now discuss.

EXHIBIT 5-3
WHAT IS A *PUBLIC* GOOD?

Definition
　　Consumption of it by one party does not prevent consumption
　　by others.

Examples
　　Knowledge
　　Lighthouse beam
　　Park
　　Road or bridge

When do these become *private* goods?
　　When *property rights* are established to overcome externality.

Only a private good, such as an apple, can be priced on a
regular market. A public good, such as knowledge, is an
example of an externality, for which the market mechanism
does not provide a price. Instead, a firm can only reap a
reward for its private investment in knowledge by maintaining
property rights over it; i.e., the firm appropriates a return to
overcome the natural externality of knowledge as a public
good.

The classic example of a public good is the lighthouse. Once it is constructed, captains can look at it and take advantage of the information to keep their ships off the rocks. If one captain looks at the lighthouse beam, another captain is not prevented from doing the same. Similarly, a person can enjoy the aesthetic qualities of a park or drive along a road or across a bridge without stopping other people from doing the same.

In contrast, a private good, such as an apple consumed by one person, prevents its consumption by anyone else. On occasion, if the park becomes very crowded or the road or the bridge congested, the public goods aspect of them ceases. Excessive use turns public goods into private goods. Each individual makes a private decision to use the good, but there are external costs (of overuse and congestion) imposed on others. This externality occurs because there was an inadequate system for pricing public goods.

The competitive market system cannot price the use of a lighthouse beam, a park, a road, or a bridge. No authority can sail around the high seas charging each captain for looking at the lighthouse beam. As ships may be simply passing by, the local harbor authority cannot raise taxes on all the ships that benefit from its lighthouse. Similarly, it is rarely feasible to charge entry fees to public parks or to have toll booths on every urban roadway and bridge. Those that do overcome the high transaction costs of a regular pricing system only if there is a high volume of traffic and relatively few entry and exit points. Most public goods cannot be priced on a competitive market, as the costs of doing so would be excessive.

Yet society benefits if these public goods are produced. In response to this market failure, a harbor authority may be set up to construct and pay for the lighthouse; the town council donates the park and pays for its upkeep; and the city, state, or federal government constructs roads and bridges. In these examples, an agent outside the market system has acted to provide the public good. It obtains the funds for this activity by some levy on the users (e.g., gasoline and motor vehicle taxes) or from the public as a whole.

Government action is one way to solve the problem of the production and pricing of public goods by paying for the costs of production through a system of subsidies. That is, government can provide the services and the funds can be raised from either general revenues or by special levies for the project. Alternatively, property rights over the public good can be assigned to either the firms or individuals to undertake the costs of their production. One method of assigning property rights over knowledge is by internalization. Creation of a market within the firm by internalization allows the firm to appropriate the knowledge it generates, knowledge which would otherwise be lost to the firm. If the firm cannot appropriate the benefits of the knowledge it generates, it will not be able to bear the costs of generation and hence will have no incentive to develop new knowledge in products, processes, information, techniques, or skills.

In the context of international business, it is necessary for a knowledge-intensive MNE to use its internal market in order to recoup the private costs of research and development. Internalization by the MNE of its firm-specific advantage in knowledge is a rational response to the natural market imperfection in the pricing of knowledge. The internal market of the MNE is an economically efficient response to this exogenous, natural, market imperfection. This conclusion can be extended to cover all cases of transaction costs; the MNE is an efficient response to any such market imperfections.

Other Types of Transaction Costs

To increase our understanding of the vital necessity for assigning property rights over knowledge or any other special advantage to the firm, consider another type of firm-specific advantage of the MNE. Some MNEs are vertically integrated, so their firm-specific advantage is in control of the supply of raw materials, marketing outlets, or both.

Multinational enterprises integrate vertically across national boundaries to reduce risk and increase efficiency. Refining, smelting, and fabrication plants can be made more efficient if they are constructed to convert fixed proportions of inputs to fixed proportions of outputs. These natural resource processing industries are highly capital intensive and must be operated at high volumes in order to obtain economies of scale. If facilities are operated below capacity, costs escalate rapidly. These characteristics have motivated firms in Europe and the United States in natural resource processing industries to become MNEs by integrating backward to reduce the risk of variations in volume, composition, and price of inputs and by integrating forward to reduce the risk of variations in sales volume, composition, and price. Their firm-specific advantage lies in the control of input sources and final demand and hence in the reduced risk and increased efficiency of their operations.

As an example, multinational petroleum companies have always sought to own secure supplies of crude oil and to control their own distributional outlets at the retail level in order to achieve maximum profitability at the refining level. With the sudden emergence of OPEC as a powerful producers' cartel in 1973 and 1974, the multinational oil firms were faced with the threat of potential disruption to their production. Yet their remaining control over distribution allowed the major integrated firms to quickly accept and adjust to the higher world price of oil. The oil MNEs were able to pass on to consumers at the retail end the higher costs of oil while at the same time maintaining their refining capacity at the high and stable volume required for substantial profitability.

When analyzing any MNE it is a useful starting point to ask what is its firm-specific advantage? Some MNEs will have one in knowledge and others in various forms of vertical integration. Still others will have variants of the knowledge advantage. These include a technological advantage; a patent right defended internationally; some internal managerial, financial, or marketing knowledge; or some other type of core skill unique to the enterprise.

In situations of the other types of natural market imperfections mentioned above, such as various sorts of transaction costs, an internal market also develops. For example, buyer uncertainty leads to internalization of customers' costs by the firm since it is cheaper for the firm to do so. Therefore, the firm develops brand name products, establishes long-term links with customers, and, in general, takes on itself the costs of organizing a market wherever the benefits exceed the costs.

As a representative type of natural market imperfection, the role of knowledge has been discussed in detail. It is now time to summarize these points. Knowledge is an invaluable asset to the MNE. Each MNE does everything it can to maintain its knowledge advantage and to generate new ones. The MNE is afraid of the risk of dissipation of its firm-specific advantage in knowledge, so it retains control for as long as necessary through its internal market. As a specialized form of information, knowledge is the oil which lubricates the engine of the MNE. Without securement of property rights over this firm-specific advantage through internalization, the engine itself will dry up and the MNE will cease to function.

The MNE has emerged in the second half of the twentieth century as a remarkable organization within which a knowledge advantage is internalized. It is a vehicle for the international transmission of knowledge; such knowledge is embodied in the final good or service which is provided by the MNE to consumers around the world. The internal market of the MNE is a mechanism which links producers and consumers in an efficient managerial system of administrative fiat. Prices are set internally, by decision makers using their experience to allocate and distribute goods and services on a worldwide basis.

DETERMINANTS OF FDI

It is now necessary to relate the concepts just introduced to the mainstream literature on the theory of the MNE. This section does this and in so doing serves to highlight the predictive nature of the theory of internalization.

INTERNALIZATION BY ENTREPRENEURS

The principles of the theory of internalization are not just confined to multinationals; they explain the activities of all firms, including small business. Consider the case of an entrepreneur.

The key function of the entrepreneur is to recognize and implement new business opportunities. To act, the entrepreneur needs superior information, whether it be acquired through insight, luck or training. Also required is the self-confidence and financial ability to act upon this information. Once the entrepreneur takes action the information upon which the judgement was made becomes a public good, as the business exists. Since the price of a public good is zero the entrepreneur is denied a reward unless the information can be internalized, i.e., protected in some manner. Methods to prevent dissipation of the information include patents, secrecy, contracts and family or collusive networks. Such entry barriers are necessary to permit the collection of any rents arising from the entrepreneurial activity of the creation of a new business.

In an international context these principles also apply. The entrepreneur seeks to retain property rights over the use of any superior information and to restrict the dissemination of knowledge about potential new business activity. Such internalization is necessary in order to avoid transaction costs in information dissipation and the difficulty of erecting suitable markets or using contractual arrangements to avoid such dissipation. Expansion abroad may be slowed down due to the difficulty of the entrepreneur trading off the need for control and secrecy against the need for a staff to evaluate the extra costs of involvement in foreign environments. However, in principle, these problems faced by the entrepreneur are identical to those faced by the strategic management team of a multinational enterprise.

Source: Mark Casson, *The Entrepreneur: An Economic Theory* (Oxford: Martin Robinson, 1982).

In a survey of the literature on MNEs, Caves (1982) has found that the MNE tends to be a multiplant firm. Its key decision is to find the boundary between the allocation of resources in either an internal market or a regular (external) market. Caves says that MNEs occur when their internal markets experience lower transaction costs than those that arise in operating an arm's-length market. As a result, MNEs are generally of three types: (1) horizontally integrated multiplant firms, (2) vertically integrated multiplant firms, and (3) diversified multiplant firms (which reduce risks).

Horizontally Integrated MNEs

Usually each MNE has a special firm-specific advantage (FSA) in the form of an intangible advantage, or asset. The FSA can be in the form of technological knowledge, management skills, or marketing know-how. In some cases the FSAs can be protected by patents, trademarks, or brand names. In other cases, the FSA may lie in a market intelligence network, channels of distribution or sourcing, expertise in marketing, or service or organizational commitment. Each and every MNE operates to gain, maintain, and utilize unique FSAs which give it a competitive edge over other MNEs and mononational firms in the countries in which it operates. The first question to ask when examining an MNE regards the nature of its unique FSA.

The natural market imperfections identified by Caves (1971, 1982) as facing horizontally integrated MNEs are of two general types. First is the public goods nature of knowledge, which leads to the appropriability problem first identified for the MNE by Johnson (1970) and Magee (1977). Second is the information impactedness and buyer uncertainty aspects of market failure raised by Williamson (1976) and in a domestic context by Teece (1982). These market imperfections are the fundamental reasons for the internalization of markets by MNEs. As an example of the application of the concept of internalization to FDI, it is of interest to study the pricing of pharmaceuticals by horizontally integrated MNEs.

There is an externality in the production and pricing of pharmaceuticals. Multinational drug firms engage in expensive R and D to develop, test, produce, and market a new product. Some estimates have revealed that it costs up to $70 million to put a new drug on the market, with most of this expense due to the animal and human testing required to guarantee the safety of the product in order to pass strict government health regulations.

These huge expenses need to be recovered by the MNE if it is to engage in further R and D. To allow MNEs to recover these costs and earn sufficient profits to encourage them to continue in this risky business, governments grant patents for drugs. Patents give the firm exclusive property rights over the manufacture and distribution of the product in the domain of the patent. In nations where patents are not respected, or when the MNE fears that licensing or a joint venture can lead to dissipation of its FSA, the MNE has an incentive to keep the proprietary knowledge within the firm. It does this by making an internal market; that is, the firm maintains control of the knowledge by using wholly owned subsidiaries to supply host nation markets with its brand name product. Multinational drug firms thereby appropriate a return on their investments and bring their new health-related products to consumers around the world.

Because of the need for internalization as a protection against dissipation of the FSA of the MNE, there is a potential for rent-seeking behavior. The MNEs have a monopoly over the use of the knowledge, and the more effective is their method of internalization of the FSA on a worldwide basis, the greater is the opportunity for rents to be earned. However, data on the profitability of MNEs in the drug industry reveal that they have not earned excess profits over time, nor is there any evidence of systematic exploitation of host nations. This is partly explained by the problem facing these MNEs, that of ongoing R and D expenses in the search for the few successful new product lines.

There is a probability distribution of successful drug innovations (just as there is for oil wells or mines). Many drugs are impossible to market as they are not sufficiently different from competitive products. Others provide little revenue to the firm because of their inability to pass health standards, regulatory codes, or other restrictions. Only a few drugs are successful, and these have to finance future investments. The dynamic FSA of an MNE in the drug industry relies on costly ongoing R and D in new product lines.

Recent policy actions in Canada have severely affected the drug industry in that nation. This is discussed in detail by Gordon and Fowler (1981). In the early 1970s both the federal and provincial governments enacted legislation for compulsory licensing by MNEs to generic producers. The MNEs were given only 3 years to sell their product in the Canadian market before they were required to license to host country generic producers, who in return paid the MNEs a royalty of only 4 percent on sales.

The effect of this compulsory licensing requirement was to virtually destroy R and D in the drug industry in Canada. It became prohibitively expensive for MNEs to maintain any R and D capacity in Canada, since patents on new drugs would not be respected for a sufficiently long period to recover development costs. Therefore, such R and D as there was in the Canadian subsidiaries fled back to the parent MNEs, where there was no risk of appropriation by the host nation of the FSA in knowledge of the MNE at such a low price. It can be observed in the context of this chapter that such environmental changes in the Canadian country-specific advantages (CSAs) disrupted the normal pattern of FDI. We can anticipate that this violation of the exogeneity of the CSAs is being repeated in other industries and nations.

Paradoxically, it is impossible for a viable Canadian-owned drug industry to develop, since the Canadian market (of 20 million people) is too small to support the huge development costs of new drugs. Canada lacks scale economies in R and D, production, and marketing in the drug industries. For more details of these points and evidence across other industries besides drugs, see Rugman (1980b and 1981). As other nations, especially developing nations (such as India), Italy, and the eastern European countries, do not respect international patents, it is not feasible for a Canadian based MNE to rely on foreign sales or production to recover its costs of drug development. Thus the lack of scale economies in Canada, coupled with the mercantilist policies of other nations, serve to shut Canada out of the world market for the development, production, and sale of drugs.

In the future, FDI in pharmaceuticals may well be reduced by the breakdown of internationally accepted patent laws. As other forms of international servicing such as licensing or exporting are not feasible because of the risk of dissipation of the knowledge advantage of the MNE, world welfare and health losses will be experienced. Only by respecting the property rights of MNEs, either U.S., Canadian, or foreign-owned, will it be feasible for drug producers to recover their position in host nations such as Canada. Without internalization it is not possible for MNEs to provide social benefits in the form of R and D, employment, taxes, and health services.

Vertically Integrated MNEs

The second type of MNEs are vertically integrated MNEs, such as oil or mineral resource firms. In the case of vertically integrated multiplant firms, the internal market can be used to establish control and minimize transaction costs. This gives another sort of FSA to the MNE. Let us consider oil firms as a case study of vertically integrated MNEs.

In the case of petroleum companies, the type of FSA that may be controlled within the MNE is always one determined by external market imperfections. Aliber (1970, pp. 19–20) puts it this way:

> Efficiencies may be realized by co-ordinating activities that occur in several different countries within the firm. Thus an international oil company co-ordinates the production, transport, refining, and the distribution of petroleum at lower costs than individual firms at each stage might be able to by using the market. The economies of vertical integration involve reduction in transactions costs, the cost of search, and the costs of holding inventories.

Petroleum firms engage in vertical integration in response to both natural and government-induced market imperfections. Their control over sources of supply and over markets is justified when an FSA needs to be generated in order to bypass a host of transaction costs involving supply uncertainties, logistics, and search costs. The optimal rate of development of an oil field requires coordination of the production (refining) and marketing function in a dynamic sense. This is best achieved within a firm, where accurate information about all these functions can be assembled. Such knowledge is not freely available, and the internalization of extraction, refining, and marketing by the MNE gives it a special type of FSA. The assignment of property rights by equity investment permits it to protect its company information and gives the firm a knowledge advantage.

Figure 5-3 illustrates this process. There are four stages of vertical integration: extraction, transportation, refining, and distribution. Control of the supplies and markets is needed to allow the crucial capital-intensive refining stage to operate at full capacity. An MNE in the oil industry can put together this package at lower costs than can be obtained through the external market. The MNEs have managed to continue this process even after OPEC disrupted the extraction stage in 1973 and 1979. The oil MNEs retained control over distribution, so they were able to pass on to consumers the higher costs of crude oil. In return, the oil MNEs required only stable supplies of oil; price did not matter. Of course, over the last 10 years the bargaining over crude oil prices has moved away from firms and toward governments. Yet the MNEs in the oil industry have still retained the general ability to overcome the set of transaction costs identified in Figure 5-3, so their role as internalizers will continue in the future.

One of the key benefits of an MNE in the oil industry is that its subsidiaries have access to the large set of crude oil supplies owned by its multinational parent. If there is a disruption to part of the supply, action can be taken by the parent to minimize the effect on any one affiliate. Also, an affiliate can always renew its contracts for supplies of crude oil. During times of crisis a firm with no ongoing relationship with a supplier of crude oil may have difficulty in obtaining adequate supplies of crude oil at any price. Another benefit for the subsidiary is access to new research and technology produced within the MNE, activities which are controlled and centralized in the parent firm, but used by all affiliates.

While there are no theoretical problems with the concept of making internal markets, practical issues may arise when it is applied internationally. The key problem is that of sovereignty. The host nation often has a viewpoint different

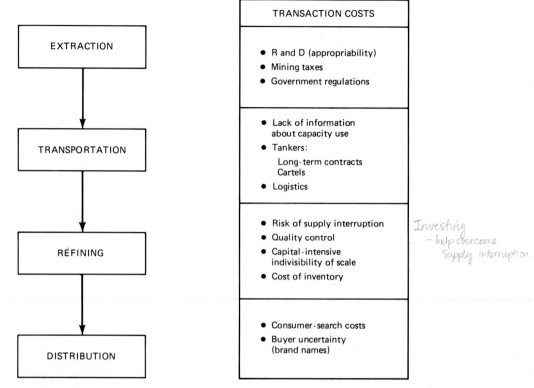

FIGURE 5-3
Vertical integration of oil MNEs. Why can MNEs decrease the transaction costs? By (1) secure supply (extraction and transportation) and (2) secure demand (marketing). This permits refining at capacity.

from that of the MNE. The host nation may view the same picture as the multinational firm and its subsidiary but interpret it differently. It is for this type of reason that FDI often puzzles governments but is accepted as a natural and beneficial phenomenon by MNEs since it reduces information and transactions costs, reduces risks, and increases efficiency. Host governments, however, may view with alarm the control that vertically integrated MNEs exercise over input sources in their countries and over markets for their final products in the home country. As described in Chapters 11 through 13, there is a high potential for conflict and confrontation between host governments and MNEs over the issue of control of resources, production, and markets. The conflict is especially severe with vertically integrated MNEs.

Diversified MNEs

The third type of multiplant MNE identified by Caves is the diversified MNE. Multinational enterprises of this type are explained by the principles of international diversification and have been discussed in detail elsewhere (Rugman, 1979). By the very nature of their international operations, MNEs are engaged in risk pooling. They are exposed to less variation in sales than are uninational firms confined to a single (domestic) market. Although international diversification is an explanation based on financial factors instead of real asset factors, it is still relevant for FDI, since risk pooling is an excellent reason for cross-industry investments.

The version of international diversification of relevance here is that in which market imperfections (in the form of information costs and government regulations) in the international capital market constrain simple portfolio diversification (which individuals could do themselves by buying into the stock indexes of various nations). Multinational enterprises rather than individual investors must do the diversification because it is prohibitively expensive for an individual to assemble an efficient world portfolio by buying into the stock markets of various nations. The individual has information and search costs. There are also political risk, exchange risk, and other environmental uncertainties to be considered.

The MNE is a potential surrogate vehicle for individual financial asset diversification since it is already operating internationally and the business cycles of nations do not move in perfect tandem. The advantages of real asset diversification of MNEs arise since MNEs avoid market imperfections by internalization. There is a type of FSA involved in the financial diversification achieved by the specific MNE. Each MNE is a portfolio of assets, with an FSA which is unique to each individual MNE. There has been a close linkage between the role of the MNE as an international diversifier and the growth of FDI in recent years.

The capital market model of Aliber (1970) appears at first sight also to be applicable to FDI. Aliber argued that a country-specific factor, foreign exchange risk, determines the international pattern of net flows of FDI. For example, if the dollar is expected to appreciate, U.S. MNEs can borrow more cheaply than other MNEs and use their lower cost of capital to finance overseas production, although precisely what motivates the MNEs to expand abroad is not made clear. In Aliber's model FDI will occur whenever the investor's valuation of exchange risk changes, and the model thus broadly explains the switchover from U.S. to European and Japanese FDI in the early seventies. It does not explain the continued expansion of European and Japanese FDI in the late seventies and early eighties, when the U.S. dollar was strong.

In an updated version of the model, Aliber (1984) stated that national Q ratios capture this CSA in exchange risk and determine the country mix of ownership. Aliber found that the Q ratios (representing the market value of a firm over its book value) for U.S. firms fell over the seventies (valuation of foreign exchange risk affects the capitalization rate and discount rate), while that of European firms increased. He attributed this to changes in relative exchange rates, as the dollar weakened over the seventies. The market value of U.S. firms increased less rapidly than the market value of European firms, drawing down the U.S. Q ratios, and reducing the relative amount of U.S. FDI.

If this model is correct, and it would be surprising if such a macro view of FDI is all that matters, we might anticipate even more FDI if exchange risk increases. However, in this book it is emphasized that a more micro level explanation of FDI is required. The investment decision of the MNE is determined primarily by an FSA, such as the need to internalize property rights in knowledge, rather than by the type of CSA identified by Aliber. If the CSAs are modeled as environmental parameters, they cannot influence the FDI decision, and if the CSAs are to be endogenized, it must be on stronger grounds than in the Aliber model. In conclusion, the FSA inherent in the international diversification motive is a stronger explanation for FDI than is the CSA explanation of Aliber's exchange risk model.

The main motivation for FDI will be cross-industry FDI in horizontally integrated MNEs with an FSA in proprietary knowledge. The exogeneity of the CSAs, assumed so far in this book, needs to be relaxed (as in Chapter 14) to encompass the swings in FDI whereby the relative advantages of U.S.-based MNEs in technology and managerial know-how have been superceded by those of Japanese and European MNEs.

ALTERNATIVE THEORIES OF FOREIGN DIRECT INVESTMENT

This section outlines two other major alternative theories of foreign direct investment (FDI) and relates them to the theory of internalization. The key models considered are: Vernon's product cycle and Dunning's eclectic model of FDI. Excellent surveys of the literature on the theory of FDI are available; some of the most recent works are by Calvet (1981), Grosse (1981), Rugman (1981), and Caves (1982).

The Product Cycle

As discussed in Chapter 2, the product cycle model was applied in an international context by Raymond Vernon of the Harvard Business School in 1966. Here we focus more on the FDI aspects of his model and less on the trade aspects as was done earlier. In Vernon's model the introduction and establishment of new products in the market follows three stages. The stimulus to develop new products is provided by the needs and opportunities of the market. The market where the firm is best aware of these needs and opportunities is the one closest at hand, the home market. New products are the result of research and development activities by the firm.

In stage one, when the product is initially developed and marketed, there is a need for close contact between the design, production, and marketing groups of the firm and the market being served by the product. This requires that production and sales take place in the home country, as shown in the upper parts of Figure 5-4.

In stage two, when the markets in other countries develop characteristics similar to those of the home market, the product is exported to foreign countries.

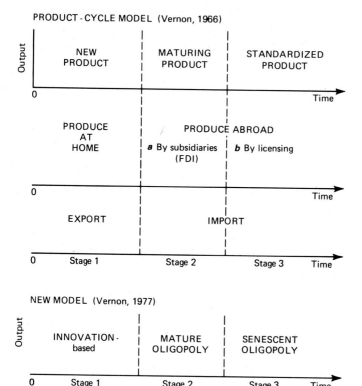

FIGURE 5-4
Product cycle. In stage 1 of Vernon's product-cycle model the new product is produced and consumed in the home nation. Exports take place. In stage 2 the maturing product can be produced abroad, perhaps in subsidiaries of the MNE. Some of the good may start to be imported by the home nation. In stage 3 the now standardized product is entirely produced abroad, even by licensing. The home nation imports all of the good that it needs. In Vernon's later model the stages are the same; only the terminology changes. [*From Raymond Vernon. "International Investment and International Trade in the Product Cycle," Quarterly Journal of Economics. 80 (May 1966).*]

The MNE will have an advantage over local firms abroad as it has already incurred and recovered the costs of developing the product. Once local firms in the host countries begin to produce competing products, the costs of production for all firms will become more important. At that point the MNE will set up local production in the host countries if this results in lower costs.

In stage three, the product becomes well established with a standardized design, and the market share of the MNE declines relative to host-country firms. In cases where the host country has strong cost advantages, the MNE will cease production at home and begin to import the product from the host country to the home country.

Vernon's model was initially developed to explain the rapid growth and worldwide spread of U.S.-based MNEs in the first two decades following World War II.

He modified the model substantially in Vernon (1971 and 1977), where the MNE in stage one is now identified as an emerging oligopoly, in stage two as a mature oligopoly, and in stage three as a senescent oligopoly. These stages are illustrated in the last row of Figure 5-4.

The model is less applicable now since MNEs have changed their character, with the European- and Japanese-based MNEs growing faster than those from the United States. Furthermore, the nonhomogeneous nature of the markets of the United States and other developed countries, in terms of the tastes and incomes of consumers, has led to the development of a greater variety of MNEs. Today's MNEs are based in many countries and consider production and marketing opportunities over a wide number of markets around the world.

The product cycle model is, however, still relevant in situations of changing market conditions, and today market conditions vary by time and country. The theory predicts that the MNEs based in (or with substantial sales in) those countries where conditions change first, will gain an advantage over those based in countries where conditions change later. The market shares of the MNEs that are the first to meet the new conditions will increase at the expense of MNEs who face the new environment at a later period. Therefore, the process of multinational activity is subject to continuous variation in the role and number of participating MNEs, all of whom must seek to generate new waves of technological or other types of firm-specific advantage, over time.

The Eclectic Approach

The eclectic approach to the theory of FDI was developed by John Dunning of the University of Reading (1977 and 1979). It provides a consolidation of the literature on FDI that draws on the industrial organization, location theory, and market imperfections approaches (see Exhibit 5-4). The eclectic theory specifies a set of three conditions that are required if a firm is to engage in FDI.

Firm-Specific Advantages   The firm must possess net ownership advantages vis à vis firms of other nationalities in serving particular (and, in practice, mainly foreign) markets. These firm-specific (or ownership) advantages largely take the form of the possession of intangible assets, which are, at least for a period of time, exclusive or specific to the firm possessing them.

Internalization Advantages   Assuming that the condition in the preceding paragraph is satisfied, it must be more beneficial for the enterprise possessing these advantages to use them itself rather than to sell or lease them to foreign firms. Thus the firm, to become an MNE, must have an incentive to internalize its FSA, for example, to secure property rights over its firm-specific advantage in knowledge. This is done through an extension of its own activities rather than by externalizing them through contracts at arm's-length prices (which may not exist in any case) with independent firms. Alternatives to internalization, such as licensing, management contracts, franchises, technical service agree-

EXHIBIT 5-4
DUNNING'S ECLECTIC THEORY OF
INTERNATIONAL PRODUCTION

Ownership-specific advantages
  Firm-specific knowledge advantages
  Management, marketing, financial skills
  Vertical integration
    Control of resources
    Control of markets
  Risk diversification

Internalizaton (by MNEs)
  To enforce property rights and overcome other
    transaction costs
  To reduce buyer uncertainty
  To overcome government regulations

Location-specific (country-specific)
  National production functions
  Government controls and regulations
  Political risk; cultural values

All three conditions are required for FDI.

ments, turnkey projects, and subcontracts are not feasible methods of appropriating the firm-specific advantage.

Country-Specific Advantages   Assuming that the conditions stated in the two preceding paragraphs are satisfied, it must be profitable to the enterprise to locate abroad, that is, to utilize these advantages in conjunction with at least some factor inputs (including natural resources) outside its home country. Otherwise foreign markets would be served entirely by exports and domestic markets by domestic production. Therefore, the location-specific advantages of the MNE are important elements in its choice of modality for servicing foreign markets.

Relevance of the Dunning Model

The net ownership, or firm-specific, advantages are required to offset the costs incurred by the MNE of operating at a distance from its home base. These costs are the costs of communicating over large distances and the costs of controlling many subsidiaries. Both types of costs occur as production decisions are made across national boundaries. Such costs of foreign operations are not incurred by a local firm. The advantage must be specific to the MNE. If assets corresponding to those conferring the advantages were available to local host-country firms, the MNE would no longer have an advantage to offset the costs of operating at a distance.

A firm possessing an advantage can either use the advantage itself or can sell or lease the advantage to other firms. This choice is usually explained in the context of transactions costs first identified by Coase (1937). There are costs involved in use of markets and in internal coordination and control. The foreign direct investment decision depends on which option presents the best net return (revenue minus cost), when the risks associated with each alternative are taken into account.

The use of the advantage in the host country is required if FDI is to take place. The cost of moving resources used in the host country must exceed the costs of controlling a subsidiary at a distance plus the costs of trade. Otherwise, the resource would be exported or moved to the home country, production would take place in the home country, and the foreign country market would be served by exports.

Firm-Specific Advantages   The range of advantages that can lead to FDI is large but can be summarized as follows:

1 Proprietary technology due to research and development activities
2 Managerial, marketing, or other skills specific to the organizational function of the firm
3 Product differentiation, trademarks, or brand names
4 Large size, reflecting scale economies
5 Large capital requirements for plants of the minimum efficient size

Internalization Advantages   The conditions that favor internalization include:

1 High costs of making and enforcing contracts
2 Buyer uncertainty about the value of the technology being sold
3 A need to control the use or re-sale of the product
4 Advantages to using price discrimination or cross-subsidization

Country-Specific Advantages   The location-specific advantages of the host country can include:

1 Natural resources
2 Efficient and skilled low-cost labor force
3 Trade barriers restricting imports

The first and second of these can result in FDI that leads to exports as well as production for the local market. The third will be associated with production for the local market only.

SUMMARY

Multinational enterprises have become increasingly important in the second half of the twentieth century. In a perfect market situation, free trade would be the most efficient means of servicing markets abroad; however, given the many barriers to trade presently affecting the market, MNEs are a necessary alternative. The ability of MNEs to create internal markets enables them to bypass the barriers to trade.

Multinational enterprises are affected by both environmental and internal factors. Tactical and strategic planning must be undertaken with these factors in mind. Environmental influences include economic, noneconomic, and government variables while internal factors refer to any skills, knowledge, or other advantages held by the MNE.

According to internalization theory, both natural and unnatural market imperfections induce internalization by MNEs. The firm must consider not only government-imposed regulations, but also such natural barriers as the pricing of a public good and other transaction costs such as buyer uncertainty.

The determinants of foreign direct investment have been studied by many authors. Their analyses break down into an explanation of three types of MNEs: horizontally integrated, vertically integrated, and internationally diversified. All three types benefit from internalization.

KEY WORDS

Unnatural market imperfections
Natural market imperfections
Transaction costs
Exogenous variable
Endogenous variable
Tactical plans
Strategic plans
Country-specific factors
Economic variables
Noneconomic variables

Firm-specific factors
Public good
Private good
Internal market
Risk pooling
Portfolio diversification
Q ratio
Vernon's product life style
Dunning's eclectic theory

QUESTIONS

1 Demonstrate with the use of a graph the symmetry between free trade and MNEs. What factors inhibit the existence of free trade? There are three major types of transaction costs; describe these. How can these factors be overcome?

2 It is stated that two sets of environmental variables are of particular concern to MNEs. Discuss these. What are the three subtypes of environmental variables? Give examples of each.

3 Distinguish between strategic and tactical planning. What are the key decisions made in each? What factors complicate these decision processes?

4 What is meant by the firm-specific advantage of MNEs? Define a firm-specific advantage. How does the MNE protect its firm-specific advantage? Give some examples of firm-specific advantages.

5 Why is the knowledge advantage of MNEs of special significance in building a theory of the multinational enterprise? Define a public good, giving examples. Contrast this with a private good.

6 Much discussion centered on the vertical integration of MNEs. Why does vertical integration occur? How does vertical integration function as a firm-specific advantage? Use an example to illustrate. What is the main problem that exists?

7 In the last section of the chapter, Vernon's product cycle and Dunning's eclectic theory are explored. Discuss the applicability of these models.

CHAPTER 6

THE CHOICE OF EXPORTING, FOREIGN DIRECT INVESTMENT, OR LICENSING

FIRM-SPECIFIC ADVANTAGES AND ENTRY METHOD

This chapter examines the choice among exporting, foreign direct investment, and licensing as the three archetypal methods of servicing foreign markets. This choice is made by a multinational enterprise (MNE), assumed to possess a firm-specific advantage (FSA) in knowledge, technology, or some other special asset embodied within its organization. Alternative methods to determine the optimal modality are presented. This form of presentation is employed here, since there are as yet unresolved problems in the operation of these models.[1]

In this chapter the MNE is regarded as a monopolist. It has a firm-specific advantage in some form of knowledge (broadly defined to include technological, marketing, and/or managerial skills). This advantage is retained within the organizational structure of the MNE. The monopolistic nature of the firm-specific advantage leads, in theory, to excessive profits (or "rents"), but these are reduced by the special costs of alternative modes of servicing the foreign markets in which the MNE operates. These special costs are inherent in running an internal market; so the profits of the MNE are always smaller than they would be if an external market for the MNE's firm-specific advantage existed.

In addition, there are administrative costs in operating an internal market. The visible hand is more expensive than an invisible hand. The second part of this chapter looks at the performance of the world's largest MNEs and finds no

---

[1]For further discussion of the theory of the MNE see Rugman (1980b, 1981). The choice between exporting and foreign direct investment (FDI) has been discussed in previous work by Horst (1973) and Hirsch (1976). This chapter proceeds in the spirit of these authors to consider the conditions favoring exporting, direct investment, and a third alternative, licensing.

121

evidence of excess profits. Finally it is clear that MNEs have many rivals; so they are really in a situation of monopolistic competition. In such a market structure excess profits are eliminated by the actions of rival MNEs. Here the firm-specific advantage is taken as a monopoly right in order to simplify the analytics.

In the discussion of the relative choices to be made by the MNE among the three available options, it is recognized that the firm runs the risk of dissipation of its firm-specific advantage if it engages in licensing, since the licensees may be able to resell information about the firm-specific advantage of the MNE to outside parties or use it themselves to compete against the MNE.[2] This problem is common to all innovation or knowledge production. Here, use is made of the economics of information and public goods to identify the specific conditions under which the MNE switches from one mode of market servicing to another. Also discussed are the potential repercussions for future sales by the multinational firm once licensing is undertaken in a world which does not have perfectly segmented markets for knowledge.[3]

THE HIRSCH METHOD

The first method of choosing among the three modes adapts and modifies substantially the model of Hirsch (1976), by extending the model to licensing and adding the concept of risk of dissipation. The variables, as defined below, are specified in present value terms. All the variables are either normal costs of production or special costs associated with one of the three modalities as the MNE chooses the best alternative.

The notation used is as follows:

C = normal costs of producing the good in the home country

C^* = normal costs of producing the good in the foreign (*) host country

M^* = export marketing costs, including insurance, transport, and tariffs (later M^* is defined as information costs only)

A^* = additional costs to multinational firms operating in the foreign country, especially environmental, cultural, and political information costs

D^* = knowledge dissipation costs associated with the risk of compromising the firm-specific advantage once a license is granted

These costs are borne by the MNE and are very high for a newly invented product but will decrease for more standardized products. The role of dissipation will also be lower if the licensee cannot readily resell the knowledge of the MNE to third parties or if the MNE has no interest in ever operating in markets served by the licensee. One way of ensuring that knowledge is not dissipated or used against the MNE is for it to police the terms of the licensing agreement; these costs can be

---

[2]Previous writers such as Magee (1977), Buckley and Casson (1976), and Casson (1979) have identified this as the appropriability problem.

[3]These models are a useful extension of the literature, since they build upon the unifying paradigm of internalization (Rugman, 1980a, b, c) and add analytical insight into the complex decision facing the MNE.

seen as part of D^*. Another way of looking at D^* is to think of it as potentially lost revenues from foreign sales when the knowledge advantage of the MNE is lost by a premature and inappropriate licensing agreement.

While potentially these variables may be influenced by many factors, the model developed here identifies only these normal or special costs as relevant for making decisions among the three modes.

The firm has three choices: it can produce at home and service foreign markets by exporting, or it can produce abroad through foreign direct investment (FDI), or it can license production to a host-country firm.

VARIABLES IN THE CHOICE OF ENTRY MODE

Country-specific costs

C Aggregate production function (home)
C^* Aggregate production function (foreign)

Special costs

M^* Export marketing costs (goods market)
A^* Additional costs of FDI (goods and factor markets)
D^* Risk of dissipation of firm-specific advantage (risk of lost sales and costs of enforcement of licensing agreements)

Using the above notation, it is possible to state the following relationship for these three modes of servicing a foreign market:

1 Export if $C + M^* < C^* + A^*$ (exporting is cheaper than FDI) and $C + M^* < C^* + D^*$ (exporting is cheaper than licensing).

2 FDI if $C^* + A^* < C + M^*$ (FDI is cheaper than exporting) and $C^* + A^* < C^* + D^*$ (FDI is cheaper than licensing).

3 License if $C^* + D^* < C^* + A^*$ (licensing costs are less than FDI) and $C^* + D^* < C + M^*$ (licensing costs are less than exporting).

The MNE will choose the mode for servicing a foreign market according to these conditions, all other things assumed constant. These choices will be optimal if the MNE has full information on each of the relevant variables. It is necessary then to develop a theory dealing with the method by which the special costs change in relation to each other over time. But first, some special cases are developed as extensions of this approach.

The work thus far has assumed that the multinational enterprise is focusing on the choice of entry mode for a foreign market. Yet direct investment abroad, or licensing, can occur in order to service not the local host market but that of the home country, or even a third market. Then the choice of production, location, and ownership strategy can be analyzed in a fashion similar to the procedure so far. To illustrate, consider the special cases of offshore production and licensing for the domestic market. When will they occur?

Assume the multinational firm is a "global scanner" and wishes to identify the most profitable means of exploiting its monopolistic advantage in its home market. It has three choices: (1) produce at home, (2) produce abroad for the domestic market, or (3) license a foreign firm to produce for export to the domestic market. The profitability of each of these methods is simply sales revenues minus production costs, less any special costs associated with international business. Since the revenues are the same for each alternative, the choice among the three depends on relative production costs in the two countries (location-specific factors) and on the special "multinational firm" costs (firm-specific factors). Thus the following situations emerge:

1 The cost of producing at home is C.

2 The cost of producing abroad for import to the home market is $C^* + M + A^*$, where M is the additional marketing cost associated with importing (such as tariffs), and A^* is the additional cost of being a foreign investor in the host country.

3 The cost of licensing a foreign firm for import to the home market is $C^* + M + D^*$, where D^* is, as before, the risk of lost profits from dissipation of the licensed knowledge.

From these can be derived the conditions for each mode of servicing the domestic market. They are as follows:

1 Produce at home if

$$C < C^* + M + A^*$$

and

$$C < C^* + M + D^*$$

2 Offshore assembly: produce abroad for import if

$$C^* + M + A^* < C$$

and

$$C^* + M + A^* < C^* + M + D^*$$

3 Trading licensee: production by a licensee if

$$C^* + M + D^* < C^* + M + A^*$$

and

$$C^* + M + D^* < C$$

These conditions are directly analogous to those associated with entering a foreign market, except that since the multinational firm itself is presumably the seller in its domestic market, it can obtain the monopolistic profits from sales to that market directly. This means it need not charge a royalty to the foreign licensee for the use of its special advantage; competition among potential licensees will ensure that the licensee's price is kept to the competitive minimum. The price and sales volume are necessarily established by the licensor as part of the agreement.

The choice of mode of servicing a domestic market can be expressed in terms of demand and cost conditions whose relative values change over time. The optimal mode of servicing thus changes over time as well. The analysis of these changes will be similar to the analysis of the evolving choice of entry method for a foreign market. The next section extends the methodology introduced here by considering the special costs of each mode in more detail.

THE NET PRESENT VALUE METHOD

Another method of choosing among the three modalities is the net present value (NPV) approach. This approach is included to illustrate the nature of a potentially more operational method.[4] The advantage of the NPV approach is that it captures some quasidynamic elements of the choice of optimal mode. The MNE should, in principle, calculate the NPV of each of the three modalities by considering the difference between the discounted revenues and costs (both normal and special). It should then choose the entry mode which has the maximum NPV for the length of time it is anticipated that the foreign market will be serviced. It is likely that the optimal mode may change over time, and the MNE can (and should) attempt to identify the basic switchover points between modes. The NPV method derived here cannot, itself, distinguish the sequence of entry modes. Rather, it provides a once-and-for-all choice of entry mode at a given point in time.

As shown above, it is a major task to consider the specification of a comprehensive model which incorporates interdependencies between the revenues and costs over time, accounts for possible reversals in the dynamic NPV choice path, and deals with other theoretical problems arising from the uncertainty of the costs and revenues in each mode. Here these issues are simplified by making the assumption of certainty of information. Then the choice of mode by the MNE is less affected by interdependencies, sequential decision making, and feedback effects. The MNE makes a once-and-for-all choice of mode at the outset of the model by calculating the NPV of each mode, given all the available information at the time of choice. Conceptually the MNE can pick an optimal sequence of modes, and then switch between them, such that NPV is maximized at each point on its finite time horizon. However, this method is probably not operational as an ongoing strategy; rather it is a guideline for the initial entry decision, which is the major investment decision facing the MNE as it involves a sunk cost in setting up the subsidiary or starting to export.

---

[4]This method was developed by Giddy and Rugman, and another version of it appears in Rugman (1980b).

The notation is as before:

R = total revenues from sales of the final product which uses the firm-specific advantage in knowledge as an intermediate good

C = total cost of labor, capital, and other normal inputs in the production function of the home nation

C^* = total costs of labor, capital, and other normal inputs in the production function of the foreign nation

M^* = export marketing costs, i.e., information costs about the foreign nation

A^* = additional costs of producing and servicing a host-nation market by FDI

D^* = costs due to the risk of dissipation of the firm-specific advantage

i = discount rate

All variables are specified for a time period t. The initial date of entry into a foreign market is defined as t_e, which may be time zero but need not be.

There are again three options open to a firm servicing a foreign market. The firm can export (E), use foreign direct investment (F), or license the knowledge advantage (L). The net present value (NPV) of each of these three options is shown as follows:

$$\text{Exporting:} \quad \text{NPV}_E = \sum_{t=t_e}^{t} \frac{R_t - C_t - M_t^*}{(1 + i)t}$$

$$\text{FDI:} \quad \text{NPV}_F = \sum_{t=t_e}^{t} \frac{R_t - C_t^* - A_t^*}{(1 + i)t}$$

$$\text{Licensing:} \quad \text{NPV}_L = \sum_{t=t_e}^{t} \frac{R_t - C_t^* - D_t^*}{(1 + i)t}$$

It is assumed that special costs M^*, A^*, and D^* all decrease over time. D^* starts as the highest relative special cost but falls at the most rapid rate; A^* is an intermediate case, while M^* starts as the lowest relative cost and falls at the slowest rate.

To determine the relative value to a firm in servicing foreign markets, it is necessary to consider the net present value (NPV) of each of the three options. The conditions are

1 Export when $\text{NPV}_E > \max (\text{NPV}_F, \text{NPV}_L)$
2 FDI when $\text{NPV}_F > \max (\text{NPV}_E, \text{NPV}_L)$
3 License when $\text{NPV}_L > \max (\text{NPV}_E, \text{NPV}_F)$
4 Do not go international if none of the NPVs is greater than zero.

Usually M^* is less than A^*, since the former special cost involves collecting information about the foreign goods market only, while A^* involves gaining information about both the foreign factor market and the foreign goods market. This follows from the special property of FDI, namely, that it involves foreign production (as well as marketing). The MNE thus faces the information costs of the foreign labor and capital markets, and their associated political and financial environments. These additional costs of the factor market are not required under the export marketing mode. Although A^* can be avoided by licensing, the third mode for most MNEs, D^* has the greatest special cost, since the MNE usually faces a high risk of dissipation of its firm-specific advantage by premature or inappropriately priced licensing. Most MNEs with genuine firm-specific advantages to safeguard will not want to put their unique monopoly position at risk. So D^* is usually greater than A^* and therefore greater than M^*.

It is apparent that the most interesting variables in these equations are the special costs associated with each mode of entry. Otherwise, normal costs of production C or C^* and revenues R are more or less the same for each alternative. For the valuation of each modality to change, it is necessary to have a theory about the relative value of special costs M^*, A^*, and D^*. As explained above, usually:

$$M^* < A^* < D^*$$

This leads to three equations for the special costs:

$$Mt^* = a + bt^c \tag{6-1}$$

$$At^* = e + ft^g \tag{6-2}$$

$$Dt^* = h + gt^p \tag{6-3}$$

The key hypothesis of the model sets the sign restrictions on the exponents as

$$c < g < p \tag{6-4}$$

It is also assumed that the fixed costs start highest for D^* but are least for M^*; so

$$a < e < h \tag{6-5}$$

If the cost relationships in Equations (6-1) to (6-3) take some other form or the relationships among the parameters in Equations (6-4) and (6-5) are different, the general *framework* of analysis presented here can still be used. Only the conclusions about the optimal mode will change. In fact, one of the key areas of analysis for the managers of MNEs is to determine the relationships among Mt^*, At^*, and Dt^* over time in order to make the correct strategic decision regarding the mode of servicing foreign markets.

The entire model is summarized in Exhibit 6-1.

EXHIBIT 6-1
THE CHOICE OF MODALITY FOR SERVICING
FOREIGN MARKETS

	1 NPV method—maximization

Exporting $NPV_E = \displaystyle\sum_{t=t_e}^{t} \dfrac{Rt - Ct - Mt^*}{(1 + i)t}$

FDI $NPV_F = \displaystyle\sum_{t=t_e}^{t} \dfrac{Rt - Ct^* - At^*}{(1 + i)t}$

Licensing $NPV_L = \displaystyle\sum_{t=t_e}^{t} \dfrac{Rt - Ct^* - Dt^*}{(1 + i)t}$

Hypothesis   At the time of entry $M^* < A^* < D^*$

	2 Cost minimization method

a $Mt^* = a + bt^c$
b $At^* = e + ft^g$
c $Dt^* = h + qt^p$
Hypothesis $c < g < p$

Given these conditions, if the MNE follows a cost-minimizing strategy (since revenues are the same for each alternative), it would be confined to a pattern of first exporting, then FDI, and finally licensing. This strategic choice of entry mode is identical to maximization under the other method, since the variables specified have the same properties. The model can be extended by relaxing some of these assumptions; for example, over time demand conditions may vary and affect the choice of mode. This possibility is discussed by Buckley and Casson (1980).

THE FOREIGN INVESTMENT DECISION PROCESS

The flowchart in Figure 6-1 summarizes the foreign investment decision process, as developed so far in this chapter. It indicates how the firm can make the theory of the chapter more operational. The flowchart makes use of the models of the MNE operating in two or more countries. An internally generated, monopolistically held knowledge advantage, produced in the home country, is transferred abroad by means of exporting, foreign direct investment, or licensing.

The models developed here assume that the MNE seeks to maximize the net present value of its firm-specific advantage in a particular foreign market. If the MNE produces at home or abroad for direct sale to the foreign market, it faces additional distance costs, which diminish with the MNE's experience in the

---

CHOICE OF ENTRY MODE: A CONCRETE EXAMPLE

An example of a switch in entry mode arose in the 1982 to 1984 period when the U.S. government used its Buy America legislation to ban the use of foreign-made cement in its highway rebuilding program. For over 40 years Canadian companies had been shipping cement to the northern states. It is mutually efficient for the United States and Canada to have this type of international trade, since the high transport costs of cement make it unprofitable to transport it more than 240 kilometers by road or rail. It is necessary for markets to be serviced either by localized plants or by imports to coastal areas or states adjacent to the Great Lakes.

The banning of Canadian cement for use in highways and bridges had a ripple effect, since it was required that all foreign cement be stored in separate silos. Thus any U.S. customers working on a federal road project had to maintain at least two silos, one for foreign and one for U.S. cement. Since most contractors have only one silo at each location, the demand for Canadian imports fell off by more than the reduced demand for road work itself.

To overcome the Buy America provisions, an increasing number of Canadian and other foreign cement producers started to switch from exporting to foreign direct investment. By 1984, at least five Canadian producers had bought U.S. plants, and European cement firms alone controlled 30 percent of the total U.S. cement-making industry. Partly in recognition of this, Canadian cement firms were exempted from the Buy America legislation in early 1984.

The European firms were possibly attracted to the large U.S. market for reasons other than protection; these included: the growth potential of the U.S. market, its lack of political risk (compared with third world markets), the stable nature of their controlled domestic markets, and the advantage in using the energy-efficient "dry" process of cement making. Whatever the reasons of the Europeans, the overriding Canadian concern was to prevent being locked out of the major rebuilding of the U.S. infrastructure in the eighties. Some estimates put the cost of rehabilitating U.S. physical plant and highways at $3 trillion—a market no cement firm can afford to miss.

Another example of a switch in entry modes is when Bombardier sold subway cars to New York City. To satisfy the Buy America provision, the Quebec-based Bombardier company uses its Vermont plant to assemble the subway cars. In a similar manner many Japanese, European, Australian, and other firms find that protective legislation in the United States forces them into joint ventures and subsidiary production rather than exporting. The benefits are in the employment of U.S. workers and the payment of U.S. taxes, but the disadvantages are foreign ownership (due to the need to prevent dissipation of any FSAs) and a probable loss of efficiency of free trade.

---

country. These costs are not borne by a host-country firm, potentially a rival producer of the same product. On the other hand, it would be very expensive for the foreign firm to develop for itself the MNE's firm-specific advantage.

In these models, revenues, normal production costs, and special international business costs all change with time. The net profit from any one mode of entry, however, changes at a rate different from that of the others; hence at some point it pays the MNE to switch modes. The MNE attempts to predict in advance which entry method will be the most profitable and when it will be so. In choosing potential switchover times, therefore, it will choose the mode that will maximize the net present value of all future cash inflows. This choice depends upon the length of time it is anticipated that the market will be serviced. Given the

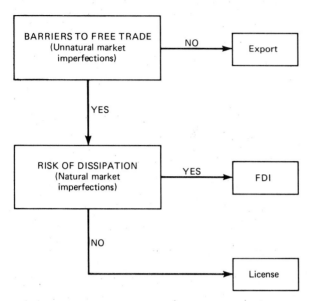

FIGURE 6-1
Flow chart of the foreign investment decision process.

conditions assumed here ($M^* < A^* < D^*$), the sequence of entry modes is most likely to be exporting, followed later by FDI and ultimately by licensing.

In terms of the flowchart in Figure 6-1, it is apparent that in a perfect world (with no information costs or barriers to trade) exporting is the first option. Yet when the foreign nation imposes a tariff or erects other barriers to entry and there is risk of dissipation to the MNE, the host nation can be best serviced by FDI, rather than by host-country production by a licensee, as $A^* < D^*$. To compensate for risk, the MNE will usually set the license fee above that charged to its own subsidiary, since with FDI, the firm-specific advantage is not at risk. Only when the host nation imposes regulations on the MNE which are greater than the benefits of FDI will the MNE turn to licensing as a mode of entry into the host nation. If the costs of regulation are less than the benefits of FDI, the MNE sticks to FDI.

DO MNEs EARN EXCESS PROFITS?

The key characteristic of the MNE is its firm-specific advantage in knowledge. In this sense, the MNE is a monopolist. Naturally there are potential competitors and seekers of the knowledge possessed by the MNE; so it attempts to retain control over its firm-specific advantage. Consequently, MNEs most often operate in markets characterized by monopolistic competition or oligopoly, where the actions of rival firms must be considered.

To retain control over the use of its monopolistic advantage, the MNE is compelled to favor use of an internal market. Contractual arrangements, such as licensing and joint ventures, are fraught with danger for the MNE. An inappropriate form of nonequity involvement has the potential to destroy the firm-specific advantage of the MNE, without which its product lines are at risk. The difficulty of having patents accepted internationally is an additional reason for internalization.

This section examines the monopolistic nature of the firm-specific advantage of the MNE, and the implications of this monopoly characteristic.[5] Using the symbols outlined previously, Figure 6-2 is developed. Based on the assumption of

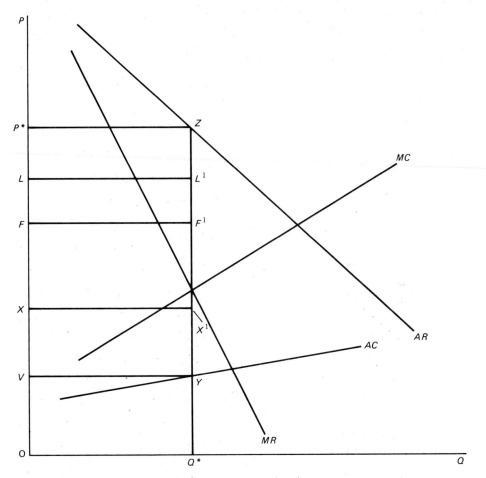

FIGURE 6-2
The choice of entry mode. For the MNE with a unique firm-specific advantage there is, conceptually, an area of rent (excess profits) available. Here it is the area VP*ZY. Yet this area is partially offset by either export marketing costs (area VXX¹Y), or additional costs of foreign direct investment (area VFF¹Y), or losses due to the risk of dissipation under licensing (area VLL¹Y).

[5]The model on which this section is based was first developed by Giddy and Rugman (1979).

a firm-specific advantage, the average revenue (demand) curve of the MNE is drawn as downward-sloping. Every MNE has an incentive to act to keep some slope on its curve, that is, to engage in product differentiation or some other activity which generates a monopoly characteristic.

The MNE has a firm-specific advantage in knowledge and can choose among the three modes of entry; exporting, foreign direct investment, and licensing. Special costs are unique to each of these modes, and here the assumed values of these are seen to determine the choice made by the MNE. There are two classifications of costs.

First, there are normal costs of production, C for the home nation and C^* for the foreign nation(s). These normal costs are best thought of as aggregate production functions with information in them about the costs of labor, capital, resources, technology, and other inputs of the respective nations. Thus, they include all normal considerations that determine a nation's comparative advantage. The MNE must consider these costs to be exogenous.

Second, there are special costs of production M^*, A^*, and D^*. These costs capture the unique costs of each mode as the MNE involves itself in one or another of the modes of entry to foreign markets. The special costs need to be distinguished from the normal country-specific (exogenous) costs of producing at home or abroad. The special costs are endogenous to the MNE and are therefore the primary decision variables in the choice of entry mode.

The firm-specific factor is not shown as a cost but is best thought of as an asset embodied in the MNE. Thus, the firm-specific factor is reflected in the revenues available to the MNE and is assumed constant for each mode. The closest the firm-specific advantage comes to being included as a cost is in the licensing mode, as discussed below.

The special costs are fixed in each time period and are modeled in this section as if they were equivalent to lump-sum taxes. Under these assumptions, the special costs do not vary with output and hence do not affect the firm's marginal cost curves. Nor can they be shifted onto consumers by the MNE; so each special cost serves to reduce the profits of the firm in a unique manner. The special costs are allowed to vary over time at different rates. This generates three separate time paths of special costs, one for each mode of servicing a foreign market. The MNE finds the optimal mode of production by setting marginal cost (normal plus appropriate special cost) equal to marginal revenue at the start of each time period. The MNE finds the mode that maximizes profits (π) in each period. Its choice depends crucially upon the relative amount of each special cost, M^*, A^*, or D^*, which are now defined in more detail.

M^* is the additional costs of export marketing, which arise from gathering information about a foreign country and its potential market. These costs are initially high but diminish over time as familiarity with the new market increases. There are also other export marketing costs, invariant with time, arising from transportation, insurance, tariffs, and other barriers to international trade. This model does not explore these other costs, which are likely to vary with output and therefore can be incorporated into the marginal cost curve of the firm. These costs are added to C, the normal cost of production in the home nation.

A^* is defined as additional information costs of foreign direct investment arising from the unfamiliarity of the MNE with the culture, politics, and economy of the host nation. These costs are separate from C^*, the normal costs of production in the foreign (host) nation.

D^* is the risk of dissipation under the licensing mode. These costs can be viewed, in general, as the potential loss associated with the risk of attempting to separate the firm's special advantage from the firm itself. If the advantage is a brand name, some sales may be lost. If, as in the present context, the advantage is knowledge, the cost equals the profits lost because of dissipation of knowledge. These risk of dissipation costs are added to C^*, the normal cost of production in the foreign nation.

The profitability of each of the modalities depends crucially upon the relative value of each of the special costs, and is best illustrated in Figure 6-2.

In Figure 6-2 the linear demand function AR represents demand for the final good at various prices in the foreign nation. For the exporting mode MC is the marginal cost or supply function for exports from the home country. Since product differentiation and control over the intermediate product (knowledge) provide the firm with at least a temporary monopoly in the sale of the good, quantity Q^* is set where marginal revenue equals marginal cost, and price P^* is found at the corresponding point on the AR function.

In Figure 6-2 the total profit from exporting is given by area P^*ZX^1X, which represents total revenue OP^*ZQ^* minus total production costs $OVYQ^*$ and the special export marketing costs, represented by area XX^1YV. The size of the one-period profit is a function of the position and slope of demand function AR, the position and slope of normal supply function MC, and the special costs associated with the entry mode. Since the host-country demand curve is unaffected by the mode of entry, the chief factors in considering the exporting alternative will be the relative production costs of producing in the two countries and the additional marketing costs M^*.

The second entry method is foreign direct investment. Its distinguishing feature is that it involves production within the foreign country by a subsidiary which is under the direct managerial control of the multinational firm. This has two implications. The first is that the multinational faces certain additional costs A^* not encountered by local host-country firms. The second implication is that retaining ownership and control of production enables the MNE to forestall dissipation of its special advantage in knowledge. In other words, internalization increases the ability of the MNE to appropriate its knowledge advantage.

The foreign direct investment case is also illustrated in Figure 6-2; MC is the marginal cost curve for the foreign nation's production. It is the same for host and home-country firms producing in that nation. MC may differ from that in the home country, as the country-specific costs (i.e., production functions) need not be identical between nations. Here, for simplicity, it is assumed to be the same.

The intersection of the marginal revenue and marginal cost curves leads to the same equilibrium monopoly quantity of Q^* and price of P^*. The profit from direct investment is given by area P^*ZF^1F, which is total monopoly profits P^*ZYV less additional costs FF^1YV to the multinational firm of operating at a distance.

The case of licensing is rather different from the first two. Here the multinational enterprise obtains its profits not directly, but indirectly, through license fees charged to the foreign firm. But how is the optimal license fee determined? What is the nature of the cost, if any, of licensing, from the viewpoint of the multinational?

Let us assume that there are several local firms willing to act as licensees for the multinational. Then the multinational firm, holding a knowledge or other special advantage, can act as a monopolist in selling its knowledge. It will sell it at such a price and in such a way as to maximize its license fees. Since several local firms are available, they can expect only a normal return on the use of the knowledge, that is, zero economic rent. This means that the local licensee would be willing to give up any monopoly profits it earns in order to obtain the knowledge, up to the point where the profits paid as license fees would be sufficient to cover the cost of generating the knowledge directly. This alternative cost of knowledge sets an upper price on the license fee.

For present purposes it is assumed that the monopoly profits in one country alone, the host country, are not sufficient to pay for the cost of generating the knowledge anew. The multinational firm is therefore able to demand a license fee equal to the full monopoly profit, if any, of the foreign firm. The licensee arrangement that the MNE establishes will then be one which generates the maximum monopoly profit. The agreement involves only one firm, to ensure a monopoly prevails. Output is set such that marginal revenue equals marginal cost; so the license fee will be the difference between average revenue (price) and average cost. As before, however, there is a special cost to the multinational associated with this mode of entry, namely, D^*.

Figure 6-2 shows the licensing revenues and net profits from licensing. It contains the same host-country demand and normal cost function C^* as before. It differs only in that the net monopolistic profits accruing to the multinational now are reduced by special dissipation costs D^* (represented by area LL^1YV); i.e., the net profits from licensing are area P^*ZL^1L.

The choice among exporting, foreign direct investment, and licensing in this model therefore depends entirely on the relative amounts of export marketing costs M^*, special additional information costs A^*, and dissipation costs D^*. The MNE will find the mode of entry that maximizes profits in the time period.

This one-period model can be expressed in algebraic terms; these supplement the diagram used here.[6] The model can then be extended to make the special costs, and other factors, vary with time. A dynamic version of this model can be developed, which leads to the derivation of Figure 6-3. The algebra of these models was developed in Giddy and Rugman (1979).

---

[6]This is done in more detail in Giddy and Rugman (1979).

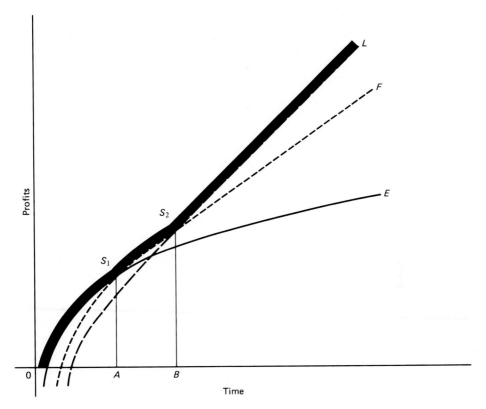

FIGURE 6-3
The sequencing of entry mode over time. A typical sequence of foreign entry for the MNE will involve exporting over time *OA,* foreign direct investment over time *AB,* and licensing thereafter.
The switchover points S_1 and S_2 are influenced by many factors, and the sequence in reality
may be much more complicated than this stylized mode.

Using the solutions of the three reduced-form equations from the Giddy-
Rugman model, it is possible to illustrate the optimal time sequence of entry
mode. This is done in Figure 6-3. Up to period A, exporting E is the optimal
modality; between A and B the best method is foreign direct investment F; and
after B licensing L is the method followed. These profit functions are entirely
theoretical, but their relative shapes and the time sequences are consistent with
the parameters of the equilibrium conditions of the model. Further work is
required to test the empirical strength of this model. Several simulations of the
model have been undertaken in which values are assigned to the parameters of the
reduced-form equations such that all the constraints imposed are satisfied. These
simulations support the sequence of entry mode illustrated in Figure 6-3. To make
this model fully operational requires further work in the specification of the
parameters, and in the gathering of data on such parameters for individual MNEs
or groupings of MNEs.

Clearly the dynamics of choice of entry mode in Figure 6-3 are much more complicated than the simple one-period case presented in Figure 6-2. In the static case, exporting generates the greatest profits, but if this modality is denied to the firm, then FDI is the next best choice, because of the assumption that $A^* < D^*$. This makes licensing the least profitable mode. Yet when special costs (and other variables) vary with time, the optimal mode can switch; a typical sequence moves from exporting, to FDI, to licensing. The reasons for this sequence depend on the hypothesis that $M^* < A^* < D^*$, and that they decrease over time in the reverse order (i.e., D^* falls at the most rapid pace). The importance of these special costs causes them to dominate the other variables and become the key determinants of profitability.

THE PROFITS OF MULTINATIONALS

One of the paradoxes revealed through the study of international business is that the earnings of MNEs are not excessive, although they are commonly perceived to be so. This section will examine data on the return on equity (ROE) for the largest MNEs in the world, in fact, the same MNEs identified in Chapter 1. In these tables no evidence is found of excess profitability. Most MNEs are found to have a ROE of between 10 to 14 percent, which is similar to the ROE of domestic firms of similar size.

These findings are also of interest when related to the theoretical work just completed. When the MNE is modeled as a monopolist, as in Figure 6-2, and elsewhere in this chapter, it is usual to expect that excess profits (or rents) will prevail for that organization, as contrasted to one in a competitive situation. We have seen, however, that there are two reasons for the disappearance of the potential excess profits that theory indicates might be available to MNEs.

First, there are special additional costs associated with whatever mode the MNE adopts in servicing foreign markets. Either M^*, A^*, or D^* serves to cut into its profits. Such special costs of multinationality are not incurred by a non-MNE firm, since it is operating only in its domestic market. There is no need for such a firm to secure information about the environmental parameters of foreign nations. Yet MNEs are constantly scanning such foreign political, cultural, and economic situations, so that their strategic planning can be accomplished in an informed and efficient manner.

Second, there are the normal administrative costs of running the internal market of the MNE. The management time, skills, and effort required to operate an internal market are considerable. The visible hand is not a free lunch. While it is difficult to quantify the costs of administrative fiat it is impossible to ignore them, as we do in a model of perfect competition where the invisible hand is operating.

Therefore, it is a reasonable hypothesis that both the special and administrative costs of internalization offset any potential excess profits available to MNEs. The evidence on profitability to which we now turn supports this prediction.

A COMPARISON OF THE PERFORMANCE OF THE WORLD'S LARGEST MNEs

Exhibits 6-2 to 6-7 report on the performance of the world's largest MNEs. The MNEs are grouped according to geographical location of the home (parent) firm. In each table, the MNEs are ranked in decreasing order of size, based on sales. Performance of the MNE is indicated by the rate of return on stockholders' equity (ROE), a conventional indicator of profitability. It is defined as the net income after tax divided by the value of stockholders' equity (net worth). The standard deviation of ROE, over the time period being considered, is used as a measure for risk of profits. For each company, the mean return on equity and mean standard deviation are recorded for the period from 1970 to 1979.

Exhibit 6-2 reports the mean ROE and standard deviation of profits for the fifty largest U.S. MNEs. The overall mean rate of return is 13.46 percent and the

EXHIBIT 6-2
PERFORMANCE OF THE FIFTY LARGEST U.S. MNEs, 1970 TO 1979

Firm	ROE mean	ROE SD
Exxon	14.90	2.96
General Motors	15.54	5.64
Mobil	13.22	2.71
Ford Motor	12.21	4.57
Texaco	12.74	3.19
Standard Oil of California	13.06	2.78
Gulf Oil	11.36	3.64
International Business Machines	18.73	2.22
General Electric	16.81	2.08
Standard Oil (Indiana)	13.68	3.37
International Telephone and Telegraph	11.05	2.00
Conoco (formerly Continental Oil)	13.96	4.08
E. I. du Pont de Nemours	12.84	3.18
Chrysler	4.26†	5.33†
Tenneco	13.17	2.24
Sun Company Incorporated	11.19	4.81
Occidental Petroleum	13.44*	12.06*
Phillips Petroleum	13.85	5.04
Procter & Gamble	17.08	0.65
Dow Chemical	18.41	5.64
Union Carbide	12.71	3.68
United Technologies	10.47*	4.08*
International Harvester	8.92	3.96
Goodyear Tire	9.68	1.89
Boeing	10.55	8.25
Eastman Kodak	17.94	1.79
Caterpillar Tractor	17.63	2.99
Union Oil of California	11.80	3.40
Beatrice Foods	15.15	0.63

EXHIBIT 6-2
(*continued*)

Firm	ROE mean	ROE SD
Westinghouse Electric	7.79*	3.85*
R. J. Reynolds Industries	17.31	0.88
Xerox	18.04	2.48
Rockwell International	11.53	2.54
Kraft Incorporated	13.59	2.39
Monsanto	12.04	4.14
Philip Morris	18.42	1.16
General Foods	13.02	4.36
Minnesota Mining and Manufacturing	18.34	2.32
Firestone Tire & Rubber	8.15*	3.43
McDonnell Douglas	12.81	1.47
W. R. Grace	11.03	3.67
PepsiCo, Incorporated	17.57	1.77
Coca-Cola	21.47	1.32
Deere & Company	14.25	3.70
Colgate-Palmolive	13.99	2.20
International Paper	12.22	5.33
Ralston Purina Company	14.51	1.66
TRW Incorporated	14.73	1.84
Allied Chemical Corporation	9.23	3.66
Weyerhaeuser	15.42	4.53
Overall mean	13.46	3.28

*Loss in 1 year treated as zero.
†Loss in 5 years treated as zero.
Definitions: ROE represents profit rate, i.e., net income after tax divided by value of stockholders' equity.
Source: *Fortune*'s "Directory of the 500 Largest U.S. Industrial Corporations."

standard deviation is 3.28 percent. The performance of the largest U.S. MNEs is good, compared with the performance of the fifty largest European MNEs, contained in Exhibit 6-3, whose overall mean and standard deviation are 8.13 and 4.49 percent, respectively, for the same period. Thus, with a considerably lower rate of return, the largest European MNEs also have the disadvantage of a higher variation in profits.

There are several possible explanations for this weaker performance. First, the European MNEs may not be as multinational as the U.S. ones, because a large proportion of foreign operations occur in neighboring countries. The MNEs may not receive the benefits of lower risk due to international diversification. Yet, conceptually, there are as many offsetting covariances within Europe as in the rest of the world. Thus, this explanation is unlikely. Second, the large number of state-owned enterprises (SOEs) in the European group may have an effect on performance. Exhibit 6-7 on page 143 lists the fourteen European SOEs as identified by Walters and Monsen (1979). It can be observed from looking at Exhibit

EXHIBIT 6-3
PERFORMANCE OF THE FIFTY LARGEST EUROPEAN MNEs, 1970 TO 1979

Firm	ROE mean	ROE SD
Royal Dutch/Shell	16.24	6.37
British Petroleum	12.10	7.86
Unilever	13.64	3.65
ENI	0.80^l	1.34^l
Fiat	3.52	3.43^b
Compagnie Française des Pétroles	11.72	12.22
Peugeot-Citroën	11.12	7.48
Volkswagenwerk	8.05^h	7.21^h
Philips	6.49	2.21
Régie Nationale des Usines Renault	2.16^h	3.59^h
Siemens	8.99	1.53
Daimler-Benz	14.65	3.68
Hoechst	8.07	3.07
Bayer	9.07	1.90
BASF	8.84	2.15
Thyssen	7.00^c	4.11^c
Societé Nationale Elf Aquitaine	12.05	7.24
Nestlé	10.25	0.88
Imperial Chemical Industries	12.81	3.21
B.A.T. Industries	13.32	1.34
Ruhrkohle	7.11^g	12.42^g
Saint-Gobain-Pont-à-Mousson	6.95	2.48
Compagnie Générale d'Electricité	6.00	2.24
Montedison	3.23^l	7.10^l
Pechiney Ugine Kuhlmann	5.81^g	3.65^g
Rhône-Poulenc	4.67^h	3.74^h
Petrofina	13.04	2.08
Thomson-Brandt	14.30	12.27
Friedrich Krupp	6.20^g	5.41^g
Mannesmann	12.35	7.64
AEG-Telefunken	4.35^k	7.72^k
ESTEL	4.72^j	5.58^j
Schneider	5.09	7.26
British Steel	2.31^l	3.66^l
DSM	10.56	9.07
BL	4.94^i	4.44^i
Michelin	10.10	2.58
Akzo	5.56^i	4.75^i
Ciba-Geigy	2.67	1.20
Robert Bosch	11.24	2.91
Gutehoffnungshutte	6.87	2.13
Volvo	11.61	6.52
Rio Tinto-Zinc	10.84	3.40
Brown Boveri	4.75^b	0.37
General Electric Co.	15.85	5.49
Metallgesellschaft	4.64	2.56
Guest, Keen & Nettlefolds	6.53	2.36

EXHIBIT 6-3
(continued)

Firm	ROE mean	ROE SD
Solvay & Cie SA	6.46	2.34
Salzgitter	2.09	3.03
BSN-Gervais Danone	4.87[g]	3.85[g]
Overall mean	8.13	4.49

[a] VEBA would have ranked fourth in terms of sales, but data for the total corporation were not available in *Fortune*; so it was excluded.
[b] Data in *Fortune* include parent only.
[c] Excludes foreign subsidiaries.
[d] Stockholders' equity includes parent only.
[e] Net profit includes parent only.
[f] Not on *Fortune*'s list.
[g] Loss in 1 year treated as zero.
[h] Loss in 2 years treated as zero.
[i] Loss in 3 years treated as zero.
[j] Loss in 4 years treated as zero.
[k] Loss in 5 years treated as zero.
[l] Loss in 6 years treated as zero.
NA indicates that the data were not available.
Figures in parentheses indicate loss.
Source: *Fortune*, "The 500 Largest Industrial Corporations Outside the U.S.," annual directory, various issues.

6-3 on European MNEs that the European SOEs perform extremely badly in economic terms and lower the overall mean performance of the European MNEs.

The poor performance of the SOEs is partly due to the fact that governments do not run SOEs as profit maximizers; instead SOEs are used to satisfy various social goals. Consequently, the management of SOEs is not rewarded on the same grounds as managers of private enterprise MNEs. Other nations (the United States, Japan, and Canada) have fewer SOEs; so the profit performance of these nations is not influenced as much as for the fifty largest European MNEs.

The industrial mix of the U.S. and European MNEs is very similar. Petroleum, motor vehicles, chemicals, electronics, and other consumer goods form a diversified group of MNEs. Technologically advanced products are the major firm-specific advantages (FSAs), followed by vertical integration (petroleum) and marketing and product development (consumer goods).

Exhibit 6-4 shows the performance of the twenty largest Japanese MNEs. The mean rate of return of 10.19 percent and standard deviation (risk) of profits of 4.13 percent place the Japanese MNEs in between the U.S. and European MNEs, in terms of performance.

The industrial mix of the Japanese MNEs is concentrated in motor vehicles (six), electronics (five), metal refining (five), and industrial equipment (three). Conspicuously absent are the petroleum MNEs so prevalent in the top fifty U.S. and European MNEs. The Japanese FSAs are not so much the actual technology embodied in the product but the use of robotics and flexible manufacturing

EXHIBIT 6-4
PERFORMANCE OF THE TWENTY LARGEST JAPANESE MNEs, 1970 TO 1979

Firm	ROE mean	ROE SD
Toyota Motor	16.21	3.95
Nissan Motor	13.01	3.52
Hitachi	11.21	3.48
Nippon Steel	7.91*	4.05*
Mitsubishi Heavy Industries	8.35	3.64
Matsushita Electric Industrial	12.25	4.43
Nippon Kokan	7.53	4.51
Sumitomo Metal Industries	7.77	3.76
Honda Motor	14.40	4.35
Kawasaki Steel	8.26	4.82
Kobe Steel	6.58	3.04
Ishikawajima-Harima Heavy Industry	8.32	3.18
Nippon Electric	8.15	4.74
Toyo Kogyo	5.79	3.92[†]
Sanyo Electric	11.53	3.29
Isuzu Motors	6.51[‡]	5.93[‡]
Sony	15.13	5.20
Kawasaki Heavy Industries	9.86[†]	4.40[†]
Bridgestone Tire	14.63	3.02
Komatsu	10.49	3.48
Overall mean	10.19	4.13

[*]Data for 1971 not available; mean and standard deviation calculated from 9 years of data.
[†]Loss in 1 year set equal to zero.
[‡]Losses in 2 years set equal to zero.
Source: *Fortune*, various issues: "The 500 Largest Industrial Corporations Outside the U.S." John M. Stopford, John H. Dunning, and Klaus O. Haberich. *The World Directory of Multinational Enterprises*. London: Macmillan, 1980.

systems, which help to hold down production costs and maintain high product quality. A related FSA is the common Japanese managerial philosophy where decision making is by consensus. This facilitates more efficient production.

Exhibit 6-5 illustrates the performance of the ten largest Canadian MNEs. The overall ROE mean and standard deviation are 11.48 and 5.64 percent, respectively. As such, the Candian MNEs place second to the U.S. MNEs, which have the highest overall rate of return. The risk of profits for the Canadian MNEs is higher than that for other MNEs, but this is due, in part, to the small sample size.

The FSAs of the Canadian MNEs are mostly in the ownership of resources and the knowledge with which to process and market them. Only one MNE, Northern Telecom, has its entire FSA in technology, although Moore's business forms embody a computer-assisted design. Otherwise, the FSAs are resource-based, i.e., for the MNEs in pulp and paper, mining and farm machinery, and alcoholic beverages.

EXHIBIT 6-5
PERFORMANCE OF THE TEN LARGEST CANADIAN MNEs, 1970 TO 1979

Firm	ROE mean	ROE SD
Alcan Aluminum	10.85	6.08
Massey Ferguson	7.68	5.88
Seagram	9.00	1.69
Inco	11.98	5.88
MacMillan Bloedel	9.75	6.32
Noranda Mines	15.14	6.66
Northern Telecom	13.72	5.88
Moore	15.86	3.24
Abitibi-Price	9.61	6.88
Domtar	11.18	7.93
Overall Mean	11.48	5.64

ROE represents profit rate, i.e., net income after tax divided by value of stockholders' equity.
Source: Various annual reports.

Finally, the performance of the twenty-four largest third world MNEs is reported in Exhibit 6-6. As many of these MNEs are newcomers to the *Fortune* "International 500," data are scarce. It is evident that many of the MNEs are growing rapidly, and the overall mean ROE of 18.8 percent should be interpreted with this upward bias in mind. The third world MNEs contain 14 SOEs, mostly petroleum firms. The predominant country, South Korea, has seven MNEs listed, and all are privately owned. The FSAs for the third world MNEs are in either resources (petroleum or mining) or the use of low-cost factor inputs employed in the manufacture of standardized products in mature industries.

EXHIBIT 6-6
PERFORMANCE OF THE TWENTY-FOUR LARGEST THIRD WORLD MNEs, 1970 TO 1979

Firm	ROE mean	ROE SD
Petróleos de Venezuela[a]	27.7[c]	NA[b]
Petrobrás[a]	19.2	3.07
Pemex[a]	0.8[d]	NA
Hyundai Group	22.1[c]	NA
YPF[a]	23.1[c]	NA
Kuwait National Petroleum[a]	47.1[f]	NA
Indian Oil[a]	15.6	3.05
Samsung Group	10.0[g]	NA
Chinese Petroleum[a]	9.3[c]	NA
Haci Omer Sabanci Holding	58.4[f]	NA
Korea Oil	16.3[c,i]	NA
CODELCO-CHILE[a]	17.9[c]	NA
Zambia Industrial & Mining[a]	11.0[g,j]	NA

EXHIBIT 6-6
(*continued*)

Firm	ROE mean	ROE SD
Lucky Group	20.9[f]	NA
Steel Authority of India[a]	7.6[h]	NA
Koc Holding	44.1[c]	NA
Hyosung Group	3.9[e]	NA
Philippine National Oil[a]	17.3[f]	NA
GECAMINES	18.1[e]	NA
Vale do Rio Doce[a]	11.7[h]	NA
Grupo Industrial Alpha	12.6[h]	NA
Pohang Iron and Steel	5.9[f]	NA
KUKjE (ICC)	14.5[f]	NA
Siderúrgica National[a]	16.8[h,i]	NA
Overall mean	18.8	NA

[a] State-owned enterprise.
[b] Insufficient years (10) available to calculate one standard deviation.
[c] 1979−1976.
[d] 1976−1970.
[e] 1979 only.
[f] 1979−1977.
[g] 1979−1973.
[h] 1979−1975.
[i] Loss in 1 year treated as zero.
[j] Loss in 2 years treated as zero.
Source: *Fortune*, various issues: "The 500 Largest Industrial Corporations Outside the U.S."

EXHIBIT 6-7
FOURTEEN EUROPEAN STATE-OWNED
ENTERPRISES

Firm	Country/State
British Petroleum	Britain
ENI	Italy
Volkswagenwerk	Germany
Renault	France
Compagnie Française Des Pétroles	France
Societé Nationale Elf Aquitaine	France
Montedison	Italy
Ruhrkohle	Germany
British Steel	Britain
Friedrich Krupp	Germany
British Leyland	Britain
NV DSM	Netherlands
Salzgitter	Germany
AG Volvo	Sweden

Source: Kenneth D. Walters, and Joseph Monsen. "State Owned Business Abroad: New Competitive Threat,"*Harvard Business Review*, 57 (March−April 1979): 160−70.

International Accounting Standards

Before we leave this discussion of the profitability of the world's largest MNEs, a standard caveat needs to be made. This is that our return on equity (ROE) figures are based on the financial statements presented by the firms themselves. These in turn are constructed in accordance with the generally accepted accounting principles (GAAP) in force in the home country of the MNE. Unfortunately, what constitutes GAAP differs from one country to another. Hence, the very foundations of our international comparisons of the ROEs of MNEs from different nations across these exhibits suffer from this limitation.

The problem of differing GAAP standards has been partly addressed by two types of international organizations; first, there are the *government* coordinating organizations such as the United Nations and the Organization for Economic Cooperation and Development (OECD), and second there are the *private* coordinating organizations sponsored by the national accounting professions such as the International Federation of Accountants and the International Accounting Standards Committee (IASC). The latter organization has published a number of accounting policy statements in an attempt to harmonize world standards and improve the comparability and consistency of financial statements across countries. The problem, however, is that the IASC policy statements in no way override the local GAAP. In many cases, they simply create another "standard" which increases the range of accounting options.

In practice, whether a company flows "extraordinary items" through its income statement or closes them directly to its stockholders' equity will have a significant impact on its ROE. Similarly, if a company can create special "reserves," it can smooth out earnings fluctuations and thus affect the variance of the rate of return to stockholders' equity. In both cases, the data in Exhibits 6-2 to 6-6 will be affected by the latitude allowed by domestic GAAP. However, having introduced this caveat, it is very difficult to do anything about it! No organization produces standardized financial statements; the closest we come are the 10-K returns filed with the U.S. Securities and Exchange Commission (SEC) to allow stock trading in the United States. Hence, without knowing any persistent bias produced in Exhibits 6-2 to 6-6 by differing accounting standards, we have to accept them at face value.

SUMMARY

The multinational enterprise can be modeled as possessing a monopolistic firm-specific advantage in knowledge, technology, or some other asset. The MNE is able to exploit this advantage abroad through exporting, foreign direct investment, or licensing.

In this chapter, several models are derived. These attempt to ascertain the optimal entry strategy for a firm servicing a foreign market. The Hirsch method determines the country-specific costs and the special costs associated with each mode of entry. The optimal entry strategy will be the least expensive one, all factors remaining constant.

The net present value (NPV) method provides a once-and-for-all choice of entry mode at a given point in time. It is possible for the NPV to change over time, and the MNE should try to identify the points at which the optimal modes change.

The final section of this chapter examines the profits and performance of the world's largest MNEs. The rate of return on stockholders' equity (ROE) and the standard deviation of the ROE are used to measure performance. Contrary to popular belief, no evidence is found of MNEs making excessive profits. Generally, the special costs identified in the first part of the chapter and the normal administrative costs of running an internal market appear to offset any potential excess profits.

KEY WORDS

Rents	Off shore assembly
Hirsch method	Trading licensee
C	Net present value method
C^*	Giddy-Rugman method
M^*	Rate of return on equity (ROE)
A^*	Standard deviation of ROE
D^*	State-owned enterprises

QUESTIONS

1   The Hirsch method of 1976 for choosing between alternative entry modes was later adapted and modified. Outline the variables of this model, giving a brief explanation of each. How do these factors change over time? How is knowledge as a firm-specific advantage affected by these variables?

2   It is stated in this chapter that the firm has three choices regarding entry mode— exporting, FDI, or licensing. Using the factors identified in the previous question, explain how this choice is made. How is the choice made optimal? How is this analysis related to production for the domestic market?

3   What is meant by the net present value method? Discuss any disadvantages of this method. What new variables are introduced into the methodology? Explain how costs change over time with this method.

4   Discuss the statement: The MNE is a monopolist. How does the MNE reduce the risk of losing its monopolistic advantage? With the use of a graph, relate this to the conditions of supply and demand.

5   Define foreign direct investment. What are the implications of foreign direct investment? How does licensing differ from foreign direct investment?

6   The Giddy-Rugman model extends the one-period model to account for variations over time. Using an illustration, explain the optimal time sequence of entry mode. What precautions must be taken when relying on this model?

7 Throughout the chapter, the MNE has been termed a monopolist because of the knowledge firm-specific advantage. Thus, it would seem likely that MNEs would earn excess profits. Is this the case? Give reasons to support your answer. What are some possible explanations for different performance rates among MNEs?

8 Discuss the different firm-specific advantages prevalent in the MNEs of different nations.

Exercise: Compare the rate of return on equity for the top ten U.S. multinational and domestic firms from Fortune 500. Is there a substantial difference? Explain your findings in terms of the concepts introduced in this chapter.

PART THREE

THE FINANCIAL ENVIRONMENT OF INTERNATIONAL BUSINESS

THE BALANCE OF PAYMENTS AND THE INTERNATIONAL MONETARY SYSTEM

INTRODUCTION

The purpose of this chapter is to discuss the implications for international management of the institutional framework within which trade and investments take place. First, however, we extend our analysis of comparative advantage, contained in Chapter 2, to include comparative advantage in investment opportunities. As a result we can discuss why capital should flow between different countries and why imperfections in the capital market work to the advantage of the multinational. Second, we discuss balance of payments statistics and accounting methodology, since most of our data are derived from this source. Third, we discuss the foreign exchange market, since this is another way of looking at the balance of payments. Finally, we discuss different methods of organizing the international monetary system and review recent historical developments as they affect international arrangements.

ESSENTIALS OF INTERNATIONAL CAPITAL MARKET THEORY

In Chapter 2 we established the principle of comparative advantage and showed how with free trade it resulted in specialization of production, and efficiency. At that stage we were principally concerned with analyzing the determinants of the pattern of trade between countries. The result was a framework with which we could analyze the effects of market imperfections and the role of the multinational. However, our analysis was *static*, in looking at trade decisions at a particular point in time. As a result, on page 30, we derived the result that the value of exports equals the value of imports. In practice, this result rarely holds, since real decisions are dynamic. By dynamic, all we mean is that the overall productive capacity of the economy can change owing to economic growth, caused by increased real investment in factories and machines. This investment can be financed by the savings of nonresidents as well as residents. In the former case of nonresident savings financial capital moves between countries. As a result, we have to consider *capital flows* in addition to the *trade flows* of Chapter 2.

The techniques used to analyze capital flows are identical to those used to analyze trade flows. In fact, Figure 7-1 is *identical* to Figure 2-4 except for the definitions involved. The production possibility frontier TT', instead of representing the possible production levels of two goods, now represents the available level of production in two different periods, labeled for convenience present and future. The indifference curves I_1' and I_T' now represent the country's preference for consuming the production of goods and services today relative to the future. For example, if no capital flows are allowed, the country has to consume from within its own resources. As a result, the best combination of resources is at point E, where the country's present and future consumption and production is at X_E and Y_E, respectively. Trade between countries would then allocate this production as exports and imports for each point in time according to the discussion of Chapter 2.

If capital flows are allowed, the analysis changes in exactly the same way as in Chapter 2 when trade flows were allowed. Then as now, the line $P_W P_{,W}$ represents the price of the good on the vertical axis relative to that on the horizontal axis. The only difference is that now the two goods represent overall production at two different points in time. This price has a special significance, since it represents the price of deferring the consumption of resources for a period of time. It is called the *interest rate*. For example, if a country or individual borrows resources and consumes them today, the price of those resources is represented by the additional resources that have to be paid back when the loan comes due. In practice, of course, rather than transferring resources directly, we transfer *purchasing power* by borrowing and lending money, which is just a claim on resources.

In Figure 7-1, with free and open capital markets, price line $P_W P_W'$ is determined in the international capital market. The slope of line $P_W P_W'$ represents one plus the world interest rate. The optimal solution for this country is to produce at J and consume at K, where the country is on the highest indifference curve I_T'. At K the country's present consumption is X_K and production X_J; it is net imports which make up the difference. In the future, consumption is Y_K and production Y_J; here the difference is made up by *net exports*. The net imports are financed by capital inflows or borrowing from other countries. These capital inflows, like all other borrowings, are promises for repayment at some future date. In our simple model of the present and the future, the capital inflows of the present to finance the net imports are paid off with the net export earnings of the future.

Figure 7-1 is fundamental to understanding international capital flows. In exactly the same way that comparative advantage in trade produced welfare gains from free trade, so too *comparative advantage in investment opportunities* produces welfare gains from free capital movements. In Figure 7-1, the country has a

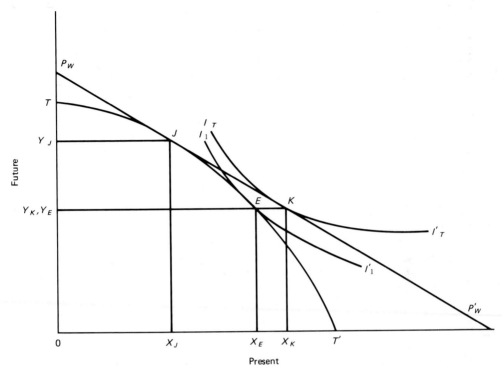

FIGURE 7-1
Essentials of capital market theory. Note: Open international capital markets are unambiguously better. In our example, present consumption is increased (from X_E to X_K) while future consumption is constant ($Y_K = Y_E$). The actual change in present and future consumption of course depends on the slopes of TT' and $I_T I_T'$.

comparative advantage in investment opportunities; that is, it can earn a relatively high rate of return by reinvesting resources today in projects that will generate relatively large amounts of resources in the future. Open capital markets imply that rather than making present sacrifices, this country can capitalize on its future opportunities by borrowing from others to finance these investments. As a result this country will finance its net imports by borrowing abroad. Moreover, this export-import imbalance is efficient, since the capital exporting country also gains by making investments to earn a higher rate of return than can be earned domestically. Just as Chapter 2 determined the efficient pattern of international trade and production so too the tools just discussed determine the efficient pattern of international investment.

Analogous to Chapter 3, governments impose quotas and tariffs on capital movements in addition to those on trade movements. For example, *withholding taxes* are imposed on interest and dividend payments to prevent capital from flowing out of a country. These taxes are similar in impact to the imposition of tariffs in changing the slope of line $P_W P_W'$ in Figure 7-1. Similarly, foreign exchange controls restrict movements of capital in and out of countries and act in the same way as import or export quotas. In all cases, the arguments in favor of restrictions on capital movements are based on the same fallacies as those used to justify restrictions on trade flows. However, they also create imperfections in the capital market that increase the value of the multinational's internal markets. The multinational, by straddling different national markets, can often minimize the effects of government-introduced distortions and thus increase efficiency. In Chapter 14 we will discuss the financial management techniques, such as transfer pricing, available to managers to minimize the imperfections introduced into the international capital market.

THE BALANCE OF PAYMENTS ACCOUNTS

A set of financial statements help managers analyze what has happened in the past and what may happen in the future. A country's balance of payments accounts are simply the financial statements prepared to help analyze a country's economic performance. Yet it is important to realize what the accounts are and are not. First, the term "balance" may indicate comparability with a firm's balance sheet. However, this is incorrect, since the balance of payments measures a flow of goods, services, and capital over a period of time, unlike the firm's balance sheet, which measures a *stock* of assets and liabilities as of a point in time. Second, the term "payments" may indicate comparability with the firm's income statement. Again, this is incorrect, since the balance of payments is not intended to determine the profit earned by a country during a period of time. Instead the balance of payments is analogous to the firm's statement of changes in financial position, or sources and uses of funds statement, which merely catalogs the flow of funds through the corporation during a particular period of time.

Balance of Payments Accounting

The construction of the balance of payments accounts, like the statement of changes in financial position, is drawn up on the basis of double-entry book-keeping. That is, every transaction involves an exchange of two distinct commodities, each of which is accounted for separately. For example, domestically a firm may buy a piece of machinery for $1 million cash. The accountant for the firm would record two transactions: a decrease in cash of $1 million and an increase in plant and equipment (the machinery) of $1 million. Over the whole of the year the accountant would construct a statement of changes in financial position by simply summing up all the changes in the different accounts and separating all items that used cash, e.g., the increase in the machinery account, from items that produced cash, e.g., a bond issue. Conceptually this produces two implications. First, the statement of changes in financial position, and hence also the balance of payments accounts, must *always* balance. Second, what is important is the change in individual accounts over a period of time, e.g., for the firm the change in its cash account.

Once the analogy between the balance of payments accounts and the statement of changes in financial position is clear, all that is needed is to point out how the presentations of the accounts differ. For a corporation the sources of funds are usually: funds flow from operations, short- and long-term borrowing, and new equity issues and accruals. Uses of funds are usually: cash, inventory, accounts receivable, dividends, and plant and equipment. The important point is that the classifications are for different types of economic transactions. Accounts payable can be netted out against accounts receivable, but long-term debt cannot be netted out against plant and equipment. The netting simply doesn't make any sense. However, this is not the case for the balance of payments accounts.

For the *sources* of funds, we can define merchandise exports, dividend and interest receipts, transfers from foreign residents, and short- and long-term borrowing. We can also define identical *uses* of funds, i.e., merchandise imports, dividend and interest payments, transfers to foreign residents, and short- and long-term lending. Hence, we can differentiate the balance of payments from the statement of changes in financial position by netting out across identical economic activities to determine net merchandise exports, net interest and dividend payments, etc. It is these individual and cumulative *net* accounts that give the balance of payments its unique appearance.

To illustrate the construction of the balance of payments accounts, consider the nine hypothetical international transactions in Exhibit 7-1. In transaction 1, our $100 million in merchandise exports gives rise to two offsetting financial transactions: the receipt of $80 million in cash and a claim on foreign residents of $20 million. This $20 million arises from the provision of trade credit; that is, the foreign purchaser takes delivery but payment will be made at some future date. To account for these transactions, the accountant will record a credit (left-hand-side adjustment) of $100 million for the trade account (exports) and debits (right-hand-side adjustment) of $80 million for the cash account and $20 million for the short-term capital flow account. The trade credit in essence is equivalent to a short-term bank loan, or capital flow, of $20 million.

Transaction 2 is just the opposite; we pay for our $80 million in imports with $70 million in cash and a $10 million short-term loan. Hence, the accountant will record a debit of $80 million for the trade account (imports) and credits of $70 million and $10 million for the cash and short-term capital flow accounts, respectively.

In analyzing these two transactions, we should make two observations. First, the terms credits and debits simply refer to the adjustments to the left- and right-hand sides of the set of accounts, respectively. Alternatively, we could refer to credits as sources of funds. In this sense, exports were a source of $100 million in funds for the first transaction, and a rundown in cash ($70 million) and increase in short-term debt ($10 million) were a source of $80 million in funds for the second transaction. Debits would then refer to uses of funds. Second, double-entry bookkeeping means that the accounting entries for each transaction always balance. This implies that summing over all transactions means that sources of funds

An Example of the Balance of Payments Accounts

EXHIBIT 7-1
BALANCE OF PAYMENTS ACCOUNTS

	Sources (credits)*	Uses (debits)*	Balance of payments	
Trade	100 (1)	80 (2)	Balance of trade	20
Services	10 (3)	15 (4)	Balance of goods and services	15
Transfers	1 (6)	5 (5)	Balance on current account	11
Long-term capital	5 (8)	15 (7)	Basic balance	1
Short-term capital	10 (2)	20 (1)	Official settlements balance	−9
Cash 70(2), 15(4), 5(5), 15(7)		80(1), 10(3), 1(6), 5(8), 9(9)		
Net Official Monetary Movements (NOMM)	9 (9)			

*In $ million.
Transactions:
1   $100 million in exports: $80 million paid in cash, $20 million in short-term loans.
2   $80 million in imports: $70 million paid in cash, $10 million in short-term loans.
3   Receipts from national shipping line: $10 million in cash.
4   Payments of dividends, and insurance: $15 million in cash.
5   Contributions to international organizations: $5 million in cash.
6   Inheritances from foreign relatives: $1 million in cash.
7   Capital market borrowing by foreign residents: $15 million in cash.
8   Domestic borrowing in foreign capital markets: $5 million in cash.
9   Sale by government of foreign securities: $9 million in cash.

will always equal uses of funds, inflows will equal outflows, or, in accounting terminology, debits equals credits. For the remaining transactions we will refer to the account entries in parentheses.

In transaction 3, $10 million in cash is received (debit cash $10 million) from nonresident use of the national shipping line (credit services $10 million). In transaction 4 $15 million in cash is paid (credit cash $15 million) for the provision of insurance by foreign companies and to service debt obligations to foreign residents (debit services $15 million). In both transactions there is an export or import of an intangible commodity (services) rather than an actual physical commodity. Hence, traditionally the services account is separated from the goods or trade account.

In transaction 5 a $5 million cash payment (credit cash $5 million) is made to an international organization as part of a continuing obligation (debit transfers $5 million). In transaction 6 $1 million in cash is received (debit cash $1 million) from an inheritance from a foreign resident (credit transfers $1 million). In these two transactions no ostensible economic service motivates the immediate payment. Hence they are classified as unrequited transfers.

In transaction 7 foreign residents receive $15 million in cash (credit cash $15 million) from the sale of long-term bonds in the domestic capital market (debit long-term capital account $15 million). In transaction 8 domestic residents receive

$5 million in cash (debit cash $5 million) from the sale of equity issues in foreign capital markets (credit long-term capital $5 million). Long-term capital movements, that is, capital supplied with a maturity date in excess of 1 year, are accounted for separately. This is because long-term capital flows ostensibly arise as a result of comparative advantage in investment opportunities rather than trade.

If we sum over the first eight transactions, we find that sources of funds or credits of $135 million equals uses of funds or debits of $135 million. However, our transactions that have involved "cash" have all been closed to an account called cash, which in fact shows a sources balance of $9 million. That is, so far we have received $9 million less in cash than we have paid out. If this statement of changes in financial position belonged to a corporation, it would simply represent a rundown in cash at the bank, which is just a reduction in the claim that the corporation has on the bank. A claim on another country is represented by its foreign exchange reserves, which are usually holdings of foreign treasury bills and foreign currency deposits held in banks. Hence, in transaction 9 we have the central bank selling $9 million of foreign treasury bills (credit NOMM $9 million) to meet this excess demand for cash of $9 million (debit cash $9 million). Any transactions by the central bank are shown separately as net official monetary movements (NOMM) or settlements, on the grounds that they represent government intervention.

Definitions of the Balance of Payments

The nine transactions of Exhibit 7-1 allow us to list the sources (credits) and uses (debits) of funds for a country. However, this sources and uses of funds statement, or changes in financial position, is more familiarly read for the balance of payments accounts as a series of partial balances. Hence we normally define five partial balances. First, the *merchandise trade balance*, or balance of trade, is simply the net exports, which in our example is $20 million. Second, the *balance on goods and services* is the combined balance resulting from adding the net services account to the net exports account. In our example, it is $15 million. Third, the *balance on current account* of $11 million adds the net transfers to the balance on goods and services. Fourth, the *basic balance* of $1 million adds the net long-term capital flows to the current account. Finally, the *official settlements balance* of –$9 million adds the short-term capital flows to the basic balance, thus indicating the magnitude of the net official monetary movements or the size of the government intervention in the balance of payments.

All these balances can be termed a balance of payments, since they represent the sources and uses of funds up to a certain category. Moreover, since they do not contain all the international transactions, these specific balances can be in imbalance, either surplus or deficit. However, since the total balance of payments "balances," any surplus or deficit, for example, on current account, must be balanced by a corresponding deficit or surplus on other transactions not included in the current account.

Interpreting the Balance of Payments Accounts

This conceptual understanding of the construction of the balance of payments accounts is important for their interpretation.

First and most fundamental, we must recognize that there is no economic reason for any of the individual balances to balance. For example, there is nothing good or bad about having a surplus on trade and a deficit on services. This would just reflect an economy with a comparative advantage in the production of merchandise such as manufactured goods as against services such as insurance, shipping, and banking.

Even the balance on current account should not necessarily balance. As we noted earlier, countries with a comparative advantage in investment opportunities would be expected to run a deficit on current account financed by capital inflows. This just reflects the great advantage of financial markets in allowing countries to escape the closed economy trap of having to consume from within their existing endowments.

A second point in the interpretation of the balance of payments accounts is that some flows are regarded as autonomous as they occur for underlying economic reasons. Traditionally, we have viewed the current account flows and the *long-term* capital flows as being autonomous. The current account flows largely arise from comparative advantage in trade, the long-term capital flows from comparative advantage in investment opportunities. Yet notice that in the construction of Exhibit 7-1, the use of trade financing of exports and imports created offsetting short-term financial flows. These flows are often called *accommodating*, since they arise automatically if payments are not made in cash.

A third interpretation of the balance of payments accounts refers to causality. From the distinction between autonomous and accommodating flows we often hear the complaint that a current account deficit forced accommodating capital inflows. This assumes that causality runs from the current account to the capital account. However, there is nothing in the balance of payments accounts that allows us to draw any such implication for causality. In fact, it may well be that autonomous capital inflows can cause an appreciation of the currency with a consequent decline in exports, increase in imports, and a current account deficit. In this second case, causality runs from the capital account to the current account, not the reverse.

In summary, we should note that the balance of payments statistics, like the statement of changes in financial position, tells us what has happened. To make inferences on whether this was good or bad requires an exogenous judgment as to what *should* have occurred. Within the overall balance individual partial balances by themselves just reflect comparative advantage. They are highly unlikely to balance, nor should they. Moreover, no implications for causality can automatically be drawn by examinaton of these partial balances.

Use of the Balance of Payments Accounts

Subject to the caveats of the previous section, the balance of payments accounts provide the basic information for analyzing a country's economic relationships with the rest of the world. The economist usually looks at the current account to determine the normal pattern of payments and receipts from ongoing economic activity. In this sense, the balance on goods and services will reflect the comparative advantage of a country in providing *current* goods and services. (The transfers account is usually relatively minor and subject to only small annual variations.) The long-term capital flows will then reflect comparative advantage in investment opportunities, since a country with tremendous resources to develop will normally find it optimal to import capital to exploit them. Hence the *basic balance* which adds the two together should reflect in aggregate a country's comparative advantage.

Economists have traditionally looked at the basic balance from the perspective that it should equal zero. This would imply that a mature economy with limited investment opportunities would export capital and run a current account surplus, whereas a young growth economy with good investment opportunities would import capital and run a current account deficit. In both cases, the division of that surplus or deficit between services and physical commodities, and then the individual commodities themselves, would again reflect comparative advantage. The basic balance would net to zero; otherwise countries would continuously increase short-term debts or run down their foreign exchange reserves.

The problem with using the basic balance in this way as the balance of payments is that financial markets have become more and more sophisticated. One result is that it is often short-term capital flows that are created in response to a comparative advantage in investment opportunities. This is particularly true when funds are raised through short-term international bank lending. The problem is that conceptually there is little difference between a long-term bond and a repeatedly rolled over short-term loan from a bank. Moreover, long-term capital flows are not always in response to comparative advantage. Often they reflect a foreign government's decision to hold foreign exchange reserves in long-term corporate securities. Hence, particularly for the United States and other reserve asset countries, the basic balance is often not what it appears to be.

The balance of payments statistics for most countries usually include bilateral country balances as well as individual statistics for particular commodities such as autos and steel. The result is that the data provide the basic information for many industry lobbying groups and government trade negotiators. The usual premise is that individual accounts should be balanced, across both countries in aggregate and individual commodities. Hence, industry lobbying groups may point out, for example, the U.S. deficit in autos and use this as a justification for protection against the Japanese until parity is reached. Similarly, politicians may point out the "intolerably" high U.S. trade deficit with Japan as a reason for "hard balling" it with the Japanese for trade concessions or political payoffs in foreign policy.

Of course, there is no economic reason for bilateral balances to be optimal across countries, let alone individual commodities. For individual commodities it obviously flies in the face of comparative advantage. For countries, it also makes no sense. For example, the United States generally runs a trade deficit with Japan. However, Japan usually runs a trade deficit with the third world countries (energy), which in turn usually run a trade deficit with the United States. All this makes good economic sense. In aggregate, trade follows comparative advantage and each country may run an overall trade balance. However, none of the bilateral balances should balance, and to force them to do so would be nonsensical. However, the arguments of trade negotiators and lobbying groups are usually not based on economic common sense in the first place, but on self-interest.

THE FOREIGN EXCHANGE MARKET

Remember that in Exhibit 7-1 the construction of our hypothetical balance of payments statistics required that many of the transactions were closed to cash. For example, the $100 million of merchandise exports resulted in cash receipts of $80 million and accounts receivable of $20 million. However, the cash *receipts* from these exports would normally be in the foreign currency, since the domestic exporter would be competing with local suppliers in the foreign market. Conversely, the $80 million of merchandise imports, which gave rise to $70 million of cash *payments*, would most likely be made in the domestic currency. In both cases, a need arises to exchange currencies. In the case of exports, the foreign currency needs to be exchanged for domestic currency, so that the exporter can meet its domestic currency commitments. For the importer, the reverse happens. The domestic currency is paid to the foreign exporter, who then makes the exchange to its own currency to meet its own domestic commitments. The market in which these participants come together to exchange currencies is called the *foreign (currency) exchange market*. The price that is determined in this market is the *foreign exchange rate*.

The nature of the transactions in the foreign exchange market was hinted at in Exhibit 7-1. In a "normal" market supply and demand curves are derived based on the cost of producing the commodity coupled with the satisfaction derived from its ultimate consumption. However, the foreign exchange market is unique in that foreign currency is supplied or demanded only as an intermediate product; the ultimate commodity consumed is the merchandise export, service, or capital flow. Hence supply and demand in the foreign exchange market, and consequently the foreign exchange rate, reflect the sum total of all international transactions. To some extent this conclusion has been moderated since the advent of floating exchange rates. Since 1973, increasingly the demand for foreign exchange has stemmed from speculation, as we will discuss in Chapters 8 and 9. However, it remains true that the foreign exchange market is a residual market and subject to more influences than normal.

We can see the result of this implication by referring back to the transactions in the lower part of Exhibit 7-1. We can break out those transactions which involve a demand for cash as transactions involving a demand for dollars, which we represent by $D(\$)$. These are merchandise trade and service exports, transfer inflows, and short- and long-term capital inflows. Similarly, the transactions which involve a supply of cash represent a supply of dollars, $S(\$)$. These are merchandise trade and service imports, transfer outflows, and short- and long-term capital outflows.

Hence, from the underlying supply and demand functions we can derive the supply and demand functions for dollars.

In Figure 7-2, we graph these supply and demand curves and add the $9 million demand stemming from official sales of foreign reserve assets $[D(\$) +]$. The vertical axis represents the price of foreign currency (FC) and the horizontal axis the quantity of dollars exchanged in the foreign exchange market. As in any market, we determine an equilibrium quantity, e.g., volume of dollars traded, and an equilibrium price, e.g., the foreign exchange rate. However, in a normal market the price is expressed in terms of the domestic currency, for example, in the United States in terms of dollars. This is because the dollar is the "numeraire," or unit of account, in the United States. For this reason in the United States we do not price houses in terms of autos, or sweaters in terms of TV sets, but instead use the dollar as a unit of account to reflect the opportunity cost of buying a particular commodity.

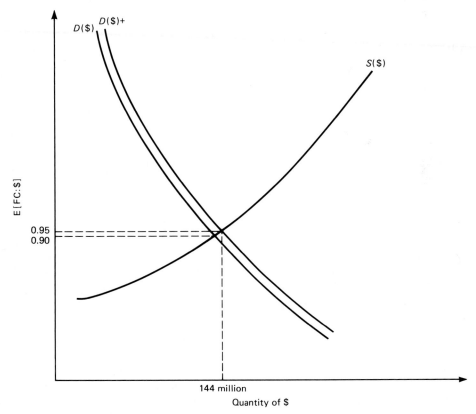

FIGURE 7-2
Equilibrium in the foreign exchange market.

Unfortunately, there is no standard unit of account internationally, since there is no international money. As a result, the price of foreign exchange is not a price as normally understood but instead is the exchange ratio of two currencies. This causes a lot of initial confusion, since any exchange ratio can be expressed in two ways. We can either express dollars in terms of deutsche marks or deutsche marks in terms of dollars. It is as if we expressed a hamburger as costing, say, $2 and then went on to say that a dollar bill cost 0.5 hamburger. Definitionally, for the U.S. dollar when it is expressed as the number of U.S. dollars per foreign currency unit, we call it the *U.S. dollar equivalent* exchange rate and will denote it as $E[US\$:FC]$. When it is expressed as foreign currency per U.S. dollar, we call it *European* terms and denote it as $E[FC:US\$]$.

Reading Exchange Rate Quotations

Figure 7-3 provides foreign exchange rate quotations from the *Wall Street Journal* for May 8, 1984. Any reputable newspaper will carry a similar, although not so extensive, list of quotations. The price quotations are based on interbank transactions in excess of $1 million charged by Bankers Trust the previous day of trading at 3 p.m. This is what is commonly referred to as the *wholesale market*, since the foreign exchange is bought and sold to maintain bank inventory levels sufficient to meet the demand coming from the bank's customers.

The *retail market*, in turn, is the purchase and sale of foreign currency to the bank's customers. This is essentially a cash market, since except for large amounts, or unusual currencies, delivery is immediate. Quotations will differ by plus or minus 2 to 3 percent from the wholesale prices. This establishes the bid-ask retail spread, which are the prices at which the bank is prepared to buy or sell foreign exchange to the retail public. For example, for pound sterling the rates would have been around 1.365 and 1.405 U.S. dollar equivalent, meaning that the bank would buy and sell pounds sterling for $1.365 and $1.405, respectively. The spread of 4 cents compensates the bank for holding an inventory of foreign currency.

In Figure 7-3 the exchange rates are quoted in both European and U.S. dollar equivalent terms. For example, for Tuesday, May 8, the pound sterling is quoted in U.S. dollar equivalent at $1.387, which is the U.S. dollar equivalent of £1 sterling. Conversely, in European terms the quote is 0.721, meaning that 1 U.S. dollar would buy that amount of pounds sterling. Whenever there is only one quotation per currency, this refers to *spot* transactions, which means that delivery will take 1 or possibly 2 business days.

With more than one quotation we have either multiple spot rates or forward rates. For example, for the Belgian franc the spot rate differs depending on whether the purpose of the transaction is commercial or financial. Hence the different spot rates result from the imposition of foreign exchange controls. The quotations in Figure 7-3 do not reflect the extent of government intervention in the foreign exchange market. Here the manager would first consult the International Monetary Fund's Annual Report on Exchange Arrangements and Restrictions and then a foreign exchange specialist, either a broker or a banker.

Foreign Exchange

Monday, May 7, 1984

The New York foreign exchange selling rates below apply to trading among banks in amounts of $1 million and more, as quoted at 3 p.m. Eastern time by Bankers Trust Co. Retail transactions provide fewer units of foreign currency per dollar.

Country	U.S. $ equiv.		Currency per U.S. $	
	Monday	Friday	Monday	Friday
Argentina (Peso)	.02683	.02815	37.274	35.527
Australia (Dollar)	.9160	.9270	1.0917	1.0787
Austria (Schilling)	.05157	.05238	19.39	19.09
Belgium (Franc)				
Commercial rate	.01807	.01807	55.355	55.355
Financial rate	.01776	.01776	56.310	56.310
Brazil (Cruzeiro)	.0006898	.0007084	1449.50	1411.50
Britain (Pound)	1.3870	1.4087	.7210	.7099
30-Day Forward	1.3896	1.4112	.7196	.7086
90-Day Forward	1.3942	1.4157	.7173	.7064
180-Day Forward	1.4022	1.4241	.7132	.7022
Canada (Dollar)	.7729	.7744	1.2939	1.2914
30-Day Forward	.7730	.7745	1.2937	1.2911
90-Day Forward	.7730	.7745	1.2937	1.2911
180-Day Forward	.7730	.7745	1.2936	1.2911
Chile (Official rate) ...	.01117	.01123	89.50	89.04
China (Yuan)	.4647	.4693	2.1521	2.1308
Colombia (Peso)	.01037	.01043	96.45	95.84
Denmark (Krone)	.09889	.1004	10.1125	9.9600
Ecuador (Sucre)				
Official rate	.01656	.01656	60.40	60.40
Floating rate	.01129	.01129	88.55	88.55
Finland (Markka)	.1720	.1743	5.8150	5.7375
France (Franc)	.1179	.1197	8.4825	8.3575
30-Day Forward	.1178	.1195	8.4925	8.3690
90-Day Forward	.1175	.1192	8.5110	8.3885
180-Day Forward	.1168	.1184	8.5605	8.4435
Greece (Drachma)	.009341	.009341	107.05	107.05
Hong Kong (Dollar) ...	.1280	.1281	7.8150	7.8055
India (Rupee)	.0912	.0913	10.9649	10.9529
Indonesia (Rupiah)	.000993	.000996	1007.00	1004.00
Ireland (Punt)	1.1125	1.1305	8989	.8846
Israel (Shekel)	.005397	.005397	185.30	185.30
Italy (Lira)	.0005844	.0005945	1711.00	1682.00
Japan (Yen)	.004371	.004410	228.80	226.75
30-Day Forward	.004391	.004429	227.75	225.76
90-Day Forward	.004427	.004466	225.90	223.91
180-Day Forward	.004487	.004525	222.85	221.00
Lebanon (Pound)	.1770	.1773	5.65	5.64
Malaysia (Ringgit)	.4358	.4367	2.2945	2.2900
Mexico (Peso)				
Floating rate	.005291	.005263	189.00	190.00
Netherlands (Guilder)	.3214	.3265	3.1110	3.0625
New Zealand (Dollar) .	.6520	.6583	1.5337	1.5191
Norway (Krone)	.1280	.1298	7.8150	7.7060
Pakistan (Rupee)	.07326	.07326	13.65	13.65
Peru (Sol)	.0003437	.0003498	2909.22	2858.69
Philippines (Peso)	.07133	.07082	14.02	14.12
Portugal (Escudo)	.007194	.007299	139.00	137.00
Saudi Arabia (Riyal) .	.2839	.2839	3.5220	3.5220
Singapore (Dollar)	.4778	.4791	2.0928	2.0871
South Africa (Rand) ..	.7935	.7990	1.2602	1.2516
South Korea (Won)	.001251	.001259	799.40	794.00
Spain (Peseta)	.006464	.006577	154.70	152.05
Sweden (Krona)	.1237	.1250	8.0840	8.0025
Switzerland (Franc) ...	.4389	.4447	2.2785	2.2485
30-Day Forward	.4420	.4477	2.2624	2.2337
90-Day Forward	.4473	.4532	2.2358	2.2065
180-Day Forward	.4456	.4617	2.1952	2.1660
Taiwan (Dollar)	.02524	.02519	39.62	39.70
Thailand (Baht)	.04351	.04351	22.985	22.985
Uruguay (New Peso)				
Financial	.01909	.01909	52.38	52.38
Venezuela (Bolivar)				
Official rate	.1333	.1333	7.50	7.50
Floating rate	.07052	.07052	14.18	14.18
W. Germany (Mark) ..	.3613	.3676	2.7680	2.7205
30-Day Forward	.3631	.3692	2.7542	2.7088
90-Day Forward	.3664	.3726	2.7295	2.6839
180-Day Forward	.3718	.3780	2.6898	2.6454
SDR	1.03986	1.04904	.961670	.953251

Special Drawing Rights are based on exchange rates for the U.S., West German, British, French and Japanese currencies. Source: International Monetary Fund.

z-Not quoted.

FIGURE 7-3
(From *Wall Street Journal*, May 8, 1984.)

The quotations for Britain, Canada, Japan, Switzerland, and West Germany all include prices for *forward market* transactions. A forward market transaction just reflects the sale of foreign currency at an agreed rate today, where delivery will take place at some future date. For example, for Tuesday, May 8, 1984, 1 deutsche mark would have bought $0.3613 if delivery was within 2 business days. However, if delivery was to take place in 180 days, the deutsche mark would have bought $0.3718. Since delivery is to take place at different points in time, there is no reason for the exchange rate quotations to be the same for forward as for spot transactions. In Chapter 9 we will see what determines the spot and forward exchange rates.

Government Intervention in the Foreign Exchange Market

Before discussing govenment intervention, we should discuss more fully the definition of the foreign exchange market. First, we can note that there will be an exchange rate determined for every pair of currencies. Hence we would not define *the* foreign exchange market but a whole series of markets. Second, we can define a composite market that consists of a weighted average of all these individual markets. The most common way of doing this is to define a trade-weighted average exchange rate, where each exchange rate involving a country's currency is weighted by the relative importance of the trading links between the two countries. Usually export weights are used, and the resulting exchange rate is often called an *effective* exchange rate. The great advantage of this is that it summarizes what is happening overall in the foreign exchange market rather than what is happening in one particular market. Finally, the International Monetary Fund's special drawing right (SDR) approximates an international unit of account, so that we could define a currency in terms of SDRs. The SDR is another composite exchange rate, where the weights are not determined by specific trade patterns but by the general importance of some countries in international trade.[1]

In Figure 7-2 we define the foreign exchange market as the overall market and express the exchange rate so determined in European terms as foreign currency (FC) per dollar. We can now answer the basic question of what causes fluctuations in exchange rates. Since the exchange rate is a price determined by supply and demand, any change is caused by a shift in one of these curves. Moreover, since shifts in these curves are themselves derived from shifts in merchandise trade, service, transfer, and capital flows, any change in the underlying international flows will have a corresponding impact in the foreign exchange market. Hence quite literally any large international transaction can move the exchange rate.

In practice, most unusually large increases or decreases in demand or supply are random, so that most of the changes "net out" and have only a small residual impact on the foreign exchange market. At times some very large transactions will cause the exchange rate, expressed in European terms, to depreciate (decrease) or appreciate (increase). For example, in the summer of 1981, the Canadian Na-

---

[1] The SDR is discussed more fully on page 169.

tional Energy Program promoted the takeover of several large U.S. energy companies by Canadian companies. The result was an unusually large supply of Canadian dollars in the Canadian-U.S. dollar foreign exchange market. This caused a noticeable decline in the Canadian dollar relative to the U.S. dollar.

One justification for government intervention in the foreign exchange market is to avoid just these effects. Consider Figure 7-2 again. The private demand and supply curves would intersect at an exchange rate of 0.9 FC:US$1. However, if this were due to an unusual transitory decline in exports or increase in imports, the government could sell $9 million in foreign exchange and use the proceeds to buy up "excess" domestic dollars offered in the foreign exchange market. This would maintain the exchange rate at its normal equilibrium rate of 0.95 FC:US$1. If 0.95 FC:US$1 is the equilibrium exchange rate, then the country's foreign exchange reserves would be replenished at some future date when exports were unusually large or imports unusually low. In this sense the country's foreign exchange reserves are a buffer stock (or inventory) used to iron out transitory shifts in supply and demand. This ensures that individuals can trade at the equilibrium exchange rates that beome fixed as a result of government intervention.

A second justification for government intervention is more technical and is related to the fact that the supply curve for dollars is derived from the domestic demand for foreign merchandise trade, service, and capital flows. The implication is that the supply curve *may* not be the normal upward-sloping supply curve of basic economics. For example, consider the situation in Exhibit 7-2. Here, we have a hypothetical situation in which at the existing export and import volumes (no capital flows), prices, and exchange rate a country has an excess supply of $100. Normally, with excess supply as in Figure 7-2, we assume that a decline in price causes a reduction in supply and an increase in demand, so that we move smoothly to a new equilibrium. However, suppose in the short run trade patterns are fixed, so that volumes are unresponsive to the new effective prices for exports and imports that result from a depreciation. In this case, if the currency depreciated to 0.95 FC:US$1, the existing import volume would now cost $526, since it now requires more dollars to come up with the constant 500 FC cost for imports. Hence excess supply gets *larger* than it was before the depreciation, and the exchange rate keeps falling!

However, the fact that imports now cost $526 and that export costs to foreigners have declined from 400 FC to 380 FC should cause domestic consumers to cut back on imports and foreign consumers to demand more of our exports. In the long run, import volume might decline to 85.5 and export volume increase to 225. Hence, with the same exchange rate of 0.95 FC:US$1 that created excess supply, we now have long-run equilibrium.

The example in Exhibit 7-2 indicates that if export and import volumes are insensitive to changes in the exchange rate, the short-run supply curve may be downward-sloping and the foreign exchange market may be unstable. This could cause excessive volatility and overshooting of the exchange rate. Hence, if the government intervenes and buys up the excess supply of $126 that is evident in the short run, then in the long run as volumes change as a result of the depreciation the need for government intervention disappears.

EXHIBIT 7-2
SHORT- AND LONG-RUN RESPONSE TO REVALUATION

	Existing		Short-run		Long-run	
	X	M	X	M	X	M
Trade volume	200	100	200	100	225	85.5
Export value, $	400		400		450	
Import value, $	500		526		450	
Surplus/deficit, $	100		126		—	

Assume: Domestic price = US$2
            Foreign price = 5 FC
            Existing $E[FC:US\$] = 1$
            Equilibrium $E[FC:US \$] = 0.95$
X = exports
M = imports

This instability argument is frequently advanced to justify government intervention to fix exchange rates or to gradually adjust them toward some anticipated equilibrium rate. Unlike other arguments, for example, to undervalue a currency to stimulate exports, the argument has some validity, especially given the short-run insensitivity of export and import volumes to effective price changes. However, the government is not the only institution capable of making foreign exchange rate forecasts. If short-term speculators feel that 0.95 FC:US$1 is a long-run equilibrium exchange rate, they will buy dollars if the exchange rate falls below that level. Only if there is insufficient speculative capital or the government is the only body capable of determining what the equilibrium exchange rate should be does there seem to be a need for government, rather than private, short-term capital flows.

Finally, it should be self-evident from the construction of our hypothetical balance of payments statistics that the foreign exchange market is "dual" to the balance of payments. That is, the balance of payments statistics are largely a catalog of transactions that have occurred in the foreign exchange market. There are some qualifications to this. For example, in the U.S. statistics earnings retained overseas by subsidiaries of U.S. corporations amounted to about $11.5 billion in 1981. However, this service inflow had no impact in supporting the value of the U.S. dollar, since there was no foreign exchange transaction. In the balance of payments statistics there is a corresponding capital outflow of $11.5 billion for direct foreign investment by U.S. corporations. Similarly, the balance of payments statistics report only net private capital flows and not the total inflows and total outflows. Hence it is impossible to work back from the balance of payments statistics to determine the volume of transactions in the foreign exchange market.

Despite inadequate accounting information, the net official monetary movements in the balance of payments statistics still represent the net size of the government intervention in the foreign exchange market over a period of time. In this sense any activity by the government intervening to repair a balance of payments problem also shows up in the foreign exchange market. These are not two independent problems, how to repair a balance of payments deficit and how to support a currency. Instead, they are simply two different sides of the same coin. For this reason, we will look at fiscal and monetary policy measures designed to correct a balance of payments problem in Chapter 9, when we also look at exchange rate policy.

ORGANIZATION OF THE INTERNATIONAL MONETARY SYSTEM

The duality that exists between the balance of payments and the foreign exchange market means that any method of structuring the international monetary system implies a policy toward exchange rate intervention. Typically, we can conceive of a continuum that runs from a laissez-faire policy of no government intervention to one in which exchange rates are fixed by government fiat.

Fixed versus Flexible Exchange Rates

In the former case, exchange rates would be allowed to *freely fluctuate* according to market forces. Consequently, there would be no need for any special international organizations and there would be little to discuss of the structure of the international monetary system. In the latter case of *fixed* exchange rates, government intervention would be required whenever market prices temporarily or permanently implied exchange rates different from those fixed by the government. Then governments would have to hold buffer stocks or inventories of foreign exchange reserves in order to intervene. If these were found to be insufficient, there would be a need for an international monetary system to provide new reserves to help a country over a balance of payments – foreign exchange crisis.

It is this classic continuum from free market to government intervention that provides the basic framework for examining the historical developments in the international monetary system. In practice, the government's monetary authorities, the central banks, rarely believe in the superiority of the free market. Traditionally, the arguments of insufficient speculative capital have been advanced to justify government intervention to smooth out temporary disturbances. More recently, however, with the emergence of substantial amounts of short-term capital movements, we have instead heard the reverse argument that "hot money" moving from one country to another causes "overshooting" and excessive fluctuations in exchange rates; that is, that there is too much speculative capital and that private judgments are so bad that the capital movements are "destabilizing."

It is almost impossible to determine whether freely fluctuating exchange rates fluctuate too much, since it is impossible to determine the standard by which to judge their fluctuation. Obviously, with changing economic conditions we would expect some fluctuation in exchange rates. Hence the justification for exchange rate policy has more often than not come from a philosophical approach to government intervention generally. Governments elected to maintain full employment, price stability, and increasing standards of living are unwilling to admit that the balance of payments and the exchange rate cannot be manipulated to further those objectives. Hence, in examining the history of the international monetary system, we are implicitly examining the changing view as to the role of government intervention in markets generally.

The Gold Standard

The *gold* (exchange) *standard* emerged partly as a result of the use of precious metals as currencies. Historically, the names of many currencies were derived from the amount and quality of the precious metal contained in their coins. For example, the currency of England, the pound sterling, denoted a pound weight of silver of "sterling" fineness. Foreign exchange rates then fluctuated according to the amount and quality of the precious metals contained in different currencies (a scale was indispensable to any foreign exchange trader!). In the nineteenth century countries began to fix the price of their currencies in terms of gold, while maintaining full convertibility of their currencies into gold. For example, in June 1816, George III of England fixed the sterling price of gold at £4.2477 per ounce; similarly the U.S. dollar price of gold was fixed at $20.67 per ounce. The result of these fixed prices was a numeraire in the international monetary system that then fixed the exchange rate as the ratio of the two currencies' value in terms of gold.

For example, if you can receive 1 ounce of gold by paying £4.2477 in London and then sell the ounce of gold in New York for $20.67, it is obvious that the dollar-sterling exchange rate $E[\text{US\$}: \pounds]$ would be 4.87. The only qualification to this would be the costs and delays incurred in actually shipping gold from London to New York, which would create a band around the exchange rate. However, by the late nineteenth century these costs had been reduced to about $\frac{1}{2}$ percent, thus effectively fixing all exchange rates in a narrow band around these relative gold values.

An implication of the fixing of the gold price of currencies is that each country's stock of currency had to be backed by gold. If this were not so, currencies inadequately backed by gold would be considered risky, since if everyone surrendered their currency they could not all be paid back in gold. *Gresham's law* would then apply in that no one would want to hold this risky currency, when they could hold a fully backed currency. As a result, the world's money supply or stock of currency was fixed as each country fixed its individual currency to its existing stock of gold.

The only exception to this general rule was Great Britain, where the pound sterling was not backed by gold to any significant extent. This was because the Bank of England was effectively the world's central bank, owing to the domination of Britain's financial markets in the international financial system. As a result, Great Britain could always meet any outflow of gold by increasing the Bank of England's rediscount rate (bank rate) and attracting short-term capital flows from other countries, which could be converted into gold. In fact, at that time, nobody even thought of converting out of sterling, since gold earned no interest, and no other currency offered the return or security offered by deposits at the Bank of England.

The great advantage of this standard was that everything was automatic and certain. Exporters and importers did not have to worry about the exchange rate or even about the currency of denomination of their merchandise, since all countries maintained their fixed parities with gold. If a country's exports declines, foreigners built up excess holdings of its currency. These holdings would then be converted to gold and subsequently into their own currency. As a result, the deficit country lost gold and its money stock declined, causing deflation. The surplus country gained gold, causing an increase in its money stock and inflation. Over time the deflation in the deficit country and inflation in the surplus country changed the competitiveness of exports and imports. Hence the balance of payments imbalance was automatically corrected.

What stood behind the gold standard was the congruency of interests of all those concerned in maintaining the security and stability of the status quo, and the monopoly position of Great Britain in ensuring that everyone played by the rules of the game. Prior to 1914, Great Britain was consistently exporting half of its annual savings through foreign investment. Moreover, the British financial markets acted as the world's financial markets in financing short-term trade throughout the world. As Nathan Rothschild pointed out in 1832:

> This country in general is bank for the whole world . . . . all transactions in India, in China, in Germany, in Russia, in all the whole world are all guided here and settled through this country.

Even accounting for some jingoistic exaggeration, it is evident that no country was prepared to alienate the Bank of England and so cut itself off from the British financial markets.

The Collapse of the Gold Standard

This ordered state of affairs came to an end in 1914 with the outbreak of World War I. A corollary of the gold standard is that no country can pursue an independent monetary policy. However, faced with the enormous materiel demands of the First World War, country after country suspended convertibility into gold and just paid for its purchases by printing more bank notes. With the conclusion of hostilities, the international monetary system had to contend with several new developments.

First, the congruency of interests had collapsed with the emergence of communist Russia. Second, the system was strapped with an enormous wealth transfer problem, as the United States demanded repayment of war debts from France, including those undertaken for France and guaranteed by Great Britain. France in turn, with a devastated economy, demanded reparations from Germany to meet these war debts. Third, many countries cut the direct link between their currency and gold and started to back their currency with foreign currency reserves, principally pound sterling. Fourth, Great Britain attempted to reestablish the traditional value of sterling in terms of gold. Since the amount of sterling in circulation had dramatically expanded, this required enormous deflation. As a result, the British economy never witnessed the sustained growth marked by most economies in the 1920s.

Officially, return to normality occurred in 1925 when Great Britain went back onto the gold standard. However, sustained speculation against sterling, particularly by the French government, combined with the financial crisis of 1929 to 1931 and the de facto renunciation of reparations by Germany conspired to cause Great Britain to leave the gold standard again in 1931. The United States followed shortly afterward in April 1933. The effect was to cause a splintering of the world's economy into trading blocks. Great Britain promoted trade within the sterling area. The United States promoted a high tariff wall and retreated into isolation. Germany reverted to strict foreign exchange controls and a virtual barter system in international trade. Even France and the remaining gold standard countries eventually abandoned the gold standard by the end of 1936. Symptomatic of the decline in international trade and cooperation was the 50 percent decline in the number of commercial trade bills discounted in London between 1929 and 1931.

The Bretton Woods System

In 1944 at the Bretton Woods conference, a new international monetary system was installed based on the twin beliefs that the flexible exchange rate system in effect from 1936 to 1939 was inherently unstable and that international cooperation was required to enforce a fixed rate system. The novelty of the Bretton Woods system was that it was a gold exchange system, with only one principal currency, the U.S. dollar, freely convertible into gold, and that only between central banks and nonresidents. (The United States still prohibited private holdings of gold by residents.) Other currencies would be freely convertible among each other, but not into gold. Moreover, each currency was to have an announced par value that could fluctuate by only ± 1 percent. Hence countries were obligated to intervene to prevent fluctuations outside the 2 percent range.

The upshot was that gold was priced at $35 (it had increased from $20.67 an ounce in January 1934) and then all principal currencies had par values relative to the U.S. dollar, which they had to maintain. The two key questions became how to finance intervention to maintain parities and how to adjust parities should it become apparent that parities were obviously over- or undervalued. Since the U.S. dollar was "as good as gold" and the United States, through Marshall aid, was providing dollar credits to western Europe, it quickly became apparent that the most efficient way of intervening to maintain a country's par value was to hold its foreign exchange reserves in U.S. dollars. These dollars would then be used as an intervention currency. This practice became pervasive with the evident decline of London and Great Britain as the preeminent financial power and the transfer of that position to New York and the United States.

To back up the new system, the *International Monetary Fund* was established in 1944. Each member had to contribute a quota based on its importance in international trade; 25 percent of the quota was in gold or U.S. dollars and 75 percent in its own currency. If the country then had to support its currency, it could automatically borrow its gold and U.S. dollars back again (the gold tranche), or with the consent of the IMF it could borrow 125 percent of its overall quota. These funds were borrowed in a convertible currency and used to intervene in support of its own par value.

The IMF quota system is essentially a domestic currency contribution that can be borrowed back in another currency and used to support a currency's par value. The same result is achieved by privately arranged *currency swaps*, as, for example, have been negotiated among the Group of Ten. Here, there is a prearranged agreement to swap, say, pounds sterling for deutsche marks between the central banks of Great Britain and Germany. If the pound was at the bottom of its parity range, the Bank of England could draw on the currency swap and use the deutsche marks to intervene and maintain parity. *Special Drawing Rights* (SDRs) are a similar sort of swap agreement, this time awarded by the IMF without any necessity to contribute domestic currency. The SDR is a composite currency, consisting of a weighted average of U.S. dollars, deutsche marks, French francs, Japanese yen, and pounds sterling. A country can give up its allotment of SDRs and receive their value in convertible currencies that can then be used for intervention purposes.

The existence of a country's IMF quota, currency swaps, and SDRs in addition to its foreign exchange reserves was intended to provide enough of a buffer stock, or enough international liquidity, to enable a country to maintain its currency's par value. Unfortunately, despite these huge increases in international foreign exchange reserves, two events were conspiring to undermine the basis of the Bretton Woods system. First, as a gold exchange system, most countries held U.S. dollars for intervention purposes. As the amount of international trade increased, they held larger and larger stocks of U.S. dollars for this purpose. However, at some point in time, the suspicion arose that the United States could not redeem these reserve assets for gold. Partly this was because of the large increase in U.S. dollar liabilities, but it was also due to the halving of the value of U.S. gold reserves as countries converted U.S. dollars into gold. Moreover, although the increased holding of U.S. dollars as reserve assets *necessitated* a U.S. deficit on current account, more and more foreign countries began to believe that the U.S. deficit on current account was a sign of weakness. The belief became widespread that the dollar was overvalued, and it was this overvaluation that was causing the current account deficit. As a result, countries became more and more uneasy about holding new foreign exchange reserves in U.S. dollars.

Second, World War II had shown the advantages of an independent national monetary policy. This, allied to the conversion of many countries to Keynesian economics, prompted increased economic intervention and a gradual increase in inflation. The problem this presented was that some currencies, notably the pound sterling and Italian lira, were fundamentally overvalued. Moreover, because of the great increase in international liquidity, the degree of overvaluation worsened as inflation built up year by year. The IMF could allow small devaluations, even a devaluation of a currency by more than 10 percent, provided that it was to correct a "fundamental disequilibrium." However, countries became loath to devalue their currency, perceiving it to be a sign of economic weakness.

The End of Bretton Woods

The Bretton Woods fixed gold exchange system eventually collapsed during the period of intense international monetary confusion of 1967 to 1973. First, the pound sterling devalued by 14 percent in 1967. Germany had earlier revalued the deutsche mark by 5 percent in 1961; so the British devaluation was not the first major change of parity since Bretton Woods. However, even in 1967 the pound sterling was still a major reserve currency in many parts of the world. The result was to cause a loss in value for those countries that had kept their reserves in pound sterling. The implication was that if sterling could devalue, then so too could other reserve currencies, notably the U.S. dollar.

The sterling devaluation was particularly significant in that Great Britain still had foreign exchange controls. It was not "normal" capital flows due to speculation that had caused Britain to devalue. Instead, the capital flows were caused by leading and lagging by major multinational corporations. Firms simply delayed exchanging, say, dollars and deutsche marks into sterling to pay their bills (lagging), and instead speeded up the process of converting sterling accounts receivable into foreign currency (leading). The sterling devaluation indicated that efficient cash management by multinational corporations could move such enormous amounts of capital around as to negate the huge increases in international reserves carefully built up since Bretton Woods.

After the sterling devaluation, speculative pressure moved to the U.S. dollar and became so intense that the United States suspended the convertibility of dollars for gold for private transactions. This created a two-tier gold market, whereby gold was exchanged between central banks at $35 an ounce but a free market was established for private transactions. Needless to say, central banks were not allowed to make sales on the free market, where the price promptly increased to reflect the international monetary uncertainty. In 1969, France was forced to devalue the franc and Germany to revalue the mark. In June 1970, Canada allowed its dollar to float. Then in 1971, amid rumors of enormous current account deficits, the United States officially cut the link between the U.S. dollar and gold on August 15. This effectively allowed the U.S. dollar to float. Simultaneously, President Nixon introduced a package of measures, including a temporary import surcharge, to correct the U.S. current account deficit.

In December 1971, the major countries met at the Smithsonian Institution to realign their par values. The hope was that the series of devaluations and revaluations had worked out the imbalances that had built up since Bretton Woods. However, once the genie is out of the bottle, it's difficult to get it back in! Without the discipline of fixed exchange rates, inflation in Great Britain had continued, so that even the Smithsonian parity overvalued sterling. As a result, there was a wave of speculation against sterling that led to sterling being floated in June 1972. Moveover, confidence in the system was so low that gold was trading at about $70 an ounce, compared with the Smithsonian fixed price of $38 an ounce. In February 1973 speculation against the U.S. dollar caused a second devaluation and the price of gold was increased to $42.22 an ounce. Uncertainty and confusion, however, remained to such an extent that the foreign exchange markets were closed for several weeks in March 1973, and when they reopened most currencies were allowed to float freely to find their own levels.

Floating Exchange Rates: The Dirty Float

The advent of floating exchange rates was formally ratified at the Jamaica IMF meeting in January 1976. The basic agreement was to permit floating exchange rates, to demonetize gold, to increase IMF quotas to $41 billion, and to set up a special $9 billion "oil facility" fund to make loans to countries having severe balance of payments problems because of the October 1973 oil crisis. The full burden of exchange intervention continued, however, to fall on the U.S. dollar, and it was not until the 1978 dollar crisis that the deutsche mark, Swiss franc, and Japanese yen emerged as true reserve currencies. Since 1978, we have witnessed the emergence of a multicurrency reserve system, rather than a single-currency reserve system.

Since March 1973, the international monetary system can be classified correctly as a managed floating system, or, as some would have it, a dirty float. If it were a truly floating system, there would be no need for any country to maintain foreign exchange reserves. However, all central banks believe that some intervention is required to dampen some of the fluctuations that they feel would otherwise occur with free floating. Moreover, since these countries intervene primarily in the market between their currency and the U.S. dollar, the U.S. dollar exchange rate is managed, even though the Federal Reserve Bank of New York generally is less interventionist than other central banks.

Consistently we have also witnessed countries attempting to revert to fixed exchange rates. In 1973, the floating of sterling was prompted by its inclusion in the European "snake," an attempt to narrow the band of fluctuation allowed for exchange rates between members of the EEC. Recently, in March 1979, the snake has returned under the guise of the European Monetary System (EMS), only to suffer the same problems of persistent currency revaluations. By March 1983, there had been no less that seven major realignments of parities between participating countries. The French and Belgian francs and Danish krona alone had devalued against the deutsche mark by 20 percent, since the inception of the EMS.

Most countries would prefer the stability of fixed exchange rates. For example, even Lord Richardson of the Bank of England stated that he hopes "that the time will come when conditions will be appropriate for us to join the EMS fully." However, like the French and Italians, the British are unwilling to give up an independent monetary policy which is the essential ingredient of a fixed exchange rate policy. As long as countries continue independent monetary policies, inflation will cause changes in international competitiveness that will affect the foreign exchange market. This makes constant realignments of exchange rates essential. Despite the professions of purity and a longing for the stability of fixed exchange rates, it is highly unlikely that we will ever return to the pre-1914 system, where governments eschewed monetary policy as an economic tool. As a result, managed floating exchange rates are inevitable.

The main problem with this inevitability of managed floating is the volatility that has characterized the foreign exchange markets since 1973. The observed volatility is in contrast to the almost unanimous predictions of economists in 1973 that floating exchange rates would result in *less* uncertainty. These predictions were based on the assumption that speculation would no longer be against a fixed value with only one way to go; instead speculation would be in an efficient market and exchange rates would move *smoothly* to new equilibrium values. Hence the current disenchantment with managed floating results in part from the original high expectations associated with it. The problem is that no one could have anticipated the enormous shocks with which the international financial system has had to contend.

Since the oil price increases of 1973, oil prices have doubled again in 1979 to 1980, interest rates have gone into the stratosphere as a result of U.S. monetary policy changes during 1979, and the third world has almost collapsed from the strain of its debt-servicing burden. Moreover, because of the growing integration of the world's economic and financial system, these shocks have affected every single country. It is thus really not surprising that exchange rates have become so volatile, given the framework within which foreign exchange market participants have had to operate. What is more disturbing is that *real* exchange rates, i.e., exchange rates adjusted for differential inflation rates, have been just as volatile as the *nominal* exchange rates. For many, this is an indication of a severe cost that is having to be paid by every participant in international trade and finance.

The main implication of a managed floating system is a continued reliance upon international reserves and swap agreements for use as buffer stocks. In Exhibit 7-3, we present a breakdown of the major components of international reserves for 1982 for all major political-economic groupings except the centrally planned economies. What is quite striking compared with 10 years or so ago is the reappearance of gold as a major reserve asset. President Nixon's decision to cut the link between the U.S. dollar and gold has allowed the price of gold to be determined by free market forces. Its subsequent appreciation in price has led to its inclusion in global reserve estimates at current market values, rather than as previously at its pegged price. By 1982, gold represented over 53 percent of the stock of global reserves, an amazing comeback once it is considered that one of the

EXHIBIT 7-3
INTERNATIONAL RESERVES 1982
(Billions of U.S. dollars)

	Gold	Nongold reserves	Breakdown of nongold reserves			
			Foreign exchange	IMF reserve position	SDRs	ECUs*
Group of Ten (plus Switzerland)	331.1	169.6	96.6	17.7	14.3	41.0
Other developed nations	41.4	40.3	37.3	1.2	1.4	0.4
Non-OPEC developing nations	32.6	73.7	70.5	1.7	1.5	
OPEC	19.1	88.6	78.7	7.5	2.4	
Total	424.2	372.2	283.1	28.1	19.6	41.4

*European currency units, an artificial European reserve asset modeled on the SDR.
Source: Bank of International Settlements.

main aims of international monetary policy during the 1960s was the "demoneti-zation of gold!"

SUMMARY

In this chapter the balance of payments, the foreign exchange market, and the international monetary system have been examined. The balance of payments accounts, like the sources and uses of funds statement, describes the flow of funds in a country over a given period of time. The overall balance is usually broken down into a series of partial balances, which include the merchandise trade balance, balance on goods and services, balance on current account, the basic balance, and the official settlements balance. However, these partial balances must be interpreted with care; since they should reflect comparative advantage, it is to be expected that they will differ across different countries.

Foreign trade requires the exchange of currencies. The market in which these currencies are exchanged is called the foreign exchange market and the price determined for each currency is the foreign exchange rate. In the last half of the chapter, factors influencing the foreign exchange market were examined. The exchange rate of a particular currency was seen to be largely influenced by the supply of and demand for that currency. Government intervention in the foreign exchange market, in response to changes in supply and demand, was also analyzed.

Finally, the international monetary system was examined. The changes in the system from the gold standard, to the Bretton Woods agreement, to the present floating exchange rates was followed and explained. The International Monetary Fund, established in 1944, has been critical to the operation of the international monetary system. The functions of its quotas, currency swaps, SDRs, etc., were studied in light of their contribution to the stability of the system.

KEY WORDS

Balance of payments accounts   Foreign exchange market
Merchandise trade balance   Exchange market stability
Balance on goods and services   Foreign exchange rate
Balance on current account   Gold standard
Special drawing rights   International Monetary Fund
Swaps   International reserves
Official settlements balance

QUESTIONS

1 Explain a country's balance of payments accounts. What are the individual balances composed of in the overall balance of payments?

2 Explain the relationship between the foreign exchange market and the foreign exchange rate. How can a change in market conditions affect the exchange rate?

3 What arguments might governments use for their intervention in the foreign exchange market? Are any of these arguments justifiable on efficiency grounds?

4 Under what circumstances does "hot money" leave a country? Are there any problems associated with this occurrence?

5 Describe the monetary system that emerged from the Bretton Woods conference. What led to the breakdown of this system?

6 How does the International Monetary Fund function? In 1982, the IMF was faced with the possibility that Mexico might default on its loans. How did it respond to this crisis? Is such a situation likely to recur?

7 What factors would you have to consider before making a decision on whether or not floating exchange rate movements were too volatile?

8 As a corporate executive, what use could you make of the balance of payments statistics?

9 Commentators often refer generally to "the foreign exchange rate." Is there only one? If not, how could you operationalize the idea?

10 In the light of current rescheduling problems associated with the debt of many countries, the opinion has often been expressed that the loans should never have been made in the first place. Many of these countries were in fact running continuous current account deficits. How would you evaluate this sort of remark if you were concerned with the *efficient* functioning of the world economy?

11 Many developing countries believe that the current international monetary system is biased against them. What measures could be taken to improve the lot of the developing countries? Would these measures be economically efficient, or can they be justified on other criteria?

12 Some commentators have argued that the dollar cannot be devalued, since other countries determine their currency's value by pegging it to the dollar. Is this true, and does it have any implications for U.S. international economic policy?

CHAPTER 8

INTERNATIONAL FINANCIAL MARKETS

INTRODUCTION

In Chapter 7 we introduced the balance of payments and the foreign exchange market to discuss the international monetary system. The purpose of this was to discuss the macroeconomic international environment. In this chapter we flesh out our discussion to include the main features of the *international financial system*. Policy makers will mainly be concerned with the international monetary system, but all participants in international business will be concerned with the workings of the international financial markets.

We begin our discussion by examining the international payments system, the foreign exchange market, and the role of the international banks. Then after discussing the nature of financial markets and financial centers generally, we discuss the international money and capital markets. With this as a background, we can discuss two topical events: the oil crisis and recycling phenomena of the 1970s and the debt burden and rescheduling phenomena of the 1980s.

THE INTERNATIONAL PAYMENTS SYSTEM AND THE FOREIGN EXCHANGE MARKET

Traditional Payments System

Every international transaction ultimately involves a settlement or payment. In this section, we will discuss ways of organizing the international payments system and the implications for the foreign exchange market. In a later section we will discuss the trade financing that arises should payment be deferred for future settlement. Suppose a British company exports machinery worth £1 million to a

German company: how could we organize the settlement? One way would be for the German company to simply maintain a sterling checking account with a bank in Great Britain. In this case, payment would be made by writing a check on this account, in the same way that payment would be made by any British purchaser. The check would be given to the British company, which would then deposit it in its checking account. The British company's bank would then present it to the German company's bank for payment through the British bank clearing system, with settlements made through the accounts that clearing banks maintain at the Bank of England. However, only MNEs and international companies with frequent foreign exchange transactions usually maintain foreign checking accounts. Moreover, these transactions would obviously have to include sterling deposits to replenish the sterling checking account balance. Hence there is a need to organize a system for international payments.

Normally, the German importer would go to its domestic bank to direct that payment be made to the British exporter. At an exchange rate of 4 deutsche marks to the pound, the German bank would debit 4 million deutsche marks from the German company's account, and then itself pay £1 million sterling to the British company out of a sterling checking account that *it* maintains in Great Britain. This sterling checking account can be either in a subsidiary or branch of the bank that conducts normal banking business in Great Britain or with a *correspondent bank*. A correspondent bank is just a bank with which another bank maintains banking relationships. In this case, having a sterling checking account in a British correspondent bank enables the German bank to make sterling payments on behalf of its domestic clients. Note that essentially, in the latter case, the German bank is just allowing its domestic clients to use its sterling checking account for their own transactions. With frequent transactions, its client would most probably go back to the first case and open a sterling account directly.

Traditionally, the correspondent banking system has been at the heart of the international payments system, with the major clearing banks in each country acting as correspondent banks with large working balances deposited in their checking accounts from foreign banks. However, with the increasingly multinational nature of banking, the functions of the correspondent bank are now more frequently being undertaken by a foreign branch of the domestic bank.

Regardless of the organization of the banking network, the international payment in fact involves two transactions. The first is the payment of 4 million deutsche marks by the German importer to its domestic bank. The second is the payment of £1 million sterling by this bank to the British exporter. Hence the German bank sees an increase in its deutsche mark deposits and a reduction in its holdings of sterling, so that its working balances of deutsche marks and pounds sterling will change. Each bank will internally set minimum cash balances or deposits to be held in its correspondent bank or branch. Hence the German bank will not necessarily immediately engage in a foreign exchange transaction to replenish its sterling holdings by selling its new deutsche mark deposits. Only if the bank's sterling deposits drop below some specified minimum balance will a foreign exchange transaction take place.

Vehicle Currency and Multilateral Payments System

Just as the German bank maintained sterling deposits with a correspondent bank in Britain to be able to make sterling payments for its German customers, so too it will hold dollar deposits at U.S. correspondent banks to be able to make U.S. dollar payments. Similarly, British and American banks will hold correspondent banking accounts in the United States and Germany, and Britain and Germany, respectively. In Figure 8-1a we illustrate this *multilateral payments system*, whereby each domestic banking system will maintain correspondent banking accounts in the other two banking systems. The number of actual correspondent banking accounts will, of course, depend on the number of banks within each banking system. Foreign exchange transactions will then occur when any particular bank's working balance in its correspondent banking accounts deviates significantly from some desired level.

The size of the working balance held in a correspondent banking account is determined in accordance with normal inventory theory by the opportunity cost of maintaining the balance and the expected size and variability of the payments to be made from it. The deficiency of the multilateral payments system is that the number of working balances equals $n(n-1)$, where n is the number of countries (assuming the simplest case of one bank per country with a correspondent banking account in each other country). Hence the number of working balances increases dramatically with the number of countries. Moreover, working balances have to be maintained between each pair of currencies, even if the volume of transactions is relatively low. The precautionary balances maintained to meet infrequent transactions tend to be relatively large.

It is to overcome these deficiencies that the *vehicle currency* payments system has evolved. Referring to Figure 8-1b, we see that to pay for this British export to Germany, what could happen is that, after the deutsche marks are deposited in the German bank, the German bank could then go through the U.S. dollar as a vehicle currency to achieve the payment in pounds sterling. If the exchange rate were two deutsche marks to the dollar, it could transfer $2 million to its correspondent bank in the United States. This U.S. bank could then in turn instruct its correspondent bank in Great Britain to make the £1 million sterling payment to the British exporter. The result is not two transactions as before but four. Hence actual transactions costs increase. However, in this system, there would be only four working balances, the British and German U.S. dollar working balances and

FIGURE 8-1
International payments system. (*a*) Multilateral payments; (*b*) vehicle currency.

the American working balances in deutsche marks and pounds sterling. Moreover, since transactions are channeled through the vehicle currency, there are no idle working balances maintained to meet infrequent transactions. Hence the total value of working balances tied up in the vehicle currency system is less than that in the multilateral payments system.

Payments Organizations

The actual mechanics of international transactions has been modernized by the development of computer networks. Between countries, the Society for World Wide Interbank Financial Telecommunications (SWIFT) has created an international telecommunications network that allows banks to electronically direct payment, rather than relying on such traditional means such as checks, mail orders, telegrams, or telexes. Within the United States in 1970, the New York Clearing House Association set up CHIPS, the Clearing House Interbank Payments System. This system ensures that any imbalances that result among banks can be cleared by electronic funds transfer on the same day that the actual transfer of funds occurs. Approximately 90 percent of all international interbank dollar transfers are cleared through CHIPS, with a 1982 average daily value of $190 billion. In 1983, the London interbank system, CHAPS, the Clearing House Automated Payments System, initiated an on-line network to provide the same clearing facilities in Great Britain.

At the present time SWIFT merely replaces checks and other means for directing payment. Hence, there is still a requirement to clear funds through CHIPS, CHAPS, or some other clearing system. However, it offers the opportunity of increasing the efficiency of the traditional correspondent banking networks and making international transactions more accessible to the smaller regional U.S. and European banks. Already a link-up has been formed with Cedel, the international securities clearing system, to allow Cedel members to use SWIFT for messages to and from Cedel. Similarly, some of the smaller banks intend to use SWIFT to market international cash management services that hitherto they were not in a position to offer internationally. Hence SWIFT could have a significant impact on international bank competition, as well as the international payments system.

The effect of the computerization of the means of payment has been to reduce the actual transactions costs of going through a vehicle currency. As a result, the savings from the concentration of working balances has tended to cause a gradual shift in favor of the vehicle currency system for international payments. In many countries the way to sell deutsche marks for French francs is now to sell deutsche marks for U.S. dollars and then sell U.S. dollars for French francs. The result is a weakening of the bilateral exchange markets not involving the U.S. dollar and a strengthening of the bilateral exchange markets involving the U.S. dollar. Moreover, this phenomenon has tended to be reinforcing. As more trades are moved through the vehicle currency, *direct* quotes become less accurate as the market has less depth, and indirect quotes become more accurate since the U.S. dollar bilateral markets increase in depth and liquidity.

Arbitrage

The use of the vehicle currency system raises an interesting question: since we are now making two trades through the vehicle currency rather than the one direct, how can we be sure that this indirect quote is accurate? Suppose, for example, we have the following exchange rates: $E[US\$:£] = 2.025$; $E[DM:£] = 4.05$; $E[US\$:DM] = 0.51$. First, we should note that to a very close approximation, we can always express the exchange rates as their reciprocals, that is, $E[£: US\$] = 0.494$; $E[£:DM] = 0.247$; $E[DM:US\$] = 1.96$, since it is a matter of convenience only that we express exchange rates in European terms or as U.S. dollar equivalents. Second, we note that using the U.S. dollar as a vehicle currency we obtain an indirect quote for pounds sterling for deutsche marks, $E[£:US\$]*\ E[US\$:DM]$, of 0.252. We call the exchange rates involved in the indirect quote the *cross rates*. In this case, the indirect quote is better and you would execute the trade using the vehicle currency. However, foreign currency arbitrageurs would *sell* deutsche marks for pounds sterling through the U.S. dollar at 0.252 and then *buy* them using the direct quote at 0.247. The arbitrageurs would make a profit of £0.005 for each deutsche mark traded. This operation of selling through the vehicle currency and buying direct, or vice versa, to make an arbitrage profit is called *triangular arbitrage*.

In practice, the foreign exchange markets are just about the most efficient markets in the world and come closest to the economist's definition of a perfect market. There are no entry or exit barriers to allow inefficient firms to remain in existence, and no firm has the ability to manipulate the prices, or exchange rates. The upshot is that triangular arbitrage ensures that the indirect quotes are always exactly in line with the direct quotes. Any profit opportunities that exist are arbitraged away before the MNE or individual investor becomes aware of them. *Geographical arbitrage*, the buying and selling of currencies in different trading centers, e.g., London and New York, ensures that quotations throughout the world are almost identical as well.

Size of the Foreign Exchange Market

The worldwide size of the foreign currency markets is notoriously difficult to tie down. However, Giddy (1979) compiled estimates from interviews to arrive at a daily value of $103 billion in 1977. This was broken down as follows: London $29 billion, Frankfurt $24 billion, Switzerland $18 billion, Amsterdam $9 billion, New York $8 billion, Paris $5 billion, Brussels $2 billion, the Far East $3 billion, and the rest of the world $5 billion. From indirect estimates based on CHIPS volume, Giddy alternatively estimated 1977 daily value at $81.7 billion rising to $133 billion in 1979. An estimate for 1982, based on CHIPS volume, would be about

EXHIBIT 8-1
FOREIGN EXCHANGE MARKET SHARES

	1969	1977	1980
Pound sterling	45.0%	17.0%	22.8%
Deutsche mark	17.0	27.3	31.8
Canadian dollar	21.0	19.2	12.2
Swiss franc	7.0	13.8	10.1
Japanese yen	2.0	5.3	10.2
Other	8.0	17.4	12.9
Total	100.0	100.0	100.0

Source: Federal Reserve Bank of New York.

$200 billion. Although New York is not very important in the worldwide foreign exchange market, the use of the U.S. dollar as the vehicle currency means that most of the settlements are made through CHIPS.

The Federal Reserve Board of New York periodically estimates the size of the foreign exchange market in New York. Exhibit 8-1 is a simplified table of the breakdown of currency trading for 1969, 1977, and 1980. Note that in 1969 the pound sterling was still a major vehicle currency in its own right. However, by 1977 the pound sterling had lost this role, and as a result the currency trading volume reflects more closely the importance of the countries for U.S. and international trade. The Federal Reserve Board also found that 99 percent of all trading was against the U.S. dollar and that 90 percent of the trading was interbank. Most of this trading is motivated by speculation on short-run interest rates and exchange rates, and the requirement of the banks to maintain minimum foreign currency working balances.

THE DEVELOPMENT OF DOMESTIC AND INTERNATIONAL FINANCIAL MARKETS

The Nature of Financial Markets

All markets and business activities are concerned with the exchange of goods and services. Financial markets are concerned with the exchange of money, which, as we discussed in Chapter 7, represents purchasing power, a claim on real goods and services. In return for lending their money, the creditor receives from the debtor a financial *security* which dictates the terms under which the money is to be repaid. These transactions between debtors and creditors are facilitated by intermediaries.

Market intermediaries are defined to be stockbrokers, investment dealers, merchant banks, etc., who act as agents in bringing together debtors and creditors. For their services they receive a fee or commission. *Financial intermediaries* are

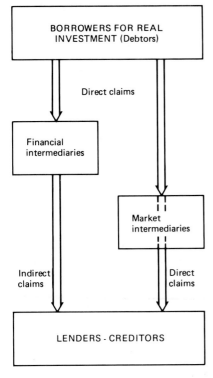

FIGURE 8-2
The organization of financial markets.

defined to be institutions like banks, insurance companies, pension funds, etc., which facilitate the exchange by placing themselves between the debtor and creditor. *They* borrow the money from the lender and in turn *they* lend the money to the ultimate borrower to create two distinct transactions. Financial intermediaries earn a profit on the *spread* between the rates at which they effectively borrow and lend money. In Figure 8-2 we schematically represent these two alternative structures for facilitating financial transactions.

We call the securities issued by the ultimate borrowers *direct securities*; typical examples are common stock, preferred stock, long-term bonds, and commercial paper. These securities can then be traded, after their initial sale, on a secondary market facilitated by the market intermediaries. Hence we see common and preferred stock traded on the stock exchange, bonds traded in the bond market, and commercial paper traded in the "paper" or money market. The market intermediaries facilitate the exchange of these securities; they in no way change the nature of the securities. Financial intermediaries, on the other hand, issue *indirect* securities, such as bank deposits, contractual savings plans by life insurance and pension funds, etc., and then invest the proceeds. In doing so they create new securities.

EXHIBIT 8-2
NATIONAL FINANCIAL MARKETS 1981

Country	GNP per capita	Total securities to* GNP	Total financial† assets to GNP
Argentina	$ 2,390	6	58
Brazil	2,050	12	51
Canada	10,300	125	353
France	11,700	30	142
West Germany	13,590	46	161
Indonesia	430	1	24
Japan	9,890	95	251
Korea	1,510	14	106
Mexico	2,130	12	40
Portugal	2,350	6	126
Sweden	13,520	78	167
United Kingdom	8,100	85	241
United States	11,530	118	209

*Securities defined as preferred and common equities plus bonds.
†Financial assets defined as broadly defined bank assets plus securities.
Source: "Selected Indicators of Financial System Depth," *International Finance Corporation.* (March 1982).

Comparative Financial Markets

Any financial market can be organized emphasizing market or financial intermediaries. In Exhibit 8-2 we provide some data on the depth or development of different financial markets around the world. Quite generally, the more developed the country's economy is the greater the sophistication of the country's financial markets.

There are two reasons for this. First, we find that as wealth increases individuals have a greater demand for financial securities. This demand is for the indirect securities of the financial intermediaries such as life insurance, pensions, and savings accounts as well as for the direct securities themselves as a tool in personal financial management for retirement and security. Second, borrowers require more sophisticated securities to tailor the financing of their real investment decisions to their unique circumstances. Hence the efficiency of the economy in allocating resources requires a more sophisticated financial system to accommodate economic growth and development.

The general relationship between per capita gross national product and the sophistication of the financial system does not, however, dictate *how* the financial system is organized. For example, Canada, the United Kingdom, the United States, and Japan all have highly developed *securities* markets, defined as the markets for common and preferred stocks and bonds. However, France and West Germany are just as wealthy with much smaller securities markets, the reason being that these countries emphasize financial intermediation. When all financial assets are included, the discrepancies are narrowed.

Development of Financial Markets

The organization of a financial system is partly motivated by ideology and partly by the accidents of history. In eighteenth century England the political philosophy of writers like John Locke and Adam Smith emphasized the rights of the individual to own property, whereas in France the Encyclopedists and Jean Jacques Rousseau emphasized statism; the subordination of the individual to the common will. As a result, with the industrial revolution England allowed the private development of capital that spawned deep and efficient financial markets. This model was subsequently exported to countries like Canada, the United States, and Australia who owed their intellectual debts to England.

As England led the world into the industrial age, the importance of London as an international financial center increased. First, because of the preeminent position of England in international trade, most short-term trade financing gravitated to London. Second, since England was the wealthiest country in the world, most countries (and American states) went to London to raise long-term capital for investment purposes. These trends tended to be reinforcing; as London developed a comparative advantage in the financial industry, foreign transactions would take place in London because of the more efficient intermediation.

On the other hand, securities markets in many countries have been retarded for two reasons. First, on grounds of ideology productive activity has been taken over by the state. In this case, there is an inevitable reduction in the number of securities, since once they become state-owned they are not traded. Second, after the First and Second World Wars, the upper and middle classes in many countries found their private wealth totally destroyed. As a result, industry was forced to raise funds from financial intermediaries who in turn raised lots of small amounts from small investors. Quite simply, the large pools of capital established through generations of inherited wealth were not available.

In the last 30 years or so we have witnessed two major developments. First, the United States, as in aggregate the wealthiest country in the world, has replaced the United Kingdom as the major capital exporter. Second, private capital in countries that do not have a sophisticated market intermediation system has gravitated to the international financial centers. This last development has been spurred by shortsighted regulations in many countries. For example, Japanese interest rate control has led to a flood of capital to the United States to obtain a fair market return. Similar attitudes in third world countries have led many wealthy local investors to invest their capital in the secure anonymity of the international financial center.

To be an international financial center requires a stable political and economic environment, a benign regulatory policy to encourage foreign transactions, an efficient and experienced financial community, and a good telecommunications industry. London has all four attributes and thus has developed into a true international financial center. New York has all the attributes, except that the regulatory environment has been far from benign. In fact, the Federal Reserve

Board has actively discouraged foreign banking in the United States. Hence domestic regulations have prevented New York from becoming the world's premier international financial market. Similar regulation in Japan has retarded the development of Tokyo. As a result, international transactions in the Pacific rim are concentrated in Hong Kong and Singapore.

The Participants in International Financial Markets

Unlike domestic market activity, the international financial markets are characterized by the size of the deals consummated. That is, there are very few small transactions; instead the markets feature the major countries, banks, and corporations of the world coming together to make significant transactions. In Exhibit 8-3, we list the major actors in the international financial markets centered in London.

In the securities market, the leading market intermediary was Credit Suisse First Boston (CSFB) which put together 92 new securities offerings to raise a total of $7246 million. Note that unlike domestic U.S. market intermediation there are no restrictions preventing banks from providing underwriting and market making functions. Hence, outside the leading U.S. investment banks and S.G. Warburg of the United Kingdom, most of the other market intermediaries are banks.

For financial intermediaries Exhibit 8-3b gives the major actors in the syndicated loan market. Many of the international loans are too large for one bank to handle, since it would unbalance the bank's loan portfolio. Hence the banks syndicate the loan by dividing it up into smaller pieces for other participating banks to take. Exhibit 8-3b gives the number of loans and their value syndicated by the major financial intermediaries. The leading bank in 1982 was Citicorp with 151 syndications, an average loan share of $56.5 million. Note that the banks are no longer so proud of their standings in the table, since many of these loans turned sour in the great rescheduling crisis of 1982 to 1983.

THE INTERNATIONAL MONEY MARKET

Definitions of International Banking

Domestic money markets are financial markets in which securities with a maturity of less than 3 years are exchanged. Conventionally, we also include nonmarketable bank deposits, since although not technically securities they are close substitutes. The international money market similarly consists of short-term securities and bank deposits. Unlike domestic money markets it is almost entirely a bank market for reasons we will discuss shortly. In determining the size of the international money market, we thus have to separate the domestic from the international parts of a bank's money market operations.

All banks act as financial intermediaries; that is, they act as agents in collecting funds from depositors or investors and lending funds to borrowers. Normally, we think of domestic banking operations as taking in dollar deposits and lending out funds as dollar loans, after keeping a dollar reserve to meet unforeseen commit-

EXHIBIT 8-3
PARTICIPANTS IN THE INTERNATIONAL FINANCIAL MARKETS

		No.	$ million			No.	$ million
	a	Top twenty market intermediaries in 1982					
1	CSFB	92	7246	11	Union Bank	16	849
2	Deutsche Bank	67	5042	12	Dresdner Bank	20	769
3	Morgan Stanley	63	3775	13	Commerz Bank	21	733
4	Morgan Guaranty	42	2011	14	Nomura	21	732
5	Salomon Bros.	40	1772	15	Amro	21	707
6	Swiss Bank Corp.	22	1741	16	Orion Royal	16	682
7	Merrill Lynch	36	1714	17	Credit Lyonaise	13	678
8	S.G. Warburg	36	1566	18	Citicorp	14	644
9	Goldman Sachs	28	1198	19	Manufacturer's Hanover	8	625
10	Societé General	25	1016	20	West LB	17	599
	b	Top twenty financial intermediaries in 1982					
1	Citicorp	151	8534	11	Barclays	70	2537
2	Bank of America	132	6245	12	RBC/Orion Royal	90	2396
3	Chase Manhattan	125	4078	13	Industrial Bank of Japan	94	2389
4	Bank of Toyko	187	3452	14	Continental Illinois	58	2349
5	National Westminster	129	3354	15	Bank of Montreal	55	2019
6	Morgan Guaranty	84	3136	16	Fuji Bank	120	1990
7	Manufacturer's Hanover	93	3065	17	Banker's Trust	62	1989
8	CIBC	49	2682	18	Midland Bank	95	1946
9	Lloyd's Bank	113	2666	19	Standard and Chartered	71	1858
10	Chemical Bank	67	2575	20	Sumitomo	111	1845

Source: Annual Financing Report 1983, *Euromoney*.

ments. However, conceptually there is nothing wrong with a bank taking in nondollar deposits and making dollar loans, or the opposite of taking in dollar deposits and making nondollar loans. In either case, the bank would just enter the foreign exchange market and exchange dollars for the appropriate currency or vice versa. Moreover, if the bank was not prepared to bear the foreign exchange risk of mismatching the currency of the deposit or loan, it could always enter into a forward contract to remove most of the foreign exchange risk.

The latter two operations are defined to be foreign banking business. There is nothing new about these operations. Banks, starting from the Renaissance in Italy, have been allowing customers foreign deposit accounts, and it was then, as now, second nature for many banks to conduct banking business from one location in multiple currencies. What is new is the final combination of business, that is, directly funding foreign currency denominated loans from foreign currency deposits. We call this *offshore*, or external, banking. We distinguish foreign from offshore banking business, mainly by the degree of government intervention. A foreign currency loan funded from domestic deposits will be subject to government intervention via interest rate controls or deposits and any mandatory reserve requirements. Similarly, a domestic loan funded from foreign currency deposits is subject to domestic credit expansion limits and all the legal requirements for domestic loans. In contrast, offshore banking, where allowed (U.S. regulations severely restrict offshore and foreign banking business in the United States), is usually subject to very few restrictions, since it is not of immediate importance to domestic credit markets or residents. The aggregation of foreign and offshore banking is commonly termed *international banking*.

The Eurocurrency Markets

Offshore banking has grown enormously since its beginnings in the 1950s. Readers may be more familiar with other names for it, such as the eurocurrency or eurodollar market. However, although the market is still centered in London, the prefix "euro-" is no longer appropriate, since there are active offshore banking centers in Hong Kong, Singapore, and a variety of Caribbean countries. Similarly, the suffix dollar is not appropriate, since although the dollar is still the principal currency intermediated offshore, there is now a significant component of the overall offshore market made up of deutsche marks, Swiss francs, and Dutch guilders.

We see that the essence of offshore banking is that a bank accepts deposits and makes loans in a foreign currency, free from the restrictions that would apply to deposit-taking and lending of that currency in the domestic banking environment. To determine the size of this market, we thus use as a working definition that a Eurodollar (Asian dollar, euromark, etc.) is a U.S. dollar deposit in a bank located outside of the United States. There are obvious difficulties in calculating the total size of the external banking market, since there are no comprehensive international reporting requirements. However, Morgan Guaranty has estimated that the gross size of the market grew from $24 billion in 1965 to $1540 billion by 1981. However, this banking market is a wholesale market involving very large individual deposits. Hence, if a bank does not immediately have a customer for a loan, it will often redeposit funds with another bank. The result is that the size of the market net of this interbank business is smaller. However, Morgan Guaranty has estimated that it has still grown from $17 billion in 1965 to $770 billion by 1981. It is the net size of the market which is of most importance, and this has still shown a remarkable growth rate of about 27 percent per year.

In Exhibit 8-4 we have some alternative estimates provided by the Bank for International Settlements, which provides a breakdown of the market by currency of denomination. The main currencies of the offshore banking market are provided. What is of particular importance to note is that when a deposit is made offshore and subsequently lent out, this represents an *alternative* to depositing it domestically and then lending it out in the domestic credit market. In this sense, the offshore banking markets are just a part of the total credit market of each

EXHIBIT 8-4
RELATIVE CURRENCY BREAKDOWN OF THE EURCURRENCY MARKET

	US$ billion			% offshore		
	1965	1970	1977	1965	1970	1977
U.S. dollar:						
External*	11.4	58.7	272.9	3.91	12.69	25.78
Domestic†	280.3	403.8	785.4			
Deutsche marks:						
External	0.9	8.1	65.0	2.16	8.56	16.15
Domestic	40.8	86.5	337.6			
Swiss francs:						
External	0.9	5.7	20.9	7.50	21.19	17.08
Domestic	11.1	21.2	74.6			
Pounds sterling:						
External	0.7	0.9	5.9	2.81	3.63	6.96
Domestic	24.2	23.9	78.9			
Dutch guilder:						
External	0.2	0.6	4.9	6.06	9.52	7.89
Domestic	3.1	5.7	57.2			
French francs:						
External	0.1	0.4	4.4	0.42	0.90	2.51
Domestic	23.6	43.8	171.1			

*External represents intermediation of the currency offshore or externally.
†Domestic is the total domestic credit market.
Source: Adapted from R. Aliber. "The Integration of the Offshore and Domestic Banking Systems," *Journal of Monetary Economics*. (1980): 509–526.

country that is intermediated (i.e., deposited and then lent out) offshore or externally. There are no offshore currencies, just currencies that are intermediated offshore. In Exhibit 8-4 it is evident that the U.S. dollar is by far the most important currency intermediated offshore, followed by the deutsche mark and Swiss franc. However, this is mainly due to the enormous size of the U.S. credit market. Both the deutsche mark and the Swiss franc have a significant proportion of their total credit markets intermediated offshore or externally.

Why Offshore Intermediation?

The main question to answer after looking at the data in Exhibit 8-4 is why has this occurred? To answer this, we have to look first at history and then at the structure of intermediation. First, bank intermediation is essentially used for short-term loans. It is only a relatively recent phenomenon that banks have started to make longer-term loans. Second, prior to the Second World War the pound sterling was the major vehicle currency and London the center for short-term international trade financing. Third, in 1957 during one of a series of balance of payments crises in Britain, the Bank of England prohibited British banks from financing international trade with short-term pound sterling loans. Fourth, to reduce the political risk of expropriation during the cold war, eastern block countries kept their U.S. dollar reserves on deposit with the Banque Commerciale pour l'Europe du Nord (telex address: EUROBANK). Fifth, most of the major currencies were still inconvertible, which meant that deutsche marks and other currencies could not be freely borrowed for purposes of trade financing.

The result of this combination of circumstances was obvious, as Bell (1973) has commented: "U.K. banks switched over smoothly and easily from financing international financial transactions in sterling to doing the same in dollars." These dollars were of course borrowed from depositors, like the eastern block countries, who for political reasons did not want to hold their deposits directly in U.S. banks in the United States. As a result, small active markets soon developed intermediating U.S. dollars outside the United States. However, it would have remained a small market had not these "Eurobanks" been able to offer higher interest rates to attract depositors, while simultaneously offering lower interest rates to borrowers.

Banks earn their profits on the *spread* between the interest rates charged borrowers and paid to depositors. In a perfect market, free from arbitrary constraints and restrictions, the offshore markets would only exist to serve the small number of depositors who wish to reduce the political risk attached to holding U.S. dollars. The enormous expansion of the offshore markets results from government intervention, which has conferred a competitive advantage to offshore intermediation. This competitive advantage stems from the fact that Eurobanks intermediating U.S. dollars do not comply with U.S. government banking regulations, since they are neither U.S. banks nor banks doing business in the United States. As a result, the offshore banking markets expand in direct proportion to the severity of domestic banking regulation.

The most onerous requirements of U.S. domestic banking regulation have been the Federal Reserve system's regulation D, establishing reserve requirements on domestic U.S. dollar demand and notice deposits, and regulation Q, controlling the interest rates set on those deposits. The effect of reserve requirements is to force a portion of the deposits to be held in non-interest-bearing reserves in the Federal Reserve system. The result is to increase interest rates on loans, since the rates have to cover the non-interest-bearing reserve, and/or lower the interest rates paid to depositors. Similarly, regulation Q has invariably kept interest rates on deposits below market rates, providing a strong incentive for depositors to shift their deposits into securities that bear market rates of interest, such as Eurocurrency deposits (or money market funds). Other restrictions such as federal deposit insurance, federal rules on loan collateral and pledging, and federal jawboning to achieve the objectives of monetary policy, have all provided an incentive to escape the regulatory burden.

The basic principle of the cost of intermediation as the spread between loan and deposit rates is illustrated in Figure 8-3, showing the supply and demand curves for external intermediation. The spread in the United States is the difference between prime and the deposit rate, which should be that for similar-size notice deposits.

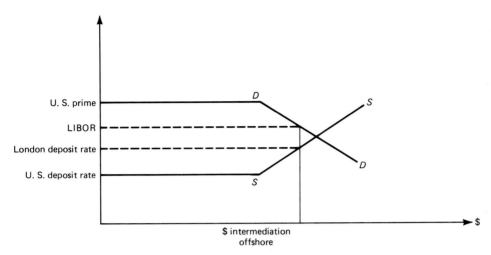

FIGURE 8-3
Offshore intermediation and the spread.

In the Eurodollar market the spread is between LIBOR, the London Inter-Bank Offer Rate, and the Eurodollar deposit rate. LIBOR is the benchmark in the offshore markets and represents the rate for wholesale transactions between the "name" banks. It is evident from Figure 8-3 that the external markets can share the gains from avoiding regulations by simultaneously offering lower loan rates and higher deposit rates. This creates the incentive to go offshore. What is indeterminate, however, is the amount of offshore intermediation. Since the spread is narrower, why doesn't all the business go offshore?

The answer, of course, is that only the most interest-sensitive transactions will shift offshore, and that which is interest-sensitive partly depends upon familiarity with the offshore markets. As the markets have become less esoteric, more and more business *has* gone offshore. However, there are extra risks attached to offshore intermediation. These are of two kinds: *sovereign* risk that arises because of the extra layer of government (deposits in London may be regulated by the British government as well as the American!) and liquidity or default risk that attaches to the regulation of the Eurobank. Sovereign risk is reduced by locating the markets in stable countries, where the government is not likely to intervene for fear of driving the market away and losing the revenues that it generates. Liquidity or default risk has partly been alleviated by a report of the Basle committee announced in 1981 by the Bank of England. This committee allocated supervisory responsibility of Eurobanks to respective national central banks, depending on whether the Eurobanks were branches or fully incorporated subsidiaries. This clarification of whether or not a lender of last resort exists for Eurobanks has either increased or decreased the risk of default depending on the credibility of the individual central banks.

The Future of the Eurocurrency Market

Our discussion of the offshore banking market has emphasized that it is one part of the total credit market for each individual currency. Hence, if a company wants to borrow U.S. dollars from a bank, it has a choice: either go offshore and get a loan in an unregulated environment or go domestic and pay a higher price but have the benefit of domestic banking regulations. This choice is advantageous for both the borrower and depositor, but for the banking industry it means that part of its business (and profits) is lost to foreign competitors operating offshore. As a result, pressure has gradually built to remove some of the competitive advantages enjoyed by Eurobanks. The U.S. Depository Institutions Deregulation and Monetary Control Act of 1980 has reduced some of the advantages by removing interest rate controls on certain bank deposits and placing most U.S. domestic financial institutions on an equal footing. Similarly, for December 1981, the Federal Reserve Board allowed U.S. banks to set up International Banking Facilities (IBFs) within the United States in the form of a "free banking zone." Although still subject to some restrictions on asset pledging and deposit insurance, the intention was to remove many of the regulations that had pushed banking business offshore.

The effect of these changes is evident in the international banking data in Exhibit 8-5, which shows external banking liabilities for the major world banking communities. The table shows external liabilities in both domestic and foreign currencies. By the end of 1982, of the $1,620.5 billion in external liabilities, $1,248.6 billion was in foreign currency and $371.8 billion in domestic currency. However, during the 3-year period 1980 to 1982, the composition changed. In 1980, the flow was $203 billion in foreign currency and $39.3 billion in domestic currency, whereas in 1982 this was reversed to become $48.8 billion in foreign currency and $76.2 billion in domestic currency. During 1981 and 1982, the new IBFs took in $47.9 billion and $123.9 billion in external U.S. dollar liabilities, respectively. In Exhibit 8-5, this is evident in the collapse of the U.S. dollar portion of external foreign currency liabilities from an annual flow of $152.9 billion to $35.6 billion, and a resurgence of external holdings of U.S. dollars in the United States from $7.4 billion to $66.0 billion. Moreover, this has occurred in an overall down market for international banking, since assets and liabilities have been growing at only half the pace of normal.

The development of IBFs in 1981 to 1982 has certainly caused a readjustment in the eurocurrency markets. Moreover, increased slippage of U.S. dollar business back to the United States by way of the IBFs is to be expected. However, the inherent advantages of the eurocurrency market in minimizing political risk and maximizing operating efficiency will ensure that a sizable portion of the $1,248.6 billion offshore in 1982 will remain offshore. Exhibit 8-5 also gives a breakdown by currency of the eurocurrency market. The U.S. dollar with $970.6 billion offshore represents 77.7 percent of the eurocurrency market. The deutsche mark and Swiss franc are the other significant currencies.

The financial instruments in the external banking markets are largely the same as in domestic U.S. banking markets. Deposits are attracted through normal fixed interest nonmarketable time deposits, and marketable time deposits called certifi-

EXHIBIT 8-5
CURRENCY BREAKDOWN OF INTERNATIONAL
BANKING ACTIVITY

	Flows*			Stocks outstanding
	1980	1981	1982	1982
Total financing	242.3	237.1	125.0	1620.4
Domestic currency financing†	39.3	47.8	76.2	371.8
Banks in:				
United States	7.4	37.5	66.0	239.7
Germany	2.9	0.1	0.3	42.1
Switzerland	5.5	2.4	-1.6	11.2
United Kingdom	6.9	4.8	7.8	30.9
Japan	7.2	1.7	1.6	14.1
Other reporting	9.4	1.3	2.1	33.8
	203.0	189.3	48.8	1248.6
Foreign currency financing‡				
U.S. dollars	152.9	148.4	35.6	970.6
Deutsche marks	14.0	10.2	1.0	116.3
Swiss francs	19.0	15.8	-3.0	62.2
Pounds sterling	7.4	0.4	-0.8	16.2
Japanese yen	-1.0	5.8	2.0	17.1
Dutch guilders	0.5	2.0	2.0	10.8
French francs	4.6	-0.2	1.6	11.3
Others	5.6	6.9	10.4	44.1

*Total net new financing per year in US$ billions.
†Nonresident loans in the domestic currency.
‡Nonresident loans in foreign currency.
Source: Bank of International Settlements.

cates of deposits (notably London dollar CDs). Loans are usually made through *eurocurrency credits*, which are essentially overdrafts repeatedly rolled over at a fixed premium over LIBOR. There is very little fixed interest term lending. The eurocurrency credits proxy for term lending, by allowing for a repeated rolling over of the loan. However, the banks as a rule will not bear the interest rate risk of a fixed interest rate. In this sense, eurocurrency loans are more like repeatedly rolled over short-term loans. As a result, market changes in interest rates are quickly fed into existing loan contracts. We will see how this has affected credit-worthiness in a later section; but note that for a borrower this is extremely risky!

THE INTERNATIONAL BOND MARKET

Foreign and Eurobonds

Banks traditionally provide short-term funds. It has only been with some reluc-tance that they have gotten into medium-term lending, and then only with loan contracts that really represent the rolling over of short-term funds. Longer-term funds are traditionally provided through the capital market, by issuing securities that can then be resold if necessary on a secondary market. Similar to our discussion of the international money market, the international bond market can be segmented into foreign bonds and Eurobonds. *Foreign bonds* are normal domestic bonds, with the twist that the borrower is a nonresident. This has been the traditional means of longer-term financing internationally; for example, the U.S. states issued foreign bonds in Great Britain throughout the nineteenth century. The proceeds of a foreign bond issue are in the currency of the capital market in which the issue is sold. By contrast, *Eurobonds* are similar to offshore banking, in that the proceeds of the issue are in a foreign currency. Moreover, Eurobonds have frequently been issued in multiple capital markets simultaneously.

Prior to the 1960s most international bond issues were foreign bonds, and with the emergence of the United States as the main capital exporting country, most foreign bonds were issued in U.S. dollars. However, with the emergence of U.S. balance of payments problems in the 1960s, successive measures were passed to try to reduce capital exports and thus support the U.S. dollar. The interest equalization tax was passed in 1963, which added a 15 percent tax to the interest received from holding foreign bonds. This effectively raised the cost of issuing foreign bonds in the United States. This was followed in 1965 by the voluntary foreign credit restraint program, which quickly became mandatory in 1968. Here, more specifically, were quotas on foreign bond issues in the United States. The result of these measures was to cut off the U.S. capital market for foreign bonds.

The important implication of these regulations was that bond contracts were difficult and expensive to write in the United States. However, U.S. dollar funds could still be raised in a bond issue *outside* of the United States, in the same way that banks could still solicit deposits outside the United States and not be subject to deposit controls. The result was the Eurobond market for longer-term funds to supplement and coexist alongside the eurocurrency market for shorter-term funds.

Functioning of the Market

The mechanics of the Eurobond market are much like those of ordinary bond markets. Funds are raised through an underwritten issue or a direct placement with some major purchasers. The issue is then listed on an exchange to facilitate secondary market trading, and a fiscal agent or trustee is appointed to look after the interests of the bondholders by monitoring the performance of the issuer. However, like the eurocurrency markets, there is only a minimal amount of regulation. Issues are listed on the London or Luxembourg stock markets, so that the prospectus requirements are minimal. Moreover, most bonds are in bearer form, so that the purchaser is not registered anywhere. It is claimed that a substantial portion of most Eurobond issues are "owned" by Swiss numbered bank accounts and the interest is never declared for tax purposes. Moreover, there is no withholding tax deducted at source, since they are issued offshore. The latter two advantages make them particularly attractive for wealthy private investors. However, since the issues are not usually registered with the U.S. Securities and Exchange Commission (SEC) they cannot initially be traded in the United States and thus are not as marketable as equivalent foreign or domestic bonds.

Initially the Eurobond market was simply a U.S. bond market offshore, as U.S. multinationals simply diverted their subsidiaries' borrowing requirements from the U.S. to the Eurobond market. However, the presence of U.S. borrowers contracted after the capital export restraints and the interest equalization tax were removed in January 1974. In their place came foreign governments and quasi-governmental agencies, and foreign corporations who did not wish to meet the rigid disclosure requirements required in the United States by the SEC. By 1982 the Eurobond market had grown to $46.5 billion and was considerably larger than the $25 billion foreign bond market. The largest group of borrowers came from western Europe with $16.6 billion, followed by the United States with $13 billion, Canada with $7 billion, and then about $10 billion from the rest of the world. In Exhibit 8-6, we have a historical series for the Eurobond and foreign bond markets. Note that for foreign bonds Switzerland is the major market, whereas in the Eurobond market, the U.S. dollar dominates all other currencies. The only time when this was not true was during 1978, when the hands-off policy of the U.S. government led to intense currency speculation against the U.S. dollar. The resulting uncertainty led to the collapse of the dollar segment of the Eurobond market.

As Exhibit 8-6 indicates, most Eurobonds are denominated in U.S. dollars or deutsche marks. However, some bonds are rather more esoteric, in having interest and principal repayments tied to so-called *currency cocktails*. For these bonds, interest and principal payments depend on the value of a prearranged group of currencies, such as those in the SDR or the European Economic Community's European Currency Unit (ECU). Moreover, some bonds even have payments tied to the value of certain commodities such as copper, oil, and gold or silver. These complexities, when added to options on maturity dates and the right to convert the bond into common shares (if issued by a company) make for some very complicated bond contracts! However, these bonds comprise only a small segment of the market and do not seem to be increasing in popularity. During 1982, 80 percent of international bond issues were traditional fixed interest rate straight issues, 15.9 percent had floating interest rates, and 3.7 percent had convertible features.

Exhibit 8-6 also gives an indication of the relative importance of the international bond and bank-lending markets over the last few years. Consistently, bank lending has been three or four times as large as international bond financing. However, during 1982 this pattern began to change as the amount of new international lending almost halved and the amount of new international bond financing jumped by over 50 percent. The reasons for this are explained in the following section.

EXHIBIT 8-6
INTERNATIONAL BOND ISSUES*

	1976	1977	1978	1979	1980	1981	1982
Eurobond issues	15.37	19.35	15.94	17.90	20.51	27.18	46.45
U.S. dollars	10.0	12.3	7.69	10.53	13.65	21.55	38.68
Deutsche marks	2.82	5.1	6.53	4.86	3.46	1.38	3.25
Others	2.55	1.95	1.72	2.51	3.40	4.25	4.52
(Private placements)	3.71	3.93	4.27	3.18	2.57	2.31	1.83
Foreign bond issues	18.93	15.61	21.38	19.18	18.93	21.58	25.2
U.S. dollars	10.63	7.58	6.36	4.59	3.09	7.58	6.03
Swiss francs	5.44	4.70	7.45	8.96	7.53	8.17	11.32
Others	2.86	3.33	7.57	5.63	8.31	5.83	7.85
(Private placements)	9.90	6.64	8.96	9.07	7.85	6.04	7.55
Net bond financing[†]	30.0	31.0	28.5	28.0	28.0	36.5	58.5
Net international lending	70.0	75.0	110.0	125.0	160.0	165.0	95.0
Net international financing[†]	96.5	102.0	132.0	145.0	180.0	195.0	145.0

*In US$ billions.
[†]Some double counting has been removed.
Source: Bank for International Settlements.

RECYCLING AND THE INTERNATIONAL DEBT BURDEN

The Problems Caused by High-Priced Oil

The financing problems of the 1980s and the successes of the 1970s are both a function of the problems that the world economic and financial system has had in adjusting to the twin oil price shocks of 1973 and 1979. We only have to look at the summary data of the Saudi Arabian balance of payments in Exhibit 8-7 to appreciate the problem. In 1975, 2 years after the quadrupling of oil prices that followed the Arab-Israeli war, Saudi Arabia had capital exports of $17.4 billion, of which $3.1 billion was through official foreign aid programs. In 1981, 2 years after the doubling of oil prices in 1979, these exports increased to $52.1 billion and $7.0 billion, respectively. Moreover, Exhibit 8-8 shows that the OPEC countries as a group had a current account surplus, which means concomitant capital flows, of $35 billion in 1975 and $114 billion in 1980. This was an enormous amount of money that had to be exported to other countries.

Conceptually, a current account surplus in one country should be matched by a current account deficit in another. However, reporting conventions and the problems in tracking down investment income receipts and payments mean that in practice the sum of the world's balances never net to zero. However, in Exhibit 8-8 we see that in 1975 the OPEC surplus was achieved as a result of the deficits among the other developed countries, the non-OPEC developing countries, and the eastern block countries ("centrally planned"). The major industrialized countries (Group of Ten) achieved a small surplus.

As discussed in Chapter 7, the existence of a surplus or deficit in a country's current account balance should, in equilibrium, indicate a comparative advantage in investment opportunities. That is, for example, a country with great opportuni-

EXHIBIT 8-7
SAUDI ARABIAN BALANCE OF PAYMENTS SUMMARY*

	1975	1976	1977	1978	1979	1980	1981
Merchandise trade balance	21.2	25.2	25.6	17.0	34.5	72.6	76.7
Oil exports	27.1	35.4	40.1	36.9	57.9	100.6	110.5
Oil output, millions of barrels	2583	3139	3358	3030	3479	3624	3586
Other exports	0.1	0.1	0.1	0.1	0.2	0.2	0.2
Imports	-6.0	-10.4	-14.7	-20.0	-27.0	-28.2	-34.0
Services and private transfers	-3.8	-7.6	-9.8	-15.3	-19.9	-25.6	-24.6
Investment income	1.8	2.9	4.0	4.3	4.9	7.4	10.5
Other receipts	1.5	1.7	2.1	2.2	2.8	3.8	4.4
Payments	-7.1	-12.2	-15.9	-21.8	-27.6	-36.8	-39.5
Current account balance	17.4	17.6	15.8	1.7	14.6	46.9	52.1
Official aid	-3 .1	-3.3	-3.9	-3.9	-3.5	-5.5	-7.0
Capital movements	-14.3	-14.3	-11.9	2.2	-11.1	-41.4	-45.1

*In US$ billions.
Sources: IMF, Saudi Arabian Monetary Agency, Saudi Arabian Ministry of Petroleum and Mineral Resources.

ties imports capital to exploit them and runs a current account deficit. However, in 1975, the world economy was not in equilibrium. The OPEC surplus resulted from two factors: first, an enormous transfer of wealth to them as a result of increased oil prices and second, the inability of the OPEC countries to spend their increased wealth. The latter problem was particularly important for the "low-absorption" OPEC countries in the Persian Gulf, which suddenly had enormous wealth but

EXHIBIT 8-8
INTERNATIONAL CURRENT ACCOUNT BALANCES

	1975	1976	1977	1978	1979	1980	1981	1982
Group of Ten:	9.8	5.3	-2.6	20.8	-23.5	-45.8	-3.5	-6.2
(United States)	11.6	-1.4	-14.1	-13.5	-0.3	1.5	4.5	-8.1
Other developed	-20.7	-22.4	-22.4	-11.8	-14.0	-22.5	-31.8	-30.1
Total developed	-10.9	-27.7	-26.0	9.0	-37.5	-68.0	-35.0	-36.0
OPEC countries	35	40	26	0	63	114	63	-3
Non-OPEC developing	-29	-19	-11	-25	-38	-65	-79	-67
Total developing	6	21	15	-25	25	49	-16	-70
Centrally planned						-11	-5	3
Total						-30	-56	-103

Group of Ten: Belgium-Luxembourg, Canada, France, Germany, Italy, Japan, Netherlands (Holland), Sweden, Switzerland, U.K., United States
Other developed: Austria, Australia, Denmark, Finland, Greece, Ireland, Israel, New Zealand, Norway, Portugal, South Africa, Spain, Turkey, Yugoslavia
OPEC: Algeria, Ecuador, Gabon, Indonesia, Iran, Iraq, Kuwait, Libya, Nigeria, Qatar, Saudi Arabia, United Arab Emirates, Venezuela, Oman
Centrally planned: Albania, Bulgaria, China, Czechoslavakia, East Germany, Hungary, North Korea, Poland, Romania, U.S.S.R., Yemen

still had small populations and no immediate needs to spend their wealth on. Moreover, the oil-importing countries, particularly the non-OPEC developing countries, could not suddenly reduce their demand for oil imports, since no immediate alternative energy sources were economically available.

The Role Played by the Eurocurrency Markets

The obvious solution to this problem was OPEC loans to the rest of the world to finance their current account deficits. However, direct loans were politically risky, since the quadrupling of oil prices had not exactly endeared the OPEC countries to the rest of the world. Hence the recycling of these petrodollars (oil imports soon switched from being priced in sterling into dollars) was diverted through financial intermediaries to bear this political risk. Consistent with the initially conservative nature of OPEC investment policy, most of their investable funds were put on deposit with the international banks. Moreover, since the increased oil prices threw the world into an economic slump, normal loan demand had fallen. Hence the funds were lent to countries to finance their current account deficits. Balance of payments financing traditionally had been the function of the IMF, but faced with bank loans without the normal "clean-up-your-act" provisions of the IMF loan, most countries borrowed from the banks.

The 1973 oil shock quickly produced international readjustment. By 1977, the industrial world entered a period of economic recovery and the non-OPEC developing countries saw their current account deficits more than halved as they increased their exports to the industrialized countries. Moreover, the OPEC countries themselves embarked on ambitious expansion programs to such an extent that by 1978 their combined current account surplus had disappeared. Moreover, the traditional current account surplus of the Group of Ten major industrialized countries had reestablished itself. In Exhibit 8-9 we have the disposition of OPEC's investible surplus. In 1974 and 1975, $13.8 billion and $4.1 billion, respectively, found its way into the eurocurrency market in London. The rest was invested in a variety of long-term and short-term instruments. Hence recycling was judged a success; there were no significant losses to the banks, and the system had shown itself flexible enough to handle large transfers of wealth.

During 1978, events began to change. The United States persisted in a very lax monetary policy to stimulate domestic demand. This created severe balance of payments problems for the United States and forced other countries to buy up U.S. dollars to prevent their currencies from appreciating. These dollars were then invested largely in the eurocurrency markets, where real interest rates declined. This prompted some non-OPEC countries to overborrow, so that despite U.S. balance of payments problems, the non-OPEC developing countries experienced increasing current account deficits.

It was in this environment of overborrowing by existing non-OPEC developing countries that first, oil prices doubled again during 1979 to 1980 and second, the United States changed its monetary policy. In 1979, the United States decided to shift from targeting interest rates to targeting money supply to bring down its rate of inflation and improve the balance of payments. The result was increasing U.S.

EXHIBIT 8-9
ESTIMATED DEPLOYMENT OF OPEC's INVESTABLE SURPLUS

	1974	1975	1979	1980	1981	1982
Identifiable investable surplus	53.2	35.2	60.6	86.5	49.5	3.1
Short-term investments	36.6	9.5	43.2	42.6	0.6	-16.2
In United States	9.4	1.1	8.3	0.3	-2.5	4.8
In U.K.	18.2	3.4	16.2	16.3	8.2	-8.2
(Eurocurrency)	(13.8)	(4.1)	(14.8)	(14.8)	(7.8)	(-9.4)
In other industrialized nations	9.0	5.0	18.7	26.2	-5.1	-12.8
Long-term investments	16.6	25.7	17.4	43.9	48.9	19.3
In United States	2.3	8.5	-1.5	13.8	18.8	7.6
In U.K.	2.8	0.9	1.0	2.5	1.1	-0.8
In other industrialized nations	3.1	5.8	8.7	17.0	19.4	6.6
With international institutions	3.5	4.0	-0.4	4.9	2.4	2.0
In developing countries	4.9	6.5	9.6	6.7	7.2	3.9

Source: Bank of England.

interest rates, so that the real interest rate rocketed up and the U.S. dollar appreciated. For the overborrowed countries the double effect was disastrous. First, much of the debt was quickly rolled over at the much higher interest rates, and second, they found themselves having to pay the debt off in rapidly appreciating U.S. dollars—all of this at a time when the tight U.S. monetary policy precipitated a world recession that slashed demand for their exports.

In Exhibit 8-8, we can see the result of the tight money policy initiated by the Federal Reserve Board in 1979. The recession it induced in 1981 restored the current account balance of the group of ten industrialized countries and wiped out the enormous $114 billion surplus of the OPEC countries. The combination of recession and even higher oil prices had further accelerated the shift away from oil imports. In just 3 years, 1979 to 1982, real oil exports by OPEC fell by 45 percent from 31 million barrels a day to 17. However, a by-product was that fewer funds were deposited in the eurocurrency markets. As Exhibit 8-9 shows, OPEC countries ran down their eurocurrency balances by $9.4 billion as the high-absorption countries sold off deposits and securities to finance their deficits and the low-absorption countries shifted their deposits to safer, higher-yielding securities in the United States.

The Non-OPEC Developing Countries' Problems

Exhibit 8-8 underestimates the OPEC countries' current account balance, since it correctly records merchandise exports but seems to underrecord investment income receipts. By 1982, investment income must have totaled around $40 billion since OPEC's net foreign asset position had climbed to $405 billion. Essentially these receipts were paid by the non-OPEC developing countries, which had seen their external debt increase from $320 billion in 1979 to about $500 billion in 1982, and their net interest payments climb to $47 billion. What was different about the situation in 1980 to 1982 was that these net interest payments no longer reflected just the inflation premium. Historically, the inflation premium had been paid by rolling over the old debt and interest payments into new debts. Now, however, the real interest rate had increased substantially from about 1 to 2 percent during 1976 to 1980, to 8 to 10 percent in 1981 to 1982. Moreover, the banks faced with rising domestic loan losses due to the recession were not prepared to make new loan commitments when it became apparent that some countries could not make real interest payments of 8 to 10 percent.

What triggered the ongoing crises of 1982 were a series of political crises. First, in 1981 came the political problems in Poland, which forced a rescheduling of Polish debt payments. Second, in April 1982 came the Falklands crisis, which increased fears of default due to the diversion of Argentine resources to military expenditures. Finally, in August 1982 came the massive flight of private Mexican capital from Mexico. Mexico was the test case. Since the mid-1970s Mexico had been borrowing enormous amounts of short-term capital to finance its oil exploration and development programs. By 1981, private bank debt alone stood at about $56.9 billion, or 85 percent of Mexico's export earnings. Moreover, the oil potential had also increased expectations of a better standard of living and increased imports. The result was that when oil prices started to decline, Mexico was unable and unwilling to take sufficient measures to fulfill its commitments.

Throughout August 1982, a "rescue" package was put together for Mexico, including $700 million in swap loans from the New York Federal Reserve Board, $1 billion in advance oil payments from the U.S. government, $1.85 billion in bridging credit from the Bank for International Settlements (BIS) and the U.S. Federal Reserve Board, $3.8 billion in credit from the IMF, and about $5 billion in new bank credits. The precedent was set that the international banks would renew and extend loans only if the international institutions took part of the burden of saving the international financial system from collapse. After Mexico came Brazil with a $1.45 billion loan from the BIS in December 1982, a $5.4 billion loan from the IMF in February 1983, and about $4.4 billion in loans from the international banks. By spring 1983 twenty-five of the non-OPEC developing countries, accounting for about two thirds of the group's bank debt, had rescheduled debt repayments. Moreover, none of their reschedulings solved the problem, as the countries had to return to the negotiating tables again to reschedule their debts in 1983 to 1984. Brazil alone rescheduled a further $5.35 billion in the spring of 1984. Rescheduling had become the norm!

Prognosis

The events of 1981 to 1984 can be explained partly by unique unexpected events and partly by structural changes that can be altered in the future. First it has to be pointed out that the changes in U.S. monetary policy produced results that could not have been predicted. Nobody in 1979 predicted the depth of the recession in 1981 to 1983 or the size of the real interest rates; both were completely uncharted territory in the post World War II era. Moreover, unlike previous periods, most of the non-OPEC developing countries' debt was bank debt, which had floating interest rates and very short maturities. Hence the real interest rates were quickly rolled over into existing debt contracts. The fact that inflation was built into the debt via high nominal interest rates, rather than indexing interest and principal repayments to inflation, also meant that the debtors were dependent on *new* debt financing just to maintain the *same* real amount of debt outstanding. The result of these structural changes was to force the nonoil developing countries to rapidly reduce the amount of debt owed, a situation akin to that of a mortgage company suddenly asking an individual to pay off 30 percent of a mortgage immediately.

The structural features of the 1981 to 1983 crisis are being remedied. In Exhibit 8-10 we show how the non-OPEC developing countries' current account deficits were financed. Noticeably, there has been a reduced amount of bank lending (mostly involuntary?) and a switch from shorter to longer maturities. This lengthening of the maturity structure of the debt helps, but what is really needed is inflation indexed, fixed real interest rate debt, and in this area the international financial markets have not been innovative. Lest we leave the impression that the problems of 1981 to 1983 were imposed upon, not caused, by the non-OPEC developing countries, we should note the conclusions of the BIS:

> The combination of recession and high interest rates in the Group of Ten countries had major adverse effects on the non-OPEC developing countries balance of payments . . . . these developing countries would in any case have had to take action to correct their external payments in 1982, since the rate at which their domestic demand, and thus their imports, had been growing in the late 1970s would have been unsustainable even in a more favourable world economic environment.

In other words, world recession and high interest rates were imposed on top of a deteriorating economic position for these developing countries.

EXHIBIT 8-10
NON-OPEC DEVELOPING COUNTRIES, ESTIMATED FINANCING
OF CURRENT ACCOUNT DEFICITS FOR 1980 TO 1982*

Item	1980	1981	1982
Current account deficit	-65	-79	-67
Financing/capital account:			
Net foreign direct investment	8	11	10
Non-IMF lending:	61	63	40
Long-term	37	48	37
Short-term	24	15	3
(bank lending)	(33)	(40)	(16)
IMF lending	2	5	5
Total lending	71	79	55
Net official monetary movements:	6	0	-12
Official reserves	0	0	-9
Other assets	6	0	-3

*In US$ billions.
Source: Bank for International Settlements.

The events of 1981 to 1983 will certainly cause the international banks to retreat from general balance of payments financing, a function which will revert to the institutions, like the IMF, that were established to do it in the first place. In addition, we can expect the banks to play a diminished role *if* the OPEC current account surplus remains depressed because of lower oil prices and reduced export volumes. However, much depends on the policy of the U.S. government and how quickly the world's economy enters a period of low inflationary economic growth. The amounts of external bank debt outstanding by the non-OPEC developing countries in Exhibit 8-11 require a long period of economic growth and stability. Otherwise, the export earnings will not be there to make the debt manageable. Some countries may decide that there is more to be gained from outright default than from staggering along with such an oppressive burden. This was the particular problem faced by Argentina in the spring of 1984, since Argentina was the one country in the world that was a major debtor *without* requiring new debt financing.

SUMMARY

In this chapter we discussed the international financial markets. The foreign exchange market was discussed first with the international payments system. The use of a vehicle currency for payments purposes was contrasted with the tradi-

EXHIBIT 8-11
NON-OPEC BANK DEBTORS
(And Nigeria)

	US$ billion		Due in 1 year	
	1982	1981	% of total	% of exports
1 Mexico	62.9	56.9	49	85
2 Brazil	60.5	52.7	35	67
3 Venezuela	27.5	26.2	61	79
4 Argentina	25.7	24.8	47	100
5 South Korea	23.2	19.9	58	37
6 Phillippines	12.6	10.2	56	63
7 Chile	11.6	10.5	40	78
8 Indonesia	9.9	7.2	41	14
9 Nigeria	8.5	6.0	34	12
10 Malaysia	6.6	4.4	31	10
11 Colombia	6.3	5.4	49	53
12 Peru	5.4	4.4	60	62
13 Thailand	4.9	5.1	60	29
14 Turkey	4.0	4.2	25	10

Source: Morgan Guaranty Trust Co. and Bank for International Settlements.

tional multilateral payments system. The implications for the size and structure of the foreign exchange market were then analyzed, along with the concepts of triangular and geographical arbitrage.

Prior to the discussion of the international financial markets, we first discussed the basic features of domestic markets. The concepts of market and financial intermediaries were introduced and applied in a comparative analysis of different domestic financial systems. This then allowed an analysis of the main participants in the international financial markets.

The history of the international money markets was briefly reviewed to emphasize the factors generating the enormous eurocurrency markets. The role of government intervention and political risk in differentiating the external and internal intermediation of a nation's credit market was emphasized. The international bond market was then discussed to complete the discussion of long- and short-term financial instruments. The different features of foreign and Eurobonds were contrasted, as was the relative importance of the international financing sources.

Finally, we discussed recent developments in the international financial markets. Here, we emphasized the recycling problem of the 1970s with the emergence of large OPEC surpluses, and deficits in most other parts of the world. The role of international bank lending was developed and the resulting bank crises of 1982 to 1983 discussed against this background.

KEY WORDS

Correspondent bank	Spread
Multilateral payments system	Sovereign risk
Vehicle currency	International banking facilities (IBFs)
Cross rates	Foreign bonds
Triangular arbitrage	Eurobonds
Geographical arbitrage	Currency cocktails
Financial intermediaries	Recycling
External/offshore banking	Petrodollars
Eurocurrency markets	Rescheduling

QUESTIONS

1 Explain the advantages of the vehicle currency system over the multilateral payments system.
2 How does triangular arbitrage ensure that all possible exchange rates are consistent?
3 What is the importance of New York to the world's foreign exchange markets?
4 Distinguish between foreign and offshore or external banking business.
5 Why did the eurocurrency markets develop, and what is sustaining them now? What is the relevance of the spread?
6 What are the most important sources of international finance? How are the different sources of finance differentiated? Distinguish between foreign and Eurobonds.
7 What caused the rescheduling crisis of 1982 to 1983?
8 How would you determine how much debt Mexico or Brazil could carry?

CHAPTER 9

EXCHANGE RATE DETERMINATION

INTRODUCTION

In Chapter 7 we discussed the structure of the international monetary system and the inherent difficulties in attempting to maintain a fixed rate system in the presence of independent national monetary policies. What we did not have time to discuss were the linkages between exchange rates and national monetary policies, or other factors at work in affecting exchange rates. In this chapter we provide the essential background required to understand what makes exchange rates tick. Without such a background, as will become readily apparent, it is all too easy for managers to make "self-apparent" observations that in fact do not make sense. For the manager in the international environment it is particularly important to be able to distinguish insight gained from a careful analysis of the facts from "obvious" explanations based upon a superficial understanding of exchange rate determination.

In structuring the correct analysis of exchange rates we have to distinguish between the long and short run. In the long run, we will assume that the international system is in equilibrium. This means that the forces working to change the system are equally balanced by forces working to preserve it. To illustrate the long-run equilibrium concept, we discuss several major international parity relationships. Although these are not all long-run phenomena, they fit together to provide an equilibrium set of relationships. In the short run the international financial system is moving from one equilibrium to another. Within this disequilibrium some international parity relationships will hold, as will some other short-run phenomena that are *required* to move us back into equilibrium.

For the international manager, it is as important to realize where the international financial system is headed as it is to realize what are the short-run phenomena that are moving it there. For the multinational enterprise we shall see that the process toward equilibrium provides unique profit opportunities. Moreover, without the MNE, the time required to move to equilibrium would be increased. In this sense, this chapter can be seen as laying the macroeconomic framework within which the major financial management decisions of MNEs, to be discussed in Chapter 18, are made.

THE INTERNATIONAL PARITY RELATIONSHIPS

The analysis of exchange rate determination requires clarification of some notation and terminology. There are many foreign exchange markets, each differentiated by the *time* at which the transaction will take place. If transactions take place immediately, we call this market a *spot* market. Hence there is a spot market for immediate delivery of foreign exchange, just as there is for oil, sugar, and many other commodities. Since we will be talking almost exclusively of financial markets, we will use the term spot market to denote the spot foreign exchange market and express the price determined in that market in European terms, the spot rate, as $S[FC:US\$]$, where FC is some foreign currency.

The banks, as a service to corporate customers, will allow future exchanges of currency at a future date at a rate agreed upon today. This market is called the forward foreign exchange market, and the price so determined, the *forward rate*, will be expressed in European terms as $F[FC:US\$]$.

Hedging

The existence of the forward market has a profound implication for individuals and corporations with short-term foreign currency denominated cash flows. With just a spot market, these cash flows would be subject to foreign exchange risk; this we define as the possibility of a change in the exchange rate from that expected on the day that the foreign cash flows have to be converted into domestic currency. However, with a forward market the individual or corporation can hedge, or cover, the foreign exchange risk. This is done by contracting with the bank today to exchange the future foreign cash flows at a rate fixed today, i.e., the current forward rate. Hence the forward market shifts the burden of foreign exchange risk from individuals and corporations to the banks and other participants in the forward market.

The forward markets thus offer the opportunity of removing foreign exchange risk from foreign currency cash flows provided two conditions are fulfilled. First, the *size* of the foreign currency cash flow has to be known for certain. Second the *time* of conversion from foreign currency into domestic currency has to be known for certain. If either of these conditions is not satisfied, it is not possible to completely remove foreign exchange risk. We will discuss hedging further in Chapter 18 in connection with the management of foreign exchange risk.

THE FORWARD MARKET HEDGE

Equipment is sold to a U.K. firm by a U.S. firm for £1 million. Payment is to be made in 90 days. Hence there is a sterling receivable outstanding.

$$S[\text{US\$}:£] = 1.523$$
$$F[\text{US\$}:£] = 1.516$$

Options:
1   Exchange into U.S. dollars in 90 days at the risk of the pound's depreciating. That is, bear the foreign exchange risk.
2   Buy U.S. dollars forward at a cost of $7000, [(1.523 − 1.516)*(1,000,000)], or 0.46 percent, [(1.523 − 1.516)/1.523]. The foreign exchange risk has been transferred to the bank for 0.46 percent, the forward premium. This is sometimes called the cost of hedging. However, this cost should really be measured relative to the expected future spot rate, not the current spot rate, since there is no reason to believe that the exchange rate will remain constant.

Swapped Deposits

The forward market also presents opportunities for *investors* in default-free fixed interest securities, since for these securities the size and timing of the cash flows are fixed and thus known for certain, for example, a U.S. investor faced with an interest rate of R on 1-year U.S. government treasury notes, and R^* on 1-year

THE SWAPPED DEPOSIT

$S[\text{FC}:\text{US\$}] = 2.23$ U.S. T-bill rate $R = 12$ percent

$F[\text{FC}:\text{US\$}] = 2.15$ German T-bill rate $R^* = 8.75$ percent

1   Invest $1 million in U.S. T-bills
     $1,000,000 × 12 percent = $120,000

2   Invest $1 million in German T-bills
     a Buy DM spot at 2.23 = DM 2,230,000
     b Buy dollars forward at 2.15
     c In 1 year receive
          DM 2,230,000 × 1.0875 = DM 2,425,125
     d Fulfill forward contract
          DM 2,425,125 ÷ 2.15DM/US$ = $1,127,965

Income earned = $127,965 or 12.8 percent

or simply $(1 + R)S[\text{FC}:\text{US\$}]/F[\text{FC}:\text{US\$}]$
              $= (1.0875)^*(2.23)/(2.15)$
              $= 1.128$, or 12.8 percent

foreign currency treasury notes issued by a foreign government. In both cases the return on the investment is guaranteed, since governments rarely default on their *domestic* financial obligations. This is because governments can always print more money to pay off debts denominated in the currency that they control. Without forward markets the investment in foreign currency treasury notes would be subject to foreign exchange risk, and thus not comparable in risk with the investment in domestic government notes. However, with forward markets the investor can contract with the bank to convert the known proceeds from the foreign investment back into domestic currency. Hence the removal of foreign exchange risk makes the two investments more comparable in risk.

The total return on the domestic investment of $1 + R$ can be compared with the total return on the covered foreign investment of $S[FC:US\$]$ $(1+R^*)/F[FC: US\$]$. A foreign investment covered or hedged against foreign exchange risk is usually called a *swapped deposit*. This investment contains two independent transactions: the investment in foreign currency treasury notes yielding $(1 + R^*)$, which is the deposit, and the simultaneous sale of domestic currency spot and purchase forward yielding $S[FC:US\$]/F[FC:US\$]$, which is the swap. The latter amount is called the *forward discount* or *premium*, depending upon whether the forward rate is less than or greater than the current spot rate, and which of the two currencies is being analyzed.

For example, suppose the spot and forward rates for the deutsche mark were 2.23 and 2.15, respectively, and the 1-year treasury notes in Germany and the United States 8.75 and 12 percent, respectively. In this case, an American investor would compare the total return of 1.12 on an investment in U.S. treasury notes with the covered return of $(1.0875)^*(2.23)/2.15 = 1.128$ on an investment in German treasury notes. Since the risk of the two investments is comparable, the U.S. investor would invest in the German swapped deposit.

Note that in comparing the U.S. and German investments the German interest rate *cannot* be considered in isolation, since it represents only part of the return to a U.S. investor. In this case, the U.S. dollar is at a forward discount of 3.7 percent against the deutsche mark, or conversely the deutsche mark is at a 3.7 percent forward premium against the dollar. That is, by just converting dollars into deutsche marks and leaving them in a zero-interest checking account in Germany and then bringing them back through the forward market 1 year later, the investor would earn 3.7 percent.

This differential return on the domestic versus swapped deposit would diminish as U.S. investors switched funds into the swapped deposit. First, funds flowing out of U.S. securities would cause their price to fall and hence their yield to increase. Second, funds flowing out of the dollar and into the deutsche mark would cause the spot rate to fall. Third, funds flowing into German treasury notes would cause their price to increase and hence their yield to fall. Finally, funds flowing back into dollars through the forward market would cause the forward rate to increase. Overall, the yield on the domestic treasury note would increase and that on the swapped deposit would decrease, as both the yield on the German treasury note and the forward discount on the dollar decreased.

Interest Rate Parity

For individuals the yield on swapped deposits is almost always slightly higher than the yield on equivalent securities. This is for two reasons. First, it is more costly to set up the swapped deposit, since more transactions are involved. Second, the swapped deposit is *illiquid*, in that there is no secondary market for swapped deposits since they involve a fixed foreign exchange contract. Hence, the swapped deposit requires a higher yield to attract investors than the more liquid domestic government note. As a result, capital importing countries have to offer a slightly higher effective yield on their short-term securities. However, this premium rarely exceeds ¼ percent, and is often negligible. For this reason, to a close approximation, we can say that the yields on swapped deposits and equivalent securities must be identical in equilibrium. This result is called the *interest rate parity* theorem and is written

$$1 + R = \frac{S}{F} (1+R^*) \qquad\qquad (9\text{-}1)$$

where for notational simplicity we drop the full description of the exchange rate.

Interest rate parity can also be derived by thinking of the problem not from the investors' point of view but from that of the borrowers. Consider, for example, the major international banks that as a matter of course raise funds and make loans in a variety of different currencies. They too have access to the forward market and can hedge foreign exchange risk. Hence, if they find that it is cheaper to raise funds from swapped deposits than by accepting domestic deposits, they will increase their funding from this source. This action will cause the differential yields to change, until there is no funding advantage from either source.

Moreover, the action of international banks and brokers as *arbitrageurs*, raising funds from cheaper domestic deposits and investing in the swapped deposits or vice versa, will also cause an equalization of yields. The latter process is often called *covered interest arbitrage*, arbitrage because no investment is required, since there is a simultaneous purchase and sale of conceptually identical deposits; interest because it is motivated by differential effective yields; and covered because the foreign deposit is covered or hedged against foreign exchange risk.

Interest rate parity is a cornerstone of the international money market, since provided capital can flow freely between countries, it must hold to a close approximation. Otherwise, international arbitrageurs could earn almost limitless profits from covered interest arbitrage. In Exhibit 9-1 we have calculated the yield on 1 year swapped eurocurrency deposits for the major currencies. As can be seen, the spread in basis points is never more than 30.6. This amount is almost negligible once the transactions costs associated with arbitrage activity are considered. Hence, to a close approximation, we can say that interest rate parity does in fact hold.

COVERED INTEREST ARBITRAGE

Spot $S[£:US\$]$ 0.67   U.K. T-bill rate 13 percent
90-day forward $F[£:US\$]$ 0.68   U.S. T-bill rate 8 percent

Forward discount on £ = (0.67 − 0.68)/0.68 = − 1.5 percent per quarter

From interest rate parity the market is not in equilibrium. The ratio of U.S. to U.K. T-bill rates gives a discount of 4.44 percent, which does not equal the annualized forward discount on sterling of 6 percent. Hence covered interest arbitrage profits are possible.

A   Day 1
   1   Borrow £1 million for 90 days at 13 percent.
   2   Exchange at spot rate for $1,492,537.
   3   Invest in U.S. T-bills for 90 days at 8 percent.
   4   Sell $1,518,382 (£ loan obligation in U.S.$).
     forward at 0.68.

B   Day 90
   1   Redeem U.S. T-bills for $1,522,388.
   2   Fulfill forward contract by delivering $1,518,382 in return for £1,032,500.
   3   Repay loan of £1 million plus interest of £32,500.

Summary

Proceeds from U.S. T-bills, **B1**	$1,522,388
Repayment of sterling loan in US $, **B2, 3,**	1,518,382
Transactions costs (estimate)	500
Arbitrage profits	$ 3,506

EXHIBIT 9-1
SWAPPED DEPOSITS
(July 18, 1983)

	Canada	U.K.	France	Germany	Switzerland	Japan
Spot[†]	1.2305	0.6497	7.615	2.5362	2.1015	238.6
Forward[†] (12 months)	1.2270	0.64809	8.135	2.4372	1.9965	230.3
Interest rate (12 months)	1.10125	1.10125	1.18	1.059375	1.04687	1.065
Effective yield $(1+R^*)S/F$	1.10439	1.10398	1.10457	1.1024	1.1019	1.10338
U.S. yield	1.105	1.105	1.105	1.105	1.105	1.105
Spread in basis points (.01)	6.1	10.1	4.27	25.9	30.6	16.1

[†]Expressed as FC per U.S. dollar.
Source: Harris Bank, *International Money Markets and Foreign Exchange Rates*.

Unbiasedness of the Forward Rate

To develop a set of international parity relationships, however, it begs the question: what determines nominal interest rates and what determines the forward rate? Prior to the period of generalized floating that effectively began in March 1973, banks essentially allowed corporations to transact business in the forward market at the spot rate. That is, the forward rate was usually just the existing spot rate. This was because under fixed exchange rates, apart from periods of intense currency speculation, the exchange rate was not anticipated to change dramatically. In this fundamental sense, the forward market was not a *speculative market*.

In fact, speculation was almost ruled out, since the banks would not allow individuals or corporations to buy or sell forward contracts for other than purely "commercial reasons." The prevailing opinion was that the forward market was provided as a service to help businesses conduct their international trade, not to help individuals speculate on currency changes. The Federal Reserve Board did not look too kindly on banks which encouraged the very speculation that its actions were designed to frustrate!

This attitude changed with the advent of generalized floating and the establishment in 1972 of the International Money Market (IMM) in Chicago. The significance of the IMM is that it established a *futures market* in foreign exchange for pure speculation. Contracts for *future* delivery of foreign currency are traded in the exact same way as the standardized contracts for delivery of pork bellies, wheat, copper, and many other commodities. For example, individuals can sell a contract to exchange £25,000 into U.S. dollars at a fixed exchange rate on any one of the closing dates in March, June, September, or December. All that they have to do is put up a margin, which varies with the size of the contract, to ensure that they fulfill the commitment.

Figure 9-1 gives recent price quotations on the IMM. The first four columns give the opening, high, low, and closing prices respectively; the fifth column, the price change, the sixth and seventh columns, the lifetime highs and lows; and the final column, the amount of "open interest" or contracts outstanding. As is apparent, most of the interest is usually in the near-term contracts.

The key to understanding the IMM futures market is that somebody else has to buy the contract. Suppose, for example, that you expected the sterling-dollar exchange rate, $E[US\$:£]$, to be $1.60 in the following April. In this case, you would *buy* a £25,000 contract for April at an exchange rate below $1.60. If you were able to buy one at $1.50 and you turned out to be correct, you would then exercise the contract in the following April by buying £25,000 for $37,500, while simultaneously executing a spot contract to convert the £25,000 into $40,000. Hence you would make a profit of $2500. However, if everybody felt that the exchange rate was going to be $1.60 or more, nobody would buy the contract. In this case, you would *sell* a sterling futures contract at, say, $1.70, and if you were correct, the reverse transactions would net you the same profit of $2500.

The economic implication of the IMM is that the actions of speculators, buying and selling futures contracts, drive the *futures rate* (the exchange rate on new

– FINANCIAL –

BRITISH POUND (IMM) – 25,000 pounds; $ per pound

June	1.3970	1.3985	1.3865	1.3880	– .0175	1.5520	1.3865	16,705
Sept	1.4040	1.4055	1.3950	1.3955	– .0170	1.5240	1.3950	2,534
Dec	1.4140	1.4140	1.4030	1.4030	– .0170	1.5100	1.3990	100
Mar85	1.4210	1.4210	1.4090	1.4110	– .0165	1.5170	1.4000	78

Est vol 6,360; vol Fri 5,532; open int 19,417, +446.

CANADIAN DOLLAR (IMM) – 100,000 dlrs.; $ per Can $

June	.7722	.7739	.7720	.7729	– .0012	.8168	.7712	8,417
Sept	.7727	.7736	.7727	.7730	– .0012	.8147	.7713	738
Dec	....	....	....	.7731	– .0012	.8048	.7719	1,635
Mar85	....	....	....	.7732	– .0012	.8050	.7738	1,439
June	....	....	....	.7734	– .0012	.7835	.7770	4

Est vol 1,553; vol Fri 1,680; open int 12,233, +228.

JAPANESE YEN (IMM) 12.5 million yen; $ per yen (.00)

June	.4405	.4407	.4390	.4394	– .0036	.4565	.4180	26,040
Sept	.4457	.4467	.4447	.4451	– .0034	.4615	.4351	2,066
Dec	.4350	.4530	.4510	.4515	– .0035	.4663	.4395	830
Mar85	....	....	....	.4577	– .0033	.4695	.4610	18

Est vol 10,527; vol Fri 8,274; open int 28,954, – 1,461.

SWISS FRANC (IMM) – 125,000 francs-$ per franc

June	.4441	.4441	.4408	.4412	– .0056	.5045	.4408	23,829
Sept	.4523	.4523	.4491	.4495	– .0055	.5020	.4491	2,048
Dec	.4610	.4610	.4576	.4579	– .0053	.5000	.4576	...
Mar85	.4695	.4695	.4661	.4661	– .0054	.5035	.4661	33
June	.4785	.4785	.4745	.4745	– .0055	.4900	.4745	7

Est vol 15,446; vol Fri 18,279; open int 26,220, – 319.

W. GERMAN MARK (IMM) – 125,000 marks; $ per mark

June	.3648	.3652	.3619	.3626	– .0059	.4002	.3568	29,003
Sept	.3698	.3703	.3670	.3677	– .0059	.4037	.3602	2,051
Dec	.3758	.3758	.3727	.3730	– .0058	.4080	.3640	528
Mar85	.3805	.3805	.3783	.3783	– .0057	.4110	.3699	23

Est vol 20,390; vol Fri 22,632; open int 31,605, – 704.

EURODOLLAR (IMM) – $1 million; pts of 100%

						Yield		Open
	Open	High	Low	Settle	Chg	Settle	Chg	Interest
June	88.28	88.33	88.20	88.21	– .09	11.79	+ .09	32,622
Sept	87.66	87.70	87.58	87.58	– .11	12.42	+ .11	25,120
Dec	87.22	87.26	87.16	87.16	– .10	12.84	+ .10	12,458
Mar85	86.87	86.89	86.81	86.30	– .10	13.20	+ .10	2,971
June	86.55	86.57	86.50	86.50	– .10	13.50	+ .10	2,345
Sept	86.26	86.28	86.25	86.24	– .09	13.76	+ .09	1,289

Est vol 12,340; vol Fri 21,046; open int 76,805, +227.

FIGURE 9-1
IMM future prices. (*Wall Street Journal, May 8, 1984.*)

contracts) to equal the overall market expectation of what the spot rate is expected to be. Hence, by reading the futures prices in Figure 9-1, we have another estimate of the future exchange rate, this time for the date when the four futures contracts mature. Moreover, although the banks do not participate directly in the IMM, the IMM has created a special class of members, exempt from margin requirements, specifically to arbitrage between the IMM futures market and the interbank forward market. As a result, the forward rate offered in the

---

FORWARD MARKET SPECULATION

1 *Buy* forward

Expected $:£ rate = $1.60
Buy £25,000 forward at $1.50

   a Fulfill contract and buy
      £25,000 at $1.50/£ = $37,500
   b Convert on spot market
      £25,000 at $1.60/£ = $40,000
Hence expected profit is $2500

2 *Sell* forward

Expected $:£ rate = $1.60
Sell £25,000 forward at $1.70

   a Buy on spot market
      £25,000 at $1.60/£ = $40,000
   b Fulfill contract and deliver
      £25,000 at $1.70/£ = $42,500
Hence expected profit is $2500

interbank market is tied to the futures rate established in the speculative IMM futures market. It is for this reason that most economists believe that the *forward rate is an unbiased expectation of the future spot rate*. That is, the forward discount or premium is actually equal to the expected change in the value of the currency.

Inflationary Expectations and the Fisher Effect

Interest rate parity implies from Equation (9-1) that the ratio of nominal interest rates is equal to the forward discount or premium. Moreover, if the forward market is efficient, this discount or premium is in turn equal to the expected change in the value of the currency. This provides a direct link between expected exchange rate changes and interest rate differentials. For example, earlier, the higher U.S. T-bill rate implied that the U.S. dollar was at a forward discount to the deutsche mark of 3.7 percent; this would then be the market's best estimate of the change in the U.S. dollar exchange rate against the deutsche mark over the next year.

However, interest rates do not drive exchange rates or expectations of exchange rate changes, the interest rates. Instead, both interest rates and expected exchange rate changes are driven by the common phenomenon of *inflationary expectations*.

Consider, for example, a man who expects the rate of inflation to be 10 percent. If he lends $1 million at 10 percent then at the end of 1 year he will receive $1.1 million. However, if he is correct about inflation, prices will have risen by 10 percent. Hence, at the end of the year the $1.1 million will only be equivalent in terms of purchasing power to the $1 million that he originally lent. In this case, the *real* rate of return, or the real interest rate, is zero, and the *nominal* interest rate of 10 percent has merely compensated the individual for the expected rate of inflation. Irving Fisher was one of the first economists to emphasize the point that conceptually the nominal interest rate can be decomposed into these two parts, the real rate of interest and the expected rate of inflation. Hence the relationship between nominal interest rates and the expected rate of inflation is often called the *Fisher effect*.

In Exhibit 9-2 we have a simple representation of the Fisher effect. Suppose that with zero inflation the investor requires a real rate of interest of 5 percent. In this case, the nominal rate of interest on the bond contract would also be 5 percent and the investor would receive a $50 interest payment at the end of the period and would still be owed $1000, i.e., the principal obligation. Moreover, if the investor was correct about no inflation, these *nominal* amounts would also be the same *real* amounts. However, suppose inflation were expected to be 10 percent. In this case, the Fisher effect states that the investor would "gross up" the nominal interest rate to reflect the inflationary expectations and the investor's required real rate of interest. The formula is

$$1 + R = (1+r)(1+I) \qquad\qquad (9\text{-}2)$$

EXHIBIT 9-2
THE FISHER EFFECT AND BOND CONTRACTS

	Nominal payments		Real payments*	
	Principal	Interest	Principal	Interest
Zero inflation	1000	50	1000	50
Nominal bond −10% inflation	1000	155	909	140.9
Indexed bond	1100	55	1000	50

*Nominal amounts deflated by $1/(1+I)$.

where R is the nominal rate, r is the real rate, and I the expected rate of inflation. With our numbers the nominal interest rate would be 15.5 percent. Hence, at the end of the period the investor would receive nominal interest payments of $155 and still have $1000 of principal outstanding.

The problem with this *nominal* bond contract is that in real terms we have mixed up the interest and principal components. We can "deflate" by $1/(1+I)$ to obtain the real amounts of interest and principal outstanding. For example, if the 10 percent expected inflation is realized, the real interest payment is in fact $140.9 and the real principal outstanding is $909. Together, they continue to make the same $1050 as under no inflation. However, the real interest component has increased, at the expense of the real principal outstanding. It is as if we are forcing the borrower to repay the debt more quickly. Note in particular that a borrower who wishes to still owe $1000 in *real terms* at the end of the period would have to borrow more money. This phenomenon became particularly important in the refinancing problem of third world debts, which we discussed in Chapter 8.

The implication of nominal bond contracts and debt agreements is that through the Fisher effect nominal interest payments increase with inflation, and debt is effectively repaid more quickly. This causes serious liquidity problems in increasing the amount of cash flow that has to be diverted to interest payments, even though in real terms the debt burden of interest and principal outstanding is constant. This effect is removed by issuing indexed debt contracts, where the interest and principal obligations are fixed in real terms but then vary with, or are indexed to, the rate of inflation in nominal terms. If the 10 percent expected inflation were realized, the indexed bond would have interest payments of $50 in real terms, increased by the 10 percent rate of inflation to $55, and the borrower would still owe $1000 in real terms, increased by the 10 percent inflation to $1100. Note that although the nominal amount owed of $1155 is *identical* to that of the nominal bond, in real terms we do not have the mismatching of interest and principal payments. Hence it has the same real interest and principal payments as would exist under zero inflation.

In the international financial markets we have both indexed and nominal bonds. The nominal bonds are usually issued in countries where inflation is not severe and where the tax system discriminates against indexed bonds. In hyperinflationary countries, however, the distortion of interest payments occurring through the Fisher effect is so obvious that even the tax authorities have had to readjust their definition of what constitutes interest income for tax purposes, and hence indexed debt is common. For our purposes, we cannot analyze the recent problems of debt capacity and refinancing in the international financial system without analyzing these inflationary effects on nominal bond contracts. Moreover, nominal bonds through the nominal interest rate provide us with a good estimate of the expected inflation rate, since the real rate of return has historically been relatively constant.

Absolute Purchasing Power Parity

The impact of expected inflation on expected exchange rate changes is more subtle than that on nominal interest rates. Consider the determination of exchange rates under the gold system. Here, prior to 1914 an ounce of gold cost £4.43 in London and $20.67 in New York. The convertibility of pounds sterling and U.S. dollars into gold meant that their exchange rate $E[US\$:£]$ was effectively fixed at $4.67. This result can be viewed in another way. Suppose the exchange rate was fixed at $4.67 and the sterling price of gold was fixed at £4.43, what would the price of gold be in New York? In the absence of significant shipping delays and costs, it is evident that someone in New York can exchange $20.67 into £4.43, buy an ounce of gold in London, and then ship it back to New York. Hence, if the price of gold in New York exceeds $20.67 an ounce by much more than these shipping costs, *commodity arbitrage* will take place; arbitrageurs will buy gold in London and then ship it back and sell it in New York for an arbitrage profit. Hence the action of commodity arbitrageurs fixes the price of gold in New York.

The principle that we have developed was termed by David Hume the *law of one price*. Simply stated, it means that in a market without restrictions on supply

---

COMMODITY ARBITRAGE AND THE GOLD POINTS

Exchange rates prior to 1914 were determined under the gold system.
Price of gold in London £4.43 per ounce
Price of gold in New York $20.67 per ounce
Hence $20.67:£4.43 or $4.67:£ is the equilibrium exchange rate.
Assuming it costs $0.30 per ounce to ship gold between London and New York, the effective dollar price of gold in London had to be

   $20.67 ± $0.30   or $20.37 to $20.97

If the effective dollar price of gold fell below $20.37 in London, gold would be purchased in London, shipped to and resold in New York for $20.67. Hence the exchange rate would have a lower bound of 4.598. Any value below that would yield after transactions cost arbitrage profits. Similarly, the exchange rate could not exceed 4.734. Otherwise gold would be purchased in New York for resale in London. These limits on the exchange rate were termed the gold points.

and demand, one price clears the market. In this case, the dollar price of gold in New York must equal the equivalent dollar price of gold in London, i.e.,

$$P_\$^g = E[\text{US\$}:\pounds]P_\pounds^g \tag{9-3}$$

In practice, the two prices of gold, in London $P_\pounds^g$ and in New York $P_\$^g$, were fixed by the governments, so that Equation (9-3) determined the exchange rate. In this case, the shipping costs just created an upper and lower bound for the exchange rate, above or below which commodity arbitrage would take place through shipments of gold. These bounds were easily determined in the nineteenth century, since the shipping costs were well known. The bounds were termed the *gold points*.

The implication of Equation (9-3) and the law of one price is that the exchange rate is equal to the ratio of the purchasing power of the two currencies in terms of gold. If we extend this principal to other traded commodities, we can see that in the absence of significant shipping costs, commodity arbitrage will always take place to ensure that the exchange rate is equal to the ratio of the purchasing power of both currencies in terms of that commodity. Moreover, the overall price level in any country is just a weighted average of the prices of all commodities in that country's currency. Hence, some people claim that the exchange rate is just the ratio of the general purchasing power of two countries' currencies. That is,

$$E[\text{US\$}:\pounds] = \frac{P_\$}{P_\pounds} \tag{9-4}$$

where $P_\$$ and $P_\pounds$ are the overall price indexes in the United States and Great Britain, respectively. This idea is called *absolute purchasing power parity* (APPP).

Whenever we look at salaries in different countries and multiply by the exchange rate to get an idea of what jobs pay in different countries, we are implicitly assuming that APPP holds, that is, that the purchasing power of that money is identical. However, in practice this is not the case. This became readily apparent to the U.S. administrators of Marshall Plan aid after the Second World War, who found that someone in Britain earning £357, or the equivalent of $1000, could actually buy goods and services worth $1625 in the United States. This was partly because the basket of goods and services differed between the United States and Great Britain. However, it was also discovered that an American living in Great Britain could buy an identical basket of goods and services for £357 that would cost $1417 in the United States. Hence, assuming PPP holds and multiplying British wages by the exchange rate $E[\text{US\$}:\pounds]$ of $2.80 was inappropriate, since it unnecessarily rewarded Americans who could spend their income in Great Britain.

The problem that this example highlights in fact has a long history; it is caused because not all commodities obey the simple law of one price. Some commodities have very high shipping or transaction costs, so that their price is determined in the local market, completely independent of world prices. For example, a haircut may cost $10 in a typical U.S. town but only 10 cents in a less developed country. Obviously, there is no commodity arbitrage; transportation costs make it uneconomic to leave the United States purely for a haircut, while immigration laws prevent the barber from coming to the United States. The result is that a country's price index reflects a weighted average of *traded* commodities, where the price closely follows Hume's law of one price, and *nontraded* commodities, where prices bear little correlation internationally. Obviously, this distinction is one of degree, where the dividing line is determined partly by international transportation costs and partly by government intervention which by quotas and tariffs can make any traded good nontraded.

Relative Purchasing Power Parity

If we return to Equation (9-4) we can modify absolute PPP by stating that the ratio of the two price levels is equal to the exchange rate times a departure from APPP, which we can call K. That is,

$$K \; E[\text{US\$:£}] \; = \; \frac{P_S}{P_£} \tag{9-5}$$

For example, if £357 buys the same basket of goods as $1417 in the United States, then the ratio on the right-hand side is 3.969. Since the exchange rate $E[\text{US\$:£}]$ just after World War II was 2.8, we can see that K equals 1.4175. This is essentially an adjustment for traded versus nontraded goods. Now suppose because of inflation the price level in Great Britain increases by 10 percent, and that in the United States by 5 percent. If the departure from APPP is constant, so that the proportion of traded to nontraded goods is constant, then the exchange rate has to change. If we let e equal the change in the exchange rate, we have

$$K \; E[\text{US\$:£}] \; (1+e) \; = \; \frac{P_S(1+I_S)}{P_£(1+I_£)} \tag{9-6}$$

but since $K \; E[\text{US\$:£}] \; = \; P_S/P_£$, we have *relative purchasing power parity* (RPPP), which states that

$$1 + e = \frac{1+I_S}{1+I_£} \tag{9-7}$$

the change in the exchange rate is equal to the ratio of the two countries' rates of inflation.

Relative PPP is much more general than absolute PPP, since it will hold regardless of the value of the deviation from APPP. Since we know that government intervention and transportation costs can cause permanent deviations from absolute PPP, we should only base our predictions on relative PPP. However, all we need to link exchange rate changes and inflationary expectations is relative PPP, since if it holds the expected exchange rate change from (9-7) is equal to the ratio of 1 plus the expected inflation rates in both countries. For convenience, we normally subtract 1 from both sides and rearrange Equation (9-7) to obtain

$$e = \frac{I_\$ - I_\pounds}{1 + I_\pounds} \qquad (9\text{-}8)$$

Note that the denominator is not equal to 1. Just using the differential inflation rates is not enough, since in high inflationary environments we are using relative PPP incorrectly and the error can be significant.

Integration of the Parity Relationships

With the discussion of relative PPP we have all the basic components of the international parity relationships. These are all pulled together in Figure 9-2. If we observe the nominal interest rate differential between countries with no restrictions on capital flows, we have two routes to an exchange rate forecast. First, because of *interest rate parity* the nominal interest rate differential is equal to the forward discount or premium. However, if a speculative market exists, this discount or premium is equal to the expected exchange rate change. Hence, in the short run, nominal interest rate differentials reflect exchange rate changes.

Second, the *Fisher effect* implies that the nominal interest rate differential *results* from differential inflation rates. This is because without restrictions on capital movements, capital will flow where the *real* rate of return is higher. Hence the real interest rate will be equalized across countries with open capital markets. Moreover from *relative PPP* this inflation differential must be offset by exchange rate changes. Otherwise the real price of traded commodities would differ across countries, and commodity arbitrage would take place. Hence in the longer term we would expect the nominal interest rate differential on longer-term securities to reflect longer-term exchange rate changes. The result that we can go directly from interest rate differentials to exchange rate changes is often called the international Fisher effect.

The upshot of putting these relationships together is that we have a consistent model for the determination of exchange rates and interest rates. Since all these values are monetary phenomena, their determination should be looked at in terms of monetary theory. Hence the inflation rate is at the heart of all these relationships. Moreover, the inflation rate itself is a function of a country's monetary policy. It is for this reason that the approach that generates these parity relationships has been termed the *monetary approach to exchange rate determination and the balance of payments*.

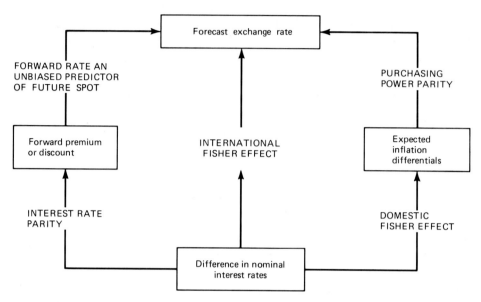

FIGURE 9-2
International parity relationships.

A Random Walk in the Exchange Market

If we refer back to the interest rate parity conditions of Equation (9-1) and substitute our assumption of an unbiased forward rate, we have

$$S_1 = \frac{1+R_1}{1+R_1^*} S_2 \tag{9-9}$$

where subscripts 1 and 2 denote the time period for the spot exchange rates and interest rates and S_2 is the expected exchange rate. The significance of Equation (9-9) is that it is a *present value* equation. The present value of the spot exchange rate is the discounted value of the expected future spot exchange rate, where the discount rate is determined by the foreign and domestic nominal interest rates. Moreover, this relationship will be expected to hold for the spot rate as of time period 2. Hence, repeatedly substituting, we determine that the spot exchange rate at any point in time is a function of interest rate expectations in both countries and the expected future exchange rate.

Equation (9-9) enables us to answer the question of why exchange rates fluctuate in a different way from that presented in Chapter 7. Once we recognize that the spot exchange rate is just another present value relationship, it follows that in an *efficient market* it will fluctuate for exactly the same reasons as other present value relationships, like those for bonds and common equities. That is, new information arriving randomly will alter the market's expectation for the future spot rate S_2, and the market's discount rate $(1+R_1)/(1+R_1^*)$. Hence it is to be expected that the spot exchange rate will fluctuate randomly in exactly the same manner as the prices determined in these other efficient financial markets.

The existence of open capital markets thus provides an additional explanation for the random fluctuation in exchange rates. In addition to the fluctuation induced by random import and export demand functions, we have changing expectations of future exchange rates and interest rates, causing short-term capital movements to enforce interest rate parity. These short-term capital movements have come to be called *hot money*, since the capital moves from one country to another in search of the highest effective yield. Since the 1973 floating of exchange rates removed much of the justification for capital controls, we have witnessed a significant increase in capital mobility and an increased amount of hot money. Hence this view of the determination of exchange rates, emphasizing an *asset-market approach* similar to that of the bond and equity markets, has increased in popularity.

IMPERFECTIONS IN THE FOREIGN EXCHANGE MARKETS—WHY SHORT-RUN DISEQUILIBRIUM MODELS OFFER OPPORTUNITIES FOR PROFITS

The international parity relationships are all *equilibrium* conditions, based upon a set of assumptions about how financial and real commodity markets operate. An implicit assumption, in fact, is that real and monetary phenomena can be separated. For example, if a country pursues a lax monetary policy and thus generates inflation, the assumption of the model is that investors protect themselves by higher nominal interest rates and that real commodity flows are unaffected, since price changes are offset by changes in the exchange rate. Hence neither borrowers and lenders nor exporters and importers are affected by inflation. It follows that real transactions, determined by comparative advantage in investment opportunities and trade, are unaffected by monetary policy and inflation.

Clearly these relationships may hold in the long run as investors incorporate their experiences with inflation into their inflationary expectations, and as exporters and importers adapt their contracting relationships to an inflationary environment. However, in the short run it is by no means certain that these real markets are capable of correctly incorporating inflationary expectations. Hence real transactions may be distorted and the exchange rate may change for reasons other than relative PPP. Hence, in this section, we consider some of the assumptions underlying the parity relationships that may not hold and the role that this leaves for management by both the government and the multinational.

Of the international parity relationships only interest rate parity must hold to a close approximation. This is because only this relationship is based upon *arbitrage* and the absence of excessive profit opportunities. However, even this relationship works only for countries without foreign exchange controls and with an active forward market. These conditions are met, however, for the main international trading countries, and de facto for other countries that fix their exchange rate in terms of these currencies.

Some have claimed, however, that the forward rate is not an unbiased expectation of the expected future spot rate and that it consistently over- or underestimates it. The argument is that the speculators in the forward market require a risk premium for undertaking the risky investment of buying or selling forward contracts. The problem is that any premium *earned* by the purchaser of a forward contract must be *paid* by the vendor. This conceivably could happen if one side of the forward market consisted of currency *hedgers*, people willing to pay a premium for removing risk, whereas the other consisted of currency *speculators*, people demanding a premium to bear risk. However, this would then imply that foreign currency hedging is all one-way; that is, people selling, say, deutsche marks forward are hedgers, whereas those buying include speculators because of a hedging gap. This gap would exist because of an insufficient supply of hedgers willing to sell deutsche marks (i.e., buy dollars) forward. In practice, no consistent premium has been found in empirical tests, and this idea of a hedging gap has proved elusive. Hence it seems difficult not to accept the idea that the forward rate is an unbiased expectation of the future spot rate.

For these reasons, most managers should accept interest rate parity and forward market efficiency as basic descriptors of the international money market. The problem comes in determining the expected future spot rate, since this causes all the other relationships to fall into place; it equals the forward rate and it causes the short-term capital movements that enforce interest rate parity. The international parity relationships place inflation differentials, via purchasing power parity, as the cause of exchange rate changes. However, this is a very simple way of looking at exchange rate changes. To see why, we need to examine purchasing power parity a little more.

Deviations from Purchasing Power Parity

Note that in deriving relative PPP in Equation (9-6) we assumed that K, the deviation from absolute PPP, remained constant. Alternatively, we could have said that a change in K with a given inflation differential would cause a further change in the exchange rate. Such an inflation-adjusted exchange rate change is often called a *real* exchange rate change. Moreover, in formulating PPP, we just about removed all factors other than differential inflation rates that could have affected the exchange rate. In practice, over the last 20 years or so the differential inflation rates have been so large that PPP has been the main factor in determining exchange rate changes. However, that is not to say that it is the *only* factor or that PPP will be just as good a predictor in a future of lower inflation as it has been in the past.

There are three main factors that determine K. First, K depends on the proportion of traded to nontraded goods and thus the proportion of prices determined internationally and domestically. Hence any innovations in transportation costs or transactions costs will cause this proportion to change and with it the real exchange rate. Second, the government distorts real exchange rates by distorting the pattern of international trade and capital flows. Hence any change in tariffs, quotas, foreign exchange controls, or implicit trade restrictions will affect the real exchange rate. Finally and fundamentally, the real exchange rate is a price that is determined by a country's comparative advantage, since this determines the underlying trade and capital flows. Hence any change in this comparative advantage in trade or investment opportunities will cause a change in the real exchange rate. Such factors would include increased labor productivity, the discovery of new raw materials, and technological changes.

Suppose, for example, a country were in equilibrium in that on an official settlements basis its balance of payments was zero. Hence there was no government intervention in the foreign exchange market. Suppose further that technological change then rendered some of its exports obsolete, so that exports declined and an official settlements deficit resulted. In this situation the real exchange rate should change. What we have to ask is, what are the adjustment mechanisms that will remove the official settlements deficit? We have already discussed the adjustment mechanism under fixed exchange rates, since this is identical to that of the gold standard. Essentially, the loss of foreign exchange reserves causes a decline in the money stock and deflation. As prices decline, exports become more competitive and increase, whereas imports become more expensive and decrease. What is of more interest is the adjustment mechanism under floating exchange rates. Will a decline in the exchange rate, resulting from a withdrawal of government intervention, solve the problem?

In Chapter 7, when we discussed the stability of the foreign exchange market, we implicitly discussed one of the main adjustment mechanisms, that is, through prices. Remember that the competitiveness of our exports depends on the domestic price level and the exchange rate, which *together* determine the price for foreign purchasers. Hence, with fixed exchange rates exports increase only if the domestic price level decreases. Conversely, if domestic deflation is ruled out on political grounds, exports will increase only if the exchange rate depreciates. For imports the argument is just reversed. Hence a depreciating currency will spur exports and retard imports. The only qualification is that mentioned in Chapter 7, that initially this could cause overshooting in the foreign exchange market or a further worsening in the official settlements balance, since there are lags to changing the pattern of exports and imports. This initial deterioration, before eventual improvement, is often called the *J curve*.

The significance of the depreciation of the currency is that it changes the "terms of trade," or the relative prices faced by a country. These changed prices, through the principles discussed in Chapter 2, will through comparative advantage alter a country's mix of exports and imports. Some commodities will now be produced locally that were previously imported, a phenomenon called *import substitution*. Some commodities will now be exported that were previously not competitive internationally. Hence the devaluation will be most successful when a country is flexible in switching resources from one product into another. If, for example, the obsolete exports were manufactured goods, the devaluation will be successful if these employees and factories can quickly be absorbed by other manufacturing firms able to produce import substitutes or competitive exports. However, if the obsolete exports were in a unique product that dominates a country's economy, then switching the resources into other industries can be a long and painful process. Hence the devaluation may not be effective.

Nonprice Adjustments

Classical economists have emphasized the relative price changes that result from a devaluation. However, in the 1930s, J. M. Keynes pointed out that there was an *income* adjustment mechanism too. Suppose the devaluation was a policy act by the government to increase exports at a time of unemployment in the domestic economy. In this case the increased exports would increase the level of national income and thus have a *multiplier* effect on other sectors of the economy, as the increased income is paid out in wages and dividends and then used to buy other goods and services. However, some of this income will leak out to be spent on imports, the exact amount depending on the Keynesian *marginal propensity to import*. It is thus conceivable that with a very high marginal propensity to import, the income effect largely offsets the positive price effect of a devaluation.

Sidney Alexander synthesized these two mechanisms in what has come to be called the *absorption* approach. Consider the national income identity

$$Y = C + I + G + (X-M) \tag{9-10}$$

where Y is aggregate production (supply); C, I, and G are consumption, investment, and government expenditures, respectively; and X and M are exports and imports, respectively. If we rearrange (9-10), we obtain

$$X-M = Y - (C+I+G) \tag{9-11}$$

where we can define $(C+I+G)$ as absorption A. Hence a balance of payments imbalance implies that aggregate supply Y does not equal domestic absorption. Simply stated, the economy is consuming more goods and services than it itself is producing.

If exports are less than imports and a country devalues, it is evident from (9-11) that national production Y has to increase by more than domestic absorption. This occurs when relative price changes cause increased production of exports and import substitutes and the resulting increased production is not offset by a more than proportional increase in domestic absorption of goods and services. Hence, from the absorption approach, a devaluation would be successful when the marginal propensity to import is low and thus the domestic absorption of goods and services does not outstrip the increased production of goods and services.

These two adjustment mechanisms, of price and income synthesized in the absorption approach, determine how quickly the economy responds to a devaluation. Note, however, that we began by assuming a decrease in exports due to technological obsolescence, and thus were concerned about a real change in the exchange rate. The opposite case would be where domestic inflation has out-stripped foreign inflation. In this case, with government intervention to maintain the exchange rate, exports decrease. The foreign price for exports increases, as domestic price increases due to inflation are not offset by a depreciation of the currency. Imports increase for the opposite reason; the domestic price of imports is constant, whereas all the domestic competitors find their prices increasing because of domestic inflation. Moreover, national income would then decline as domestic production is outcompeted by imports and foreign demand for exports declines.

If the official settlements imbalance comes about for the latter reason of exchange rate intervention in the face of domestic inflation, then we are artifi-cially subsidizing imports and penalizing exports. However, the shift of resources out of the export sector will still take place. If the exchange rate is then devalued, we are just restoring the natural pattern of trade and capital flows. In this case, if the overvaluation has not been maintained for too long, the economy should quickly respond as resources can more easily be reallocated.

The upshot of this discussion is that the need to reallocate resources creates a lag in the removal of an official settlement's imbalance, and the movement of the exchange rate to its equilibrium value. Hence purchasing power parity cannot be expected to hold continuously. Studies done for the EEC economies have sug-gested that the effects of a devaluation are completely removed within 2 to 3 years. The corollary to these studies is that it takes 2 to 3 years for the resources to be reallocated in response to a devaluation, and that during this period there is a deviation from relative purchasing power parity. Hence we can envisage a situa-tion analogous to that of a ship sailing across the Atlantic. Its captain knows its ultimate destination but periodically will have to plot a new course as the ship gets blown off course by currents and storms. For exchange rates, as well as knowing how off course they are at a point in time, we also have to determine what the original course was!

EXCHANGE RATE FORECASTING

In the first two sections of this chapter we have developed the international parity relationships and discussed the short-run adjustment mechanisms. In this section we will discuss the essentials of constructing an exchange rate forecast. For the MNE dealing in an environment of floating exchange rates, it is important to come up with a forecast of the exchange rate for three basic reasons. First, it is required to determine the long-run allocation of funds; i.e., it is a required input for the MNE's capital budgeting decision. Second, it is required for short-run funds positioning, to ensure that funds are not located in a devaluing currency where their lost value is not compensated for by higher interest rates. Third, it is required for control purposes to ensure that management in foreign subsidiaries are held accountable only for factors that they can control. We will elaborate on all these uses of the foreign exchange forecast in Chapter 18. Here we note that a foreign exchange forecast is an important input for the efficient functioning of the MNE.

There are four types of foreign exchange forecast. First, there is the *opinion-gathering* forecast, which relies on a sampling of the views of experts. This type of forecast is quite common with the proliferation of investment newsletters. However, it is not an independent forecast, since we have no specification of how the experts derived their forecast. Second, we have the *technical* or *chartist* forecast, which attempts to forecast future values, based on some pattern evident in the exchange rate's past values. Most technical analysts forecast future values for a whole range of commodities, from orange juice, gold, and shares of IBM to the value of the deutsche mark. In fact, most technical analysts will forecast without knowing what the actual commodity is! That is, all they require for their forecast is a chart of past values, plus some other statistics such as volume of trading.

Theoretically, it is hard to justify technical analysis as a credible forecast, since the forecast violates the most basic assumptions of the *efficient markets hypothesis* (EMH). The weakest form of the EMH states quite simply that all relevant information contained in a price series is already reflected in the current market price. If this were not so, individuals could make money by utilizing some simple trading rule, for example, sell on two consecutive price increases. Moreover, this would then imply that the person buying would lose money. At its most basic, the EMH simply asserts that there is no "free lunch" in financial markets.

The observation that the foreign exchange market is efficient produces the result discussed earlier that exchange rates follow a random walk. If the prices do reflect all available information, then since new information must arrive randomly, the price or exchange rate will move randomly to incorporate that information. Hence the volatility of exchange rates, like that of stock prices, is an inevitable by-product of an efficient market. Unfortunately, it then implies that charting these random movements has no value whatsoever.

Analysis of simple trading rules, used by technical analysis in the stock market, has found that such rules do not allow an investor to earn an abnormal rate of return. Preliminary studies of the foreign exchange markets have shown that exchange rates do behave in a similar manner to stock prices, the implication being that forecasts based on technical analysis should not be able to "beat the market."

The third type of forecast is the *monetarist model* based upon purchasing power parity. We have seen that provided that comparative advantage, transactions costs, and government intervention are all constant, exchange rate changes should follow inflation rate differentials. It follows that a forecast based upon inflation differentials, with a qualification added to reflect government intervention, should be reasonably good. In fact, most monetarist models use the change in a country's foreign exchange reserves to adjust for any government intervention. Thus a loss in foreign exchange reserves indicates government intervention to support the value of the currency. The size of the foreign exchange reserves left, and this intention to support the exchange rate, would then qualify any forecast based on inflation differentials alone.

The fourth type of forecast is the *fundamental* or *econometric* forecast. This type of forecast is largely a by-product of a major macroeconomic forecast for an economy as a whole. Hence, for example, as a by-product of its forecast of the U.S. economy, the Wharton economic forecasting unit will produce a forecast of the value for the U.S. dollar. Statistically, most of the econometric forecasts are based on multiple regression analysis or multiple discriminant analysis. The construction of these types of forecasts is inherently Keynesian in relying upon the standard Keynesian constructs of marginal propensities to import and the corresponding income multipliers. More recently, as the market for foreign exchange forecasts has expanded, fundamental forecasts have been constructed independently of the main economic models. In this framework, monetarist models can then be viewed as simple econometric or fundamental models.

EFFICIENT MARKETS HYPOTHESIS

In discussing technical forecasts, we noted that if the foreign exchange market is efficient, such a forecast based simply on past values should not be able to beat the market. Technical analysis is particularly suspect, since it violates the *weak-form* version of the EMH in that it uses only published past prices. However, the econometric and monetarist models violate the *semistrong* version of the EMH, because you should not be able to use *any* information that is publicly available to make excess returns. All the data used in monetarist and econometric forecasts are publicly available. The efficient markets hypothesis is particularly relevant to the foreign exchange market, since we have a forward rate that with a speculative futures market should equal the expected future spot rate. Hence we have a free short-term forecast available in every morning newspaper that publishes spot and forward rates.

EFFICIENT MARKETS HYPOTHESIS

Form	Type of information already reflected in market prices
Weak	Prices reflect *all* the information contained in the record of past prices.
Semistrong	Prices reflect all publicly available information.
Strong	Prices reflect all information available, that is, private information that can only be acquired by expensive research, as well as publicly available information.

Source: H. Roberts. "Statistical versus Clinical Prediction of the Stock Market," unpublished University of Chicago paper, May 1967.

The idea that the forward rate is a *free* forecast that is as good as any other average forecast is obviously a threat to those advisory services *selling* foreign exchange rate forecasts. It was in response to this idea that Chase Econometrics explicitly discussed the construction of their foreign exchange forecast in February 1976 in *Euromoney*, a professional trade journal. In Exhibit 9-3 we outline the main variables included in the Chase Econometric's forecast at that time, and the reasons for including them. The Chase rebuttal of the use of the forward rate was based upon an explanation of the construction of their forecast and their claimed ability to beat the market. That is, they provided evidence that they correctly forecasted exchange rate values, when the forward rate did not.

Testing Forecast Accuracy

More recently, Richard Levich (1981) has analyzed the predictive abilities of thirteen foreign exchange forecasters for *Euromoney* magazine, in what is becoming an annual ratings contest. He uses two tests, one to determine whether a forecaster's mean absolute forecast error is greater or less than that of the forward rate. This test is designed to test overall *forecasting accuracy*. The second test is to determine whether the forecast is on the right side of the forward rate. That is, if

EXHIBIT 9-3
CHASE ECONOMETRIC'S FORECAST VARIABLES
(February 1976)

Variable	Reason
Trade balance	Supply and demand of currencies for trade purposes
Inflation	PPP impact on future trade balance
Real expected growth	Keynesian import multiplier. Increased income means increased imports
Capacity utilization	Used with above, if low with high growth then capacity increases, *good*; if high with high growth then demand pulls inflation, *bad*
Foreign exchange reserves	Government flexibility to intervene in foreign exchange market
Productivity	Affects long-run comparative advantage and real exchange rate
Wage performance	Affects future price performance and through PPP the exchange rate
Government deficit	Monetization of national debt affects future inflation rate
Short interest rates	Through Fisher effect produces an exchange rate forecast

the forecast is higher than the forward rate and the exchange rate actually is higher than the forward rate, then the forecast is regarded as a success. The idea here is to test not the accuracy of the forecast but whether or not the forecaster forecasts in the right *direction*.

The results of Levich's analysis are what we would expect from the efficient market's hypothesis. *As a group*, forecasters do not possess any ability to consistently beat the forward rate. Their mean absolute forecast errors are generally greater than that of the forward rate, and they do not consistently forecast the direction of exchange rate movements any better than the forward rate. This is what we would expect, since these same forecasting techniques are used by hedgers and speculators in establishing the forward rate in the first place.

However, within this group some forecasters are better than others. In the 1981 tests Predex and Conticurrency exhibited significant forecasting abilities. In 1982, the overall forecasting standards declined, as the rise of the U.S. dollar took all the forecasters by surprise. However, the Wharton forecast and Predex's short-

---

SPECULATION IN THE FUTURES MARKET

The Chicago Mercantile Exchange established the International Money Market (IMM) in May 1972. Trading is conducted through public outcry in eight currencies; deutsche mark, Swiss franc, pound sterling, Japanese yen, Canadian dollar, Mexican peso, French franc, and Dutch guilder; volume in the latter three currencies is negligible. Each contract is completely standardized, for example, pound sterling is for £25,000, and all are for delivery on the third Wednesday of March, June, September, or December. All prices are quoted in terms of U.S. dollars.

The mechanics are for an individual to open an account with a broker, who will then execute the transaction against the Clearing House. To execute a trade, an individual has to post two margin accounts to ensure fulfillment of the contract. An initial margin is set by the exchange for every standardized contract. This margin can be posted in interest-bearing government securities. Contracts are then *marked to market every day*, so that gains and losses are realized daily. In the futures market the fact that contracts are marked to market each day ensures that contracts will be met. In the forward market, the lack of this monitoring leaves the bank open to the risk of nonfulfillment. Hence the market is simply closed off to smaller investors and companies.

There is a direct link between the IMM futures market and the interbank forward market. The arbitrage that results keeps the forward and futures rates consistent. Following the IMM, there have been foreign currency futures markets established on the New York Futures Exchange, (NYFE), the London International Financial Futures Exchange (LIFFE), and the Toronto Futures Exchange (TFE). However, trading volumes on these markets have been low as transactions continue to flow to the IMM.

The IMM is a purely speculative market; it is not particularly well suited for the commercial customer that wishes to remove foreign exchange risks. First, the daily settlement is at the least annoying. Second, the contracts are standardized, whereas most commercial transactions are not for "round lots." Third, the delivery dates are fixed. The latter two restrictions mean that, in practice, the futures market cannot remove all foreign exchange risk and is thus dominated by the interbank forward market.

term forecast (again) achieved statistically significant forecasting results. Again this is consistent with EMH; market efficiency does not say that individuals with superior ability cannot make excess returns but just that everybody cannot have superior ability.

As a qualification to Levich's assessments, we should note that he rated fundamental or econometric forecasters. He did not include an assessment of the accuracy of technical or chartist forecasts. Goodman (1979) has performed such an assessment and found that a mixture of technical forecasts could have beat the market. However, his statistical analysis is not as rigorous as Levich's, and it remains to be seen whether or not his preliminary results stand up to more comprehensive analyses.

The evidence on foreign exchange forecasting is that the market is efficient, and thus the forward rate is at least as good as the average forecast sold by advisory services. However, some advisory services do have expertise, in the same way that some security analysts can pick undervalued stock. Where does this leave the MNE? Well for one thing, MNEs have the resources and the need to produce superior forecasts. Hence most MNEs would most probably find it advantageous to forecast exchange rates. However, the cost of this exercise must be weighed against its benefits. These can be determined by the accuracy of the in-house forecasts using Levich's statistical techniques.

FOREIGN EXCHANGE OPTIONS MARKET

The fact that the futures contract is marked to market each day is also a limitation for the small speculator, who would like to limit the downside risk and remove the annoyance of frequent margin calls. It is to meet these twin needs that foreign currency call and put options have been introduced. Call options give the purchaser the right to buy a specific amount of foreign currency at an agreed price (the exercise price) and the put option the purchaser has the right to sell. Like the IMM futures contracts, the contracts are standardized with fixed amounts and maturity dates on the third Wednesday of March, June, September, and December. The exercise price is set by the exchange, with all prices expressed in U.S. dollar equivalent values. Trading is conducted on the Montreal and Philadelphia Stock Exchanges.

Foreign currency options give the small investor a chance to speculate on foreign exchange rates. The purchase of the option involves an initial cash outlay and no further commitment; so the loss is strictly controlled. If the exchange rate subsequently exceeds the exercise price fixed in the contract, the holder can buy the foreign exchange at the fixed exercise price and then simultaneously execute a spot transaction selling the foreign currency for a certain profit. The fact that contracts are standardized with the same maturity as IMM futures contracts encourages speculation across the different speculative contracts. To protect the exchange which guarantees execution of all contracts, all investors selling or "writing" call options have to post margin accounts with the options clearinghouse.

Foreign currency options have proved to be very popular. Currently about half of the Philadelphia Stock Exchange's volume comes from European traders. The largest class of individual customers seems to be corporate treasurers hedging general exchange risk, not specific transactions.

THE MNE AND EXCHANGE RATE DETERMINATION

So far we have not discussed the role of the MNE in exchange rate determination, the reason being that we have sought to emphasize the dual relationship between the balance of payments and the foreign exchange market. Moreover, we have justified the trade and capital flows that determine the balance of payments and the resulting exchange rate, on the basis of comparative advantage and government intervention. However, just as we could not justify all trade and capital flows from the simpler concepts of comparative advantage, in that we needed the MNE to explain some flows, so too it becomes apparent that the MNE is needed for a full explanation of the exchange rate.

Consider, for example, a non-MNE world. In this case, some information-rich commodities will be imported, because the exporting producer will not accept the risks of foreign licensing. Hence the importing country will have to export more to provide the foreign exchange resources to maintain the same foreign exchange rate. However, with the MNE the import is replaced by a foreign subsidiary. Hence, instead of the continuous burden of imports, we have some initial capital inflows to build the subsidiary, followed by a series of capital outflows as dividends are remitted. However, this dividend, representing a return on investment, would in effect be included in the price of the import anyway through the product's gross margin. Hence the outflow for dividends will be considerably smaller than the corresponding outflow for imports. In effect, all the other costs included in the import's value, such as labor and materials, are now being sourced internally, with a commensurate reduction in the burden on the foreign exchange rate.

This line of reasoning inexorably leads to the conclusion that MNEs through a reduction of trade will affect the equilibrium exchange rate. However, the effects are by no means clear-cut. For one thing the increase in local demand for labor may affect the local wage rate, which will itself affect comparative advantage as some labor-intensive exports are no longer competitive in the world market. Second, the time pattern of inflows and outflows is altered, since with an MNE subsidiary we will initially have capital inflows, followed by capital outflows, rather than the continuous outflow on imports. Third, at least among the industrialized countries, internalization produces a proliferation of MNEs of all nationalities, so that the net effect is uncertain. Finally, in the less developed countries, government intervention may have prohibited the imports anyway, particularly when they are of western consumer luxuries. Hence the effect of the MNE is often just the capital flows, with no offsetting import reduction.

That the MNE through altering the pattern of international trade affects exchange rates should be reasonably obvious. Moreover, this effect is entirely positive, since the MNE is substituting for markets that are not operating efficiently. What is questionable is whether MNEs contribute to the instability of exchange rates. We have already noted that MNEs through leading and lagging intracorporate payments contributed substantially to the speculation against sterling in 1967. There is no doubt that such techniques today contribute to the amount of short-term capital movements or hot money. From the point of view of governments, intent on preserving a particular exchange rate value, this is obviously undesirable and explains why many countries have regulations that dictate collection and payment periods on international transactions.

However, just because governments find such practices undesirable should not blind us to *why* such practices exist. MNEs lead and lag payments to protect themselves from imminent losses from currency devaluations. Such losses would not be imminent if the exchange rates were allowed to adjust freely to changed economic circumstances. In a freely floating exchange rate environment, the MNE's leading and lagging techniques are not significant, since exchange rate expectations are then formed on the basis of an efficient foreign exchange market. If governments intervene to fix exchange rates, different from what they would be in an efficient market, it creates an economic incentive for participants to gain at the government's expense. Rather than criticize the MNEs, it makes more sense to criticize the government for intervening and distorting market prices. It is noteworthy that criticism of the MNE is largest in countries that fix the value of their currency in the belief that they know more than the market about its appropriate value.

In summary, we can say that MNEs undoubtedly affect exchange rates, both by affecting the flows of international trade and through short-term capital movements. However, no negative connotations should be attached to this phenomenon, since in both cases the MNE is simply substituting for a failure in the market, either for technological reasons or by government fiat.

SUMMARY

In this chapter we have discussed the economic theory of exchange rate determination. Initially, we examined the long-run relationships characterizing an equilibrium in the international economic and financial system. Here, we noted that the key concepts of interest rate parity, forward market efficiency, purchasing power parity, and the Fisher effect all combined to present an integrated theory of exchange rate determination. This approach emphasizes the monetary theory underlying the balance of payments and the foreign exchange rate. Recent refinements to this theory have tended to look at the foreign exchange market as an asset market, where the exchange rate, like any other asset price, e.g., bond prices, is determined as a present value relationship. We saw, as a result, that exchange rates should then be expected to fluctuate randomly in the same way that bond and equity prices do.

In the second section we described how the international system is rarely in long-run equilibrium. Instead, there are constant changes in technology, government intervention, labor productivity, etc., that cause the basis for trade to change. As a result, there are persistent deviations from purchasing power parity as the exchange market moves back to equilibrium. During this disequilibrium period, the adjustment forces are the standard price and income adjustments of normal economics, synthesized as the "absorption approach" by Alexander.

In the final sections, we looked at the problem of forecasting exchange rates, given an efficient foreign exchange market. The techniques and results of opinion gatherers, chartists, monetarists, and econometricians were contrasted against this efficient market's background. Finally, we considered the role of the multinational in foreign exchange markets.

KEY WORDS

Forward market	Relative purchasing power parity
Spot market	Fisher effect
Futures market	Hot money
Hedge	Real interest rate
Covered interest arbitrage	Nominal interest rate
Arbitrageurs	Import substitution
Law of one price	Marginal propensity to import
Gold points	Efficient markets hypothesis
Absolute purchasing power parity	

QUESTIONS

1 Explain the forward exchange market and spot market. How can these markets be used as a hedge against future fluctuations in exchange rates?
2 What are the economic implications and significance of the international money market?
3 How does inflation affect the nominal interest rate? How can debts be arranged such that the rate of inflation does not affect the real cost of borrowing at all?
4 International organizations often pay their employees stationed overseas a salary based on purchasing power rather than their domestic salary translated into foreign currency. What are the reasons for this practice?
5 Describe four methods of foreign exchange forecasting. List the advantages and disadvantages of each type.
6 Do MNEs have a destabilizing effect on exchange rates? Explain.

PART FOUR

THE REGULATION OF INTERNATIONAL BUSINESS

THE INSTITUTIONAL ENVIRONMENT OF INTERNATIONAL BUSINESS

INTERNATIONAL ORGANIZATIONS AND INTERNATIONAL BUSINESS

The environment of international business is affected by organizations that work to regulate and expand world trade and investments. This chapter examines the major institutions involved in the regulation of international trade, international financial investment, foreign direct investment, and licensing. These agencies affect the strategy, tactics, and day-to-day operations of a firm engaged in international business, especially since their goals are often complex and even contradictory.

The chapter focuses on the international manager operating in a world system of nation states and international agencies—two types of bodies that present conflicting signals concerning trade opportunities. While nation states frequently regulate trade to achieve domestic goals, there exist today many international organizations whose objective is to promote trade and generate a movement toward world economic integration. The post-World War II movement toward trade liberalization and the type of international trading arrangements which exist today are now examined.

GENERAL AGREEMENT ON TARIFFS AND TRADE (GATT)

The General Agreement on Tariffs and Trade (GATT) was established in 1947 by twenty-three founding member nations. Today it has 100 members which include virtually all high-income, noncommunist countries, several of the communist countries of eastern Europe, and many low- and middle-income countries. The founding members of the GATT recognized that increases in tariffs worldwide during the later 1920s and 1930s had restricted world trade and deepened and prolonged the Great Depression. The GATT has three primary purposes: to serve as a forum in which nations can discuss trade issues, to provide an institutional context for negotiations to reduce trade barriers, and to facilitate negotiations between its members over trade disputes that have arisen between them. The GATT has established a number of principles to achieve its objectives to lower trade barriers and harmonize trade relations between nations.

The most important principle of the GATT is one of *nondiscrimination*. Broadly speaking, the principle of nondiscrimination requires that each member country must impose the same tariff rate to all member countries. This rate is referred to as the *most favored nation* (MFN) rate. Changes in tariffs negotiated between two countries must be applied to all member countries. There are three important general exceptions to the nondiscrimination principle (and many specific exceptions). First, the British Commonwealth preferences were retained. The importance of this exception has decreased over time as MFN tariff rates have been lowered relative to British Preferential rates. Second, groups of countries can band together in customs unions, free trade areas, or trading associations which charge lower tariffs between member countries than those imposed on countries outside the group.

Third, high-income countries have the right to grant General Preferential tariffs (GP) to low- and middle-income countries without extending these lower tariffs to other high-income countries. This concession was implemented to foster the growth and development of developing countries through trade. Developing countries are also in a special position in that the tariff concessions required of them during formal GATT negotiations are usually small. Also, they are allowed to retain their own often highly restrictive trade barriers if these barriers protect domestic industries. Developing countries, however, have little bargaining power within the GATT to achieve their specific trade goals. In particular, their exports of textiles, garments, footwear, wood products, and some processed agricultural products have come under highly restrictive quotas imposed by high-income countries.

The principle of nondiscrimination is designed to prevent one member country from raising tariffs against another country to impede trade without raising the tariff against all other countries. Nondiscrimination sometimes makes the negotiations for lowering tariffs more difficult and complicated but gives each nation a powerful incentive not to raise tariffs to block imports from a specific country. Such an increase could affect several of its trading partners since the increase would have to be applied to imports from all countries and they could jointly gang up on the offending country.

The second principle of the GATT is *tariff binding*. The member countries of the GATT have agreed to bind their tariffs at ceiling level. A country can charge a lower rate, but if they want to charge a rate above the bound rate, it must negotiate to "pay" for this action by lowering rates on other products or by allowing other nations to restrict some of its exports into their markets. Tariff binding acts as a powerful incentive not to raise tariffs to restrict imports of a given product.

Another important role of the GATT is as a forum for discussions about the settlement of international trade disputes. When the nations involved in a dispute cannot settle it by negotiations with each other, they can appeal to GATT. A committee of experts from member countries will then be set up to investigate the facts of the dispute and to facilitate the negotiations among the parties involved. If a settlement is not reached, the committee can make recommendations, and if these are not followed, countermeasures against the country not following the GATT rules can be authorized. This arbitration power is important because prior to GATT there was no mechanism in operation to settle disputes. Such disputes in the 1930s resulted in mutual retaliation and very high levels of trade barriers. One major aim of GATT was to avoid the repetition of such costly international tariff wars. While trade wars have been avoided, GATT has not been called on to resolve any really major trade disputes, and it is difficult to believe that it could do so, successfully, if it had to.

The seven rounds of GATT negotiations have achieved a substantial reduction in the levels of tariffs since 1947, especially for manufactured goods. As a consequence, there has been a continual and sustained increase in the volume of world trade. At the end of the Kennedy round of tariff cuts in 1967 the weighted average nominal tariff for major trading nations stood at 7.7 percent on industrial goods, 9.8 percent on semifinished products, and only 2 percent on raw materials. After the Tokyo round, average nominal tariffs were below 5 percent. It should be noted, however, that effective rates of protection are usually higher than these nominal rates.

Agricultural products have been an exception to the success story in manufacturing. Agriculture is an industry protected by special policies in most countries. Trade barriers in the form of tariffs, quotas, health standards, and other restrictions are still common in this sector.

During the Tokyo round of negotiations, for example, the European Economic Community (EEC) refused at the outset to negotiate concerning their Common Agricultural Policy (CAP). The CAP not only contains highly restrictive measures against agricultural imports (such as floating tariffs), but also enables the EEC to subsidize exports of its agricultural products. The Japanese policy toward trade in agricultural products (including high-variable tariffs, standards, and quotas) has been a continual bone of contention between the United States, Canada, and Japan.

The Tokyo round of negotiations, completed in 1978, was the first to consider nontariff barriers to trade. With the reductions in tariffs these barriers have become more important, and for some products, NTBs are the main restrictions on trade. The application of NTBs to restrict trade often violates the two fundamental principles of the GATT: nondiscrimination and binding. Quotas and voluntary export restraint agreements, the most important NTBs, are often applied on imports from one country or a group of countries. The size of a quota may be varied from year to year, in effect raising and lowering the degree of the protection. The governments of low- and middle-income countries feel that these exceptions to the principles of the GATT discriminate against them unfairly and allow the affluent to take advantage of the poor. High-income countries have erected quotas and special measures of protection on an increasing variety of products (e.g., clothing, textiles, footwear) produced by an ever-lengthening list of low- and middle-income countries just at a time when many of these countries have turned toward exports of labor-intensive manufactures to spur economic growth.

Trade in *services* has largely been left out of the GATT negotiations yet it is an increasingly large component of international trade. Exports of services—technology, finance, communications, media, data, information, and transportation—have become more important for high-income countries as they have progressively moved toward a postindustrial economy. Yet there is no international organization, concerned with the regulation of this trade, which could serve as a forum for reducing distortions in the international marketplace. Moreover, national regulation of trade in services is often based on highly charged, nationalistic considerations rather than economic ones so that negotiation is difficult. The United States is pressing for international negotiations to reduce the barriers to trade in services either by including them within the GATT or through a separate organization.

Finally, it is worth remembering that since the GATT deals only with trade in goods and is not concerned with trade in services or international investment except as they impact on trade, GATT has not considered the special role of MNEs in world trade. Yet MNEs offer alternatives to trade, as is discussed in the theoretical and policy sections of this text.

In addition to the GATT, a host of international organizations, agreements, and institutions are also involved in the regulation of international trade, finance, and the MNE. In the last decade, these have become increasingly important to the MNE in its international operations. Some of the more important of these multilateral agencies and institutions are now discussed.

UNITED NATIONS CONFERENCE ON TRADE AND DEVELOPMENT (UNCTAD)

The first United Nations Conference on Trade and Development (UNCTAD) was organized in 1964 and was attended by representatives of 119 countries. The countries involved felt that current international trade arrangements benefited primarily the developed countries and worked to the disadvantage of the developing countries. The Conference was established as a permanent UN organization and held five additional conferences to 1982. It now has a membership of 136 countries. These conferences have been used by the developing countries to press for trade concessions from the developed countries, as well as for other changes that would aid in their development.

The exports of the developing countries are mostly primary products, and trade in these goods is subject to price instability as market conditions change. The terms of trade, which refer to the quantity of imports that can be purchased with a given amount of exports, have also been turning against the developing countries, according to some economists, but not others. These countries allege that the terms of trade for primary products were declining relative to manufactured products, although the evidence on this is ambiguous. In response, the developing nations have attempted to increase the proportion of manufactured exports in their exports and to seek preferential entry into the markets of developed nations for all their exports, especially manufactured products. In addition, they have demanded that buffer stocks of primary products be set up to stabilize world prices at a "fair" level.

The main request at the early UNCTAD sessions, for a system of tariff preferences on the part of developed countries favoring the export of their manufactured goods from developing countries, was resisted by developed countries. The latter felt that preferences could have an adverse effect on some of their low-technology, labor-intensive industries, causing substantial unemployment in those industries, for example, in textiles. Despite the initial resistance, a system of preferential tariffs, with quota limitations on the amount imported from the developing countries, was eventually implemented. Today, exports which fall under GP tariffs from developing countries face lower tariffs than do exports of these products from developed countries.

At the more recent UNCTAD sessions, the developing countries have pressed for establishment of commodity agreements covering their major exports of raw materials and agricultural products. These types of agreement are discussed in a separate section. During a meeting in 1976, a proposed code of conduct covering the international transfer of technology was presented.

THE NEW INTERNATIONAL ECONOMIC ORDER (NIEO)

A resolution of the UN general assembly in May 1974 formalized many of the issues raised by UNCTAD in a declaration calling for a new international economic order. This declaration asked for measures to ensure a redistribution of world resources to "eliminate the widening gap between the developed and developing countries." It called for action in the areas of commodity price stabilization, preferential entry of manufactured exports from developing nations, transfer of appropriate technology, favorable financial arrangements, and regulation of MNEs, among other interventionist policies. The subsequent lack of action on this agenda is not surprising, although it had disappointed the developing nations. In addition to the NIEO declaration, UNCTAD has also stimulated a North-South dialogue; the North representing the industrialized nations and the South the less developed countries.

The countries of the less developed South are currently facing significant problems in their economic development programs and international trade. Their call for a restructuring of the world economic system has largely fallen on deaf ears, at least as far as tangible results are concerned. As discussed in a later section of this chapter, their desire for commodity buffer stocks to stabilize and raise prices has not been met. Beyond General Preferential tariffs, the demands for the North to further lower trade barriers have also not been satisfied. This chilly reception has been partially the result of the two conflicting arguments advanced by the South.

First, the countries of the South maintain higher tariffs and more restrictive NTBs (with Singapore and Hong Kong as notable exceptions) than do the countries of the North. Arguments based on reducing trade restrictions on efficiency grounds work both ways. If the North were to remove its trade restrictions, the South would benefit by an amount roughly equal to the amount of aid they are presently receiving ($25 billion). If the countries of the South also dropped their trade barriers, their terms of trade would deteriorate so far that they would be substantial net losers. The South's argument for a restructuring of world trade to increase efficiency, if followed by all countries, would hurt the South. Moreover, the projected increase in output in the South will only serve to turn the terms of trade further against it and lead to immiserizing growth, an effect that only the North could reverse by unilaterally dropping its trade restrictions.

Second, the South argues for a redistribution of world income based on equity considerations. Restructuring of world trade to even income distribution between countries leads to two problems. First, the South desires "Trade not aid," but world trade restrictions already work in favor of the South, and intervention to cause further shifts in the South's favor would only decrease world efficiency. Second, as shown before, restricting trade for purposes of income distribution is *not* the best means from an economic point of view. Direct transfers (aid) is the preferred method. The North, however, has become increasingly parsimonious with its aid money. Aid from high-income countries as a percentage of their GNP fell from 0.51 percent in 1960 to 0.35 percent in 1981.

COMMODITY AGREEMENTS

Commodity agreements are attempts by the major producing and consuming nations of a particular primary product to stabilize the price of the product. Price stability, in turn, leads to more stable incomes and can help to foster a planned program of growth and development. The mechanisms most commonly used in implementing a commodity agreement are buffer stocks or the use of quotas. These are generally applied to support agricultural, mining, or other resource-based products and exports.

When buffer stocks are used, floor and ceiling prices are set by agreement and a fund is set up to cover the costs of operating the buffer stock. When the price falls below the floor, purchases are made to add to the stock, and when prices are above the ceiling, sales are made from the stock. These purchases and sales are designed to keep the price within the set range and to stabilize incomes. Like many types of agricultural support programs, however, it is very difficult in practice to operate a successful commodity price stabilization scheme. While support is assured as prices fall, in a period of rising prices it is rare to find many participants willing to keep prices from rising by the sale of the buffer stocks. Instead, suppliers prefer to have higher income in boom periods and usually want support only to avoid the downside risk of a poor market. In the long run, most stabilization schemes have been found to be an ineffective means of income maintenance. An additional problem has arisen over which countries should contribute the capital to finance such a stabilization fund.

Export quotas can be used to keep the price up by limiting supply when the price starts to fall below some minimum level. Import quotas have also been used in some agreements to divide up sales and help maintain prices. The quotas are subject to the same problems as buffer stocks in that they intervene in the competitive market and become an inefficient device for stabilizing prices and incomes.

Unsuccessful commodity agreements include: tin, wheat, sugar, coffee, cocoa, olive oil, and textiles. The tin agreement was started in 1956, has thirty-five member countries, and uses buffer stocks. These stocks were largely depleted during 1976 and 1977, when the price often rose substantially. The buffer stocks were financed by the seven major producing countries, and output quotas were occasionally used in addition to the buffer stocks.

The cocoa agreement has forty-two members and uses buffer stocks and export quotas. Coffee, with forty-eight members, and sugar, with forty-four members, have both used quota restrictions on exports.

A number of other difficulties are encountered in trying to establish and maintain a commodity agreement. Producing and consuming nations often disagree over the floor and ceiling prices. Another cause for disagreement is the appropriate financial contribution from each member to the fund used to finance the buffer stocks. Finally, exporters fail to agree on the basis for sharing any export quotas.

Once an agreement is in operation, it is very difficult to adjust the floor and ceiling prices. This can lead to a breakdown of the agreement if the price becomes very high and the buffer stock runs out, or if the price remains very low and no more additions to the buffer stock can be financed. Such breakdowns are seldom permanent, but it may be some time before the agreement is renegotiated. Because of these types of breakdowns, most of the agreements have not been very effective in stabilizing prices.

To improve this situation, UNCTAD proposed in 1976 an agreement covering ten core commodities. It would operate through buffer stocks which would be financed from a joint fund. The commodities covered included: coffee, cocoa, tea, sugar, cotton, rubber, jute, hard fibers, copper, and tin. An agreement to establish a common fund was reached in 1981, but the amount is much smaller than originally planned; UNCTAD has also proposed that the prices of commodities be tied to the export price of manufactured products.

An alternative method of protecting developing countries from price fluctuations of their main exports is for the developed countries to provide financial assistance when the prices become very low. Even more desirable would be for a realistic program of world income redistribution to be implemented. Given the difficulties of achieving such income redistribution within nations, where single governments have sovereignty, it will be even more difficult to achieve on an international scale where there is no effective world government and where an "appropriate" redistribution of income would be almost impossible to define, much less effect.

The EEC and fifty-seven developing countries have established an Export Review Stabilization Plan (STABEX), which covers forty-four commodities. The plan comes into operation when the export receipts of a developing country fall below the average of the last 4 years. The poorer the country, the smaller the fall has to be before it receives any assistance. For the poorest countries, this assistance is in the form of aid. For the more affluent countries, it is a loan that will have to be repaid when commodity prices rise.

PRODUCERS' ASSOCIATIONS

A producers' association (or cartel) is an organization of the countries that produce and export a particular commodity. It usually includes all the major exporting countries but need not include all the minor exporting countries. It excludes countries that produce for local consumption only and do not export. Producers' associations differ from commodity agreements, since only the exporting countries are included, with the consuming nations excluded from the association.

The objective of a producers' association is to stabilize and increase the prices received for the commodity involved. At its simplest level such associations can serve as meeting places and act as clearing houses for information. However, this gives the associations very little authority to increase prices over what they would be otherwise. To be more effective, an association must be able to set production and export quotas that are binding on its members. This allows supply to be restricted, resulting in an increase in price. For a small number of primary products, the formation of a cartel may be possible and yield the members benefits. With the exception of oil (and for a time, uranium and tin), however, producers' associations have not been successful.

The Organization of Petroleum Exporting Countries (OPEC), the best-known producers' association, was established in 1961. Until 1970, it prevented reductions in the revenue to the producing countries but was not able to increase prices. This was partly because the interests of the middle-eastern oil states and the foreign (mainly U.S.) multinational firms largely coincided. This common interest was broken during the early 1970s, when there was a sudden decrease in the world supply of crude oil. Immediately after the 1973 Arab-Israeli war, Arab oil-producing states instituted an oil embargo against a number of western developed countries. This temporary reduction in supply led to a substantial increase in the price of crude oil. OPEC learned the power of their political oil agreement and thereafter continued to maintain an artificially high world price for crude oil. The disruption of Iranian production in 1979 due to the revolution allowed for further price increases.

A situation of oversupply of crude oil developed during the early 1980s. This was the result of reduced demand due to the recession in the western countries and also to the increased use of alternative energy sources. The development of crude oil supplies outside of OPEC also had an effect and resulted in some price reductions. To continue to be effective in maintaining prices, OPEC needs to develop a workable system of export quotas; this would allow it to restrict supply. Such a system has not yet been developed and is the major problem facing OPEC at this time.

The experience of OPEC illustrates that market conditions may not be a major factor in the apparent success of a producers' association; more important is the political power and identification of common interests by the members of the cartel. Such common interests are notoriously difficult to maintain over a period of time by producer nations; this indicates that producers' associations will probably have limited success in the future.

Even with OPEC, often cited as the most successful cartel, there is continued controversy over the relative impact of the cartel and natural market forces on the price of oil from 1973 to 1983. MacAvoy (1982), for example, concluded that 90 percent of the price increases over this period would have happened without cartel action as a result of natural supply and demand conditions in the world market.[1] Griffin and Teece (1982), however, have disputed this conclusion, and while agreeing that fundamental supply and demand conditions did not play a part, they found that actions by the cartel to restrict supply and to drive up price were the major influence.[2]

Notwithstanding the difficulty of forming and maintaining a cartel (as described in Chapter 9), a number of producers' associations have been established. In general these have failed in attempts to stabilize and increase prices. These recent producers' associations are

Council of Copper Exporting Countries (CIPEC), established in 1974
Association of Iron Ore Exporting Countries (AIEC), established in 1975
The International Bauxite Association (IBA), established in 1974
The Association of Natural Rubber Producing Countries (ANRPC), established in 1970
Union of Banana Exporting Countries (UBEC), established in 1974

LAW OF THE SEA CONVENTION

The Law of the Sea Convention agreed on in 1982 was the culmination of many years of negotiations concerning the future development of ocean resources. The area of conflict centered on the distribution of seabed wealth rather than the efficient management of offshore resources. The majority of nations, especially

---

[1]Paul W. MacAvoy, *Crude Oil Prices: As Determined by OPEC and Market Fundamentals*, Cambridge, MA: Harper and Row, Ballinger, 1982.
[2]James Griffin and David Teece, *OPEC Behavior and World Oil Prices*, London: Allen and Unwin, 1982.

the developing ones, argued for a world division of the "common heritage of mankind."

The four major seabed-producing nations, the United States, Britain, West Germany, and Japan, were most concerned with the optimal rate and type of exploitation of the resources. Their commitment to the demands by other nations for equitable distribution of the income from offshore resources varied. Since these producing nations, especially the United States, have a stronghold on the technology needed for seabed mining, they achieved their objective of prolonging the negotiations over many years. Ultimately the United States failed to accept the convention.

The terms for the exploitation of manganese nodules, rich in minerals, especially nickel, was a major obstacle in the path of the convention. The role of U.S.-based MNEs in ocean mining was a source of division, yet, despite nonparticipation of the United States, the final agreement incorporated many principles of free trade and common ownership of wealth. It is an agreement which recognizes the interdependence of world economies, even in the offshore domain.

TRADE AREAS AND ECONOMIC UNIONS

Countries can enter into agreements to eliminate or reduce trade barriers between themselves in a free trade area or customs union and can also agree to coordinate some of their economic policies, as in a common market. These three types of agreement are an exception to the nondiscrimination rule of GATT.

Free Trade Area

A free trade area occurs when countries eliminate tariff and quota barriers on the movement of all or specific goods between them, with each member country retaining its own system of external tariffs and quotas against nonmember countries. These tariffs may be different for each country such that rules about the country of origin of goods are required to avoid goods entering the area through a country with a low external tariff. These agreements are allowed by GATT if 85 percent of the trade is free.

Customs Union

A customs union combines the elimination of tariffs between members with the adoption of a unified system of tariffs against nonmember countries. This new system of tariffs replaces the individual tariffs of the member countries. Because of the common external tariff, the problem of goods entering the area through the country with the lowest tariff does not arise.

Common Market

A common market combines the features of a customs union with the removal of barriers on movement of factors of production (labor and capital) between countries. This leads the common market to attempt to implement homogenous economic, social, and political policies, although the emphasis is usually on the economic factors. A common market may also try to have consistent regulations concerning trade and business among member countries. Differences in these regulations can give rise to nontariff barriers to trade.

EUROPEAN ECONOMIC COMMUNITY

The European Economic Community (EEC) was established in 1957 with the signing of the Treaty of Rome. It is the best-known example of a common market. The six original members of the EEC were France, West Germany, Italy, Belgium, the Netherlands, and Luxembourg. In 1973 the United Kingdom, Ireland, and Denmark joined the EEC, and Greece joined in 1981. Negotiations with Spain and Portugal were in progress in the early 1980s.

In the EEC, tariffs between member countries on manufactured goods were eliminated and a common external tariff was adopted and was fully implemented by 1968. In addition the EEC has been working on the reduction of nontariff barriers to trade between member countries, but this has been a much slower process than the elimination of tariffs and some significant nontariff barriers still remain. One major area of concern is that of policies covering transportation.

Formal restrictions on the movement of labor between member countries have been eliminated. However, certain technical and professional qualifications granted in each country are not yet recognized by all other member countries. Nonrecognition reduces the mobility of certain types of labor. While attempts are being made to eliminate this barrier in some professions, such as law and medicine, progress in this direction may be very slow because of substantial resistance by some countries.

Restrictions on the movement of capital have been reduced. Although formal restrictions have been removed, difficulties still arise from differences in company law. Also, the exchange rates of all member countries are not fixed with respect to each other. The EEC has experienced great difficulty in implementing a common monetary unit, as a result of different rates of growth of productivity in member nations. The problem caused by fluctuating exchange rates still affects capital mobility.

The EEC operates through a number of institutions:

The Commission has fourteen members, who serve as the main administrative body of the community organization, which consists of over 12,000 employees. The role of the Commission is to draw up policies for the Council of Ministers to consider.

The Council of Ministers is composed of ten people, one from the government of each member country. It is responsible for making the major policy decisions for the community. It can act only on proposals submitted by the Commission.

The European Parliament is basically an advisory body. It is now elected by a direct vote and is not appointed by the governments of member countries as it was previously. In 1979 the first direct election was held to fill 410 seats in the

European Parliament. The budget of the EEC, which is drawn up by the Council of Ministers, must be approved by the Parliament. The Parliament has used this power to force some changes in the spending plans of the Council of Ministers.

The Court of Justice is composed of one member from each country of the EEC. It is the supreme appeal court for EEC law. Member countries can be brought to the court by other members or by the Commission for failing to meet treaty obligations. The Commission or the Council of Ministers can be brought to the court by firms or institutions for failure to meet their obligations under the Treaty of Rome.

The EEC has its own budget with which to finance its operations and programs. Its revenue consists of all import duties and agricultural levies plus a fraction of the value-added tax levied in all member countries. This fraction is subject to a fixed upper ceiling which limits the total budget. In 1980 and 1981 there was concern that increases in the cost of EEC programs, particularly the Common Agricultural Policy, would cause the total costs to exceed this limit, unless changes were made to the policy.

The EEC has a number of programs; the most important of these is the Common Agricultural Policy. This provides for free internal trade in agricultural products between EEC members and is supposed to ensure that farmers in the EEC make a reasonable income. Operating through a system of minimum target prices, the Common Agricultural Policy controls imports by a variable import tariff which increases the world price to just above the minimum price. To support the price, internal buying authorities exist to purchase any EEC surplus at an intervention price which is slightly below the target price. These surpluses have been sold on the world market at prices substantially below the EEC price for internal consumption.

The Common Agricultural Policy has two major problems: a disproportionately large amount of the income from tariffs on agricultural products has come from imports into Britain, and most of the benefits of the price supports have been received by farmers in France and Germany. The cost of the policy has become very large, limiting EEC spending on other programs. Recently the cost has threatened to exceed the EEC budget, which has initiated much discussion of the cost problem. By convention, price increases must be approved by all member countries, although in 1982, majority voting was used on this issue, since Britain had threatened to prevent any more increases.

There are many other programs of the EEC, some of which are briefly described as follows:

1 The EEC has been working to achieve consistent national government regulations and to introduce EEC-level regulations in a number of areas affecting social, welfare, and economic policies, such as quality standards. This harmonization of regulations will help to reduce nontariff barriers to trade.

2 Antitrust regulations have been established at the EEC level. Interfirm agreements which restrict competition within the EEC are not allowed. Only registered agreements that improve production or technology and do not reduce competition are permitted. Misuse of a dominant position by a firm (such as price discrimination and refusal to deal) is not permitted. Such agreements can be declared null and void, and fines can be imposed for violations. A number of cases have been heard under this law, and these provide some information on what is and is not allowed.

3 A European patents law has been established. Under this, a patent in ten European countries can be obtained by means of a single application and issuance procedure. This single application results in ten separate patents, each subject to the laws of one of the EEC countries and enforceable in each individual country. Work toward developing a single patent that would replace the individual patents of member countries is continuing.

4 Additional items that the EEC is working on include development of a common policy on export credits and standardized regulations concerning the representation of unions on the boards of directors of firms. Individual countries within the EEC have their own policies toward foreign direct investment, and little has been done toward harmonizing them. The policies of the EEC toward developing countries are discussed in the section on commodity agreements.

MAJOR TRADE GROUPS

In addition to the EEC, a number of trading groups have been formed between countries. These groups have had varying degrees of success. Some of the more notable trading groups are as follows:

European Free Trade Area (EFTA), established in 1960. Initial members: Austria, Denmark, Norway, Portugal, Sweden, Switzerland, United Kingdom. Members joining later: Faroe Islands, Finland, Iceland. Britain and Denmark left when they joined the EEC.

Benelux, established in 1960. Members: Belgium, the Netherlands, Luxembourg. These countries joined the EEC.

Nordek, The Nordic Council, established in 1953. Members: Denmark, Finland, Iceland, Norway, Sweden.

Latin American Free Trade Association (LAFTA), established in 1960. Members: Argentina, Bolivia, Brazil, Chile, Colombia, Ecuador, Mexico, Paraguay, Peru, Uruguay, Venezuela. This association was originally intended to be a free trade area; however, progress in removing internal tariffs has been slow. In 1980 the name of the organization was changed. The abbreviation of its Spanish name is ALADI. Also in 1980 the same members disbanded LAFTA and signed a treaty to establish the Latin American Integration Association (LAIA), which has established new goals for tariff reduction and other policies to integrate their economies.

Andean Common Market (ANCOM), established in 1969. Initial Members: Bolivia, Colombia, Chile, Ecuador, Peru. Changes: Chile left in 1976; Venezuela joined in 1973. It is a subgroup of LAFTA and has a restrictive policy toward foreign-owned investment, which is still functioning.

Central American Common Market (CACM), established in 1960. Members: Costa Rica, El Salvador, Guatemala, Honduras, Nicaragua. This was intended to be a customs union; however, there are political obstacles to increased co-operation.

Caribbean Common Market (CARICOM), formed in 1973, developed out of the CARIFTA. Membership was extended to also include: Bahamas, Belize, St. Kitts-Nevis-Anguilla.

Arab Economic Unity Agreement, established in 1964. Members: Iraq, Jordan, Kuwait, Syria, Egypt. Other signatories: Sudan, Yemen.

East African Community (EAC), established in 1967. Members: Kenya, Tanzania, Uganda. Because of political turmoil in Uganda, the association was ineffective and was dissolved in 1977.

Economic Community of West African States (ECOWAS), established in 1975. Members: Benin, Gambia, Ghana, Guinea, Ivory Coast, Mali, Mauritania, Niger, Nigeria, Senegal, Sierra Leone, Togo, Upper Volta.

Organization Commune Africaine Malgacke (OCAM), established in 1965. Members: Cameroon, Central African Republic, Chad, Congo (Brazzaville), Congo (Democratic Republic), Dahomey, Gabon, Ivory Coast, Madagascar, Niger, Ruanda, Senegal, Togo, Upper Volta.

Association of Southeast Asian Nations (ASEAN), established in 1967. Members: Indonesia, Malaysia, Philippines, Singapore, Thailand.

New Zealand-Australia Free Trade Association (NAFTA), established in 1966. Members: Australia, New Zealand.

Council for Mutual Economic Assistance (COMECON), established in 1949. Members: Bulgaria, Czechoslovakia, Cuba, East Germany, Hungary, Mongolia, Vietnam, Poland, Romania, Soviet Union. Partial participant: Yugoslavia. A number of problems have restricted the achievement of COMECON. The currencies of the member countries are not readily convertible; as a result, trade has been largely bilateral and not multilateral. Some attempts have been made to integrate the economic plans of the member countries. Integration has not been very successful, partially beause of the complexity of such an undertaking and the limits of planning ability.

EAST-WEST TRADE

East-west trade refers to trade between the western nations and the centrally planned, communist nations. This differs from the bulk of world trade, which is between western nations, for two reasons: (1) restrictions on this type of trade are imposed by the nations on both sides, and (2) the communist nations do not conduct trade in the same manner as do western nations.

The eastern countries all have a problem in obtaining a sufficient amount of hard currency to pay for their imports. To control their balance of payments problems, they often restrict imports and subsidize exports. They also try to achieve a bilateral balance in their trade with other countries.

In eastern nations the economy is subject to government control and planning. Foreign trade is not conducted by individual firms, but through foreign trade organizations (FTOs), which are organized along product lines. Trade cannot be conducted with the enterprise actually using or providing the product but must go through the appropriate FTO. In certain technical areas this is now being relaxed by some of the eastern countries, and more direct contact with the enterprise involved is allowed. The degree to which this occurs varies between different eastern countries.

Western countries have export controls that restrict the flow of goods to eastern countries. These vary between the individual western countries and also according to the destination of the exports. The export of certain types of strategic goods requires a specific license, regardless of the country of destination. For a wide range of goods destined for eastern countries, a specific license is required. The export of most types of strategic goods to eastern countries is not allowed. United States policy blows hot and cold depending on the administration in power; in general, U.S. restrictions have been consistently stringent regarding the export of armaments and high-technology goods to eastern buyers.

The restrictions of other western countries have been stricter than those of the United States. This stance allows firms based in those countries to move goods to eastern countries that U.S. firms are not permitted to export. Trade by U.S.-controlled foreign subsidiaries with eastern countries is also restricted by U.S. law. This, however, has gradually been reduced, partly as a result of complaints and pressure from other western governments that are host countries to some of these subsidiaries. The transfer of unpublished technical data through U.S. subsidiaries remains restricted.

Due to problems in obtaining hard currency, eastern countries make use of bilateral contracts where payment is not in hard currency. One arrangement is for the firm selling to the eastern country to take payment in goods exported from that country. The firm must then find a buyer for the goods. There are trading houses in Europe that will undertake to find buyers in such cases. Another arrangement is for the firm to take payment in the form of credit with the importing country. These credits are useful only to someone who wishes to purchase exports from the country involved. Again, there are trading specialists who arrange the sale of credits between firms dealing with the country involved.

Businesses that are not willing to consider arrangements of this type and insist on payment in hard currency will find themselves at a disadvantage to those firms willing to use these types of arrangements in trade with eastern countries. When such arrangements are used, the firm must ensure that the payment is sufficient to cover the costs of the extra transactions involved.

Eastern countries also make use of the trade credit with western countries. Some of this credit is export credit from western governments. Individual western governments differ in the amount and type of credits they will provide for trade with eastern countries; the United States is the most restrictive in this respect. Eastern countries also seek to make use of normal commercial credit from private sources; however, the Polish crisis of 1981 through 1982 illustrates the problems facing the international banking community when a nation is in danger of defaulting on its foreign debt. This has led to the development of country risk analysis by major international banks, which will be discussed in the section on political risk analysis.

BILATERAL TRADE AGREEMENTS

Bilateral trade agreements include any agreement between two nations that concerns trade between them. Three main types can be distinguished:

1 Agreements to maintain a bilateral balance of trade. These usually cover the exchange of specific products at specified ratios. A clearing account may be used to allow for temporary imbalance up to a specified limit. An example is the U.S.-Canadian automotive agreement, or Autopact, which removed tariffs on autos traded between the nations if certain conditions of investment, trade, and value added were met by the automobile manufacturers. The Canadians have objected that the agreement did not include auto parts, on which Canada has been running a large trade deficit for several years.

2 Bilateral agreements between potential home and host countries, used to encourage FDI. These are generally between developed and developing countries. The home country will provide the investor with insurance against certain types of loss. The host country agrees to provide compensation on a government-to-government basis. The host country retains the right to control which investments it will accept.

3 Bilateral agreements covering trade in specific products, reducing or limiting the barriers to trade in those products between the two countries.

INTERNATIONAL MONETARY FUND

The IMF (International Monetary Fund) was established in 1944 at the Bretton Woods conference. Its basic objectives were to (1) promote exchange rate stability, (2) maintain orderly exchange arrangements, (3) avoid competitive currency depreciations, (4) establish a multilateral system of payments, (5) assist in the elimination of foreign exchange restrictions, and (6) create stand-by reserves that could be made available to member countries under appropriate conditions.

Under the Bretton Woods system, members agreed to state a fixed parity for their currency and to maintain the actual value within a range of plus or minus 1 percent of parity. The parity could be changed, but only when there had been a fundamental change in the economic conditions affecting the exchange rate. A change in the parity value of more than 10 percent required prior consultation with the fund.

The 1971 Smithsonian Agreement changed these rules to allow for fluctuations around parity of plus or minus 2¼ percent. In 1973 the parity system was terminated, and since then the major currencies have been floating. The currencies of some minor countries are still tied to the currency of their major trading partner.

Special Drawing Rights (SDRs) were devised in the late 1960s and were initially allocated to member countries in 1970, 1971, and 1972. Since then there have been several more such allocations. Special Drawing Rights are essentially a paper currency established by the IMF to provide additional foreign exchange reserves and increase the liquidity of the international payment system. Their value was originally tied to the U.S. dollar but is now based on a composite value of five currencies. Their value is calculated daily, and the percentages used are to be revised every five years, giving the SDR a fairly stable value. Special Drawing Rights are mainly used between governments or between governments and the IMF. However, attempts have been made, thus far unsuccessfully, to create a private SDR market, particularly in SDR denominated bonds.

In 1963 the IMF introduced a Compensatory Financing Facility to help provide developing countries with balance of payments assistance when their export receipts suffered a temporary shortfall. In 1969 a Buffer Stock Financing Facility was introduced to help members meet their obligations in the financing of international commodity agreements. In 1974 the Extended Fund Facility was introduced to finance structural difficulties, followed by the supplementary financing facility to finance energy difficulties (the oil facility). In 1976 the Trust Fund was established to manage the sale of IMF gold, now that gold was demonetized.

When a country is facing balance of payments problems, it can request temporary loans from the IMF to reduce its short-run imbalance. In return for these funds, the IMF requires a country to undertake a program of fiscal and monetary restraint designed to correct its payments situation. Typically the recipient country is anxious for the IMF loan but reluctant to disrupt its economy (and reduce the government's popularity) by imposing the required measures. Negotiations between the IMF and the recipient country can be prolonged and acrimonious. Consequently, most developing countries regard the IMF as a tool of the rich designed to enforce their will on the poor.

During the early 1980s the IMF received considerable attention as its loan facilities were needed by country after country. The IMF itself faced a barrier since its capital available for these loans was fixed at $35 billion and had not been increased significantly in a decade. World trade and imbalances in world trade as a proportion of this fixed capital has increased fourfold. Finally in early 1983 the loan capital of the IMF was increased to $60 billion, over the strong objections of several high-income countries, particularly the United States. Their main fear was that this dramatic increase in capital would lead to a multiplied increase in world liquidity and worldwide inflation. It was necessary, however, in order to prevent several countries from defaulting on their international debt. This default could possibly have caused the collapse of the existing world financial system.

BANK FOR INTERNATIONAL SETTLEMENTS

The Bank for International Settlements (BIS) was founded after World War I to increase international financial cooperation and to facilitate transactions between governments. It remained intact after World War II and served as a private forum in which consultations between its members could be carried out in secret without the glare of publicity of the IMF. The BIS is the central bank of the world's major central banks. In this capacity it clears foreign exchange transactions between central banks. It also collects data on international financial flows and financial instruments such as Eurodollars and Eurobonds.

In 1982 the BIS emerged from relative obscurity when it extended loans to a few countries which were about to default on their international loan obligations. These actions went beyond its traditional role as a central banker and some feel beyond its mandate. At the time, however, the IMF's capital was strained to the breaking point and the BIS intervened. With the increase in IMF capital in 1983, the BIS will probably revert to its earlier role.

WORLD BANK GROUP

The World Bank Group consists of three institutions: IBRD, IDA, and IFC. The International Bank for Reconstruction and Development (IBRD) was established in 1944 at the Bretton Woods conference. Its purpose was to provide financial assistance for postwar reconstructions and for development. Its main role has been in the development area.

The IBRD provides loans to the governments of developing countries, which are to be used to develop the economic infrastructure of the country. The recipient country must be a member of the IMF. The loans are made for specific projects, usually when private capital is unavailable except at high cost. They cover the costs of the hard currency imports needed for the project and must be repaid in the currency lent. They are usually at an interest rate below the prevailing world level, but the borrower must be creditworthy. The term of the loans varies from 15 to 30 years, and sometimes longer.

The International Development Association (IDA) was established in 1960 to provide credit to developing countries on more liberal terms than those offered by IBRD. The countries must still be creditworthy and be unable to obtain funds from other sources on reasonable terms. In addition, these loans are usually restricted to countries with a per capita income of less than US $250. The loans are usually for specific projects. No interest is charged, but there is a service charge of 0.75 percent per annum. The loans can be negotiated for a period of up to 50 years with no payments on the principal starting until 10 years after the project is started. The repayments can be in the currency initially lent or can be in any other convertible currency.

The International Finance Corporation (IFC) was established in 1956. It provides risk capital, usually loans but sometimes equity, to private firms in member developing countries. The term of the loans is usually 7 to 12 years. Consideration is given to the economic priority of the project for the country, the availability of capital from private sources, and the soundness of the project. The IFC also seeks to encourage the development of local capital markets in individual countries and tries to stimulate international flows of capital.

An International Centre for the Settlement of Investment Disputes was established in 1967 as part of the World Bank Organization. Its purpose is to provide a center for conciliation or arbitration of disputes between private investors (usually firms) and host country governments. The first request for assistance was received in 1972, but since then the center has been little used.

SUMMARY

An international business manager must be aware of the international organizations that exist today, for these organizations can affect the strategy, tactics, and day-to-day operations of a firm.

Since World War II there has been a general liberalization of trade. This trend has been greatly influenced by the establishment of the General Agreement on Tariffs and Trade (GATT), whose main objectives have been to reduce tariffs, encourage nondiscrimination, and settle disputes. Although GATT has experienced, considerable success, some countries have entered into agreements which, while lowering trade barriers amongst themselves, have broken GATT's nondiscrimination rule. The three types of agreement are: free trade areas, customs unions, and common markets.

While many trade groups exist, the best known is undoubtedly the European Economic Community. Since its establishment, it has been able to eliminate tariffs, reduce nontariff barriers, eliminate restrictions on labor movement between countries, reduce restrictions on the movement of capital, and develop common policies.

Another recent theme in international trade has been the concern over developing countries. The objectives of organizations such as the United Nations Conference on Trade and Development (UNCTAD) and resolutions calling for a New International Economic Order (NIEO) have been to provide lower tariffs for the exports from developing countries and to seek a redistribution of world resources. Commodity agreements and producers' associations are two other means by which developing countries have sought to improve their position in international trade.

International trade activity has increased substantially in recent years. While some trade—for example, east-west trade—is subject to considerable government restriction, barriers to trade are generally being reduced.

KEY WORDS

Developed countries
Developing countries
Buffer stock
Commodity agreement
Producers' association

Free trade area
Customs Union
Common market
Bilateral trade agreements

QUESTIONS

1 Established in 1947, the General Agreement on Tariffs and Trade now has over 100 members. Why was GATT formed? Discuss the primary objectives of GATT. What is meant by the principle of nondiscrimination? What exceptions to this principle apply?

2 What was the reason for the organization of UNCTAD? Outline the main request of these sessions. What are the difficulties faced in establishing and maintaining a commodity agreement?

3 As discussed in the chapter, the less developed countries of the South are currently facing significant problems in their economic development. Discuss the reasons for the demands not being met. What problems arise as a result?

4 What lessons can be learned from the experience of OPEC? What has been the general result of producers' associations?

5 Three types of agreements are outlined as exceptions to the nondiscrimination rule of GATT. Briefly describe these. The best known of these is the EEC. Discuss the success of the EEC and the institutions and programs through which it operates.

6 How does east-west trade differ from that of the rest of the world? Will countertrade increase if east-west trade increases? Why or why not?

7 Outline the three main types of Bilateral Trade Agreements. Give examples where possible.

8 How should a U.S.-based MNE, concerned with the international business environment, respond to such modern issues as:

   a The North-South dialogue and the call through the United Nations' New International Economic Order (NIEO) for a redistribution of world income.

   b The implementation of codes of conduct for MNEs in both developing and developed nations.

CHAPTER 11

SOURCES OF CONFLICT BETWEEN MULTINATIONALS AND GOVERNMENT

INTRODUCTION

The very nature of the MNE makes conflict with government inevitable. The MNE's basic objective is to maximize its overall value based on the worldwide revenues arising from sales of products using its firm-specific advantage (FSA). To achieve this goal, the MNE may wish to maximize profits, increase market share, or operate on other aspects of its performance. All these objectives require the successful use of its FSA. Such FSAs can occur in areas such as product and process technology, marketing expertise and brand names, control over supplies of raw materials and other inputs, access to global markets, knowledge, and management know-how.

In its drive to maximize value, the MNE uses its assets to its best advantage on a worldwide basis. This strategy leads MNEs into conflict with three types of government: host-country governments, home-country governments, and multilateral government organizations. Each of these may have goals that differ and often conflict with those of the MNE. In spite of such conflicts, however, government usually still seeks the involvement of MNEs in trade, investment, and technology transfer as a result of the contributions that they can make to the economic and social welfare of the nation state. Naturally, demands of this nature can place a strain on the operations of the MNE.

During the 1960s and early 1970s, MNEs were perceived as having sufficient power to overcome government restrictions on their pursuit of profits, control of resources, operations, and markets. Governments in host and home countries, as well as multilateral regulatory agencies, often felt powerless when compared to MNEs. The worldwide operations, assets, and sales of MNEs often dwarfed the size of national economies and dominated world production and markets for some

253

products. However, host and home governments retained their sovereignty and possessed the ultimate legal power over the operations of MNEs. This power was often seen as empty since the net benefits of MNEs to the national economy were generally perceived as positive. Thus the costs of outright rejection of MNEs were outweighed by the benefits to be gained by their presence. Furthermore, MNEs could threaten to withdraw their operations if government did not acquiesce to their demands.

Attempts to regulate MNEs to increase the benefits of their operations to the nation state often seemed equally futile. Because of their size, diversity, and global reach, MNEs were perceived to have the ability to circumvent government regulation. They were also accused of attempting to influence the framing and application of laws which impinged on their operations. Some governments believed that they had lost control over their national economy to MNEs.[1] The balance of power between MNEs and national governments often appeared to be firmly, and unfairly, on the side of the MNEs.

Figure 11-1 illustrates this concern over the influence of MNEs as expressed by many host nations. Multinational enterprises are perceived by these nations as vehicles for the transfer of cultural, political, and economic values from the home nations of the MNEs. The subsidiaries of the MNEs, indeed, do transmit information from the parent MNEs but are also useful conduits for a reverse flow of information from the host nation. Unfortunately, it is unlikely that the parent MNEs succeed in transmitting this potentially valuable understanding of foreign nations into the mainstream of thought in the home nation.

More recently the balance of power has shifted from the MNE toward the nation state.[2] Today, MNEs are sometimes unable to achieve their own internal strategic objectives in the face of government regulation. They are often constrained by conflicting demands placed on them by host and home governments and multilateral regulatory bodies. Codes of conduct, regulations, and public scrutiny restrict the ability of the MNEs to operate efficiently. This shift in the balance of power between MNEs and governments has been gradual. Nonetheless, it is a key trend in international business, and its causes and consequences are explored over this and the next two chapters.

THE OBJECTIVES OF MNEs, NATIONAL GOVERNMENTS, AND MULTILATERAL ORGANIZATIONS

As described in Chapters 5 and 6, the objective of the MNE is to maximize its return on a firm-specific advantage through its international operation in trade, licensing, and foreign direct investment. Multinational enterprises act as monopolists possessing a combination of advantages, such as information, skills, control over resources, inputs and factors of production, and access to final goods markets. The objective of the MNE is to choose the mode of international operation—

---

[1]Raymond Vernon, *Sovereignty at Bay*, New York: Basic Books, 1971.
[2]Raymond Vernon, *Storm Over the Multinationals*, New York: Macmillan, 1977.

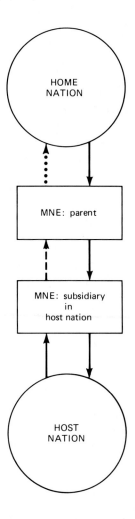

FIGURE 11-1
The MNE exercises control over its subsidiaries. Many host nations perceive this control (solid line) as a mechanism for the
transfer of the home nation's values. The MNE can reverse the
flow of information from its subsidiaries to the parent (broken
line). It is difficult for many MNEs to convey this intelligence
about foreign nations to the home nation (dotted line).

trade, licensing, or foreign direct investment—that maximizes the net present
value to the MNE of its monopoly rents earned on the firm-specific advantage. In
this maximization process there are two interdependent components that proceed
simultaneously.

First, MNEs strive to improve the efficiency of their internal markets, which
were formed to supersede the natural and government-imposed barriers to the
free flow of goods and services—to this end, the MNEs allocate resources within
the firm to their most profitable use so as to maximize the surplus of revenues over
costs.

Second, MNEs strive to retain as much of this surplus as possible. They have no
incentive to share such rents with any other stakeholders in the international
environment, whether they are competitors, governments, or individuals in the
host or home country. Yet, as demonstrated in Chapter 6 on the performance of
MNEs, the costs of running the internal market act to offset these monopoly rents.

In practice, MNEs do not on average earn profits above those of non-MNEs. MNEs are able to maximize return to the enterprise from use of their firm-specific advantages by a process involving control over worldwide allocation of their resources and retention of any remaining operating surplus.

Host governments often have different, and sometimes opposing, goals to those held by MNEs operating in their country. The major objective of a host-nation government in this context is to maximize the net benefits accruing to it from the activities of MNEs operating within its borders.[3] This generalization can be extended to multilateral organizations that seek to maximize the benefits of activities of MNEs to their constituent members.[4] Sovereign governments, however, place the net benefits derived from MNEs within the context of the broader economic, social, political, and cultural goals of their nations. In order to achieve such goals, government regulation of the national economy and its interface with the world economy may distort the global allocation of resources. The MNEs operating in the host nation may respond to these market distortions by allocating resources efficiently within the enterprise. This process may reduce the host government's control over its economy and reduce the benefits which accrue to it from the MNE's operations.

In addition to control over the allocation of resources by MNEs, national governments desire to retain as much as possible of the surplus generated by MNEs. Governments want their "fair share" of the profits. Such a generalization applies to all the activities of MNEs—trade, licensing, and FDI—and to the governments of all the nations in which MNEs operate.

Since the goals of national governments and multilateral bodies in their relations with MNEs differ from each other and conflict with the goals of MNEs themselves, there is much potential for dispute. MNEs can be subject to different, and mutually incompatible, demands on the control over the allocation of their resources and the distribution of their profits. This is particularly true during recessionary periods. For example, in 1981 falling world demand for nickel forced Inco to cut production. Both the Canadian and Indonesian governments pressured Inco to maintain production levels in their countries at the expense of employment in other countries.

On most occasions, a national government recognizes that the activities of MNEs lead to net benefits for its country, yet a problem remains over the distribution of these benefits. Control of the MNE's resources among host country, home country, third countries, and the MNE is also a source of conflict. If MNEs operated in efficient markets, these twin problems of the distribution of net benefits and allocation of resources would not arise since there would be no perceived monopoly rents to distribute and resources would flow naturally to their most efficient use. If such conditions existed, of course, there would be no need

---

[3]For the moment we are assuming that government acts as a custodian of the general national public interest, not as an agent for some specific interest group.

[4]The exceptions to this generalization, particularly the charge that multilateral organizations may seek to regulate MNEs to the advantage of one or a group of their constituents, are explored further on.

for MNEs since they exist in response to market imperfections. In the real world, MNEs do not operate in industries for products which are produced, distributed, and sold in efficient, competitive markets. Therefore, there is usually some surplus that accrues from their operations, and they have some discretion in the allocation of their resources.[5]

The sources of conflict between MNEs and governments as discussed in this chapter are outlined in Figure 11-2.

Home-Country Governments

In the struggle over the distribution of the surplus of revenues over direct costs (perceived surplus) and over control of the allocation of resources by MNEs, the interests of the MNE's home-country government are often aligned with that of the MNE itself. The profits an MNE earns on its international operations usually accrue to its shareholders in dividends and capital appreciation, to its workers in

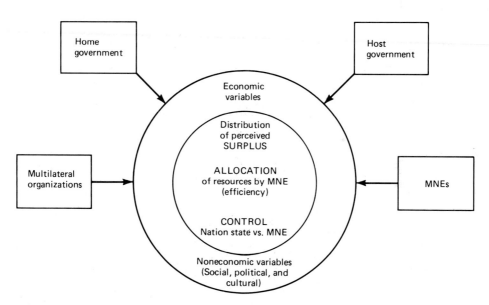

FIGURE 11-2
Sources of conflict. The three sources of conflict (in the circle) are over distributional issues, allocation issues, and control issues. Conflicts arise between MNEs and three types of government: home, host, and multilateral. The resolution of these conflicts is difficult owing to different perspectives over economic, social, political, and cultural variables.

[5]This generalization is not true in the two cases. First, in the one in which the costs of international operation through exports, licensing, or FDI are such that no monopoly profit is generated. Referring back to Figure 6-2, we see that this is the case in which one of OX, OF, or OL is equal to OP* and the rest are greater than OP*, i.e., OP*=MIN (OX, OF, OL). Second, the one referred to in Chapter 6, where the costs of operating the internal market increase total costs to the MNE up to, or above, OP*.

higher wages and to the entire home-country population through taxation of corporate profits in the home country.

To the extent that the owners and managers of MNEs are ethnocentric and identify their interests with those of their home country, they will attempt to match the interests of their enterprise with the national interest of their home country. They may do this even if this action constrains the efficiency of their enterprise. For example, if demand falls, the MNE may be more willing to reduce output and employment in its subsidiaries abroad rather than cut back at home. Clearly this impinges on the overall efficiency of the MNE and reduces profits. However, the interests of the home nation loom larger for the MNE than the interests of foreign host nations.

Despite the general coincidence of interests between the MNE and its home country, certain groups in the home country may be adversely affected by the operations of MNEs and may lobby government to restrict the MNE's activities. International trade changes the relative prices of goods in the market, thereby decreasing the real incomes of some consumers. Similarly, trade changes the relative return to factors of production. Since labor and capital are usually immobile in the short run, some owners of capital and labor may bear a disproportionate share of this burden. The same situation applies in the cases of licensing and foreign direct investment to the extent that they are substitutes for trade.

In theory, since the home country as a whole gains from the operations of MNEs, the winners could compensate the losers such that nobody loses and at least some groups gain. Unfortunately, such a redistribution of the gains between stakeholders has been notoriously difficult within the framework of the capitalist market system. In fact, such compensation rarely takes place. Moreover, for the losers (the unemployed workers, bankrupted owners, and depressed regions), losses are immediate, severe, and of paramount importance. For the winners (the owners, employees, suppliers, and customers of MNEs), gains are diffused and often difficult to perceive and quantify. The losers have every incentive to lobby government to restrict the activities of the MNEs, but the winners are apt to be less aware of their gains or vocal in representing their interests. Therefore, even though overall gains exceed losses from the activities of MNEs, home-country governments may act to restrict their activities in response to some pressure groups.[6]

In spite of their arguable tendency toward ethnocentric decisions, the cost of ignoring world economic realities in allocating resources may force MNEs to allocate resources away from the home country. Slack economic conditions or high labor costs at home may lead the MNE to invest money and create jobs abroad. Again, home governments have sometimes acted to halt this outflow of investment capital and job opportunities. For example, until the mid-1970s, Japan followed a policy which placed strict limits on capital exports to retain scarce capital for investment in Japan.

[6]Interestingly, the American textile industry, the first industry in a then developing country, was founded on existing British technology. At that time it was a capital offense to take textile machinery or plans out of England.

The government and people of the home country view, in some ill-defined sense, the MNE as belonging to the nation. Its firm-specific advantages are seen to be at least an indirect product of the nation as a whole. Hence home governments may believe that MNEs should use their assets to derive the greatest possible gains for the home nation and to act in the national interest even if profits are reduced. For example, in France, the major decisions by French-based MNEs are often made in close consultation with the government. France thereby ensures that it derives a large share of the benefits from its MNEs.

Despite these potential conflicts, from a purely *economic* viewpoint, the goals of the MNE and the home country are often mutually compatible. However, the home country has *noneconomic* goals, which may be contrary to those of the MNEs based within its borders. In the case of national defense, there is a clear potential for confrontation between private and public benefits and costs. While export of products of strategic use to the enemy, licensing and technology needed to produce such products, or investment in facilities abroad to produce them, may present opportunities for profits, it may not be in the interest of the home country and its allies. This situation is clear-cut; the MNE must bow to the national interests of its home country and restrict its international operations, even if this action precipitates retaliation.

Circumstances can arise, however, in which the MNE has operations in two host countries who are hostile to each other (but neutral toward the home country), as happened with U.S.-based MNEs during the early years of World War II. They had operations in Germany and France while German MNEs operated in the United States. In this case balancing home and host-country national interests against the MNE's own interest is difficult, if not impossible.

A similar situation can occur if, for political reasons, the home-country government tries to control the operations of subsidiaries in other host countries. This issue of extraterritoriality has plagued the operations of U.S.-based MNEs and their relations with government at home and abroad. In the late 1960s the French government, for example, temporarily seized control of Fruehauf (France) to ensure that it filled an export order for China in the face of a U.S. prohibition on the sale. Fruehauf was caught squarely in the middle between two mutually incompatible sets of regulations. Another example arose when the United States broke diplomatic relations with Cuba and banned a wide range of exports from the United States to that country. Similarly, in 1982 the U.S. government tried to punish the Soviet Union for its political activities in Poland and Afghanistan by limiting exports of technology-intensive products from the United States. It attempted to extend this limitation to goods produced by U.S. MNEs abroad or produced using technology licensed by U.S. MNEs to firms in other countries. U.S.-based MNEs were caught between conflicting pressures, since several European nations required that U.S. subsidiaries, located in their nations, comply with the law and politics of the host nations.

Despite these problems, the interests of the MNEs and their home governments largely coincide. Most of the perceived surplus generated by MNEs through their international activities ultimately comes back to the home country through increased profits, dividend remittances, and fees from licensed technology. The major problem between the home government and MNEs is due to the role of the MNE in integrating the economy of its home country with that of the rest of the world. There is a consequent loss of control by the home country over the goods, services, and capital being generated by its economy. Arguably, this loss of control would occur even if MNEs did not exist and all international economic interactions were by arm's-length exports, licensing, or financial investment. To the extent that MNEs facilitate international interaction, they expose the home country to economic forces outside their national boundaries and control. Without MNEs, however, the net benefits to the home country of increased international interaction would be reduced.

Host-Country Governments

The relationship between MNEs and host-country governments is usually more complex than that between MNEs and their home governments. While the latter is often characterized by pride and appreciation mixed with a vague uneasiness, the former often borders on a love-hate relationship. Although host governments and their constituents may recognize that MNEs bring net benefits to their economies, they often feel that the net gain is too small. The issue is clouded since the calculation of the costs and benefits of MNEs to the host country is a difficult, subjective, and value-laden exercise. Often the feeling persists in the host governments of both developed and less developed countries that somehow they have come out on the short end of the stick.

The problem of MNE-host country relations is further complicated by the fact that many of the costs of MNEs to host countries are social, political, and cultural rather than economic, while the benefits are largely economic. Therefore, quantification of the impact of MNEs on the host country is virtually impossible and subject to wide interpretation depending on the values placed by the different stakeholders. Moreover, the valuation of the net benefits of MNEs in general, or a single MNE in particular, changes with varying economic, social, and political events in the host country. The policies of a host government toward MNEs shift as the strength and attitudes of its various constituents change over time.

Economic Conflicts   The economic basis for the controversy and disputes between MNEs and host governments is easy to recognize. As demonstrated in Chapter 2, in a static, purely competitive world, increased flows of trade, technology, or investment unequivocally lead to increased economic welfare for all parties: the agents of the transfer, the recipient, and the source. In such a world, there should be no controversy over the economic role of international trade and investment. There would also be no MNEs since MNEs can exist only in a dynamic world of imperfect competition. Current economic controversy is based on the distribution of the perceived surplus generated by the MNE, the effects of the operations of MNEs on the host economy over time, and control over the allocation of resources by the MNE.

The framework developed in Chapter 6 is useful in analyzing this controversy since its sets out the determinants of MNE operations in host countries. The goal of host countries in their relations with MNEs is to maximize the benefits accruing to them from these operations. Host governments believe that the profits accruing to MNEs from operations—trade, licensing, and FDI—in host nations arise from the use of local resources, namely raw materials, labor, capital, and access to the nation's markets. From this viewpoint, a large part of the perceived surplus generated by MNEs should accrue to the host country, as should control over MNE allocation of resources, both in and out of the country. Yet MNEs believe that any surplus is generated by the efficient use and allocation of a firm-specific advantage over which proprietary rights need to be applied. This dispute over the control of resources and the distribution of any surplus is at the heart of the economic basis of the controversy between MNEs and host governments.

The struggle over the perceived surplus is complicated by the difficulty in placing a specific monetary value on it. Two factors make this valuation difficult and controversial. As previous chapters have shown, one of the fundamental reasons that MNEs use internal markets is that the external markets for the firm-specific advantages of MNEs are imperfect. The external markets are not in a competitive equilibrium and do not value the assets correctly.[7] In the stylized, one-period framework shown in Exhibit 6-1 and the multiperiod framework shown in Figure 6-3, the valuation of the three operational modes of MNEs is clear-cut. In practice, however, neither the demand curve in these diagrams nor the various cost functions are known with any certainty. They are both subject to wide and often unknown variation, uncertainty, and risk.

As described in Chapter 6, the incorporation of uncertainty and risk into the MNE's calculations of the NPV of the various modes of entry, while conceptually straightforward, is rather messy in practice. Uncertainty and risk lead to two problems in the valuation of the MNE's operations by the host-country government.

First, the host-country government may have a perception different from that of the MNE of the expected demand and the various costs associated with the venture and the dispersion of possible outcomes around their expected values.

Second, the attitude toward risk, and hence the discount factor placed on the expected stream of benefits, may differ between government and MNE. Typically, the host government perceives the risks associated with an MNE's operations to be lower than does the MNE. Therefore, the government has a more risk neutral attitude toward a single project. It also perceives the costs of an MNE's operations in the host country to be lower than does the MNE. In terms of Chapters 5 and 6, the special additional costs of FDI, A^*, are undervalued by the host government. Consequently, there is often a valuation gap in the assessment of the NPV of the perceived surplus between the MNE and the host government. There is contro-

---

[7]The other major reason for internalization as described in previous chapters is that transfer of FSAs internally may be less costly (more efficient) than transferring them via the external market no matter how inefficient it is.

versy over both the size and distribution of the surplus. This analysis is especially applicable to the situation between an MNE and the host government before operations have commenced.

The controversy is further complicated once the operation is in place. Here two factors are at work. Once the venture is in full operation, the costs to the MNE fall. Many internal operational and external information costs are up-front costs that do not recur after the first few years of operation. This characteristic of the time path of costs and revenues is accounted for in the NPV calculation performed by the MNE prior to starting the venture and choosing the most suitable mode of operation. Yet, when the host-country government evaluates the surplus from the MNE's operations after the venture is in place, it may believe that the profits are excessive. The host government may not be receptive to the logic that profits in any one year are not an appropriate measure of the surplus accruing to the MNE over the life of the venture.

This situation results from different viewpoints concerning the timing of the flow of benefits from the venture. From the perspective of the MNE, the major costs are incurred at the beginning of the venture, while the benefits accrue later. For the host country, the benefits in terms of increases in employment, increased capital investment, technology transfer, and access to international markets accrue largely when the venture is first initiated, while the costs, in terms of capital outflow, come later.

Once the venture is in place and operating successfully, it is tempting (with hindsight) for a host government to argue that the project's risk of failure was low and hence its return to the MNE should not have included a high risk premium. From the MNE's viewpoint, however, the success of this venture may not influence the underlying probability distribution of possible outcomes on its worldwide investments. High profits on its winners are necessary to offset the low profits on its losers. MNEs believe that it is incorrect, dysfunctional, and unfair for host governments to appropriate profits from successful ventures, unless they are prepared to subsidize less successful ones. When host governments move in on successful projects, they are shifting the probability distribution against the MNE. In the long run, future investment will be discouraged. This has happened in Canada when the National Energy Program of 1980 served to discourage new foreign investment in the oil and gas sectors.

These problems between MNEs and host governments which arise from differences over the time path of costs, benefits, and risk for MNEs and host governments are compounded by shifts in bargaining power over time. Prior to making an investment, MNEs are usually in a relatively strong bargaining position since they can withhold the investment if their demands are not met. Once the investment is in place, however, withdrawing it may be too costly. In this situation, the host government can hold the subsidiary hostage to its demands. This phenomenon of the "obsolescing bargain" is described further in Chapter 13.

The winners and losers in the MNE's operations do not always occur in the same host country. The MNE hopes that the countries in which its ventures are successful will subsidize the countries in which its ventures are not. This belief is not easy for host governments to accept. Yet if host governments attempt to appropriate the "excess profits" of successful ventures alone, MNEs are likely to reduce the overall level of their international operations, to the detriment of all nations.

One response to this discriminatory treatment is for MNEs to play off host governments against each other. For example, MNEs often shop around when selecting the site for a new factory to benefit from the maximum allowances and tax breaks available. They also react when one of their ventures does not live up to expectations. Then MNEs are prone to lobby the host government for concessions, increased tariffs, reduced taxes, and capital transfer in order to increase the profitability of their unsuccessful subsidiary. This reaction is understandable but is inconsistent with the theoretical position that there is a normal distribution of business ventures, in which profitable ventures offset the unsuccessful ones. Moreover, government intervention along these dimensions usually decreases economic inefficiency contrary to the raison d'être of MNEs.

In addition to the effects of timing, uncertainty, and risk of differences in the valuation of the perceived surplus, a gap may arise as a result of different valuations placed on the social costs and benefits arising from the venture. This problem looms even larger for developing nations than for developed ones.

In all countries, but particularly in developing ones, the economy suffers from distortions which make market forces difficult to operate. Market prices often do not reflect the actual costs of the resources used by the MNE in production or the prices that would prevail in a marketplace. Other market imperfections are: tariffs and price controls which distort input and output prices, artificially high minimum wages in the industrial sector which overstate the resource cost of labor, capital rationing which understates the value of capital, foreign exchange restrictions which distort the resource cost of imports and exports alike, government subsidies on electricity, fuel, and transportation which lead MNEs to undervalue their costs to the economy, the market structure which may lead to prices above the competitive level, and finally the discount rate used in aggregated costs and benefits which may differ between the MNE and the host government.

The disparity between the private costs and revenues that accrue to the MNE and the public costs and benefits realized by the host country can be large. It is possible for an investment by an MNE to be viable from the point of view of the MNE, that is, have a positive NPV, yet have a negative NPV from the viewpoint of the host country. In this case, the MNE will find the host government unreceptive to its proposal. The reverse situation may occur with a venture bringing positive net benefits to the country, but with a negative private NPV for the MNE. In this case, the venture will not be undertaken by the MNE without subsidies or other incentives from the host government to correct the market imperfection. In less extreme cases, the MNE may find that the host government is less receptive to its proposed venture or less positive toward its existing operations than it had expected as a result of a difference in valuation.

In theory, this problem of difference in valuation can be resolved by the technique of cost-benefit analysis (CBA). Essentially CBA adjusts the private costs and benefits of a venture to public costs and benefits and uses the host nation's cost of capital (time preference for money) as the discount rate. Although simple in theory, the use of CBA can be very complex in specific situations. A detailed description of CBA is beyond the scope of this book.[8] Nevertheless, managers of the MNE should be aware that prices in the markets for inputs, labor, capital, foreign exchange, and output can be distorted so that they do not reflect the scarcity value of the good in the market. When this occurs, a valuation gap between private and public evaluations of a venture occurs and that gap may cause conflict between the MNE and the host government.

Noneconomic Conflicts   The social, political, and cultural sources of conflict between MNEs and host governments are more difficult to describe, much less analyze and resolve, than the economic sources of conflict. Social, political, and cultural factors can have an important, sometimes overriding, influence on host-government relations with MNEs. Just as host governments may feel that international economic integration through the operations of MNEs leads to loss of economic control, they may also believe that the increased international social, cultural, and political interaction leads to loss of control over those aspects of life in their countries. This fear is particularly strong in host countries whose political and social systems and cultural values are different from those of the home country of the MNE, since MNEs can act as agents of change either inadvertently or by design.

The economic impact of MNEs also has social, political, and cultural ramifications on the host country. Investment by MNEs may lead to the rise in economic (and hence social and political) fortunes of a new entrepreneurial group at the expense of those in power. The opposite may occur; MNEs may further strengthen the power of the dominant group. MNEs may pay higher wages than locally owned firms, and their operations may be perceived as signaling general wage increases in the industrial sector. Groups that benefit from the operations of MNEs in the host country may view their interests as coincident with those of MNEs, shift their allegiance toward MNEs and away from the country or its government, and lobby government to be more supportive in its policies toward MNEs.

The size and multinational spread of MNEs may also lead to a feeling within the host nation of subservience, weakness, and inferiority. Some people in the host nation may come to believe that they are unable to develop, produce, and sell products on their own in competition with MNEs or without their aid. Ethnocentric policies within MNEs may compound this problem by allocating R and D to the home country and reserving senior management positions for home-country nationals. Products provided by MNEs may not be valued by host governments or be inappropriate to the cultural values, level of income, or development strategy of the country. For example, the host country's national economic strategy may be

---

[8]There are many books on CBA. The interested student is referred to E. J. Mishan, *Cost Benefit Analysis*, New York: Praeger Publishers, 1971.

to promote savings and investment and to satisfy basic nutritional and health needs. This may conflict with a sales strategy of an MNE to promote consumption of luxury consumer products.

To summarize, there are feelings of economic, social, political, and cultural dominance by MNEs and loss of control of the nation to them. It is also believed that the surplus of revenues over costs from the operations of MNEs in the host country is unevenly divided. These feelings and beliefs may lead to attempts by host-country governments to use the law to regulate the behavior of MNEs. Such actions are constrained by the ability of MNEs to shift investment, trade, and technology between nations, moving from those in which they earn low returns to those in which the returns are higher. The strategies and tactics followed by host governments to regulate MNEs and the response of MNEs to these actions are described in Chapter 12.

Multilateral Organizations

From the end of World War II to the early 1970s, the overall objectives of multilateral economic regulatory bodies were to increase the efficiency and equity of the world economic system. These multilateral bodies acted in order to foster growth and redistribute world income through increased trade (the GATT); to facilitate capital flows and adjustment to international payments imbalances (the IMF); to increase investment, trade, and technology flows to low-income countries (the World Bank, UNCTAD, UNIDO); and to aid workers in various countries (ILO). These multilateral bodies were not concerned with MNEs per se, but only their relation to the more general mandates of economic regulation (and deregulation, as in the case of GATT).

Through the 1960s and 1970s, as the number and size of MNEs increased, the public and governments around the world became more aware of their impact.[9] A consensus began to emerge that nation states, individually, were ineffectual in regulating many of the activities of MNEs as their operations extended beyond national boundaries. This concern was fostered by several trends in the international economic and political environment. As countries around the world, especially in Japan and Europe, recovered from the ravages of World War II, they began to question the economic and political dominance of the United States. Some U.S.-based MNEs were perceived as extensions, symbols, even as flag bearers, of U.S. economic, cultural, and political imperialism and hegemony. This feeling was heightened by media attention in host nations to the application by the U.S. government of extraterritoriality to some activities of U.S.-based MNEs. Furthermore, the U.S. government was too often insensitive to the feelings of host nations and tended to extend its economic and political power.[10]

---

[9]See, for example, J. J. Servan-Schreiber, *The American Challenge* (1968) and Kari Levitt, *Silent Surrender* (1970).

[10]The much publicized, if seldom used, Hickenlooper Amendment, which necessitated the cutoff of aid money to countries that expropriated U.S.-owned subsidiaries, is the most notorious example of such protection.

In the late 1960s and early 1970s, the interdependence of interests and activities of the U.S. government and U.S.-based MNEs had a potentially disruptive impact on national interests abroad. This impact was underlined by a series of tax and direct control measures instituted by the U.S. government to restrict the outflow of foreign direct investment and accelerate the inflow of funds from profits earned abroad. These measures were used in an attempt to alleviate the U.S. balance of payments situation. Similarily, the Burke-Hartke bill, although never passed, was designed to limit foreign investment and technology transfer by MNEs and to protect U.S. labor at the expense of investment and labor abroad.

To the extent that nations outside the United States had relied on capital and technology from U.S.-based MNEs, these initiatives highlighted their potential vulnerability and generated international repercussions. The reaction was initially limited in volume. Immediate regulatory actions were directed at U.S.-based MNEs by host nations. The effects were not easily discerned on actual capital flows and the balance of payments of countries in which these MNEs operated. In the long run, the climate for U.S. foreign direct investment was clouded. In addition, it was recognized that the U.S. government exercised far less control over the operations of U.S. enterprises than did the governments of other advanced countries. The potential vulnerability of economies outside the United States to U.S. government policies toward U.S. enterprises became an increasing concern. U.S.-based MNEs often acted as lightning rods for resentments outside the United States toward American political and economic power and inside the United States by those concerned with the gradual decline of U.S. economic dominance and their relative economic well-being.

At the same time that the role in the international economy of U.S.-based MNEs was under increasing scrutiny and attack, the more general role of private enterprise itself, as a means of organizing and fostering economic activity, was being questioned. In most countries, the size of government relative to the national economy increased from 1960 to 1980 as the growth of public consumption and investment outpaced the growth of private consumption and investment.[11] This growth in the relative size of government and the scope of economic regulation of private enterprise was accompanied by increased government ownership of industry. Government ownership and economic regulation barred MNEs from some industries, placed them in direct competition with government-owned enterprises in others, and generally subjected them to increased government regulation.[12]

Government-business interaction at the national level often spilled over into more government regulation and ownership at the international level. This trend was accelerated in the late 1970s with the demands of low-income countries, in the "South," for a restructuring of the world economy into a New World Economic Order, that should reallocate resources from North to South. This attitude toward

---

[11]See World Bank, *World Development Report 1982*, Tables 4 and 5.
[12]See Raymond Vernon (ed.), *Big Business and the State*, Cambridge, MA: Harvard University Press, 1974.

private enterprise was typified by the *Brandt Report* of the Brandt Commission, where the proposed role of private enterprise in world economic development was reduced to the point of virtual absence.[13]

After World War II, the number, size, and importance of multilateral political and economic organizations increased. These organizations were usually founded at the request of the United States and the major western European countries and initially functioned under their direction and in their immediate interests. Over time, their constituency was broadened, and, as the political and economic fortunes of the United States declined relative to other high- and low-income countries, the dominance of these organizations by the U.S. government decreased. Some member countries of these organizations began to perceive that their multinational character could and should be used to counterbalance and deal with the power and reach of MNEs.

The emergence of MNEs, based in Europe, Japan, Canada, and some middle-income countries in the 1970s, also influenced the international regulatory environment of MNEs. The multinational enterprise was no longer viewed as an entirely American phenomenon that could be dealt with on a bilateral or multilateral-U.S. basis, but as a more general phenomenon that required truly multilateral initiatives. The U.S. government opposition to multilateral initiatives toward MNEs also declined, since these initiatives were no longer perceived as attempts directed solely at U.S. economic policy and U.S. enterprises. In addition, the United States itself began to have problems with MNEs based in other countries and to some extent felt the need for regulating their activities. The governments of the home countries of these new MNEs, however, became somewhat less supportive of attempts to regulate their behavior.

By the late 1970s, all these trends converged to bring about a number of initiatives directed toward the regulation of MNEs by multilateral organizations such as the Organization for Economic Co-operation and Development (OECD), the International Labor Organization (ILO), and the UN Commission of Transnational Corporations (UNCTC). By the early 1980s, these initiatives were in various stages of completion and implementation. They had largely taken the form of voluntary codes of conduct and information gathering on several aspects of the operations of MNEs. The major components of the OECD Code of Conduct are summarized in Exhibit 11-1. Multinational enterprises were required to satisfy requirements in the areas of ownership, financing, technology transfer, use of labor, local sourcing, and so on.

The reaction of MNEs to these initiatives has ranged from unawareness and indifference to hostility and obstruction. In general, they have viewed regulation of their international activities as unnecessary, unwarranted, and inimical to both their interests and those of the world economy. In their view, these regulations are designed to correct problems that existed in the past, when U.S.-based MNEs were dominant and had quasimonopoly positions in some industries. They main-

---

[13]See W. Brandt, *North-South: A Program for Survival*, United Nations: International Commission on International Development Issues, 1980.

EXHIBIT 11-1
OECD GUIDELINES FOR MULTINATIONAL ENTERPRISES (MNEs) AND LABOR RELATIONS

Objective:	Improve the foreign investment climate by encouraging positive contribution to economic and social progress which MNEs can make while minimizing the difficulties arising from their operations
Key provisions—MNEs should:	1 Disclose to the public significant financial and operational information on a regular basis
	2 Meet standards concerning working conditions and labor relations, provide notice and consultation regarding major changes in operations, avoid discrimination in employment
	3 Refrain from actions which adversely affect competition by abusing dominant positions of market power
	4 Take into consideration national balance of payments and credit objectives in financial activities
	5 Provide full information for tax purposes
	6 Contribute to national science and technology objectives, permit rapid diffusion of technologies

tain that these problems have largely disappeared with the rise of MNEs based in other countries, the diffusion of technological capabilities, access to international capital, fierce worldwide competition, the rise in strength of firms in host countries, and the increased capabilities of national governments to regulate private enterprise in general and MNEs in particular. Nevertheless, regulation by multilateral organizations of many aspects of the operations of MNEs has become an increasingly important factor in the business environment of MNEs.

SUMMARY

The goals of MNEs and their strategies to achieve these goals can place them in conflict with the governments of the countries in which they operate. The essential economic basis of this conflict is over control of the allocation of the resources of MNEs and over the distribution of the perceived surplus from their operations both within the host country and on a global basis. This conflict has led host and home governments to attempt to regulate the operations of MNEs within their borders.

MNEs serve to link the economies of the countries in which they operate and hence are often the focal point of the struggle between nations over the allocation of international resources and division of the world economic "pie." As a consequence of the international nature of their operations, which makes control by any one nation difficult, multilateral organizations have come to take an increasingly large role in the regulation of MNEs.

In the future, the operations of MNEs will come under increased national and international regulation based on the economic, political, and social goals of the countries in which they operate and on the goals of the constituents of multilateral organizations. International businesspeople need to understand the basis of this drive toward increased regulation of its operations, the ways in which regulations are framed and implemented, and how to operate in the face of the regulations.

The regulation by national governments and multilateral organizations will constrain the ability of MNEs to allocate resources within the enterprise and achieve overall global profit-maximizing goals. Regulation may also intensify competition between MNEs and between MNEs and firms based in the countries in which they operate.

In response to these trends, MNEs will have to develop new firm-specific advantages which will enable them to continue to operate internationally. Unless MNEs develop new strategies for the deployment of such advantages, they will have to withdraw from international operations and evolve back to their bases in their home countries. These changes can already be observed in some MNEs that are unable to cope with increased government regulation and international competition.

KEY WORDS

Home-country government	Equity-distributional goals of nations
Host-country government	Private cost-benefit analysis
Multilateral organizations	Public cost-benefit analysis
Perceived surplus—monopoly rents	Ethnocentric organization

QUESTIONS

1 How do the basic efficiency objectives of MNEs conflict with the equity or distributional goals of host-country governments and multilateral organizations? In your answer, discuss the differing objectives of each group. What are the three sources of conflict?
2 Discuss the dominant characteristics of the host-country government-MNE relationship. What possible explanations can be given for these characteristics?
3 Host-country governments often claim that they are entitled to a large part of the perceived surplus generated by MNEs operating within their countries. What is the basis for these claims? What arguments can the MNE use to refute this claim?
4 Uncertainty and risk lead to two problems in the valuation of the MNE's operations by the host-country governments. What are these problems? How are the problems complicated once the operation is in place?
5 The technique of cost-benefit analysis can be used to resolve problems in valuation. Discuss this technique. What factors must the MNE manager be made aware of?
6 How can the economic impact of MNEs affect the social, political, and cultural aspects of a host country? Give examples, where possible. Discuss how the host-country government might respond to these aspects.
7 Why have multilateral organizations been more effective in regulating MNEs than individual nations? In your answer, explain the involvement of these organizations.

CASE: Nestlé and the Infant Formula Controversy

Introduction

In May 1979, the United Nations World Health Assembly adopted the International Code of Marketing of Breast-milk Substitutes. It was hoped that this would put an end to the emotional controversy surrounding the marketing of infant formula in less developed countries. In practice, the issue was not resolved until 1984.

Nestlé's Background

Nestlé SA, a Swiss-based multinational, is the second largest food processor in the world. Starting as a baby milk food producer in 1867, it diversified into foreign markets and in the 1930s began the development of instant drinks such as Nescafé. By 1979 four product lines, infant formula, condensed milk, powdered milk, and chocolate, accounted for 35 percent of its sales. In addition to its food production, its operations now also include hotels, pharmaceuticals, and cosmetics. In 1979 it had principal subsidiaries in over forty countries, and 95 percent of its sales came from foreign markets. Its sales for that year were 21,639 million Swiss francs (about $12 billion); of this, infant formula sales of $250 million represented only 2.5 percent of total sales.

The company's postwar strategy was threefold: to develop new product lines; to diversify production by acquisitions in Europe and North America; and to undertake foreign expansion, mainly into developing nations. Nestlé undertook the risk of foreign direct investment to satisfy the demands of host nations for local production facilities and host nation employment. The substitution of host production for imports saved scarce foreign exchange; this was especially desired by developing nations. Nestlé also attempted to train host nationals, maintain high quality standards, and adapt its product lines to local conditions.

Infant Formula Issue

As early as December 1969, at a meeting of the United Nation's Protein-Calorie Advisory Group (PAG), health professionals expressed concern over the world-wide decline in breast-feeding and the possibility that aggressive marketing of infant formula was contributing to that decline. By November 1973 PAG produced a document (PAG Statement 23) calling for the cooperation of the industry, governments, and medical profession in overcoming the basic dilemma that faced less developed countries—how to stop the trend away from breast-feeding while making infant formula available for mothers unable to breast-feed. Governments were asked to provide the financial assistance to make available nutritious, low-cost breast milk substitutes. The industry was asked to avoid aggressive marketing practices. The PAG was unsuccessful in gaining the cooperation of these bodies, so consumer advocacy groups, on learning of the issue, took up the cause.

The Consumer Boycott

Numerous consumer, development, and church groups objected not only to the marketing efforts of infant formula producers, in particular Nestlé, but also to their lack of corporate responsibility. Promotion of the formula had included the following:

- Mass media advertising, in which the underlying message was that healthy babies were the result of bottle-feeding with infant formula. This message was promoted by posters, giant billboards, and radio commercials.
- Free samples provided through doctors, hospitals, and clinics.
- Mothercraft nurses. These uniformed (but untrained) "nurses," in the employ of Nestlé, worked at village clinics promoting formula to mothers. They were direct sales representatives rather than health workers.

The consumer groups claimed that mothercraft nurses were perceived by many villagers to be real nurses. On this basis, Nestlé was accused of false promotion. Furthermore, mothers who stopped breast-feeding and used the free samples often stopped lactating. Therefore they were forced to continue bottle-feeding and had to buy formula once the free sample was finished. It was further argued that mothers thereby denied their babies the natural immunity and nutrition from their own breast milk.

In addition to these specific business complaints, these groups accused Nestlé of corporate social irresponsibility. Infant formula was marketed in less developed countries as a powder to be mixed with sterile water. In many third world countries, water is a scarce commodity and the means with which to sterilize it (a stove or firewood) are equally scarce. Furthermore, the formula and water had to be mixed in the correct proportions, and there was virtually no refrigeration for storage of the formula. While instructions for the preparation were written on the package, many mothers were illiterate and mixed the formula incorrectly. Finally, in an attempt to economize, many mothers diluted the mixture.

Advocacy groups claimed that Nestlé was directly responsible for the disease, malnutrition, and death that resulted from the incorrect and unsterile use of formula. It was estimated that up to 10 million babies were affected annually. In late 1973, these claims against infant formula producers were published in *The New Internationalist* in an article entitled "The Baby Killer." This article was subsequently altered and translated into German under the title "Nestlé Kills Babies." Although Nestlé sued for libel and won, the article was successful in its attempt to focus attention on Nestlé.

As a result of these articles and other public attacks on Nestlé, the Infant Formula Action Coalition was formed in 1977. This group organized a boycott of all Nestlé products sold in the United States with the hope that Nestlé would be pressured into changing their role in third world countries. Nestlé was picked as the focus for the boycott as it had over 50 percent of the third world market for infant formula. However, the boycott organizers aimed to use Nestlé as a lever to stop the aggressive sales promotion of infant formula by all companies operating in the third world.

Nestlé's Response

Nestlé and other infant formula producers had not responded to the initial PAG call for cooperation in November 1973. However, after the controversy over the *New Internationalist* article, Nestlé did modify its marketing practices in the third world: there was greater control over the distribution of samples, direct contact between company representatives and new mothers was eliminated, and all advertising had to meet the approval of public authorities. In addition, in 1975 Nestlé, with seven other infant formula producers, formed the PAG-sponsored International Council of Infant Food Industries (ICIFI). This group agreed to follow a code of conduct based on the PAG Statement 23.

Once the boycott was launched, Nestlé met with INFACT twice, but each encounter drove them further apart. Nestlé, at this point, agreed that breast-feeding was best and that their purpose was to provide a nutritious substitute or supplement. By 1978, all mass media advertising of infant formula was terminated. In spite of these concessions, an agreement was not reached with INFACT until early 1984.

WHO Code

The controversy was finally brought to a conference on infant feeding in 1979 cosponsored by two UN organizations: the World Health Organization (WHO) and UNICEF. The result of this conference was the adoption of the International Code of Breast-milk Substitutes in Geneva in May 1981. By 1984 Nestlé had agreed to comply with all the WHO guidelines, to carry warnings on its labels about the improper use of infant formula, not to use material that was promotional, to limit free samples to cases of medical need and where mothers could not breast-feed, and to end personal gifts to health workers in third world nations.

To some extent the issue was never resolved. Advocacy groups are still not fully satisfied with Nestlé, although the boycott was suspended in early 1984. The results of the 7-year boycott are also unclear. Nestlé said that the boycott had little commercial impact and that its sales had increased during the peak years of the protests. However, the company says that it was willing to settle the issue due to its concern about the company image, rather than sales. Nestlé maintains that it endorsed the WHO code immediately, but the boycott committee claims that it took several years to make Nestlé comply fully with the code. Perhaps these conflicting viewpoints will never be resolved.

QUESTIONS

1 Do you believe that Nestlé exhibited sufficient corporate responsibility? Why or why not? If not, how should Nestlé have marketed infant formula in third world countries? How much should a multinational spend on reducing host nation information costs when it extends its product line there?

2 What were the concerns of each group of stakeholders (interest groups) in the boycott? What were their strategic objectives and what tactics did they use to achieve them? What do you think of these tactics?

3 Can host governments be held partly responsible for allowing a private firm access to its public through government institutions (clinics and hospitals)? Do you think that there is any difference between the responsibilities of third world governments and governments of "advanced" nations in this regard?

4 How should the management of Nestlé react to the consumer boycott in order to maintain their market share of all their product lines? Consider this from viewpoints of the chief executive officer, marketing manager for infant formula, production manager for infant formula, managers of different products, and regional managers.

CHAPTER 12

GOVERNMENT REGULATION OF MULTINATIONAL ENTERPRISES

INTRODUCTION

Host-country governments have a stake in the successful operation of multinational enterprises (MNEs) in their economies. MNEs can provide the host country with capital, process and product technology, management and marketing skills, access to imported inputs, and markets for exports. In response to the perceived nature of MNEs, host-country governments often regulate the operations of MNEs within their borders. They do this by attempting to increase the benefits flowing from the operations of MNEs in the country as a whole or to specific groups within the country. To achieve the twin goals of sovereignty and increased net benefits, governments employ a wide variety of regulations and incentives ranging from outright nationalization to substantial subsidies to attract investment by MNEs.

MNEs also benefit from their operations in host countries. Host countries provide MNEs with markets for their products and factors of production—labor, capital, raw materials, and semimanufactured products—with which to produce them. MNEs also use host nations for their natural resources and, on occasion, as a base for exports. In their operations worldwide, the strategy of MNEs is to maximize total system profits by allocating internal resources to make best use of their firm-specific advantages and to retain the surplus from their worldwide operations. Multinationals attempt to respond to the international economic environment with a wide variety of tactics aimed at reducing or circumventing the impact of government regulation.

In some nations, government-MNE relations are characterized by confrontation and mutual distrust. Some MNEs view government regulations as unwarranted, disruptive intrusions in their operations and abrogations of the rights of private property that violate natural law. Some host governments are apt to regard MNEs as evils, if necessary ones, dedicated to exploitation and profit gouging, all-powerful and beyond national control. Such views serve to poison relationships between host countries and MNEs.

Today, such stereotypes are being replaced with more reasoned assessments of the value, rights, and responsibilities of both MNEs and host-country governments. Although the fundamental causes of the conflict remain, the approach to resolving the issues has moved toward negotiation and bargaining within a more rational framework. While highly charged rhetoric is still heard, especially at international forums, it is largely confined to times of abrupt economic and political change, or during economic recessions when tensions increase and long-standing grievances erupt.

The role of the three types of regulation is outlined in Figure 12-1. The manner by which they regulate MNEs is discussed in this chapter.

HOME-COUNTRY REGULATION

As described in Chapter 11, the interests of MNEs and their home countries usually coincide in large measure. The economics of the enterprise, especially economies of scale in production, research, product development, information gathering and processing, and strategic planning functions usually dictate that these activities be centralized in one country. Since the MNE typically begins operations in its home country, it will tend to centralize these operations at home.

Organizational slack and inertia tend to develop in any enterprise, especially those in the concentrated, oligopolistic industries characteristic of MNEs. This slack can retard the organizational change necessary for an MNE to allocate resources outside the home country, even when economic efficiency and overall profitability might be increased by such a move. Moreover, the tendency of the executives of MNEs toward ethnocentricity in their outlook and decisions often

THREE REGULATORS

FIGURE 12-1
The regulation of MNEs. Most of the regulation of MNEs is done by host nations, and these regulations constrain the actions of its subsidiaries. Multilateral organizations reinforce the host nations' regulation by acting as agents for the dissemination of information about MNEs.

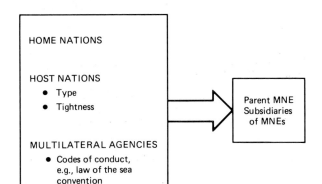

works to the advantage of the home country, even if to the long-run disadvantage of the MNE itself. There is evidence that some MNEs have retained operations in their home countries after the time when they could best be performed abroad. For example, some U.S. MNEs in the electronics industry retained production operations in the United States even when they could have been performed less expensively abroad. Most U.S. textile firms have refused to invest heavily abroad even when failure to do so has led to their gradual decline. Also, the nationalistic aspirations of the home country are often shared by executives of its MNEs.[1]

Home-Country Bargaining Power

The government of the home country is in a strong position in its relationship with locally owned MNEs. Typically, the largest proportion of the assets of MNEs are located in their home country and are potential hostages in any dispute. In the extreme case of an outright confrontation, the option of withdrawing operations from the home country is rarely available. In less extreme cases, the policies of home-country governments, as embodied in their laws and regulations, can be applied forcefully to MNEs based within its borders and to executives of MNEs who are usually citizens of the home country.[2]

For these reasons, home country–MNE relations tend toward mutual support and cooperation in the pursuit of common goals rather than to distrust and confrontation. Laws and regulations in the home country are seldom directed specifically at the MNE, but apply equally to all firms that operate in the economy. If specific regulations are directed toward MNEs, they tend not to be overt, codified in laws and regulations, but rather are applied through administrative guidance, mutual advice and agreement. Home-country governments are apt to act through personal contact and to privately suggest a course of action to MNEs based in their countries rather than use the force of law.

The most publicized exceptions to this generalization have occurred in the relations between the U.S. government and U.S. multinationals. In these cases—involving profit and capital repatriation, technology transfer, extraterritoriality, trade, and employment creation abroad—regulation has been proposed and effected under the glare of national and international publicity.[3] Governments in Europe, the United Kingdom, and Japan have also regulated the operations of MNEs based in their countries, especially in periods of balance of trade or balance

---

[1]As an extreme example, an executive of a Japanese MNE recently pointed out a huge sign of a Japanese enterprise that dominated Singapore's skyline. He remarked, "We tried to do it the wrong way the first time."

[2]In the case of the uranium cartel, however, one American executive of Gulf Oil who was running one of the Canadian subsidiaries took Canadian citizenship to avoid the long arm of the U.S. Senate and courts.

[3]As an extreme example, in 1982 during Israel's invasion of Lebanon, President Reagan banned the export of cluster bombs to Israel. One American producer was not officially informed of this prohibition and continued to export even though American soldiers were operating in the area. This oversight was eventually detected (by the news media), and exports were halted, too late for one American soldier who was killed and several others who were wounded by these bombs.

of payments crises. In Japan, for example, until the mid-1970s, outward invest-ment by Japanese trading firms was tightly limited by the Ministry of International Trade and Industry (MITI). Some Japanese MNEs ran afoul of government trade regulations, as happened in the mid-1970s, when several Japanese trading compa-nies were charged with hoarding commodities in order to manipulate prices in Japan.

Regulation of Trade

The regulation of MNEs by their home governments is primarily directed toward their activities in the home countries, where they are subject to the laws governing the operations of any enterprise. National governments can regulate the interna-tional operations of MNEs when their operations abroad have an impact on the home market. The problem for international managers is that almost any aspect of their international operations might be construed as having an impact on the home economy. Moreover, host-country governments may regulate MNEs so that some of their activities abroad are not in the best interests of their home countries and contravene laws at home.

Striking examples of this conflict between MNEs and host and home govern-

---

THE URANIUM CARTEL: AN EXAMPLE OF MNE–HOME GOVERNMENT CONFLICT[4]

The production, trade, and use of uranium is subject to complex national and international regulations because of its strategic importance. After a boom in the mid-1950s, uranium prices on the world market plummeted (from $12 per pound in 1955 to $4 per pound in 1972) as U.S. demand to fill its strategic stockpile decreased. From 1959 to 1967, world production of uranium fell almost 70 percent, while stockpiles of unsold uranium increased, causing massive drops in production, profits, employment, and exports in producing countries. In light of the change in demand and the ramifications of this change, a uranium cartel was established.

In February 1972 a meeting was held in Paris, under the guise of a Uranium Marketing Research Organization which was attended by government representatives from Canada, Australia, France, South Africa, and executives from Rio Tinto Zinc (RTZ). This meeting led to the formation of a clandestine uranium cartel, known as the Club, in mid-1972. The immediate problem for the cartel was that for the 1972 to 1977 period, the available supply of uranium exceeded projected demand by four times. The uranium cartel established production and sales quotas, set prices and rigged bids, and allocated market shares.

Over the period of the cartel's operations during 1972 to 1975, the price of uranium on the world market, in Canada, and in the United States rose from $4 per pound to $20 per pound. After the cartel was disbanded, prices rose to a high of $42 per pound. The impact of the cartel, if any, on the world price of uranium is uncertain.

---

[4]See Lecraw (1977a) for a more detailed description of the cartel. Some of the most fascinating documents on international business are appended to a series of hearings before subcommittees of the U.S. Congress on the cartel.

ments occur in international trade. However, conflict also arises in transfers of technology and foreign direct investment (through joint ventures and forced mergers to achieve industry rationalization). Export agreements and cartels formed solely to serve the export market are typically exempt from national competition laws against such practices. But exports for one country are imports for another. It is often difficult to unhook the export market from the home market since world prices tend to affect prices in the economy at home.

Regulation of Foreign Direct Investment and Licensing

Home governments may also act against MNEs because of their foreign direct investment (FDI) and technology licensing activities. These activities have an impact on the trade of the home country and on competition within it. The most obvious case occurs when an MNE acquires an enterprise abroad which is a potential or actual competitor in its home market either through exports or foreign direct investment. Joint ventures abroad can have similar effects. In some cases such acquisitions have been struck down. Licensing of technology can also serve to limit international trade and domestic competition. An MNE can license an enterprise abroad to use its product or process technology and, as part of the licensing agreement, restrict the sale of products, based on that technology, to the licensee's home market or to a set geographic region. Cross-licensing by MNEs based in different home countries can be used to divide international markets and restrict international investment. Licenses used for this purpose have also been struck down in some instances.

International Competition

The number of competitors at the international level is greater than at the national level. The restriction of international competition and trade is difficult to achieve and sustain. Even in such an overt and tightly run cartel as the uranium cartel (a cartel which operated with explicit approval and support of the governments of the producing countries), cheating was so widespread that it threatened to blow the cartel apart. Most agreements between enterprises to restrict competition operate in the shadows outside the law. Information exchange is limited, and chiseling on quotas and prices is endemic. Even if detected, cheating is difficult to punish.

Restrictive provisions incorporated into technology transfer agreements are also difficult to enforce. Pilkington's revolutionary process for producing plate glass was licensed by the British firm to almost every producer in the world. These licenses contained strict provisions concerning which markets the licensees were permitted to serve. Yet despite Pilkington's monopoly position in this technology and its associated power to withdraw licenses and act under patent laws, licensees regularly violated the market restrictions in their agreements and Pilkington was largely powerless to act against them.

During the 1970s and into the 1980s, there was an increase in the number of MNEs, as well as the number of home countries in which they were based.[5] These trends decreased the overall level of industrial concentration at the international level and increased the sources of capital and technology. The firm-specific advantages of MNEs based in different countries often vary. MNEs compete on different FSAs and follow different strategies to exploit them. These differences increase the difficulty that MNEs have in recognizing that it would be to their mutual benefit to overtly or tacitly coordinate their activities.

In some industries and in some markets, MNEs still exercise considerable market power, either individually or jointly. Many of the most dynamic industries such as electronics, computers, biological and pharmaceutical products, machine tools, and robotics have become highly fragmented. Although overall industry concentration has fallen, within segments, MNEs can exercise significant market power.

In the future, as MNEs based in different home countries gain experience competing with each other in international markets, the existing level of competition may change. In the 1970s the number of joint ventures and cross licenses between MNEs rose dramatically. These joint operations could lead to increased coordination and cooperation in the future as well.

An increased level of global competition has induced firms at the national level to merge and rationalize their operations, often with the encouragement of national governments. MNEs that were competitors in one national market have found partners for themselves. An interesting question in international business and the relationship of MNEs with home governments, is whether partnership in markets in host countries abroad will lead to cooperation at the enterprise level in other markets, including home markets. For example, will joint ventures and cross licensing between U.S. and Japanese auto manufacturers reduce the level of competition in the U.S. auto market?

Governments at the national level, as well as international organizations, have become more aware of the potential for MNEs to restrain competition. As a result, many have enacted (and in some cases enforced) laws directed at the activities of MNEs. These are designed to regulate competition in both domestic and international markets. The form of future regulation is unknown, and the effects of such regulations by home countries on the operations of MNEs cannot be predicted with any degree of certainty. Consequently, the international manager will be operating in an increasingly uncertain environment at home and abroad.

HOST-COUNTRY REGULATION

As described in Chapter 11, the potential severity and range of conflicts between MNEs and host-country governments are much greater than the possible conflicts

---

[5]See the annual issue of *Fortune* magazine for the International Top 500 and Dunning and Pearce, *The World's Largest Industrial Enterprises: 1962–1978* (Gower Press, 1981, 1983).

between MNEs and their home-country governments. Essentially, these conflicts arise over the control of the resources of the MNE in the host country and the division of the perceived surplus from operations. Since the goals of MNEs and host governments often differ, one or both sides must give up some measure of control plus some of its desired share of the surplus. The mechanisms through which such bargaining is determined are described in detail in Chapter 13. This section describes some of the means by which host governments act to increase their control over the operations of MNEs and acquire a share in any surplus that accrues from multinational operations.

Instruments of Host-Government Regulations

The means by which host governments regulate MNEs can be analyzed along two dimensions: the instruments used to regulate MNEs and the tightness of the regulation. The instruments of regulation include instruments that affect the macroeconomic environment such as taxes, tariffs, capital costs, wages, exchange rates, and prices and those that affect the firm's microeconomic environment, such as local ownership requirements, local value-added regulations, capital rationing, hiring quotas, export requirements, and import licensing. They also include controls on technology, foreign exchange, prices, and restrictions on transfer pricing.

Governments can use one or both types of regulatory instruments to achieve their goals. For example, an objective may be to increase the level of local ownership in an industry. This goal might be achieved by requiring that MNEs invest in joint ventures with local partners or by asking them to increase the availability of capital, technology, and management training to local entrepreneurs. Similarly, governments might act to achieve a balance in the external accounts by moving toward an equilibrium exchange rate, instituting foreign exchange restrictions, or requiring MNEs to obtain licenses for their imports.

In general, regulation of the behavior of MNEs (and the national economy) via macroeconomic policies is difficult and can be accomplished only over a long period of time. Such regulation, however, tends to lead to a more efficient allocation of resources, involves fewer distortions in the economy, and requires a lower level of bureaucratic regulatory involvement. The effects of direct regulation on the internal operations of MNEs are more immediate and certain. In the long run, however, they often lead to further distortions in the economy, have unanticipated consequences, and place heavy requirements on scarce bureaucratic resources for continuous monitoring, supervision, and control.

Multinational enterprise−host government relations differ depending on the type of government regulation. While some MNEs flourish in host countries where there is a high degree of government involvement in their internal activities, others do not. They operate best in countries in which the government confines its regulation to the macroeconomy. For example, some MNEs thrive under the low level of microeconomic regulation in Singapore and the reliance of that government on macroeconomic regulation. Some of these MNEs refuse to operate in

Indonesia, where the government regulates the most minute details of their operations. Other MNEs find the exact opposite to be attractive.

The basis of government regulation in host countries is thus an important variable for the operations of MNEs. Changing economic or political conditions alter it as does a new government with a different regulatory philosophy. Managers of MNEs must be sensitive to their regulatory environment and to trends in that environment.

The Tightness of Regulation

The second dimension of host-government regulations, the tightness of the regulatory environment, also directly affects the operations of MNEs. The strictness of the enforcement of the laws concerning MNEs can be independent of the type of regulatory method used by the government.

The governments of both Singapore and Hong Kong regulate the behavior of MNEs through their macroeconomic environment. Singapore's government has chosen to take an active role in regulating tariffs, wage rates, and infrastructure development to push the economy in the direction it desires. The government in Hong Kong, on the other hand, has tended to let the free market operate with only minimal government intervention. Korea and India both regulate the microenvironment of MNEs. In India, this regulation is far tighter than in Korea and has caused such firms as Coca-Cola, IBM, and Exxon to withdraw some of their operations from India. The tightness of the regulatory environment and future trends in the degree of tightness are of considerable interest and concern for MNEs.

An important factor in the tightness of the regulatory environment of MNEs lies in the application of government regulatory policy. There are often differences between government policy statements, the embodiment of these policies in laws and regulations, and their application. When these differences exist, international managers are faced with the problem of assessing the regulatory environment and operating within it. On the one hand, despite harsh statements toward MNEs, the government may, in fact, be quite lenient and benign toward MNEs. In such circumstances, MNEs, scared off by the government's rhetoric, may miss attractive opportunities to utilize host-country resources. The ITT, for example, has operated successfully in many countries despite strong rhetoric specifically directed against it.

On the other hand, MNEs who believe they can "do business" in the face of hostile statements by a government with stringent, but unenforced, laws may find that suddenly these laws are applied (even applied retroactively) to their operations. The difference may lie in the other direction as well. Government policy statements and regulations may be directed at encouraging the operations of MNEs, yet bureaucratic application of the laws can range from cumbersome, to obstructionist, to hostile.

In situations of conflict between government policy and its application, MNEs must rely heavily on information provided by local managers living in the host country. No amount of analysis at headquarters or fly-in visits by top-level executives can substitute for first-hand experience based on daily interaction with government bureaucrats. In many MNEs, however, information and decisions flow from headquarters down to the subsidiary, not from subsidiary to headquarters.

The problem arising from differences in laws and their application is compounded by the fact that while government policies and laws are directed toward all MNEs, they are often applied to only some industries or some MNEs. In extreme cases, some MNEs may be expelled from a country while others are invited in. These inconsistencies in host-government regulation can be analyzed on the basis of the relative bargaining power of MNEs and host governments. This method of analysis is described in Chapter 13.

In summary, specific host-government regulation of MNEs should be analyzed within the context of the two general methods of regulation—microeconomic and macroeconomic. Attention must also be paid to the tightness of these regulations. Managers of MNEs should bear in mind that there is often a lack of congruence between a government's stated policy toward MNEs, the embodiment of that policy in laws and regulations, and its application in practice. One of the most valuable functions of subsidiaries in the host country is to provide their headquarters with information on the actual, day-to-day, regulatory environment in the host country.

Problems With Host-Country Regulation

Host governments use a wide range of instruments to regulate the operations of MNEs within their countries. These regulations are directed at all three of the major activities of the MNE: trade, licensing, and foreign direct investment (FDI). Regulations specifically directed at MNEs have focused mainly on their direct investment activities. Regulation of foreign investment includes: outright prohibition of any investment by MNEs, prohibitions on investment in certain sectors of the economy, schemes to phase out the equity position of MNEs over time, and requirements for varying degrees of participation by national residents in joint ventures with MNEs.

Almost inevitably, government regulation of direct investment by MNEs varies over time, with changes in the economic, social, and political environment of the host country. Sometimes MNEs with operations already in place in the host country respond with outrage to these changes in the rules of the game and attempt to block their formulation and implementation. Other MNEs respond in a more cooperative manner and accept increased host-government involvement in their operations. Some MNEs respond less directly and, while accepting local partners, have been able to organize their operations to retain control of the allocation and use of their resources.[6]

---

[6]See Lecraw (1983) for evidence on the ability of MNEs to allow local equity participation yet retain control of their subsidiary's operations and profits.

Regulation of Equity Participation   Host governments act to increase local equity participation in operations of MNEs for several reasons. Local equity participation may increase local control over the MNE's resources in the host country and increase the share of the perceived surplus accruing to the country as a whole or to certain groups within the country. Local partners may also gain access to information concerning the operations of the local subsidiary and help their governments to obtain a better idea of what goes on within the "black box" of MNEs and be in a better position to regulate its activities. Host governments may also require local ownership participation for political reasons. A high level of foreign ownership is often a political liability for the government in power. Governments may take a strong stance toward foreign ownership to enhance their position with the population as a whole and particularly with groups that benefit from local ownership requirements.

Host governments typically use several means of direct regulation to induce greater local ownership in the subsidiaries of MNEs. Prior to the initial investment, they may require a specified percentage of local equity participation. The amount depends on the industry in which the subsidiary operates and, more recently, on whether the subsidiary's output is to be sold on the domestic market or exported. Similarly, at the outset of foreign direct investment, the government may impose a time schedule over which the MNE must reduce its share of equity to the point where local owners eventually have a majority interest or even sole ownership. Instead of mandating a level of local equity ownership, host governments may make additional incentives contingent on local ownership. These incentives include reduced tax rates and reduced duties on imports. Since the ownership conditions in such cases are specified at the outset, the response of MNEs is relatively straightforward as they can make their NPV calculations on the viability of the investment with some degree of certainty.

The situation becomes complicated and indeed rancorous when governments change the local ownership requirements or the rewards system after the foreign investment is in place.[7] MNEs feel that this change in the rules of the game once it is in progress is unfair and immoral. It is seen to represent expropriation of assets that rightfully belong to the MNEs. As already described, this conflict is often due to differences in timing of the flows of costs and benefits of direct investment from the viewpoint of the host government and the MNE. In the first years of operation, the costs to the MNE are often high and the benefits are low. At this time the costs to the host country are low and the benefits are high. The situation reverses after the investment has been in place for a time.

The issue here is twofold: (1) whether host governments have the fundamental right to require MNEs to divest of some or all of the equity in their subsidiaries and (2) at what price the sale should be made. Some MNEs would rather cease operations in the host country than sell part of their equity to local partners,

---

[7]Host governments need not act directly to allocate equity to local partners. They can use the tax system or price controls to reduce the profitability of the venture for the MNE to the point at which it agrees to sell out to local interests.

regardless of the selling price. For example, IBM ultimately withdrew most of its operations from India rather than accept Indian equity participation in its core operations. For such MNEs no price is sufficient to compensate for loss of ownership and control of the subsidiary. In most instances, however, the issue is over the appropriate price that an MNE should be paid for the equity position it is being forced to relinquish.

Host-government initiatives to reduce the level of foreign ownership by MNEs in their economies were not confined to developing countries. For example, to promote plans in electronics and telecommunications, France has forced several MNEs to sell their subsidiaries and be merged with government or privately owned French firms. This is part of France's drive to nationalize key sectors of its industry. The Japanese government has long discouraged FDI and made majority ownership by MNEs virtually impossible. Japan is one of the few nations where nonequity forms of foreign investment (such as licensing and joint ventures) exceed the amount of foreign direct investment. Japan has also forced U.S. auto manufacturers to cease operations in Japan and has placed direct and indirect restrictions on the operations of MNEs that had at one time majority-owned subsidiaries in Japan after World War II.

In the 1970s Canada established a Foreign Investment Review Agency (FIRA) to screen foreign direct investment. This agency has erected barriers to prevent foreign-owned firms from acquiring other firms, even if they were already foreign-owned. It also reviews applications for all new subsidiaries to determine if they are in Canada's national interest based on the net benefits they will bring to Canada. Canada's National Energy Program (1981) discriminated against foreign-owned petroleum firms by its tax and ownership provisions. One result was the purchase of the Belgian-owned Petrofina and British Petroleum by the government's agency, Petrocan.[8]

Multinational enterprises cannot expect host-government requirements for local equity participation to remain stable over time. Changing economic conditions and political and social pressures inevitably cause shifts in government attitudes, laws, and the application of those laws. Such changes increase the uncertainty and risk for MNEs in their operations in host countries. Prediction of these changes is difficult since similar changes in conditions lead to radically different shifts in government policy. Worsening economic conditions in Canada have caused the government to loosen its restrictions on MNEs and encourage new foreign investment. Yet, worsening economic conditions in other countries have led governments to expropriate the subsidiaries of MNEs.

The concept of the *"obsolescing bargain"* can serve as a useful framework for analysis of trends in regulation by host governments. If the perceived or actual net benefits brought to the host country by the MNE changes over time, the MNE must expect changes in the host-government attitude and, ultimately, regulation of its operations. For the reasons described in Chapter 11, these net benefits often

---

[8]The price paid for Petrofina was the subject of considerable controversy since it was about 150 percent of its share value on the stock exchange.

are, or are perceived to be, highest at the start of the MNE's operations in the host country and decline over time. The MNE's relative bargaining power is usually greatest prior to its initial investment and declines over time as well as a result of dissipation of its firm-specific advantages and an increased level of expertise in the host country. Moreover, as the size of the MNE's operations increases in the host country, its importance to the local economy increases as well, and with it, the host government's concern over controlling this increasingly important force in its economy. Unless the MNE can continually act to maintain its relative bargaining power, it must expect the host government to intervene in its operations to an increasing extent over time. An MNE can follow some combination of three strategies to maintain control over its operations: it can increase the net benefits it brings to the host country, it can increase perception of the host government of the net benefits due to its operations, and it can act to retain and develop its FSAs. The tactics to be successful in these strategies are described in Chapter 13.

RESPONSES BY MNEs

MNE Reponses to Local-Ownership Regulations

Multinational enterprises can respond to local ownership regulations by reducing their level of investment in host countries or by changing the nature of their operations to retain control over the critical aspects of their business. Some MNEs can retain effective operating control with only a minority equity position and, through manipulation of transfer prices, can retain any surplus within their enterprise.

Some MNEs fear that firm-specific advantages, particularly proprietary technology, may be diffused through joint-venture partners. The reaction is to reduce the level of technology transfer to such subsidiaries or to withdraw from the country entirely. Marketing-intensive MNEs also bargain for majority ownership to retain product quality and worldwide brand reputation. In general, technology-intensive and marketing-intensive MNEs desire 100 percent equity ownership not only because they fear loss of control to local minority partners, but also because they place little value on the resources brought to the venture by local partners.

Regulations concerning the level of local equity ownership are the most important set of host-government regulations directed specifically toward the subsidiaries of MNEs. Other forms of government regulation, such as local value-added requirements, technology licensing regulations, and regulations on transfer pricing of inputs and outputs, debt, and technology, although not specifically directed toward MNEs, are disproportionately applied to them because of the nature of their operations.

Value-Added Regulations

Governments often set tariffs not only to raise revenues and reduce imports, but also to encourage the development of local industries. Many MNEs invest in host countries when their tariffs make exports from the home country noncompetitive in the local market. Often these "tariff-jumping" investments are little more than assembly operations using imported raw materials, semifinished products and components. Value added in the host country is low.

MNEs often claim that these components are not available in the host country in sufficient quantity and that the quality of local inputs is low and the price high. To encourage local production and to increase the value added in the host country, host governments often raise tariffs on imported inputs to increase local sourcing. The effect of such tariffs is uncertain. The landed cost of importing may still be lower than comparable domestically produced inputs, if they are available at all. Quotas can also be used, but here the problem is to place quotas on only the inputs that can be produced locally at a competitive price and quality. MNEs may be able to avoid these tariffs and quotas through manipulation of transfer prices. Tariffs and quotas set to force increases in the value added in one industry may have unintended and undesirable effects on their availability and price for other industries. Another solution to the problem of increasing local value added is for the host government to regulate local value added directly. It can mandate that a given percentage of the cost of production or local sales price must be produced locally.

Although simple in theory, value-added requirements are difficult to monitor and enforce. Government must obtain, verify, and analyze highly detailed data at the firm level in order to determine whether each subsidiary is in fact meeting the requirements. As an example of one possible strategic response, an MNE could set up a separate local operation to "manufacture" some previously imported input. This subsidiary would essentially import the input at a low price and sell it to its parent's other subsidiary after "local processing" as a host-country product. Alternatively, the MNE could continue to import its inputs from its parent at home, but at low transfer prices. It could then charge itself high prices for capital equipment, technology, management fees, interest on intracompany debt, and suppliers' credits or simply record high local profits. All these "local" costs and profits typically count in the calculation of local value added.

Local value-added requirements are essentially a combination of a quota and a tariff which raise local costs and prices. MNEs will try to avoid incurring these costs, often in direct conflict with host-government plans and objectives.

TECHNOLOGY TRANSFER

The ability of MNEs to generate and transfer technology is one of their strengths and the most obvious benefit to host countries. Despite this, technology transfer by MNEs is surrounded by controversy and conflict and is increasingly the subject of government regulation. As described in Chapter 11, some groups, most notably labor, may perceive that technology transfer by MNEs harms the home country. They lobby the home government to limit its exports of technology. Yet the most serious and widespread problems for MNEs with technology transfer arise with host governments in both developed and less developed countries. Host governments have erected an increasing array of regulations to control the flow of technology by MNEs.

The usual perception of technology is limited and static: a formula, blueprints, a machine, a product. Modern industrial technology includes these, but it involves much more. It is multidimensional and dynamic. The value and strength of IBM's technology is not just in its machines and software programs, but in its sales force, production workers, service support, management, financial strength, and ongoing research and development which brings a continuous stream of new products onto the market. The value of a specific product or process technology usually seldom resides simply in some well-defined entity, but in the complex expertise that surrounds this entity. It also resides in future improvements and innovations to both the specific technology and the surrounding support activities.

To transfer this package of technology through an external market is seldom practical. Therefore, internal markets are used by MNEs to protect their proprietary rights in technology. Neither buyer nor seller can know the value of technology, once it is removed from the support activities that surround it within the MNE and from the flow of future technology generated within the MNE.[9] These characteristics of modern industrial technology lead MNEs to centralize their R and D activities within the firm and to transfer their technology within the enterprise rather than through the market.

Host governments sometimes perceive these practices of MNEs as contrary to the best interests of the host nation. In response, they have imposed regulations to change this behavior. To the host country, the price at which technology is transferred within MNEs is apparently arbitrary since no market or "arm's-length" price exists. However, this host-country viewpoint ignores the rationale of internalization. Attempts to unbundle the package of technology often fail. Host governments also impose arbitrary limits on technical service fees, royalties, and management fees.

Some host governments have tried at times to force MNEs to locate some R and D activities within their countries to help upgrade the levels of the jobs available in that country. It is difficult for the MNE to relocate R and D. It may require a reorganization of the administrative structure of the MNE and even a fundamental shift in its strategy. The Canadian government, for example, has encouraged MNEs to locate the entire worldwide R and D, production, and marketing of one line of their products in Canada, that is, to give their Canadian subsidiary a "world product mandate." For the MNE to act in accord with this initiative, it requires decentralization of its R and D, production, and marketing operations by product line. The policy would serve to scatter the operations of the MNE around the world. Not surprisingly, few MNEs have followed this Canadian policy.

Host governments also fear that through their technological capabilities, MNEs are able to dominate local firms, thus stunting the development of technology in those firms. In response, host governments have acted to reduce the flow of

---

[9]See Killing (1980) for a description of the market for technology and the problems of uncertainty and asymmetric information between buyer and seller.

technology through MNEs by either excluding them from the host market entirely or by forcing them to license technology at "arm's length" to local firms. Japan has followed this strategy with success. Increasingly, governments in high-income countries have come to regulate MNEs in high-technology industries. In Canada, however, there is an increasing awareness that Canada has gained access to technology more rapidly and at a lower cost through MNEs than it would have if it had had to rely on the external market.

Host governments in low-income countries have additional concerns with technology transfer by MNEs. They often find that their factor proportions of labor and capital and their consumer demand patterns are at variance with the product and process technology employed by MNEs. This technology is often ill suited to their factor costs, the size of their markets, and the quality and availability of locally produced inputs. These host nations also look askance at MNEs' product technology, finding it inappropriate to local income levels and the basic needs of low-income earners. Yet, when MNEs transfer more appropriate (but older) capital equipment and produce more standardized products, they are accused of fobbing off second-best product and process technology to third world countries. Indeed, several third world countries have banned the import of second-hand machinery, although this machinery is typically smaller-scale and more labor-intensive than the technology the MNEs have developed for use at home.

The concern about the power of the MNE arises as a result of its power in the three areas of technology, capital, and management. These encompass a local firm. This domination of the MNE comes from the package of advantages it has in these three areas. Attempts by host nations to regulate one of these will be unsuccessful, as the MNE can rely on its other advantages to compensate. Indeed, it is practically impossible for a host nation to unbundle this package of technological, capital, and management skills owned by the MNE. About the only worthwhile strategy for host nations is to attempt to acquire one of the three advantages from different MNEs, for example, capital from U.S. MNEs, technology from German MNEs, and managerial skills from Japanese MNEs. This reinforces the point that competition among the MNEs provides a better means of control than does regulation.

The role of MNEs in generating and transferring product and process technology to third world countries is, and will remain, a source of conflict between host governments and MNEs. The ability of host governments to monitor and regulate the flow of technology by means of MNEs has increased significantly over the last decade. Host governments have also acted to develop the technological capabilities of their indigenous firms in the hope of generating appropriate technology, sourced on an international basis. The impacts of these host-country initiatives on MNEs remains unknown. Appropriate technology for some products and processes has been developed outside MNEs and is now more widely available and used in low- and middle-income countries. Host-government policy toward the technology provided by MNEs can be ambivalent at best and obstructive at worst. There is reason to believe that when host governments become involved in technology choice, the resulting technology is less appropriate to the economic conditions of their countries.

REGULATION OF INTRAFIRM TRADE

Transfer Pricing: Theory

Transfer prices are internal prices set by the MNE when conducting intrafirm trade. The transfer price may or may not approximate an arm's-length (market) price. On many occasions the arm's-length price itself may not exist. This occurs when the MNE has made an internal market, and no regular market exists. Transfer pricing can also be used by the MNE to minimize global taxes or circumvent foreign exchange controls, which prevent repatriation of funds.

Tax rates on profits and tariff rates on imports vary between nations. The MNE will set a high transfer price on exports to a host-country subsidiary when the host nation's tax rate exceeds the home country's. This has the effect of reducing profits and hence taxes, in the host country. If tariffs are present, however, the subsidiary will incur greater tariff costs as tariffs are levied on the declared value of the imports. Thus the MNE will consider both taxes and tariffs in the transfer pricing decision. Generally, a high transfer price will be used when the savings on host-country taxes exceed the additional tariff costs. A low transfer price will be used when the savings on tariffs exceed the additional income taxes paid. Horst (1971) illustrates this in a model for transfer pricing using taxes and tariffs (see Exhibit 12-1).

Foreign exchange controls, dividend taxes, and depreciating foreign currencies also influence the transfer pricing decision. Foreign exchange controls can "lock in" a subsidiary's profits. A high transfer price will circumvent currency controls and repatriate profits from the host country. Dividend taxes, in effect, tax profits twice and thus encourage the MNE to repatriate funds using a high transfer price rather than dividends. A rapidly depreciating foreign currency also encourages a policy of high transfer pricing. The high transfer price provides more timely conversion into stronger currencies to decrease the foreign exchange losses which can occur if funds are left for too long in the depreciating currency.

It is commonly recognized that everyone has the right to arrange their business affairs in such a way as to minimize taxes. The MNE extends this concept into an international context. The reasons for the MNE setting a transfer price different from the market price are all government-induced: taxes, tariffs, and controls. The transfer pricing mechanism, then, is an efficient response in which the MNE attempts to minimize its losses from exposure to exogenous market imperfections.

Transfer Pricing: Evidence

Host-country regulation of the intraenterprise trade conducted by MNEs focuses largely on the appropriate level of transfer prices charged between the subsidiaries of the MNE in different countries. This problem is particularly acute for

EXHIBIT 12-1
THE HORST (1971) MODEL

The Horst model describes the situation where the parent MNE exports to a host-country subsidiary. The parent's before-tax profit is domestic sales S_P plus export sales x less domestic costs C_P or

$$E_P \text{ (before tax)} = S_P + Ax - C_P$$

where A = the transfer price
         x = the quantity of intrafirm trade

The subsidiary's before tax profit is domestic sales S_H or

$$E_H \text{ (before tax)} = S_H - Ax - C_H$$

Thus far there is no reason for the transfer price to differ from the market price. Enter the government with taxes and tariffs. Each profit equation is multiplied by the after-tax profit retention rate $(1 - \text{tax rate})$, and the subsidiary's import costs are grossed up by the tariff rate $(1 + \text{tariff rate})$. Thus:

$$E_P = (1 - T_P)(S_P + Ax - C_P)$$
$$E_H = (1 - T_H)[S_H - (1 + t)Ax - C_H]$$

where T_P = the home-country income tax rate
         T_H = the host-country income tax rate
         t = the host-country import tariff rate

Global after-tax profits are determined by adding E_P and E_H and after much algebraic manipulation the following relationship results:

$$\frac{(T_H - T_P)}{(1 - T_H)} \gtrless t$$

The equation states that if the relative differential tax rate $(T_H - T_P)/(1 - T_H)$ exceeds the tariff rate t, then a high transfer price will be used because savings on reduced host-country income taxes exceed the extra costs of tariffs. Conversely, if $(T_H - T_P)/(1 - T_H)$ is less than t, a low transfer price is used as tariff savings exceed additional host-country income taxes.

---

technology-intensive MNEs and, to a lesser extent, for MNEs selling branded products. Studies of the transfer pricing problem have found that MNEs reduce transfer prices on imports into the host country when host nation tariffs are high or when local profit taxes are low. MNEs also set transfer prices above the arm's-length price when the host government imposes capital and dividend repatriation restrictions or currency controls. Transfer prices of exports from the home country are increased when host-country profit taxes are high. The net effect is to squeeze the profits of the subsidiaries in the host nation. This is a natural response by MNEs to such environmental factors as tax rate differentials, tariffs, or controls.

Transfer prices charged by decentralized MNEs reflect arm's-length prices to a greater extent than do those of MNEs with more centralized control systems. Imports and exports to and from subsidiaries of MNEs involved in joint ventures also tend to be transferred at arm's-length prices as the joint-venture partner has some idea of the subsidiary's cost data. The partner is unwilling to accept reduced profits in the host country.

Host governments impose regulations that attempt to control the procedures and levels at which transfer prices can be set. As explained earlier, in theory, the level preferred by governments is the arm's-length price at which the good or service is sold or purchased in the home country of the MNE. This assumes that such prices can be observed, which of course they cannot be for integrated MNEs with internal markets. Another price acceptable to governments is the "international price" of the good or service, as reported to customs officers. The arm's-length price in a third world country market at the same level of trade is also used by some governments as a measuring rod, albeit a hypothetical and arbitrary one.

For pure undifferentiated commodities, at least one of these three valuations of the appropriate transfer price may be available. If, as is often the case, prices on these three markets differ, MNEs may be allowed to pick one if it uses this pricing formula consistently. In other instances, MNEs and host governments negotiate to determine which of the prices will be used. Problems can arise when the governments in the two countries between which intraenterprise trade is conducted insist on the use of different transfer prices or nonexistent arm's-length prices.

Unfortunately, the intrafirm trade of MNEs is largely in differentiated products, for which there are no arm's-length market prices. In these cases, some proxy for the fair, arm's-length, market price must be determined by governments attempting to regulate transfer pricing. The procedure for determining this price varies from country to country and is usually unsatisfactory to both parties.

A typical practice is to take the cost of production and add a "normal" profit. Two obvious problems with this are to (1) arrive at the "cost of production" and (2) determine a "normal profit" that will satisfy both the MNE and the host government. If production cost is the marginal cost, should the government use the marginal cost plus production overhead, or the marginal cost of production plus full corporate overhead? Should the normal profit be the "risk-free" rate, the MNE's average profitability, or its profit rate on the particular product?

Even if these questions could be resolved in theory (which is difficult, if not impossible), in practice the actual calculation of the appropriate costs and profits is difficult. These problems can lead to a highly arbitrary assessment of the presumed gap between transfer prices and arm's-length prices. The case of pharmaceutical products illustrates this point.

Competitive Practices

Some host governments appear to view MNEs as all-powerful monopolists, using proprietary R and D, brand names, financial muscle, access to channels of

---

TRANSFER PRICING IN PHARMACEUTICALS

For some pharmaceutical products, the direct cost of production is less than 5 percent of the sales price. In 1973, the U.K. Monopolies Commission calculated the actual production cost of the active ingredients of F. Hoffmann-LaRoche's tranquilizer Librium (chlordiazepoxide) to be £9 per kilo (1.2 percent of sales price) compared to the company's transfer price of £370 per kilo (50.3 percent of sales price). When local production costs in the United Kingdom were added in, the difference in the cost figures was £437 to £76 per kilo. There were also differences between F. Hoffmann-LaRoche and the Commission on the costs of research in the United Kingdom, the valuation of Librium's appropriate contribution to central R and D and to central overheads. When the two separate cost calculations were added up, and subtracted from the sales price, the company showed a profit of 0.2 percent on sales; the commission showing a profit of 55.2 percent of sales. On a worldwide basis, the price of Librium in the United Kingdom was not excessive. In fact, the sale price of Librium was 169 percent higher in the United States than in the United Kingdom.

Not surprisingly, no consensus on prices and costs was reached between F. Hoffmann-LaRoche and the Commission. Equally unsurprising, there has been increased public concern over drug prices in Europe, the United States, Canada, and many developing countries. The transfer pricing practices of MNEs in this area are widely misunderstood. Since the knowledge advantage of the MNEs is at stake, MNEs prefer to use their internal markets to price R and D intensive pharmaceuticals and will pull out of host nations which threaten to disrupt their knowledge advantage.

---

distribution, and other means to gain and entrench market power. Multinational enterprises do tend to operate in concentrated industries, both at home and abroad. It is an unresolved issue, however, whether the operations of MNEs in an industry have led to increased industrial concentration beyond some natural level, or whether MNEs simply inhabit concentrated industries.[10]

Multinational enterprises have engaged in a wide variety of anticompetitive practices that could lead to further increased industry concentration, barriers to entry, and sustained supranormal profits. In response, host governments have acted to regulate some of the anticompetitive practices of MNEs. Some of these regulations are directed toward all enterprises that operate in the host country, while others are directed specifically at MNEs. This distinction between regulation of the general competitive environment and regulations specifically directed toward MNEs is somewhat arbitrary. Regulations that are directed toward all enterprises may only apply to MNEs when they are the sole firm in a particular industry, or the only firm engaging in the particular practice being regulated.

Host-country regulation of the competitive environment in general and of MNEs in particular has increased over time. In the future, the international manager should expect even greater government regulation of the competitive activities of MNEs.

---

[10]See Caves (1982), Chapter 4 for an excellent discussion of the effect of MNEs on industrial structure.

SUMMARY

Both host and home-country governments stand to gain from the operations of MNEs in their countries. They seek to maximize the net benefit through regulation and control of those operations. While the interests of the home governments and MNEs generally coincide, the host country – MNE relationship is often one of discord.

Home-country governments tend to be in a strong bargaining position in their relations with locally owned MNEs. Most of their regulations focus on the activities of the MNE in the home country and international operations are regulated only when they have an impact on the home market. However, both foreign direct investment and licensing abroad can affect trade and competition in the home country and, as such, are often subject to home-government restrictions.

Conflicts arise between host governments and MNEs over the control of operations in the host country and the division of the surplus that accrues from those operations. Host governments attempt to regulate the MNEs through the use of instruments which affect both the macroeconomic and microeconomic environments. Operations of the MNE are also affected by the tightness of these regulations. Instruments with which the host country attempts to control FDI include regulations on local ownership, local value-added requirements, and regulation of technology flows and payments. While host-country governments usually favor technology transfer, they recognize problems associated with it. Recently, regulations concerning the flow of technology via MNEs have increased significantly.

Finally, host-government regulations are directed at the appropriate level of transfer prices to be charged by the subsidiaries of MNEs in several countries. Often arm's-length prices do not exist for products traded within the MNE and the host government and MNE have difficulty in agreeing on an acceptable price.

KEY WORDS

Technology transfer
Cross-licensing
Microeconomic regulations
Macroeconomic regulations

Transfer price
Value-added regulations
Arm's-length price
Cartel

QUESTIONS

1 Discuss the statement: The government of the home country is in a strong position in its relationship with locally owned MNEs. Why is this true? Are there any exceptions to this rule?

2 The uranium cartel provides a good example of a home government – MNE conflict. Find an example of another major home government – MNE conflict, discuss the reasons for the conflict, and suggest possible courses of action for both the home government and the MNE.

3 The conflicts between MNEs and host-country governments are often much more serious than those between the MNE and home government. Why? Discuss the instruments of regulation used by the host-governments. How does the type of regulation and its tightness affect the relationship?

4 What should the managers of MNEs bear in mind when facing host country laws and regulations? Outline the strategies the MNE can follow to maintain control over its operations.

5 To increase local input, the host government can regulate local value added directly. What is the difficulty with value added requirements? Give examples, where possible, of how the MNE could respond to these requirements.

6 Why is technology transfer a source of conflict between host governments and MNEs? Describe how host governments may respond to this.

7 Transfer pricing is one means by which the MNE can minimize global taxes and foreign exchange controls. Explain how transfer prices work. What variables affect the transfer-pricing decision? What "evidence" is discussed in the chapter?

8 Discuss the statement: Nations can choose to be either rich and dependent or poor and independent. Give examples of nations in each category. Are there any nations that have managed to become both rich and independent? If so, what lesson for international business can be drawn from their experience?

CASE: FIRA—Canada's Foreign Investment Review Agency

Foreign ownership of the Canadian economy is of great concern to Canadians, yet few agencies have received more criticism than Canada's Foreign Investment Review Agency (FIRA), founded in 1974. Described as being too tough, too lax, inconsistent, unfair, and a hindrance to FDI, FIRA has always been one of Ottawa's problem children.

Much of the criticism stems from FIRA's inconsistent policies, which seem to bend with the political winds. New data released for the period April to June 1983 indicate an approval rate of 98 percent for acquisitions (takeovers) and 97 percent for new businesses. Since FIRA began screening takeovers in 1974, the acceptance rate had been about 85 percent. Yet just 2 years earlier, in 1981, the number of unsuccessful new business cases doubled to 30 percent and the approval rate dropped to 71 percent. Indeed, such fluctuations in approval rate raise the questions of whether FIRA is a barrier to FDI and what evidence is available to support its interventionist viewpoint.

As expressed by FIRA officials, there is no reason to expect approval rates to be higher or lower during a certain period or to follow a particular trend over time. Each proposal is dealt with separately to assess its "significant benefit" to Canada. These criteria include the provision of jobs, enhanced technology, increased exports, and regional effects. Since the economic definition of significant benefit is so broad, it is surprising that any proposals are rejected. A closer look at the political atmosphere during these times can shed some light on the shifting approval rates.

In 1980 Herb Gray was appointed as Minister of Industry, Trade and Commerce, the department responsible for the administration of FIRA. Mr. Gray advocated a strong nationalistic platform and greater control of foreign investment. At the same time, Canada implemented the National Energy Program (NEP), aimed at reducing foreign ownership of the petroleum sector from 70 to 50 percent by 1990.

In a period of recession, with high unemployment and a declining Canadian dollar, such nationalistic tendencies had harmful effects. In 1981 the capital account in the Canadian balance of payments recorded a net outflow of $10 billion, five times that of the previous year.

The increase in rejection rates in 1981 (U.S. allowed cases as a percentage of resolved cases) expresses a barrier felt by U.S. investors and results in deteriorating Canada-U.S. trade relations. The industries hardest hit were those with high-technology potential. As they are less likely to submit themselves to FIRA's complex review procedure, they risk the dissipation of their knowledge or technology FSA.

The result? The firms go elsewhere to protect their FSA. J. P. Lippincott of Canada, a U.S.-owned publishing firm is an example of this. Lippincott's U.S. parent was overtaken by another U.S. firm and was forced to have its Canadian subsidiary reviewed. It was forced to sell its operations to a Canadian buyer. However, FIRA disallowed their case, feeling it represented too much competition for Canadian publishers. Twelve jobs and $3 million in sales were lost in Canada as a result of FIRA's decision.

The chief problem is not in the agency itself, but in the FIRA Act, which is vague, inconsistent, and unenforceable. The agency, as a result, is the scapegoat for the failings of this legislation.

In September 1982 Herb Gray was dropped as the minister responsible for FIRA. His replacement, Ed Lumley, formerly responsible for International Trade, was viewed in the business community as less nationalistic. The changes were visible; FIRA speeded up its review process and soon established a higher approval rate.

The damage, however, may be irreversible. Canada's Foreign Investment Review Agency is now seen as a potentially harmful "wild card" in the investment decisions of many foreign businesses. Besides adding time to the decision-making process, FIRA can go so far as to close businesses, as with J. P. Lippincott. Perhaps more important is the psychological deterrent inflicted by FIRA. Investors view Canada as something of a socialist nation, where "the government is always on your back."

An open economy, such as Canada's, cannot afford to alienate foreign investors. Capital inflows are needed to support the ailing Canadian dollar. The uncertainty surrounding FIRA erects a barrier to go elsewhere and industries may well do so.

Canada needs to be more precise about its policy intentions. On both political and economic levels FIRA is too important to be ignored. Ottawa's options are to send a welcome signal to foreign investors, narrow its definition of "significant benefit," reduce the secrecy presently surrounding the FIRA review process in an attempt to gain the confidence and support of foreign investment, or abolish FIRA altogether.

SHORT QUESTIONS ON FIRA CASE

1 Has FIRA become more of a barrier to FDI in recent years? Refer to actual data on approval rates and interpret these rates properly.

2 What firms, and in what sectors, are being rejected or approved?

3 Should FIRA be amended or abolished?

DISCUSSION QUESTIONS ON FIRA

1 If you are on the strategic management team of a U.S.-based corporation considering expansion abroad, will the existence of FIRA change your foreign investment decision? To support your decision, specify the type of product line your corporation is producing, the size of your firm, and so on.

2 Still from the viewpoint of a U.S. MNE, do the provisions of secrecy surrounding the screening process at FIRA provide you with any comfort? How many details of the firm-specific advantage(s) of your corporation are you prepared to reveal to the Canadian bureaucrats? What price will you accept for such dissipation of knowledge? Are there ways in which you can use FIRA to introduce your firm to other Canadian agencies where support and subsidies may be available?

CHAPTER 13

INTERNATIONAL BUSINESS RESPONSE TO GOVERNMENT REGULATION

INTRODUCTION

Government intervention and regulation is an important determinant of the political and economic environment of MNEs. Governments regulate both national and multinational enterprises (MNEs) to try to increase benefits accruing to the nation state. They also regulate the distribution of these benefits to the specific stakeholders within the nation. The efficient operation of enterprises, within the jurisdictions of governments, is affected by regulations as enterprises must adjust to them in order to maximize profits, subject to such environmental constraints.

As discussed in Chapter 12, the extent, type, and application of government regulations vary from country to country, industry to industry, and firm to firm. They also vary over time. The response by firms to a specific government regulation depends on the characteristics of the firm and its business strategy. Some firms attempt to influence the regulatory activities of government. Others treat government regulation as an immutable fact over which they have no control and, therefore, seek to maximize their returns in relation to these regulations. Such considerations apply to enterprises operating solely within one nation, as well as to multinational enterprises engaged in international operations in trade, licensing, or international production.

As explained in Chapter 6, each MNE chooses between some mix of the three major modes of servicing international markets—trade, licensing, and direct investment—to maximize the net present value of return on its firm-specific advantages. If the NPV of the best of these alternatives is negative in any country, the MNE may cease operations there completely. Clearly, government regulations can affect the relative NPV of a firm's activities in trade, licensing, or direct investment. The task of the manager of an MNE is not only to respond to government regulations in order to maximize profits in one mode of international operations, but also to determine whether changes in the international regulatory and economic environment require changes in the mode itself or even complete withdrawal of its operations from a nation.

For example, tariffs in a foreign market may reduce the NPV of the exporting mode and induce the MNE to serve the market by licensing or direct investment. Restrictions on royalties for technology may induce the firm to serve the market by exports or FDI. Regulation of FDI or codes of conduct directed toward MNEs may lead to divestment and an increase in joint ventures or licensing agreements. The MNE is not locked into any one form of entry mode; one of the advantages of the MNE is its versatility.

Government regulation is merely one factor, although an important one, in the MNE's worldwide economic, social, political, and technological environment. All the responses to government regulation described below, therefore, should be related back to their impact on the relative NPV of the three modes of international operations. Managers in international business must constantly bear in mind, when responding to government regulation, that switching to another mode of operations can be a better strategy than remaining with the current mode.

THE ANALYTICAL FRAMEWORK FOR RESPONSE

As described in Chapter 11, whichever mode or combination of modes an MNE chooses for its operations abroad, the fundamental basis for the conflict between its interests and those of the countries in which it operates are concerned with the division of the *perceived surplus* from its operations and *control* of the resources it deploys. Recently, the concept of relative bargaining power has been employed to analyze the determinants of the outcome of this conflict.

In a bargaining framework, the outcome of the negotiations between MNEs and host-country governments is determined by four groups of factors. The goals of the MNE and the goals of the host government determine their bargaining *position*. The characteristics of the MNE and the characteristics of the host government determine their relative bargaining *power*. This analysis is not straightforward since the characteristics of both the MNE and the host government strongly influence their respective goals in the negotiations. The analysis is further complicated by the fact that neither the goals nor the relative bargaining strengths of MNEs and host governments are static. They change over time, sometimes in predictable patterns, but sometimes abruptly, without warning.

Exhibit 13-1 illustrates the major topics discussed in this chapter. It highlights the areas of concern to MNEs and host governments as they bargain and use tactics to achieve their different goals.

MNE GOALS AND BARGAINING POWER

The overall goal of an MNE is to maximize the risk-adjusted NPV of its firm-specific advantages through its worldwide operations in trade, licensing, and FDI.

EXHIBIT 13-1
BARGAINING BETWEEN MNEs AND GOVERNMENTS

	Host country	MNE

Goals	Appropriate technology
	Higher share of surplus
	Power—control over its
	  nation (sovereignty)
	Increase national welfare
	  (employment, etc.)
		To sell products, use
		  local inputs
		To make profit
		To be a good corporate
		  citizen

Bargaining power	Market access
	Natural resources
	Human resources
	Alternative sources
	Regional associations
		FSA in
		  Technology
		  Marketing
		  Capital
		  Market access
		  Management
		  Size

Tactics	Intervention and
	  regulation
		Local ownership
		Stimulating local
		  enterprise
		Employment
		Exports and intrafirm
		  trade
		Location of operations
		  and organizational
		  complexity
		Legal defences
		Support of home-country
		  government

Secondary to this goal but often critical to its achievement is the goal of retaining control over the allocation of its resources within the enterprise. The greater the NPV of one mode of international operations relative to other modes, the greater is the MNE's incentive to structure its operations and relations with host-country governments to retain the profitability of that mode. Government regulation can reduce the NPV of that mode or force the MNE to switch into another mode.

If the NPV of exporting far exceeds that of licensing or FDI, for example, the MNE will respond vigorously to attempts by foreign governments to reduce the NPV of exporting (by tariffs, NTBs, price controls, etc.). In this situation, the MNE will also be unreceptive to attempts to induce it to license or undertake FDI. Such a situation might arise in the case where the MNE's firm-specific advantage is its access to relatively inexpensive raw materials coupled with the technical expertise of its workers in the home country. If these advantages are not available in the host country, the MNE would resist government regulations to locate production there or to license local producers.

If the host government imposes local value-added requirements in order to encourage investment and local production, the MNE might respond by setting up a minimum level of local final assembly and finishing. It might also manipulate transfer prices on its exports to its subsidiary in the host country to increase reported local value added. Some Japanese automobile manufacturers have followed this strategy in their operations in low- and middle-income countries. Similarly, if licensing or FDI is the preferred mode, the MNE will try to retain this mode of operation and resist government regulations that reduce their NPV.

The bargaining power of the MNE is high when its firm-specific advantages are valuable to the host country. These firm-specific advantages can be in product and process technology, management skills, access to markets for inputs and finished products, and access to capital and other scarce factors of production. The MNE's bargaining power is also greater when its firm-specific advantages are tightly held; that is, few firms in the world exist that can supply such advantages. We now discuss how the bargaining power of the MNE varies according to the type of firm-specific advantages it possesses.

Technology Advantage

The possession of a firm-specific advantage in product or process technology is often seen to be the most important determinant of the bargaining power of MNEs, particularly those based in high-income countries. If the host nation values access to this technology, it must either allow the MNE to operate in its country through its desired mode or forego the benefits of increased efficiency through technology and increased consumer satisfaction. The bargaining power of the MNE is particularly strong if it is a technological leader in its industry. If this is the case, then few, if any, other firms possess comparable technology. Ongoing R and D can keep the MNE in this monopolistic position, with the result that new products and process improvements which are valued by the host country continuously come on stream.

As described in Chapter 6, technology-intensive MNEs risk losing control of their firm-specific advantage in technology. Such MNEs are apt to demand restrictions on licensors to circumscribe geographic markets or allow the diffusion of their technology to potential competitors. They value cross-license agreements for access to the licensor's technology, and flowback of any improvements is made by the licensor. When technology-intensive MNEs undertake FDI, their goal is often 100 percent ownership in order to retain control over their technology and reap the full benefits from it. Moreover, technology-intensive MNEs rarely need the contributions of local partners in such areas as management, market access, or local marketing skills since the products of these MNEs are usually sold on the basis of *product* quality and performance, not price or access to channels of distribution in the host nations. For these reasons, technology-intensive MNEs set goals of complete ownership in their foreign subsidiaries and often possess the bargaining power to attain them.

Marketing Advantage

Marketing-intensive MNEs with branded, quality products often follow the same pattern of international operations as technology-intensive MNEs. Their bargaining power is usually high since, if the host country values their products, they are the sole suppliers. In low- and middle-income countries, however, the host government may view highly branded products as inappropriate to local income levels. In addition, it may consider the advertising and marketing expenses incurred by MNEs as wasting the nation's resources. As a consequence, the host government may block imports entirely, demand that the MNE take a minority position in FDI or impose severe limitations on licensing fees or royalties. In Indonesia, for example, the government has encouraged some local firms to break the trademarks of internationally recognized products and sell a "brand" name product without compensation to the MNEs which own the trademarks.

The firm-specific advantage of marketing-intensive MNEs may be dissipated if their product is not of uniform, high quality. In order to ensure quality control, the goal of marketing-intensive MNEs is usually majority, if not 100 percent, ownership. Moreover, marketing-intensive MNEs seldom value the marketing expertise of local partners in host countries. The brand names of MNEs are rarely country-specific, so that their products can be sold without high expenditures being required to gain knowledge of local channels of distribution and consumer behavior. Coke is sold around the world under the same name, slogans, and advertisements. Yet, Coca-Cola divested in India rather than take a minority position which might have led to a loss of control over its formula, product quality, and brand name. In the less risky environment of the Philippines, Coca-Cola licenses its products to San Miquel, an experienced producer of high-quality, branded beer.

Capital Advantage

At one time the access of MNEs to large amounts of relatively cheap capital was one of the three pillars which formed the competitive advantage of MNEs; the other two were product and process technology and management skills. In the late 1960s and early 1970s, however, the internationalization of capital markets allowed many national governments and large national enterprises to gain access to capital markets at terms comparable to those available to MNEs. In addition, U.S.-based MNEs operating in high-income countries increased their borrowing on local capital markets. In this case, the direct investments of MNEs may have substituted for funds available to local firms, rather than appreciably increasing the total investment capital available in the economy of host countries. Empirical studies on this issue are inconclusive.[1]

Several studies of the impact of MNEs on local capital markets and the balance of payments, particularly in low- and middle-income countries, have found that the long-run effect of investment by MNEs on the host country's balance of payments is often negative. There is a short-run inflow of capital followed by a large outflow. These studies tend to ignore the growth of real income which permits the recipient nation to repay its debt. Measuring the impact of MNEs is a

---

[1]See Richard Caves, *Multinational Enterprise: An Economic Analysis,* Cambridge: Cambridge University Press, 1982, chapter 6 for a discussion of this issue.

complicated undertaking and the methodology of studies in this area is often questioned.[2] Yet the conclusions (however ill-founded) have influenced the attitudes of host governments toward the desirability of MNEs as net sources of capital.

Developments such as these have eroded the bargaining power of MNEs that relied on access to cheap home-country capital. In the middle and late 1970s, however, the escalation of oil prices led to severe balance of payments and external debt problems in many countries. This situation once again increased the bargaining power of MNEs with external capital for investment. For example, Canada's interest for foreign investment has increased with its needs for external funding for major investment projects. When imbalance on external accounts places restrictions on economic development, governments are often more willing to trade off short-term capital inflows against possible long-term outflows.

Market Access Advantage

Over the past 15 years, access to export markets, particularly those in their home countries, has become an important bargaining chip of MNEs. Following the example of Japan, more and more low- and middle-income countries have turned toward a development strategy based on export-led growth. Unlike Japan, however, countries such as Taiwan, Korea, Singapore, Hong Kong, Mexico, and Brazil did not have large enterprises that were experienced in international trade. Consequently, these countries turned to MNEs to provide access to international markets.

Some MNEs have also set up "export platforms" in low-wage countries. These offshore assembly platforms produce inputs to the production processes of the MNEs at home and also provide final goods for sale through the MNEs' existing channels of distribution and sales networks. Export platform investments are characteristic of the electronics and garment industries, but recent trends have seen investment expansion into parts and finished goods for a wide range of consumer products and industrial equipment.

Investments by MNEs in export platforms can have a dramatic effect on a country's exports. Thailand's exports of electronics rose from a few million dollars to several hundred million dollars in just 3 years, all through the efforts of MNEs. In Singapore, 91 percent of its exports are by foreign-owned enterprises.

Access to export markets is such a strong bargaining chip for MNEs that with it they are often able to attain 100 percent equity ownership. If an MNE sources some of the inputs for its home production process from an offshore assembly platform, it must retain control over product quality, logistics, and scheduling for the operation to be successful. Such product and managerial control requires 100 percent ownership. Moreover, since the host country typically provides only low-cost labor, the MNE does not need to obtain local expertise in management, technology, or marketing. In terms of the model given in Chapter 6, the export

[2]Ibid., chapter 6.

marketing costs M^* or the additional costs of FDI A^* are minimal for such MNEs.

MNEs can also use their firm-specific advantage of access to export markets and worldwide commercial intelligence to engage in countertrade. This involves access to host-country markets through imports or FDI, in exchange for exports by the MNE. Countertrade has long been a feature of exchange between centrally planned and market economies. Increasingly, however, low- and middle-income countries such as Indonesia, India, China, and Sri Lanka have implemented policies that exchange access to their markets for exports, in an attempt to alleviate trade imbalances. High-income countries have also used countertrade, most notably in computers, aircraft, and military procurement contracts.

Some MNEs have developed a strategic plan in which their most important firm-specific advantages will be their worldwide commercial intelligence, international marketing and sourcing expertise, and access to products and global markets. While this has always been the situation for Japanese trading companies, U.S. and European MNEs are now moving away from international production alone. They are reformulating strategies around an expertise in international commercial intelligence and trade. This trend may see MNEs evolve from stereotypes, only undertaking foreign investments, toward more complex organizations in which trade, licensing, investment, and intelligence services form a more balanced mix of international activities.

Management Advantage

MNEs also possess firm-specifc advantages in management skills. Without the efficient use of modern management techniques and strategies, the MNE's firm-specific advantage in other areas (technology, marketing, access to capital markets, and access to worldwide markets for inputs and products) may be of little value. The operation of the internal market of the MNE is a complex process, but one which provides the MNE with unique managerial skills.

The host nations in which MNEs operate, particularly low- and middle-income countries, are often short on general management expertise. The ability of management to increase the value of technology often argues against its "arm's-length" transfer by way of the market and in favor of transfer through exports or direct investment. While the management capabilities of nationals in host countries have been increasing in recent years, the lack of sophisticated managerial capacity can still be a bottleneck for economic development.

The value to the MNE of firm-specific management skills as a bargaining chip is constrained in four ways: (1) "management" is intangible—its value is difficult to quantify and perceive; (2) foreign management can be equated with loss of control over the national economy; (3) foreign management of local enterprises may have the effect (or be perceived by host governments to have the effect) of consigning local workers to menial, uninteresting, and unproductive tasks as a means for MNEs to continue their dominance; and (4) although host governments may accept the proposition that foreign enterprises possess superior technology, access to capital, and so on, they balk at the proposition that foreigners per se are superior to their nationals in anything but training, experience, and education. Host governments believe that these qualities can and should be gradually transferred to nationals through in-house human resource development.

One study on government intervention in the operations of MNEs concluded that the complexity of the management tasks facing an MNE in its operations in the host country may deter government intervention.[3] Host governments may fear that intervention in complex operations will decrease the value of the subsidiary to both the MNE and their nation.

Size Advantage

The size of an MNE may influence both its bargaining power and its goals in international operations. Often relatively small firms view the international component of their operations as only an adjunct to their operations in the home country. Small firms seldom have the management resources to devote to international operations. They export only in response to orders received from abroad, at the purchaser's initiative.[4]

Small firms license technology as long as licensing fees exceed the marginal costs of transfer. They take minority equity positions in subsidiaries abroad, often in lieu of licensing fees, since they have neither the capital nor the management resources to operate the total production, marketing, finance, and control of a foreign subsidiary. Nor do they fear the adverse effects of their technology on firms in markets in which they have little interest.

HOST-COUNTRY GOALS AND BARGAINING POWER

The goals of host-country governments in their relations with MNEs and the means by which they seek to achieve these goals have been described in Chapters 11 and 12. The general economic goals of host nations are to maximize the returns to their countries from the operations of MNEs within their borders and to exercise control over the flow of the MNE's resources, particularly in and out of their countries. Depending on the economic conditions within their countries, they may also have goals of increasing local ownership, decreasing imports or, more specifically, some types of imports, increasing exports, increasing investment, developing human resources, developing indigenous technology, and so on.

In addition to these purely economic goals, host governments may desire to change or preserve the social, political, and economic structure of the country. The host government then sets its objectives in its bargaining with MNEs to achieve these complex goals. This process may require the government to trade off an increase in the net benefits from the operations of MNEs on one dimension in order to increase net benefits on another. For example, the goal of increased local equity ownership may conflict with a goal of increased investment, employment,

---

[3]See Thomas Poynter, "Government Intervention in Less Developed Countries: The Experience of Multinational Corporations," *Journal of International Business Studies*, 13:1, 1982.

[4]Czinkota and Johnston (1983) does not support this conclusion.

or efficiency in resource utilization. An increase in national technological capabilities may require reduction of inward technology transfer by MNEs. The host country will then negotiate with MNEs to move as far out on its utility curve as possible given its often ill-defined, national utility function. At one time, for example, communist countries with centrally planned economies rejected, on ideological grounds, involvement with MNEs, particularly involvement through FDI. For pragmatic reasons this attitude has been moderated in recent years, and, with the exception of Albania, communist countries have accepted the need to cooperate with MNEs, with strict supervision of their activities. There has been a tendency for command economies to prefer licensing arrangements with MNEs, rather than FDI. This is the case, for example, in Yugoslavia.

Host-country bargaining power increases when the value of its country-specific advantages to the MNE increases. These country-specific advantages may be comprised of some of the factor endowments, such as human and natural resources and capital factors of production. They also include familiar cultural and social systems, cooperative political parties and other factors which reduce or minimize the M^* or risk of dissipation D^* costs facing the MNEs. The bargaining power of the host country increases as its control over these country-specific factors increases, especially if they are not available in the same degree to the MNE from other sources.

To the extent that host governments exercise control over access to their economy, they can act as monopoly purchasers of the goods and services provided by MNEs. For example, the governments of several countries have acted as the sole purchasing agent for some imported pharmaceutical products. They have negotiated prices below those prevailing on world markets. Japan has closed its markets to many imports and FDI and has closely supervised technology licensing agreements. In doing this, Japan was able to negotiate licensing fees on highly favorable terms.

In order to exercise its sovereign rights in its external relations with MNEs, the host government must have the will and the power to impose on its people its perception of the trade-off between the costs and benefits of regulating MNEs.

At one time the government of India, for example, placed strict regulations on MNEs operating there. India was willing to make its trade-off between short-run inflows of capital and technology in exchange for reduced foreign ownership and the development of indigenous technology. This position has moderated in recent years as a result of the inefficiencies resulting from India's policy of self-reliance. Singapore, on the other hand, has continually encouraged FDI with minimal restrictions. Government policies have focused on setting the economic environment so that MNEs will maximize their local value-added contingent on maintaining economic efficiency. The Canadian federal government has had to moderate its policies toward MNEs at one time or another in response to criticism by the provinces about the adverse impact of such measures on the local economies. The provinces have been more concerned with the loss of employment, income, and other economic benefits than with the somewhat intangible costs of foregone political sovereignty.

We now consider several of the key factors which influence host-country bargaining power.

Market Access

The more attractive the market in the host country, that is, the greater the NPV of the MNE's preferred mode of operations, the greater is the bargaining power of the host-country government. If host governments can control access to their domestic market through the use of tariffs and nontariff barriers, regulations on FDI, and the level of licensing fees, their bargaining power increases.

As described elsewhere, GATT circumscribes the ability of member countries to change tariffs and NTBs to trade for the purpose of regulating their economy, or when negotiating with MNEs over market access. Some middle-income countries, even though members of the GATT, have violated GATT regulations in attempts to achieve a wide range of objectives, some of which involve their relations with MNEs. Nonmember countries, of course, are free to regulate trade barriers as they wish.

At present there is no international institution comparable to the GATT for services (including technology licensing) or foreign direct investment. After the successful completion of the Tokyo round of GATT negotiations, the United States tried, in the early 1980s, to bring about a similar agreement for trade in services and for foreign investment. It has made little headway, however, in its efforts because of the worldwide recession and associated mercantilist sentiment of many nations. The United States has also tried to use provisions in the GATT to halt other countries from using their regulation over FDI by MNEs to increase their exports. For example, the United States referred to GATT its dispute with Canada over policies of the Foreign Investment Review Agency (FIRA) that screen FDI and only allow foreign investment in exchange for commitments to exports, local procurement, and so forth.

Natural Resources

If the host country has deposits of natural resources that are valuable to MNEs, its bargaining power increases. The host-country government may then use its control over access to natural resources to bargain with MNEs and achieve some of its goals of local ownership and control, mineral royalties, local staffing, profit and dividend remittance rates, and others. The more attractive the natural resources to the MNE, the greater the host country's bargaining power. However, achievement of these goals may decrease the efficiency with which MNEs utilize these resources and decrease the nation's net benefits from them as measured in purely economic terms.

Human Resources

MNEs may seek to locate subsidiaries in host countries to have access to abundant, inexpensive human resources. Such export platform investments are typically located in low-wage countries and oriented exclusively toward the export market. Possession of attractive human resources is a precondition for attracting export platform investments. The number of host countries which can provide low-wage labor is large, and MNEs are able to search among host nations to find the one which will give the greatest incentives to invest. Moreover, once the host country has relied on its cheap labor to attract FDI and MNEs, it may find itself in the position of having to restrain wages in order to retain these footloose investments.

Alternative Sources

The more alternative sources available to the host nations for capital, technology, management, and access to export markets, the greater its bargaining power over MNEs. The increase in the number of MNEs and the number of home countries in which they are based over the past 20 years have resulted in an increase of the bargaining power of host governments. Recently, Brazil, for example, invited proposals from several computer firms to determine which one would produce minicomputers in that country for its domestic market. The MNE chosen submitted the most attractive package of local ownership participation, exports, and local sourcing.

Host countries can also follow policies which develop expertise in technology, management, and export marketing in locally owned firms. MNEs based in middle-income countries are already a significant factor in national and international markets.[5] While at present they are most active at the lower end of the technology spectrum and in low-income markets, their capabilities have increased rapidly. Such MNEs have begun to operate, if only on a very small scale, through FDI in high-income markets. In the not-too-distant future "third world" MNEs may become a significant competitive force and serve to balance and erode the bargaining power of other MNEs both at home and abroad.

Regional Associations

Host governments may be able to increase their bargaining power if they can form regional associations with neighboring countries. These associations can take several forms, from common markets to agreements on a common set of investment incentives and regulations for MNEs. Regional common markets have been formed in Europe (the EEC) and among several groups of low- and middle-income countries (see Chapter 10). If successful, they can increase the attractiveness of their joint market for MNEs and hence their joint bargaining power. Similarly, if a group of countries can jointly set incentives and regulations for MNEs, the ability of MNEs to play one country off against another is reduced, thereby increasing the joint bargaining power of individual countries within the group.

---

[5]Poynter, op. cit.

In summary, the bargaining power of both MNEs and host governments lies in their respective possession of firm-specific and country-specific factors that are valuable to each other. The more tightly held these are, the greater the bargaining power of the respective party. This generalization applies across all three modes of MNE-host country interaction: exporting, licensing, and foreign direct investment.

MNE TACTICS TO INCREASE AND UTILIZE BARGAINING POWER TO REDUCE GOVERNMENT INTERVENTION

Three propositions form the basis of the analysis of host-government intervention and regulation of MNEs and the response of MNEs to such regulation. First, both MNEs and host governments possess assets valuable to the other. Second, the ability of both host governments and MNEs to provide or withhold these assets gives them some degree of bargaining power with the other. Third, MNEs and host governments use their bargaining power to maximize returns from their economic interaction.

This section describes the tactics used by MNEs to increase and utilize their bargaining power to reduce host-government intervention and regulation in their operations. It assumes that the multiple goals of MNEs and host countries differ and that mutually beneficial resolutions of the bargaining process are possible. For example, the MNE might increase the number of local managers in its subsidiary above the level it desires (a cost to the MNE, but a benefit to the host nation) in exchange for increased tariff protection (a benefit to the MNE and a cost to the host country).

In the bargaining situation between MNEs and host governments, MNEs gain advantage from the simplicity of their ultimate goal: risk-adjusted value maximization. In theory, the goal of host governments is equally simple; maximization of the risk-adjusted return to the country. In practice, however, it is often extremely difficult for the host government to know and follow the best strategy and achieve its often multidimensional goals. Host governments often set a wide variety of subgoals, the achievement of which, they hope, will contribute to the overall goal of maximum return through efficiency. In reality, in host countries there are many influential interest groups whose interests differ, so host governments often set distributional objectives ahead of efficiency.

Host governments are often unwilling or unable to let market forces operate to achieve efficiency. Instead they may set more emphasis on specific goals: export expansion, import reduction, local value added, upgrading of natural resources, local ownership, technology transfer, employment, and managerial representation. MNEs are often in a position to structure their operations to further host-country achievement of some of these goals in exchange for increased profitability. Ultimately, though, there is a conflict of interests between MNEs interested in profits gained through efficiency and host governments driven by distributional considerations as well as economic, cultural, social, and political goals.

Local Ownership

Almost every government in the world would prefer to have less rather than more foreign ownership in the national economy. If by some alternative means nations could acquire the package of technology, capital, management, and access to markets which the MNEs are able to provide, host governments would restrict the entry of MNEs. The U.S. government is one government to perceive that foreign ownership has low costs. This is due to the U.S. philosophical commitment to private enterprise, the size and scope of U.S.-based MNEs, and the small amount of FDI in the United States, relative to the size of its economy. Even in the United States, however, the influx of FDI in the late 1970s and early 1980s has led to outcries of foreign domination and "unfair" foreign competition.

For MNEs which desire 100 percent ownership of subsidiaries abroad to increase their control over resource transfer, intercompany pricing, management structure and control, dividend flows, proprietary technology and total profits, it is becoming increasingly difficult for MNEs to operate in this fashion. Under host-government pressure, some MNEs have relinquished total ownership and even taken minority positions. Some MNEs have found it possible to retain control over the key variables in their subsidiaries abroad and to earn satisfactory profits. Other MNEs have preferred to divest entirely rather than reduce their equity ownership below what they perceive to be a critical minimum level.

Joint ventures are one method of reducing political risk, or other aspects of the A^* costs. Local partners both reduce the profile of the MNE in the host country and give it allies in negotiations with government over other regulatory controls. MNEs have also formed joint ventures with local host governments. Such arrangements can be advantageous as they constrain government intervention in other areas of the MNE's operations and give it a direct pipeline into the government for the expression of its needs and opinions. Moreover, governments are typically less interested in short-run profitability and dividends and more interested in long-term growth than is the case with private joint venture partners. They are also less interested in the day-to-day management of their joint venture. Such a strategy of joint ownership with host governments will backfire if the MNE becomes too closely identified with the political party in power and there is a subsequent change of government. Thus it is better to identify with the nation as a whole, both through representation to government and opposition parties and groups.

Since the MNE must relinquish some measure of control and profits to local joint venture partners, its strategy should be to retain control of those variables that are critical to the success of its operations.[6] The MNE can also structure its operations in order to earn a return on its firm-specific advantages by other means; sale of inputs to the joint venture, sale of the output on export markets through sales subsidiaries located outside the host country, technical service, management and royalty fees, and so on.

[6]See Wells (1982) for a description and analysis of these third world MNEs.

One study of MNE operations in middle-income countries concluded that there was a direct positive relationship between the MNEs' control over the variables critical to the success of their operations and their evaluation of the success of their joint-venture investments.[7] The same study revealed that joint ventures in which the MNEs had ownership of greater than 70 percent or less than 30 percent were more successful from the MNEs' point of view than joint ventures in which ownership was divided more evenly. There is the potential for MNEs to trade off reduced equity ownership for other benefits while at the same time retaining the control necessary to make the venture successful from their point of view.

Stimulating Local Enterprise

One of the most frequent complaints by host governments against MNEs is that they operate as enclaves within the national economy. Host governments sometimes have instituted policies that force MNEs to increase local value added either through sourcing inputs through local producers or increasing the local value added within the subsidiary itself. These regulations range from direct requirements for local value added to tariffs or import bans on certain inputs. This second method has the effect of making local sourcing necessary. These regulations affect exports of the MNE to the host country and its manufacturing operations there.

Host-country measures designed to stimulate local production through trade restrictions are often the prime motivation for MNEs to undertake direct investment in local operations. As long as trade restrictions or natural barriers to trade protect the local foreign market sufficiently, MNEs may be able to pass the higher costs of increasing local value added on to the local consumers in the form of higher prices.

On a more positive note, MNEs have often found that after some initial difficulties, local producers have responded to their sourcing needs with products that have met all their requirements. In Pakistan, for example, the government placed limitations on food imports by multinational hotels. The first trips to the local food bazaar were unproductive and even frightening. When the hotels turned directly to local producers and specified the quality they required and guaranteed price and volume, supply was forthcoming at the desired quality and at prices below those of imports. Another positive aspect of this strategy is the way local suppliers can also act as allies and advocates of MNEs in their relations with host governments.

Another form of increasing local value added is the further processing of natural resources prior to export. This presents greater problems for MNEs in natural resource industries. For many natural resources there is a world price in the unprocessed form and at each stage of processing. If the full cost of local processing per unit of output is greater than the difference between the unproces-

---

[7]See D. Lecraw, "Bargaining Power and the Success of TNCs in LDCs," *Journal of International Business Studies* (Spring/Summer 1984).

sed and processed commodity, local upgrading is uneconomical. Someone must make up the difference, either the MNE in reduced profits or the host government in reduced royalties on its deposits.

A more basic problem in the upgrading of natural resources arises when MNEs that have expertise in mineral extraction and marketing of the raw mineral product have expertise in neither the processing of the mineral nor the sale of the upgraded product on world markets. Copper mining companies in western Canada have successfully resisted government attempts to smelt and refine copper in British Columbia. After more than 15 years of delay, study, and negotiation, copper producers in the Philippines were finally forced to form a consortium to undertake smelting and refining of some of their output prior to export.

Employment

Host governments often require that MNEs employ host-country nationals in positions other than those of production workers and clerical staff. Malaysia, for example, has gone so far as to set quotas by job classification for foreigners as well as *bumiputras* (indigenous Malays). Some MNEs have responded positively to the aspirations of host countries for increased local representation at the upper levels of management of the subsidiary, if for no other reason than to reduce the expense of maintaining expatriate personnel abroad. As an extreme example, in 1980, rents in Hong Kong for "reasonable" apartments ranged from $3000 to $10,000 per month. When travel expenses, other living expenses, overseas salary bonuses, dependent education costs, and so on were added together, the cost of maintaining one expatriate in Hong Kong was roughly five times the cost of employing the person at home and fifteen times that of hiring a local senior manager.

Host-country nationals may also have expertise in production, marketing, finance, and local taxation laws and practices not available within the MNE. They are more likely to have insights into the operation of the host-country government and the means by which MNEs can best manage the government-business interface. Local nationals can also become strong and effective advocates of the MNE's interests with government.

A study of government intervention in Indonesia, Kenya, Zambia, and Tanzania revealed that host government intervention decreased when the proportion of senior management positions filled by nationals was between 50 and 89 percent.[8] Intervention increased when nationals filled less than 50 percent or more than 90 percent of all management positions. The study concluded that the host governments of these four countries were discontented with MNEs that had below 50 percent of their staff comprised of nationals, but when the percentage rose above 90 percent, they perceived these subsidiaries as prime targets for local ownership due to the simplicity of their operations.

[8]Ibid.

Exports and Intrafirm Trade

Historically, all governments have valued exports as a spur to the development of their national economies. With the rapid increase in oil prices after 1973, most countries have increased their efforts to accelerate export expansion. Multi-national enterprises often have expertise in trade in both directions and have access to channels of distribution, brand names, and established sales forces that may increase their attractiveness to host governments as potential exporters. A commitment to increase exports may reduce other forms of host-government intervention.

Exports from one country are by necessity imports for another, most often the home country. This is an instance in which the MNE may become caught between conflicting pressures of the countries in which it operates. This conflict may be particularly severe if increased exports from one country imply decreased production in another. Labor leaders and some government officials in Canada were incensed a few years ago when Inco (the Canadian nickel MNE) increased production abroad (at the urging of the host governments), at the same time laying off workers in Sudbury, Ontario. MNEs must be concerned not only about government intervention in one host country, but about all host countries and in their home country as well.

MNEs may also be able to reduce host government intervention by increasing their level of intrafirm trade, imports of inputs, and exports of outputs. If host governments attempt to intervene, they may be warned off by the consequences this intervention might have on the trade within the control of the MNE.

Increasing intrafirm trade as a defence against government intervention may be a two-edged sword. The greater the intrafirm trade, the greater is the MNE's dependence on operations in the host country for exports and imports of inputs and final goods. This increased dependence may force the MNE to acquiesce to host-government regulation rather than risk disruption of its worldwide trade network. The MNE can reduce its vulnerability to actions by one host government by diversifying its sources of supply among several countries.

Location of Operations and Organizational Complexity

One key strategic decision faced by MNEs concerns the division of their resources between home and host nations. Host countries typically vary in their valuation of different types of operation. Sales offices to promote imports are least valued, while increasing value is placed on the following: assembly operations; full-production operations; production combined with exports; R and D facilities; and subsidiaries involving the whole array of production, sales, R and D, and exports. As the MNE moves up this chain of increasing commitment in the host country, the host government views the MNE's contribution to the economy in a more favorable light. The host government is less eager to upset the increasingly complex activities through its own intervention.

A strategy of increasing the range and complexity of its operations in host countries may impose substantial costs on the MNE. First, some activities are best carried out in one country rather than another because of costs of production and transportation and the availability of labor, capital, and natural resources. Second, some activities such as R and D administration and control are better centralized in one place rather than scattered around the world. Third, full-scale decentralization of all operations implies costs of organization and control that may outweigh the benefits of increased bargaining power with host governments.

For example, the Canadian government's enthusiasm for MNEs to locate the "World Product Mandate" for one product in Canada (i.e., complete R and D, production, and international sales and management for a new product line) has not been greeted enthusiastically by most MNEs. Despite these costs, however, over the past 10 years there has been a trend toward increased decentralization and polycentralization among many MNEs.

If the MNE can develop its firm-specific advantage in technology such that it generates a continuous stream of new product and process technologies, it can increase its bargaining power with host governments since, if they intervene in its operations, this may reduce the flow of technology. A technology leader will also enjoy a monopolistic position such that the host government cannot turn to other suppliers without incurring substantial costs.

Legal Defences

MNEs can fight government intervention in the courts. This alternative is usually taken only as a last resort, when negotiation has failed. Court action focuses the glare of publicity on the MNE's operations and places the negotiating process into a confrontational mode. The framing and application of national laws may also discriminate against MNEs. In one notable example, F. Hoffmann-LaRoche defended its pricing and transfer pricing policies and its profitability in courts around the world. Despite worldwide publicity, strong negative reactions, and statements by governments, these actions were successful from LaRoche's point of view. They delayed imposition of price and profit controls on two of its products, Librium and Valium (diazepam), in many cases until its patents on these products had expired.

Support by Home-Country Governments

The interests of MNEs and their home governments are often closely aligned. MNEs can turn to their home-country governments for support in their negotiations with host governments. The most often cited instances of this support, such as U.S. intervention in Chile, French intervention in Algeria, and British intervention in Libya, have not proved to be very effective, especially in the long run. Intervention by foreign governments in support of MNEs often serves to catalyze public opinion in host countries against the MNE. Other types of public intervention have included pressure on the World Bank, the IMF, the U.S. Export-Import Bank (and similar institutions in other home countries), and threats to block home markets and reduce aid financing.

Although instances of home-government pressure in support of MNEs have received much (usually unfavorable) publicity, they have been relatively few in number and have had little practical impact, except in the short run. Of greater importance, if less noticeable, has been the more low-key, private representations by foreign governments to host governments in support of the positions of their MNEs. These have been particularly effective in competitive bidding situations for large export contracts such as large turnkey projects. For example, at a crucial phase of the negotiating process between a Japanese consortium and the Philippine government over a $250 million project, Japan announced a new aid program of $100 million for the Philippines and clinched the sale for the consortium.

An MNE may be able to increase the range of government support on which it can draw by forming joint ventures with MNEs based in other countries. Such joint ventures may also increase access to concessional financing from the home governments of each partner.

Interaction with Government

A key determinant of the success for the MNE in the bargaining process is its relationship with the host government. Much depends on the perception by the government and government bureaucrats of the net benefits of the MNE's operations in the host country. As described in Chapter 11, there is often a problem in differences in the perception of these net benefits by government and MNE. Some of these differences can be reduced by close, continuous contact between the staff of the MNE and government officials at all levels. Informal, relatively low level contact on an ongoing basis is often more effective than the grand tour by the company president replete with airport receptions, banquets, and speeches. These activities may help at crucial stages of the negotiations—to open or close them—or if there is an impass.

During meetings with government, the staff of the MNE should aim to develop the understanding of government bureaucrats of the MNE's operations, its problems and prospects, and how these are affected by government policy. They should also emphasize the long-run nature of their relationship and the flow of net benefits over time. This interaction will also give the MNE's staff an appreciation of the viewpoint and goals of the host government and what it values and what it does not. If a working relationship can be developed, the MNE may be able to influence government regulatory policy and its application and to forecast changes in policy that will affect the MNE's operations.

Bribery   The question of bribery should also be examined in this context. Despite several sensational cases and well-publicized stereotypes, bribery exists in all countries in one form or another and is not the exclusive province of MNEs. The international bagperson, with hand reaching in pocket on arrival at the airport, has declined in prominence. But bribery is still an important factor in international business in its somewhat subtler guise.

A strategy with bribery as a component is not an easy one to follow and requires country-specific knowledge on the correct type, amount, route, and target. This all requires intimate, long-term knowledge of how business is carried out in the specific host country. Bribery has also been made more complicated by laws and regulations in some home countries.

Some MNEs will not enter into bribery at all and will prefer to withdraw, some go along with local customs, others use their financial power to bull their way into a market by this means, others distance themselves from this activity through agents or by commission sales, and others distinguish between grease (paying to speed up services which should be performed by government employees) and bribery (paying government employees to act against the interests and laws of their countries). Often bribery does not have the desired result as when the bribe taker sells out again to a higher bid or takes the bribe but does not perform the service. If one is willing to cheat one's country, why not the foreign MNE?

Bribery is a complex, uncertain and risky business practice and may be best left alone. It is often better, in the long run, for the MNE to influence government by providing the host nation with positive net benefits than to rely on subversive activities.

POLITICAL RISK ANALYSIS

The relative bargaining powers of MNEs and host governments provide a useful framework for analyzing the differences in the level of host-government intervention in the operations of different MNEs operating in the same country. The relative bargaining power framework of analysis is also useful in analyzing the average level of host-government intervention among countries. Nations with low bargaining power tend to intervene less in the operations of MNEs than those with high bargaining power. This analysis can give the MNE some degree of certainty and predictive ability in relations with host governments.

MNEs must also be prepared for, and respond to, abrupt changes in host-country intervention. These sudden changes often accompany radical changes in government in host nations. Radical changes in host and home-government policies toward MNEs have been a fact of international business for many years. Only recently, however, with the series of communist takeovers in some host countries and the fiasco of the U.S. and Japanese MNEs in Iran, has the importance of this facet of international business been realized by MNEs and incorporated to some extent into their strategic planning.

Despite the new-found prominence of political risk in the minds of international businesspeople, the number of forced divestments may have peaked in the mid-1970s. A study by Kobrin for the UN Centre on Transnational Corporations identified 1705 forced divestments that took place in 79 developing countries over the 20-year period from 1960 to 1979.[9] These forced divestments represented

---

[9]See Kobrin (1981) for a treatment of the subset of managing political risk.

less than 5 percent of all foreign affiliates in these countries. For purposes of comparison, Kobrin grouped the 1705 separate nationalizations into 559 acts of nationalization. Over two-thirds of these acts occurred in the 7-year period from 1970 to 1976. During the 3 years from 1977 to 1979, the rate of nationalization fell by a factor of 3, to less that 17 acts per year compared to 60 at the peak. Kobrin attributed this decline to four factors:

1 The nationalization of large-scale mining and petroleum production was virtually complete by 1975.

2 The ability of developing countries to achieve their goals by regulation rather than nationalization has improved dramatically since the mid-1970s.

3 The incidence of postindependence nationalization has abated.

4 The OPEC price increases and consequent economic problems have increased the needs of many developing countries for FDI.

Despite the decline in forced divestments, political risk analysis and forecasting have become major growth areas within the staff of MNEs and for international business consultants. Almost every journal directed toward international business-people now reports, analyzes and, in some cases, ranks the "political risk" of the host countries in which MNEs operate. Several specialized publications by political risk advisory services are also available.

The methodology behind these various sources of information on political risk varies greatly from in-depth country reports to brief impressions of events. They use complicated scoring systems to quantify political risk or rank the country risk based on the spread over LIBOR of the country's borrowings on the Eurodollar market. Several large MNEs have developed their own in-house political risk assessment capabilities.

At best, these evaluations of the country's political risk serve as general background information against which each MNE must assess its own position. To avoid trade, licensing, or FDI with a particular country because the perceived level of political risk is too high may exclude the MNE from realizing profitable opportunities. Both risk and return need to be evaluated in the assessment of an international business project. High political risk need not deter investment provided there is a high rate of return to compensate for the risk. Political risk opens windows rather than shuts them.

Host-country regulation, intervention, and nationalization vary widely depending on industry and firm characteristics. There are many profitable investment and trade ventures possible with eastern European nations or with developing countries. As one observer pointed out, for every American businessperson on a plane out of Iran in 1979, a Swiss businessperson was on the return flight to take the American's place.

The ability to evaluate and take risks due to access to information and risk diversification can be used to generate powerful firm-specific advantages by MNEs. The problem for the MNE is to realize its potential in this area. The MNE needs to undertake enterprise-specific political risk analysis and incorporate the results of this analysis in a systematic way into its strategic global planning. Kobrin (1981) concluded that MNEs, in general, had not acted to realize this potential.

SUMMARY

These last three chapters have examined the relationship between international businesses and governments of the nation states in which they operate. The specifics of MNE-government relations are as changing as today's newspapers. In these chapters, a basic framework has been set out which can be used to analyze and predict what may appear to be random events.

Chapter 11 described the sources of conflict between MNEs and national governments and MNEs and international organizations. This conflict is focused on the goals of each stakeholder in maximizing returns from the operations of MNEs or in controlling the allocation of resources. Chapter 12 described the mechanisms by which national governments and international organizations have sought to achieve these goals. In this chapter the response by MNEs to these controls has been described, using a bargaining power framework of analysis.

Five vitally important conclusions for the international businessperson emerge from these three chapters:

1 In general, the operations of MNEs through trade, licensing, and foreign direct investment increases world efficiency in the use and allocation of resources and hence generates net benefits for the nations in which MNEs operate.

2 There are inherent conflicts between MNEs and the nation states in which they operate; these arise from the fundamental nature of the multinational enterprise. Conflicts develop between host countries and the MNE over the distribution of the net benefits generated by its operations.

3 It is the right and duty of each stakeholder in the operations of MNEs—the governments of host and home nations, international organizations, and MNEs—to try to achieve their own legitimate economic goals.

4 Discussions, negotiations and bargaining between MNEs, host and home governments, and international organizations can lead to resolution of the problems and conflicts that arise between MNEs and government in an orderly, rational, and practical fashion. This occurs even though the goals and aspirations of no one stakeholder are ever satisfied.

A final, important point must be understood by both international businesspeople and government officials engaged in regulating MNEs. The basis for interaction and cooperation between MNEs and the nations in which they operate is that each party receives net benefits from the transaction. MNEs and governments that use their bargaining power to its extreme limits will almost inevitably force other vitally important stakeholders in these operations to reassess the value of continued participation.

There is a double constraint. MNEs that use their short-term bargaining power to exploit one or more of the nations in which they operate will find that, in the long run, these nations will turn to alternative sources for technology, capital, and access to markets. Nation states that use their sovereign power to expropriate the assets of MNEs within their boundaries without due compensation will find that the benefits of international production are reduced. This inevitable mutual constraint should help to temper relations between MNEs and the countries in which they operate.

KEY WORDS

Offshore assembly platform	Nation state
Countertrade	Decentralization
Political risk	Market access

QUESTIONS

1 Discuss the basis of conflict between the interests of the MNE and the host nation. What are the four groups of factors which determine the outcome of the negotiations? How is this analysis further complicated?

2 Discuss the implications of the following statement: Government regulation can reduce the NPV of one mode, forcing the MNE to switch to another mode. How might the MNE react to such regulation? What types of firm-specific advantages contribute to the high bargaining power of the MNE?

3 The importance of using appropriate management techniques and strategies cannot be overemphasized. Yet, in this chapter it is stated that the lack of sophisticated managerial capacity can still be a bottleneck for economic development. Discuss how the value of a firm-specific advantage in management skills is constrained. Can you suggest ways that the MNE might overcome these constraints?

4 What are the general economic goals of host nations? How do these goals affect the bargaining power of the MNE? Under what circumstances is a host country in a strong bargaining position? Discuss how the country-specific advantage affects the strength of the bargaining position.

5 Three propositions are discussed which form the basis of the analysis of host-government intervention, regulation of MNEs, and their response to such regulation. What are these? Discuss tactics which the MNE can use to reduce such intervention.

6 MNEs have relinquished degrees of ownership because of increasing host-government pressure. What methods are available to the MNE wishing to reduce political risk? What precautions must the MNE take to avoid problems in this area?

7 Stimulating local enterprise by host governments has become increasingly pervasive. Discuss how the MNE can increase local value added. What problems arise when attempting to do this?

8 Kobrin's study of forced divestments identified 1705 cases. Over two-thirds of these acts occurred during 1970 to 1976, with a dramatic decrease in 1977 to 1979. What factors can be attributed to this decline? How can an analysis of political risk assist the management of the MNE?

PART FIVE

FIVE

STRATEGY AND MANAGEMENT OF INTERNATIONAL BUSINESS

Having studied both the environmental and internal factors affecting the existence of MNEs and other firms which operate internationally, we now focus on the practical management of international business. Part 5 shows how the principles learned so far can be applied to the actual running of the MNE. We find out here how the internal markets are being operated and why it is essential to manage them effectively in order to maintain a high level of performance in the MNE.

This section examines the four key functional areas of the MNE: marketing, production, management of human resources, and finance. Linking these areas is an important preliminary chapter on the strategic planning and strategic competition of the MNE. Chapter 14 on global strategy serves both to introduce and to integrate in a general manner the specialized nature of the four functional chapters. In turn, each of these functional chapters is written from a strategic perspective. In this manner the details of each area can be studied not in isolation, but to discover the way in which they contribute to the successful positioning of the MNE relative to its global competitors.

Throughout this part of the book, attention is directed toward three types of MNEs: those that are ethnocentric (home-oriented), polycentric (host-country-oriented), and geocentric (world-oriented). This distinction, introduced earlier, is now very useful in understanding the relationships between strategy and structure in the MNE and in determining how each of the functional areas should be operated in an effective manner.

CHAPTER 14

GLOBAL COMPETITIVE STRATEGY

INTRODUCTION

Global competitive strategy is defined as the formulation of plans to place the MNE in a position where it can survive and prosper relative to its global competitors. The successful implementation of such strategy depends on the effective performance of the internal market of the MNE and the resilience of the MNE to changes in environmental forces.

One central theme of this book is the fact that MNEs exist as a response to market imperfections, both natural and government-induced. The theory of internalization, as developed in Chapters 5 and 6, explained this relationship. This chapter relates this theoretical analysis to the actual strategic planning of MNEs. It shows how the theory developed earlier can be applied to understand the strategic management of the key functional areas of the MNE. Organizational structure is discussed in Chapter 17. Here it is demonstrated how a global strategy is built and used by MNEs in a world which is becoming increasingly competitive. The threats to MNEs from foreign rivals are considered, as are the new windows of opportunity which open to those MNEs that plan effectively on a long-run global basis.

Strategy in international business is influenced by many considerations. A key one of these is the environment within which MNEs operate. The environment itself, and government-induced changes in it, influence the options open to the MNEs. Not all MNEs can respond efficiently to these environmental parameters. Those that do not lose their competitive edge to rival MNEs or to local host-country firms. Over time MNEs must respond to changes in government regulation which may affect their firm-specific advantages (FSAs) and their capacity to exploit these FSAs in appropriate world markets.

We have noted in earlier chapters the growing propensity for governments to monitor and regulate trade, international investments, and licensing. Such government intervention in the world system of exchange and capital flows makes life difficult for MNEs as this uncertainty requires changes in the strategic planning of both established and nascent MNEs. Fortunately, it may also open opportunities for MNEs in trade, investment, and licensing. Up to now (for simplicity), the environment, including government regulation, has been taken as given. In this chapter this assumption is relaxed, and we consider the complexities of a changing world environment.

These changes are modeled here as environmental information costs which the MNE needs to assess and respond to. In the context of strategic planning it is necessary for the MNE to overcome information costs and other transaction costs about key environmental parameters. This process then allows the MNE to formulate, implement, and control a successful global strategy. Basically it does this by adapting the managerial and organizational structure of its internal markets to assimilate new information in a rapid manner.

The new model developed here will allow us, in the following chapters, to consider the functional areas of the MNE and how to operate them. We find that the MNE is often forced to bargain with the governments of many nations as these influence its environment and constrain its strategic options.

PORTFOLIO MATRIX STRATEGY FOR THE MNE

In the 1970s, a popular method of corporate strategy analysis used the portfolio matrix designed by the Boston Consulting Group. Indeed it has been estimated that about half of the 500 largest U.S. corporations used a version of the BCG portfolio matrix by 1979. The analysis of such a portfolio of businesses is a useful starting point in the formulation of strategy at the corporate level and for the review of the performance of corporate units (or subsidiaries of the MNE). However, it is too limited to be used for the formulation of global competitive strategy across industries. Bearing this in mind, this section reviews the basic techniques of portfolio analysis.

A simplified version of the BCG portfolio matrix appears in Figure 14-1. The BCG matrix is focused on the contributions that various businesses bring to the cash flows of the corporation. It relates company market share, on the horizontal axis (abscissa), to market growth of the industry on the vertical axis (ordinate).

The four cells of the matrix define products (or business units), that are either "cash cows" with a large market share and a stable market growth, "dogs" with a low market share and slow growth, "stars" with large market share and anticipated fast growth, or "question marks" (also called "wildcats" or "problem children") with small market share but possible rapid growth. The simplistic strategy for a corporation to follow is to divest its dogs, harvest the cash flows from its cash cows to finance growth of stars, and help improve the market position of its wildcats.

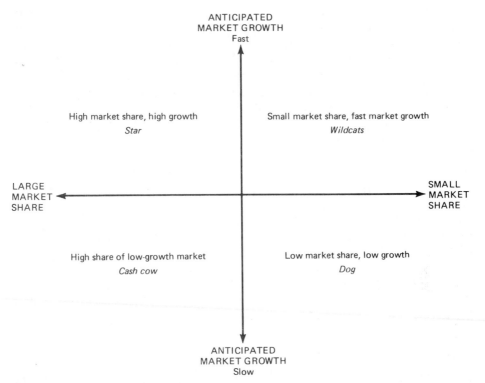

ANTICIPATED
MARKET GROWTH
Fast

High market share, high growth

Star

Small market share, fast market growth

Wildcats

LARGE
MARKET
SHARE

SMALL
MARKET
SHARE

High share of low-growth market

Cash cow

Low market share, low growth

Dog

ANTICIPATED
MARKET GROWTH
Slow

FIGURE 14-1
A business portfolio matrix. Policy strategy: Find an optimal mix of business, i.e., balance port-folio of business. Practical use: divest dogs and use cash cows to finance expansion of stars or wildcats.

In practice, the real world is more complicated than this, so the BCG matrix must be interpreted and used with caution. The BCG matrix emphasized market share and growth due to underlying assumptions that there are experience curve effects and associated scale economies arising from production. These aspects are developed further in Chapter 16 on production. Given this caveat, Figure 14-1 can be modified in a straightforward manner for an international context.

The overseas subsidiaries of the MNEs are often viewed as cash cows. They are usually branch plants producing a standardized product for the host-country market. This is a simplistic view since the nature of the host-country markets can help to turn a cash cow in one market into a dog or star in others. The strength of host-country environmental factors and foreign rivals makes international strate-gic planning more difficult than domestic strategy. The international version of the BCG matrix means that product lines are analyzed across markets, not just against each other as in the domestic version.

The BCG matrix was designed for domestic firms. For example, if there is a change in the environmental parameters, as when a host nation imposes more regulations on the MNE, blocks remittances, does not respect patents, or otherwise increases the costs of operating, the MNE may find the cash cow turning into a dog. Provided there is no strategic reason to keep a presence in that market, the MNE has the option of divesting (liquidating) the dog to either the host government or local participants. When Canada imposed its National Energy Program in 1980, one result was to drive down the share prices of subsidiaries of oil MNEs, making them more vulnerable to takeovers by Canadians. Indeed, several subsidiaries were bought out by Petrocan, a state-owned Canadian agency.

Another international implication of the matrix comes from remembering the competitive position of the MNE. In order to fight rival firms for world market share, it may be necessary for the MNE to retain a division with slow market growth simply to defend its interests and preempt entry by rivals. Similarly, it may be worthwhile for the MNE to seek out relatively small market niches, again, before its rivals get into such product or country market segments. Global competitive strategy is much more complicated than domestic strategy because of the greater number of players in the game and the diversity of geographic markets involved.

The construction of a portfolio of business units is much more complicated than the simple BCG matrix allows, even in a domestic context. In addition to company market promotion and industry growth, it is necessary to consider other domestic factors affecting the product portfolio. These include: profitability and growth of business units, synergistic effects, diversification effects if a unit reduces profit variability, and cash flow balance, whereby some profitable units can finance expansion of other units.

None of these elements are easy to introduce domestically, and it is even more difficult on an international dimension. For example, it is not clear why the cash flows of divisions should be balanced. The MNE can usually secure capital in host markets, or internationally. Furthermore, the delicate balance between risk and return is ignored. The MNE can face high risk in a division if it is compensated by a high expected return. The other way the BCG matrix needs to be modified is to have a product-country portfolio. This will help to provoke strategic thinking by certain types of firms, especially MNEs operating as conglomerates.

More advanced portfolio planning frameworks have been developed by consulting firms building on this growth-share matrix. These include the attractiveness screen to find the firm's position versus industry attractiveness as developed by McKinsey and others, the product cycle framework used by Arthur D. Little, Inc. and statistically based forecasting models using the profit impact of market strategies (PIMS) model. These variants of the BCG approach cannot be discussed here because of lack of space. For more information on them, see Porter (1980, especially Appendix A; 1983).

A final danger with the BCG approach and its variants is that it is primarily suitable to explain acquisitions and to analyze the operations of conglomerates. However, the great majority of MNEs are not conglomerates. Rather, most MNEs exist for reasons of horizontal or vertical integration; that is, they are in related lines of business. MNEs are involved in international operations to defend their worldwide market shares and exploit firm-specific advantages. They are not primarily financial conglomerates. While many MNEs benefit from international diversification, they do so indirectly, rather than as a deliberate strategy.

It is now necessary to consider our forthcoming study of the organizational structure of the MNE, since the implementation of any strategy will be influenced and intimately related to the structure of the firm. To link this chapter with Chapter 17 on structure the following analogy may be useful.

Running the MNE

Strategy is like effective jogging. To secure the optimal aerobic benefit, a jogger needs to prepare properly, usually starting with a series of scientifically designed stretching exercises, followed by an appropriate warmup, the actual run itself, and finally, a cooling down period where further stretching is required. Failure to follow this routine will lead to strained muscles or even a total system failure—the collapse of the runner.

In the same way, the MNE needs to organize itself such that it creates an appropriate firm-specific advantage, for example, through its R and D division. The firm-specific advantage is to be consistent with the overall strategic goals of the MNE. The actual tactical implementation of the firm-specific advantage (the heart blood of the MNE) occurs when the organizational structure of the MNE is running at a fine pitch, within some upper and lower boundaries determined by the age and vital signs of the organization. The aerobic "fix" for the MNE comes when it has warmed up by a successful product launch and is into its cash cow phase of production and sales. There, the product line is contributing to the overall strength and future fitness of the organization. The MNE also needs to know how to cool off product lines when the firm-specific advantage has been lost and the product line has become standardized. It must also know how to kick off its running shoes and divest potential dogs.

CORPORATE BUSINESS STRATEGY FOR THE MNE

Strategy for the MNE is defined as long-term planning, basically qualitative and pragmatic, which integrates and directs the functional areas into an overall company goal. The strategic policy of the MNE incorporates an assessment of both changing environmental and internal factors and is understood (or at least recognized) by the top- and middle-level managers who implement it. In addition, there is an intimate relationship between an MNE's strategy and its organizational structure, a theme explored throughout this chapter. The key elements of the strategic planning process in the MNE are identified in outline form in Figure 14-2.

In order to maximize its value and profits, the goal or "mission" of the MNE is to develop, produce, and gain world markets for the product lines which best use its firm-specific advantage(s). The FSAs, sometimes called *competitive* or *differential* advantages, arise in the areas of proprietary knowledge, technology, marketing skills, and so on. These FSAs are exploited in particular world markets,

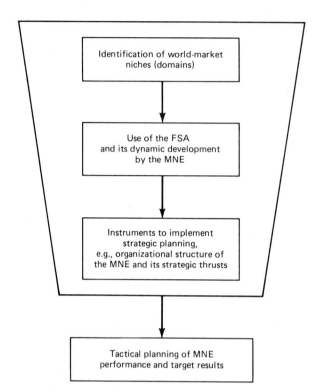

FIGURE 14-2
The strategic planning process in the MNE. (*Adapted to an international dimension from Boris Yavitz and William H. Newman. Strategy in Action. New York: Free Press, 1982, 123.*)

often for products tailored to those markets. These market niches are broad segments of world demand. MNEs use their internal information-gathering capabilities as a basis to forecast and monitor these global markets. Also assessed is the possible entry of rival firms into the actual and potential worldwide markets of the MNE. New FSAs are achieved by strategic thrusts, or initiatives, which launch new product lines into appropriate markets and attempt to do so at opportune times, given the perceived strategies of rival firms.

The strategic planning of the MNE pays special attention to the actions of different stakeholders, such as home and host governments, producers, consumers, rival firms, and workers. In recent years, the need for social responsibility of MNEs has become more apparent. Now the MNE has to satisfy not only its managers, workers, bankers, suppliers, and customers, but also the community at large, especially as represented by home and host governments.

The implementation of the strategic plan of the MNE depends on the type of organizational structure it has, since the top management must understand fully the goals of the MNE in order to carry them out. The extent to which structure follows strategy largely determines the success of the strategy. For a strategy to be successful, the four key functional areas must be operated in a tactically efficient manner to achieve the performance and target results of the MNE. The specific details of the many aspects of the strategic planning process of the MNE are now explained in more detail.

Strategic Business Units and the MNE

Strategic management is often formulated and carried out by strategic business units (SBUs). A SBU consists of either a single line or a set of homogeneous product lines with similar FSAs, where the FSA is based on a technological, manufacturing or marketing advantage. The SBU serves a special and unique market and faces common rivals in the marketing and dynamic development of its product lines.

In the context of this book, the MNE can have several SBUs. Each MNE has at least one FSA, and often there are many actual or potential competitors in the same industry. If the MNE has several SBUs, it must consider how the best interests of each SBU can be achieved within its overall strategic plan. The implementation of a successful global competitive strategy must build on the strengths of the SBUs and integrate these advantages into an evolving company-wide strategy over time.

The performance, or target results, of the MNE's corporate strategy now needs to be measured in a broader manner than discussed earlier, for example, in Chapter 6, where performance of MNEs was restricted to an evaluation of return on equity. The performance of SBUs is now evaluated against the background of the MNE's overall strategic plans, not as independent profit centers. For example, for reasons of defensive investment, some foreign subsidiaries or SBUs may not be highly profitable. However, if they secure the worldwide market share of the MNE, preempt entry by rivals into new markets, or otherwise reduce the risks faced by the MNE, their performance may be very valuable in a strategic context.

There is a difference between business unit strategy and corporate strategy. The SBUs need to know how to develop, maintain, and utilize their firm-specific advantages for their product lines. Corporate strategy deals with the optimal integration of units. It assigns a responsibility to each business unit, defining the market segment (niche) in which it will operate, and the FSA it can exploit. In MNEs which have one particular FSA, the two categories are combined in the firm's primary product line. For example, most MNEs set up miniature replicas abroad to produce the primary product line of the MNE for the local market of the host nation.

A successful SBU needs to find an appropriate niche, or domain, for the product line and then maintain and exploit its FSA in that market, time appropriate strategic thrusts as it moves to achieve the goal of the MNE and turn in a successful performance, as defined by corporate headquarters. All four of these elements are related parts of the strategy of the business unit.

The key contribution of the SBU to the strategic planning of the MNE lies in the information and market knowledge that it has acquired. This market intelligence must be conveyed back to the parent MNE to have an impact on strategic planning. Thus the SBU should not neglect the synergistic benefits which come from developing and exploiting abroad several closely related FSAs in new market niches. Indeed, the MNE may become a specialist in servicing certain overseas markets once it has overcome the information costs and uncertainty associated with doing business in representative foreign nations.

The MNE can also learn to handle uncertainty by building an environmental assessment into the manager's conception of the strategic plan. In addition to head office forecasting of political and country risk, constant monitoring of the host-nation environment by subsidiary managers can provide vital information and help in the appropriate revision of corporate strategy. The internal market of the MNE can be reversed. Information can flow from the subsidiaries to the parent where strategic planning is undertaken. Such intelligent use of the strengths of the MNE limits the firm's exposure to uncertainty and reduces threats from foreign governments and potential rivals. It also permits the MNE to take advantage of new opportunities arising from changes in such environmental factors.

A MODEL OF GLOBAL STRATEGIC PLANNING

Figure 14-3 outlines the main elements to be considered in the process of global strategic planning. It is based on the analysis given in Chapter 5 but develops the conceptual foundations and operational phase of the strategy in more detail.

First, it is necessary for the management of the MNE to assess both environmental and internal variables. The environmental variables consist of the economic, political, cultural, and social factors of relevance in both the home and host nations serviced by the MNE. While all these variables were assumed to be constant (exogenous) in the preceding chapters, in order to simplify the theory of the MNE, changes in these parameters can now be considered. In particular, the manner in which the MNE negotiates with governments and possibly with other firms needs to be worked into the strategic planning process. The result is an increase in information costs which the MNE must not only assess but also interpret and react to. Indeed, it may be necessary to attempt to forecast changes in the environment in order to minimize unanticipated effects on the FSAs.

The internal variables, especially the FSAs of the MNE, need to be assessed on their own terms. Other potential FSAs, which may develop in the future, should also be kept in mind when engaged in strategic planning. The MNE needs to know precisely why its product lines are successful and how it can retain its advantages in the future, in the face of competitive threats by rivals. This competitive analysis requires an objective analysis of the MNE's technological edge, its ongoing R and D, the efficiency of its four functional areas, and its capacity to respond to new entrants and changing world market conditions.

These two elements—environmental and internal assessment—require an appropriate organizational structure. Information must reach the strategic planners in a speedy manner. The managers of the internal communications network of the MNE must screen out superfluous environmental information from its monitoring agencies and be competent enough to distill all relevant changes, spot key trends,

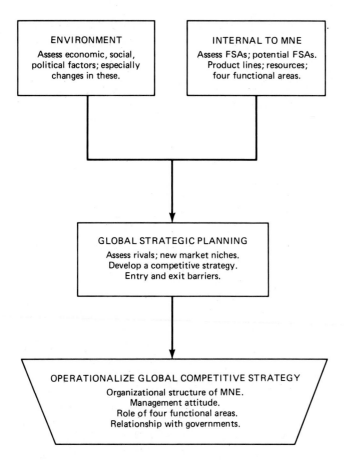

FIGURE 14-3
Strategic planning in the MNE.

and advise on new opportunities as they arise. Information about the firm's goals must also flow from the head office down since this is essential for the implementation of the strategic plan within the MNE. This two-way flow of information is the hallmark of a successful MNE.

The actual global strategic planning is done at the highest levels of the MNE. The reaction to changing environmental conditions occurs against an ongoing assessment of the internal operations of the MNE, especially in relation to those of its major established and potential competitors. In fact, the analysis of rivals and potential entrants is the essence of strategic planning. In a successful global competitive strategy, factors threatening the worldwide market share and profits of the MNE will be anticipated. The full resources of the MNE will be used to beat off challenges to its firm-specific advantage, and attempts will be made to develop new firm-specific advantages ahead of its rivals. The new FSAs will be brought on stream according to the strategic thrusts decided upon by the planners. It is important to turn the strategic goals into action through the use of an appropriate structure within the MNE.

One of the most important strategic decisions is the choice of entry mode in servicing foreign markets. There is a need for the MNE to constantly reassess its choice between exporting, foreign direct investment, and licensing. As conditions change, it may become necessary to switch modalities. There are, of course, sunk costs involved in having an overseas subsidiary, but this particular type of exit barrier must be objectively evaluated and the option of divestment must never be forgotten. There are also entry barriers in the form of political and other risks to be considered. These also change over time. All in all, the dynamics of entry mode are complex, but they cannot be neglected in strategic planning.

The operation of the strategic plan for the MNE is itself a complicated process. Its success depends on the structure of the firm. A good strategic plan will take into account the organizational structure of the firm and build on whatever strengths it has. If the MNE has a matrix structure, much of the effective decision making is delegated to the middle-level managers who combine responsibilities for products and regions. In this case, the MNE needs to have a truly geocentric management attitude where the managers develop an awareness of their strategic role and respond to changing opportunities.

The attitude of management and the identification with corporate goals will vary from MNE to MNE. However, the successful firm will organize to develop a flexible and responsive system in which the strategic goals are understood and accepted by the managers who have to operationalize them. The coordination of the four functional areas will be easier if there is a common concern for the achievement of dynamic competitive advantages. This will come about only if both managers and workers identify with the goals of the MNE and recognize the threats from foreign competitors as the world environment changes. The MNE operates in markets which are contestable, and its dynamic viability is constrained by rivals. These points are further developed in the next section, on global competitive strategy.

Another area where the global competitive strategy of the MNE can be compromised, unless there is successful planning, is in its relationship with governments. As explained in Chapters 11 to 13 on the interaction of MNEs and governments, the MNE must consider the interests of many stakeholders. It often faces trade-offs between the conflicting demands of home and host governments. The MNE is perceived by the host country to be an agent of its home nation, in particular, from the country in which its original firm-specific advantage developed. Because of the nationalism of all host countries, foreign MNEs are not loved. Their activities are often viewed sceptically by host governments. Some host nations are more hostile than others, but all of them constrain the efficient operations of the MNEs.

In addition to looking for changes in host-government attitudes (or for changes in the government), the MNE needs to be well positioned to bargain with govern-

GLOBAL STRATEGIC PLANNING: The Case of Chrysler and Honda Motors

Chrysler is a U.S.-based multinational, engaged in the manufacture of passenger cars and trucks. Honda Motors is a Japanese multinational which produces motorcycles, automobiles, and power products. Both companies are the third largest domestic automaker in their home country. Both spend an almost equal proportion on R and D (Chrysler 2.31 percent in 1981, Honda 3.13 percent in 1981). Yet the performance of the two companies is far from similar.

While Honda's worldwide sales are only 45 percent of Chrysler's, its market share has continued to increase, while Chrysler's has fallen. During 1978 to 1981, Chrysler's market share dropped from 11.3 percent to 10.2 percent. Honda's, on the other hand, almost doubled from 2.4 percent to 4.6 percent. During the same period, Chrysler suffered severe losses in its Return on Equity, while Honda's ROE averaged 14.7 percent during this time. These performance measures are typical not only of these two firms, but of the automobile industry as a whole and reflect the great contrasts between American and Japanese automakers.

The answer to this disparity lies in the Japanese management style and its global strategy. This emphasizes concepts such as quality control circles and lifetime employment. It is this style which promotes participative management and a human-oriented approach, and it is this style which gets results like those of Honda. Honda developed a comprehensive marketing strategy and an expanded product line to attract new customer segments. As well, Honda erected entry barriers with scale economies by centralizing manufacturing and logistics. The combination of these factors serves as a strong competitive force in Honda's global strategy.

GLOBAL STRATEGIC PLANNING: The Case of Texas Instruments and Matsushita

Texas Instruments (U.S.) and Matsushita Electric (Japan) are MNEs in the consumer and industrial electronics industry. Both companies experienced phenomenal growth during the 1970s and much of this success stemmed from their firm-specific advantage in R and D. Matsushita also possesses worldwide marketing skills and a unique (Japanese-style) management philosophy. For years, Texas Instruments was known for its success in adapting a matrix structure along its diverse product lines. Recently, however, both MNEs have experienced difficulties which are evident from their profit figures. For Texas Instruments, net income declined (as a percentage of sales) from 5.8 in 1976 to 2.6 in 1981.

Both Texas Instruments and Matsushita have been "victims" of their own success. Texas Instruments placed too much emphasis on R and D and ignored other critical factors in an effective global strategy, such as an integrated marketing effort and a sound organizational structure. Instead, its strategy focused only on technological innovation, "the more the better." By constantly increasing the amount of R and D, with inadequate regard for the marketplace, Texas Instruments had to write off very large investments in products that did not sell. Matsushita made a similar mistake in relying on only one component of a successful global strategy, namely, salesmanship, only to be beaten by competitors.

These examples serve to illustrate the necessity of having a complete, integrated global strategy. Research and development alone is not enough. Nor is salesmanship. For a global strategy to work, these factors (R and D, marketing, a sound organizational structure) must work together. Both firms are presently undergoing major reorganizations in an attempt to coordinate these activities and make their global strategy more effective.

ments. The MNE has a certain flexibility in being able to go to different regions, so it can attempt to secure the best deal for itself in the form of tax allowances, construction grants, employment grants, and so on. This process must be combined with a sense of corporate social responsibility, which again is recognized by successful geocentric MNEs.

PORTER'S MODEL OF COMPETITIVE STRATEGY

Perhaps the most influential model of business strategy, and one which is readily applicable in an international context, is that by Michael E. Porter (1980). Porter, of the Harvard Business School, has developed a model of competitive strategy which extends the components of business strategy from a concern with general and environmental factors to a more specific focus on the nature of competition facing a firm.

His model integrates the work of industrial organization theory where the linkages of structure, conduct, and performance are explored, often in an economic context, with that of business strategy formulation, in which concepts of strategic planning seek to match the internal strength of the company (its firm-specific advantages) to its external environment (the CSAs). In this new approach strategic planning has its roots in the competitive aspects of industrial organization. It fills a gap in the structure-conduct-performance view of the world, in which conduct can be viewed as the economic aspects of a firm's strategy—aspects typically ignored or skimmed over in purely economic analysis but of critical importance in corporate planning.

Porter shows that competition in an industry is influenced by five factors: the rivalry among existing firms, the threat of new entrants, the threat of substitutes, the bargaining power of buyers, and the bargaining power of suppliers. These are illustrated in Exhibit 14-1.

To some extent, all of these competitive forces reflect structural (environmental) factors facing the firm (MNE) and together determine the attractiveness of the industry and the performance of the firm. However, the firms can influence all of these factors by the appropriate strategy; strategy unlocks the environmental constraints.

EXHIBIT 14-1
PORTER'S FIVE TYPES OF COMPETITIVE FORCE

I	Industry competitors: rivalry among existing firms
2	Potential entrants: threat of new entrants
3	Substitutes: threat of substitute products or services
4	Suppliers: bargaining power of suppliers
5	Buyers: bargaining power of purchasers

Source: Adapted from Porter, Michael E., *Competitive Strategy*, New York: The Free Press, 1980, Chapter 1, especially Figure 1-1.

Rivalry exists when a competitor sees the opportunity to improve its position. Intense rivalry results from many factors, including numerous or equally balanced competitors, high fixed costs, and high strategic stakes. Since these factors can and do change, companies can attempt to defend or improve their position, for example through strategic moves, such as offering a new service or product development.

The threat of new entrants depends largely on the ability of the industry to erect entry barriers which exclude newcomers. Substitute products can act as a competitive threat by placing a limit on potential returns through price ceilings. Two categories of substitutes deserve the most attention: those that are subject to trends improving their price performance and those that are produced by industries earning high profits.

Competition can also be influenced by the bargaining power of buyers and suppliers. Purchasers compete by forcing down prices or demanding higher quality or more service. Alternatively, a supplier can use its market power to raise prices or lower quality. Thus a firm's choice of buyer and supplier must be viewed as a major strategic decision. The complexities of this are greater for MNEs, since they often face government purchase and local content requirements, which constrain the strategic choices open to the MNE.

Porter finds that there are several diagnostic components necessary for successful competitive analysis. The firm must be able to define and recognize its future goals, current strategy, assumptions used, and capabilities. Once these elements of competitor analysis are known and understood, there is a platform for the implementation of a global strategy.

Competitor Analysis

Competitor analysis is a process used to develop a profile of the likely strategic changes that a competitor might make in reaction to a firm's strategic moves and general industry conditions. Four components must be examined in competitor analysis: the future goals, current strategy, assumptions, and capabilities of the competitors in an industry.

A knowledge of future goals helps to predict the competitor's response and its degree of satisfaction with its present position. The second component, assumptions, are examined to identify "blind spots" or biases that affect the way managers in competing firms see their environment. Statements of the competitor's current strategy expose key operating policies in each functional area. Capabilities, the fourth component, determine the competitor's ability to react to strategic moves.

Integration of the four components enables a firm to develop a profile of each of the competitors, which can be an important input for forecasting future industry conditions. It identifies where the firm has advantages over competitors and how it can overcome weaknesses.

In general, all of these concepts are readily applicable in an international context. This section now continues to outline the Porter model to determine how it

EXHIBIT 14-2
ENTRY AND EXIT BARRIERS

Entry barriers	Exit barriers
Scale economies	Specialized assets—difficult to liquidate
Product differentiation	Fixed costs—difficult to terminate
Capital requirements	Strategic costs
Switching (supplier) costs	Information barriers
Distribution channels	Manager's emotions
Government regulation	Government and social expectations

relates to MNEs. In particular, the international aspect of entry and exit barriers are of great importance and are examined in more detail. These barriers are listed in Exhibit 14-2.

Entry Barriers and Strategy

Porter finds that *barriers to entry* stem from six sources. Several of these relate to production constraints, which are discussed in more detail in Chapter 16.

First, the existence of scale economies which force a newcomer to start up a product line at a large scale if it is to be cost-competitive. Potential rivals also experience strong resistance from existing firms, to the extent that a newcomer may not be able to capture a sufficiently large share of the market to realize sufficient scale economies.

The second barrier is that of product differentiation. This forces potential entrants to overcome product loyalites and brand names. It may involve considerable expense, for example, in large advertising and R and D expenditures.

Third, there are capital requirements which entail large up-front expenditures to enter a new market.

Switching costs, the fourth barrier, are one-time costs involved in switching from one supplier to another or breaking down the long-term relationship between existing rival firms and their suppliers. Such costs can be reduced if the entrant can find cost or performance improvements over existing suppliers, but this is a difficult task.

Access to distribution channels acts as the fifth barrier. The newcomer must gain acceptance in marketing channels, which can require a large amount of time and effort.

A sixth barrier exists in the form of government regulations. These interact with the other barriers and serve to limit entry into certain industries by imposing requirements such as mandatory licensing to host firms, export quotas, or provisions to purchase from local suppliers.

In addition, fear of retaliation from existing rivals is a powerful entry barrier. Such a threat is signaled by factors such as the existence of a large powerful firm with a history of retaliation by devices such as price wars or predatory pricing. Whatever their form, these barriers change with time. Their intensity is influenced by the strategy that the firm chooses to follow.

Porter develops three generic strategies which can be followed by an established firm to protect its market position. These are: cost leadership, involving strict cost control; product differentiation based on brand names; and focus, which is the creation of a "unique" product or area of sale, that is, the creation of a market niche. There is clearly some degree of interaction amongst these strategies, but each strategy alone, although involving different skills, resources, and risks, provides some degree of protection against the structural environment of the five competitive forces. Of course, there are also risks involved in these strategies. For example, a cost leadership approach can be undercut by a newcomer with low-cost learning. Similarly, product differentiation narrows differences in product lines and leads to the risk of imitation. Finally, competitors may be able to hit upon submarkets in the chosen niche, thus destroying the focus of the MNE.

The extent to which international competition can erode profitability depends on several factors, some on the demand side and some on the supply side. There are several major reasons for demand-side erosions of profitability, stemming from demographic changes, changes in tastes, or changes in consumer incomes. On the supply side there may be technological substitution and other changes affecting performance. From this it is clear that it is vitally important for the MNE to develop a planning system which allows it to assess and respond to changes in information affecting its FSAs and strategy.

Exit Barriers and Strategy

Despite the existence of falling profits, there are important factors which keep firms producing in an industry. These are termed *exit barriers* and result from six sources.

The first one is the presence of specialized assets, especially for large, capital-intensive firms in the steel, heavy-engineering, or mineral resource industries. These are difficult to place elsewhere and lower the liquidation value of a plant or business.

A second factor reducing liquidation value is the fixed costs associated with slowing down and stopping production. These include labor settlements and payments for pension funds and are complicated by low employee productivity.

Third, strategic exit barriers may inhibit the firm from divesting, as the unprofitable business may still be important to the success of the overall company. Exiting may hurt the company's image and endanger its access to capital markets.

Fourth, information barriers can make it difficult for management to obtain accurate data to assess performance and exercise the judgment to exit.

The fifth exit barrier is somewhat more intangible. It is the reluctance of management to leave a business, as a result of subjective emotions and pride, the fear of having "nowhere to go," and the personal identification of managers with certain projects.

Finally, governments and society often impose exit barriers, such as the wish to minimize the adverse employment effects of a plant closing down.

Given these structural barriers, Porter finds that there are four strategies which can be followed when an industry is in decline. The first one is a leadership strategy which involves taking advantage of a declining industry to earn high profits. Second, a niche can be developed by identifying a segment of a declining industry that will maintain stable demand and profits. Harvesting is the third strategy. It involves the optimization of cash flows by such tactics as reducing the number of distribution channels used. Finally, there is always the option of quick divestment by selling early, when uncertainty about the future is greatest. The choice of any strategy depends ultimately on the capabilities of the firm in its environment.

Operation of a Global Strategy

One of the first points to remember in the operation of a global strategy is that entry and exit barriers are commonly related (e.g., scale economies which directly result from specialized assets). To optimize profits, the best situation for the MNE is one in which entry barriers are high while exit barriers are low. The MNE faces most, if not all, of the domestic entry and exit barriers. Indeed, they pose greater problems in an international dimension.

For example, consider the role of government regulations and social concerns, Porter's last entry or exit barrier. The MNE must deal not only with the home government, but with a variety of host-nation governments, many of which have mutually conflicting views and policies. How does a U.S. MNE deal with the British and Argentinean governments when they are at war, or with middle-eastern nations, or with the nationalism of even close neighbors such as Canada or Mexico?

An effective global competitive strategy must adapt to changes in environmental limitations on the MNE's activities. For instance, it is necessary to accomodate such country-specific factors as cost differences, the regulatory role of host governments, and different resource structures. Although the competitive forces are structurally the same, they are more complex on an international scale.

The impediments, or entry barriers to competition, are broader on a global level. There are economic impediments, such as higher transportation and storage costs, the need for a large sales force, and increased sensitivity to lead times. Managerial barriers are also greater, including such factors as changing technology and the need for a differentiated marketing effort. Institutional or government impediments are greater still. The decision to compete globally necessitates the search for more information, which in itself is costly.

Offsetting these costs are opportunities available to a global firm that are not there for a domestic firm. For example, for some product lines the relevant market may be global only, and not exist domestically. This is especially true for firms from small nations. Only by selling on a worldwide basis will there be opportunities for economies of scale, or the possiblity of sourcing from several countries, or a spread of costs over several markets.

Porter also identified unique strategic issues pertinent to a global competitor. These environmental structures include industrial policies, relationships with host governments, and the difficulty in accurately analyzing foreign competitors' positions.

In light of all these considerations, the decision for the MNE in its competitive strategy rests on whether it is necessary to compete globally to exploit the MNE's firm-specific advantage. As discussed earlier, Porter advocates four strategic alternatives: competing with a full product line; choosing a global focus (a niche); choosing a national focus emphasizing market differences among nations (which requires a polycentric attitude by management); or competing through a protected niche, where measures such as tariffs or national policy offer unexpected opportunities. Whatever the strategic choice, the MNE needs to consider the high barriers which exist on a global level rather than in any single nation. Although the structural factors and market forces may be the same in conceptual terms, in practice they exist on a much more complex level.

World Product Mandates   To pursue the problem of host government constraints on strategic planning one step further, let us look at the issue of world product mandates. These are charters given by the MNE to one of its foreign subsidiaries to develop, produce, and market a new product line. Some host nations are willing to give a subsidy for R and D only to the subsidiaries of MNEs which can demonstrate that they have received such a mandate. In Canada, Black and Decker has secured such mandates for sander machines, as has Westinghouse for water turbines.

From the viewpoint of the host nations, such discriminatory subsidies make sense, since the requirement for international marketing by the subsidiary will help the nation's exports of technologically intensive products. Yet, from the viewpoint of the MNE, decentralization of its R and D capacity may not be desired. Furthermore, the creation of a new international marketing division in a subsidiary presents many challenges to its overall organizational structure. The subsidiary will develop more autonomy, and the ongoing FSA of the MNE may be put at risk.

Prahaled and Doz (1981) have investigated a way in which the MNE can attempt to use its organizational structure to control its subsidiaries in undertaking world product mandates, but ultimately its ability is constrained by government actions. Recent work by Rugman and Bennett (1982) and Poynter and Rugman (1982) has investigated these and related problems in more detail. It has been found that most MNEs are not willing to accept world product mandating because of the risk of dissipation of the FSA and the increased complexity (and thus higher cost) of parent-subsidiary relationships.

However, host nations will continue to come up with such tax incentives or, alternatively, penalties, as they attempt to regulate MNEs, often for reasons related more to income redistribution than to efficiency. There is a tendency to want a bigger share of the golden egg laid by the MNE goose. These conflicts between MNE and host governments were explored in detail in Chapters 11 to 13. Here it is necessary only to note that the MNE must incorporate these constraints into its global strategic planning.

PROBLEMS OF GLOBAL COMPETITIVE STRATEGY

The decline in tariff and nontariff barriers to trade and the dissemination of technology among countries and firms has led to the development of global industries. In these industries a firm's competitive advantage in any one country is dependent on its performance in all the countries in which it operates around the world. The firm's strategy in marketing, production, product development, trade, and investment must be integrated on a worldwide basis if it is to survive in any one market. Automobiles, steel, and telecommunications are examples of global industries.

Global industries require a firm to compete on a worldwide, coordinated basis or face strategic disadvantage. Some industries that are international in the sense of being populated by multinational companies do not have the essential characteristics of a global industry. Thus industries with multinational companies are not necessarily global industries.

A global enterprise sells a fairly uniform product all around the world. In Porter's model, the MNEs, on the other hand, view each of its businesses as

---

EXAMPLES OF GLOBAL COMPETITION

Caterpillar and Komatsu

By forging a global strategy, Caterpillar Tractor Company maintained its world leadership in the large-scale equipment business, despite heavy competition. Caterpillar faced increasing pressure from Komatsu, Japan's leading construction equipment producer. Komatsu exported products from centralized facilities with labor and skill cost advantages. Despite this, Caterpillar gained world market share through four defensive moves: a global strategy of its own, a willingness to invest in manufacturing, a willingness to commit finances, and a blocking position in the Japanese market.

How did Caterpillar implement this global strategy? The solution was in erecting two barriers to entry. The first was a global distribution system which served to block off competition. The second consisted of production economies. As a result, no competitor was able to match Caterpillar's production and distribution costs.

L. M. Ericsson

L. M. Ericsson of Sweden is a telephone-equipment producer whose strategy for success arose from exploiting a technological niche. Ericsson began by investing in developing countries and small European markets that did not have access to national suppliers. Later, the company developed a series of standardized modules, adaptable to many telephone systems. This strategy resulted in scale economies which continued to grow with the number of systems. Consequently, Ericsson built an entry barrier to competitors.

independent entities. Thus the MNE has less chance of selling a uniform or standardized product, because of its attention to host-country variety. Of course, what Porter has identified is a polycentric MNE. There are other types of MNEs.

The two boxes in this section apply the Porter model to two case studies of global competitive strategy, where competitor analysis is used by the MNE. More details of these cases can be found in Hout et al. (1982).

SUMMARY

In this chapter, the issues of formulation and organization of effective strategic planning were discussed. The chapter revealed the conditions under which a global strategy is required, how it is formed, and when it is implemented by MNEs in a competitive world. Rather than continuing to assume that the environment is given, the chapter considered changes in the environment in an international setting. Global competition is more complex than domestic competition, and this chapter examined the strategies required for success in the changing international environment.

A major consideration in global competition is the entry and exit barriers which exist. These serve to restrict the activities of MNEs wishing to enter or exit from an industry and reinforce the necessity of adopting an effective global strategy. Several cases at the end of the chapter illustrate this point. The MNE, in designing its global competitive strategy, must assess its firm-specific advantage and know how to retain it in the light of international rivalry.

KEY WORDS

Portfolio matrix strategy
Corporate business strategy
Strategic planning process
Strategic business units
Business unit strategy
Global strategic planning

Environmental and internal variables
Global competitive strategy
Barriers to entry
Barriers to exit
World product mandates

QUESTIONS

1 Relate the theory of internalization to the MNE's global competitive strategy. How does the environment in which the MNE operates influence its strategic alternatives? How can the MNE successfully implement a global strategy?

2 The portfolio matrix strategy designed by the Boston Consulting Group received much recognition in the 1970s. Discuss how successful it is when adapted to MNEs. What modifications are necessary and what factors are overlooked by the matrix method?

3 What are the key elements of the strategic planning process of the MNE? Discuss the factors of special importance to the MNE during this process.

4 You are attempting to evaluate the performance of a Strategic Business Unit which has not been entirely profitable. What factors would you consider in your assessment? What should its contribution to the MNE be based upon?

5 Discuss the elements of strategic planning in the MNE. In what areas can the global competitive strategy be compromised? Use one of the cases, or an example you are familiar with, to illustrate global strategic planning.

6 The model of competitive business strategy developed by Porter (1980) has received much attention. What are the elements of this model as they relate to MNEs? How can competitor analysis, as described by Porter, assist the MNE in its strategy?

7 What is the impact of entry and exit barriers on the MNE's strategy? Give a few examples to illustrate your point. What are the options available to the firm to protect its position? What risks are involved?

8 You are acting in a consulting role for a large MNE. Elaborate upon the evolution of global strategic management. What advice would you give to a firm which is considering the adoption of such a strategy?

Exercise: Discuss the distinction·between a multinational industry and a global industry. To illustrate your answer, use examples of firms from the Fortune 500.

CHAPTER 15

MARKETING MANAGEMENT

INTRODUCTION

This chapter deals with the issues confronting the marketing manager in international business. The functions involved in multinational marketing mirror those necessary in domestic marketing but are often complicated by environmental differences in the countries served by the MNE. The marketing functions include identification of the needs of potential and actual customers (the function of marketing research), the design of products and/or services to fill these needs (a matter of product planning with emphasis on the trade-off between standardization and differentiation), the pricing and promotion of the offering (including advertising and personal selling), the selection and coordination of channels of distribution, and the provision of follow-up services to ensure satisfactory performance.

In the standard marketing literature these functions are often summarized as "the 4 Ps": product, price, promotion, and place (distribution). Although it is possible to argue that, in general, international marketing also falls within the parameters of these 4 Ps, it is necessary here to consider the increased scope and complexity of marketing when many countries are involved.

For example, the financing function often takes on a very important role in international marketing because of the relative scarcity of accessible credit and financing. Similarly, for industrial products in particular, the assessment of needs comprises much more than just an understanding of what the prospective buyer says is wanted. In many cases, especially in developing countries, the marketing function must incorporate a broad assessment of whether the desired product really will provide the kind of benefit the buyer perceives. In these and related situations a narrow concern for the 4 Ps is insufficient for the proper execution of the required marketing functions.

This chapter deals with important issues by identifying the main tasks and problems facing the international marketing manager. It identifies the tools and techniques which enable the manager to deal with these issues, concentrating on those unique to the international marketing function. Only a brief treatment of each area can be provided. The interested student is encouraged to develop further in-depth knowledge by continuing on to the more specialized courses and texts in international and export marketing. Nevertheless, this chapter should serve to make the reader conversant with the issues, tools, and some of the solutions relevant for the international marketing manager. The chapter covers two basic situations for which the marketing function assumes identical proportions. One is the multinational case where production facilities are located in many different countries. The other case is represented by the large exporter whose production facilities might be located in only one country (the home country) but whose marketing effort is directed from wholly or partly owned sales subsidiaries in the market countries.

The discussion will first deal with the two cornerstones of marketing strategy, market segmentation and foreign product positioning. The emphasis will then shift to the implementation of this strategy as it is reflected in the 4 Ps.

MARKET SEGMENTATION

International market segmentation is used to adapt to customer heterogeneity both between nations and within countries. Whether a single-country or multi-country markets are contemplated, there is usually considerable heterogeneity among the buyers across and within countries. This can be recognized by the astute marketer. By differentiating the offering between countries and target segments, a much better fit is achieved between the offerings and the various segments.

Bases for Segmentation

Several standard bases for segmentation are useful in foreign markets, despite potential data problems. Exhibit 15-1 identifies three classifications of standard bases for segmentation.

Geographical subdivisions of the total market are a natural first cut considering the importance of national borders and different country market characteristics. As for within-country segmentation, data availability often constrains the marketer to the use of demographics. Many countries segment naturally into different ethnic groups, the "melting pot" of the United States being somewhat of an oddity rather than the norm in the international context. Demographics, socioeconomic status, and geographical location serve together as strong criteria for segmentation in many countries. Eastman Kodak's International Photographic Operations, for example, develop regional groups of various countries based on geo-

EXHIBIT 15-1
STANDARD BASES FOR MARKET SEGMENTATION

Traditional:	Geography
	Demographics (such as age, number of children, marital status, sex)
	Socioeconomics (such as income, social class)
Behavioristic:	Usage background
	Brand loyalty
	Channel choice
Behavioral:	Benefits sought
	Life-style and psychographics
	Personality
	Attitudes
	Ideal point segmentation

graphical location and then identify target segments within each member country in a region on the basis of income and family-size data. The more modern segmentation variables common in present-day analyses of consumers—life-styles, benefits sought, usage rates, loyalty, status, or attitudes—tend to be less useful in foreign markets. This is due to difficulties in collecting the requisite primary data.

Criteria for Viable Segments

The chosen segmentation variables and the consequent division of the total market into subgroups should satisfy the following criteria.

First, the segments should be "measurable." It is necessary to measure the size and purchasing power of each segment. One standard approach is to identify the number of families in a country above a certain income level using national and UN data on the distribution of disposable income. Such "income elasticity" evaluations provide a rough figure on segment potentials under the assumption that variations in incomes are associated with differences in consumption levels. Durable consumer goods marketers (Ford, Sony, and General Electric, for example) can get a relatively good reading on potentials by comparing a given country with existing markets using such income data. For industrial goods (Corning Glass, L. M. Ericsson) and consumer convenience producers (Coca-Cola, Proctor & Gamble) such income data need to be complemented by information on industrial activity and country-specific consumption data, respectively.

Second, the segments should be accessible. That is, the identified subgroups should be reachable in terms of both communication and physical distribution. The infrastructure of a country determines whether this requirement can be met. In India, physical distribution often becomes a problem because of relatively poor access to certain sections of the country. Some countries (like Sweden) prohibit the use of TV advertising, preventing the kind of saturation campaigns for the introduction of a new product associated with U.S. consumer markets.

Third, the target should be substantial. Generally, it makes little sense to target a segment with few members or very low potential. Tailoring marketing mixes to separate segments tends to be expensive. The advantages of standardization, large-scale economies, and learning-curve effects are reduced. The potential sales volume in a segment needs to be substantial enough to pay for the "tailoring" done. On the other hand, the emergence of flexible manufacturing systems (FMS) where scale economies can be obtained even for short series, and the chance to learn about new foreign markets by establishing a small foothold there sometimes makes a less substantial target segment attractive. The small-scale entry of Nissan and Toyota into the declining import market for autos in the U.S. in the early sixties is a case in point.

Target Marketing

Once segments have been identified in the host-country market, the targeting alternatives available to the marketer involve a "shotgun" or "no-target" approach (usually advisable as a strategy only in the initial stages of involvement), a "concentrated" approach where only one or two segments are targeted, or a "differentiated" approach with most of the uncovered segments adapted to.

In developing the cost-benefit analysis for choosing either of these strategies, the manager needs to pay strict attention to the firm-specific advantages that can be sustained in the different markets. Not all countries and segments will be served equally well by the particular company skills embodied in the final product line offered for sale. For example, the "safety" advantage of the Volvo car, which is emphasized in North American markets, carries less weight in the Japanese market, where safety is a minor concern. Furthermore, even though certain segments may be of potentially great value, the firm might not be able to target this particular segment because the product desired cannot be supplied without extensive changes in production and marketing procedures. One example is the global market for digital watches left unattended by the dominant Swiss manufacturers for years. The electronics technology demanded for efficient manufacturing of these new products was simply not within the Swiss watchmakers' domain.

In the international arena, the concentrated approach is often the most profitable one, since it allows a focused attempt to sell in a relatively homogeneous subset of the market. The Japanese approach to foreign markets often amounts to an initial focused entry in a niche of the market left unguarded by existing firms, and then a gradual spreading of the attack from the secured beachhead.

The Japanese entry into the North American automobile industry is evidence of this tactic. When American automobile producers were focusing on larger cars, the Japanese began to export compacts and subcompacts to the United States and Canada. By the time the Americans could respond to this competition the Japanese producers had a secure position in the small car market and were expanding their product line to include larger, more luxurious models.

FOREIGN POSITIONING

To target a specific segment, the marketer needs to be skillful at developing the marketing mix. This task, referred to as product positioning in domestic markets, takes on some special characteristics in foreign markets.

The Procedure for FP

The basic idea behind the foreign positioning (FP) concept is that products consist of bundles of attributes which are capable of generating a stream of benefits to the buyer and user.

Viewed in a multidimensional space (commonly denoted the perceptual space or product space), a product is then graphically represented as a point defined by its attribute scores. Other products are represented by other points. If the points are close, the products tend to have similar attribute scores and are thus fair substitutes; i.e., they tend to compete heavily. The farther away a point is from another, the less the direct competition tends to be (since they differ considerably on the salient attributes). The location of a product's point in this product space is its positioning. An example of a positioning map is given in Figure 15-1. It shows how the market views a number of automobiles from different countries in terms of sportiness and ride characteristics.

"Made-in" Labels

One reason FP is different from domestic positioning is that the country of origin of a product is identified with an explicit label on the product. This is tantamount to a branding of the product. Sellers have the option of making such branding a cornerstone of their marketing campaign ("From the land of the Vikings . . .") or conversely of attempting to transcend the label ("Dodge Colt, built by Mitsubishi"). In a narrow sense, foreign positioning refers to this choice.

We are all familiar with the problems foreign products might encounter in a country. According to newspaper reports, the Japanese buyer for many products is most favorably disposed to domestic offerings. In other cases, notably cosmetics and women's apparel, European or U.S. manufacturers seem to have an edge. Sweden might still enjoy an advantage in specialty steels, Germany in chemicals and autos, and the United States in electronics. In some European countries, Japanese products are still eyed with suspicion. In the United States, Japanese products seem to have captured the imagination of buyers to the extent that many refuse to even consider products from other countries, including the United States itself.

These crude generalizations can apply to large or small segments of the population (or the relevant market). As country stereotyping occurs, a given manufacturer from one country marketing in another will do well to accommodate such

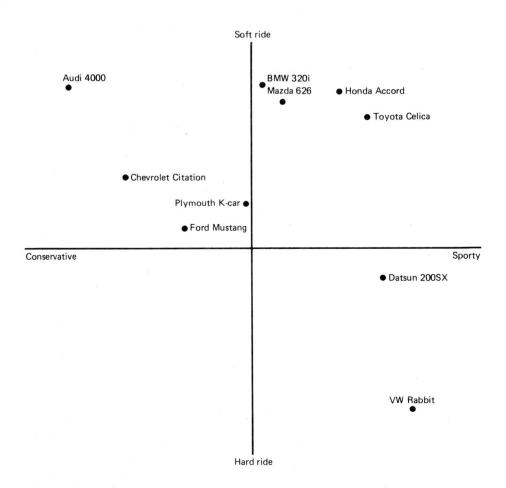

FIGURE 15-1
Product positioning map: automobiles.

phenomena. In some cases the balance tilts positively; in others the overriding result is negative. In order to be optimal, the marketing mix needs to be calibrated carefully. For example, if a negative stereotype persists, is there need for a new brand name which hides the country of origin (Nike athletic shoes, made in South Korea and Taiwan)? Is there need for advertising with explicit counterargumentation, attempting to dispel the people's negative stereotypes of the home country ("An Italian car? Fiat—the best selling car in Europe")? Are introductory discounts required to enter the distribution chains (South Korean TV sets in the United States)? In many cases hardly any one of the mix ingredients will go unaffected by the country-of-origin label and the decision about how highly to profile it.

Standardization versus Adaptation

Another reason that FP is different from the standard case of product positioning relates to the importance of balancing the desire for standardization against the need for adaptation of the product to the specific needs of the foreign market. The standardization benefits have been well documented. They include scale economies, experience effects, and consequent lower unit costs, making maximum use of a good idea and maintaining consistency in marketing across many countries and markets ("Coke refreshes"). The adaptation argument has even more proponents and perhaps an even longer history. It generally maintains that the identical product cannot be sold everywhere, except in rare circumstances.

The development of "world products" such as the Ford Fiesta and the Canon AE-1 camera represents efforts to avoid costly adaptation in favor of standardization. Such "global strategies" become particularly appropriate when tastes and preferences among the population of various countries have been sufficiently homogenized that local variation is minimal. With increasing interdependence and instantaneous satellite communications (especially via television) such an assumption appears increasingly valid. It should be recognized, however, that these standardized products will not necessarily aim at the identical markets in the various countries. The AE-1 is a technically advanced, semiprofessional item in the Japanese camera market but a high-convenience, easy-to-use product in some western markets (including the United States). These differences need to be reflected in the pricing, promotion, and advertising strategies for the various countries. For example, sports stars (John Newcombe, Bruce Jenner) are used as spokesmen for the AE-1 in the United States while professional photographers are depicted in Japanese commercials.

emphasize a different set on attributes in each segmented area

Managing the FP

The introduction of FP into the manager's arsenal leads to a particular set of questions that need to be answered explicitly. First, to what extent are the particular biases known a priori? Is there need for more research to attempt to chart the stereotypes vis-à-vis our country?

Second, do the biases affect primarily the factual *beliefs* about our product, or is there a larger *emotional* component? If the stereotyping is primarily perceptual, an informational campaign is called for. At issue is the fact that the offered product is mispositioned in the product space. If the informational campaign could use relatively large amounts of promotional media and techniques such as comparative advertising, perceptions might well be altered. In most cases, however, the changes are slow and based more upon actual product experiences than promotion as such. In these cases, promotion serves basically in a supportive role rather than as an initiator of change.

In cases where the biases are anchored in emotional evaluation, the most successful strategy might well be to completely change one's approach and use subcontracting (licensing), a joint-venture arrangement, or a similar setup. This would avoid a direct identification of country of origin. The seller does in fact have to decide whether bucking the trend is worthwhile.

Again, the objective of the manager in answering these questions is to ensure that the product positioning achieved is the strongest possible under the circumstances. Successful application of the positioning concepts would mean that sales of the product to a well-defined target market, capitalizing on the firm-specific advantages, are ensured and that direct competition from domestic and foreign competitors is minimized. Lack of attention to these principles leads to a haphazard positioning, possibly in some niche of the market not of much interest to most customers and of low use satisfaction among the few buyers because of misperceptions. In this respect short-run sales increases could be very misleading indicators of long-term success. Examples include the difficulties of sustaining operations in the North American auto market by British carmakers, the lackluster international performance of presumably high-quality products from Philips and GE, faced with Japanese competition as well as the competitive difficulties encountered by consumer goods companies such as Unilever and Nestlé trying to break into the North American market.

THE INTERNATIONAL ENVIRONMENT AND THE MARKETING MIX

This section examines the 4 Ps of marketing; product, pricing, promotion, and place (distribution) as they apply to international marketing. In international marketing, the determinants of the appropriate marketing mix are complicated by local environmental factors. These affect both the marketing strategy of the MNE and the management of the marketing function.

In principle, the generation of an optimal marketing mix flows logically from the international segmentation and positioning strategies decided upon. But although the principles are straightforward, their implementation in foreign markets is fraught with possibilities for mistakes and problems. For example, the price settled upon as correct for one country might suddenly be made too high (or low) because of fluctuating exchange rates. Where the pricing is determined at headquarters, attempts at correcting these swings often meet resistance in the distribution channels. Dealers may take possession of cars at lower delivered prices but still maintain previous retail prices (as happened in the U.S. market after 1981 when the U.S. dollar soared to new heights).

Product and promotion decisions suffer from the same lack of head office control. Special regulations force certain product adaptations and make others very expensive to undertake. The imposition of tariffs of varying levels for semiprocessed versus finished products makes the location of some manufacturing activity (e.g., final assembly) in the market country worthwhile. The required investment and subsequent sales often make some product modifications viable while others are too expensive for small market segments.

Promotion is probably the tactical area hardest hit by the conversion to an international perspective. A number of promotional tools, well developed and skillfully used in the home market, might well be unavailable in foreign markets (for example, commercial TV and radio are unavailable in Scandinavian countries) or simply of no value in communicating with the targeted segments (direct mail solicitations are of little use in the interpersonally oriented Japanese markets). Differences in language and culture make communication a much greater problem than it is in the home market. The attainment of a targeted position with some kind of standardized message is always questionable. In terms of adaptation, the promotional effort is often the area in most need of a complete adjustment to the country market's special requirements.

Finally, distribution decisions carry special relevance in the international context. Mistakes in this area, such as the wrong choice of local outlets for the product, easily waylay even a well-directed and -targeted marketing effort along the other three tactical dimensions. U.S. soft drink companies, for example, have found that grocery stores, a major outlet in the home market, carry relatively little weight in many Asian markets, where the majority of sales go through specialized stores. In international marketing, distribution becomes the alpha and the omega of marketing tactics.

The upshot of these complications is that a completely standardized marketing mix is never optimal. Rather, as Sorenson and Wiechmann have shown, most companies maintain standard *procedures* but leave the specific *content* of the decisions for local adaptation. The specific procedures and contents of each of the 4 Ps will now be examined in more detail.

PRODUCT DECISIONS

Product decisions represent the most complex decisions in the marketing mix. Product decision making involves several subsets of activities, including design, standardization, or adaptation to local markets, the development of a line of related products, and management of the product through its life cycle.

Managing the Product Life Cycle

In most country markets it is generally hypothesized that products follow a life cycle (see Figure 15-2). In the international context it is common for a product to be in the mature stage of the life cycle in one country and in the introductory stage in another. Color television is in the maturity stage in most developed countries, while in the LDCs it is still in the introductory stage. A carefully coordinated marketing program with a nonstandardized product design is therefore required.

The development of well-adapted product designs involves several kinds of market information. Determining the actual stage in the PLC is the starting point. A mistake here usually means that the product entry falters. For example, an early 1960s full-scale entry into the German market by laundromat operators proved premature since the requisite educational process had not yet been completed and washing was still a matter of work at home. The initial entry in the United States of Shiseido, the largest Japanese cosmetics marketer, underestimated the promotional spending necessary to break loyalties formed toward the existing brands in a mature market. The company withdrew.

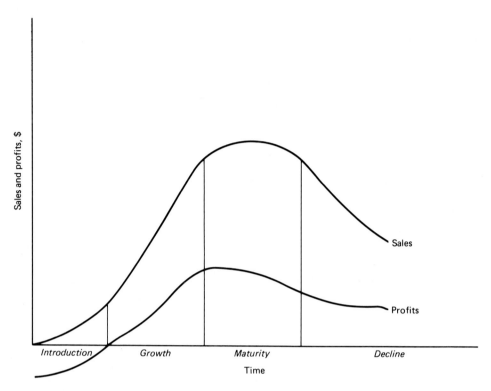

FIGURE 15-2
The product life cycle.

2   A second step in the analysis centers on the degree to which the brand, as opposed to the product, is in an introductory stage in the country or is already well known there. When the Japanese entered the TV market in North America, Sony was still an unknown brand while the product (color TVs) was already in a very competitive growth stage. The marketing strategy adopted employed both heavy advertising to make the brand well known and product design features (Trinitron) to claim superiority over existing competitors. By contrast, when Sony introduced the Walkman, the market itself was new and the previous success of Sony products could be used in advertising to guarantee performance and ensure rapid acceptance.

Perhaps the most risky undertaking for a company is the entry into a country market still in the introductory stage with an unknown brand name. Apple's success in the Japanese market is one example where these obstacles were overcome (although their very success spanned domestic competition with consequent declining market share).

One solution here is to adopt a very gradual penetration posture, beginning with a relatively minor investment and successively increasing the commitment as the market unfolds. This approach was taken by Kikkoman, the Japanese soy sauce maker, in entering the U.S. market. The problem with the gradual approach is the possibility of competitive imitation before the brand has been firmly established.

The speed at which products are introduced in different country markets has escalated over the past two decades. At one time products were first introduced in high-income, high-wage markets such as the United States and only later introduced in Europe, Japan and middle- and low-income countries (the international product life cycle has been discussed earlier in Chapters 2 and 5). The reduction of tariff and nontariff barriers to trade, rapidly rising income in previously lower income countries, and the formation of free-trade areas has condensed the product cycle. By the early 1980s, the launch of many new products was occurring almost simultaneously around the world. International marketers who missed this trend often found themselves closed out of foreign markets which they once dominated. When Gillette delayed introduction of its Trac II razor in Japan, Schick was able to seize the dominant position in the Japanese market.

The third step in the PLC analysis involves the assessment of whether product designs and promotional programs employed in existing markets will also work in the corresponding stages in new countries. Can the introductory campaign be used again with only minor changes (e.g., language), or will a whole new design be necessary? At one extreme virtually no adaptation takes place. Volvo initially introduced their car in the United States with standard Swedish design and a simple translation of their advertising slogan. As the American car buyer failed to react, Volvo quickly abandoned this approach, made product modifications, and hired an American ad agency.

At the other extreme, completely new designs and campaign material are developed. This approach is usually justified only when major country markets are considered. For TV manufacturers the difference in picture tube density between Europe and the United States has prohibited strong competition between manufacturers from different countries, although it has not prohibited the Japanese producers from entering both markets. As noted before, the promotional programs are the ones most often in need of complete revamping. As for product features, most cases involve an adaptation of existing models to the special requirements of the new countries. Japanese needs for a smaller refrigerator have been accommodated by G.E., and Italy's Fiat makes more rust-resistant cars for the northern European countries. Such product adaptation becomes particularly important in the mature stage of the PLC when the buyers in the various countries have developed more differentiated needs and their product knowledge is thorough.

In general, the maturity phase is probably the most difficult one to manage profitably for the foreign marketer. In this phase, much of the production technology has been standardized. The international product life cycle also generates an increasing quantity of products from countries with low labor costs or other related advantages. For the western firm without maintainable FSAs, the solution is usually to shift the production base offshore or simply get into a new product.

EXHIBIT 15-2
FIRM-SPECIFIC ADVANTAGES IN MARKETING

Established brand name

Exclusive distribution

Customer loyalty

Experienced sales force

Advertising skills

Marketing research

Source: Johny K. Johansson. "Firm-Specific Advantages and International Marketing Strategy," Dalhousie Discussion Paper in International Business, No. 24, Centre for International Business Studies, Dalhousie University, 1983.

Exhibit 15-2 lists some of the marketing FSAs that the firm can exploit during its strategic planning over the product life cycle.

Product-Line Stretching

The design and presentation of the product help to position it in the product space. In the usual case the firm would not be content with a single offering on the market. It would like to develop a line of related products. In traditional marketing terms, this is done to better satisfy the varying desires of the different customer segments. In the international framework, there is an added element of competitive attack and defense that enters into the product-line decisions. Entry into foreign markets is often gradual, starting from a beachhead segment, then spreading to additional segments through product-line additions. This is the strategy employed by the Japanese auto makers in many foreign markets, with product lines gradually stretched from the early small entries to larger and higher-performance vehicles.

This stretching strategy serves several purposes. By expanding the existing skill base, consistency in the offered line is maintained while new segments are reached. The same promotion and distribution channels used in the main product line can be employed to piggyback the new offerings without losing existing customers. By moving into unfilled niches, new introductions of competing products, attacking the firm's existing positions, can be preempted. The new products, together with the existing offerings, can be built as a wall around a particular position in the market, making a direct attack by competitors more difficult. Customers can then move upscale along the firm's product line rather than switching from one product space to another as their needs change. Mercedes' introduction of the 240 SL sportscar served to buffer the major model against encroachments from high-performance Corvettes and Porsches, while the introduction of a smaller sedan protects it from competition of smaller and cheaper substitutes (including Volvo, Saab, and BMW).

In these line-stretching decisions, the major drawback tends to be the high risk of cannibalization. As relatively close variants of a product are introduced into a market, the risk grows larger that the new product will cut into existing sales. The buyer of the 240 SL might very well have bought the standard Mercedes sedan had the sportscar not been available. With the strong increase in international competition over the last few years, such cannibalization is now viewed with less fear. The problem facing the firm in many of today's western markets is that if they do not position a product close to their existing ones, some competitor will.

PRICING DECISIONS

The second of the 4 Ps of the marketing mix is pricing. There are several common pricing practices and issues relevant to managers marketing abroad. These relate to legal problems in pricing, cost-plus pricing, price escalation, experience curve pricing, and skimming versus penetration pricing.

Dumping and Legal Problems of Pricing

Pricing is notorious for its complicated legal aspects. In most countries there is antitrust legislation to protect competition. Concurrently, however, there are often contradictory regulations or "orderly marketing" agreements which function as price cartels, effectively diminishing price as a competitive weapon. Market sharing agreements between EC steel producers have had this effect. To some extent, so have the "voluntary" Japanese auto import restrictions in the United States which have made prices on Japanese cars relatively inflexible. There is concern in most countries about low pricing by foreign firms in their markets. This is the question of dumping.

Dumping refers to the practice of selling goods in foreign markets below their full costs of production plus freight and tariff charges. This practice has received extensive scrutiny under the General Agreements on Tariffs and Trade. Many nations around the world are interested in protecting their domestic firms from predatory pricing by foreign suppliers. The issue is complicated because many nations give subsidies for exports and it is difficult to assess the precise cost effect of such subsidies. Dumping is a natural practice when foreign markets are viewed as recipients of unsold inventory. In such a case, any amount retrieved above direct variable costs can justify sales for the individual firm. The domestic producers find that such a practice is highly destructive, although in the short run consumers benefit. Domestic producers want the price to be motivated by cost figures over and above variable costs (i.e., include fixed costs); otherwise they cannot compete.

The greatest difficulty in enforcing dumping regulations is the assessment of the actual costs. When Sony was accused of dumping television sets in the United States, the authorities were unable to conclusively assess Sony's costs. Instead, a "cease and desist" agreement was reached. Since the legal proceedings can take considerable time (the TV case was still not completed after more than 6 years), much of the competitive damage can be completed by the time a verdict is reached. Because of these uncertainties, the domestic firm threatened by dumping tends to view legal proceedings as a "slow-down" tactic while more constructive counterstrategies (such as cost cutting and product redesign) are undertaken.

Cost-Plus Pricing

The emphasis of dumping on a cost-justified price basis has been used as one rationalization for developing a pricing system based on cost allocations—a cost-plus procedure. In the long run, a firm finds it best to set its price at a level where costs are covered. It would also seem reasonable to allow a certain added figure (the plus) for reasonable profit margins. Such pricing procedure lends itself naturally to a good defense in dumping charges. On the other hand, it is often not clear precisely what the firm's costs for a specific product are, especially where indirect costs and overheads need to be allocated. The practice needs to be augmented to allow demand factors to enter into the pricing decision.

Even in cases where international markets are not seen as a dumping ground for unsold inventory and a more mature and considered effort is underway, a version of average cost pricing is still practiced. This full cost allocation has the advantage of enabling the firm to establish profit centers for different country and product line combinations. This is a common practice among U.S. auto manufacturers in Europe, with manufacturing in Germany and the United Kingdom and subsidiary sales offices in the individual countries. In some industries the development of global strategies has led to an avoidance of cost-plus pricing. Caterpillar's operation in Japan is a strategic attack on their competitor Komatsu's home market and is accompanied by an aggressive price discounting policy.

Price Escalation

When products are exported, costs tend to be higher. The reality of greater transport distances, tariff charges, customs duties, and the necessary product adaptation makes it natural that a price escalation occurs.

From a competitve viewpoint, such a price disadvantage could be a strong disincentive to sell a firm's product in a foreign country. The fact that it is marketed here has to do with the firm-specific advantages of the firm. Simply put, the FSAs need to be sufficient to offset the price disadvantage.

In the case where only marginal costs are used as a basis for the cost-plus-based formula, prices might become lower in the foreign markets than at home. This happens frequently in intensely competitive markets. Volvos are more expensive in the Swedish home market than in North America. Experience curve effects on unit costs in the higher-volume North American market compensate for the relatively lower price there.

Experience Curves and Marketing

From a theoretical viewpoint, the best justification against dumping is to show that the price closely follows the movements of marginal costs and revenues. One empirically tested phenomenon which has been used to demonstrate this fact is the so-called experience curve (the experience curve is discussed in more detail in Chapter 16).

The experience curve shows that a fall in unit costs occurs as output increases. As more units of a given product are produced, learning and experience develop the firm's skill in manufacturing. With a large market share the gain is faster than the competition's, translating into lower unit costs for the product. This suggests that the firm might do well to aim for large cumulative production over a few years; so it should consider entering foreign markets in order to increase production.

Under this scenario, entry into a new country market might well be accompanied by a lower price than that maintained even in the home market. With increased output and lower unit costs, the anticipated gains might be offset by a lower introductory price in the new market. Whether or not this price will later increase is determined by the rate at which the experience accumulates and the ability of the firm to retain its market share. Where the firm is operating on a steep experience curve, the relatively large gains from increased output will be great enough to make up for the small margins due to low prices.

Experience curve pricing has been adopted primarily by companies entering an existing market in the maturity stage. Many Japanese firms such as Fujitsu (computers) and Komatsu (construction equipment) use this strategy in important foreign markets, since it allows them to maintain a penetration price level.

Skimming versus Penetration Pricing

One standard pricing practice which emerges from the application of the product life cycle (PLC) concept distinguishes between a high "skimming" price and a low "penetration" price. In the introductory stage of the PLC, customers often care little about price and are more concerned with other attributes of the product. Therefore, a high price can be sustained and used to skim the cream off the top of the market. Sony's Betamax video cassette was initially priced in this manner both at home and in the United States. Because of the price escalation phenomenon, such a strategy often becomes natural in foreign markets. For example, high tariff rates make American cigarettes high-price entries in many foreign markets.

Alternatively, the introductory price might be set low so that the risk of a trial purchase is lessened and a larger number of potential customers are attracted. By maintaining this low price, the market is penetrated more quickly and the growth stage of the PLC is attained earlier. If a penetration price strategy is followed, competitors are less likely to become a problem. This is partly because of the speed of product acceptance and partly because the lower price keeps profits down and market attractiveness low. The Japanese penetration of the U.S. subcompact car market is an example of penetration pricing. However, firms already in the market may react violently to the erosion of their market shares, resulting in a full-scale price war.

The experience curve aids the practice of penetration pricing, a low introductory offering generating high sales and market shares. In international competition, if products are standardized and firms from newly industrialized countries (NICs) are able to enter the market, the long-term viability of a skimming price is in serious question. Because of this difficulty, companies are often forced to develop a high level of product differentiation in order to sustain a price differential and make innovation a profitable alternative. Casual jeans are a case in point. Low-priced competition from Taiwan, Hong Kong, and Singapore has made designer jeans a natural development where differentiation allows the maintenance of higher prices and profitability (especially with the basic manufacturing located in the low-cost NICs).

PROMOTIONAL DECISIONS

The promotional decisions facing the international marketer can generally be subdivided into mass communication (advertising) and interpersonal communication (personal selling and sales management).

MNEs and exporters use both of these methods to varying degrees. They are sufficiently important to have attracted a number of separate treatments. Although in the present context these methods will be seen as complementary, they are better discussed separately according to the nature of the product. Advertising will be discussed with reference to consumer goods, and personal selling with reference to industrial goods. These distinctions should not be taken too literally. Both means of communication are useful for either consumer or industrial products.

Advertising as a "Pull" Strategy

Mass communication messages are traditionally broadcast to the people at large, the ultimate consumers in terms of marketing. Advertising efforts are primarily directed at generating demand from ultimate consumers which will then be made known to the channels of distribution. This is a "pull" strategy.

Advertising management is usually divided into three problem areas. The first is how much to spend to stimulate demand (the budgeting problem), and the second is which media to direct the firm's message (the media-selection problem). The third problem concerns what the message is and how it should be formulated.

Advertising Budget

The area of advertising budgeting is ripe with simple rules of thumb for decision makers. Three of these rules are to spend "all you can afford," "in proportion to your competitors," or "a given percentage of last year's sales." The lack of adherence to economic principles (spend until the marginal cost equals the marginal revenue) reflects the problem in identifying the appropriate cost and demand functions. It is difficult to find out how effective advertising is in terms of sales volume.

The foreign marketer is in an even more difficult position than the domestic one. One common approach is to let the advertising budget in a country be self-sustaining by spending a certain percentage of last year's sales. The sales generated will pay for future spending. In this fashion, possibilities of control are enhanced and revenue generation is rewarded.

adapted to host market

The percentage applied cannot necessarily be the same in each country market, as Kikkoman, the Japanese soy sauce marketer, discovered upon entering the U.S. market. The advertising/sales ratio in the home market hovered around 1:30 for approximately a 3 percent figure. In the United States, with its much higher levels of advertising spending, the company was not successful until the corresponding figure reached 12 percent of sales.

Many multinational companies with standardized promotional messages tend to cut costs by providing local subsidiaries with various advertising materials. The well-known "Put a tiger in your tank" campaign by Exxon is one instance of cost reduction. The problem with such shared resources is that local adaptation in terms of copy (language) and layout is often required.

Media Selection

The basic issue here is how the media used in the home country can also be used effectively in the foreign setting. The most striking example of the difficulty is commercial TV, which is extremely important in the United States and Japan yet has lower significance in many other countries.

The problem is compounded by the coverage figures of the various media and the degree to which the selected target market(s) can be reached with a given media schedule. In general, the media selection is necessarily country-specific. In Europe considerable overlap of station coverage exists. Differences in language make a consistent spillover effect hard to count on. In India, the two most important media are film theaters and outdoor advertising. This occurs because literacy rates are generally low and wide language differences exist within the country (there are some 14 distinct languages on the Indian subcontinent, as well as numerous local dialects); so verbal cues must be kept to a minimum while visual displays become important.

Media must be selected with the help of local advertising agencies. This is recognized by most multinational marketers, who rely on local talent to identify the appropriate schedules. In response to this problem, several large advertising agencies in high-income countries have set up international branch operations to service their multinational clients and to augment their firm-specific advantages. The spread of advertising technology has been very rapid over the last two decades, and the international marketer can utilize the services of advertising agencies that combine the latest marketing techniques with intimate knowledge of the tools necessary to be successful in the local markets. In addition, these firms can often provide sophisticated market research on demand conditions and market segments in the host country.

Advertising Message

The most important and interesting question in overseas advertising relates to the message. What should be said? How should it be said? By whom should it be said?

These questions are not easy to answer even in domestic markets. In an international setting, questions arise about the language, credible spokespersons, features, and projected image. These are choices which require familiarity with the local market.

The case for standardization is most easily made for brand and company names. Coca-Cola, Sony, and Volkswagen are well known throughout most world markets. The Sony Walkman was introduced in Europe as the Soundabout with no apparent success until the Japanese name Walkman was adopted globally. At the same time, examples of less successful standardization exist. Nova, the Chevrolet car, had to be renamed in Spanish-speaking countries after it was discovered that the name meant "won't go" in Spanish. Nissan's sportscar, the 240Z, is called Fairlady in Japan, a name deemed inappropriate for the North American market. Volvo's standard sedan of the sixties was called the Amazon in Europe and sold successfully but was renamed the B18 upon its introduction to North America. Less drastic changes preserve the recognition element of the name. The U.S. shampoo Pert is called Pret in French markets.

The slogans are adapted more readily to local country markets, partly because language symbolism varies a great deal. The "young generation" theme of Pepsi Cola in the North American market has not been used globally. The "We are driven" appeal of Datsun and the "What a feeling" theme of Toyota were developed specifically for the North American markets. There are exceptions. The "Tiger in the tank" and "Coke refreshes" are two. Others include Sony's stress on "innovation" and Marlboro's "cowboy image." In the majority of cases, some adaptation is necessary. Even a "Tiger in the tank" does not carry the U.S. message in a country like India, where the animal takes on a more mythical-religious dimension than one of pure power.

The spokesperson chosen for the product also requires a careful adaptation to local sentiment. Takamiyama, the Hawaiian Sumo wrestler, can sell any product in Japan but loses all effectiveness in other countries. The same is true of Arthur Godfrey. There are exceptions, such as Bjorn Borg for tennis equipment and film stars such as Paul Newman for Nissan. The problem is partly one of recognition, partly one of projection. Its is not clear how Orson Wells or Peter Ustinov would come across in Asian countries where their very size is more exceptional than in western countries.

The case for a standardized advertising campaign across countries and regions continues. The advantages are obvious in terms of lower overall costs, greater consistency, spillover of goodwill, and use of company-specific advantages such as a common brand name. Whether a standardization such as "Coke refreshes" is effective is difficult to answer. The evidence seems to be that *some* adaptation to local conditions is desirable. The degree to which this adaptation should occur remains to be settled.

The Personal Selling Equation

Personal selling problems are country- and product-specific. The firm's salespersons should all have some rudimentary knowledge of a country's people, culture, and language. The importance of salespersons as an integral part of the firm's total "push" strategy is self-evident. The ways in which such people need to operate in a foreign country are, perhaps, less clear.

According to many sources, the best salesperson for a firm is a host-country native. Delegations from headquarters and accompanying sales meetings are necessary, especially for large-scale contracts and agreements. Limited sales objectives can be achieved by standardized and repetitive calls by a native salesperson. The task is to provide support service and spare parts for the product once sold, generate new orders from existing customers, and develop future prospects with profit potential. Overseas assignments differ in fact, but not in principle, from this general description.

PLACE (DISTRIBUTION) DECISIONS

International distribution decisions tend to fall into two subcategories. There are those decisions which concern the physical handling of the product (the physical transportation aspect). There are also those decisions which have to do with managing the product through the channel from the producer to the ultimate buyer (the channel management decisions).

The importance of physical distribution in international trade can hardly be exaggerated. Most of the theoretical and practical work in international trade has focused on transportation costs (shipment loading, warehousing, etc.), which are seen as the cornerstone of the decision framework. These issues are discussed in Chapter 4. The channel management issues are rarely discussed. Nevertheless, it is the channel management decisions that are most important for international marketing purposes.

The channel management issues that need to be dealt with include questions of what type of organizational unit to employ or create in various countries. Should the firm rely on an independent distributor in the foreign market? Should a more intensive commitment be made in the form of a wholly owned subsidiary so that the marketing effort can be executed and controlled in accord with the MNE's or exporter's strategic plans? How should the payment schedules be formulated—straight ownership or commission? Should territorial exclusivity be granted? These are but a few of the questions.

Channel Management

Entering the foreign market and developing the trade relationship with units active in the physical handling of the product leads to the question of channel management. The firm must develop safeguards and control mechanisms to ensure a smooth functional distribution channel from production to the ultimate buyer.

There are several approaches to this. They include intensive personal preparation, visits to potential distributors in the host country, training programs for local channel representatives, direct investment in a local sales office, and assembly and manufacturing.

These steps are not mutually exclusive but portray an increasing commitment over time to the country market. An illustrative example of the sequence involved is Nissan's entry into the U.S. market. In the early 1960s a small staff of Japanese managers and one technician organized a handful of American sales and service representatives. Two locations in Los Angeles and New Jersey were used as distributing points for cars shipped from Yokohama. As sales grew, the dealer network was gradually strengthened by addition of new dealerships and systematic training of service personnel. Parts management became more sophisticated as inventory, warehousing facilities, and personnel were added. Toward the end of the 1960s, the construction of a new building as headquarters of Nissan Motor Sales USA signified the establishment of a wholly independent sales subsidiary with company-owned distributorships on the two coasts, a dealer network which penetrated the Midwest and was capable of supporting dealers carrying only Datsun automobiles. Finally, in the 1980s, protectionism increased and the company started assembly of trucks in Tennessee.

From a marketing perspective these various organizational choices help to determine the degree to which the company's marketing effort in the country can be directed from a centralized point at headquarters. The firm must consider whether effective marketing requires company-owned sales branches or independent distributors. For many large companies such as Nissan, the former alternative is preferred, with the expatriate sales manager working directly with the local representatives providing service, support, and directives from headquarters.

Smaller companies and larger companies in smaller markets will usually work with independent distributors responsible for organizing and implementing the marketing of the product in the host country. Mitsubishi cars were introduced into the North American market through the Chrysler dealer network. In other cases, the lack of knowledge and contacts necessitates a licensing tie-up. Many Swedish machine tools are sold in Japan through Gadelius K.K., a Swedish trading company with extensive experience in the Japanese market.

A Sales Subsidiary

A well-focused foreign marketing effort tends to require that the company open its own sales offices abroad. The company pushes the product through the distribution channels. The effort is backed by a unit more responsive to headquarter control and directives than independent distributors.

Such a sales office needs to be staffed with host-country nationals in addition to expatriates. The main role for the expatriate is often that of translating headquarter orders and communications into workable statements for the domestic staff who carry the burden of contact with the local buyers. The careful selection of nationals reduces the need for expatriates. IBM Japan has a Japanese president and very few expatriates on the staff.

The most common arrangement outside Japan is for top management in the subsidiary to consist of home-country expatriates. This is true for most U.S. MNEs in western Europe as well as most Japanese ventures abroad. Only in the cases of joint ventures with host-country companies is this principle reversed. Honeywell and Bull's joint computer venture in France is headed by French personnel. Toyota's and GM's subsidiaries in the United States will be headed by U.S. managers. The Japanese will provide technical skills and process know-how.

The important point is that channel activities should be handled by local people, whose ease of access to marketing channels makes for the requisite understanding and building of an ongoing, productive relationship. The major tasks of the sales office tend to be handling the promotional campaigns and the provision of continued support to existing representatives. The basis for its existence is the consistency of supplies from the home country. Building trust in the channels of distribution is a factor of continuing importance not only within marketing but for all facets of overseas management.

SUMMARY

In this chapter, the focus has been on those issues in marketing strategy and tactics which make international marketing management different from that in domestic markets. As the reader will have learned, the basic function is analogous to that in domestic markets. In a sense, good marketing is good marketing in any country. However, the specifics of the strategic and tactical evaluation vary greatly depending upon the values and attitudes that underlie the product and service requirements in foreign markets. Unless proper allowance is made for these differences, the marketing effort will not be successful.

The chapter has dealt with the question of adaptation versus standardization of the marketing effort, in particular the product and the advertising policies. It also covered the complicating factor of being an outsider in the foreign country and the difference country stereotyping can make in the positioning strategy. The discussion has demonstrated the important influence of the product life cycle in the competitive strategy against domestic producers as well as other MNEs. Simply shipping surplus products to another country is bad business, at least in the long run. At the same time, a local polycentric adaptation that comes naturally to a completely market-oriented business might not justify its costs. Striking the right balance between standardization and adaptation is the art of skillful marketing management.

KEY WORDS

Market segmentation	Price escalation
Foreign positioning	Experience curve pricing

Country stereotyping   Standardized advertising programs
Product attributes   Personal selling
Product life cycle (PLC)   Distribution channels
Product-line stretching

QUESTIONS

1 The two cornerstones of marketing strategy have been identified as market segmentation and foreign product positioning. What bases for segmentation have been identified? What criteria must be satisfied? Discuss some possible segmentation bases for:
   a Industrial products in Europe
   b Consumer goods in southeast Asia
2 Three strategies have been named for the purpose of target marketing. Identify these. What must the manager consider in choosing one of these strategies? Which strategy is most profitable in an international market?
3 Referred to as "product positioning" in domestic markets, discuss the special characteristics of foreign positioning. In your answer, define foreign positioning.
4 The complexities inherent in foreign positioning lead to several questions which must be answered by the marketing manager. What are these questions? What is meant by successful application of the positioning concepts? Can you think of some examples of unsuccessful application?
5 Both the marketing strategy of the MNE and the management of the marketing function are more complex in an international setting. Discuss why this is so. In your discussion, focus on the 4 Ps of the marketing mix.
6 "Product decisions represent the most complex decisions in the marketing mix." Discuss this statement, with particular emphasis on the product life cycle. How has the product cycle changed in recent years? What firm-specific advantages can the firm exploit over the product life cycle?
7 The development of a line of related products is termed "product-line stretching." What is the purpose of this stretching strategy? What is the major drawback?
8 Much concern has been expressed over the issue of dumping. Define dumping. What difficulties arise in enforcing dumping legislation? Are there any defenses available? Discuss other arguments for/against dumping.
9 What is a "pull" strategy in advertising? Discuss the three problem areas in advertising management. How are these problems made more difficult for the foreign marketer? How do they differ from personal selling?
10 "It is the channel management decisions that are most important for international marketing purposes." Discuss this statement. How can the MNE ensure a smooth distribution channel? Why is it important that channel activities be handled by local people?

CHAPTER 16

STRATEGIC PRODUCTION MANAGEMENT

The focus of this chapter is on the strategic implications of production management. Particular attention is devoted to the modern methods of flexible management used in Japan and the implications that these have for MNEs today. Several examples of successful production management by MNEs are given. Also explained is the way in which MNEs make use of experience curves, economies of scope, and other such modern production techniques and strategies.

THE NATURE OF INTERNATIONAL PRODUCTION

The nature of production management in the MNE is similar in many respects to that of the domestic firm. Both are concerned with the efficient use of factors of production such as labor and capital, and the manner by which productivity can be improved by reducing costs. Both need to engage in ongoing investment in product and process research and development (R and D) in order to generate successful new product lines and increase production efficiency. Both need to consider the appropriate degree of horizontal and/or vertical integration of their operations. Both need to organize their production management in order to use logistics and inventory control to optimize transportation, inventory, and stockout costs.

In an international context, all these basic problems of production management are more complicated than production in one country. In its use of labor, the MNE must take into account different wage rates and cultural values. The nature of industrial relations in each nation in which subsidiaries operate must be understood. With regard to financing, the choice between local and international borrowing and the use of internally generated funds to minimize the cost of capital is complicated by consideration of foreign exchange risk, international tax laws, and controls on capital. The MNEs need to know where they are on their production experience curves in each country and globally and how to exploit them with an appropriate organizational structure.

The role of MNEs, in both advanced and developing nations, is of social importance, to the extent that the basic production management of the firm can be constrained by host-government regulations and expectations. In particular, this may affect decisions about R and D, technology transfer, labor relations, capital sources, and mobility and marketing practices. Many MNEs wish to centralize development and control of R and D in order to retain their firm-specific advantage in proprietary knowledge. Host nations frequently demand that R and D be decentralized to the subsidiary level. This raises problems for the MNE concerning the autonomy of its subsidiaries and the manner in which the internal market can be operated efficiently under such constraints. MNEs are also under pressure from host governments to use local sourcing for their supplies, to use local workers, train managers and supervisors, and help improve the production environment in the host nation.

In a similar manner, pressures from host-country governments or interest groups can affect the MNE's strategic choice about the optimal method of vertical or horizontal integration. For example, many resource-based MNEs are criticized by host governments for backward integration in the mining industry. They claim that the extraction of minerals does little for employment or development in the host nation. Forward integration is also criticized on the basis that by controlling the markets, MNEs have the power to homogenize consumer tastes to the detriment of the national identities, as perceived by host countries. Horizontal integration is also criticized for introducing similar product lines on a worldwide basis and for undercutting the existence of local firms, most of which lack the scale economies experienced by MNEs. One of the major topics discussed in this chapter is the learning (experience) curve and its application to international production.

Even such relatively prosaic issues as inventory control and logistics costs take on increased complexity when placed in an international context. International constraints on the free movement of goods include the normal transaction costs of imperfect information due to the need to operate across great distances. These require a major investment in the internal communications network of the MNE, a network that needs to take into account possible disruption by foreign governments. Besides these normal information costs, which make inventory and logistics a more subtle puzzle, there are major problems facing the MNE in terms of government-imposed market imperfections. There are often huge amounts of paperwork, red tape, and bureaucratic inertia to cut through when dealing in foreign markets. There is seldom an easy way around such problems. These characteristics of international production operations can act as barriers to entry initially, but for the experienced MNE they can protect its market segment from potential new competitors.

All such information and regulatory barriers raise the costs of international production over that of locally owned firms, since they increase the cost of operating the internal market of the MNE. This chapter identifies such production costs and examines methods by which the MNE can minimize the constraints on its efficient management of production. But first we look into the role of the experience curve in the fascinating world of modern production management.

THE EXPERIENCE CURVE

An important aspect of modern production management is the concept of the experience curve. The experience curve is the relationship between accumulated production and unit manufacturing costs. It was first observed by the Boston Consulting Group. It has been found that, for many large corporations, unit costs decrease by 5 to 30 percent with each doubling of accumulated production.

Figure 16-1 demonstrates an experience curve for an assumed 25 percent cost saving. Cost reduction comes from economies of scale, the growing familiarity of

FIGURE 16-1
The experience curve. For each doubling of output, the experience curve predicts a 25 percent reduction in unit costs from their previous level. The experience curve levels out as each subsequent doubling of output decreases unit costs on a diminishing marginal basis.

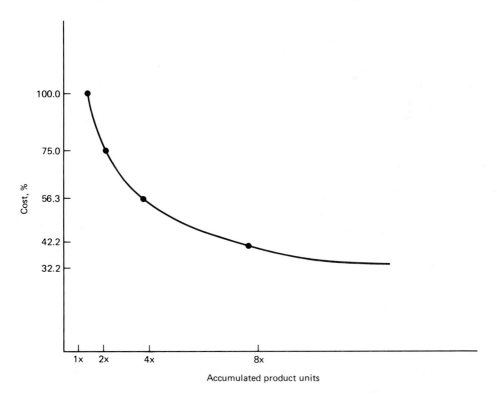

labor with the production process, lower inventory per unit output, lower wastage, and more effective use and redesign of products.

The experience curve has several implications for international business. First, if an MNE fails to obtain cost reductions as it increases output, it will probably fall behind its competitors who benefit from an experience curve effect to the extent that they can lower prices while maintaining profits. Second, if the MNE does not grow at least at the same rate as its competitors to retain its market share, its competitors will have an opportunity to achieve cost reductions through the experience curve effect. Third, if cost reductions result from increased market share, the MNE with a dominant market share will be able to defend itself against rivals, since they cannot experience the cost reductions associated with greater accumulated production. Fourth, the experience curve operates as a barrier to entry for new firms. A new entrant will have little accumulated production experience and it will have higher unit costs.

Another way of visualizing the implications of the experience curve for international business is to think of the MNE as a network of businesses, linked by information through its internal market. Within the context of this network the MNE is attempting to move down an experience curve by global production. It does this by sharing information and ideas among several subsidiaries so that worldwide cost savings result from global integration.

The Product-Process Matrix

The experience curve can become "kinked" by new technologies and/or innovations to the production process. Competitors or new entrants to an industry may be able to leap along (or beyond) the experience curve because of technology-induced cost savings. The use of the experience curve in production planning needs to be tempered by this technological consideration.

Hayes and Wheelwright (1979) have suggested that the life cycle of the product should be matched to the appropriate process life cycle stage. The product-process matrix in Exhibit 16-1 shows the appropriate matchings. This matrix indicates how the MNE can utilize both the experience curve and its technology to obtain an optimal balance between the two.

The use of the experience curve in production planning is equivalent to moving along the horizontal axis only; that is, the product moves through the various life cycle stages while maintaining the same production process. Cost savings in the experience curve context are still possible. However, other opportunities for cost savings are forgone, such as technology improvements in automation and materials handling.

The danger of proceeding vertically down the matrix is a loss of both flexibility in response to product changes and cost savings through the experience curve effect. Product flexibility is reduced when the MNE locks itself into a particular production process without reference to its product mix or their individual stages in the product life cycle. The experience curve effects may be underutilized by

EXHIBIT 16-1
THE PRODUCT-PROCESS MATRIX

Process life cycle stages	Product life cycle stages			
	Low volume, small batch	Low volume, many products	High volume, few products	High volume, high standardization
Job shop	Commercial printer			
Disconnected line flow		Heavy equipment		
Assembly line			Auto	
Process continuous flow				Chemicals

Source: Robert H. Hayes and Steven G. Wheelwright. "The Dynamics of Process-Product Life Cycles," *Harvard Business Review*. (March–April 1979): 127.

moving through the process life cycle without recognizing that each stage has its own experience curve.

Although individual circumstance can dictate otherwise, generally the optimal direction is a diagonal path through the product-process matrix which combines process change and experience curve cost savings. The example in Exhibit 16-1 uses different industries rather than the evolution of one MNE's product line. In this context, the product-process matrix is viewed as an entry-exit strategy. The technological kinks in the experience curve present both opportunity and danger for the MNE.

The MNE seeking to diversify into new products can use the matrix to assess the competition already existing in a product's market. If the competition has not matched its product with the proper process, a technological kink can be created to minimize the experience advantage of the competitor. The MNE can move in with the proper process technology that matches the stage of the product life cycle. The other side of the coin is protecting the markets of the MNE. The MNE should match process with product life cycles to discourage competitive entry and maintain its experience curve advantage.

The product-process matrix can also be applied to the evolution of a single product line. Consider the product life cycle of a sailboat manufacturer. The MNE begins to manufacture one type of sailboat slowly (low volume, small batch). As demand grows in both quantity and variety of sailboats, the MNE may continue the job shop process and benefit from the experience curve or make a process change to a disconnected line flow. In this way the new product life cycle stage (low volume, many products) is matched with the appropriate technology. Experience curve and technology benefits are obtained. Similarly, when a few types of sailboats become popular and profitable (high volume, few products) another technological change to assembly-line process production ensures the appropriate product-process match. Finally, one particular style of sailboat (such as Canada's Laser) becomes immensely popular (high volume, high standardization). At this stage the MNE will find it desirable to use a continuous-flow process technology.

The product-process matrix is both an entry/exit strategy and an outline for matching the appropriate process technology with current product life cycle stage. With this approach, both experience curve and technologically induced cost savings are possible.

THE NEW PRODUCTION ENVIRONMENT

Since the late 1970s, production management has gone through a revolution. Flexible manufacturing systems (FMS), which use modular assemblies, robots, and computer-assisted control of inventories, along with many related innovations, are speeding up the production process and making it more efficient and flexible. Pressure to adopt these new techniques affects all firms, but especially MNEs, since they are open to international competition. Recently, the past dominance of U.S.-based firms in production technology has eroded and major advances have come from Japanese or European firms rather than from Americans. Indeed, the U.S. technological edge has been slipping since the early seventies in an increasing number of industries, and many U.S.-based MNEs have suffered a declining market share because of their inability to adapt to the changing realities of modern production methods.

The use of robots by Japanese automobile manufacturers is a good example of the competitive threat posed to producers worldwide by the introduction of a new technology in a major industry. The superior quality and reliability of Japanese automobiles is partly related to the transformation of Japanese auto production brought about by robotics. The Japanese have more robots that any other nation. In automaking, robots are programmed to carry out, tirelessly and precisely, a wide variety of mechanical tasks, to the extent that relatively few workers are required. As a result, the productivity of Japanese automakers is relatively high and quality control is enhanced.

Robotics also allows the manufacturer to capture small market niches by adapting the basic module to local tastes. It is possible to program robots to undertake different tasks such that a large number of relatively small batches of components can be produced cheaply and assembled at the optimal time. The planning of subassemblies is simplified when it is known with certainty how many units can be produced by the robots, when they will be needed, and how quickly a finished unit can be built. If robots are used intensively, inventory control is not disrupted by labor disputes caused by poor industrial relations. Robots don't go on strike. The savings in production smoothing are substantial and lead to both lower prices for consumers and better wages for workers. The successful use of robotics and related technological advances requires the support of labor, and

Japanese MNEs have been able to move ahead with automation partly because of their management style and the long-term stability of employment in these firms.

Experience curve (and what we shall later define as economies of scope) effects can also be achieved at lower volumes by robotics, since the subassemblies are produced in large quantity. Product differentiation is feasible without significantly increased costs. The final goods produced by robots can contain a high degree of product variety at low unit cost. Sales to many market niches add up to a large volume as the consumer tastes of different nations are served. Adaptability is the name of the game in the world marketplace, and robots can be programmed to adapt more rapidly than human labor. Workers take time to be retrained, and many still have ethnocentric attitudes. It is clear that the use of robotics is a useful tool for the MNE.

Flexible Manufacturing in the Internal Markets of MNEs

MNEs have many advantages in achieving improved production management. Indeed, by definition, the MNE is an international producer; so, presumably, it is motivated to produce efficiently across its national units. One of the methods used by MNEs to increase production efficiency has been to use a flexible manufacturing system. An FMS is a production system in which the MNE uses subassemblies of components from several subsidiaries. This permits the MNE to source from the lowest-cost factory, depending upon the country-specific costs of each nation. Worldwide production and sales give the MNE an opportunity to use FMS to realize scale economies, provided there are relatively few barriers imposed by host governments.

AUTOMATING AMERICA: ROBOTIC GO-SLOW

In Japan, over 30,000 robots are in use. In the United States, this figure is only about 7000. As the use of robotics increases, employees are seeking protection for their jobs. Why does this fear exist? The answer is simple. One robot can do the work of between 1.7 and 6 people. In the United States, where wage rates are high, such wage savings are essential for survival in the competitive global environment. Both quantity and quality of output are higher with robots.

What can U.S. managers do to pave the way for robotics? Foulkes and Hirsch suggest several steps:

1 Developing a displacement policy
2 Gaining line-management support
3 Educating employees in robotics
4 Working in cooperation with unions

A gradual introduction is optimal, and continually seeking employees' ideas and suggestions makes the use of robotics a more pleasant and profitable venture. In the end, it is "people who make robots work."

Source: Fred K. Foulkes and Jeffrey L. Hirsch. "People Make Robots Work," *Harvard Business Review*. (January–February 1984): 94–102.

Recent advances in communications and management information systems have increased the abilities of the MNE to control and monitor production around the world. This allows for reduced inventory levels and costs and simplifies control of scheduling of output and inputs. Standardization of parts can also be increased and their interchangeability improved. Scale economies are realized by this standardization of production, yet the MNE remains responsive to changing market conditions by using these new flexible manufacturing technologies. The MNE can make a centralized decision to adapt a basic subassembly quickly to new conditions in a host market while still optimizing its overall production system. Today's improved communications network provides the information which makes the internal market work more efficiently.

Flexible factories allow a geocentric MNE to respond rapidly to new market demands as niches open up in host-country markets. The MNE can provide customized products at low prices once it has organized itself with a flexible manufacturing system. This type of MNE has plants that are highly automated, uses computer-assisted design and control processes, implements robotics to a major degree, and has modular production techniques. These permit the MNE to produce standardized subassemblies which benefit from the economies of long production runs while having the flexibility to adapt shorter batches of products for local markets with specific tastes. This overall dual advantage is called economies of scope.

Economies of Scope

Economies of scope is a term which captures many of these aspects of successful international production. *Economies of scale* are cost reductions due to increased volume of production of one product. *Economies of scope* are cost reductions resulting from the production of similar products, but with the volume of any one product held constant. Economies of scope arise from the sharing or joint use of inputs across several product lines. Scope economies are observed when multiple products are produced more cheaply in combination than separately.

In an international context it is useful to think of the "economies" as referring to production, where scale economies can be realized by long runs of basic, standardized subassemblies or modules. "Scope" refers to production across different product lines as determined by marketing information. This calls for decentralization, flexibility, custom products, and production that is tied to demand. The marketing intelligence of the MNE reduces the information costs of selling in different markets, since the firm can supply customized products quickly with its flexible manufacturing systems.

The internal market of the MNE facilitates achieving economies of scope. Within the MNE, both production and marketing costs are reduced to such an extent that it is cheaper to organize production within the firm than to have separate firms produce each product and trade them on the external market. In this way it can be seen that economies of scope are a subset of internalization theory; so there is no need to examine them here in any further detail.

ECONOMIES OF SCOPE AS A NEW COMPETITIVE STRATEGY

With the latest advances in computer-based manufacturing technology and the increasing competition for product customization, managers must change their traditional way of thinking. Economies of *scale* (experience curve and task specialization) give way to the new capabilities of economies of *scope*. These capabilities include:

- · Greater flexibility in production design and mix
- · Rapid response to market shifts
- · Increased control and predictability
- · Reduced waste
- · Faster throughput
- · Distributed processing capabilities on easily replicable software

Competition is no longer based exclusively on *price*. The new process technology is based on efficiencies gained by variety, rather than volume. Technologies have four attributes:

1 Independence of product design
2 Programmable
3 Flexible
4 Dedicated

Strategic Lessons

The costs of not adopting such a strategy are high and the ramifications spread throughout all elements: marketing, accounting, finance, strategy, and structure. The adaptation is not an easy one. Manufacturers must look at how manufacturing decisions affect strategic options, rather than vice versa.

Source: J.D. Goldar and M. Jelinek, "Plan for Economies of Scope," *Harvard Business Review*. (November–December 1983): 141–148.

As an example of the type of MNE which is successful in the 1980s, let us now examine production in the Japanese auto industry and compare it with that of the U.S. auto industry.

THE JAPANESE SECRET

The nature of global competition has changed such that today, innovative technology is often what gives a firm a distinctive advantage. A prime example of this is in the automobile industry, where U.S. producers find themselves at a serious disadvantage to Japanese producers because of changing rates of product and process technological advancement. The Japanese have superior product and process technology, while the U.S. technological edge of the 1950 to 1970 period has eroded.

The Japanese advantage in production costs and product quality stems from the superior organization and administration of their production systems. One result is that the Japanese have significant cost advantages in U.S. markets. This has been found by Abernathy et al. (1981). Japanese cars were estimated to cost some

23 percent less than U.S.-made cars for a 1980 subcompact. This is due mainly to better management practices which have increased Japanese productivity. This has lowered relative labor costs per unit of output. The Japanese also have an edge in product design and innovative use of subassemblies, flexible manufacturing systems, and so on. As a result, Japanese autos have earned higher customer loyalty because of their reputation of high quality for their price.

The primary source of the Japanese advantage lies in the use of well-designed manufacturing and product strategy. Their strategy is based on manufacturing excellence, low labor costs, and high productivity. The focus is on *process yield*, a combination of management practices and systems, connected with production planning and control. These reflect the Japanese superiority in operating processes.

Based on extensive research of U.S. versus Japanese production management conditions, it is found that productivity is higher in Japan for micromanagement reasons. For example, see Hayes (1981) and Wheelwright (1983). The management and operation of the production process itself is the source of the Japanese advantage. It does not just occur because of a better corporate culture, quality circles, lifetime security of employment, or other macrofactors in the socioeconomic and cultural environment. Nor is it all due to better high-technology equipment and computer-assisted robotics. All these are important, but the key characteristic is the ability of Japanese firms to manage them effectively.

The Japanese manager has a different orientation than the typical western manager. Western managers learn to distinguish themselves from others through their performance. The resulting divisional competition for the firm's scarce resources can be at the expense of corporate goals. In contrast, the Japanese manage by consensus; so teamwork skills are emphasized. Japanese managers are rotated frequently throughout the functional areas, and seniority plays a major role in personal advancement. In this way, personal competition between managers is minimized.

Japanese styles also minimize the friction between workers and management. The usual separation of operative and strategic decisions which occurs in western nations does not occur in Japan. Operative decisions relating to the work force, quality, and production planning are viewed as being inexorably linked to long-term strategic goals. The worker, considering the value of his or her lifetime employment, is accorded the same attention that a comparable capital expenditure would receive. Attention paid to workers is reciprocated in productivity increases.

There is a near obsession with quality. The practice of *jidoka* halts production when a defect occurs so that all may be made glaringly aware of its causes and remedies. Quality and cost are often viewed as opposing objectives in western nations. In Japan, quality is seen as a way to reduce costs through fewer reworks, less scrap, and fewer quality inspectors. The idea is to prevent defects, not just to detect them. Quality is linked to long-term strategy as the means to ensure customer loyalty and hence the stability and growth of sales.

Production planning and implementation operate with the precision of a fine

Swiss watch. Zero inventories and a disruption-free production process are the goals. Zero inventories reduce costs in warehousing, handling, financing, and management's time in tracking stocks and movements. "Buffer" inventories are perceived as hiding inefficiencies.

To facilitate zero inventories, there is the Japanese concept of *kanban*, or "just in time." Suppliers will make deliveries many times in a single day rather than once a month. Production is a "pull" system. Shipments of finished products create demand down through the production chain. At no stage in the production process will intermediate or semiprocessed goods be made until there is demand in the subsequent stage.

In summary, effective management, Japanese style, entails linking short-term operative decisions to long-range strategic planning, involving workers and managers in this process, and being meticulous in the execution of production. This attention to detail by management results in high-quality goods, produced at a high volume and low cost, but customized for individual consumer preferences.

These are not special attributes unique to Japanese culture but are the characteristics of any successful MNE. Effective management is necessary for the internal market to function efficiently. There is good and open communication at all levels

---

PRODUCTION QUALITY IN AIR CONDITIONERS: A U.S.-JAPANESE COMPARISON

A recent case study by D. A. Garvin of U.S. and Japanese air-conditioner manufacturers compared their product quality. It was found that quality is a costly and powerful competitive weapon.

Quality was measured in two ways, "internal failures" (defects observed before the product leaves the factory) and "external failures" (problems incurred after the unit is installed). The results were not surprising. Garvin grouped companies according to quality performance. Japanese firms were far superior to their American counterparts, with an average assembly-line defect rate almost ten times lower.

Quality *pays*. The best producers had the highest output per labor-hour while warranty costs were lower. On average, the Japanese manufacturers had warranty costs of 0.6 percent of sales, while U.S. firms ranged between 1.8 and 5.2 percent of sales. Other studies, using the PIMS data base, indicate that higher quality means higher market share.

Five sources of quality were pinpointed. The first was *programs*, *policies*, and *attitudes*, which include greater visibility and a commitment from upper management, both of which were stronger in Japanese firms. *Information systems* must emphasize timeliness and attention to detail. The third element is *product design*, where the Japanese utilize reliability engineering and extensive testing of products before their release. *Production and work force policies* stress well-maintained equipment, well-trained workers, and rapid detection of deviations. The final source is *vendor management*, where quality must remain the primary objective.

There are encouraging signs. Both Hewlett-Packard and Ford are placing greater emphasis on quality control, with subsequent declines in failure rates. The answer to U.S. production problems lies in a long-term commitment from all levels of management.

Source: David A. Garvin. "Quality on the Line," *Harvard Business Review*. (September–October 1983): 64–75.

and a recognition by all individuals of the firm-specific advantage of the firm. American and other MNEs can be just as successful as the Japanese if they have effective production management.

PRODUCTION BY GLOBAL FIRMS

Despite the example of successful Japanese MNEs, Levitt (1983) has argued that global firms develop standardized products produced in one country for sales around the world. These standard products are marketed to consumers on the basis of low price rather than by attempting to satisfy perceived variations in local tastes by tailoring products to each country market. Levitt concluded that this globalization of markets will make the MNE dated, since it must adapt to host-country preferences, at high cost. Levitt further concluded that a global operation is more effective when it does not try to adapt. It can use a common technology to produce a standard product at a low price, which it then markets as if world demand is homogeneous.

Similar points on global corporations can be derived from Porter's model of global competitive analysis, which was outlined in Chapter 14. However, Porter argued that emphasis on cost savings by standardization is only one of three strategies by which a firm can compete on a global basis. The global firm still faces potential rivalry by new entrants willing to service host-nation variety in tastes. The advantage of the MNE (as opposed to the global corporation) is that it can use information from its subsidiaries to learn about changing markets in host nations, thereby adapting to today's competitive world markets.

Levitt's assertion that tastes around the world are sufficiently homogeneous such that price is the overriding consideration contains a high degree of ethnocentric thinking. The major markets for most products of interest to MNEs are in high-income nations rather than in developing nations. Most trade, by either exporting, foreign direct investment, or licensing, is north-north rather than north-south. The high-income nations are experiencing the ability to indulge in heterogeneous tastes. This is where the new market niches are found for many products.

MNEs have an advantage in gaining information about host-country markets over the quintessential ethnocentric-minded, global corporations whose standardized products service consumers assumed to be homogeneous. In reality, product variety and adaptability, ensured by flexible manufacturing systems, are the requirements of the 1980s, and these are the natural attributes of the MNE. The MNE, through its internal market, is adaptable to changes in the world environment, and it will survive despite competition from global corporations in certain standardized products in the declining phase of the product life cycle.

PRODUCTION SMOOTHING

Business cycles, competition, product substitutions, and government-induced changes in exogenous variables (such as tariffs) cause demand to fluctuate over

INTERNATIONAL PRODUCTION MANAGEMENT:

MICHELIN TIRE

The experience of Michelin Tire in expanding to North America illustrates the problem of internationalizing without either a strategic plan or a full assessment of the role of major stakeholders in a new project. In 1969, Michelin decided to locate a new plant in Nova Scotia, Canada. The decision was based on the low degree of financial risk resulting from Canadian government tax concessions and grants for the project. However, Michelin overlooked the power of stakeholders like the U.S. government and the U.S. tire industry.

The location in Nova Scotia was based on several country-specific advantages—Canadian financial support ($85 million in loans and grants), importing and exporting benefits (draw-backs and duty-free trade), and a lack of political risk. In addition, Michelin possessed firm-specific advantages (R and D, technology, quality control, production, marketing, manage-ment, and financing) which made production in Nova Scotia advantageous. Rather than evaluating alternative locations (Quebec, the United States), Michelin forged ahead into the Nova Scotian market without sufficient strategic planning.

The choice of Nova Scotia as the location followed from a chance airplane contact in 1967 between the president of Michelin and a representative of Industrial Estates (IEL, the develop-ment agency for the Province of Nova Scotia), who stressed the advantages of such a location in serving both U.S. and Canadian markets. Michelin expected to export tires from Canada to the United States. There was a very low tariff on such trade, and the U.S. tariffs on imports of tires from Europe were very high.

Michelin's rapid movement into Nova Scotia resulted in retaliation from the American government and a new prohibitive tariff to protect American industry. Michelin's error came in failing to evaluate its alternatives and in not anticipating any retaliation. In February 1973, the U.S. government responded by imposing countervailing duties to the IEL loan of $50 million at a subsidized rate of 6 percent, which was seen to represent an export subsidy. An appeal was heard in 1982, but the damage was done. There are now several Michelin plants in the United States and their radials are now being used on many U.S. cars. The Michelin experience illustrates the danger of foreign entry without a strategic plan.

time. The MNE, through its internal markets, must smooth production and avoid, to some degree, the periodic conditions of under- and overcapacity. This section explores how this process of production smoothing is undertaken by the three major types of MNEs.

Ethnocentric   For the ethnocentric MNE, production smoothing is actually demand smoothing. The MNE will carefully select its markets and promotional methods so that demand will not exceed its capacity; otherwise stockouts will occur and competitors will move in. When demand declines in one market, it will reduce output as quickly as possible, but it does so at the risk of losing customers in future periods.

Polycentric   The polycentric MNE will try to use small-capacity production facilities and carry larger inventories and/or use overtime production to meet periods of increased demand. While both methods are costly, the cost is often less than that of underutilized capacity in a larger production facility. For cultural reasons, monetary rewards may not be valued as an inducement to work overtime. Thus, in all nations, the reward for overtime must reflect the local value system. This may require that the MNE allows time off with pay during slack periods in exchange for overtime. Layoffs to reduce production may be illegal or viewed unfavorably by a host government and labor unions. The polycentric MNE can also rely upon subcontracting production and the use of appropriate operations research techniques in satisfying demand.

Geocentric   The geocentric MNE manufactures the same product in a variety of nations. By constructing a source-market matrix (discussed later), based on incremental manufacturing and logistics costs, the MNE can efficiently shift capacity and output on a global basis. The MNE can also specialize production into four types of functions: low unit cost, seasonal, stockpile, and flexible plants.

The *low unit cost* plant is intended to produce at full capacity. When foreign markets experience excess demand or oversupply, the lower unit costs are expected to compensate for the added logistics or inventory costs, respectively.

In situations where a product's demand is seasonal and variations in demand can be forecasted accurately, a *seasonal plant* would eliminate the need for temporary yearly layoffs. An extensive search may be required to locate a community with a stable seasonal work force. The fishing villages of eastern Canada and Norway and communities with large resident student populations may provide seasonal workers in winter and summer, respectively.

A *stockpile plant* may complement a low unit cost plant or operate independently. Certain countries offer inventory tax deductions or subsidies for warehousing which will compensate for the logistics cost of shipping. Sweden, for example, offers a tax deduction equal to 60 percent of the inventory carrying value.

Flexible plants are designed to shift production quickly into new or existing products. They are job shop rather than mass production oriented. The MNE can react rapidly to the introduction of new products by competitors or unexpected changes in demand with flexible plants. Excess consumer demand or production shortfalls due to strikes or nationalizations in one country can also be filled using a flexible plant in another country.

LOGISTICS

Logistics is the coordination of the movements and storage of inputs and outputs. The objective of the MNE is to minimize such costs. It also needs to ensure that supplies are secured and demand for the final product is satisfied. Logistics activities include order processing, shipment of output, forecasting, purchasing, and production scheduling. Logistics also includes the functions necessary to facilitate these activities, namely, transportation, storage, packaging, materials handling, and site location.

INTERNATIONAL PRODUCTION MANAGEMENT:

FORD EUROPE

In 1967, Ford decided to integrate its operations in the United Kingdom and Germany into one unified operation, Ford of Europe. The purpose was to obtain cost savings of about $100 million. The British and German operations were consolidated to achieve efficient mass production, focusing on cost efficiencies (avoiding duplication, buying in volume, etc.) and emphasizing high-growth countries. This adoption of a global strategy and production smoothing was indicative of Ford's move away from a polycentric organization to a geocentric structure.

The change did not occur smoothly. Problems associated with the integration involved a lack of appreciation of nationalism and difficult labor relations. These were compounded by poor product quality, insufficient inventories, difficulty in meeting delivery dates, and communication breakdowns. Decreasing market share in both the United Kingdom and Germany resulted from this situation.

The problems resulted from attempting to integrate production in the two countries too quickly. Ford Germany lacked an adequate supply of parts owing to quality problems and strikes in Britain, its only supplier. Sales dropped as a result of inadequate inventory levels and a premature product launch. The launch of the Cortina/Launus in Germany was executed incorrectly because of deteriorating quality-control standards, an inadequate supply, and poor timing. These strategic errors resulted in a loss of Ford's firm-specific advantage in quality and reliability. The integration would have been smoother if done in two stages. First, Ford could have focused on producing subassembly parts only, ensuring that quality-control standards could be met. The second stage would have involved assembly of the final product.

Ford's concern was with strengthening the major problem areas—product quality and production scheduling. To accomplish this, more attention should have been paid to national differences and quality standards. Alternative suppliers and improved management-labor relations were also required. Ford management did not consider the diverse needs of different markets and the cultural differences which exist between them. Their strategy of going global too quickly realized all the disadvantages of integration rather than the advantages.

Ethnocentric Logistics for the ethnocentric MNE is confined to exporting in the most cost- and time-efficient manner. The basic modes available for transportation are air, sea, rail, and road freight. Rutenberg (1982) identifies fifteen costs and incentives to consider in each transportation mode. These include holding extra inventory for a freight forwarder, packaging, paperwork, freight costs, customs fees, storage and delivery fees, repackaging, and others, all involving two or more nations with different bureaucratic, economic, and commercial systems.

Polycentric The polycentric MNE, being positioned to usually serve the host nation's market only, has a tendency to deemphasize logistics. This may make the MNE's foreign subsidiaries slow to respond to new product launches by competitors and vulnerable to excess consumer demand or production stockouts. These problems may be ameliorated by diverting production from another foreign subsidiary. However, if the MNE has neglected the importance of a logistics system, shifting production may not only be costly, it might even be impaired.

Geocentric The geocentric MNE will have a separate logistics department which coordinates all activities between a multitude of foreign subsidiaries' markets, production locations, and input sources. The complexities of such coordination can be enormous. Even for a relatively small MNE with few foreign operations, logistics coordination can easily become 100 different costs. Computer capability and a knowledgeable staff are required for the efficient operation of a logistics department.

Multiple sourcing and the use of specialized plants (i.e., low unit cost plants) which use round-trip transportation loading and unloading further complicate logistics. A source-market matrix provides the logistics planner with a summary of global production and logistics cost.

A Source-Market Matrix

To help plan its production management, the MNE can design a source-market matrix. This relates the supply of products of various subsidiaries to the demand for these products in various markets. Each cell in the matrix in Figure 16-2 contains information about the incremental costs of producing one extra unit of output and the logistics costs of transporting that unit from one subsidiary (source) to another market.

Assuming one subsidiary in each source nation, its production costs will vary because of country-specific factors, such as local wage rates. Logistics costs will also vary because of environmental factors, such as the optimal transport mode and level of tariffs.

The purpose of the matrix is to provide a framework for the MNE to evaluate production and logistics costs in relationship to market demand. The MNE's objective is to avoid both excess production, which builds up inventory costs, and also underproduction, which can lead to stockouts. It has to optimize production by many subsidiaries across many markets. The source-market matrix is one device to focus attention on the integrated nature of its production management.

The source-market matrix in Figure 16-2 simplifies the total matrix that a large MNE may have by focusing on the relationships between three nations. Some MNEs operate subsidiaries or affiliated companies in over one hundred countries. In addition, the matrix could be further subdivided into major regions within the host nations. For instance, the German plant could be located closer to a market segment in France than the French plant itself.

Each cell in the matrix is further divided into over- and under-capacity production costs, as these will differ significantly between plants, partly because of overtime wages. The matrix needs to be updated periodically to reflect other changes in production and logistics costs in the various nations in which the MNE operates.

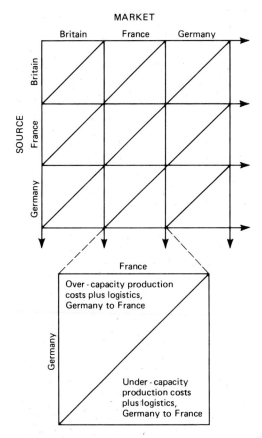

FIGURE 16-2
The source-market matrix.

PRODUCTION AND MIS

The coordination of information within the internal market of the MNE is an expensive and difficult task. It is helpful if the MNE has a good management information system (MIS). One method of reducing the internal costs, in terms of production planning, is to keep down the level of intermediate inputs (inventory) on hand at any one time in any one plant. To achieve this objective, excellent plant monitoring devices are required, such as computerized stock control systems.

Nakane and Hall (1983) have proposed such a method of stockless production. This is achieved by careful production planning. The entire production process is subject to controls and rules which bind it to firm scheduling through the use of automated procedures and information systems. This is achieved by job shop centers (grouping of similar machines). These are used to plan a work flow in which final assembly pulls production along all the stages. In order to function well, this system needs a good relationship with suppliers, since small and more frequent orders are placed. The disadvantage of this system is that any interruption destroys the whole production process, which is unresponsive to short-run changes.

Buss (1982) has found that when many subsidiaries exist, the information systems used in each nation can differ considerably. These differences stem from diverse products and markets which are at various stages in the product life cycle. The degree of parent involvement can also vary, ranging from complete control to no involvement. Many changes in information technology and the MNE's external environment are now occurring, making it necessary for MNEs to rethink their approach to management information systems (MIS).

Four trends are especially relevant to many U.S. (and other) MNEs: the growing interdependence of affiliates, the increasingly hostile legal and regulatory environment, unionization of data-processing departments, and rapidly changing technology. Companies have traditionally made several mistakes in attempting to deal with these areas, ranging from poorly defined objectives to misunderstanding data-processing capabilities. To implement successfully a new MIS, the MNE must begin by assessing the firm's status in this area and move on to identify problem areas which exist.

Success in managing international information systems depends, to a great extent, on active participation by senior international managers. Where guidelines exist, these should be used by management to assess and examine the present capabilities of the MNE. The managers need to create the right organizational framework, defining the roles of key players, in order to take advantage of the new and more productive technologies available. To make an international information system work, everyone in the MNE must be involved.

THE FUTURE OF INTERNATIONAL MANAGEMENT

Robinson (1982) develops five propositions about current business management: markets are becoming increasingly international; the rate of commercially viable technological innovation is slowing, but its diffusion is spreading more rapidly; the rate of increase in world per capita production of goods is slowing; pressure from employees for participative decision making is increasing; and the economies of scale in industrial production may be reduced. (Robinson did not discuss economies of scope). There is also increasing political-legal pressure by governments to restore local control. Robinson examines what these events mean for future corporate management strategists.

The most important implication is that many firms which had previously ignored the international dimension of business can no longer afford to do so. Firms will need to develop new skills in management within a more complicated foreign political-economic environment. They will need more knowledge, new product research for overseas markets, international production training, and so on. Corporate policies must reflect these international dimensions. If technological innovation is indeed slowing, survival will depend upon a firm's ability to work down its experience curves faster than competitors. To do this, there are certain preconditions, such as a stable work force, open communication between produc-

INTERNATIONAL PRODUCTION MANAGEMENT:

CUMMINS ENGINE COMPANY

In 1972, Cummins Engine Company was contemplating whether to allow a Japanese manufacturer, Komatsu, to license and produce the new, superpowerful K engine. The initial project to design the engine in the United States required an investment of $44 million. The proposed joint venture with Komatsu would reduce the size of the investment and help develop a friendly relationship with a powerful world competitor.

Komatsu had three major firm-specific advantages which could benefit Cummins: innovative and insightful management, superb product quality, and an emphasis on world markets. The licensing agreement was mutually beneficial, as Komatsu gave Cummins access to the Japanese market and its lower cost of capital and Cummins contributed their technical expertise. For Cummins, several strategic questions had to be answered, including the impact of substituting foreign production for domestic production, the competitive and economic situation abroad, the financial advantages, any strategic disadvantages, and the transfer price for its firm-specific advantage in technology.

The venture with Komatsu did not proceed as smoothly as hoped. There were poor communications and a delay in doing a proper cost-benefit analysis of producing in Japan. After subsequent analyses, the decision was made to source from Japan. There was much hesitation about the decision, mostly stemming from the feeling that Cummins's firm-specific advantage in quality would be endangered through inadequate attention by the Japanese. As well, other problems existed. Labor unrest could result in sourcing problems, which meant problems in control and pricing. Finally, the uncertainty of the Japanese economy and industry in general was seen as a major barrier.

The experience of Cummins illustrates the shortcomings of licensing or joint venture agreement. Cummins traded their technology advantage for the financial advantages offered by Komatsu and the high profits which could result from an expanded market. The uncertainty and risk of the Japanese market forced Cummins to reevaluate its strategic alternatives. This licensing trade-off could have been reduced by another form of foreign involvement, foreign direct investment, but that involved financial risks to Cummins as barriers imposed by the Japanese government. The advantages of the Japanese market were not easy to realize, and the question remained whether the risks experienced were matched by the returns.

tion centers and managers at the head office, avoidance of work stoppages, development of job flexibility, and enlarging market shares on a worldwide basis.

Enlarging the market share can be done by going abroad to exploit lower labor costs and new markets. The effect is to transfer the firm's position on the experience curve, ensuring maximum growth. Transferability of production abroad depends upon many factors: capacity to train foreign personnel, product and process maturity, skills of trainees, etc. As the development of commercially viable technology slows, manufacturing will shift to less developed countries. Firms will be forced to move their production operations overseas. Success in this area will depend on divisibility of production processes, transportation costs, and political power.

As firm-specific advantages erode, it may become necessary for MNEs to divest themselves of some of their unprofitable subsidiaries in an increasingly international marketplace. MNEs must closely reexamine any firm-specific advantages arising from experience and organization. In the future MNEs may retain an advantage in the use of *information* about production, marketing, and financial management. However, many MNEs may be selling off production subsidiaries.

MNEs will also require an awareness of nonmarket biases such as operating-control bias, engineering bias (preference given to the newest and most complex technology regardless of commercial viability abroad), distance bias (tendency to assign higher risks to operations farther removed from one's experience and home base), and the bias of past success. To overcome such problems of international management, both domestic firms and MNEs must organize their production, and other functions, in an efficient manner. Their internal markets must be constantly reappraised, so that new product lines and information skills are developed in time to succeed in the more competitive world markets of the future.

SUMMARY

The basic problems of domestic and international production management are similar, but they are more complex in an international dimension. Pressures from host-country governments, along with other international constraints and opportunities, make production for, and in, foreign nations a complicated venture in which uncertainty is experienced. This chapter examined how the MNE can overcome these potentially costly complications to increase production efficiency.

Several facets of effective production such as the experience curve, production smoothing logistics, and the source-market matrix were explained. These were analyzed from three viewpoints: ethnocentric, polycentric, and geocentric, exploring the complexities of each.

The environment affecting production management is undergoing rapid changes, as seen in such developments as flexible manufacturing systems (FMS), robotics, and computerized inventories and control systems. These are particularly relevant to MNEs, since they face increasing worldwide competition in which they must fight to maintain production economies and experience curve effects.

The very fact that the MNE is an international producer helps to promote efficient worldwide production through the use of FMS, state-of-the-art management information systems, and flexible factories. By integrating these elements, the MNE can benefit from lower production costs arising from economies of scope and lower factor costs. These are the economies of long production runs combined with the flexibility of shorter batches required to market customized products. It is through such economies that the MNE ensures product variety and adaptability and overcomes ethnocentric attitudes which falsely assume a global commonality of tastes.

The chapter also briefly explores some of the keys to Japanese success in production. It dispels the belief that this success is due solely to a superior corporate culture or intricate quality control circles. Instead, it is also due to management systems which link short-term operative decisions to long-term strategic decisions. The result is a detailed attention to implementing the production nuts and bolts of the firm's overall strategic plan.

KEY WORDS

Experience curve
National experience curve
Robotics
Flexible manufacturing systems
  (FMS)
Economies of Scope
Globalization of markets

Internal market
Production smoothing
Source-market matrix
Product-process matrix
Logistics
Management information systems
  (MIS)

QUESTIONS

1 Discuss the distinction between domestic production and international production. Give examples of areas where these differences may be seen. What is the special role of MNEs in international production?

2 Discuss the experience curve effects, as first observed by the Boston Consulting Group. What are the implications for international business? How does this relate to Porter's barriers to entry, as discussed in Chapter 14?

3 Describe the relationship between the experience curve and the product-process matrix. How does this relate to the strategy of the MNE in dealing with competitors? What cost savings are available with the product-process matrix? Use a diagram in your answer.

4 Production management has gone through major changes in the 1970s, with the adoption of flexible manufacturing systems (FMS). Why are FMS of special importance to MNEs? In your answer, define FMS. How have the Japanese fared in this new production environment? Explain. What factors are necessary to ensure success in the use of FMS?

5 Much discussion has revolved around economies of scale. In this chapter, economies of scope are introduced. What is the distinction? What are the implications of scope economies? How can the MNE gain the benefits of scope economies?

6 Why is the "Japanese secret" of such importance in this chapter? What is the primary source of the Japanese advantage? Define "process yield." Discuss why productivity is higher in Japan.

7 Discuss the concept of production smoothing. How does this concept relate to the three managerial attitudes described by Perlmutter? What methods are available to assist the MNE in the area of production smoothing?

8 What activities are included in logistics? How do these activities change when comparing ethnocentric, polycentric, and geocentric MNEs? Discuss. What can cause problems to arise in this area?

9 Discuss the importance of management information systems. What trends are evolving which make it necessary for the MNE to rethink its approach to these systems? What is the key to success?

10 What are the implications for the future of international production management? How can the MNE successfully adapt to changing environmental forces?

ORGANIZATION OF HUMAN RESOURCES

THE HRM FUNCTION IN THE MNE

The effective management of human resources is of critical importance to the MNE (as it is for all firms). The employees of an MNE are the ones who develop and maintain its firm-specific advantages (FSAs) in marketing, production, R and D, and finance. Moreover, the FSA of an MNE may lie in the *management* of its human resources: organization, motivation, control, and compensation. Conversely, overall management and the level of development of the MNE's human resources may place constraints on the utilization of its FSAs. For example, an MNE may have an FSA in engineering technology yet be unable to operate successfully abroad because of a lack of managers experienced in international operations or, perhaps, in operating with joint venture partners. Inadequate or underutilized human resources may foreclose strategic alternatives for the MNE to exploit its FSAs by international operations.

The human resources of the MNE both shape its strategy and are a vital component in the successful implementation of its strategy. In the short run, human resources can constrain the strategic alternatives which the MNE can pursue successfully. In the long run, the development of human resources must be an integral part of the MNE's overall strategy. Unless the human resource management (HRM) function is closely involved in the MNE's operations and strategy formulation, there can be a mismatch between the firm's strategy and its capabilities to develop and carry out that strategy. To avoid such disasters, the MNE must devote considerable time and care to the selection, training, development, evaluation, and compensation of its personnel. This helps the MNE to ensure that the HRM function plays an integral role in the formulation and implementation of its strategy.

The HRM function is more difficult for the MNE than for domestic firms, since MNEs operate in many countries, with different cultures, languages, value systems, and business environments. The problem of diversity is compounded by geographical and psychic distances between the operating units and headquarters. This complicates the process of communication, information gathering, and evaluation and control. This chapter explores the methods by which the MNE organizes itself to overcome such problems in the management of its HRM. To do this, HRM is related to the factors in the external environment that the MNE faces in its international operations and to factors affecting its internal environment and corporate strategy.

The focus of this chapter is upon the organizational design and strategic management concepts necessary to operate the HRM function. Relatively little emphasis is given to explaining the HRM function itself. These issues (organizational structure, staffing, compensation, training and development, performance appraisal) are explained in mainline HRM courses. Here we shall simply point out some of the international aspects of these issues. In particular, we relate these conventional areas of HRM to the particular problems of HRM of the multinational, in contrast to the normal HRM focus in domestic firms. We are concerned with the manner in which the HRM function is complicated in an international dimension and how the MNE is constrained in its strategic planning by such costs of managing its internal markets.

ENVIRONMENTAL FACTORS IN HRM

The MNE faces a host of external environmental factors in its international operations which have an impact on the management of its HRM function. They include: the skills, attitudes, and motivation of its personnel given the populations in the countries in which it operates, government policies and institutional practices (such as labor laws on compensation, hiring and firing, unionization, management-worker relationships), and consideration of ethics, social responsibility, and business-government interaction. The diversity faced by the MNE across these operational dimensions can impose costs on the firm; but with skill (and a little luck), diversity can be turned into a strength (an FSA) much as diversity in production sites, finance, or R and D becomes strength for the MNE.

At the risk of oversimplification, four generic strategies in the management of the human resources can be identified in response to the diversity of the firm's external environment. Each entails costs and benefits for the MNE, and hence success in employing one or the other (or some combination) will depend on the MNE's characteristics and its overall objectives.

First, the MNE can employ the same HRM procedures and techniques in all the countries in which it operates. For an MNE following this ethnocentric strategy, HRM is the same as if all the operations of the MNE were located in one country.

A second strategy, closely related to the first, is to fit the HRM function of all units of the MNE into one mold by socializing all personnel to *the* corporate system in attitudes and behavior.

A third strategy is to decentralize the HRM function on a country-by-country (polycentric) basis to align HRM in each country with the local external environment.

Finally, an MNE may manage its human resources on a global (geocentric) basis to facilitate intrafirm mobility of human resources by harmonizing the overall enterprise management of human resources while at the same time responding to local environmental factors.

Whatever HRM strategy the MNE follows, it will incur additional costs of operating its internal market and will experience a poorer performance if it adopts an inappropriate HRM strategy. This can occur if it follows a strategy which is not sensitive to its external environment in the countries in which it operates, does not mesh with its overall corporate strategy, or does not correspond to its resources and skills. Conversely, successful management of the HRM function may increase the efficiency of the firm's internal markets in utilizing its firm-specific advantages, or it may help the MNE develop a new firm-specific advantage in the area of HRM.

INTERNAL FACTORS IN HRM

The management of relevant internal factors must be decided upon in an objective and fruitful fashion. The organizational structure of the MNE will influence the implementation of the strategic planning determined by its senior managers. The choice of functional, product, or regional organizational structure is an important signal about the management attitude of the MNE. Related to its organizational structure is the management style it has adopted. Management style is an important determinant of the way in which both managers and workers, across different nations, identify with the corporate philosophy of the MNE.

Several components of the MNE's internal environment are particularly important: organizational structure; evaluation, control, and reward systems; management style; corporate philosophy; and business strategy. Each of these will be discussed as the chapter progresses.

Organizational Structure

There are several generic organizational structures that a non-MNE can use: organization by function (marketing, production, finance, etc.), by product (laundry detergent, hand soaps, shampoos, etc.), by division (soaps, health care, foods, etc.), or in a few cases by a matrix. For an MNE, the organizational structure becomes more complicated. The central problem lies in where to locate the firm's international activities within each functional area (e.g., international finance within the finance function), by products or by geographical area. Not only is there no one ideal organizational structure for all MNEs, but for any one MNE there may be no ideal structure. Each organizational structure has different costs and benefits associated with it, and the MNE must evaluate which structure is most appropriate given its external environment, strategy, and human resources.

One of the prime responsibilities of the HRM function is to evaluate the organizational structure of the MNE and how it functions in relation to the firm's strategy and external environment. Once an organizational structure has been chosen, the evaluation, control, and compensation systems must be designed to operate efficiently within that structure. Staffing and staff development also must be tailored to the organizational structure. For example, if the international function is located within each division, managers in each division must be trained in the international dimension of the firm's operations and the entire international operation must be coordinated and controlled.

Other Internal Strategic Factors

Particular attention must be paid to executive development and compensation. It takes many years to train a potentially valuable senior manager capable of contributing to the strategic planning or top-level management of the MNE. For example, assume that each placement in a product area and/or region takes about 3 years before there is a benefit in terms of experience and lessons learned. It becomes apparent that even an exposure to a minimum of ten such postings in the MNE will take up most of the career span of an executive. Therefore, each posting must be chosen carefully, such that it contributes to the long-run development of the manager. For a technician, line manger, or production worker, such strategic considerations are clearly less important than for the senior general manager.

A key characteristic of successful MNEs is that they have the ability to develop and maintain a well-trained management team capable of effective strategic planning. Failure to expand the management team has been identified by Penrose (1958) as a critical limit to the growth of the firm. Continual executive development in the MNE is necessary to overcome this constraint. This requires that the senior management team be expanded at a gradual rate. The rollover of senior managers is accomplished more easily in a firm with a common corporate style with which the cadre of senior executives can identify.

The successful MNE will monitor these environmental, internal, and strategic factors in the long-run planning of its human resource function. It will plan to foster the development of its senior managers. Finally, it will ensure that its key people receive sufficient incentives and rewards that they remain loyal to the MNE and continue to serve it at the peak of their managerial careers.

ORGANIZATIONAL STRUCTURES OF MNEs

The strategic planning of the MNE will only be as successful as its organizational structure allows it to be. In this section, we shall explore several basic types of internal organizational frameworks, in which MNEs are organized either by a functional structure such as an international division or in one of three ways:

1 By product lines
2 By nations or regions
3 By a matrix structure

The bottom line in organizational structure is to decide upon the degree of centralization or decentralization. While functional areas can be either centralized (finance) or decentralized (marketing), here one needs to have a feel for the overall strategic organization of the MNE. Most MNEs are multiproduct firms and they operate in many nations. Resolving these two dimensions, product lines and regions, in an appropriate organizational structure is crucial to the operations of an efficient internal market.

The classic method of distinguishing managerial attitudes, following Perlmutter (1969), identifies three types of attitudes:

1 Ethnocentric—home-oriented
2 Polycentric—host-nation-oriented
3 Geocentric—internationally oriented

The three archetypes are used here to simplify some of the issues of choice of organizational structure. The MNE must choose how its organization can be most effectively divisionalized: by product line, by area (region), or by function.

Functional Organization

It is not necessary here to consider, in any detail, organization by function. This form is mainly used by firms with a narrow and highly integrated product mix, and most MNEs are multiproduct firms. Chandler (1962) was one of the first to observe that the growth of large companies, like General Motors, Du Pont, General Electric, and Sears, is market-driven and results in an increased number of product lines. This leads to a shift away from a functional organization to a multidivisional structure. Today, most MNEs are multidivisional.

In a functional organizational structure, managers have worldwide responsibility as line executives. The major functional areas are typically production (often including R and D), finance, human resources, and marketing. The advantages to this type of centralized structure are that management's attention is concentrated on internal functions, it enables a small group to control the organization without duplication, and there is no conflict between profit centers. There are some major disadvantages, however. Functional organizations are unsuitable for multiproduct organizations. Managers may end up reporting to two or more people, and inevitably communications break down.

Here, it is better to be realistic and ignore simple divisionalized functional structures, except for the most famous example of this, the international division.

International Division

The role of the international division can vary by MNE. Its structure is outlined in Figure 17-1. It shows that the general manager of the international division has the same level of authority as a general manager of one of the major product-line divisions of the firm. Foreign subsidiaries are organized by region and report to

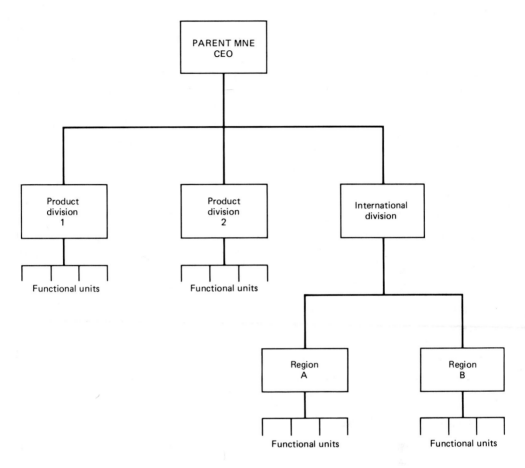

FIGURE 17-1
The international division.

the international division. The general managers in the regions control the activities of their functional units (marketing, production, finance).

The main advantage of the international division is that it provides an organizational "umbrella" or base for the international operations of the firm. This enables the firm to balance the interests of the subsidiaries to the benefit of the company as a whole. In this division, knowledge of the international aspects of the firm's business is concentrated in a separate, centralized division which provides a focal point for learning about international operations. Decisions regarding purchasing, inventory control, and so on can be made on a secure and economic base. Most important, the international division enables the firm to make investment decisions on a global basis.

Inasmuch as the international division provides the subsidiaries with guidance, it also reduces their autonomy. The division may become extremely dependent on the domestic product divisions for access to their products. Conflict may occur between domestic divisions and the international division in such areas as transfer pricing. Since the international division is an autonomous (rather than an integrated) unit, there may be a failure to use existing managerial knowledge to its utmost potential. It is not possible to use it to transfer aspects of the firm-specific advantage, owing to the risk of dissipation of proprietary knowledge and the lack of a control system for the evaluation of intra-affiliate transactions.

An international division is often appropriate for a firm which is just starting international operations, since it allows the centralization of the firm's international expertise in one place. An international division is also often used by firms whose international operations are not closely linked with its domestic operations in the home country, such as some banks and hotels.

In some firms, the international division provides a service function, pumping in information about foreign markets to product-line managers, who may or may not take up the challenge of foreign sales. In other MNEs with foreign subsidiaries, the international division has a stronger administrative responsibility. It can act as a bridge between foreign subsidiaries and the parent firm. It can attempt to mediate differences between product-line managers and regional managers. In some large MNEs, the international division can be replaced by product, area, or matrix structures. In others, however, this structural change does not occur.

For MNEs, if the international division is ignored, this leaves the choice between products and regions, which in turn generates a discussion of the three Perlmutter types of organizational structure, by ethnocentric product line, by polycentric area, or by a matrix structure which combines product and area responsibilities.

Product-Line Organization

An ethnocentric firm may view the world as one market for its product and organize by product line, as in Figure 17-2. The MNE is organized into world product groups, such as for product division 1. Within each product division, activities are centralized, but there is little, if any, linkage between the world product groups. Therefore, in any host nation the MNE appears to be decentralized. One advantage of organization by product lines is that full-scale economies are realized. The MNE can focus on its FSAs and avoid dissipation of proprietary knowledge by control of the product lines.

The product division structure works best when there are diverse product lines, many end users, and a requirement for high-technological expertise. Scale economies and experience curve effects can be realized while high shipping costs, tariffs, and other costs are reduced. Unlike an international division, there is less conflict between domestic and foreign divisions or any duplication of effort. Most important, organization by product line enables the MNE to compete on a global basis, as the product division managers can respond quickly to actions by competitive rivals.

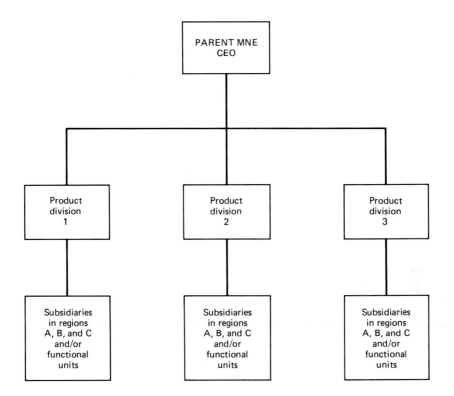

FIGURE 17-2
Organization by product line (ethnocentric).

One major drawback to the product-line structure is that responsibility for international operations must usually be given to managers with product expertise but little or no international experience. This can result in a lack of emphasis on host-nation markets and foreign political and cultural conditions. Local marketing and political information is missed. Coordination in any one region is complex, communication with foreign subsidiaries is difficult, and the special needs of international markets can be neglected. In today's nationalistic and competitive world, an ethnocentric MNE is looking for trouble; so product-line management on an international basis must be used cautiously.

Area Organization

A polycentric firm is organized by area, that is, by geographical region, as in Figure 17-3. The senior manager of Region A runs that region in a decentralized manner as an independent profit center. The regional manager controls the product lines of the operating companies in that region. Product-line managers control functional units such as marketing, production, and finance. Again, there

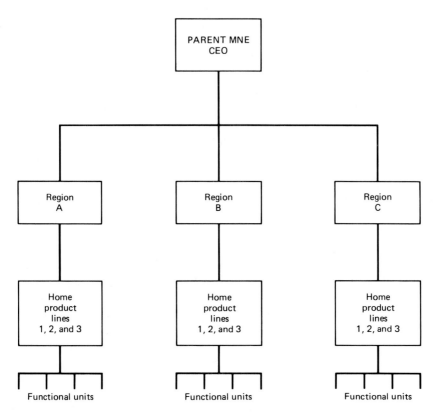

FIGURE 17-3
Organization by nation (polycentric).

is little integration of worldwide operations, yet the MNE is responsive to the needs of the host nations. Indeed, the polycentric MNEs may be at an advantage in forestalling adverse movements of host-nation environmental parameters. This advantage of reducing host-nation information costs needs to be set against the possible loss of scale economies, when product lines are fragmented or at least not optimized. A polycentric structure works best when the MNE has many mature, standardized product lines, in which the risk of dissipation of the FSAs is at a low level. Then, the focus can be upon marketing and servicing the host nations by autonomous regional managers who can determine the best delivery system for the product lines of the MNE.

The major advantage of organizing by area is the ability to differentiate markets and obtain an optimal marketing mix. There is greater emphasis on regional subsidiaries as profit centers. The unique characteristics of foreign subsidiaries and foreign regions are more easily recognized. Organization by area, therefore, enables the MNE to reduce host-country political risk since it is aware of, and responsive to, local interests. Management's job is also simplified as regional matters are dealt with quickly. One final advantage is that regional expertise can be fostered and built upon in the management team.

A major weakness of the area form is that too much emphasis is placed on the regions and there is little worldwide integration. Organization by area is especially difficult if there is a diverse product line. Coordination along different product lines is extremely difficult, if not impossible. In this case, a large international staff is required. In the end, organization by area may require duplication of functional and product specialists. This is a costly undertaking.

Matrix Structure

A geocentric firm integrates its worldwide operations and, being world-oriented, attempts to serve the stakeholders in each nation. The usual method of doing this is by a matrix structure.

The matrix structure for the MNE is more complicated than that for a domestic firm. The typical matrix for a domestic firm looks at two relationships, those between functional areas and those between the product lines. The MNE must also consider a third dimension, namely, regions. Therefore, the matrix for the MNE, sometimes called a grid structure, is really a cube. However, since it is difficult to juggle all these dimensions, this region simplifies by examining the relationships between regions and product lines. The functional areas are not explored.

A geographically based matrix organization is illustrated in Figure 17-4. It shows how the MNE attempts to jointly relate responsibilities for both product lines and regions. The matrix structure has some of the benefits of decentralization, as the managers are aware of regional needs and know the product lines.

FIGURE 17-4
Geographical matrix organization.

Products → Regions	Country A	Country B	Country C
Product 1			
Product 2			
Product 3			

When pressures exist along more than one dimension (e.g., along product and country lines), a matrix organization may be optimal. The main advantage to implementing a matrix is that there is greater emphasis on markets, competition, and environmental aspects. Matrix organizations adapt well to changes in these parameters.

The weakness of the matrix structure is that, unless adhered to closely by all executives, it will be destroyed. The success of the matrix depends upon the ability of those using it to give and take direction in at least two dimensions: product areas and functions. Because of the complexity, only MNEs with adequate financial resources can use it. The major disadvantage of the matrix structure is that it is extremely complex for smaller MNEs to implement successfully.

A Challenge to Matrix Managers

To make a matrix work requires that the managers be coordinated in a centralized manner. This needs an expensive superstructure and a willingness to use consensus group decision making. Only large MNEs can afford to train managers in the dual roles required to operate a matrix structure properly.

The matrix organization of the MNE is a hard act to pull off. It is extremely difficult to operate, as it requires sensitive and well-trained middle managers, who assume responsibility for both products and nations. Essentially they have two bosses, as indicated in Figure 17-5. In this figure, matrix manager 1 may be the product-line boss and matrix manager A the regional boss. The middle manager has to work out how to resolve the often conflicting demands of product lines and nations. To do so, the MNE needs to supply the manager with excellent information and provide incentives and rewards for this responsibility. It is no wonder that MBA students see themselves cut out to be matrix managers.

The ultimate choice for any MNE is between centralization and decentralization of its functional areas. Organization by product line, region, or matrix must also meet the special requirements of each functional area. For example, control of the finance function is usually centralized in the treasurer's office, since only there can all the offsetting taxes and other regulations be assessed and the foreign exchange exposure minimized. On the other hand, the marketing function is often decentralized, since host-country information about consumer tastes is so important. The successful MNEs have organizational structures which resolve the competing demands of functional divisions, product lines, and regions. It is not an easy task, but it is essential in the implementation of an effective global competitive strategy.

GROWTH OF ORGANIZATIONAL STRUCTURES FOR MNEs

It is dangerous to be dogmatic about the correct form of organizational structure for the MNE, since this varies over time and reflects the changing state of global competition. However, the previous discussion drew out some general principles, and these are now elaborated in the context of strategic management.

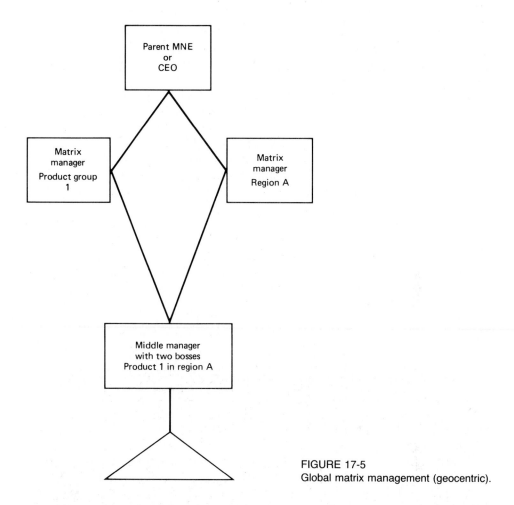

FIGURE 17-5
Global matrix management (geocentric).

There is causality between strategy and structure; structure follows strategy, and the correct type of structure is vital for the successful implementation of the chosen strategy of the MNE. For a typical MNE there is an evolving international commitment. At first a domestic firm begins foreign sales through its functional or product divisions. It has export units. Later it may use its joint venture partners or licensing partners to service foreign markets. As the firm becomes more involved overseas, it may then start an international division. This alleviates some problems, such as the need for centralized control over the foreign operations of the firm and the need for specialized information about individual foreign markets. Yet it also raises new problems, such as the relationship of the new international division with other functional and product divisions and the relative power of each group. It is also not clear how the firm protects itself against dissipation of its firm-specific advantages if there is no integration of the international operations into its strategic planning.

Such problems can lead the firms into integrated global structure, i.e., attempts to organize by world product lines or by geographic areas. These lead to problems in coordination and trade-offs between selling standardized product lines at as low a cost as possible versus servicing host-country needs with a variety of customized product lines. To reconcile these problems, the matrix structure has been designed and even tried out by some of the larger MNEs. However, it is no panacea. IBM moved successfully from an international division to a global structure, whereas Pfizer chose to retain its international division. Dow Chemical tried a matrix structure but abandoned it, whereas Dow Corning was able to operate its matrix successfully. The inevitable conclusion is that the MNE goes through a series of organizational structures as it attempts to find out which is best suited to its strategy. As its strategy develops, so too may its structures change.

The 1970s saw a shift in many U.S. MNEs from a traditional organizational structure (an independent international division) to one of worldwide, or global, product divisions. Indeed, by 1980 only about 20 percent of MNEs used an international division while about one-third used a global product-line structure. The perceived benefits occurred in three areas: better cost efficiency, improved communication and resource transfer, and most important, the development of a global strategic focus. In studies reported by Davidson and Haspeslagh (1982), however, it was found that these benefits, if existing at all, were often costly and short-lived. MNEs like Westinghouse had moved all the way from an international division to a global product structure (in 1971) into a global matrix structure (in 1979).

The price of cost efficiency in a global product division lay in vulnerability to transportation and labor problems when single-plant sourcing was used. In the area of resource transfer, it was found that global product companies transferred fewer products, at a slower rate, than those organized by international division or matrix. Global product companies typically lack local responsiveness. They have a tendency to be ethnocentric, risk-averse, and defensive in their attitude about foreign operations. This results in a deterioration of foreign sales. Even the choice of the right manager can be a problem, as few product managers have international expertise.

In studies reported by Bartlett (1983), it was found that some companies, rather than reorganize to a global structure, followed an internal system stressing people management. The system was developed in three phases: the establishment of internal groups, building channels of communication for decision making, and developing norms to support these decisions. The key to the system lies in its flexibility. Rather than changing the organizational structure each time a problem or opportunity presents itself, the emphasis is on changing behavior.

This is not to say that a global product structure cannot work. If properly adapted to the company's strategy, it can be very successful. Rather, the message is one of caution. A company should examine other structures (matrix and international division) within the context of its strategic planning before adopting a global structure too quickly. The process should be an evolutionary one, rather than one of rapid structural change. In this way, the correct balance of people is

---

CITIBANK

A classic example of the successful adaptation of structure to implement a change in strategic planning was the reorganization by Citibank, in 1974, of its method of servicing MNEs. Citibank's strategic planners identified the provision of specialized financial services and loans to the world's largest MNEs as a niche which it could service. The organizational structure of Citibank (or First National City Bank, as it was then called) did not permit it to service both the parents and subsidiaries of MNEs in a satisfactory manner.

Owing to the polycentric nature of Citibank before 1974, whereby its international division (the International Banking Group) decentralized major responsibility to senior officers in each geographic region, it could not develop a strategy of servicing MNEs on an integrated basis. The autonomy of Citibank's regional managers led to internal conflicts between its international group and the U.S.-based Corporate Banking Group, which was responsible for servicing the parent MNEs but not the overseas subsidiaries of the MNEs. To overcome the neglect of the needs of subsidiary managers of MNEs (despite the existence of its many overseas branches), Citibank abolished its polycentric international banking group and replaced it with a geocentric World Corporation Group (WCG).

Citibank's WCG was given sole responsibility for all 450 of its multinational clients. The WCG handles both parent and subsidiary, thereby undercutting the alienation of the MNE subsidiary managers. The WCG is staffed by a cadre of highly motivated specialists, knowledgeable about the special nature and financial needs of MNEs. Global account managers in the WCG work with the parent MNEs while field account managers handle the subsidiaries. The matrix structure makes managers in the WCG responsible for both the product lines of MNEs and regional loans to subsidiary MNEs.

The Citibank structure mirrors the structure of many of its multinational clients and permits it to respond quickly to their needs. This retains the firm-specific advantage of Citibank. MNEs are satisfied with this arrangement and have developed some dependence upon the expert knowledge of Citibank in key areas such as foreign exchange transactions, the management of cash balances, transfer of funds, and short-term borrowing. The integrated structure of Citibank's WCG, plus its successful track record with the MNEs, acts as an entry barrier to potential rivals such as Bankamerica and major foreign banks. More details of this case appear in Rutenberg (1982).

---

achieved between the holy trinity of product, area, and functional dimensions.

It is also worth keeping in mind that Japanese-based MNEs have very simple, even informal, organizational structures, typically by function. Their success in international markets does not seem to have been hampered by their lack of interest in organizational design, perhaps because their strategic planning has made effective use of well-trained and motivated operatives and managers.

STAFFING THE MNE: HOME OR HOST NATIONALS?

The MNE must identify the human resources necessary to implement its strategy and either develop them within the firm or hire them from outside. Developing staff who are not only capable within functional areas but also have experience and training in the international environment is a key success factor in the global competitive strategy of the MNE. For this reason, it is appropriate to speak of strategic human resource management in which the HRM function is an integral component of the MNE's process of strategy formulation and implementation.

For simplicity, the managers to be allocated to various divisions of the MNE can be grouped into two categories: home nationals and host nationals. For most MNEs, the actual number of home-country nationals required abroad is, in practice, quite small. Reynolds (1972) found that relatively few Americans were employed abroad by U.S. MNEs—only about 100,000 in the early seventies. This was less than 10 percent of all the employees in foreign subsidiaries and held across all industries. At that time General Motors had over 200,000 workers in its foreign subsidiaries but only 300 were Americans. Local managers are preferred, since they know and understand the host nation's culture, society, and political and economic systems.

It is also expensive to locate a home-country national abroad. By using later (1979) data, Reynolds estimated the cost to the MNE at over one-half million dollars, on average, for a 3-year posting of one U.S. executive. U.S. tax laws are not particularly helpful in foreign placements, since U.S. citizens are taxed on their worldwide income (unlike citizens of many other nations in which MNEs are based). This discourages executive mobility, since there are substantial costs to executives when they are transferred in terms of international relocation and family adjustment. While the MNE can pay for the direct costs of relocation, it is frequently impossible to compensate for the indirect psychological costs.

The choice facing the MNE is relatively easy when viewed in this framework (which ignores the constraints imposed upon individual labor markets by government regulations, labor power planning, union strength, etc.). It can either hire host-country nationals and train them to be specialists in the functional or product area required, or it can use home-country people who can operate in a global context. Unfortunately, although MNEs operate across cultures and require international capabilities in their managers, most people are monocultural.

There are several advantages to the ethnocentric policy of staffing the MNE with home-country nationals. First, the propriety of the firm-specific advantage(s) is enhanced. Home nationals will have an orientation, both learned and inherent, toward the parent company. The home-country identification increases control and improves communication. Thus, to a certain extent, the D^* costs (risk of dissipation of firm-specific advantage) of foreign operations are reduced.

Certain A^* costs (additional costs of foreign operations) are also reduced. If the host national does identify more with the host country, a number of inefficiencies can arise. The host national may, unconsciously or otherwise, prioritize the host nation's interests before that of the MNE. For example, in an effort to reduce indigenous unemployment, overutilization of labor or local sourcing in preference to cheaper global sourcing could occur. Another inefficiency is the suboptimal use of the firm-specific advantage(s). Host-nation orientation may result in adherence to indigenous business practices despite the availability of more efficient FSAs in marketing or management.

Direct A^* cost savings, as opposed to the forgone cost savings of efficiency, are also possible under an ethnocentric staffing policy. The underavailability of skilled managerial/technical personnel may necessitate the added cost of in-house training programs. In an age of rapidly advancing technology, translations of technical terms may not even exist in the host-country language. The disadvantages of ethnocentric staffing are the advantages of polycentric staffing (and vice versa) and will be discussed in this context.

A major advantage of polycentric staffing is that host-country nationals are closer to the host-country environment. Host-country managers are better able to manage local workers and deal with local trade unions than are home-country nationals. There is often less antipathy toward local managers by workers, although this feeling should not be overestimated by the MNE. Workers and management are often locked into competing positions, and in some nations with a poor record of industrial relations, such as Britain, a manager will always be a manager, no matter the nationality. In some cultures, personnel will accept direction from foreign managers which they would not accept from their compatriots.

Polycentric staffing reduces the problems of cultural differences and possible racial prejudice. A manager from the home country who is not sensitive to the local culture, especially in a developing nation, can be a walking time bomb for the MNE. This may occur, for example, when mineral resource and petroleum-based MNEs move engineers and other technicians into management positions without sufficiently training them to general management practices, particularly people management.

Finally, there is the geocentric staffing strategy. The single greatest advantage to geocentric staffing is that the best person for the job is chosen, regardless of nationality. The implication is that third-country nationals which are neither home nor host nationals can be chosen. Depending on the circumstance, geocentric staffing will have the disadvantages of both ethnocentric and polycentric staffing. In addition to these, however, is the cost and time of such a program. Language orientation and training, transfers, and compensation complexities all serve to increase the A^* costs of this strategy. The benefits of the program are also both distant and uncertain. For these reasons, a formalized geocentric staffing strategy is rare in practice.

Senior Management in the MNE

Everyone is human and has flaws. Effective senior executives are trained to manage people. In the MNE, this requires the development not only of an international viewpoint but also of a sensitivity to cross-cultural attitudes and the ability to foresee and resolve potential conflicts. It is difficult and costly for the MNE to train managers who have both technical expertise and the ability to manage the personnel operations of its overseas subsidiaries. To reduce this problem, at the very least, the MNE must have an effective general management training program in which executives become aware of the different value systems involved in foreign assignments.

If the MNE has an international division, its senior positions will probably be

---

IBM

IBM is a good example of the way in which the MNE can make effective use of its personnel. IBM has a policy of recruiting and developing host-country nationals for both research and management positions. It even decentralizes much of its R and D, using local technicians, engineers, and managers, while retaining centralized control over the ultimate use of the R and D. IBM also engages in local purchasing and attempts to keep a balance of trade by nation. It has host nationals, including local political figures, on its boards, and it attempts to act as a good corporate citizen in each host nation.

This geocentric concern for the social and economic welfare of all its managers and workers has resulted in an extraordinary loyalty to IBM among its personnel at all levels. There are excellent management-labor relations and a common corporate culture. Managers identify with the mission of IBM as the leader in the computer industry. Partly because of this method of human resource management, IBM has been successful in retaining its world market share in the face of ever-increasing global competition.

---

staffed by home nationals, as will the MNE with a strong global product division. These MNEs tend to be ethnocentric unless they take time to foster a global perspective in their managers. The MNE with an area (or regional) organizational structure is polycentric in nature. It staffs its area divisions with host-country nationals. Finally, the MNE with a matrix structure tends to use host-country nationals who have to be trained to adjust and understand the product line for which they are responsible.

The Boston Consulting Group (BCG) matrix developed in Chapter 14 also has some important implications for staffing decisions in the MNE. The skills required to build a star, harvest a cow, or divest a dog are quite different. Entrepreneurial ability, flair, and initiative are required to expand market share and develop a new product line. The manager must be an energetic builder and conqueror. When the market has stabilized, more emphasis must be placed on administrative skills, experience, and procedures. A more passive and conservative manager is required. Bureaucratic skills and a sound operational and organizational ability are more useful than aggressive entrepreneurial innovation.

At the final stage, terminating a dog is a most difficult operation, but one which the MNE must perform with a minimum of disruption in order to avoid spoiling the market for future ventures. Divestment requires diplomatic skill. The manager must be attuned to the attributes and expectations of the host nation's politicians and workers and be able to smooth over a difficult process. This requires an experienced manager with considerable personal charisma. Indeed, running a subsidiary which is being divested may be the most challenging and valuable managerial position open in the MNE.

WORKER PARTICIPATION

The MNE must also be aware of, and sensitive to, the industrial relations climate in each of the host nations in which it operates. Recently U.S. MNEs have been concerned about legislative proposals submitted to the European Economic Community (EEC) in an effort to involve workers in the management of MNEs. The best-known of these was the Vredeling proposal on employee information and consultation. This proposal would have forced MNEs to disclose information about their global operations and strategic plans to workers participating as members of the board and to consult actively with workers on issues affecting them. A version of the proposal was first endorsed by the European Commission on October 1, 1980. However, the ultimate proposal accepted in 1982 was much weaker than the original.

The impetus behind the original endorsement came mainly from the international trade union movement. Organizations like the International Confederation of Free Trade Unions (ICFTU) and the European Trade Union Confederation (ETUC) have been fighting since the early 1970s to constrain the global power of MNEs. Support also came from some of the major European nations where unions are intimately involved with political parties and governments. In 1979, Commissioner Vredeling used his work on labor law to grant unions some of their demands for access to information from the headquarters of MNEs.

Most U.S. MNEs and trade associations feel that the existing system for informing workers is good enough and they are opposed to worker democracy and most aspects of the Vredeling proposal. MNEs use the examples of poor industrial relations and constrained decision making of Caterpillar and Ford to illustrate how the Vredeling proposal would lower efficiency. A number of MNEs were not so adamantly opposed to the proposal and reacted more positively. This was due to their knowledge of industrial democracy is such bellwether countries as Sweden and West Germany.

JAPANESE STYLE MANAGEMENT

Of particular interest to a course in international business is the recent analysis of successful Japanese HRM. The Japanese style of management has been analyzed comprehensively by Pascale and Athos (1981). They apply the seven S framework of organizational effectiveness, first developed at McKinsey and Company by Peters and Waterman (1982). In turn, this framework is an extension of the philosophy of quality circles developed by American scholars and practitioners in the fifties but only implemented on any scale by the Japanese. In a *quality circle*, workers are involved in the discussion of problems and solutions to quality control and in other aspects of production management. This discussion of the seven Ss is useful, as it provides important lessons on how to run a successful MNE.

The seven Ss are identified as

1 Strategy
2 Structure
3 Systems
4 Staff
5 Style
6 Skills
7 Superordinate goals

It has been argued that the hardware, strategy, and structure, of prime importance to North American firms, need to be modified by paying greater attention to the software of organizational management systems, style, staff, skills, and shared goals.

Theory Z

The basic theme of the Japanese model of effective management organization is that the workers and managers identify with the goals and operations of the firm. They are more cooperative and involved than the aggressive *organization men* identified by Whyte (1956). Whereas organization men sought to fight their way up the corporate hierarchy in a competitive, even hostile, environment, the emphasis in Japanese style management is on harmony rather than on competition. Managers identify with the firms and colleagues in a cooperative and communal manner. This style partly reflects the Japanese culture compared with the more aggressively competitive American one. Theory Z by Ouchi (1981) has a similar approach but with the emphasis being on American firms which have successfully used a Japanese management style.

Ouchi emphasizes that each step takes time. Success depends upon the company's ability to coordinate people, rather than technology, to achieve productivity. A corporate philosophy is necessary for a type Z company to have long-term thinking as a top requirement. This philosophy includes the organization's objectives, operating procedures, and environmental constraints. Some of the most successful U.S. MNEs have a Japanese-style management organization. These include IBM, Procter & Gamble, Eastman Kodak, Intel, Eli Lilly, Boeing, Delta, Hewlett-Packard, United Airlines, Dayton-Hudson, General Electric, Westinghouse, Texas Instruments, and International Harvester. The key to the success of these firms lies in coming to grips with the conflict between human and economic goals.

All these firms have generally good management and employee relations. Their underlying feature is the interdependence between the company and the employees. This is characterized by a participative approach to decision making and a wholistic concern for people. Each type Z company has developed a unique corporate culture. The employees work together (like a clan) and operate on a basis of mutual trust and respect. There is corporate loyalty, a corporate culture, and identification with superordinate goals.

Beyond Theory Z

Japanese management style as examined by Pascale and Athos and Ouchi emphasizes that success depends upon the ability to coordinate people, as well as develop technology, in an environment of harmony and trust. The use of quality circles is required to involve workers in the effective management of the firm. The keys to Japanese success, however, are not simply human and cultural variables but also those of production. This focus on production management, as discussed in Chapter 16, is sometimes called micromanagement.

What does all this mean? Simply that successful management of the MNE requires an integration of all four functional areas: human resources, production, marketing, and finance. Human resource management, alone, is not what has led to the rise of Japanese firms. An effective international business strategy relies on all four areas being expertly managed.

Searching for Excellence

The emphasis on the motivation of managers and workers in the organization has also been stressed by Peters and Waterman (1982). They find that the excellent U.S. companies have developed corporate loyalty and pride in their employees and that responsibility for the performance of the corporation is accepted at all levels as employees respond to incentives and accept the shared values of the company. Such corporate loyalty is helped along by the socialization associated with regular "beer busts" but, more importantly, by the recognition of the importance of individual contributions which improve the quality of the corporation's products and services.

Peters and Waterman found that excellent companies have eight common attributes: they have a bias for action; they maintain closeness to their customers; they develop autonomous champions with entrepreneurial ability; they achieve productivity through people (i.e., respect for their individual employees); they have a hands-on and value-driven approach to management; they stick to businesses they know how to run; they have a simple form and lean staff; and they are centralized in company values and goals but decentralized in production, development, and sales.

While these attributes are becoming the clichés of modern management motivation, it is clear that successful corporations need to develop excellent relationships with their employees. Many of these successful U.S. corporations are also MNEs. However, it is not clear that the Japanese and U.S. "team player" concept will necessarily apply to all other MNEs, especially European MNEs (such as the British ones), where many cultural characteristics emphasize the nonconformist nature of the individual. Enlightened management will recognize that employees are as heterogeneous as customers.

SUMMARY

Chapter 17 explains the human resource management (HRM) function in an international context, emphasizing the importance of organizational design and effective HRM in the strategic success of the MNE. This chapter starts by examining the environmental, internal, and strategic HRM factors important to the MNE.

The MNE faces two classic choices in its staffing: using home nationals or host nationals. Either choice offers advantages and disadvantages, and the choice rests not only on the type of strategy and structure used by the MNE but also on its stage of its international involvement. Whatever the choice, the MNE should beware of developing an ethnocentric attitude. IBM illustrates the successful adoption of a geocentric attitude toward HRM.

Whatever the level of management (strategic, managerial, or operational), the MNE must carefully consider the human and cultural factors in its international operations to have a chance of success against a rival host-country firm. Failure to consider cultural factors can invite disaster in international business. Finally, the chapter analyzed Japanese management style. The seven S framework is discussed, as is the type Z organization. Both illustrate the emphasis placed on human management in successful Japanese (and U.S.) organizations.

KEY WORDS

Human resource management	Compensation
Host-country national	Training and development
Home-country national	Performance appraisal
Ethnocentric/polycentric/geocentric attitudes	Seven S framework
Staffing of the international division	Type Z organization
Strategic staffing	Product-line organization
Centralization of staffing function	Area organization
Recruitment and selection	Matrix structure

QUESTIONS

1 The management of human resources is made more complex on an international scale. Give some examples of this. Discuss strategies which may be effective for the MNE in the face of such complexities.

2 What are the costs and benefits associated with human resource management under different types of organizational structures? What is the responsibility of the human resource management function in relation to the MNE's structure?

3 Perlmutter identifies three types of managerial attitudes. Discuss how these relate to the organizational structure of the MNE. Give an example to assist in your answer. Use an illustration of the appropriate structure.

4 How do the concepts of strategy and structure interface in the management of human resources? Discuss the evolvement of organizational structure. Why have so many firms shifted to global product divisions? What are the risks, if any?

5 Discuss the advantages and disadvantages of home-country versus host-country management in staffing the MNE. How does the organizational structure used by the MNE determine its staffing? Relate these to Perlmutter's managerial attitudes.

6 What is the Vredeling proposal? Discuss the implication of proposals such as this. Why are MNEs generally opposed to the Vredeling proposal?

7 In Chapter 14, the portfolio matrix developed by the Boston Consulting Group was examined. Discuss the implications of this model on human resource management. In particular, discuss the managerial qualities necessary to operate a "star," "cash cow," and a "dog."

8 Compare and contrast the Japanese management style with the American style of management. In your answer, discuss the framework developed by Pascale and Athos. What are the key components of Ouchi's Theory Z?

9 Is it possible for the MNE to possess a firm-specific advantage in the management of human resources?

CHAPTER 18

INTERNATIONAL
FINANCIAL MANAGEMENT

INTRODUCTION

The financial manager of a domestic corporation essentially has four areas of responsibility: financial planning and control, working capital management, capital expenditure analysis, and the financing of corporate operations. For the firm with only intermittent international contacts the international financial problems are usually restricted to working capital management problems, such as the additional sources of funds available for export financing or the additional funds management problems of foreign currency inflows. However, the multinational firm is faced with added international dimensions to all of the four main areas of financial management.

The international dimensions added to financial management take one of two forms. First, we have the complexity of different cultures organizing different ways of doing basically the same thing. We can call this an *institutional* dimension. One example is the difference in tax structures across countries; whereas, for example, in North America emphasis is placed on personal and corporate income taxes in raising government revenues, in Europe emphasis is placed on value-added taxes (a form of sales tax). Another example is in sources of financing. In many countries the stock market, if it exists at all, is moribund and risk capital is provided through either government loans and guarantees or bank loans. In both of these cases, international financial managers do not have to solve a new problem; instead they require new institutional knowledge to solve a conventional problem.

The second dimension to international financial management can be called the *incremental* dimension. This consists of a set of incremental or additional problems that do not have their counterpart in the problems of conventional financial

405

management. One example is the additional problem of managing cash flows internationally, when the cash flows are denominated in different currencies and face different national restrictions on their convertibility. A second example is the additional problem of analyzing a capital expenditure proposal, when there is a distinct possibility of expropriation or foreign exchange controls. The former case of *foreign exchange risk* and the latter case of *political* or *country risk* both add a new dimension to the conventional financial management problem.

In this one chapter it is not possible to fully analyze the institutional dimension to international financial management. Partly this reflects the simple page and time constraints involved, but mainly it reflects the fact that such knowledge is extremely current, and thus quickly becomes dated. Instead, we focus on the incremental dimension of international financial management. Hence, successively, we discuss financial planning and control, working capital management, capital expenditure analysis, and corporate financing for a multinational corporation. Schematically, this is illustrated in Figure 18-1.

FINANCIAL PLANNING AND CONTROL IN A MULTINATIONAL

There are two points to recognize in discussing financial planning and control within a multinational. First, the separate national subsidiaries and branches will institute their own planning and control systems as part of normal domestic financial management practices. Second, we then have to justify the creation of a different or a supplementary system to take into account that this subsidiary is part of a multinational organization. The problem is to justify this second layer of reporting and management, since it undoubtedly imposes on the multinational an extra layer of costs that would otherwise reduce its competitiveness.

FIGURE 18-1
International financial management functions.

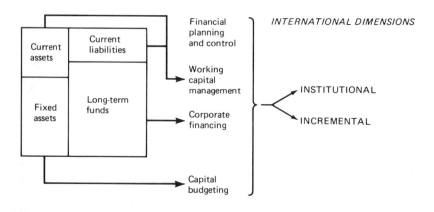

Polycentric Solution

In the solution to this problem we have two extremes. The first is sometimes referred to as the *polycentric* solution, which essentially treats the multinational enterprise (MNE) as a holding company and decentralizes decision making to the national subsidiary level. In this case, central reporting and control amounts to the portfolio analysis of the separate operating units. Financial statements would be prepared according to generally accepted accounting principles (GAAP) in both the subsidiary and the parent's home country. The subsidiary's performance would be evaluated against that of similar domestic and foreign concerns. Most decision making would be decentralized, except for major new projects and financing, which, since they affect the value of the parent's holding, would be scrutinized by head office.

The advantages of the polycentric approach are the normal advantages that accrue to decentralization. Decisions are made on the spot by those most informed about market conditions. Hence the national subsidiaries should be more flexible, more motivated, and altogether more efficient and competitive. However, to a large extent this reduces the role of the multinational to that of being a portfolio manager, picking undervalued foreign subsidiaries instead of stocks. Moreover, unlike the portfolio manager, who can sell a stock that is performing badly, the multinational that adopts a polycentric approach may have difficulty rectifying inadequate performance by a subsidiary, particularly when this suddenly manifests itself as heavy-handed interference by the parent. There have even been cases when the polycentric approach resulted in competition between different national subsidiaries and lower overall profits within the multinational.

Ethnocentric Solution

The opposite extreme is that of the *ethnocentric* corporation, which treats all foreign operations, whether they are subsidiaries or branches, as if they were extensions of domestic operations. In this case, all operations are integrated into the planning and control system of the parent company. The advantages of such a system are that somebody is always looking at the overall picture. As a result, the multinational will have a detailed rule book that describes exactly what local managers can and cannot do. Usually, this results in the complete centralization of the finance function. Excess cash, over some predetermined amount, is concentrated in particular countries for investment in marketable securities. Financing sources, even collection and payment periods, are centralized so that funds can be raised at the lowest cost within the organization, and transfer prices are set to minimize global tax payments.

The ethnocentric approach often results in severe problems in planning and control. For example, to minimize global taxes the parent might sell an intermediate product to a subsidiary at a very high price. As a result, that subsidiary's profit and taxes on that profit would be reduced. However, the parent company's profits, and also its taxes, would be increased. By the manipulation of these *transfer prices*, the multinational can reallocate taxable income away from high tax jurisdictions and into low tax jurisdictions, thereby reducing its overall tax burden. The problem is that the financial statements of the subsidiary then become almost meaningless. We might have a very profitable subsidiary that is reporting very large losses because of an arbitrary allocation of debt and artificially high transfer prices. How can we then control and assess the performance of that subsidiary?

SHIFTING PROFITS BY TRANSFER PRICING: A SELLS TO B

	"Arm's-length" price		Transfer price	
	Country A	Country B	Country A	Country B
Sales	$10,000 *Exports* $12,000		$12,000 *Exports* $12,000	
Costs of sales	8,000	→10,000	8,000	→12,000
Profit	2,000	2,000	4,000	Nil
Tax (A:40%, B:50%)	800	1,000	1,600	Nil
Net profit	$ 1,200	$ 1,000	$ 3,400	$ Nil

Transfer prices affect the after-tax profits resulting from *internal* MNE transactions. Using the "arm's-length" price, the MNE has paid global taxes of $1800.

By increasing the transfer price, the MNE increases its revenues and profits in country A, thereby increasing its taxes in Country A. However, its costs in country B are increased and thus its profits reduced. Overall its *after-tax* profits are increased, because of the lower tax rate in country A. (*Note*: For simplicity we assume no tariffs that could otherwise affect after-tax profitability.)

The solution to the above problem is more documentation. Ethnocentric corporations produce multiple sets of financial statements. There will normally be at least three, one for local reporting requirements, one for the consolidated financial statements, and one "real one" for managerial decision making. In practice, there may also be two more, one for each of the two sets of tax authorities and possibly even another one for minority shareholders in the foreign subsidiary. It then becomes an enormous task to keep track of all the flows within the multinational, particularly when each transaction may then have several prices attached to it. This problem becomes acute if tax authorities attempt to seize the additional sets of financial statements and then apply a mix of data to assess the highest possible amount of tax.

Geocentric Solution

Between these two extremes lies the *geocentric* corporation, where the management is aware of the international implications of management decisions. In a basic sense this is the true multinational; it recognizes the advantages of being a multinational, and yet tempers this knowledge with the understanding that centralization destroys flexibility and initiative. The particular solution adopted by any company depends on two main factors. First, the nature and location of the subsidiary determines the gain from decentralization. For example, British investment in North America has predominantly been via holding companies, the polycentric approach, since the quality of local management largely rewards decentralization. Conversely, investment in developing countries is more likely to be centralized. Second, the gains from centralization are dependent on widely divergent tax rates, financial systems, and competitive environments. Where subsidiaries are located in industrialized countries, the integration of the financial and economic systems and the force of bilateral tax treaties is likely to reduce the gains to centralization. Conversely, if some subsidiaries are located in countries with inadequately developed financial markets or widely divergent tax codes, the gains to centralization are proportionately higher.

Foreign Exchange Translation

The financial planning and control problem thus revolves around a solution to the centralization-decentralization dilemma. However, regardless of the degree of centralization, we still have the basic problem of consistency across the financial statements of different countries. That is, in order to compare the performance of, say, a German or British subsidiary with a U.S. one, we have to translate all the financial statements into a common denominator. This problem, *foreign exchange translation*, has been one of the most controversial issues in accounting in North America for the last 10 years. The emphasis hitherto has been on *financial reporting*, that is, how to consolidate financial statements in the annual report to stockholders. This has been the subject of two statements, No. 8 in 1976 and No. 52 in 1981, of the U.S. *Financial Accounting Standards Board* (FASB). However, even more important than the reporting issue is the relevance of these translation methodologies for performance evaluation and control, that is, *managerial reporting*. It may very well be that the consolidated statements that conform to generally accepted accounting principles (GAAP) still give a set of financial statements that are inadequate for purposes of performance evaluation and control.

To illustrate a complicated technical issue, consider the financial statements in Exhibit 18-1. The column "Foreign" provides the end-of-year financial statements for our foreign subsidiary drawn up in accordance with historical cost GAAP. The main implications of this are that depreciation as an allocation of historical cost is fixed, as is that part of the cost of goods sold which was in inventory at the beginning of the year. In the construction of the example we have assumed first in first out (FIFO) inventory policy. We have also assumed that the exchange rate has devalued by 10 percent during the year. That is, whereas at the beginning of the year one FC would buy $1, at the end of the year it would buy only $0.909. (Alternatively, $1 would buy 1 FC and 1.1 FC, respectively.)

Our problem is to translate the "foreign" financial statements, drawn up in FC into dollars, so that we can consolidate them and/or compare them with equivalent subsidiaries elsewhere. The two translation methodologies in Exhibit 18-1 are the temporal method of statement No. 8 of the Financial Accounting Standards Board (FAS No. 8) and the current rate method of FAS No. 52. The two methodologies differ over their choice of exchange rates when translating different balance sheet and income statement items. The current rate method, which became GAAP in the United States in 1981, is the simplest of the two; it simply translates all balance sheet and income statement items at the current exchange rate (end of year for annual financial statements). The foreign exchange gain or loss from the income statement and balance sheet is then closed to the firm's retained earnings.

The only complexity that FAS No. 52 introduced into this current rate method comes in drawing up the foreign subsidiary's statements in the first place. These statements have to be drawn up in the subsidiary's *functional currency*, which is the predominant currency in which the subsidiary transacts business. In practice, this should be the same as the currency of the country in which the subsidiary is located. However, to determine the functional currency, accounting managers will have to look at the currency that determines the firm's cash flow; this will mean looking at the firm's revenue and expense stream. This may cause the functional currency to be different from the local currency.

The current rate method's main advantages are simplicity and the fact that most of the relationships in the foreign financial statements are preserved on translation. That is, for example, the fixed asset turnover ratio in the statements in Exhibit 18-1 remains at 2.18, regardless of whether it is calculated from the foreign currency or from translated financial statements. Hence, financial control, both centrally and locally, will be using the same ratios. This obviously simplifies the control process. However, simplicity is not necessarily a virtue if it brings with it distortions that make it difficult to analyze comparable situations. This problem was recognized in FAS No. 8, the translation methodology that was GAAP in the United States between 1976 and 1981.

Temporal Method   FAS No. 8, or the temporal method, recognizes that with historical cost accounting the dollars in the financial statements are not of equal value. That is, for example, the fixed assets may have been recorded 10 years ago when the plant was originally built. However, the accounts receivables represent trade credit that was extended only 30 days ago, the problem being that with inflation these dollar assets will not be comparable. To remedy this defect of historical cost accounting, FAS No. 8 distinguished between monetary items and nonmonetary items. Monetary items like cash, accounts receivable, accounts payable, short- and long-term debt, and notes payable represent current values and thus should be translated at the current exchange rate. Nonmonetary items

EXHIBIT 18-1
FOREIGN EXCHANGE TRANSLATION

Income statement	Foreign	Temporal FAS No. 8		Current FAS No. 52	
Sales	165	C	150	C	150
Cost of goods sold	105	C/H	100	C	95.45
General expenses	27.5	C	25	C	25
Depreciation	7.5	H	7.5	C	6.82
Net operating income	25			C	22.73
Interest	7.75	C	7.05	C	7.05
Foreign exchange gain/loss	—	P	4.45	P	(6.82)
Net income	17.25	P	15.0	P	8.86
Dividend	16.5	C	15.0	C	15.0
Retained earnings	0.75	P	0	P	(6.14)
Balance sheet					
Accounts receivable	27.5	C	25	C	25
Inventory	55	H	50	C	50
Fixed assets	75.75	H	75	C	68.86
Accounts payable	27.5	C	25	C	25
Long-term debt	55	C	50	C	50
Stockholders' equity	75	H	75	C	75
Retained earnings for year	0.75		—		—
Plug	—	P	—	P	(6.14)

C = exchange at current rate, assumed to be 0.909 due to 10 percent devaluation and 10 percent inflation.
H = exchange at appropriate historic rate, assumed to be 1.
P = plug or adjustment due to translation.

like plant and equipment and inventory, however, would not reflect current values due to historical cost accounting. As a result, they should be translated at the historic exchange rate that existed when the expenditures were recorded. The same distinction between monetary and nonmonetary items is extended to the income statement, where depreciation and part of cost of goods sold are translated at historic exchange rates, since they are tied via historical cost accounting (and inventory policy) to the balance sheet accounts, plant and equipment and inventory.

FAS No. 8 implicitly recognizes that the inflation that distorts historical cost financial statements also causes exchange rates to change, that is, purchasing power parity (PPP) holds. Hence, by translating monetary and nonmonetary accounts at different exchange rates, we are minimizing the distortionary effects of inflation. For example, fixed assets and depreciation are translated at historical exchange rates, the reason simply being that they are recorded in the statements in terms of historical values. Hence, if PPP holds, the combination of the two valuation assumptions should approximate their current dollar values. Similarly, current liabilities are expressed in the accounts at current market value; thus exchanging them at the current exchange rate will approximate their current dollar value too. Hence FAS No. 8 correctly translates foreign financial statements once it is recognized that with historical cost accounting the foreign currency values are not all equal.

The implication of FAS No. 8 is that since monetary accounts are the only ones affected by the current exchange rate, foreign exchange gains and losses depend upon whether the firm has a net monetary liability or asset. For most firms monetary liabilities exceed monetary assets, since they borrow (incur monetary liabilities) to invest in fixed assets. In our example, the combination of a devaluation of the foreign currency with the net monetary liability produced a *foreign exchange gain* of $4.54. This is thoroughly logical. With the devaluation the foreign currency debt now requires fewer dollars to pay it off. Conversely, if the FC had revalued (the dollar had devalued), the net monetary liability would have produced a *foreign exchange loss*, since now more dollars are required to pay off the foreign currency debt.

The foreign exchange gain or loss produced by FAS No. 8 is in fact similar to the purchasing power gain or loss, discussed in Chapter 9, that results from issuing debt under inflation. If there is high inflation in the country of your foreign subsidiary, you can expect two things: first interest rates will be higher to reflect that inflation and second the exchange rate will be expected to devalue. Hence, by borrowing in that currency, you will *expect* to incur higher interest costs and positive foreign exchange gains. The combination of the two just equates the cost of foreign borrowing with that of domestic borrowing, which with reasonably efficient international capital markets, should be the same.

FAS No. 8 ran into a storm of protest from U.S. multinationals, for the simple reason that when it was introduced in 1976 the U.S. dollar had just begun to weaken. As a result, foreign exchange losses on translation wiped out the foreign profits that were being produced as a result of the lower interest rates being paid on foreign currency debt. This was how it should have been! However, at the time, it appeared to many treasurers of U.S. multinationals that FAS No. 8 was just forcing them to realize foreign exchange gains or losses due to random and transitory foreign exchange changes. Hence, under pressure, the FASB withdrew FAS No. 8 and replaced it with FAS No. 52. Unfortunately, with FAS No. 52, foreign exchange gains and losses vary with stockholders' equity, not net monetary liabilities. Hence, when the U.S. dollar appreciated in 1981 to 1984, the same companies that had recorded translation losses under FAS No. 8 in 1977 to 1980, now produced translation losses under FAS No. 52!

Summary of Translation Methodologies and Control

U.S. multinationals now have to use FAS No. 52 for reporting purposes. However, it makes no sense to compound the error by using it for control purposes as well. If the foreign subsidiary's statements are produced under historical cost GAAP, they should be translated using FAS No. 8 principles. If the firm wishes to remove the foreign exchange gain or loss that results from the change in value of the net monetary liabilities, then its cost, the interest bill, should also be removed.

This is because they are simply two sides of the same coin. The firm's *operating* results can then be compared with those of other foreign subsidiaries. For control purposes, this makes the most sense, since debt is usually not under the control of local managers anyway. If the foreign subsidiary's statements are prepared under inflation-adjusted GAAP, either replacement cost or general price level adjusted, then FAS No. 52 can be used, since all items in the financial statements then represent their current values.

The upshot of this discussion is simply that control should be based on consistent financial policies adopted across all the subsidiaries in the multinational enterprise. If historical cost accounting is the basis of the internal financial statements used for control purposes, FAS No. 8 should be used to translate the statements to a common denominator. Similarly, if current cost accounting is the basis, FAS No. 52 should be used. What makes no sense is a mishmash of the two, since any credibility that the financial statements originally possessed is subsequently destroyed on translation.

Once the basis for translation has been determined, the parent corporation can assign *budgets* to individual subsidiaries and then evaluate performance relative to budget. Most studies have found that multinationals control their subsidiaries through normal financial analysis, such as the Du Pont return on investment approach, and performance relative to budget. In the latter case, the only real question is whether or not the local corporation should be held accountable for exchange rate changes. It makes sense to motivate managers by holding them responsible only for factors that they control. In this case, firms should use the forward rate or the expected exchange rate to evaluate performance, since the manager has no control over the subsequent change in the exchange rate. However, in practice most companies use actual exchange rates in setting and evaluating performance, thus implicitly holding local management responsible for factors over which they can exert no control. This makes little sense but is justified by trying to keep local management aware of the importance of exchange rate changes.

WORKING CAPITAL MANAGEMENT

Working capital management is defined to be the management of short-term asset and liability accounts (less than 1 year's maturity). The solution to a working capital problem is affected by the institutional framework of each country. For example, credit policy affects the competitiveness of a firm's sales, more lenient terms effectively representing a lower price. This credit can be viewed as a short-term loan provided to the purchaser of the product. Hence credit policy will be affected by the institutional framework for documenting short-term loans.

In France credit is often regularized as a promissory note, since it is then accorded a higher priority in any subsequent bankruptcy proceedings. As a result, in Europe, generally, money markets have developed to buy (discount) and sell short-term promissory notes. However, if a European company then attempted to regularize credit by means of a fixed-interest promissory note with a Muslim customer, problems could result. This is because it may be against the civil as well as the religious laws of the customer to receive or pay interest on debt. In this case, the firm would instead make the sale by increasing the sale price and extending the period of payment without any explicit interest charge. In both cases, the necessary credit has been made to make the sale; the only difference is the legal or institutional framework that documents it.

Similar modifications have to be made to the solution to cash management and other working capital problems. However, the really interesting problems are the incremental problems faced by the multinational. In this section, we will discuss two main incremental problems; foreign exchange exposure and funds positioning.

EXPOSURE MANAGEMENT

Exposure just means "affected by." Hence foreign exchange exposure is a general title that considers the management of foreign exchange risk or the extent to which exchange rate changes affect the firm. In the previous section, we saw how exchange rate changes would produce foreign exchange gains or losses on the translation of the financial statements of a foreign subsidiary. This exposure is called *translation exposure*. However, changes in exchange rates can also affect the real economic value of subsidiary operations and the value of particular cash inflows and outflows. The extent to which the value of a foreign subsidiary is affected by exchange rate changes is called *economic exposure* and the extent to which a particular cash flow is affected, *transaction exposure*. Since the value of a subsidiary is simply the present value of all the cash flows generated by that subsidiary, we can see that transaction and economic exposure are really only differentiated by the timing of the receipt of the cash flows. In general, transaction exposure is subsumed within economic exposure.

In considering exchange rate exposure, we must answer two questions. First, should we do anything about it? Second, if we do attempt to remove exposure, should we take real measures, that is, change real variables like the investment in inventory and plant and equipment, or financial measures? The first question is very difficult to answer. Most studies have shown that translation exposure has very little impact, if any at all, on common stock prices. Hence, if we accept the standard objective of the firm as the maximization of its market value, on the grounds that this maximizes the owner's wealth, then translation exposure is irrelevant. This seems appropriate, particularly when translation exposure can be completely reversed as a result of a change in accounting standards, as, for example, occurred when the FASB went from FAS No. 8 to FAS No. 52.

However, since FAS No. 8 sensitized firms to the problems of translation exposure, most firms have attempted to remove it. On the other hand, economic exposure is important, since by definition the value of the subsidiary operations is affected, and yet most firms do not manage economic exposure on the grounds that they find it "hard to define." In the middle ground, transaction exposure may or may not be important, and some firms manage it while others do not. However, the firms that manage transaction exposure are not necessarily those for whom it is important!

To simplify the latter remarks, it may help, first of all, to consider how exposure can be removed. In considering exposure, we first have to define the *time horizon*, since we are really talking about the effect of exchange rate changes between two points in time. Second, we have to determine the *amount* exposed. Once this is done, the mechanics of removing exposure by financial means are similar for all three types of foreign exchange exposure. Suppose, for example, the amount exposed is FC 55 million and the time period is 1 year. This could be translation exposure, since, for example, under FAS No. 8 the net monetary liability in Exhibit 18-1 is FC 55 million, transaction exposure if a FC 55 million cash inflow is expected at the end of the year, or economic exposure if that is the expected FC value of the foreign subsidiary.

Hedging to Remove Exposure

The financial solution to the removal of foreign exchange exposure is to *hedge*. Hedging is defined to be to "bet on both sides of a gamble so as to remove the risk of loss." In our example, the gamble involves the domestic value of the FC account due in 1 year's time, which is uncertain because of the exchange rate uncertainty. Hence hedging requires that we create an FC inflow to match against the *existing* FC outflow. We can do this in one of two ways, through either a *money market hedge* or a *forward market hedge*.

A money market hedge simply involves the firm borrowing in foreign currency the present value of the amount to be hedged. Hence, if the FC interest rate is 12.2 percent, the firm would borrow FC 49.0 million, since FC 49 million invested at 12.2 percent would accumulate to FC 55 million in 1 year's time. The firm would then *immediately* exchange the funds into its own currency. For example, if the exchange rate, $E[US\$: FC]$, were 1.0, the firm would receive \$49.0 million. At the end of the year, any foreign exchange gains or losses on the domestic value of the FC *inflow* are completely offset against corresponding foreign exchange losses or gains on the domestic value of the FC *outflow* required to repay the principal and interest on the foreign currency debt. In this way, the money market hedge realizes domestic currency *immediately* and removes all foreign exchange exposure on the domestic value of the FC inflow due in 1 year's time.

The forward market hedge obviously requires that a functioning forward market exists. If it does, the offsetting FC outflow can be created by selling FC forward against the domestic currency. In our example, the firm could go to the bank and buy a *forward contract* to sell FC 55 million in 1 year's time at the current forward rate. If the forward rate, $F[US\$: FC]$, were 0.909, then the contract would commit the firm to exchange FC 55 million into \$50 million in 1 year's time. If the exchange rate changes, any foreign exchange gains and losses on this forward contract would then be offset against the foreign exchange losses or gains on the FC inflow. Hence, similar to the money market hedge, the forward market hedge removes all foreign exchange exposure. The only difference between the

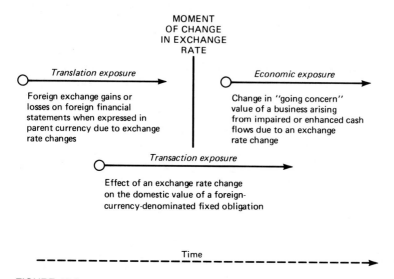

FIGURE 18-2
Three types of foreign exchange exposure. (*Adapted from Exhibit 5.1 in David Eitemann and Arthur Stonehill. Multinational Business Finance, 3rd ed. Reading, Mass.: Addison-Wesley, 1982.*)

two is that the forward market hedge provides $50 million in 1 year's time, whereas the money market hedge gives $49 million immediately.

Choosing between Hedges

In choosing between the two hedges, let us assume that we are hedging transaction exposure; for example, the FC 55 million may be a cash inflow from some export or an expected divided remittance from a foreign subsidiary. In this case, with the money market hedge we are receiving domestic currency *today* and the forward market hedge domestic currency in 1 year's time. To compare the two, we have to take into account the time value of money and either discount the proceeds of the forward market hedge backward or compound the proceeds of the money market hedge forward into the future. Suppose the domestic interest rate were 2 percent, in this case the value of the two hedges would be identical and the firm would be indifferent toward the two.

The comparison is illustrated in Figure 18-3. The money market hedge starts with the FC 55 million, discounts it back to today to FC 49 million, and then exchanges it at the current spot rate into $49 million. The forward market hedge simply exchanges the FC 55 million into $50 million at the current forward rate. The problem then is one of comparing these two dollar amounts; $49 million today versus $50 million in 1 year's time. If the current interest rate is 2 percent, the firm could use the forward contract and FC proceeds as collateral for a loan of $49 million. Alternatively, it could invest the $49 million at 2 percent to receive $50 million in 1 year's time. Hence both hedges are of equivalent value.

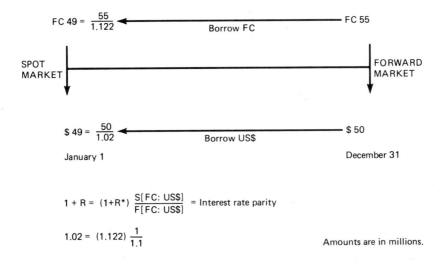

$$FC\ 49 = \frac{55}{1.122} \xleftarrow{\hspace{2cm}} FC\ 55$$

Borrow FC

SPOT
MARKET

FORWARD
MARKET

$$\$\ 49 = \frac{50}{1.02} \xleftarrow{\hspace{2cm}} \$\ 50$$

Borrow US$

January 1   December 31

$$1 + R = (1+R^*)\ \frac{S[FC:\ US\$]}{F[FC:\ US\$]} = \text{Interest rate parity}$$

$$1.02 = (1.122)\ \frac{1}{1.1}$$

Amounts are in millions.

FIGURE 18-3
Hedging exchange rate exposure.

This indifference result should not be too surprising, since in our example we have assumed that *interest rate parity* holds. That is, from Equation (9-1), 1 plus the domestic interest rate, 1.02, is equal to 1 plus the foreign interest rate times the ratio of the spot to forward exchange rate, or (1.122)(1/1.1). Here the exchange rates, consistent with Equation (9-1), have been expressed in their U.S. dollar equivalent values, $E[FC:US\$]$. As previously discussed, covered interest arbitrage will always force interest rate parity to hold, but does this then mean that the hedging choice is irrelevant? Certainly not!

First, the corporation will face different borrowing and lending costs from those of the international arbitrageurs who enforce interest rate parity. In particular, the firm's borrowing or lending position is particularly relevant, since it usually makes no sense to borrow foreign currency, through the money market hedge, just to invest the proceeds in a dollar deposit. Second, interest rate parity presupposes a functioning forward and money market. In some countries, one or both may not exist or they may be subsidized or regulated, in which case, there may be a bias in favor of one hedge. Hence it always pays to consider both types of hedge.

A final comment on hedging is of the relevance of hedging translation exposure. In our example we assumed a FC 55 million cash inflow, so that either hedge removed any foreign exchange uncertainty surrounding *cash flows*. However, if one had been hedging translation exposure of FC 55 million, this would not have been the case. For the money market hedge, offsetting an arbitrary FC accounting value, we created an FC inflow in repaying the foreign currency debt. Similarly, for the forward market hedge to fulfill our forward commitment to sell FC 55 million for $50 million, we would have to buy the FC in the first place. In both cases, we created *real* cash flows from dollars into FC to offset the "notional" accounting values that were exposed to foreign exchange gains and losses. Needless to say, many treasurers have balked at the idea of creating this *real* transaction exposure to offset some *nebulous* translation exposure that may or may not be of any importance. Moreover, the transaction gains and losses are taxable, whereas translation gains and losses are not. Therefore, the hedge requires *even greater* pretax transaction exposure to offset the translation exposure.

Economic Exposure

In hedging economic exposure, we have this same problem of creating transaction exposure to offset value exposure that does not immediately involve cash flows. However, with economic exposure the more fundamental question to ask is whether a 1-year horizon is relevant. From the construction of our interest rate parity example the foreign currency has both higher nominal interest rates and a depreciating currency. This is what we would expect from a country with higher inflation. Moreover, inflation tends to increase the value of the foreign subsidiary, since the nominal value of its plant and equipment will also increase with inflation. Hence, there may in fact be *no* change in the domestic value of the foreign subsidiary after the exchange rate change. All that is happening is that, through purchasing power parity (PPP), the exchange rate is offsetting the inflationary increase in value of the foreign subsidiary.

This line of reasoning leads to a definition of economic exposure that consists of either short-run deviations from PPP or the failure of PPP to hold in the long run. In the short run, there may in fact be deviations from PPP. However, these are unlikely to have much of an impact on market value, since this represents the present value of all *future* cash flows, wherein the most immediate cash flow is not important. Moreover, such fluctuations in market value are likely to be completely random, thus reducing the incentive to hedge, since it can be fully diversified away. We call this type of exposure *residual economic exposure*.

The failure of PPP to hold in the long run represents *real economic exposure*. However, hedging is not very useful, since the change takes effect over a reasonably long period of time, whereas hedging is intrinsically a short-run tool. To counter real economic exposure we usually change real variables. Hence Ford of Europe changed its production strategy from individual integrated national carmakers to an integrated European carmaker. Individual components were sourced internationally, not nationally, so that geographic diversification reduced the real economic exposure to individual subsidiaries. Other multinationals faced with real economic exposure have changed their marketing strategies, so that high-cost producers focused on market segments with low price elasticities of demand, and low-cost producers focused on the more competitive markets, the upshot being that real economic exposure is countered by long-run production and marketing strategies, not by short-run financial management techniques.

Transaction Exposure

From this general discussion it would seem that neither translation nor economic exposure need be hedged; this leaves only transaction exposure. The problem with hedging transaction exposure is that for large companies the number of transactions involved could become large, particularly for a multinational with a large number of international transactions. As a result, a policy of consistently hedging all such transactions would be exceedingly complicated. Moreover, there are good reasons to suspect that such a policy is not worthwhile. First, for such a large corporation, there are inherent diversification benefits, in that a lot of the fluctuation in exchange rates nets out. That is, an increase in one exchange rate just offsets a decrease in another. Hence *overall* there may be little exposure. Second, with efficient foreign exchange markets the forward exchange rate is just equal to the expected spot exchange rate. However, with a policy of consistently hedging, we still don't know what the forward exchange rate will be on the date that we have to hedge. In fact, it may be just as uncertain as the spot rate. Finally, hedging is costly in that there are large administrative costs in establishing a fully functional exposure management team, in addition to the marginally higher costs of actually implementing the hedging techniques.

The upshot is that attitudes toward hedging are changing. After FAS No. 8, most firms hedged transaction and translation exposure. Today, firms are more likely to hedge by exception. That is, they will hedge a very large foreign currency inflow, since exchange rate changes could then have a material impact on its value. However, they will not have a policy of consistently hedging every foreign currency inflow. In the same way, a small corporation will hedge its infrequent foreign currency cash flows. After a period of initial interest in economic exposure, most firms are now coming to realize that hedging is not the best tool to manage it.

Leading and Lagging

An additional short-run exposure management technique is the infamous use of leading and lagging. This technique involves the short-run manipulation of accounts payable and accounts receivable. For example, suppose you have a U.K. subsidiary that does international business and has both sterling and foreign receivables and payables. If sterling is expected to depreciate from $1.60 to $1.50 ($E[US\$:£]$), what do you do? Obviously, a fixed £1000 obligation will have its value reduced from $1600 to $1500. Hence, if you owe the money, you would delay payment, i.e., lag payables, and if you are owed the money, you would speed up collection, i.e., lead receivables. Conversely, if the U.K. subsidiary has fixed foreign currency obligations, e.g., $1000, its value in sterling will increase from £625 to £666.7. Hence you would delay foreign currency receipts and speed up foreign currency payments. The net result is seen in Exhibit 18-2. The multinational will instruct its U.K. subsidiary to convert as much of its sterling monetary assets into cash as possible and use the proceeds to pay off foreign currency liabilities, with the excess exchanged into domestic currency. The British company will delay collecting foreign currency receivables (lag) and speed up foreign currency payables (lead).

This short-run manipulation of credit policy may have harmful side effects. Factoring sterling receivables, i.e., "selling" them to a financial institution, and speeding up collection by dunning letters, etc., may result in the loss of sales.

EXHIBIT 18-2
LEADING AND LAGGING RECEIVABLES

Denomination of credit	$1.60	$1.50	Decision
Receivables:			
Sterling (£1000)	+$1600	+$1500	Lead
Foreign currency ($1000)	+£ 625	+£ 666.7	Lag
Payables:			
Sterling (£1000)	−£ 1600	−$1500	Lag
Foreign currency ($1000)	−£ 625	−£ 666.7	Lead

However, the overall result is to reduce holdings of sterling monetary assets prior to devaluation and thus reduce possible losses. Before generalized floating, leading and lagging by multinational corporations was claimed to be the main force behind international monetary instability. As explained in Chapter 7, this was mainly because with fixed exchange rates it was a one-sided bet. If there was no devaluation, nothing was lost, whereas if there was a devaluation a lot was to be gained. Since generalized floating, leading and lagging has been reduced in importance, since the gamble involved is no longer so one-sided. However, countries that attempt to peg or fix their exchange rates are aware of the enormous potential that leading and lagging has to frustrate their exchange rate policy. Hence such countries often have rigid controls on payment policies and credit periods. For example, Denmark has a 30-day limit on leading and lagging import payments and export receipts, respectively.

FUNDS POSITIONING

The second major incremental problem in working capital management is that of *positioning funds*. For a domestic corporation, branch plants and subsidiaries will usually have cash ceilings. Excess cash will automatically be concentrated in a banking account at the parent level where it will be managed, conditional on the firm's short-term expected sources and uses of funds. The parameters of the funds-positioning problem for a domestic corporation are usually easy to determine: a cash management routine, usually provided by commercial banks, to concentrate cash and ensure that cash transfers are made efficiently, and a cash budget, to determine how much is excess and for how long. With these the firm can determine what type of money market securities to purchase.

The Problems of International Funds Positioning

For the multinational firm this simple problem takes on nightmarish proportions. First, there is the basic *political constraint* that cash cannot simply be moved in and out of many countries, because of foreign exchange controls. These controls range from outright prohibition, whereby the foreign exchange market is controlled by the government and foreign currency can simply not be bought and sold without the government's approval, to various weaker forms that verge on simple taxation. For example, some countries have a priority system whereby a certain amount of currency is allowed out per month, or a multiple exchange rate system whereby different exchange rates are appropriate for funds leaving or entering for different purposes. The simplest example of the latter was the U.K. dollar premium market, where investment funds leaving the U.K. had to be exchanged into dollars at a rate that depended on the availability of investment dollars. Moreover, the U.K. government took a cut from all foreign currency exchanged into sterling as a result of the liquidation of foreign investment positions. Hence, the supply of investment dollars was reduced, and a premium resulted.

The second constraint is that as well as general political problems, there is a *basic tax problem* in that different countries apply different taxes to cash flows leaving their jurisdiction. These taxes are called withholding taxes, since a fixed percentage of the cash flow is withheld on exchange into another currency. Generally, most countries have a basic set of withholding taxes, which are then altered according to bilateral tax treaties that have been negotiated with individual countries. As a result, we may have a 25 percent withholding tax on dividends, 10 percent on interest payments, and 0 percent on royalties. However, for country A the rates may have been negotiated to 15, 15, and 10 percent, whereas for country B they may have been negotiated to 10, 20, and 15 percent. Normally, the tax treaties negotiate bilateral rates downward, but few tax treaties are consistent. The result is that the tax is not only a function of how you define the cash flow, but it is also a function of where the cash is coming from and going to.

Implications for Funds Management

The implication of this problem is quite severe. The raison d'être for most multinationals is internalization, the fact that they have special skills at organizing production and marketing certain products. Without the restrictions just mentioned, it is almost a matter of indifference where profits show up within the organization and how cash flows are labeled. However, with these restrictions it becomes very important. Political risk and withholding taxes vary tremendously depending on whether the parent charges the foreign subsidiary a licensing or royalty fee for the use of technology, interest payments for the use of intercorporate debt, dividends as a return on the parent's equity investment, or management fees to represent the subsidiary's fair share of corporate overhead. Hence the multinational has to structure its involvement in different countries in a way that allows it the maximum amount of flexibility in moving funds around, while simultaneously minimizing these leakages to tax that occur when funds are exchanged into other currencies.

The latter problem of liquid asset management is one that is amenable to solution by modern operations research techniques. Essentially, we have a problem in that funds have to be concentrated from certain subsidiaries for central investment, subject to a series of constraints on maneuverability and withholding. This problem can be solved by *network* techniques or by *linear* and *goal programming* techniques. Many algorithms are available to solve these technical problems. The more interesting problem is to manage the political risk. Here it is important to differentiate between the political rhetoric and fact. Many countries will present a public image of being hard on multinationals, while privately being soft; the image being required for domestic (and possibly international) consumption, while the economic managers (often trained in western economics or business schools) are softer because they know only too well the importance of the multinational's contribution.

It is in this environment that funds positioning becomes important. Instead of publishing very large profits, the multinational can *unbundle* its services and charge separately for R and D, management services, debt provisions, etc. Hence, by the time that all these *expenses* are deducted, the GAAP profit may be very low. Hence, for public consumption the multinational's profit is low, that is, no "gouging," while the firm is still making a satisfactory rate of return. An implication here for the outsider is never to put too much faith in the financial statements of foreign controlled subsidiaries!

Funds Positioning Techniques

Of particular importance in funds positioning is the prevalence of transfer price manipulation. By consistently *overbilling* for the provision of goods and services to the foreign subsidiary, and underbilling for its exports, the multinational can artificially reduce the subsidiary's profit and tax. This was illustrated at the beginning of the chapter. The rampant misuse of transfer pricing in this manner has caused widespread concern. Several countries have now abrogated to themselves the right to determine fair "arm's-length" prices on intracorporate transactions. Moreover, some U.S. states are now taxing on worldwide corporate income on the basis that the multinational is a unitary firm, and any allocation of profit to a particular location is almost arbitrary. Despite the misuse of transfer pricing to reduce taxes, it remains an extremely useful tool for circumventing foreign exchange controls. This is because most countries are unlikely to block exports, and yet they are also rarely able to determine the "arm's-length" prices for those exports.

Another popular technique to circumvent or reduce political risk is a *fronting loan*. We have implicitly discussed this already in connection with the offshore financial markets. In the 1950s the eastern bloc countries feared expropriation of their dollar holdings if they invested them directly in the United States. Hence they deposited them with European banks, who in turn invested them in the United States. The United States was not likely to expropriate the European banks, even if they became aware of the ultimate ownership of the investments. In the same way, if a multinational fears expropriation, it could deposit funds with a major international bank, which in turn would lend funds to the multinational's foreign subsidiary. In this way, the foreign government would have to expropriate the multinational *and* the bank's loan. This it is often unlikely to do, since it may in part be dependent on the international banking community for balance of payments or development financing. In this way, the multinational has shifted part of the political risk onto an institution that is better able to bear it.

A final technique is for the use of international subsidiaries set up in tax havens. If a subsidiary sells its output at a very low cost to another subsidiary in a tax haven, which then in turn sells it at a very high price to another subsidiary, the result is to locate all the profits in a low-tax jurisdiction. This is transfer pricing in the extreme. In reaction to the lost tax revenues, most countries now tax "passive" income earned by subsidiaries of their resident corporations overseas. However, most countries still allow their multinationals to exploit the bilateral tax treaties to minimize withholding taxes. As a result, most major U.S. corporations have international financing affiliates located in places like the Dutch Antilles. Their purpose is to raise funds for the multinational, while avoiding any withholding taxes on the interest payments on the funds so raised. This is because the Dutch Antilles have negotiated tax treaties with most countries with *zero* withholding taxes.

Funds positioning is thus important, in both moving funds around a multinational and reducing political and foreign exchange risk. Often the actual solution represents a compromise. Funds are structured so as to minimize political risk and yet at the same time the structure does not minimize the withholding taxes due once the funds are reallocated within the multinational. This overall solution has to remain somewhat subjective, since the analysis of political risk is still, of necessity, subjective.

TRANSFER PRICING THROUGH TAX HAVENS: A SELLS TO C TO B

	Country A		Country C		Country B
Sales	8,000	Exports	12,000	Exports	12,000
Cost of sales	8,000	→	8,000	→	12,000
Profit	—		4,000		—
Tax (A=40%, B=50%, C=0%)	—		—		—
Net profit	0		4,000		0

The example is identical to that earlier in the chapter, except that sales are routed through a subsidiary located in a tax haven, country C. In this extreme case, there is no tax paid at all.

CAPITAL EXPENDITURE ANALYSIS AND CORPORATE FINANCING

Capital expenditures are major projects where the costs are to be allocated over a number of years. Examples are the building of new plants, the refurbishing of existing equipment, and major acquisitions. In all cases, the fact that the firm generally has to live with the results for a long period of time has resulted in the development of rigorous, mathematical techniques of analysis. In the domestic environment, discounted cash flow techniques, such as net present value (NPV) and internal rate of return (IRR), now predominate in modern, well-run corporations. However, the traditional methods such as payback period and accounting rate of return are still often used, either as a first-cut approximation technique or to provide additional information. Financial theory is quite clear in showing that net present value is the best method for the evaluation of capital expenditures. This applies whether the expenditures being analyzed are domestic or foreign. Hence the basic techniques appropriate to domestic analysis can be applied in toto to capital expenditure analysis in multinationals, and to foreign projects generally.

However, one basic question naturally arises, which is who does the analysis, the parent or the foreign subsidiary? For domestic companies, initial analysis is usually done at the subsidiary or branch level and then passed up to head office for approval and modification. The head office modification is usually concerned with coordinating the activities of all the subsidiaries. This ensures that incremental revenues and costs are indeed incremental to the firm and not the subsidiary doing the analysis. In the same way, we have a basic need for the parent corporation to coordinate the activities of its foreign subsidiaries. It may be that, quite independently, two subsidiaries both decide to build a new tire plant and sell to the same market. Without coordination, they would compete against each other and the expected profits would not materialize. Hence the parent corporation has a basic coordinating role to play, to ensure that projects are undertaken to the benefit of the *whole* firm.

In the latter role, the parent will often have to turn down a positive NPV project from one subsidiary in favor of a higher NPV project from another national subsidiary, since among *competing* projects the multinational should always choose the one with the highest NPV. The same arguments apply in reverse to plant closures. A plant is always closed when to continue in operation creates a negative NPV. That is, the value of keeping the plant operating is *less* than the proceeds to be received from closing it down. If a choice exists between closing two plants, the shutdown should always be of the plant with the largest negative NPV. This obvious conclusion is particularly relevant once we realize that it is quite possible that a plant or subsidiary may be generating accounting profits, and yet still have a negative NPV. All that this means is that the real profits are not as high as could be generated by closing the plant down and using the resources elsewhere.

The plant closure problem became particularly acute during the recessionary period 1980 to 1983, when the reduction in overall demand meant that many firms had excess capacity and were faced with the choice of where to cut. In many cases, multinationals closed down foreign operations and switched production to the domestic market, even when the foreign operations had a history of operating profits. The foregoing discussion indicates that this is not necessarily an intrinsic bias of the parent corporation in wanting to protect its own nationals. Instead, it could be the logical result of the multinational acting as efficiently as possible, with no nationality bias whatsoever.

Conceptual Problems in Capital Budgeting for MNEs

The coordinating role of the parent in reviewing capital expenditure proposals is required because of the greater amount of information available to it. However, the capital expenditure decision can also differ between the parent and subsidiary perspectives because of faulty valuation techniques and political risk. In outlining why these differences occur, we first review the basic NPV criterion. The most popular technique separates the financing and operating parts of the problem, by discounting *operating* cash flows by a weighted average cost of capital that embodies the *financing* decision.

$$NPV = \sum_{t=0}^{T} \frac{-I_t + C_t}{(1+K_A)^t} \qquad (18\text{-}1)$$

where

$$K_A = k_e \frac{S}{V} + k_d (1-t_x) \frac{D}{V} \qquad (18\text{-}2)$$

The definitions of the terms are:

I_t	=	investment cash outlays in year t
C_t	=	cash inflows in year t
T	=	terminal date or end of project
K_A	=	weighted average cost of capital
k_e	=	cost of equity capital
k_d	=	cost of debt financing
t_x	=	tax rate
D/V, S/V	=	debt and equity ratios, respectively
NPV	=	incremental net present value for the project

Equations (18-1) and (18-2) are standard to any introductory finance course.

Political Risk

In examining what determines the NPV, we can note that disagreement between parent and subsidiary can arise because of discount rate K_A, investment cost, and annual cash flows. Political risk can affect all these values. For example, the risk of foreign currency controls can cause some of the future cash flows to be largely ignored by the parent. From the parent's perspective, if funds can no longer be remitted, their value is substantially reduced, since they are not available for dividend payments or to reinvest elsewhere within the multinational. Conversely, once foreign exchange controls are in place, the parent will treat blocked funds as being less valuable. Hence, from the parent's perspective, the cost of any future investments in the country, financed by these blocked funds, is reduced. In both cases, the subsidiary is not directly concerned with the problem of foreign exchange controls, and it will discount all cash flows that are incremental from *its* perspective.

Similarly, political risk may cause the parent to increase the discount rate or required return to reflect that risk. However, if the subsidiary doesn't agree with that perception, it will not increase the discount rate, and as a result its calculation of the present value of the cash inflows and NPV will be higher. Moreover, if foreign exchange controls are enforced, the local capital markets can be isolated from the international capital market. From the subsidiary's perspective, the result may be lower local real interest rates, which make local investment opportunities seem attractive. However, again the parent looking at global opportunities may decide that it would make more sense to try to get capital out of the country for reinvestment elsewhere.

All of these three possible areas of disagreement can cause the NPV to diverge between parent and subsidiary. The use of transfer pricing and other funds-positioning tools will serve to partially reduce the effectiveness of foreign exchange controls, but a discrepancy will still exist. The problem is one of which NPV to accept, particularly if the subsidiary's decision is go and the parent's is "no go." There is a clear theoretical solution to this problem for wholly owned subsidiaries. Since the objective of the firm's management should be to maximize the value of the firm, it should act in the interests of the parent company's stockholders and adopt the parent perspective. Quite simply, if the funds cannot be remitted, they are of no value to the multinational's stockholders.

Forcible reinvestment due to foreign exchange controls is in many ways similar to the dividend paradox of domestic finance. If a company has never paid *and* will never pay dividends, obviously its value is zero. This is because both the existing *and* the future investors will receive nothing from owning it. Hence its value at all points in time must be zero. The paradox is usually resolved in that no firm can expect to retain all its funds forever; it will eventually run out of investment opportunities and start paying dividends. However, there is no reason for a country not to maintain foreign exchange controls forever. Hence the foreign subsidiary may be getting bigger and bigger every year, but if no cash is expected to be received from owning it, its value is zero. In practice, the sensible solution is to apply a "shadow cost" to forcibly reinvested funds, for example, 30 cents on the dollar. This value would then reflect the likely duration of the controls and the opportunities for local investment. However, again this merely narrows the gap between the parent and subsidiary; it does not remove it. Ultimately the parent's

NPV is the overriding criterion, so that the decision must be made from the parent's perspective.

NPV Application Errors

The second reason why parent and local NPVs may differ is faulty application of the NPV framework. The most common errors are in incorrectly choosing t_x and K_A. The tax rate t_x is relevant in two places, the incremental tax that results from the incremental profits and the incremental tax shield that results from debt financing. Here, the errors usually come from a failure to determine the incremental tax rate. From the subsidiary's perspective, the tax rate is the extra tax that it pays *locally*. However, the parent must also consider any incremental tax that it will pay, once dividends are *remitted*.

Questions concerning tax are difficult in the domestic environment. The compounding of tax jurisdictions and philosophies makes for horrendous problems in the analysis of international projects. At this junction, suffice it to note that in most jurisdictions there are two principles for taxing foreign source income. First, income is taxed only once it is remitted (deferral privileges). Second, foreign taxes paid are applied as a credit against any domestic taxes that might be due. The problem that this introduces is that suppose we have a subsidiary in a low-tax jurisdiction that remits all profit to the parent. In this case, the subsidiary will use its low tax rate in Equations (18-1) and (18-2), whereas the parent will recognize the incremental tax that it will pay on the remittance, since the domestic tax rate is higher than the subsidiary's foreign tax rate. Hence the parent's NPV will be lower, because some of the subsidiary's NPV has in fact gone in taxes to the parent company's tax authorities.

Finally, in determining the discount rate K_A, several problems emerge. First, it is not at all uncommon that discount rates differ by several percentage points. The reason is obvious: inflation differs across different countries, and hence the inflationary premium built into the discount rate will differ. What the firm can *never* do is use a discount rate from one country to evaluate cash flows denominated in another currency. The correct procedure is to calculate the real discount rate and then "gross it up" for the inflationary expectations of the relevant country.

Second, debt ratios differ across different subsidiaries, and hence the weights in Equation (18-2) may alter the cost of capital. This will inevitably occur if the multinational maximizes the use of debt financing in a country with subsidized borrowing rates. However, the debt ratio of that country is then *not* appropriate from determining the cost of capital, since the excess debt can only be carried because that subsidiary is part of a multinational. Similarly, the third mistake is to use the local real cost of debt to determine the cost of capital.

In both of these final two examples, if the firm uses local debt norms and local debt costs, it is *negating* the advantage of being a multinational. That advantage is the ability to raise debt internally wherever it is cheapest. As a result, in a country with a high debt cost the firm may have very little debt, whereas in a country with subsidized interest costs it will have a large amount of debt. In both instances there is no effect on the *overall* cost of funds to the multinational. Hence local debt norms and interest costs should be *ignored*, unless local regulations restrict the use of debt funds to projects within that country. In the latter case, as the firm accepts a local project it can also raise more subsidized foreign debt; if the money cannot be removed from the country by transfer pricing or whatever, then its cost is relevant in Equation (18-2).

In general, the financing options open to a multinational are larger than those of a domestic firm. The Eurobond market and foreign bond markets give the multinational the ability to raise funds where their cost is cheapest. Moreover, the extensive national network of the multinationals enables them to take advantage of local incentive programs. These range from regional investment incentives, tax holidays for new investments, export insurance, to loan guarantees, etc. The net result of this greater access to funds is a lower overall cost. However, in the analysis of any *particular* project the discount rate should reflect only the subsidized rates that would not be available unless the project were undertaken. The latter three application errors are frequently made, since they involve subtle points of what constitutes "incremental" to an individual project. However, they all serve to drive a wedge between the parent and the subsidiary, and often result in considerable acrimony between the respective staffs, as particularly the local staff comes to believe that head office just doesn't understand.

Equity Costs

The final component of the capital expenditure analysis decision in Equations (18-1) and (18-2) is the role of k_e, the cost of equity capital. There are two problems that are of interest internationally; first how do you determine it? and second does it give the multinational an advantage?

There are two main techniques for determining the cost of equity capital. The first is through discounted cash flow techniques and the second is through risk premium techniques. The former can be applied without any adjustments to a multinational firm; so the reader is referred for a discussion to any introductory finance textbook. The latter, however, has an international dimension which we will develop.

We know that the costs of issuing various types of securities is a function of their risk; for example, debt normally has a fixed promised coupon rate and thus commands a lower required return than equity which has no promised return whatsoever. Hence the cost of equity in Equation (18-2) is a function of the risk of the foreign investment. Moreover, risk can never be considered in isolation, since investors largely hold *diversified* portfolios, that is, portfolios consisting of a large number of securities. Hence the risk that determines k_e in Equation (18-2) is the risk judged from the point of view of an investor holding a diversified portfolio.

Solnik looked at the impact on the risk of a portfolio of randomly allocating securities to portfolios of various sizes, assuming different policies. The main result is illustrated in Figure 18-4. The upper line indicates that if the portfolio is

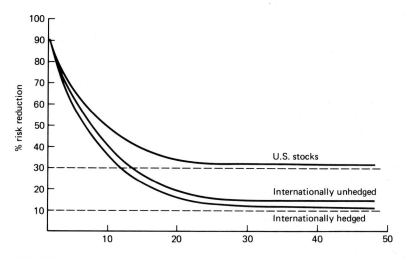

FIGURE 18-4

International diversification. Percentage risk of average security removed by holding it in a diversified portfolio of varying size. [*From Bruno H. Solnik. "Why Not Diversify Internationally." Financial Analysts Journal. (July/August 1974): 48–54.*]

made up entirely of U.S. securities, the portfolio's risk is dramatically reduced as the size of the portfolio is increased. Beyond twenty securities the benefit of further diversification rapidly diminishes. This result is standard; it holds in most countries and indicates that some risk is diversifiable since it represents factors unique to individual securities, whereas some risks are not. The latter risks are usually called undiversifiable, systematic, or market risks.

Solnik's contribution was to include foreign as well as domestic securities in building portfolios. His results confirm other studies in showing that there are gains to *international diversification*. In Figure 18-4, we see that including foreign securities unhedged as well as U.S. securities results in even greater gains to diversification. Moreover, if we remove the exchange risk by hedging the investment in foreign securities, there are slightly more gains to diversification. The implication is that some of the domestic market risk is in fact diversifiable if the investor holds an internationally diversified portfolio.

A by-product of Solnik's observation is the derivation of the international capital asset pricing model (ICAPM),

$$k_{ej} = r + [E(R_w) - r] \; ß_j \tag{18-3}$$

where k_{ej} is the cost of equity for the jth firm, which is a function of the risk-free rate in its own country, plus a risk premium. This risk premium is the product of the world risk premium (the real expected return on the world portfolio minus the risk-free rate) and the security's beta coefficient measured with respect to the world market portfolio. Full discussion of the ICAPM is beyond the scope of a textbook in international business, but those familiar with the domestic CAPM will note that we have just replaced the domestic market portfolio by the world market portfolio. Also note that we have not included a term reflecting exchange risk. This is because from Figure 18-4, we note that exchange risk is largely diversifiable, in that the gains from diversification are pretty much the same regardless of whether the individual hedges or not.

The ICAPM provides an alternative way of estimating the required return, since both beta and the world risk premium can be estimated. It also provides some controversial insights into investment behavior. First, multinationals, being largely headquartered in countries with deep capital markets, should have lower overall equity costs than local corporations trapped in segmented local capital markets. This is because the risk premiums on their equities should be lower as a result of the diversification gains. Second, in practice world capital markets are segmented, so that private investors cannot fully diversify internationally. As a result some have claimed that multinationals serve as a proxy for foreign portfolio investment, since multinationals are diversified internationally in their real cash flow streams. Hence multinationals would have lower cost of equity capitals than domestic corporations.

Both of the foregoing conclusions are controversial, as is the ICAPM. However, what they demonstrate yet again is the ability of the multinational to create value by internalization. If governments create barriers to capital flows, particularly equity flows, to try to keep risk capital at home and maintain national ownership, they impose a cost on domestic corporations; in this case, higher equity costs. The multinational, by diversifying internationally, can take advantage of this opportunity that has been *created* by governments to create value. This it will do by exploiting its advantage of having a lower overall cost of capital, which allows it to enter a market and be more competitive.

Institutional Features

So far we have been considering the technical question of *how* to evaluate capital expenditures, for without the correct framework we cannot possibly expect the right answers. However, capital expenditure analysis and financing for multinationals is also innately more complicated, simply because of the more complicated institutional environment within which it has to be made. We have touched on some of the issues already. Taxes are particularly complicated, so much so that even in international finance books the reader is advised to consult with the tax experts. There remain two other additional institutional factors that usually have to be considered in evaluating major foreign investments: government subsidies and controls and political risk insurance.

Government intervention affects either the profitability of the project or its financing. In considering foreign investments, many countries, for example, Australia and Canada, have foreign investment review agencies, the intent being to ensure that foreign investment benefits the local economy. As a result, foreign investment is often contingent on additional factors such as local employment quotas, local sourcing of components, the transfer of technology, and a degree of local ownership. All this introduces factors which complicate capital expenditure analysis. Although these factors may be involved in some individual domestic projects, internationally the problem is that they are often all compounded into one analysis.

Frequently, the result is to force multinationals to come up with some very hard numbers. For example, if technology is locally licensed, what is the possible impact of its being leaked to different countries? If you have to train local middle management and sell shares locally, how does this affect the probability of forcible divestiture at some future date? In many cases, the result of such local content regulations is to expropriate all the advantages possessed by the multinational. One of the particular problems here is local ownership requirements. The parent's viewpoint is dominant on the assumption that the objective of the firm is to maximize its market value, which is owned by shareholders in its home country. However, once we have joint ventures and significant minority shareholdings traded locally, this neat solution breaks down. The problem now becomes whose market value should be maximized? The result is that, whereas minority ownership reduces the political risk of expropriation, it restricts the multinational's freedom of action. It is therefore not surprising that where political risk is lowered minority shareholdings get bought out. Hence Ford bought out its British minority shareholdings in 1961, and conversely Shell bought out its minority American shareholdings in 1984.

However, government regulation is not all bad. Outside North America, the interventionist approach of most governments creates unique opportunities for the multinational. For example, most countries provide concessionary financing contingent on the use of certain local resources. The British Export Credits Guarantee Department (ECGD), which is equivalent to the U.S. Exim bank, has some of the cheapest money around for export financing as long as you use British equipment. Hence, by structuring an investment to use British equipment, rather than equivalent equipment from elsewhere, the multinational might be able to borrow $10 million at 4 percent interest, instead of a market rate of, say, 12 percent. In effect, this subsidized loan represents a straight gift by the British taxpayers. This value has to be factored into the analysis. The inclusion of subsidies also occurs in domestic capital expenditure analysis, for example, with the proliferation of small business financing programs. However, in an international project, rather than being unusual, it is *rare* not to have to determine the value or cost of a particular government program.

Political risk insurance is available in most countries for exports and foreign direct investment. In the United States, the Overseas Private Investment Corporation (OPIC) was established in January 1971 to provide insurance for U.S. foreign investment against blocked funds, expropriation and war, and revolution and insurrection. The terms of political risk insurance are quite similar across different countries. Usually there has to be approval by the host government of the investment, some type of bilateral agreement on foreign investment, and coverage is limited to some multiple of the initial investment for up to 20 years.

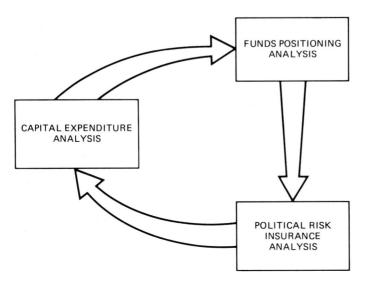

FIGURE 18-5
Multinational capital expenditure analysis.

Coverage for specific types of risk can be separated and insured separately. In the United States, it is estimated that about 70 percent of foreign investment in less developed countries is insured through OPIC.

The problem introduced by political risk insurance is to create another option available for analysis. Instead of analyzing the project on its own, it now must be analyzed with and without political risk insurance. In effect, the company has to decide the incremental value of political risk insurance. Moreover, this is not the end of the analysis. Earlier we discussed funds positioning as a technique to minimize political risk. Hence we have to consider how we can restructure the foreign investment, e.g., fronting loans, long-term contracts at high transfer prices, as an *alternative* to taking out political risk insurance. In Figure 18-5, we schematically illustrate the process. The multinational evaluates the project and then iteratively must consider the impact of funds positioning and political risk insurance. The decision then reflects the optimum structuring of the proposal under analysis.

SUMMARY

To understand international financial management we have to distinguish between two main dimensions. The first is the *institutional* dimension, which basically provides a different framework within which the same familiar problems are solved. The second is the incremental dimension, where the international financial management solves a problem which does not exist within domestic finance. With this approach we analyzed the four main areas of financial management: financial planning and control, working capital management, capital expenditure analysis, and corporate financing.

In international planning and control we initially discussed the twin problems of centralization-decentralization within a multinational and foreign exchange translation. We showed that there are no easy answers to either problem. In particular, we briefly reviewed the complex technical question of foreign exchange translation, since without being able to translate foreign financial statements into a common denominator, no control is possible. Here we contrasted the FAS No. 8 and FAS No. 52 solutions with the theory of exchange rate determination discussed in Chapter 9.

In international working capital management, we discussed the two main incremental problems of foreign exchange exposure hedging and funds positioning. We analyzed the money and forward market hedges, along with other hedging techniques, and considered the fundamental question, is this whole hedging exercise valuable? In funds positioning we analyzed the problems of political risk and heterogeneous tax rates and regulations, to consider how to structure a project so as to maximize the return of cash flow. Liquid asset management was considered in the context of different withholding taxes and controls and foreign exchange movements.

Finally, we considered capital expenditure analysis and corporate financing. Here, we focused on the incremental problems that arise from a more complex valuation problem, resulting from additional valuation principles and more complicated financial environments. We showed how political risk insurance and funds positioning interacted with the overall solution to the capital expenditure analysis problem.

KEY WORDS

Polycentric, ethnocentric, geocentric
Foreign exchange translation
Foreign exchange gain/loss
Purchasing power gain/loss
Centralization-decentralization
Budgets
Foreign exposure management
Money market hedge
Forward market hedge
Leading and lagging
Residual economic exposure

Translation exposure
Transaction exposure
Real economic exposure
Fronting loan
Funds positioning
Withholding tax
Parent-subsidiary perspective
OPIC
Political insurance
International capital asset pricing model
International diversification

QUESTIONS

1 What factors should you consider in organizing the control process in a multinational?
2 How would you compare different foreign subsidiaries in order to evaluate performance?

3 Contrast the economic principles underlying FAS No. 8 and FAS No. 52. When would either one be an acceptable translation methodology?

4 What do we mean by foreign exchange exposure? Differentiate between the three main types.

5 How could you hedge a £10,000 receivable due in 3 months? How would you evaluate the choices?

6 What is the relevance of funds positioning?

7 How does the multinational's problem in evaluating capital expenditures proposals differ from that of a domestic corporation?

8 Why should we adopt the parent perspective even if it means turning down a project with a positive NPV from the perspective of the subsidiary?

9 How does the availability of political risk insurance change the structure of the capital expenditure analysis process?

BIBLIOGRAPHY

Abernathy, William J. *The Productivity Dilemma: Roadblock to Innovation in the Automobile Industry*. Baltimore, Md.: Johns Hopkins University Press, 1978.

Abernathy, William J., Kim B. Clark, and Alan M. Kantrow. "The New Industrial Competition," *Harvard Business Review*. (September–October 1981): 68–79.

Agmon, Tamir, and Charles P. Kindleberger (eds.). *Multinationals from Small Countries*. Cambridge, Mass.: MIT Press, 1977.

Agmon, Tamir, and Seev Hirsch. "Multinational Corporations and the Developing Economies: Potential Gains in a World of Imperfect Markets and Uncertainty," *Oxford Bulletin of Economics and Statistics*. 41 (November 1979): 333–344.

Alexander, Sidney, "The Effects of Devaluation: A Simplified Synthesis of Elasticities and Absorption Approaches," *American Economic Review*. (March 1959): 22–41.

Aliber, Robert Z. "A Theory of Direct Foreign Investment," in *The International Corporation*, Charles P. Kindleberger (ed.). Cambridge, Mass.: MIT Press, 1970.

_____. "The Multinational Enterprise in a Multiple Currency World," in *The Multinational Enterprise*, John H. Dunning (ed.). London: George Allen and Unwin, 1971.

_____. "The Integration of the Offshore and Domestic Banking Systems," *Journal of Monetary Economics*. (1980): 509–526.

_____. *Exchange Risk and Corporate International Finance*. New York: Wiley, 1978.

_____, and C.P. Stickney. "Accounting Measures of Foreign Exchange Exposure: The Long and Short of It," *Accounting Review*. (January 1975): 44–57.

Anthony, Robert. *Planning and Control Systems: A Framework for Analysis*. Cambridge, Mass.: Division of Research, Graduate School of Business Administration, Harvard University, 1965.

Ball, Donald A., and Wendell H. McCulloch, Jr. *International Business*. Plano, Tex.: Business Publications Inc., 1982.

Bank for International Settlements. *Annual Reports*, successive years.

Baranson, Jack. *Technology and the Multinational: Corporate Strategies in a Changing World Economy*. Lexington, Mass.: Lexington Books, D.C. Heath, 1978.

435

Barnett, John S. "Corporate Foreign Exposure Strategy Formulation," *Columbia Journal of World Business*. (Winter 1976): 87−97.

Bartlett, Christopher. "MNCs: Get Off the Reorganization Merry-Go-Round," *Harvard Business Review*. (March−April, 1983): 138−146.

Behrman, J.H., and W.A. Fischer. *Overseas R&D Activity of Transnational Companies*. Cambridge, Mass.: Oelgeschlager, Gunn and Hain, 1980.

Bell, Geoffrey. *The Eurodollar Market and the International Financial System*. New York: Wiley, 1973.

Bergsten, C.F., T. Horst, and T. Moran. *American Multinationals and American Interests*. Washington: Brookings Institution, 1978.

Bilkey, Warren J. "An Attempted Integration of the Literature on the Export Behavior of Firms," *Journal of International Business Studies*. (Summer 1978): 33−46.

Bilson, John F.O. "Rational Expectations and the Exchange Rate," in *The Economics of Exchange Rates*, Jacob A. Frenkel and Harry G. Johnson (eds.). Reading, Mass.: Addison-Wesley, 1978: 75−96.

_____. "Leading Indicators of Currency Devaluation," *Columbia Journal of World Business*. (Winter 1979): 62−76.

Boarman, Patrick N., and David G. Tuerck (eds.). *World Monetary Disorder: National Policies vs. International Imperatives*. New York: Praeger, 1976.

Boddewyn, Jean J. "Foreign Direct Divestment Theory: Is It the Reverse of FDI Theory," *Weltwirtschfliches Archiv*. (1983): 345−355.

Booth, Laurence D. "Hedging and Foreign Exchange Exposure," *Management International Review*. (Spring 1982): 26−42.

_____. "Capital Budgeting Frameworks for the Multinational Corporation," *Journal of International Business Studies*. (Fall 1982): 113−123.

Booth, Laurence D., and Ronald Vanderkraats. "Empirical Tests of the Monetary Approach to Exchange Rate Determination," *Journal of International Money and Finance*. (December 1983).

Boston Consulting Group. *Perspectives on Experience*. Boston, Mass.: Boston Consulting Group Inc., 1972.

Brada, J. "Technology Transfer between the United States and Communist Countries," in *Research in International Business and Finance*: *Technology and Economic Development*, R. Hawkins and J. Prasad (eds.). Greenwich, Conn.: JAI Press, 1981.

Brash, D.T. *American Investment in Australian Industry*. Cambridge, Mass.: Harvard University Press, 1966.

Brenner, Michael J. *The Politics of International Monetary Reform*, Cambridge, Mass.: Ballinger, 1976.

Brooke, Michael Z., and Lee H. Remmers. *The International Firm*. London: Pitman Publishing Ltd., 1977.

_____. *The Strategy of the Multinational Enterprise*, 2d ed. London: Pitman Publishing Ltd., 1978.

Brown, Brendon. *Money, Hard and Soft*. New York: Wiley, 1978.

Buckley, Peter J., and Mark Casson. *The Future of the Multinational Enterprise*. Basingstoke and London: Macmillan, 1976.

Buckley, Peter J., and Mark Casson. "The Optimal Timing of a Foreign Direct Investment," *The Economic Journal*. (March 1980).

Buckley, Peter J., and Howard Davis. "The Place of Licensing in the Theory and Practice of Foreign Operations," in *Research in International Business and Finance: Technology and Economic Development*, R. Hawkins and J. Prasad (eds.). Greenwich, Conn.: JAI Press, 1981.

Buss, Martin D.J. "Managing International Information Systems," *Harvard Business Review*. (September–October 1982): 153–162.

Buzzell, Robert D. "Can You Standardize Multinational Marketing?" *Harvard Business Review*. (November–December 1968).

Calvet, A. Louis. "A Synthesis of Foreign Direct Investment Theories and Theories of the Multinational Firm," *Journal of International Business Studies*. (Spring/Summer 1981): 43–59.

Casson, Mark. *Alternatives to the Multinational Enterprise*. London: Macmillan, 1979.

_____. *The Entrepreneur: An Economic Theory*. Oxford: Martin Robertson, 1983.

_____ (ed.). *The Growth of International Business*. London: George Allen and Unwin, 1983.

Caves, Richard E. "International Corporations: The Industrial Economics of Foreign Investment," *Economica*. 38 (1971): 1–27.

_____. *Multinational Enterprise and Economic Analysis*. Cambridge and New York: Cambridge University Press, 1982.

Caves, Richard E., and Harry G. Johnson (eds.). *Readings in International Business*. London: George Allen and Unwin, 1968.

Caves, Richard E., M.E. Porter, and A.M. Spence. *Competition in the Open Economy: A Model Applied to Canada*. Cambridge, Mass.: Harvard University Press, 1980.

Chandler, Alfred J., Jr. *Strategy and Structure: Chapters in the History of the American Industrial Enterprise*. Cambridge, Mass.: MIT Press, 1962.

Chandler, Alfred, and H. Daems (eds.). *Managerial Hierarchies*. Cambridge, Mass.: Harvard University Press, 1980.

Coase, Ronald H. "The Nature of the Firm," *Economica*. 4 (1937): 386–405.

Contractor, Farok J. "The 'Profitability' of Technology Licensing by U.S. Multinationals: A Framework for Analysis and an Empirical Study," *Journal of International Business Studies*. 11 (Fall 1980).

_____. "In Defence of Licensing: Its Increased Role in International Operations," *Columbia Journal of World Business*. (1981).

Coombs, Charles A. *The Arena of International Finance*. New York: Wiley, 1976.

Cooper, Kerry, Donald Fraser, and R. Malcolm Richards. "The Impact of SFAS #8 on Financial Management Practices," *Financial Executive*. (June 1978): 26–31.

Corden, W.M. "The Theory of International Trade," in *Economic Analysis and the Multinational Enterprise*, J.H. Dunning (ed.). New York: Praeger, 1974.

_____. *Trade Policy and Economic Welfare*. Oxford: Oxford University Press, 1974.

Cornell, Bradford. "Spot Rates, Forward Rates, and Exchange Market Efficiency," *Journal of Financial Economics*. (August 1977): 55–65.

Cornell, Bradford, and J.K. Dietrich. "The Efficiency of the Foreign Exchange Market under Floating Exchange Rates," *Review of Economics and Statistics* (February 1978): 111–120.

Cory, Peter F., and John H. Dunning. "The Eclectic Theory of International Production and MNE Involvement in Eastern Europe and Latin America," in *Multinational Corporations in Latin America and Eastern Europe*, P. Marer and J. Lombardi (eds.). Bloomington, Indiana, 1982.

Crockett, Andrew D., and Morris Goldstein. "Inflation under Fixed and Flexible Exchange Rates," *Staff Papers*. (November 1976): 509–544.

Czinkota, Michael R., and Wesley J. Johnston. "Exporting: Does Sales Volume Make a Difference?" *Journal of International Business Studies* (Spring/Summer 1983): 147–153.

Daniels, John D., Ernest W. Ogram, and Lee H. Radebaugh. *International Business: Environments and Operations*, 3d ed. Don Mills, Ontario: Addison-Wesley, 1982.

Davidson, William H. *Global Strategic Management*. New York: Wiley, 1982.

Davidson, William H., and Phillipe Haspeslagh. "Shaping a Global Product Organization," *Harvard Business Review*. (July–August 1982): 125–132.

Davies, Howard. "Technology Transfer through Commercial Transactions," *Journal of Industrial Economics*. 26 (Fall 1977).

Davies, Stanley M. *Managing and Organizing Multinational Corporations*. New York: Pergamon Press, 1979.

_____. "Organizational Design," in *Handbook of International Business*, Ingo Walter and Tracy Murray (eds.). New York: Wiley, 1982.

Denis, Jack, Jr. "How Well Does the International Money Market Track the Interbank Forward Market?" *Financial Analysts Journal*. (January–February 1976): 50–54.

Dornbusch, Rudiger. "The Theory of Flexible Exchange Rate Regimes and Macroeconomic Policy," *Scandinavian Journal of Economics*. (May 1976): 255–275. Reprinted in *The Economics of Exchange Rates*, Jacob A. Frenkel and Harry G. Johnson (eds.). Reading, Mass.: Addison-Wesley, 1978.

_____. "Expectations and Exchange Rate Dynamics," *Journal of Political Economy*. (December 1976): 1161–1176.

Dufey, Gunter, and Ian Giddy. *The International Money Market*. Englewood Cliffs, N.J.: Prentice-Hall, 1978.

_____. "Forecasting Exchange Rates in a Floating World," *Euromoney*. (November 1975): 28–35.

Dukes, Ronald. *An Empirical Investigation of the Effects of Statement of Financial Accounting Standards No. 8 on Security Return Behaviour*. Stamford, Conn.: Financial Accounting Standards Board, 1978.

Dunning, John H. *American Investment in British Manufacturing Industry*, London: George Allen and Unwin, 1958.

_____. "Multinational Enterprises, Market Structure, Economic Power and Industrial Policy," *Journal of World Trade Law*. (November/December 1975): 575–613.

_____. "Trade, Location of Economic Activity and the MNE: A Search for an Eclectic Approach," in *The International Allocation of Economic Activity, Proceedings of a Nobel Symposium held in Stockholm*, Bertil Ohlin et al. (eds.). London: Macmillan, 1977. Reprinted as Chapter 3 in his *International Production and the Multinational Enterprise*. London: George Allen and Unwin, 1981.

_____. "Explaining Outward Direct Investment of Devloping Countries: In Support of the Eclectic Theory of International Production," *Weltwirtschaftliches Archiv*. 49 (1980).

_____. "Explaining Changing Patterns of International Production: In Defense of the Eclectic Theory," *The Oxford Bulletin of Economics and Statistics*. 41 (1979): 269–296. Reprinted as Chapter 3 in his *International Production and the Multinational Enterprise*. London: George Allen and Unwin, 1981.

_____. "Explaining the International Direct Investment Position of Countries: Towards a Dynamic or Developmental Approach," *Weltwirtschaftliches Archiv*. 11:1 (1981a): 30–64.

Eiteman, David, and Arthur Stonehill. *Multinational Business Finance*, 3d ed. Reading, Mass.: Addison-Wesley, 1982.

Elinder, Erik. "How International Can European Advertising Be?" *Journal of Marketing Management*. (April 1965): 7–11.

Ensor, Richard. "The World's Best Foreign Exchange Dealer," *Euromoney* (September 1980): 92–99.

Ernst and Whinney. *International Accounting Standards* (September 1982).

Euromoney. "Annual Financing Report 1983." (March 1983).

Folks, William R., Jr. "Optimal Foreign Borrowing Strategies with Operations in the Forward Exchange Markets," *Journal of Financial and Quantitative Analysis*. (June 1978): 245–254.

Folks, William, and Stanley R. Stansell. "The Use of Discriminant Analysis in Forecasting Exchange Risk Movements," *Journal of International Business Studies*. (Spring 1975): 33–50.

Forsyth, David J.C. *U.S. Investment in Scotland*. New York: Praeger, 1972.

Fortune. "The 500 Largest Industrial Corporations Outside the U.S.," annual directory, various issues.

Foulkes, Fred K., and Jeffrey L. Hirsch. "People Make Robots Work," *Harvard Business Review* (January–February 1984): 94–102.

Frankel, Jacob A. "The Diversifiability of Exchange Risk," *Journal of International Economics*. 9 (1979): 379–393.

_____. "A Monetary Approach to the Exchange Rate: Doctrinal Aspects and Empirical Evidence," *Scandinavian Journal of Economics*. (May 1976): 200–224. Reprinted in *The Economics of Exchange Rates*, Jacob A. Frenkel and Harry G. Johnson (eds.). Reading, Mass.: Addison-Wesley, 1978.

_____. "Efficiency and Volatility of Exchange Rates and Prices in the 1970's," *Columbia Journal of World Business*. (Winter 1979): 15–27.

Franko, Lawrence G. *Joint Venture Survival in Multinational Corporations*. New York: Praeger, 1971.

_____. "Patterns in the Multi-National Spread of Continental Enterprise," *Journal of International Business*. (Fall 1975).

Gabriel, Peter. *The International Transfer of Corporate Skills*. Cambridge, Mass.: Harvard University Press, 1966.

Garvin, David A. "Quality on the Line," *Harvard Business Review*. (September–October 1983): 64–75.

General Agreement on Tariffs and Trade. Activities in Geneva: GATT annual.

Giddy, Ian H., "An Integrated Theory of Exchange Rate Equilibrium," *Journal of Financial and quantitative Analysis*. (December 1976): 863–892.

_____. "Why It Doesn't Pay to Make a Habit of Forward Hedging," *Euromoney*. (December 1976): 96–100.

_____. "Measuring the World Foreign Exchange Market," *Columbia Journal of World Business*. (Winter 1979): 36–48.

Giddy, Ian H., and Gunter Dufey. "The Random Behavior of Flexible Exchange Rates: Implications for Forecasting," *Journal of International Business Studies*. (Spring 1975): 1–32.

Giddy, Ian, and Alan M. Rugman. "A Model of Trade, Foreign Direct Investment and Licensing," mimeographed, Graduate School of Business, Columbia University, December 1979.

Giersch, Herbert (ed.). *On the Economics of Intra-Industry Trade*. Tübingen: J.C.B. Mohr (Pal Siebick), 1979.

Globerman, Stephen. "Technological Diffusion in the Canadian Tool and Die Industry," *Review of Economic Statistics*. 57 (November 1975).

_____. "Foreign Direct Investment and 'Spillover' Efficiency Benefits in Canadian Manufacturing Industries," *Canadian Journal of Economics*. 12 (February 1975).

Goldar, J.D., and Mariann Jelinek. "Plan for Economies of Scope," *Harvard Business Review*. (November−December 1983): 141−148.

Goldstein, Henry N. "Foreign Currency Futures: Some Further Aspects," *Economic Perspective*. Federal Reserve Bank of Chicago (November−December 1983): 3−13.

Gonzalez, Richard, and Anant Negandhi. *The United States Overseas Executive: His Orientation and Career Patterns*. East Lansing, Mich.: Michigan State University, 1967.

Goodman, Laurie. "New Options Markets," *Quarterly Review*. Federal Reserve Bank of New York (Autumn 1983): 35−47.

Goodman, Stephen. "Foreign Exchange Forecasting Techniques: Implications for Business and Policy," *Journal of Finance* (May 1979): 415−427.

_____. "Technical Analysis Still Beats Econometrics," *Euromoney*. (August 1981): 48−59.

Gordon, Myron, and David Fowler. *The Drug Industry: A Case Study of the Effect of Foreign Control on the Canadian Economy*. Toronto: James Lorimer, 1981.

Gray, H. Peter. *International Trade, Investment, and Payments*. Boston: Houghton Mifflin, 1979.

_____. "The Theory of International Trade among Industrialised Nations," *Weltwirtschaftliches Archiv*. 116: 3 (1980).

_____. "Toward a Unified Theory of International Trade, International Production and Foreign Direct Investment," in *International Investment and Capital Movement*, J. Black, and John H. Dunning, (eds.). London: Macmillan, 1982.

Grosse, Robert. *Foreign Investment Codes and Location of Direct Investment*. New York: Praeger, 1980.

_____. "The Theory of Foreign Direct Investment," *South Carolina Essays in International Business* no. 3 (December 1981).

_____. "Codes of Conduct on Multinational Enterprises: A Solution?" *Journal of World Trade Law*. (July, August 1982).

Grubel, Herbert G. *International Economics*, 2d ed. Homewood, Ill.: Irwin, 1981.

Grubel, Herbert, and Harry G. Johnson (eds.). *Effective Protection*. Geneva: GATT, 1971.

Grubel, Herbert G., and Peter J. Lloyd. *Intra-industry Trade: The Theory and Measurement of International Trade in Differentiated Products*. London: Macmillan, 1975.

Gruber, William, Dileep, Mehta, and Raymond Vernon. "The R&D Factor in International Trade and International Investment of U.S. Industries," *Journal of Political Economics*. 75 (February 1967).

Hayes, Robert H. "Why Japanese Factories Work," *Harvard Business Review*. (July−August 1981): 56−66.

Hayes, Robert H., and Steven G. Wheelwright. "The Dynamics of Process-Product Life Cycles," *Harvard Business Review*. (March−April 1979): 127−136.

Hedley, Barry. "A Fundamental Approach to Strategy Development," *The Boston Consulting Group*. London: December, 1976.

Heenan, David A., and Warren J. Keegan. "The Rise of Third World Multinationals," *Harvard Business Review* (January−February 1979).

Heenan, David A., and Howard Perlmutter. *Multinational Organization and Development*. Reading, Mass.: Addison-Wesley, 1979.

Helleiner, G.K. "The Role of Multinational Corporations in the Less Developed Countries' Trade in Technology," *World Development*. 3 (1975): 161−189.

Hennert, Jean-François. *A Theory of Multinational Enterprise*. Ann Arbor: University of Michigan Press, 1982.

Hilley, John L., Carl R. Beidleman, and James A. Greenleaf. "Does Covered Interest Arbitrage Dominate in Foreign Exchange Markets?" *Columbia Journal of World Business*. (Winter 1979): 99−107.

Hirsch, Seev. "An International Trade and Investment Theory of the Firm," *Oxford Economic Papers*. 28 (July 1976): 258−270.

Hofer, Charles W., and Dan Schendel. *Strategy Formulation: Analytical Concepts*. Minnesota: West Publishing Co., 1978.

Hogendorn, Jan, and Wilson Brown. *The New International Economics*. Reading, Mass.: Addison-Wesley, 1979.

Holzman, F.D. *International Trade under Communism*. New York: Basic Books, 1976.

Hood, Neil, and Stephen Young. *The Economics of Multinational Enterprise*. London: Longman, 1979.

Horst, Thomas. "The Simple Analytics of Multi-National Firm Behaviour," in *International Trade and Money*, Michael B. Connolly and Alexander Swoboda (eds.). Toronto: University of Toronto Press, 1973.

_____. "American Taxation of Multinational Firms," *American Economic Review*. 67 (June 1977): 376−389.

Hout, Thomas, Michael E. Porter, and Eileen Rudden. "How Global Companies Win Out," *Harvard Business Review* (September−October 1982).

Hufbauer, Gary C. *Synthetic Materials and the Theory of International Trade*. Cambridge, Mass.: Harvard University Press, 1966.

_____. "The Multinational Corporation and Direct Investment," in *International Trade and Finance: Frontiers for Research*, P.B. Kenen (ed.). New York: Cambridge University Press, 1975.

Hume, David. *Essays and Treatises on Several Subjects*. London, 1772.

Hymer, Stephen H. *The International Operations of National Firms: A Study of Direct Foreign Investment*. Cambridge, Mass.: MIT Press, 1976.

Ibbotson, Roger G., Richard Carr, and Anthony Robinson. "International Equity and Bond Returns," *Financial Analysts Journal* (July−August 1982): 61−83.

Ingo, Walter, and Tom Gladwyn. *Multinationals under Fire*. New York: Wiley, 1981.

Isard, Peter. "How Far Can We Push The Law of One Price?" *American Economic Review*. (December 1977): 942−948.

Jacque, Laurent L. "Management of Foreign Exchange Risk: A Review Article," *Journal of International Business Studies*. (Spring/Summer 1981): 81−103.

Johansson, Johny K. *Japanese Marketing Strategies*. Stockholm, Sweden: Marknadstekniskt Centrum, February 1981.

Johansson, Johny K., and J.E. Vahlne. "The Internationalization Process of the Firm: A Model of Knowledge Development and Increasing Foreign Market Commitments," *Journal of International Business Studies*. 8:1 (Spring/Summer 1977): 23−32.

Johanson, Jan, and Jan-Eric Vahlne. *The Internationalization Process of the Firm*. University of Uppsala, Department of Business Administration. December 1974.

Johanson, Jan, and Paul Wiedersheim. "The Internationalization of the Firm—Four Swedish Cases," *Journal of Management Studies*. (1975).

Johnson, Harry G. "The Efficiency and Welfare Implications of the International Corporation," in *The International Corporation*, Charles P. Kindleberger (ed.). Cambridge, Mass.: MIT Press, 1970.

_____. *Comparative Cost and Commercial Policy Theory for a Developing World Economy*, Wicksell Lectures. Stockholm: Almqvist & Wiksell, 1968.

Jones, R.W. "The Role of Technology in the Theory of International Trade," in *The Technology Factor in International Trade*, Raymond Vernon (ed.). Universities-National Bureau Conference Series no. 22 (New York: National Bureau of Economic Research, 1970).

Keegan, Warren J. *Multinational Marketing Management*, 2d ed. Englewood Cliffs, N.J.: Prentice-Hall, 1980.

Keynes, John M. *The General Theory of Employment, Interest and Money*. London: Macmillan, 1936.

Kiechel, Walter III. "Playing the Global Game," *Fortune* (November 16, 1981).

Killing, Peter J. "How to Make a Global Joint Venture Work," *Harvard Business Review*. (May–June 1982): 120–127.

Kindleberger, Charles P. *American Business Abroad: Six Lectures on Direct Investment*. New Haven: Yale University Press, 1969.

Kindleberger, Charles P., and Peter H. Lindert. *International Economics*, 7th ed. Homewood, Ill.: Irwin, 1982.

Knickerbocker, Fredrick T. *Oligopolistic Reaction and Multinational Enterprise*. Boston: Division of Research, Graduate School of Business Administration, Harvard University, 1973.

Kobrin, Stephen J. "Political Assessments by International Firms: Models or Methodologies," *Journal of Policy Modelling*. (1981).

Kohlhagen, Steven, W. "The Performance of the Foreign Exchange Markets: 1971–1974," *Journal of International Business Studies*. (Fall 1975): 33–39.

_____. *The Behavior of Foreign Exchange Markets—A Critical Survey of the Empirical Literature*. New York: New York University Monograph Series in Finance and Economics, no. 3, 1978.

_____. "The Forward Rate as an Unbiased Predictor of the Future Spot Rate," *Columbia Journal of World Business*. (Winter 1979): 77–85.

Kojima, Kiyoshi. *Direct Foreign Investment*. London: Croom Helm, 1978.

Kotler, Philip. *Marketing Management: Planning, Analysis and Control*, 4th ed. Englewood Cliffs, N.J.: Prentice-Hall, 1981.

Kotler, Philip, and Liam Fahey. "The World's Champion Marketers: The Japanese?" *American Marketing Association Conference*. (Chicago, August 5, 1982).

Krauss, Melvyn B. *The New Protectionism*. New York: University Press, 1978.

Kreinin, M.E. *International Economics*, 4th ed. New York: Harcourt, Brace, Jovanovich, 1983.

Kreuger, Anne O. "The Political Economy of a Rent Seeking Society," *American Economic Review*. (June 1974).

Krugman, Paul. "A Model of Innovation, Technology Transfer, and the World Distribution of Income," *Journal of Political Economy*. 87 (April 1979).

_____. "Vehicle Currencies and the Structure of International Exchange," *Journal of Money, Credit and Banking*. (August 1980): 513–526.

Kubarych, Roger. *Foreign Exchange Markets in the United States*, rev. ed. Federal Reserve Bank of New York, March 1983.

Lake, A.W. "Technology Creation and Technology Transfer by Multinational Firms," in *Research in International Business and Finance: An Annual Compilation of Research*, vol. 1, *The Effects of Multinational Corporations*, R.G. Hawkins (ed.). Greenwich, Conn.: JAI Press, 1979.

Lall, Sanjaya. "The International Allocation of Research Activity by U.S. Multinationals," *Oxford Bulletin of Economics and Statistics*. 41 (November 1979).

_____. *The Multinational Corporation*. London: Macmillan, 1980.

_____, and Paul Strecten. *Foreign Investment, Transnationals and Developing Countries.* London: Macmillan, 1977.

Lall, Sanjaya, et al. *The New Multinationals: The Spread of Third World Enterprises.* Chichester, U.K.: Wiley, 1984.

Lecraw, Donald J. "The Uranium Cartel: An Interim Report," *Business Quarterly.* (Winter 1977).

_____. "Direct Investment by Firms from Less Developed Countries," *Oxford Economic Papers.* 29:4 (1977).

_____. "Performance of Transnational Corporations in Less Developed Countries," *Journal of International Business Studies.* (Spring 1983): 15–33.

_____. "Bargaining Power and the Success of TNCs in LDCs," *Journal of International Business Studies.* (in print 1984)

Lessard, Donald. "World National and Industry Factors in Equity Returns: Implications for Risk through International Diversification," *Financial Analysts Journal.* (January–February 1976): 32–38.

Levich, Richard M. "On the Efficiency of Markets for Foreign Exchange," in *International Economic Policy: An Assessment of Theory and Evidence*, J. Frenkel and R. Dornbusch (eds.). Baltimore: John Hopkins Press, 1978.

_____. "Are Forward Exchange Rates Unbiased Predictors of Future Spot Rates?" *Columbia Journal of World Business.* (Winter 1979): 49–61.

_____. *The International Monetary Market: An Assessment of Forecasting Techniques and Market Efficiency.* Greenwich, Conn.: JAI Press, 1979.

_____. "Analyzing the Accuracy of Foreign Exchange Forecasting Services: Theory and Evidence," in *Exchange Risk and Exposure: Current Development in International Financial Development*, Clas Wihlborg and Richard Levich (eds.). Lexington, Mass.: Heath, 1980.

_____. "How to Compare Chance with Forecasting Expertise," *Euromoney.* (August 1981): 61–78.

Levitt, Theodore. "The Globalization of Markets," *Harvard Business Review.* (May–June 1983): 92–102.

Lietaer, Bernard A. "Managing Risks in Foreign Exchange," *Harvard Business Review.* (March/April 1970): 127–138.

Logue, Dennis E., Richard Sweeney, and Thomas Willett, "The Speculative Behavior of Exchange Rates during the Current Float," *Journal of Business Research.* 6:2 (1978): 147–158.

Magee, Stephen P. "Information and the Multinational Corporation: An Appropriability Theory of Direct Foreign Investment," in *The New International Economic Order*, Jagdish N. Bhagwati (ed.). Cambridge, Mass.: MIT Press, 1977.

_____. "Contracting and Spurious Deviations from Purchasing-Power Parity," in *The Economics of Exchange Rates*, Jacob A. Frenkel and Harry G. Johnson (eds.). Reading, Mass.: Addison-Wesley, 1978, 67–74.

Makin, John H. "Fixed versus Floating: A Red Herring," *Columbia Journal of World Business.* (Winter 1979): 7–14.

Mansfield, Edwin. "Technology and Technological Change," in *Economic Analysis and the Multinational Enterprise*, J.H. Dunning (ed.). London: George Allen and Unwin, 1974, chapter 6.

Mansfield, Edwin, and A. Romeo. "Technology Transfer to Overseas Subsidiaries by U.S.-Based Firms," *Quarterly Journal of Economics.* 95 (December 1980).

Mansfield, Edwin, A. Romeo, and S. Wagner. "Foreign Trade and U.S. Research Development," *Review of Economics and Statistics.* 61 (February 1979).

Mansfield, Edwin, J. Teece, and S. Wagner. "Overseas Research and Development by U.S.-Based Firms," *Review of Economics and Statistics*. 46 (May 1979): 187–196.

Maslow, Abraham. *Motivation and Personality*. New York: Harper and Brothers, 1954.

Mason, Hal R., Robert R. Miller, and Dale R. Weigel. *International Business*, 2d ed. Toronto: Wiley, 1981.

Mattson, Lars-Gunnar. *Systemforsaljing*. Stockholm, Sweden: Marknadstekniskt Centrum, April 1975.

McKinnon, Ronald I. *Money in International Exchanges (The Convertible Currency System)*. New York and Oxford: Oxford University Press, 1979.

McManus, John. "The Theory of the International Firm," in *The Multinational Firm and the Nation State*, G. Paquet (ed.). Toronto: Collier-Macmillan, 1972.

Miller, Edwin L. "The International Selection Decision: A Study of Some Dimensions of Managerial Behavior in the Selection Decision Process," *Academy of Management Journal*. 16:2 (1973): 239–252.

Miller, Edwin L., and Joseph Cheng. "A Closer Look at the Decision to Accept an Overseas Position," *Management International Review* 18:3 (1978): 25–33.

Moxon, Richard W. "Export Platform Foreign Investments in the Theory of International Production," Mimeographed, 1980.

Nakane, Jinichiro, and Robert W. Hall. "Management Specs for Stockless Production," *Harvard Business Review*. (May–June 1983): 84–91.

Newbould, G.D., Peter J. Buckley, and J.C. Thurwell. *Going International*. New York: Wiley, 1978.

Niehaus, Jurg, and John Hewson. "The Eurodollar Market and Monetary Theory, *Journal of Money, Credit and Banking*. (February 1976): 1–27.

Officer, Lawrence H. "The Purchasing-Power-Parity Theory of Exchange Rates: A Review Article," *IMF Staff Papers*. (March 1976): 1–60.

Organization for Economic Cooperation and Development (OECD). *The Impact of the Newly Industrializing Continuum on Production and Trade in Manufacturers*. Paris, 1979.

Ouchi, William G. *Theory Z: How American Business Can Meet the Japanese Challenge*. Reading, Mass.: Addison-Wesley, 1981.

Parry, Thomas G. "Technology and the Size of the Multinational Corporation Subsidiary: Evidence from the Australian Manufacturing Sector," *Journal of Industrial Economics*. 23 (December 1974).

Pascale, Richard Tanner, and Anthony G. Athos. *The Art of Japanese Management: Applications for American Executives*. New York: Simon and Schuster, 1981.

Penrose, Edith. *The Theory of the Growth of the Firm*. Oxford: Basil Blackwell, 1958.

_____. "International Patenting and the Less-Developed Countries," *Economic Journal*. 83 (September 1973).

Perlmutter, Howard V. "The Tortuous Evolution of the Multinational Corporation," *Columbia Journal of World Business*. (January–February 1969): 9–18.

Peters, Thomas J., and Robert H. Waterman, Jr. *In Search of Excellence: Lessons from America's Best-Run Companies*. New York: Harper and Row, 1982.

Porter, Michael E. *Competitive Strategy*. New York: The Free Press, 1980.

_____. "Industrial Organization and the Evolution of Concepts for Strategic Planning: The New Learning," *Managerial and Decision Economics*. 4:3 (1983).

Poynter, Thomas A. "Government Intervention in Less Developed Countries: The Experience of Multinational Companies," *Journal of International Business Studies* 13:1 (Spring/Summer 1982): 9–26.

_____, and Alan M. Rugman. "World Product Mandates: How Will Multinationals Respond?" *Business Quarterly*. 47:3 (October 1982): 54−61.

Prahalad, C.K., and Yves L. Doz. "An Approach to Strategic Control in MNCs," *Sloan Management Review*. (Summer 1981): 5−13.

_____. "Headquarters Influence and Strategic Control in MNCs," *Sloan Management Review*. (Fall 1981): 15−29.

Pugel, T.A. "Technology Transfer and the Neoclassical Theory of International Trade," in *Technology Transfer and Economic Development*, R.G. Hawkins and A.J. Prasad (eds.). Greenwich, Conn.: JAI Press, 1981.

Ragazzi, Giorgio. "Theories of the Determinants of Direct Foreign Investment," *IMF Staff Papers*. (July 1973): 471−498.

Reynolds, Calvin. "Career Paths and Compensation in the Multinational Enterprise," *Columbia Journal of World Business*. (November−December 1972): 77−87.

Robinson, Richard D. *National Conditions of Foreign Business Entry*. New York: Praeger, 1976.

_____. *International Business Management*. New York: Holt, Reinhart, & Winston, 1978.

_____. "Positioning the Corporation to Meet International Competition," *UMBC Economic Review*. (1982): 42−47.

Robock, Stefan H., and Kenneth Simmonds. *International Business and Multinational Enterprises*, 3d ed. Homewood, Ill.: Irwin, 1983.

Rodriquez, Rita M. *Foreign Exchange Management in U.S. Multinationals*. Lexington, Mass.: Lexington Books, 1980.

_____. "Corporate Exchange Risk Management: Theme and Aberrations," *Journal of Finance*. (May 1981): 427−439.

Rogalski, Richard J., and Joseph D. Vinso. "The Price Level Variations as Predictors of Flexible Exchange Rates," *Journal of International Business Studies*. (Spring−Summer 1977): 71−81.

Ronstadt, Robert. *Research and Development Abroad by U.S. Multinationals*. New York: Praeger, 1977.

Rugman, Alan M. *International Diversification and the Multinational Enterprise*. Lexington: D.C. Heath, 1979.

_____. "Internalization as a General Theory of Foreign Direct Investment," *Weltwirtschaftliches Archiv*. 116:2 (June 1980a): 365−379.

_____. *Multinationals in Canada: Theory, Performance and Economic Impact*. Boston: Martinus Nijhoff, 1980b.

_____. "A New Theory of the Multinational Enterprise: Internationalization versus Internalization," *Columbia Journal of World Business*. (Spring 1980c): 23−29.

_____. *Inside the Multinationals: The Economics of Internal Markets*. London: Croom Helm, New York: Columbia University Press, 1981.

_____. "A Test of Internalization Theory," *Journal of Managerial and Decision Economics*. (September 1981b).

_____ (ed.). *New Theories of the Multinational Enterprise*. New York: St. Martin's Press, 1982.

_____, and Jocelyn M. Bennett. "Technology Transfer and World Product Mandating in Canada," *Columbia Journal of World Business*. (Winter 1982): 58−62.

_____, and Lorraine Eden (eds.). *Multinationals and Transfer Pricing*. New York: St. Martin's Press, 1985.

Rutenberg, David P. *Multinational Management*. Boston: Little Brown, 1982.

_____. "Maneuvering Liquid Assets in a Multinational Company: Formulation and Deterministic Solution Procedures," *Management Science*. (June 1970): 671–684.

Safarian, A.E. *Foreign Ownership of Canadian Industry*. Toronto: McGraw-Hill, 1966.

Salvatore, Schiavo-Campo. *International Economics: An Introduction to Theory and Policy*. Cambridge, Mass.: Winthrop, 1978.

Scammell, W.M. *International Monetary Policy: Bretton Woods and After*. New York: Wiley, 1975.

Shapiro, Alan C., and David P. Rutenberg. "When to Hedge Against Devaluation," *Management Science*. (August 1974): 1514–1530.

_____. "Managing Exchange Risks in a Floating World," *Financial Management*. (Summer 1976): 48–58.

_____. "Defining Exchange Risk," *Journal of Business*. (January 1977): 27–39.

Sodersten, Bo. *International Economics*. London: Macmillan, 1970.

Solnik, Bruno H. "Why Not Diversify Internationally," *Financial Analysts Journal*. (July/August 1974): 48–54.

_____. "International Parity Conditions and Exchange Risk," *Journal of Banking and Finance*. (August 1981): 281–293.

Sommers, Montrose, and Jerome Kernan. "Why Products Flourish Here, Fizzle There," *Columbia Journal of World Business*. (March–April 1967): 89–97.

Sorenson, Ralph Z., and Ulrich E. Wiechmann. "How Multinationals View Marketing Standardization," *Harvard Business Review*. (May–June 1975): 54–63.

Stanley, Marjorie T., and Stanley B. Block. "Response by United States Financial Managers to Financial Accounting Standard No. 8," *Journal of International Business Studies*. (Fall 1978): 85–99.

Steiner, George A. *Strategic Planning: What Every Manager Must Know*. New York: Free Press, 1979.

Stern, Robert M. "Tariffs and Other Measures of Trade Control: A Survey of Recent Developments," *Journal of Economic Literature*. 2:3 (September): 71.

Stokes, Houston H., and Hugh Neuburger. "Interest Arbitrage, Forward Speculation and the Determination of the Forward Exchange Rate," *Columbia Journal of World Business*. (Winter 1979): 86–98.

Stopford, John M. "Changing Perspectives on Investment by British Manufacturing Multinationals," *Journal of International Business Studies*. 7:2 (Winter 1976).

_____, John H. Dunning, and Klaus O. Haberich. *The World Directory of Multinational Enterprises*. London: Macmillan 1980.

_____, and John H. Dunning. *Multinationals—Company Performance and Global Trends*. London: Macmillan, 1983.

_____, and Louis T. Wells, Jr. *Managing the Multinational Enterprise: Organization of the Firm and Ownership of the Subsidiaries*. New York: Basic Books, 1972.

Teece, David J. *The Multinational Corporation and the Resource Cost of International Technology Transfer*. Cambridge, Mass.: Ballinger, 1976.

_____. "A Transaction Cost Theory of the Multinational Enterprise," University of Reading Discussion Paper in International Investment and Business Studies, no. 66 (September 1982).

Telesio, Piero. *Technology Licensing and Multinational Enterprises*. New York: Praeger, 1979.

Thorelli, Hans B. "The Information Seekers: Multinational Strategy Target," *California Management Review*. (1980–1981).

Tichy, Noel M., Charles J. Fombrun, and Mary Anne Devanna. "Strategic Human Resource Management," *Sloan Management Review*. (Winter 1978): 47–61.

Tilton, John E. *The International Diffusion of Technology: The Case of Semi-Conductors*. Washington: Brookings Institution, 1971.

Triffin, R. *Gold and the Dollar Crisis*. New Haven, Conn.: Yale Press, 1960.

Tsurumi, Yoshihiro. *The Japanese Are Coming: A Multinational Spread of Japanese Firms*. Cambridge, Mass.: Ballinger, 1976.

United Nations. *Multinational Corporations In World Development*. New York, 1973.

_____. *Transnational Corporations In World Developments: A Re-examination*. New York, 1978.

Vernon, Raymond. "International Investment and International Trade in the Product Cycle," *Quarterly Journal of Economics*. 80 (May 1966).

_____. *Sovereignty at Bay: The Multinational Spread of U.S. Enterprises*. New York: Basic Books, 1971.

_____. Storm over the Multinationals. Cambridge, Mass.: Harvard University Press, 1977.

_____. "The Product Cycle Hypothesis in a New International Environment," *Oxford Bulletin of Economics and Statistics*. 41 (November 1979).

_____. "Gone Are the Cash Cows of Yesteryear," *Harvard Business Review*. 58 (November–December 1980): 150–155.

Vernon, Raymond, and Yain Aharoni. *State-Owned Enterprises in the Western Economies*. London: Croom Helm, 1981.

Walters, Kenneth D., and Joseph Monsen. "State Owned Business Abroad: New Competitive Threat," *Harvard Business Review*. 57 (March–April 1979): 160–170.

Wells, L.T., Jr. "A Product Life Cycle for International Trade?" *Journal of Marketing*. 32 (July 1968): 1–6.

_____ (ed.). *The Product Cycle and International Trade*. Boston: Division of Research, Graduate School of Business Administration, Harvard University, 1972.

_____. *Third World Multinationals*. Cambridge, Mass.: MIT Press, 1983.

Westerfield, Janice M. "Empirical Properties of Foreign Exchange Rates under Fixed and Floating Rate Regimes," *Journal of International Economics*. (June 1977): 181–200.

Wheelwright, Steven C. "Japan—Where Operations Really Are Strategic," *Harvard Business Review*. (July–August 1983): 67–74.

Whitman, Marina. "The Payments Adjustment Process and the Exchange Rate Regime: What Have We Learned?" *American Economic Review*. (May 1975): 133–136.

Whyte, William H., Jr., *The Organization Man*. New York: Simon and Schuster, 1956.

Williamson, J. "Surveys in Applied Economics: International Liquidity," *Economic Journal*. (September 1973): 684–746.

Williamson, Oliver F. *Markets and Hierarchies: Analysis and Antitrust Implications: A Study of the Economics of Internal Organizations*. New York: Free Press, 1976.

Yavitz, Boris, and William H. Newman. *Strategy in Action*. New York: Free Press, 1982.

Yeager, L.B. *International Monetary Relations: Theory, History and Policy*. 2d ed. New York: Harper & Row, 1976.

Yoshino, Michael Y. *The Japanese Are Coming*. Cambridge, Mass.: Harvard University Press, 1976.

NAME INDEX

SUBJECT INDEX